Islamic Theology, Philosophy and Law

Studien zur Geschichte und Kultur des islamischen Orients

Beihefte zur Zeitschrift „Der Islam“

Herausgegeben von

Lawrence I. Conrad
und Benjamin Jokisch

Neue Folge

Band 27

De Gruyter

Islamic Theology, Philosophy and Law

Debating Ibn Taymiyya and Ibn Qayyim al-Jawziyya

Edited by
Birgit Krawietz
and Georges Tamer

in collaboration with
Alina Kokoschka

De Gruyter

MIX
Papier aus verantwortungsvollen Quellen
FSC® C016439
FSC
www.fsc.org

ISBN 978-3-11-028534-5
e-ISBN 978-3-11-028540-6
ISSN 1862-1295

Library of Congress Cataloging-in-Publication Data

A CIP catalogue record for this book has been applied for at the Library of Congress.

Bibliografische Information der Deutschen Nationalbibliothek

Die Deutsche Nationalbibliothek verzeichnet diese Publikation in der Deutschen Nationalbibliografie; detaillierte bibliografische Daten sind im Internet über http://dnb.dnb.de abrufbar.

Druck: Hubert & Co. GmbH und Co. KG, Göttingen
∞ Gedruckt auf säurefreiem Papier

Printed in Germany

www.degruyter.com

Table of Contents

Section 3: Philosophy

Section 4: Inclusion and Exclusion in Islamic Theology and Law

Section 5: Creative Reception Outside the Arab World

Acknowledgements

This edited volume represents a collective, multi-layered and trans-Atlantic enterprise: half of the papers presented here were originally delivered at the international workshop "Neo-Hanbalism Reconsidered: The Impact of Ibn Taymiyya and Ibn Qayyim al-Jawziyya", held at the "Zentrum Moderner Orient" (ZMO) in Berlin on October 23–25, 2007. The authors of the articles which were not presented during the conference agreed to contribute their work at a later date. That the publication of the volume took much longer than expected by the editors is caused by exceptional circumstances which we were not able to control.

First of all, we would like to express our gratitude to the "Deutsche Forschungsgemeinschaft" (DFG) for funding the workshop and of Birgit Krawietz's research on Ibn al-Qayyim. Lutz Rogler, then research fellow at the ZMO, was a gracious part of the success of the workshop event. We are indebted to the ZMO and its director, Prof. Dr. Ulrike Freitag, for allocating additional money for native-language review of a portion of the manuscript. We are also indebted to Mitch Cohen (Berlin) who embellished most of the articles. The then ZMO-student assistants Alina Kokoschka, Türkan Yılmaz, and Katharina Zöller, further Bettina Gräf, at that time assistant of the director, and likewise Silke Nagel, a ZMO-staff member, helped tremendously before, during and after the workshop. Alina Kokoschka, doctoral student at the Berlin Graduate School Muslim Cultures and Societies, collaborated in editing the volume, and co-authored the introductory article. We wish to thank her for her greatly appreciated efforts. Allen Tuazon, doctoral student at the Department of Near Eastern Languages and Cultures at The Ohio State University and Research Assistant of Georges Tamer, assisted with editing the contributions, improved the style of many of them, and prepared the index. We wish to thank him for his dedicated and scrupulous work. We are indebted to Annabelle Böttcher and Werner Ende for their valuable intellectual input. In this sense, we also thank Nadine Westphal from the German Israeli Foundation project "Patterns of Argumentation and Rhetorical Devices in the Legal and Theological Works of Ibn Qayyim al-Jawziyya" for her tremendous help in thoroughly reviewing the contributions as well as formatting and editing the final version. Arts and Humanities and the Department of Near Eastern Languages and Cultures at the Ohio State University generously provided funding and a publication subvention, for which we are very grateful.

Finally, we greatly appreciate the friendly and professional handling by the publisher Walter de Gruyter, and especially the input and feedback of Dr. Gertrud Grünkorn, Editorial Director Humanities, for accepting the volume in the series "Studien zur Geschichte und Kultur des islamischen Orients".

Birgit Krawietz, Berlin, & Georges Tamer, Columbus, May 2012

Appropriation of Ibn Taymiyya and Ibn Qayyim al-Jawziyya

Challenging Expectations of Ingenuity

Alina Kokoschka and Birgit Krawietz

For many centuries, the Damascene Muslim scholar Ibn Qayyim al-Jawziyya (d. 1350) has been viewed mainly as the devoted pupil of his teacher Ibn Taymiyya (d. 1328), academic attention falling, however grudgingly, primarily to the master himself. Having originated among Arab contemporaries, this contrasting attribution henceforth gained wider currency until early Salafi reformers, for their own purposes, "rediscovered" both authors. Their work suddenly precious and meaningful, Ibn al-Qayyim's and Ibn Taymiyya's standing abruptly increased in the context of the Islamic heritage. Nevertheless, the persistent impression of Ibn al-Qayyim's submissiveness, even within Western scholarship from the late 19th century until recently, is all the more perplexing inasmuch as this period witnessed an astounding surge both of printed works by Ibn al-Qayyim and of significant Arabic secondary literature discussing him. Our introduction focuses on the exaggerated binary perception regarding both these authors, which is a strangely twisted phenomenon. It can be surmised that there are some deeper, structural reasons at work for such an attitude of disregard for Ibn al-Qayyim, on the one hand, and either admiration or demonization of Ibn Taymiyya on the other. As such, we also suggest taking into account the historical development of European ideas of ingenuity and their potential impact. This relativising approach enables us to then argue in favour of alternative, modified conceptions of scholarly potential within the framework of Muslim cultures and societies in the widest sense. Taking Ibn al-Qayyim as a case study, we employ the concept of appropriation to highlight, analyse and appreciate similarly important intellectual activities. In fact, this attitude may in itself be influenced not only by writings in anthropology, art history, literature studies and so forth, but also by general Western outlooks that have meanwhile changed. As such, appropriation both counteracts the persuasiveness of prior *creatio ex nihilo* narratives and stresses the important role of imaginative cultural brokers.

The phrase "appropriation of" in the main title of this introduction points in different directions: Ibn al-Qayyim is tremendously influenced by the ideas and enactments of Ibn Taymiyya, yet also selectively reshapes them; further, he creatively integrates countless manuscripts from his own voluminous library. Beyond this, Ibn Taymiyya himself owes a great deal to his predecessors, to the scholars of his time and even to his opponents – a fact that may have been blurred to a considerable degree both by his harsh vituperations and his tendency to conceal quotations and borrowings as such. A strong case in point is Anke von Kügelgen's demonstration, in this edited volume, of how much Ibn Taymiyya actually absorbed from philosophy. He shares this strategy with many other Ḥanbalī and later Salafi authors, all of whom are very anxious to acquit themselves of any trace of recent influence and to re-root or transplant their message in early Islamic times. Likewise, the overall feature of productive appropriation characterizes negotiation with Ibn Taymiyya and Ibn al-Qayyim by other scholars up to (post-)modern times, notably, but not exclusively by Salafis; even the negotiations of semi-scholars and all sorts of laypeople share this characteristic. In his article "Appropriating the Past. Twentieth Century Reconstruction of Premodern Islamic Thought", Ahmad Dallal discusses his understanding of such a "reconstruction" as "not intended to carry any negative or pejorative connotation". He tries to "avoid the equation of reconstruction and distortion" and suggests it would be better "to shift the focus of examination from the assumed absolute origins of this tradition to the continuous process through which it is regenerated".[1] In this sense, we perceive Ibn Taymiyya and Ibn al-Qayyim as the twin peaks of Ḥanbalī/Salafi literary output that currently enjoys the greatest popularity, for whatever reasons; yet, we propose to distinguish between the very different circumstances of the productivity of these two – and consequently also other – scholars. This does not ignore scholarly findings like those of El-Rouayheb,

1 Dallal, Ahmad: Appropriating the Past. Twentieth Century Reconstruction of Premodern Islamic Thought, in: *Islamic Law and Society* 7 (2000), pp. 325–358, here p. 326, where Dallal encourages us to "identify the mechanisms through which a tradition is endowed with different meanings at different historical moments".

who traces the (un)popularity of Ibn Taymiyya over five centuries, discusses assumed proto-Salafis' and early revivalists' commitment to this figure, and stresses that his importance must be historically relativized: "From a little-read scholar with problematic and controversial views, he was to become for many Sunnis of the modern age one of the central figures in the Islamic religious tradition."[2]

The present volume provides glimpses into some of the grandest fields of Islamic intellectual history – such as theology, jurisprudence and philosophy – by elucidating some of their subgenres. Although an edited volume on the same two authors was published relatively recently,[3] the exploration of their writings is far from exhausted (and, as a matter of fact, gained considerable momentum with regard to Ibn al-Qayyim only at the turn of the 21st century): research needs to be done, in a collective effort, on various levels. Hence, this volume addresses: (i) the oeuvre of Ibn Taymiyya and Ibn Qayyim al-Jawziyya; (ii) ways in which their works are intertwined; (iii) modes in which these two writers of Islamic law and theology make use of prior authors; (iv) the manner in which they both (re)construct and normatively refer to an ideal(ized) early Islamic past; and (v) the processes by which they themselves become appropriated by later authors who are not necessarily full-fledged scholars.

To avoid the widespread feature of biological metaphors (most famously enshrined in the notion of Ibn Taymiyya being the "father" of Islamic fundamentalism)[4] and to steer clear from implying respon-

2 El-Rouayheb, Khaled: From Ibn Ḥajar al-Haytamī (d. 1566) to Khayr al-Dīn al-Ālūsī (d. 1899). Changing Views of Ibn Taymiyya Among Non-Ḥanbalī Sunni Scholars, in: Yossef Rapoport and Shahab Ahmed (eds.): *Ibn Taymiyya and His Times*, Karachi 2010, pp. 296–318, here p. 305.

3 Rapoport and Ahmed, *Ibn Taymiyya and His Times*, Karachi 2010; Bori, Caterina and Holtzman, Livnat (eds.): *A Scholar in the Shadow. Essays in the Legal and Theological Thought of Ibn Qayyim al-Ǧawziyyah*, in: *Oriente Moderno* 15 (2010).

4 Sivan, Emmanuel: Ibn Taymiyya. Father of the Islamic Revolution; Medieval Theology & Modern Politics, in: *Encounter* 60 (1983), pp. 41–50; Jansen, Johannes J. G.: Ibn Taymiyyah and the Thirteenth Century. A Formative Period of Modern Muslim Radicalism, in: *Quaderni di Studi Arabi* 5–6 (1987–88), pp. 391–396; Krawietz, Birgit: Ibn Taymiyya, Vater des islamischen Fundamentalismus? Zur westlichen Rezeption eines mittelalterlichen Schariatsgelehrten, in: Manuel Atienza, Enrico Pattaro, Martin Schulte, Boris Topornin and Dieter Wyduckel (eds.): *Theorie des Rechts in der Gesellschaft*, Berlin 2003, pp. 39–62, here pp. 50–55; Rapoport, Yossef and Ahmed, Shahab: Introduction, in: idem (eds.), *Ibn Taymiyya and His Times*, pp. 3–20, here p. 4.

sibility for any sort of ensuing appropriation by others, we refrain from labelling Ibn Taymiyya and Ibn al-Qayyim as the double-helixed DNA within the nucleus of (post)modern Salafism or anything like this; rather, we opt for the model of a repository that is selectively employed by different actors for all sorts of purposes in accordance with their respective agendas. Therefore, agency in the production of meaning is attributed respectively to all multifarious parties. By such processes of combined adoption and exclusion, in which all sorts of techniques of compilation and blending are applied, the material transforms and constantly takes on new qualities. Obviously the rich scholarly output of these two postclassical masters significantly contributes to Islamic law, theology and also philosophy.[5] However, it even serves as a huge repository for various ends, transcending – and, according to many, descending from – the confines of higher Islamic learning. To highlight some such manoeuvres in detail is likewise the concern of this book. It cuts vastly across centuries, depicting three decisive timescapes: the period of the *salaf ṣāliḥ*, the imagined age of the pristine and most-authentically-inspired first three generations of Islam; the period of Ibn Taymiyya and Ibn Qayyim al-Jawziyya; and, finally, from the age of printing onwards to the Internet. Hence, this introduction focuses on (1) 20th-century Western secondary literature on Ibn al-Qayyim, (2) the topos of Ibn Taymiyya's – if not general Ḥanbalī – intransigence, (3) the paradigm of Ibn al-Qayyim being the eternal pupil and (4) a more differentiated conception of creative scholarship.

1. Western Secondary Literature on Ibn al-Qayyim in the 20th Century

As a matter of fact and for reasons that still require reflection, the beginning of the 21st century has witnessed a sudden surge in publications regarding Ibn Qayyim al-Jawziyya. In due course, the present volume incorporates these findings. However, it is worthwhile to also take a closer look at what happened or, rather, did *not* happen previ-

5 We do not use the expression (late) medieval; compare Leder, Stefan: Postklassisch und vormodern. Beobachtungen in der Mamlūkenzeit, in: Stephan Conermann and Anja Pistor-Hatam (eds.): *Die Mamlūken. Studien zu ihrer Geschichte und Kultur; zum Gedenken an Ulrich Haarmann (1942–1999)*, Schenefeld 2003, pp. 290–312. See also Kahl, Hans-Dietrich: Was bedeutet "Mittelalter"?, in: *Saeculum* 40 (1989), pp. 15–38.

ously: that is to say, 20th century Western scholarship on this author hardly exists. Even Henri Laoust (1905–1983), the frontrunner of Ibn Taymiyya studies, and, some decades later, the "voice in the wilderness" of George Makdisi (1920–2002) – who explored the Sunni revival and the decisive role of Ḥanbalism – did not have much to say about Ibn al-Qayyim.[6] Of course, the excessive media hype since the killing of Anwar al-Sadat in 1981 has widely broadcasted allegations of Ibn Taymiyya's proto-fundamentalism and of his siring of modern terrorism; however, this did nothing to encourage scholarly publications on his "well-known" student. Neither did this occur in the wider research about Salafism or Muslim reformers. Although it has been common wisdom for a long time that Ibn Taymiyya and Ibn al-Qayyim were rediscovered and appropriated especially by early Salafi writers in the decades around the turn of the 20th century,[7] we can speak neither of a sketchy outline of the oeuvre of Ibn al-Qayyim nor of in-depth studies of major traits. As a rule, Ibn al-Qayyim is referred to only in passing, this acknowledgment being more ceremonial than expressing genuine interest in his writings.[8] Most importantly, throughout the 20th century, not a single book on him was published[9]; meanwhile, other (mediocre) premodern Muslim writers received extensive monographic treatment.

6 See Sourdel, Dominique and Sourdel-Thomine, Janine: Henri Laoust 1905–1983, in: *Revue des études islamiques* 52 (1984), pp. 3–16; Laoust, Henri: Ibn Ḳayyim al-Djawziyya, in: *EI*², vol. 3, pp. 821–822. Although George Makdisi in his Ibn Taymīya. A Ṣūfī of the Qādiriya Order (in: *The American Journal of Arabic Studies* 3 (1975), pp. 118–129) ventured to point out – see also his article on The Hanbali School and Sufism, in: *Boletin de la Asociacion Española de Orientalistas* 15 (1979), pp. 115–126 – the Sufi dimension of Ibn Taymiyya's thought at a time when the Hanbali scholar was still perceived as an arch-enemy of Sufism, he did not wrestle with Ibn al-Qayyim, whose work is so strongly immersed in Sufi topics, rhetoric and emotional dispositions. The Sufi influence on Ibn al-Qayyim has more recently been demonstrated by Anjum and Schallenbergh. In general, there are various reasons why "the entire school of Ḥanbalī thinkers suffered from an unjustified negligence by Western research for many decades", as is told by Bori and Holtzman, Introduction, p. 36.

7 His work was appropriated, by, for instance, Muhammad ʿAbduh, Muḥammad Rashīd Riḍā, and certain members of the Iraqi al-Ālūsī family; this is not to mention earlier scholars, such as Ibrāhīm al-Qūrānī, Shāh Walī Allāh al-Dihlawī and Muḥammad al-Shawkānī.

8 Bell as the foremost exception is tackled here a bit later.

9 We are speaking here only about official publications on the book market; otherwise worth mentioning is an unpublished dissertation by Nawir Yuslem Nurbain: *Ibn Qayyim*'s *Reformulation of the Fatwā*, Ph.D. thesis, Montreal 1995.

However, several (shortened) translations (of more spiritually-oriented writings) have been published since the last decade of the 20th century. Noting the content of these works, however, causes one to question their analytical capacity. The most frequently discussed topic is prophetic medicine (*al-ṭibb al-nabawī*), an issue dealt with by Ibn al-Qayyim especially in his *Zād al-maʿād*.[10] Almost as popular are renderings of Ibn al-Qayyim's monograph on the soul, his *Kitāb al-Rūḥ*;[11] another focus is moral psychology with a Sufi flavour.[12] Obviously, it can be easily determined that the initiative to translate Ibn al-Qayyim into European languages comes from within Muslim circles or institutions. Nevertheless, despite their primary appeal to Muslim audiences, such translations will also influence Western academia in the long run. There is only one translation project in which no Muslim background is discernable, namely Dieter Johannes Bellmann's German version of Ibn Qayyim al-Ǧauziyya: *Über die Frauen. Liebeshistorien und Liebeserfahrung aus dem arabischen Mittelalter*.[13] This loosely assembles "reports about women" (*akhbār al-nisāʾ*), i.e. (pseudo-)historical narrations on the characteristics of women, with a special emphasis on their jealousy, their infidelity and prostitution. Bellmann mentions that the ascription of the monograph to Ibn al-Qayyim is dubious and discusses remarks identifying Ibn al-Jawzī (d. 1201) as the correct author[14]; yet, in his bizarre epilogue he cannot help but indulge in an

On Nurbain's contribution, see Krawietz, Birgit: Transgressive Creativity in the Making. Ibn Qayyim al-Ǧawziyyah's Reframing within Ḥanbalī Legal Methodology, in: Bori and Holtzman, *A Scholar in the Shadow*, pp. 43–62.

10 Translated by Muhammad Al-Akili as *Natural Healing with Tibb Medicine. Medicine of the Prophet*, Philadelphia 1993; translated by Penelope Johnstone as *Medicine of the Prophet*, which was published in Cambridge, UK by – notably – The Islamic Texts Society, 1998; yet another edition has been offered by Raymond J. Manderola under the title *Healing with the Medicine of the Prophet*, Riyadh 1999.

11 Ibn Qayyim al-Jawziyya: *The Soul's Journey After Death. An Abridgement of Ibn al-Qayyim's Kitab ar-Ruh with a Commentary of Layla Mabrouk*, London 1987; idem: *Le paradis. Hadi el arwah ila bilad el afrah; résumé par Fdal Haja and trad. Hébri Bousserouel*, Paris 1995.

12 *Patience and Gratitude. An Abridged Translation of ʿUddat as-sabirin wa dhakhirat as-shakirin*, edited by ʿAbdassamad Clarke and Nasiruddin al-Khattab, London 1997, reprint 1998.

13 Munich 1986.

14 [Pseudo-] Ibn Qayyim al-Ǧauziyya, Taqī al-Dīn: *Über die Frauen*, Munich 1986, p. 463. Holtzman, Livnat: Ibn Qayyim al-Jawziyyah, in: Joseph E. Lowry and Devin J. Stewart (eds.): *Essays in Arabic Literary Biography*, Wiesbaden

exploration of the tension between the rigid posture of Ibn al-Qayyim as a religious scholar and the juiciness of the stories of this anthology.[15] It is an oddity that, of all things, Western 20th-century scholarship chose for translation a single monograph that Ibn al-Qayyim not only did not write, but that also runs highly contrary to his concerns. Nevertheless, one could perhaps take this incident as symptomatic of the fact that, for a long time, Western publications could hardly make sense of Ibn al-Qayyim at all, whereas – in contrast – research on Ibn Taymiyya has, for decades now, followed clearly defined interests, however political, polemical, or not strictly scholarly they might be.

When we reckon the number of articles, book chapters and the like in Western research on Ibn al-Qayyim, we cannot come up with more than about a dozen contributions throughout the 20th century.[16] It becomes obvious that few people involved in Western Islamic Studies have examined Ibn al-Qayyim in even a minor way. Of these examinations, Joseph Normant Bell's book *Love Theory in Later Hanbalite Islam* is highly important, inasmuch as it not only provides a chapter on Ibn Taymiyya[17] but also devotes two chapters to Ibn al-Qayyim's relevant writings,[18] furthermore undertaking the first Western attempt of chronologizing some of the latter's work. One also has to note Livingston's article on "Ibn Qayyim al-Jawziyyah. A Fourteenth Century Defense

2009, pp. 202–223, here p. 206, clarifies: "Ibn al-Jawzī composed a work entitled Aḥkām al-nisā' (Laws regarding Women), whose content is different from Akhbār al-nisā'. Nevertheless, Akhbār al-nisā' appears in a list of Ibn al-Jawzī's works in several biographies, which leads to the conclusion that it is indeed his work." It is not the first time that people have confused these two Ḥanbalīs with similar names; see Ḥijāzī, ʿIwaḍ Allāh Jād: *Ibn al-Qayyim wa-mawqifuhu min al-tafkīr al-islāmī*, Cairo 1960, pp. 26–27; Abū Zayd, Bakr b. ʿAbd Allāh: *Ibn Qayyim al-Jawziyya. Ḥayātuhu, āthāruhu, mawāriduhu*, Riyadh 1412/1991/92, pp. 24–29, 202–208.

15 [Pseudo-] Ibn Qayyim al-Ǧauziyya, *Über die Frauen*, pp. 448–450, 465.

16 It is probable that we have missed a publication or two, but the ones we *have* mentioned are those that usually resurface in the discourse of Islamic Studies. We exclude from this counting the laudatory accounts of Abdul Azim Islahi: *Economic Thought of Ibn al Qayyim (1292–1350 A. D.)*, Jeddah (International Center for Research in Islamic Economics, King Abdulaziz University) 1984 (Research series in English; p. 20), and Saiyed Ahsan's very short general article Ibn Qayyim al-Jawziyah, in: *Islam and the Modern Age* 12 (1981), pp. 244–249.

17 Albany, New York 1979, pp. 74–91.

18 Bell, *Love Theory*, pp. 92–124 et passim. [Pseudo-] Ibn Qayyim al-Ǧauziyya, *Über die Frauen*, pp. 456–459, only enumerates and quickly comments on some of Ibn al-Qayyim's most important works without any footnotes or references to time; his afterword, therefore, cannot count as such an attempt.

Against Astrological Divination and Alchemical Transmutation"[19] with a follow-up article two decades later.[20] A third person who must be given credit for his early publication on Ibn al-Qayyim is Moshe Perlmann, who narrates a sort of rough outline of Ibn al-Qayyim's work "Rescuing the Distressed from Satan's Snares" (*Ighāthat al-lahfān min maṣāyid al-shayṭān*). Perlmann's devil article is basically a useful overview of the table of contents with some additional information.[21] In similar fashion, in 1935 Cooke provides an explanatory overview of the contents of the "Book on the Soul".[22] Apart from that, there are only two issues that have drawn serious attention to Ibn al-Qayyim from 20th century scholarship, viz., the aforementioned genre of prophetic medicine in the important research of Irmeli Perho,[23] including embryology[24] and a discussion of the rituals and

---

19 Livingston, John W.: Ibn Qayyim al-Jawziyyah. A Fourteenth Century Defense Against Astrological Divination and Alchemical Transmutation, in: *Journal of the American Oriental Society* 91 (1971), pp. 96–103. Compare Yahya J. Michot: Ibn Taymiyya on Astrology. Annotated Translation of Three Fatwas, in: *Journal of Islamic Studies* 11 (2000), pp. 147–208.

20 Livingston, John W.: Science and the Occult in the Thinking of Ibn Qayyim al-Jawziyya, in: *Journal of the American Oriental Society* 112 (1992), pp. 598–610. Compare Yahya Michot: Between Entertainment and Religion. Ibn Taymiyya's Views on Superstition, in: *The Muslim World* 99 (2009), pp. 1–20.

21 Perlmann, Moshe: Ibn Qayyim and the Devil, in: *Studi orientalistici in onore di Giorgio Levi della Vida*, 2 vols. 2, Rome 1956, pp. 330–337; it is based on the edition by Muḥammad Ḥāmid al-Fiqī. However, Perlmann's monograph "Samau'al al-Maghribī Ifḥām al-Yahūd. Silencing the Jews" (in: *American Academy of Jewish Research Proceedings* 32 (1964), pp. 1–104) does not specifically identify the exact proportions of Ibn al-Qayyim's quotations of the work in his *Hidāyat al-ḥayārā*, although it draws attention to the fact and presents an Arabic edition of the text. His remarks on Ibn al-Qayyim could already be read much earlier in his "Ibn al-Qayyim and Samau'al al-Maghribi", in: *Journal of Jewish Bibliography* 3 (1942), pp. 71–74.

22 Cooke, Francis T.: Ibn al-Qaiyim's Kitāb al-Rūḥ, in: *The Muslim World* 25 (1935), pp. 129–144. The latter topic has more recently engaged scholars like Geneviève Gobillot and especially Tzvi Langermann. See the latter's contribution in this volume.

23 Perho, Irmeli: *The Prophet's Medicine. A Creation of the Muslim Traditionalist Scholars*, Helsinki 1995.

24 Weisser, Ursula: Ibn Qaiyim al-Ǧauzīya über die Methoden der Embryologie, in: *Medizinhistorisches Journal* 16 (1981), pp. 227–239; Bummel, Julia: *Zeugung und pränatale Entwicklung des Menschen nach Schriften mittelalterlicher muslimischer Religionsgelehrter über die "Medizin des Propheten"*, http://www.sub.uni-hamburg.de/opus/volltexte/1999/244/, accessed Sept. 04, 2011.

ethics of the raising of children.[25] This very slow-beginning and still-scattered perception of Ibn al-Qayyim as an author in his own right hardly reminds one of Ibn Taymiyya, and the profile that emerges is very different. However, some topics are associated with both authors simultaneously, such as legal methodology – as tentatively analysed by Kerr[26] – and, of course, the complex field of the veneration of saints and visitation of graves,[27] which persistently haunts people around the globe and fuels the perception of Ibn Taymiyya and Ibn al-Qayyim as notorious troublemakers.

In conclusion for the century under discussion, the writings of Bell, Bummel and Perho in particular can be qualified as profound and as effectively preparing the ground for later research. Bummel, for instance, enhanced the analysis of the emerging importance of Ibn al-Qayyim in the field of bioethics.[28] Despite this, the extremely low number of contributions on Ibn al-Qayyim in Western languages throughout the 20th century[29] stands in stark contrast to the multiple

25 Adamek, Gerhard: *Das Kleinkind in Glaube und Sitte der Araber im Mittelalter*, Ph. D. thesis, Bonn (Universität Bonn) 1968; Giladi, Avner: *Children of Islam. Concepts of Childhood in Medieval Muslim Society*, New York 1968, pp. 10–34 et passim; idem: Gender Differences on Child Rearing and Education. Some Preliminary Observations with Reference to Medieval Muslim Thought, in: *al-Qantara* 16 (1995), pp. 291–301, here pp. 295–299, 301, and idem: Some Notes on Taḥnīq in Medieval Islam, in: *Journal of Near Eastern Studies* 47 (1988), pp. 175–179, here pp. 175, 177–178.

26 Kerr, Malcolm H.: *Islamic Reform. The Political and Legal Theories of Muhammad 'Abduh and Rashid Rida*. Berkeley and Los Angeles 1966, pp. 68, 77–79, 88–89, 99–100, 191–196. Compare Al-Matroudi, Abdul Hakim: *The Ḥanbalī School of Law and Ibn Taymiyyah. Conflict or Conciliation*, London and New York 2006, pp. 132–136.

27 Taylor, Christopher S.: *In the Vicinity of the Righteous.* Ziyāra *and the Veneration of Muslim Saints in Late Medieval Egypt*, Leiden 1999, chapters 5–6, pp. 168–218.

28 The strategic use of Ibn al-Qayyim's writings enabled Saudi Arabian scholars, and scholars from other countries, to expand the period before the ensoulment of the embryo to up to 120 days in their debates about abortion. On this linkage, see Eich, Thomas: Die Diskussion islamischer Rechtsgelehrter um pre-marital screening und die Abtreibung behinderter Embryonen, in: Thomas Eich and Thomas Sören Hoffmann (eds.): *Kulturübergreifende Bioethik. Zwischen globaler Herausforderung und regionaler Perspektive*, Freiburg and Munich 2006, pp. 152–178, here pp. 163, 166–170, 174.

29 Bori and Holtzman, writing as late as 2011, comment on the situation as follows: "Yet, a student of Ibn al-Qayyim embarking upon research on the thought of Ibn Qayyim al-Ǧawziyyah will eventually start with a meagre handful of stud-

publications on Ibn Taymiyya on the one hand and the high demand from Arabic readers on the other. Ibn al-Qayyim's works are reprinted again and again;[30] the main and growing bulk consists of mostly uncritical Salafi editions that flood the book market, which has simultaneously been injected with an increasing amount of translations. Ibn al-Qayyim's monographs pile up in bookshops from Berlin to Jakarta; they have become – in various forms – a pervasive feature especially on the Internet.[31] Many Muslim authors quote and have appropriated not only Ibn Taymiyya but also Ibn al-Qayyim; hence, there is also a considerable number of academic publications on Ibn al-Qayyim in Arabic that unfortunately cannot be reviewed here for lack of space. However, with this high level of activity in mind, it seems all the more necessary to look back in astonishment. Why, for a whole century, has Western scholarship nearly unanimously avoided paying attention to Ibn al-Qayyim, especially at a time when his (re)invented relevance was already generally known? One might argue that Ibn al-Qayyim's Arabic is not easily accessible to the average reader, especially because of his frequent quotations from Koran and Hadith. Furthermore, Ibn al-Qayyim hardly ever manages to keep his story short, most of his monographs being greatly repetitive, meandering, multi-layered and spread over more than one book volume. Although these factors may represent certain impediments to quickly accessing Ibn al-Qayyim and to continuing to read him, we surmise that such a lasting blindness may rather have deeper, structural reasons. Our fourth section will unpack these and suggest them for discussion. Beforehand, we must revisit the fact that both our authors met not only considerable resistance in their own period and negligence in later centuries, but – for distinctive and only partly overlapping reasons – have had remarkably bad press in modern Western scholarship.

ies, then painstakingly hunt for more references to Ibn al-Qayyim mainly in works dedicated to Ibn Taymiyyah", Bori and Holtzman, Introduction, p. 15.

30 Detailed studies of such printing patterns over time that also include publishing locations, the involved publishing houses and key figures, as well as the changing emphasis on various topics, are still desiderata.

31 On this, see for example the article by Annabelle Böttcher in the present volume.

2. The Topos of Intransigence

In his *Encyclopaedia of Islam* entry on the Ḥanbalīs that was published in 1971, Laoust diagnoses an "often intransigent rigidity of the dogmatic position of Ḥanbalism".[32] This expresses both a familiar value judgement and popular perception. Consequently, nine years later, Makdisi in his turn deplores the widespread contempt for Ḥanbalī authors, "who are variously regarded as conservative to the core, rigid, intransigent, even fanatical".[33] He attributes this trend primarily to the 19th century, "the great enemy of Hanbali studies"[34], and identifies Goldziher as the figurehead of such disregard.[35] Here is not the place to dwell on the genesis of this attitude in Arabic sources. Suffice it to say that nowadays in Arabic the idiomatic phrase "don't behave like a Ḥanbalī" (*lā takun ḥanbaliyyan*) means to be not too rigid or fussy. The famous Ḥanbalī preacher Ibn al-Jawzī, for instance, is also regarded as "l'un des plus intransigeants *ʿulamāʾ* de son temps".[36] Intransigence was, of course, neither invented nor monopolized by the Ḥanbalī school, but is a recurrent pattern in Islamic history. Already the Khārijīs (*khawārij*), who had seceded from the camp of the caliph ʿAlī, were unwilling to compromise: "for many Muslims, early Kharijis were the first intransigent group to emerge among Muslims."[37] Again Laoust speaks of "l'intransigence khârijite"[38] and henceforth it is the Khārijīs with whom Ibn Taymiyya is most often compared. Like him, the leaders of early Khārijite thinking were "no arm-chair

32 Laoust, Henri: Ḥanābila, in: *EI*², vol. 3 (1971), pp. 158–162, here p. 158.

33 Makdisi, George: The Hanbali School and Sufism, in: *Boletin de la Asociacion Española de Orientalistas* 15 (1979), pp. 115–126, here p. 115.

34 Makdisi, George: Hanbalite Islam, in: *Studies on Islam*, translated and edited by Merlin L. Swartz, New York and Oxford 1981, pp. 216–274, here p. 219 [translated from "L'Islam Hanbalisant", in: *Revue des études islamiques* 42 (1974), pp. 211–244; 43 (1975), pp. 45–76].

35 Makdisi, Hanbalite Islam, p. 223; compare Krawietz, Vater des islamischen Fundamentalismus?, p. 58.

36 Hartmann, Angelika: La prédication islamique au moyen age. Ibn al-Ǧauzī et ses sermons (fin du 6/12e siècle), in: *Quaderni di Studi Arabi* 5–6 (1987–88), pp. 337–345, here p. 338.

37 Saeed, Abdullah and Hassan Saeed: *Freedom of Religion, Apostasy and Islam*, Aldershot and Burlington 2004, p. 24.

38 Laoust, Henri: *La profession de foi d'Ibn Baṭṭa. Traditionniste et jurisconsulte musulman d'école hanbalite mort en Irak à ʿUkbarâ en 387/997*, Damascus 1958, p. xlix.

theologians."[39] It tends to be overlooked, however, that Ibn Taymiyya himself also severely criticized the Khārijīs, stressing that no Companion of the Prophet was among them and that no *ṣaḥābī* had ever forbidden anyone to fight them.[40] Stubbornness and unwavering defence of his peculiar convictions have become the trademark of this scholar *cum* activist. And hence, Brunschvig, too, qualifies Ibn Taymiyya as "a la vez intransigente y anticonformista."[41] It is stated that contemporaries must already have perceived the singlemindedness with which he was "completely dedicated to a cause", so much that Donald Little in 1975 asked the famous – and not completely ironically intended – question "Did Ibn Taymiyya have a Screw Loose?"[42] Though Ibn Taymiyya's "intransigence led to repeated imprisonment",[43] the related multiple inquisitions (*miḥan*) – in the hallowed tradition modelled by the eponym of the Ḥanbalī school of law, Aḥmad b. Ḥanbal (d. 855) – contributed to Ibn Taymiyya's halo. Indeed, the latter appears as the natural heir par excellence to this imagined typically Ḥanbalī trait: "Ibn Ḥanbal's rigor and personal courage were most spectacularly emulated by the Damascene jurist Taqī al-Dīn b. Taymiya."[44] What captivates contemporaries and later admirers of Ibn Taymiyya is the paradigmatic situation of wholehearted insistence on and standing up for one's beliefs. It is no surprise, then, that Ibn Taymiyya has become the most famous prison inmate of Islamic history, appropriated as an icon of reference for political prisoners. While some cherish Ibn Taymiyya for his "unsurpassed moral courage, intensity, and intellec-

39 Watt, W. Montgomery: Khārijite Thought in the Umayyad Period, in: *Der Islam* 36 (1961), pp. 215–231, here p. 218.

40 Jansen, Johannes J. G.: Ibn Taymiyyah and the Thirteenth Century. A Formative Period of Modern Muslim Radicalism, in: *Quaderni di Studi Arabi* 5–6 (1987–88), pp. 391–396, here p. 392.

41 Brunschvig, Robert: Los teólogos-juristas del islam en pro o en contra de la lógica griega, Ibn Ḥazm, al-Ġazālī, Ibn Taymiyya, in: *al-Andalus* 35 (1970), pp. 143–177, here p. 169.

42 Little, Donald: Did Ibn Taymiyya have a Screw Loose?, in: *Studia Islamica* 41 (1975), pp. 93–111, here p. 105.

43 Schallenbergh, Gino: Ibn Taymīya on the *'ahl al-bayt*, in: Urbain Vermeulen and Jo van Steenbergen (eds.): *Egypt and Syria in the Fatimid, Ayyubid and Mamluk Eras*, vol. 3 (Proceedings of the 6th, 7th and 8th International Colloquium organized at the Katholieke Universiteit Leuven in May 1997, 1998 and 1999), Leuven 2001, pp. 407–420, here p. 408.

44 Cooperson, Michael: *Classical Arabic Biography. The Heirs of the Prophets in the Age of al-Ma'mūn*, Cambridge 2000, p. 109.

tual vigour",[45] for others he mutated into a convenient code word for evil, most often based on the snowballing hearsay of experts, such as Irshad Manji: "And if that doesn't attest to Ibn Tammiya's contemporary reach, get this: Sayyid Qutb's exiled brother, Muhammad, taught Osama bin Laden in Saudi Arabia".[46]

However, both camps agree that Ibn Taymiyya sometimes implemented his teachings by vigilantism, enacting his doctrines in a twofold manner.[47] His intransigence emerges not only in the trials as such, but also in his excesses against, for example, Christians and those Muslims he perceived to be deviant. His is a case of radical activism[48] in the form of jihad and intervention in public space against individual evildoers (*al-amr bil-maʿrūf*): "Ibn Taymiyya is an activist, convinced that God calls upon Muslims to undertake the responsibility of combating external enemies as well as internal evils."[49] As such, his life appears as a constant construction site, as a rushing back and forth between different fronts, and as a ceaseless migration between the spheres of political intervention, teaching, personal enmities and chastisement of colleagues and contemporaries, intrigues against the establishment, military interventions and key points of contention as expressed in certain fatwas or epistles. Because of his special combining of political activism with intellectual production and his simultaneous combat on numerous battlefields, Ibn Taymiyya's life has attracted extraordinary biographical attention.[50] It is probably due to his various interventions, his harsh rhetoric of "us *versus* them" and his pointed statements that the life of

45 Sivan, Ibn Taymiyya, p. 42.

46 Manji, Irshad: *The Trouble with Islam Today. A Muslim's Call for Reform*, Toronto 2005, p. 147.

47 An example is already his first public appearance. In 1294, Ibn Taymiyya organized a riot against a Christian scribe named ʿAssāf al-Naṣrānī, who was accused of blasphemy against the Prophet Muḥammad, Henri Laoust: La biographie d'Ibn Taimīya d'après Ibn Kaṯīr, in: *Bulletin d'études orientales* 9 (1942–1943), pp. 115–162, here p. 118. Ibn Taymiyya's treatise *al-Ṣārim al-maslūl ʿalā shātim al-rasūl* was written in this context, see Turki, Abdelmagid: Situation du "tributaire" qui insulte l'islam, au regard de la doctrine et de la jurisprudence musulmanes, in: *Studia Islamica* 30 (1969), pp. 39–72.

48 Makari, Victor E.: *Ibn Taymiyyah*'s *Ethics. The Social Factor*, Chico 1983, p. 27: "To strive in the divine way was for him to stand up and to take action in the name of God."

49 Michel, Thomas: Ibn Taymiyya's *Sharḥ* on the *Futūḥ al-Ghayb* of ʿAbd al-Qādir al-Jīlānī, in: *Hamdard Islamicus* 4 (1981), pp. 3–12, here p. 7.

50 Bori, Caterina: The Collection and Edition of Ibn Taymiyya's Works. Concerns of a Disciple, in: *Mamlūk Studies Review* 13 (2009), pp. 47–67, here pp. 51–52.

Ibn Taymiyya has fuelled the imagination of so many observers. His biography seems to follow familiar scripts, and appears as if it were destined for film. The ensuing oversimplifications and shortcut interpretations of his multifaceted writings have been criticised;[51] hence there are various differentiated readings in the realm of academia. Michael Cook emphasizes that albeit "his notorious disposition to rock the boat", Ibn Taymiyya made "no attempt to cultivate street-power".[52]

3. The Paradigm of the Eternal Pupil

Against the backdrop of the histrionic life of his master, the biography of Ibn al-Qayyim (and, indeed, that of any other scholar) looks much less spectacular, more so as Ibn Taymiyya is "so eccentric, charismatic, original, and captivating, and his writings so voluminous, that next to him a person with a more gentle profile like Ibn Qayyim al-Ǧawziyyah runs the risk of looking dull."[53] This impression unfolds on various levels and it applies to the person as much as to the oeuvre. There is no need to replicate here the distinctive but intertwined biographical trajectories of both authors. Suffice it to mention that, unlike Ibn Taymiyya, his pupil Ibn al-Qayyim did not spend his life fighting on several fronts. The latter's inquisitorial experience in and outside prison (*miḥna*)[54] and the fierce criticism he encountered for issuing fatwas and defending theological stances in line with his famous teacher also elevated him – in the eyes of admirers – to the ranks of heroic resistance and moral courage. Taken as a whole, however, his life is very much a life of writing. Ibn al-Qayyim is described as being well aware of the shortness of man's lifetime; he therefore worked incessantly, even when separated from his private hometown library.[55] Instead of revisiting their entangled life

51 The call for a painstakingly close reading has notably been made by Yahya Michot; compare, for instance, his: Ibn Taymiyya's "New Mardin Fatwa." Is Genetically Modified Islam Carcinogenic?, in: *The Muslim World* 101 (2011), pp. 130–181.

52 Cook, Michael: *Commanding Right and Forbidding Wrong in Islamic Thought*, Cambridge 2000, pp. 149–150. See the chapter by Abdessamad Belhaj in the present volume.

53 Bori and Holtzman, Introduction, p. 16.

54 Krawietz, Birgit: Ibn Qayyim al-Jawzīyah. His Life and Works, in: *Mamlūk Studies Review* 10 (2006), pp. 19–64, here p. 24.

55 Al-Baqrī, Aḥmad Maḥmūd: *Ibn al-Qayyim min āthārihi al-ʿilmiyya*, Beirut 1404/1984, p. 142.

histories, we trace in the following the idea of "minorness" in virtually everything – apart from the amount of written output and spiritual devotion[56] – when it comes to Ibn al-Qayyim, a pattern that resurfaces on a regular basis. The pervasive perception of being second(ary) is fed by several factors, such as Ibn al-Qayyim's unabashed admiration for Ibn Taymiyya, his apparently uncritical subordination to his ideas, his personal modesty and humbleness, as well as his editorial and intellectual curating of Ibn Taymiyya's heritage.

After Ibn Taymiyya had returned from Egypt, Ibn al-Qayyim became his most ardent follower and spent one and a half decades with him in Damascus, leading to nearly two years in prison – physically apart, but with a shared vision. Contrary to the custom of studying with several different teachers, Ibn al-Qayyim was obviously overwhelmed by Ibn Taymiyya,[57] so much so that he "dedicated the next fifteen years of his life to study only with Ibn Taymiyyah, and he soon succeeded in establishing himself as the latter's senior disciple."[58] This strong intellectual and emotional attachment seems to have tied Ibn al-Qayyim to his hometown during the earlier period of his life.[59] Anjum points out that the relationship even transcended Ibn al-Qayyim's status as a master student of Ibn Taymiyya and that especially the *Madārij al-sālikīn*, his famous commentary on a Ḥanbalī Sufi manual, provides vivid insights into this lasting, deeply felt affection, since it "also addresses the question of the relationship of Ibn Qayyim al-Ǧawziyyah's spiritual vision to his teacher Ibn Taymiyyah."[60] Therein, he expresses "exceeding reverence and love for his teacher, Ibn Taymiyyah (...) perhaps more than in any other work",[61] so that Anjum suggests a comparison to "the

---

56 Krawietz, Ibn Qayyim al-Jawzīyah, pp. 22–23.

57 For his other teachers, see Holtzman, Ibn Qayyim al-Jawziyyah, pp. 206–207; Abdul-Mawjûd, Salâhud-Dîn Ibn Alî: *The Biography of Imâm ibn al-Qayyim, translated by Abdul-Râfi Adewale Imâm*, Riyadh 2006, pp. 43–51. Holtzman struggles to extend the list, so that Ibn al-Qayyim meets the familiar pattern of expectations.

58 Holtzman, Ibn Qayyim al-Jawziyyah, p. 210.

59 Abdul-Mawjûd, *Biography*, pp. 63–67, apparently feels awkward that Ibn al-Qayyim has not lived up to the widespread norm of searching for knowledge in other locations (*ṭalab al-ʿilm*) and accordingly tries to appease his readers; Krawietz, Ibn Qayyim al-Jawzīyah, p. 23.

60 Anjum, Ovamir: Sufism without Mysticism. Ibn Qayyim al-Ǧawziyya's Objectives in *Madāriǧ al-sālikīn*, in: Bori and Holtzman, *A Scholar in the Shadow*, pp. 161–188, here p. 162.

61 Anjum, Sufism without Mysticism, p. 163.

type of intense spiritual affection that we have become familiar with in the case of Rumi and Shams-i Tabrizi."[62] It was out of the question that Ibn al-Qayyim would openly criticize a theological standpoint taken by Ibn Taymiyya.[63] Another factor sustaining this idea of "minorness" is Ibn al-Qayyim's modest family background. His agnomen (*laqab*) as "the son of the Superintendent of al-Jawziyyah Law College" is "an indication of the father's occupation and social status."[64] However, while the term 'superintendent' may sound somewhat acceptable in English, 'janitor' may be the expression that comes closer; that is to say, Ibn al-Qayyim's own career is one of enormous social climbing, even though he – not least because of his loyalty to Ibn Taymiyya – definitely did not make it to the top. As a constant reminder, his low social background as "the son of a janitor of the Jawziyya" was permanently inscribed in the scholar's agnomen.[65] One may speculate as to whether Ibn al-Qayyim suffered from these circumstances; one may also surmise as to whether his compulsive acquiring of manuscripts and quest for role models and spiritual emulation – be that of Ibn Taymiyya or of the Prophet Muḥammad – might have had something to do with this lowly origin. Ibn Taymiyya's superior command of scholarship and unabashed self-confidence must have had a special appeal for Ibn al-Qayyim. Nevertheless, in contrast to the arrogant Ibn Taymiyya, he comes across in the sources as constantly struggling with a lack of self-confidence, in no way eager to indulge in harsh accusations of oth-

62 Ibid, p. 164, n. 9.

63 Nevertheless, he would do so on some jurisprudential issues; ibid, p. 164.

64 Holtzman, Ibn Qayyim al-Jawziyyah, p. 208. Compare Irmeli Perho, Climbing the Ladder. Social Mobility in the Mamluk Period, in: *Mamlūk Studies Review* 15 (2011), pp. 19–35, here p. 19.

65 Perho, Climbing the Ladder, p. 20, includes caretakers of mosques (sg. *qayyim*) among "the lowest paid employees of the religious institutions, but even though they worked among the scholars, they were not necessarily scholars themselves" and in her conclusion, p. 34, she stresses, "that social advancement cannot have been easy, and a successful climb up the social ladder was an exception rather than a rule." A laudatory biography tries to put these circumstances in another light by labelling the occupation of the father as "director" and offering further cover-up reading: "It is sufficient source of his pride that he should be in charge of this school because of the great influence it had amongst all the schools of that time" and that, afterwards, "his offspring and his grandchildren became famous with this ascription", Abdul-Mawjûd, *Biography*, pp. 24–25. The fact that the father had some rudimentary knowledge of hereditary regulations has confused some writers, as if he had already belonged to the lower strata of scholars, Krawietz, Ibn Qayyim al-Jawzīyah, p. 21.

ers, but rather filled with extraordinary humbleness and piety.[66] At any rate, it is hardly imaginable that Ibn Taymiyya would have put up with someone as noisy and uncompromising as himself. Among his group of followers it was him who was undoubtedly in charge,[67] while Ibn al-Qayyim ranks regularly as his most famous disciple.[68] The habitus of subordination to Ibn Taymiyya may have curbed Ibn al-Qayyim's individual ambition and caused a sort of writer's block even when he was no longer juvenile, as is insinuated. For instance, the translators Michael Abdurrahman Fitzgerald and Moulay Youssef Sitine comment, it "appears that only after his teacher's death did Ibn al-Qayyim begin his own prolific period as a writer." At this point Ibn al-Qayyim must have had a coming out of sorts: "This stage of his life was also marked by much travel, learning and teaching, as well as several pilgrimages to Mecca, where he even lived for some time."[69] By the time of Ibn Taymiyya's death in 1328, Ibn al-Qayyim was already at the age of 37 or 38. He wrote the overwhelming majority of his contributions after this date;[70] one wonders with what exactly he had been occupied before then[71] and why his own scholarly production witnessed such a large incubation period before the extraordinary amount of text production of his later decades. We do not know whether he might have written parts of his work already during Ibn Taymiyya's lifetime and refrained for whatever reason from publishing them. It has long been assumed that Ibn al-Qayyim played the central role in the collection and arrangement of Ibn Taymiyya's works, although exactly how and by whom the widely scattered pieces were assembled still needs more investigation.[72] Ibn Taymiyya is one of those scholars who brilliantly mastered various genres of the religious sciences.[73] He himself, how-

---

66 Holtzman, Ibn Qayyim al-Jawziyyah, pp. 210–211.

67 Bori, Caterina: Ibn Taymiyya *wa-Jamāʿatuhu*. Authority, Conflict and Consensus in Ibn Taymiyya's Circle, in: Rapoport and Ahmed, *Ibn Taymiyya and His Times*, pp. 23–52, here 25, 28, 30 et passim.

68 One hesitates to call the others famous. This applies only to some traditionalist Shāfiʿīs who somehow sympathized with Ibn Taymiyya; ibid, p. 37.

69 *Ibn Qayyim al-Jawziyya on the Invocation of God. Al-Wābil al-Ṣayyib min al-Kalim al-Ṭayyib*, translated by Michael Abdurrahman Fitzgerald and Moulay Youssef Sitine, Cambridge 2000, p. xi.

70 Holtzman, Ibn Qayyim al-Jawziyyah, p. 206.

71 On his occupations and pursuits, see Abdul-Mawjûd, *Biography*, pp. 69–71.

72 Bori, Collection, p. 58 et passim.

73 Weismann, Itzhak: *Taste of Modernity. Sufism, Salafiyya, and Arabism in Late Ottoman Damascus*, Leiden and Boston 2001, p. 263.

ever, did not invest any energy or diligence into pre-structuring his posthumous fame either by means of systematic presentation, by convenient arrangement or by attentive care to his works. It is uncertain whether he regarded all the pieces of writing he haphazardly handed out in response to fatwa requests as really part of his oeuvre – indeed, it is uncertain whether he thought in such terms at all. He developed the issuing of religious legal advice into a central means of self-articulation in order to express his own intellectual concerns; the short form of "the fatwa became for him a major vehicle for the expression of his ideas".[74] Ibn Taymiyya at times even gave different titles to one and the same piece of his writing[75] and there are many other circumstances that impede a precise mapping of his output. Nevertheless, an astonishing amount of his writing has survived the centuries, although already his contemporaries did not have a clear overview of it. Certain aspects of Ibn Taymiyya's work might have failed the test of time were it not for the devoted efforts of his admirers, be they Ibn al-Qayyim or others. It is a lucky historical coincidence that such an impulsive author, who constantly shifted from one topic to the other and from one front to the next, was preserved, (re-)arranged, systematized and further developed by willing admirers.

Any description of Ibn Qayyim al-Jawziyya seems to start with the remark that he was a prolific writer. However, this does not quite imply that he was productive in the fullest sense of the word; rather, without stating it too bluntly, the expression conveys a certain reservation about the quality of his output. Some scholars have no qualms about airing their disregard for him. The main assumption behind both approaches is the epigonal character of his person and oeuvre. In probably involuntary irony, the editors of *Aḥkām ahl al-dhimma* hail Ibn al-Qayyim as "the second master of Islam" (*shaykh al-islām al-thānī*) in conjunction with the first master of Islam (*shaykh al-islām al-awwal*) Ibn Taymiyya.[76] The label "polygraph" is likewise problem-

74 Weiss, Bernard: Ibn Taymiyya on Leadership in the Ritual Prayer, in: Muhammad Khalid Masud, Brinkley Morris Messick, and David Stephan Powers (eds.): *Islamic Legal Interpretation. Muftis and Their Fatwas*, Cambridge, MA, and London 1996, pp. 63–71, here pp. 63–64.

75 Ibn Taymiyya: *A Muslim Theologian's Response to Christianity. Ibn Taymiyya's* al-Jawāb al-ṣaḥīḥ, edited and translated by Thomas F. Michel, Delmar 1984, p. 68.

76 Ibn Qayyim al-Jawziyya, *Aḥkām ahl al-dhimma*, p. 11. Another service by Abū Zayd, *Ibn Qayyim al-Jawziyya*, pp. 129–156, delves into the relationship between Ibn Taymiyya and Ibn al-Qayyim.

atic, inasmuch as it relieves readers of the burden of pondering the question *wes Geistes Kind der Autor ist* and trying to make sense of his writings. That is to say, this label may restrict, from the start, a perspective on a writer's consistence, inner convictions, developing agendas, decisive turns and so forth in favour of a tempting logic of sheer numbers. This is dangerous and misleading, all the more so since in 1979 Bell already identified certain phases of and the influences dominating Ibn al-Qayyim's works, signalling that "the various shifts in stress or disciplinary framework discernible in the writings of Ibn al-Qayyim correspond to fairly distinct periods in his career."[77] Therefore, turning him into a copy of Ibn Taymiyya and perceiving him mainly as his master's voice – an allegation already lodged by his contemporaries – blocks important avenues of research. Though even from the start this allegation of imitation and slavish adherence loomed large on the part of the enemies, Abū Zayd still feels the need to dedicate a section of 17 pages to maintain that "Ibn al-Qayyim is no copy of his master (*laysa nuskha min shaykhihi*) Ibn Taymiyya."[78]

From the beginning and to this day, however, the allegation of mere replication could not be strictly upheld, given Ibn al-Qayyim's scholarly stature and output. As such, we find the similarly widespread and, in fact, complementary narrative of a sort of against-all-odds-creativity. It is pointed out that, at the most, he managed to find a niche for himself while still generally following the path of Ibn Taymiyya: "Ibn Qayyim absorbed all the ideas of his master and took extraordinary pains to revive the popularity of his works but at the same time he carved out a separate identity for himself."[79] In that sense, the "separate identity" conceded to or defended for Ibn al-Qayyim seems to consist primarily of the empty spots that Ibn Taymiyya's sweeping brush left untouched or that the latter took no interest in covering. This identity henceforth appears as scattered individual topics associated with the name of Ibn al-Qayyim and resurfacing in 20th-century Western scholarship on a piecemeal basis, as has been demonstrated, such as the issue of children or prophetic medicine. Despite the importance granted to those works, their status is still minimized by the impression of a second-class originality, in the sense that Ibn al-Qayyim managed to use the energy that was left to him – i.e., not already

77 Bell, *Love Theory*, p. 101.

78 For historical details, see Abū Zayd, *Ibn Qayyim al-Jawziyya*, pp. 139–156.

79 Ahsan, Sayyid: *Life and Thoughts of Muhammad Ibn Abd al-Wahhab*, Aligarh 1988, p. 33.

absorbed by catering immediately to the demands of Ibn Taymiyya and later to the ordering of the latter's legacy of scattered writings – to scratch out a little corner for himself. In view of such perceptions, we deem it no longer sufficient – especially on the part of Ibn al-Qayyim connoisseurs – to join the "yes-he-can" mantra while it remains somehow tainted both by the impression that he was basically spellbound by Ibn Taymiyya and that he was caught in eclecticism of sorts. Bori and Holtzman deplore that Ibn al-Qayyim's "broad literary corpus remains almost unexplored" and diagnose: "Although some of Ibn Qayyim al-Ǧawziyyah's works were recognized as unique and, in some cases, were used as the almost exclusive source for research, Ibn al-Qayyim was almost never credited for them as an independent and substantial thinker." The crux is that his framing as a "diligent pupil of Ibn Taymiyyah (…) implies a lack of originality on Ibn al-Qayyim's part that makes him unworthy of proper scientific research."[80] Yet, is independence really the precondition of originality? What exactly is independence supposed to mean? Relativizing the validity of such a claim by unpacking its historical influences and cultural constructedness, the idea of creative independence will be challenged in the next section. And, if originality proves not to be an absolute criterion, what could be more viable criteria?

4. Challenging Expectations of Ingenuity via Appropriation

In their introduction to *Ibn Taymiyya and His Times*, the editors Yossef Rapoport and Shahab Ahmed assert: "Ibn Taymiyya was, by almost universal consensus, one of the most original and systematic thinkers in the history of Islam."[81] The nearly "universal consensus" they have in mind here is at most a modern, academic one brought about by Sunni revivalism after half a millennium of negligence in Arabic sources.[82] As for the last part of the statement, the systematic character attributed to Ibn Taymiyya has to be relativized, since he usually did not produce structured overviews – even less so in the

80 Bori and Holtzman, Introduction, p. 15.

81 Rapoport and Ahmed, Introduction, p. 19.

82 This has been demonstrated in the same volume; see El-Rouayheb, Changing Views, pp. 270, 311. A study comparable to his is lacking for Ibn al-Qayyim.

realm of jurisprudence[83] – but displayed a series of creative outbursts. Bori stresses that Ibn Taymiyya "did not have a systematic mind", but was "unsystematically explosive both in the quantity and the quality of his works".[84] This is very much in confluence with his typical format because it perfectly fit his mode of performance, for "fatwa literature does not attain the degree of systemization that is found in the great treatises and, as a rule, does not admit of such highly extended argumentation as is found in *uṣūl al-fiqh*-work."[85] The engagement on behalf of Ibn Taymiyya (and his work), above all by Ibn al-Qayyim but also by other followers and admirers, should be regarded as a huge accomplishment in itself: (i) socially, by recognizing and asserting Ibn Taymiyya's importance, i. e. backing someone who was often not acknowledged by the establishment and partaking in his protests; (ii) materially and practically, by identifying, collecting and ordering his scattered notes; (iii) and not least, intellectually, by curiously exploring the breaches made by him, spelling out implications, and developing and systematizing his ideas.[86] Nevertheless, we do not want to pursue these "auxiliary" functions and their merits any further here, because it is not yet the decisive point we finally want to make; in addition, the above argumentation again bears the risk of ending up in the double bind of apologetics. Coming back to the cited axiomatic statement of Rapoport and Ahmed, we are hesitant to endorse even the remaining middle element, namely the claim that Ibn Taymiyya was "one of the most original (…) thinkers in the history of Islam."[87] We do not undertake to flatly deny this assertion of supreme originality, but rather to note the broader intellectual climate in Western literature that reinforces such value judgements.

In an article on Mamluk *belles lettres* and the role of poetry therein, Thomas Bauer argues that it is simple-minded to evaluate this literature *per se*, because one should also consider the historical develop-

83 Krawietz, Transgressive Creativity, pp. 43–49.

84 Bori, Collection, p. 55.

85 Weiss, Ibn Taymiyya on Leadership, p. 64.

86 It must be added that well-versed modern scholars like the Egyptian Muḥammad Abū Zahra (d. 1974) may appreciate Ibn Taymiyya's writings "because they are clear, illustrative and illuminating, never complicating or obscuring things" (*fa-innahā wāḍiḥa mushriqa nayyira lā taʿqīd fīhā wa-lā ibhām*), Abū Zahra, *Ibn Taymiyya. Ḥayātuhu wa-ʿaṣruhu wa-ārāʾuhu wa-fiqhuhu*, Cairo 1952, p. 521. The majority of his readers would not endorse this, but would rather bemoan his utter conciseness – to put it mildly.

87 Rapoport and Ahmed, Introduction, p. 19.

ment of taste and its related predilections and displeasures in Europe.[88] He stresses the specific importance of colonial trajectories and their impact on the perception of Oriental poetry and concludes "that Mamluk Arabic literature is not characterized by stagnation and a lack of innovation but rather by a steady and gradual development". The latter, "however, did not evolve towards the same endpoint as Western literature of the nineteenth and twentieth centuries." Dismissing certain segments of this literature as stagnant primarily has to do with "the lack of developments that mimicked and confirmed Western models."[89] Both features – i. e. steady development and nonconformity with long-prevailing Western models of innovation – very much apply to the case of Ibn al-Qayyim. We suggest, therefore, that the thorough disregard for Ibn al-Qayyim and his persistent portrayal in the Western secondary literature as an epigone is not a coincidence having to do solely with his specific case,[90] but rather may be strongly influenced by the tenacious Romantic notion of the genius and the exaggerated hailing of invention, especially since the era of colonial expansion and industrial capitalism. In the course of the 18th century, originality and "its moral antonym plagiarism"[91] became the cornerstone of debates about artistic genius. Only the invention of the concept of the "original genius" transformed the appropriation of texts – for example in the form of repetition – into a "problem"; in the Baroque period, for instance, exact repetition was taken for granted as an element of the fine arts.[92] The idea of the "original genius" is often dated back to Robert Wood's "Essay on the Original Genius and Writings of Homer",[93] which also strongly influenced conceptions of creativity across Europe.[94] Here,

88 Bauer, Thomas: Mamluk Literature. Misunderstandings and New Approaches, in: *Mamlūk Studies Review* 9 (2005), pp. 105–132, here pp. 105, 108.

89 Bauer, Mamluk Literature, p. 116.

90 Another candidate would be Jalāl al-Dīn al-Suyūṭī (d. 1505).

91 Buelow, George J.: Originality, Genius, Plagiarism in English Criticism of the Eighteenth Century, in: *International Review of the Aesthetics and Sociology of Music* 21 (1990), pp. 117–128, here p. 117.

92 Glasmeier, Michael: "Loop. Zur Geschichte und Theorie der Endlosschleife am Beispiel Rodney Grahams", key note speech, May 5, 2011 in the course of the conference "Wiederaufgelegt. Zur Appropriation von Texten und Büchern in Büchern" (May 5–7, 2011), organized by Annette Gilbert, Peter Szondi-Institute, FU Berlin.

93 Wood, Robert: *An Essay on the Original Genius and Writings of Homer. With a Comparative View of the Ancient and Present State of the Troade*, London 1769.

94 Compare Fredriksson, Martin: The Avant-Gardist, the Male Genius and the Proprietor, in: *Nordlit* 21 (2007), pp. 275–284, here p. 278.

the very same mechanism is of course applied if we take Wood's essay as the founding event.[95] This attitude has long been questioned in arts and music – with DaDa collages and ready-mades to Street Art and digital music – as they are practised, and should likewise be questioned not only in studies of music, literature, and arts but also in such "alien" subjects as Islamic Studies. However, these "alien" fields have hitherto shown a certain predilection for innovators who present themselves with the air of novelty and give the impression that they are not indebted to others – so as to leave other competitors behind.

Although Ibn Taymiyya does not claim *creatio ex nihilo* creativity for himself, he greatly devalues recent and older competitors. He presents himself as being committed to the *salaf ṣāliḥ* as the first three generations of Islam, and this move functionally allows him to brush aside and devalue what so many generations of scholars had gathered. Distancing himself from those closer to his own time in favour of earlier referees thereby enhances his legitimacy. With his *salaf ṣāliḥ* formula, Ibn Taymiyya offered a thorough and effective clean-up program. No wonder, then, that this has become and is regularly used as a powerful tool by "reformed" Muslim scholars and/or activists around the globe, especially when they return to their local communities with the impetus to tidy up the deviations of lived Islam in the name of the holy sources and the knowledgeable early forefathers. The West – of which Oriental and later Islamic Studies in its different variants are part – has for some time fostered and socially rewarded the encouragement and applauding of ostentatious self-posing, the by-passing of traditions or predecessors, and even the ignoring of those who have lent a helping hand, and this has affected reception of such behaviour in Western contexts. Against such a background, a figure like Ibn al-Qayyim, combining some general Muslim notions of a sober habitus, respect towards elders, courtesy, immersion in pious practices, and so forth, appears as the complete antithesis of well-deserved stardom. His status is greatly aggravated by his endless quotations and extraor-

95 For a more thorough account of "when imitation became plagiarism" see Buelow, Originality, and Jaffe, Kineret S.: The Concept of Genius. Its Changing Role in Eighteenth-century French Aesthetics, in: *Journal of the History of Ideas* 41 (1980), pp. 579–599. Compare Brunner, Anette: Der zum Himmel erhobene Blick als Ausdruck enthusiastischen Schöpfertums. Die Darstellung der Invention im Künstlerbildnis der Goethezeit, in: *Paragrana. Internationale Zeitschrift für Historische Anthropologie*, suppl. 2 (2006), pp. 57–72.

dinary personal humility – an attitude that in some modern settings might be perceived as downright pathological. Ibn al-Qayyim would never voice criticism of Ibn Taymiyya even if some occurred to him. It is inadequate on the part of Western Islamic Studies to expect that Ibn al-Qayyim should explicitly distinguish himself via criticism of Ibn Taymiyya in order to signal being his own man. It is also inept to demand this kind of criticism as a starting point from which his scholarly merits can be inferred. It cannot be overlooked that figures like Ibn al-Qayyim are much less appreciated among non-Muslims and that his habitus is taken as an unmistakable sign of inferiority, often triggering contempt. In contrast, Ibn Taymiyya's cocky aggressiveness and air of superiority represent the ultimate alternative model to the devotional piety and intellectual long-windedness of Ibn al-Qayyim. This does not mean that Ibn Taymiyya is highly esteemed everywhere, but he is definitely "respected" – either as a great theologian/scholar/activist or as a powerful, dangerous villain (whose violent "impact" is felt even centuries later). Despite the wide range of congruence in terms of doctrine and methodology shared by the two authors, in recent times Ibn Taymiyya has met modern European-bred Western expectations of ingenuity to a much greater degree; he bears, after all, their "unmistaken" insignia, like self-aggrandizement and cultivation of sudden inspiration. It is a strange coincidence of history that this duo represents such contrasting ends of the scale in matters of habitus and self-presentation. However, apart from the strikingly complementary symbiosis between Ibn Taymiyya and Ibn al-Qayyim, we surmise that there are other phenomena that are relevant to Islamic Studies which likewise emanate from the same overall cultural disposition: we propose, for example, the utter Orientalist/Western fondness for and strange aestheticization of "independent" Islamic jurisprudence (*ijtihād*), the prevalent lamenting rhetoric about the closing of its door and about the evil principle of imitation (*taqlīd*). However, space does not allow us to follow up on this or similar other narratives. Hence, we must finally turn to a constructive reconfiguration of Ibn al-Qayyim's intellectual calibre and propagate an alternative or, rather, complementary model of scholarly ingenuity. The widespread impression of eclecticism can be challenged by suggesting the concept of the appropriation of especially postclassical Arabic writings on theology, jurisprudence and philosophy. While in the field of cultural and social studies, literature studies, or arts the angle has shifted toward a new approach to creativity and originality, an equivalent is still lacking in Islamic Studies.[96] From this perspective, the study of Muslim practices of citation and legitimization offers a deeper understanding of them, especially with regard to changing modes in the era of digital data.[97] We suggest exploring and highlighting this unfolding appropriation, including paths not taken by Ibn al-Qayyim, his creative quoting practices and genre transgression, as well as presenting him as the epitome of appropriation.

4.1. Unfolding Appropriation

Ibn al-Qayyim's outward conformity with and praise of Ibn Taymiyya should not be taken as a blanket compliance with all the latter's opinions, insofar as he is extremely picky about which of his master's ideas he actively takes up, pursues and propagates. Where he is not enthusiastic about the latter's topics, arrangements and pitches, he simply does not mention them: he sees no need to openly criticise. The paths Ibn al-Qayyim did not take in relation to Ibn Taymiyya's writings, however, have not hitherto been systematically explored; they are, at most, alluded to. Therefore, instead of watching for Ibn al-Qayyim to explicitly distance himself from Ibn Taymiyya, we surmise that interpreters should pay more attention to his silent omissions, slight variants and quotations from Ibn Taymiyya that quite often disclose a slightly shifted meaning by way of translocation and a specific combination with other authors. A diligent context-sensitive comparison of their writings allows the reader to discern the emergence of subtle divergent drafts of this kind.[98] On the other end of the scale, Ibn al-Qayyim grossly adopts "alien" elements and incorporates large quantities, if

96 For an overview, see Aigner, Anita: Einleitung. Von 'architektonischer Moderne' zu 'Architektur in der Moderne'. Kulturelle Grenzüberschreitungen, in: idem (ed.): *Vernakulare Moderne. Grenzüberschreitungen in der Architektur um 1900. Das Bauernhaus und seine Aneignung*, Bielefeld 2010, pp. 7–35, here especially pp. 11–13.

97 Carmen Bauer has shown the proximity of digital techniques, like threads in online forums, and Muslim practices of argumentation: Zurück zum Quellcode. Salafistische Wissenspraktiken im Internet, in: *inamo* 57 (2009), pp. 37–42, here p. 39.

98 Compare Frenkel, Yehoshua: Islamic Utopia under the Mamluks. The Social and Legal Ideals of Ibn Qayyim al-Ǧawziyyah, in: Bori and Holtzmann, *Scholar in the Shadow*, pp. 67–87, here p. 81, with regard to cemetery rituals, and especially the chapter by Hoover in the present volume.

not huge building blocks, of more or less direct quotations. Appropriation is the central rubric under which we look at the immense scale of discernable processes.

We understand appropriation as a set of practices that – consciously or unconsciously – occupy meaning. An object, figure, sign, formulation, topic, narrative, style and so forth is turned into something that, within the logic of the personal life practice, is "made one's own (*proprius*)" and by this "appropriate". This is beyond any notion of "copy and paste" or of mere repetition or imitation. Thilo Schwer distinguishes three different types varying in the degree of appropriation and creativity: (i) small "seemingly obstinate" gestures of identification with the object, (ii) individual combination and "recoding", and (iii) encompassing modifications, after which the original object cannot be recognized anymore.[99] "Recoding" in particular has the power to question hierarchies of appropriate and inappropriate, "high" and "low", "orthodox" and "heterodox". So what is being appropriated in our case of the two Shaykhs of Islam? There are, for instance, (i) concepts, styles, arguments, terms, (ii) biographies and historical figures, (iii) narratives, (iv) practices, and (v) material, like manuscripts. Ibn Taymiyya appropriates Greek philosophers' writings; Ibn al-Qayyim appropriates the writings of Ibn Taymiyya, but not necessarily his style; Muslim authors and activists appropriate both of them in order to underline their Salafi or Wahhabi claims and a myriad of detectable facets. Translation and thereby transformation of meaning is another issue pertinent to this broad set of possibilities.[100] While the ideas of intertextuality in a Kristevan sense are the basis of our understanding, this approach must be extended to include a notion of the subject/agent, thereby tracing practices rather

99 Schwer, Thilo: Persönliche Aneignung versus kommerzielle Verwertung im Möbeldesign, in: Birgit Richard and Alexander Ruhl (eds.): *Konsumguerilla. Widerstand gegen Massenkultur?*, Frankfurt and New York 2008, pp. 55–68, here p. 55. Referring to A. I. Sabra and others, Tzvi Langermann depicts appropriation as the first phase within a process that leads to a "naturalization" of science (The Naturalization of Science in Ibn Qayyim al-Ǧawziyyah's *Kitāb al-Rūḥ*, in: Bori and Holtzman, *A Scholar in the Shadow*, pp. 211–228, here p. 211). We, however, work with a much broader and complex understanding of appropriation pertinent to art history, anthropology and others fields that avoids the expression naturalization.

100 See especially the chapters of Arif, Böttcher, Özervarli, Preckel and Riexinger in this volume, although the findings of Translation Studies have not yet been applied in research on Ibn Taymiyya and Ibn Qayyim al-Jawziyya.

than merely analysing results.[101] To understand current appropriation of works of Ibn Taymiyya and Ibn al-Qayyim in, for example, Malaysia and Indonesia, the tool of intertextuality is not sufficient; an intertextual approach requires transparency in order to even perceive, much less analyze the different layers of influence and references. This is not possible with the "invisible" editors who produce the pamphlets that are sold on street corners.

4.2. Quotation and Compiling

To start, the religio-legal literature of the so-called Koranic sciences is full of quotations from the holy sources of Koran and Hadith. In varying quantities, but especially by Ḥanbalī scholars, such quotations are constantly interpolated in the course of an oral or written production and presentation of sense. A particularly striking example is the legal sub-genre of Fatwa literature, whose condensed line of argumentation is often structured and fed according to the hierarchy of the sources of jurisprudence the author acknowledges. In order to constantly explore and expand the realm of pious knowledge, various techniques of quoting and compiling are applied. While it is true that Ibn al-Qayyim quoted Ibn Taymiyya excessively, scholarly attention has not focused enough on the plethora of other authors he cites or employs.[102] He himself had assembled an impressive number of manuscripts from various disciplines in his library, and the implications of this possession and passion have not yet been explored in detail. At any rate, in those times "the concept of authorship and 'copy-right' was quite different from our understanding" and Ibn al-Qayyim is definitely a "great recycler" of the work of others and – to a great degree – also of himself.[103] This feature of multiple and even lengthy quotations has led Holtzman to label Ibn al-Qayyim as a "mimetic"

101 For example, Holthuis endeavours to assemble prototypes of the different manifestations of intertextual relations between literary texts in the sense of a taxonomy; Holthuis, Susanne: *Intertextualität. Aspekte einer rezeptionsorientierten Konzeption*, Tübingen 1993, pp. v, 34.

102 Ibn Ḥazm is but one example. Holtzman scrutinizes Ibn al-Qayyim's reading of Fakhr al-Dīn al-Rāzī in this edited volume. On Samau'al al-Maghribi see our n. 21.

103 Krawietz, Ibn Qayyim al-Jawzīyah, p. 62.

writer.[104] Yet, using all sorts of manuscripts as a huge repository was in accordance with the conventions of the time and did not detract from his scholarly status. One cannot imagine his contemporary, expert readers taking such blended, compiled works as mere copies; they, too, were used to such additions and most probably were quite sensitive to reading between the lines and paying close attention to nuances. They could not have expected him to state his viewpoint bluntly from the beginning. We need to know more whether, to what degree, and how the process of "merely" copying manuscripts was distinguished from rearranging them and fusing additions to them – in this case, we must know exactly how work was organized and distributed in the studio of Ibn al-Qayyim (and other scholars). Modern electronic devices now allow for a much more diligent deciphering of such processes – a fact that may greatly enhance research on this author and lead to a refined appreciation of his imaginative composing skills.

4.3. Genre-Transgression and Transformation

The topical systematization of Hadith compendia provided convenient corridors for the development and differentiation of new genres. The constitution of new genres and sub-genres has been and still is an ongoing process of Islamic – or Islamicate – writings. However, along with the Western idea of the original genius came the demand to follow a "pure" style adhering to a certain genre. Congruently, many people have low regard for cultural techniques such as pastiche, collage, and montage, inasmuch as they are the outcome of a "polluting" mixing of objects from distinct categories. The act of selecting, discarding, compiling and contextualizing does not count as the outcome of a creative mind but as a "service". Hence, as has been shown, Ibn al-Qayyim is portrayed as a service provider on behalf of his master. Yet, such techniques are the very basis of pious Islamic writings within the frame of Koranic sciences proper and even beyond. As a postclassical scholar with a personal inability or unwillingness to be concise, Ibn al-Qayyim produced a considerable number of highly complex and compact works that often do not fit into one genre alone. His later huge compendia, especially, embody an ongoing process of synthesizing different elements in multiple variations and rearrangements.

104 Holtzman, Ibn Qayyim al-Jawziyyah, p. 205 et passim.

Thereby, he often transgresses familiar boundaries and genre-categories and deliberately blurs and possibly even constitutes or co-develops new genres.[105] In an article in 2006, Krawietz attempts to subsume Ibn al-Qayyim's oeuvre under genre-headings, only to ultimately find that his contributions cannot be deciphered and evaluated within a corset of clear-cut genre-categories.[106] His fusing creativity, increasing manoeuvres of criss-crossing, redirecting, compiling, and "reframing" are perhaps a much truer expression of his scholarly merits than anything else that has hitherto been discussed in this introductory chapter. Frenkel has pointed out that such techniques of Ibn al-Qayyim's work are detached from predictable topic-genre correlations, since "there is no clear evidence that he preferred particular genres for specific themes; rather, he addressed the same topic in several works, regularly manipulating this line of reasoning in order to serve his aim."[107] It is therefore important to keep in mind that genres should be conceptualized as dynamic entities with a heterogeneous internal structure.[108] We are confronted with texts that, on the surface, are reproductive and try to deny their subjectivity, although they constantly and in a rather subversive manner produce new significance.[109] It must be added that our Ḥanbalī author seems to derive intense spiritual blessing from this type of creative textual journeying. Frenkel has emphasized: "Through the extensive use of Hadith quotations and citations from earlier scholars, Ibn Qayyim al-Ǧawziyyah virtually obliterated the boundaries of time and space, creating connections between remote eras and areas."[110] In this sense, writing – or more precisely rewriting, which entails a process of detecting new dimensions by which the divine guidance, through innumerable perspectives, holds the world together – provides him and

105 Perho, *The Prophets's Medicine*.

106 Krawietz, Ibn Qayyim al-Jawzīyah, p. 62 et passim. Krawietz, Transgressive Creativity, analyses the degree to which his *Iʿlām al-muwaqqiʿīn* oscillates between the format of an *adab al-muftī* treatise and an *uṣul al-fiqh* manual. Various later writings of his are much more genre-transgressive than this early example.

107 Frenkel, Islamic Utopia, p. 70.

108 Zymner, Rüdiger: Gattungen aus literaturwissenschaftlicher Sicht, in: Stephan Conermann (ed.): *Was sind Genres? Nicht-abendländische Kategorisierungen von Gattungen*, Berlin 2011, pp. 7–21, here p. 18.

109 Conermann, Stephan and El Hawary, Amr: Ausklang. Das Problem der Gattungsbestimmung in transkultureller Perspektive, in: Conerman, *Was sind Genres?*, pp. 316–324, here p. 322.

110 Frenkel, Islamic Utopia, p. 86.

his pious readers with ongoing enchantment. The aesthetics of "repetition" and constant divine realization powerfully evoke his increasing Sufi leanings. It requires further research to analyse the degree to which a pattern of transgression prevails in his oeuvre or whether one should argue with, for example, de Certeau, that Ibn al-Qayyim had no space of his own so that the only remaining possibility was, "sich innerhalb einer vorgegebenen Struktur einzunisten."[111]

5. Master of Appropriation

An oeuvre of such vast dimensions could have been produced only by fusion on a large scale, especially since Ibn al-Qayyim emerged as "author" relatively late in his life. He is such a great recycler that any of his contributions can be expected to show up in more or less transformed shape somewhere else in his writings. Ibn al-Qayyim's wide reading, erudition, intellectual landscape and capacity to combine and blend are extraordinarily consistent, even daring. There is no scope in this chapter, unfortunately, to determine either the pattern of selected topics and overall concerns he recycles and appropriates or how they evolve during his lifetime.

A last shift in perspective is due. We do not deem it incidental that the publications of Ibn al-Qayyim on the Arabic book market have witnessed such a tremendous surge. The Ibn al-Qayyim available in printed edited versions at the turn to the 20th century can hardly be compared to the omnipresent figure at the turn to the 21st century; that is to say, the gradual evolution of this phenomenon with its multiple or revised editions, short versions etc. can provide telling insights into the patterns of audience interests. Concerning the reconstruction of his oeuvre and its authentic shape, today's editions not only make Ibn al-Qayyim's works much more accessible than the dispersed manuscripts of previous times, allowing for helpful insights; they simultaneously and contrariwise increase the already existing obscurity and disorder.[112] On the other hand, his oeuvre is used as a kaleidoscopic repository by an increasing number of readers, with few or no scholarly credentials, from a broader range of social strata, who nevertheless project their agendas onto his work and infuse his agendas, likewise,

111 De Certeau, *Kunst des Handelns*, p. 92.
112 Krawietz, Ibn Qayyim al-Jawzīyah, p. 63.

into theirs. Since the voluminous compendia seem to be too overwhelming for casual readers, the modern book market offers all sorts of single chapters, piecemeal selections, shortened versions or anthologies with other authors. While such editors often hail themselves for the service done to religious knowledge, for the most part readers – and not only the average ones – become all the more confused. Not infrequently, a 20th century or (post)modern consumer even combines his own musings or his leftover university manuals with quotations from Ibn al-Qayyim; as a consequence, a rising flood of publications claiming Ibn al-Qayyim as the author, including many paperbacks, is pouring forth. Accordingly, the authenticity of the contents of the shorter publications, in particular – but also of several larger synthetic works – must be thoroughly tested. At times, these pious self-appointed editors dress up their medleys with fancy titles deliberately reminiscent of famous, authentic titles of Ibn al-Qayyim's or someone else's real oeuvre. Ardent readers often seek a profound elevation of spirit. Religiosity flourishes and sells – especially if not protected by copy-right regulations. Ibn al-Qayyim is an extreme example of a premodern Arabic scholar being dismembered, in terms of scholarly corpus, into the minutest entities imaginable then reconstructed in multiple ways. Perhaps one should not join in the bashing of "Salafi primitivists"[113] but acknowledge – from a scientific point of view – that such maneuvers can raise awareness of the highly structured nature of Ibn al-Qayyim's work, which still itself displays many seams of composition and integration. "Ibn al-Qayyim lite" is available everywhere and has entered the rhetoric of many contemporary Muslim authors, such as Yūsuf al-Qaraḍāwī (himself a great recycler or, better, appropriator). Such processes of nostrification led to a completely different breadth of effect in the Muslim audience which in turn reacts with enhanced or modified structures of needs and desires. On the Internet, Ibn al-Qayyim may still not generate more hits than Ibn Taymiyya, especially due to political polemics, but the contexts in which – one meanwhile hesitates to say – his "teachings" are employed are tremendously variegated and diverse. Ibn Qayyim al-Jawziyya has in almost no way been "the first man on the moon", but we suggest depicting him as the master of appropriation.

***

113 We take this expression from Christopher Melchert in the present volume.

Apart from what they themselves understand as their own scholarly merits, the ensuing contributions from an international committee of authors demonstrate considerably different dimensions of these processes of appropriation – from most subtle variations to considerable changes of function. Authors have been grouped to highlight thematic and disciplinary links. We aim to attain a differentiated perspective by further elucidating, by means of these chapters, the concept of appropriation. Part one comprises contributions to theology, more specifically to the role of human agency: Sait Özervarli compares "Divine Wisdom, Human Agency and the *fiṭra* in Ibn Taymiyya's Thought", a key topic in this genre; in "Debating the Doctrine of *jabr* (Compulsion): Ibn Qayyim al-Jawziyya Reads Fakhr al-Dīn al-Rāzī", Livnat Holtzman traces one of the important sources of Ibn al-Qayyim; Gino Schallenbergh's "Ibn Qayyim al-Jawziyya's Manipulation of Sufi Terms: Fear and Hope", demonstrates *inter alia* how the classical theological problem of free will versus predestination is (directly or indirectly) likewise addressed in the subgenre of Sufi writings on the mystical path. Part three is dedicated to "Ibn Taymiyya and Philosophy". In "The Poison of Philosophy: Ibn Taymiya's Struggle For and Against Reason", Anke von Kügelgen analyzes the ways in which Ibn Taymiyya appropriated Greek philosophy and the thinking and/or methodology of its Muslim heirs, debating whether his strategy is compatible with his outspoken vendetta against philosophy. With "The Curse of Philosophy: Ibn Taymiyya as a Philosopher in Contemporary Islamic Thought", Georges Tamer has written a complementary article that deals with Ibn Taymiyya's perception in modern times and ultimately speculates whether or not Ibn Taymiyya should be portrayed as a philosopher or as a theologian. The other three parts do not focus on mainly one genre, but traverse variant fields and vast spacial and temporal distances: part two, on the "Career of Books" (while the term 'book' has to be understood for the earlier periods as monograph), ranges from our Ḥanbalī authors' century to later ones up to the beginning of the 21st. Geographically, it travels from 14th century Damascus to the Indian subcontinent and to contemporary Indonesia. In "The Relation of Ibn al-Qayyim's *Kitāb al-Rūḥ*: Some Literary Aspects", Tzvi Langerman provides insight into his ongoing research on a specific book of Ibn al-Qayyim, which is perhaps the monograph with the most sympathetic reception in non-partisan, wider Sunni circles. Christopher Melchert, in "Ibn Taymiyya and Ibn Qayyim al-Jawziyya to the Ḥanbalī School of Law", measures quoting patterns by other Ḥanbalī authors and thus tests the significance of both authors, examining why Ibn al-Qayyim made an even lesser impact than Ibn Taymiyya. The contribution by Syamsuddin Arif entitled "Ibn Qayyim al-Jawziyya in the 'Lands Below the Wind': An Ideological Father of Radicalism or a Popular Sufi Master?" deals with translations into other 'Oriental' languages, since Indonesia is the demographically largest Muslim country in the world and Indonesian translations from the Arabic also have a great impact on the religious landscape in neighboring Malaysia. In "Screening Ṣiddīq Ḥasan Khān's Library: The Use of Ḥanbalī Literature in 19th-Century Bhopal", Claudia Preckel turns to Ḥanbalī influences on the Indian Ahl-i Ḥadīth-movement; she depicts the collection, translation and overall appropriation activities of the spouse of the third female ruler of the North Indian Local Dynasty of Bophal as a decisive agent in that process. Part five examines appropriations "Outside the Arab World": Martin Riexinger highlights "Ibn Taymiyya's Worldview and the Challenge of Modernity: A Conflict Among the Ahl-i Ḥadīth in British India", while Annabelle Böttcher, in her contribution entitled "Ibn Taymiyya and Ibn Qayyim al-Jawziyya as Changing Salafi Icons", considers contemporary Germany. Part four, "Inclusion and Exclusion in Islamic Theology and Law", assembles articles on either law or theology under the shared rhetoric of punishing deviance as well as the "us *versus* them" mentality with which both Ḥanbalī authors are so persistently associated: Abdessamad Belhaj presents "Law and Order According to Ibn Taymiyya and Ibn Qayyim al-Jawziyya: A Re-Examination of *siyāsa sharʿiyya*"; Dominik Schlosser elaborates on "Ibn Qayyim al-Jawziyya's Attitude Toward Christianity in *Hidāyat al-ḥayārā fī ajwibat al-yahūd wal-naṣārā*", while Jon Hoover speaks out "Against Islamic Universalism: ʿAlī al-Ḥarbī's 1990 Attempt to Prove that Ibn Taymiyya and Ibn Qayyim al-Jawziyya Affirm the Eternity of Hell-Fire". Needless to mention, the current arrangement could easily have been shaped otherwise.

Section 1: Human Agency

Divine Wisdom, Human Agency and the *fiṭra* in Ibn Taymiyya's Thought

M. Sait Özervarli

Ibn Taymiyya, although a follower of the traditionalist path of *aṣḥāb al-ḥadīth* in theology and of the Ḥanbalī School in jurisprudence, was generally an independent-minded thinker with a critical approach to other views and did not follow his predecessors blindly. Unlike earlier traditionalist scholars, he sought to present an alternative theology based on the Koran and the Sunna, while engaging with the discourse of philosophical theology. His focus on philosophical debates led him to a deeper rationalistic approach despite his traditionalist background and a confrontational stance on intellectual issues and figures. The large number and variety of his students also show that people of different backgrounds had confidence in his scholarship. Among his students were Shāfiʿīs, like al-Dhahabī and Ibn Kathīr; the Sufi ʿImād al-Dīn al-Wāsiṭī; moderate Ḥanbalīs, like Ibn Mufliḥ or al-Ṭūfī; and many others.

Ibn Rajab (d. 795/1393), the leading Ḥanbalī biographer, underscores that although the traditionalist groups greatly respected Ibn Taymiyya, they were not happy with his debates with theologians and philosophers or his indulgence in discussing their issues. He points out that a number of Ibn Taymiyya's contemporary Ḥanbalī scholars did not approve of and tried even to prevent him from some of his views, which they regarded as contradicting the main position of the school.[1] Especially his legal decisions demonstrate his self-determination in expressing his own views no matter how different from previous ones. In an essay based on three interesting fatwas of Ibn Taymiyya, Benjamin Jokisch displays persuasively how the scholar reached new conclusions by employing different analogies and referring to some partial consensuses.[2] In previ-

1 Ibn Rajab, Zayn al-Dīn ʿAbd al-Raḥmān b. Aḥmad: *Dhayl ʿalā ṭabaqāt al-ḥanābila,* Beirut n. d., vol. 2, pp. 393–394.

2 Jokisch, Benjamin: *Ijtihad* in Ibn Taymiyya's *Fatāwā*, in: Robert Gleave and Eugenia Kermeli (eds.): *Islamic Law. Theory and Practice*, London and New

ous works of mine I gave examples of Ibn Taymiyya's critical approach in theology, on issues such as arguments for the existence of God, Divine Will and human responsibility, causality etc.[3] In this chapter I will highlight Ibn Taymiyya's focus on the extent of divine wisdom in creation and its relationship to human free will and agency in connection with human nature (*fiṭra*). Moreover, I will identify the place of the love of God, which in his thought provides a more profound acknowledgement of divine wisdom than rational argumentations do.

1. God's Wisdom and Human Capacity

An important point of emphasis by Ibn Taymiyya regarding God's relationship with the universe and human beings is the issue of wisdom (*ḥikma*) in divine actions. All Muslim theologians accepted that the actions of God were purposeful and meaningful and that they did not happen accidentally or for no reason. Not all of them, however, viewed the existence of causes and aims for God's actions: the Ashʿarīs in particular, unlike the Muʿtazilīs, argued that causes would limit the supremacy and authority of God and would mean dependency on those causes. According to the Ashʿarīs nothing should imply any kind of underestimation of God's omnipotence or impose upon Him a necessity to perform an action. They put more emphasis on His power and considered that a possible correlation may lead to a sort of limitation of divine infinity. God's power could not be limited or surpassed, in the Ashʿarī approach, for the sake of wisdom. Causation may explain His wisdom in understanding various divine actions in a better way, but it would generate a direct or indirect dependency on that specific cause for God. God may be seen as needing that cause in

York 1997, pp. 119–137 and Jokisch, Bejamin: *Islamisches Recht in Theorie und Praxis. Analyse einiger kaufrechtlicher Fatwas von Taqī 'd-Dīn Aḥmad b. Taymiyya*, Berlin 1996. For a long list of Ibn Taymiyya's distinctive fatwas, see Ibn Rajab, *Dhayl ʿalā ṭabaqāt al-ḥanābila*, vol. 2, pp. 404–405, and al-Karmī, Marʿī b. Yūsuf: *al-Kawākib al-durriyya fī manāqib al-mujtahid Ibn Taymiyya*, edited by Najm ʿAbd al-Raḥmān Khalaf, Beirut 1986, pp. 141–145.

3 Özervarlı, M. Sait: *İbn Teymiyye'nin Düşünce Metodolojisi ve Kelamcılara Eleştirisi*, Istanbul 2008, pp. 118–161; idem: The Qurʾānic Rational Theology of Ibn Taymiyya and His Criticism of the *Mutakallimūn*, in: Yossef Rapoport and Shahab Ahmed (eds.): *Ibn Taymiyya and His Times*, Karachi 2010, pp. 78–100. See also Hoover, Jon: *Ibn Taymiyya's Theodicy of Perpetual Optimism*, Leiden and Boston 2007.

order to act, or as being incomplete without the cause. Moreover, the Ashʿarīs assume that the view of causation in divine actions would also turn the act of creation into a rotation within a vicious circle without end.[4] The Muʿtazilīs, however, see this cautious approach as unnecessary and worry that such arguments would leave God's actions aimless with no explanation. For them causation does not bring any limitation to God's attributes, provided that the causes are not necessary.[5]

In January 1315, Ibn Taymiyya was asked whether God considers any cause or purpose in His creation and, if so, whether the cause would become pre-eternal or not; or, if not, whether this means He is occupied with absurdity. These conditions highlight the complex, multifaceted nature of the issue. Ibn Taymiyya explains his position, taking a middle way between the positions of the Ashʿarīs and Muʿtazilīs.[6]

In his response, Ibn Taymiyya points out the comprehensive character of the issue since it is related to divine actions, attributes, names, and principles, and reminds us that it has become one of the most debated topics. Following a summary of the views of various schools, Ibn Taymiyya criticizes both philosophers and theologians for using the wrong or deficient arguments. In his view, acknowledging causes and aims in God's actions results neither in the pre-eternity of the cause, nor in the limitation of His authority. Because God's actions are related to the universe and the created beings, therefore their causes can only be created. The pre-eternity of such causes is not imaginable for Ibn Taymiyya, since they are generated and employed through God's will. If the causes had an eternal nature, there would not be any origination or creation in the physical existence.[7]

---

4 For the Ashʿarī view of divine wisdom, see al-Bāqillānī, Abū Bakr: *Tamhīd al-awāʾil wa-talkhīṣ al-dalāʾil*, edited by ʿImād al-Dīn Aḥmad Ḥaydar, Beirut 1987, pp. 50–52; al-Rāzī, Fakhr al-Dīn: *Kitāb al-Arbaʿīn fī uṣūl al-dīn*, edited by Aḥmad Ḥijāzī al-Saqqā, Cairo 1986, vol. 1, pp. 350–354; al-Taftazānī, Saʿd al-Dīn: *Sharḥ al-Maqāṣid*, edited by ʿAbd al-Raḥmān ʿUmayra, Beirut 1989, vol. 4, pp. 301–302.

5 For the Muʿtazilī view, see Ibn Mattawayh, Abū Muḥammad Ḥasan b. Aḥmad: *al-Majmūʿ fī al-Muḥīṭ bil-taklīf*, edited by Jean Joseph Houben and Daniel Gimaret, Beirut 1986, vol. 2, pp. 179–180.

6 Ibn Taymiyya, Taqī al-Dīn: *Majmūʿat al-Rasāʾil wal-masāʾil*, edited by Muḥammad Rashīd Riḍā, Beirut 1983, vol. 5, p. 285; Ibn Taymiyya, Taqī al-Dīn: *Majmūʿ Fatāwā*, edited by ʿAbd al-Raḥmān b. Muḥammad b. Qāsim al-ʿĀṣimī al-Najdī, Riyadh 1991, vol. 8, p. 81.

7 Ibn Taymiyya, *Majmūʿat al-Rasāʾil wal-masāʾil*, vol. 5, pp. 286–290; Ibn Taymiyya, *Majmūʿ Fatāwā*, vol. 8, pp. 82–85, 377–381.

The Muʿtazilīs overlooked the omnipotence of God in order to prove His justice, and the Ashʿarīs ignored justice in order to demonstrate His omnipotence, and therefore, Ibn Taymiyya argued, both schools failed to present a complete picture of divinity, since both qualities need to be equally underlined. In his view, since all His actions wisely and purposefully take place of His free will, He cannot be determinedly in need of purposes or become perfected by them. If He were considered to be in need of purposes, then he would also be regarded as being in need of attributes, which is pointless. The purposes are parts of actions, and mutually brought into being by God without any preceding source. Therefore, there is no obstacle to the existence of causes, motives, or purposes in His actions.[8] Moreover, he says, if there is no other argument, God's infinite knowledge would be enough to prevent aimless acts by Him. The idea of an aimless creation would be against the divine essence and qualities.[9]

It is clear that Ibn Taymiyya held a more rational approach to divine actions than other Sunni theologians and particularly the Ashʿarīs. As Fazlur Rahman pointed out:

> Ibn Taymiyya reinstates into Muslim theology the doctrine of the purposiveness of the Divine behaviour, a doctrine so strenuously denied by Ashʿarism, Maturidism, and Zahirism as compromising the omnipotence of God's will and His dissimilarity to His creation. This purposiveness is God's involvement in the destiny of man and from this he directly deduces the idea of God as the Commander or the Sharīʿa-Giver. He next strives to distinguish the planes at which the Will and Wisdom of God are respectively meaningful.[10]

Furthermore Ibn Taymiyya does not see a real problem with divine wisdom in apparently evil situations in nature or human life. A lack of comprehension of the hidden purposes behind evil should not affect a broad approach regarding divine wisdom. We cannot deny our definite knowledge about many purposeful actions in the universe because of some cases, certain details of which may have not been discovered. If the being of a thing is more important than the partial harms it causes,

---

8 Ibn Taymiyya, Taqī al-Dīn: *Minhāj al-sunna al-nabawiyya fī naqḍ kalām al-shīʿa wal-qadariyya*, edited by Muḥammad Rashād Sālim, Cairo 1989, vol. 1, pp. 145–147; Ibn Taymiyya, *Majmūʿat al-Rasāʾil*, vol. 5, p. 337; Ibn Taymiyya, *Majmūʿ Fatāwā*, vol. 8, p. 146.

9 Ibn Taymiyya, Taqī al-Dīn: *Kitāb al-Nubuwwāt*, Beirut 1985, pp. 258–259 and 271–274.

10 Rahman, Fazlur: *Islam*, Chicago 1979, pp. 113–114.

he argues, it would not be acceptable to reject it by highlighting its harmfulness. As he wrote:

> We know that God is All-Wise and everything He does and everything He commands. Our lack of knowledge in the wisdom of some particulars does not undermine what we know of Him from His being All-Wise. We do not reject what we do not know regarding the details of His Wisdom out of what we know from His Wisdom. [For example] We know that whoever knows the knowledge of the expertise of mathematicians, physicians, and grammarians, while not possessing their qualities which make them deserving to be called mathematicians, physicians, and grammarians, this will not undermine what they say because of a lacking in one's knowledge of its perspective. Therefore, the servants of God are more distant from having knowledge about God and about His Wisdom in His creation than what common people have of knowledge about mathematics, medicine and grammar.[11]

He declares that those who oppose divine wisdom are in contradiction with many verses of the Koran (21:17), (23:115), (75:36), and so on.[12]

In all creatures, even in harmful beings and painful situations, Ibn Taymiyya finds wise aspects, and he responds to arguments regarding the existence of absolute evils and their effects on innocents. According to Ibn Taymiyya, the extent of divine blessings minimizes all kind of evil appearances, because humans are not able to see all the facets of created beings. He considers the evilness of those apparently wicked existents, therefore, as "relative" due to their role in the universal being and the ultimate goodness of creation.[13]

Likewise in Ibn Taymiyya's view, divine wisdom also requires humans to be real owners of their actions despite their being created by God. In classical Muslim theological texts, human actions are discussed in a separate section titled *khalq afʿāl al-ʿibād* that refers to various theories. While the Muʿtazilīs attribute actions fully to men and the Jabrīs to God, the Ashʿarīs and Māturīdīs accept the role of both in human actions. The Ashʿarīs in their acquisition (*kasb*) theory, for instance, argue that human actions are created by God and only acquired by humans through a power offered to them just at the time of action. Therefore, in their theory humans are not the real owners

11 Ibn Taymiyya, *Majmūʿ Fatāwā*, vol. 6, p. 128.
12 Ibn Taymiyya, *Majmūʿ Fatāwā*, vol. 16, pp. 297–299.
13 Ibn Taymiyya, *Majmūʿ Fatāwā*, vol. 14, pp. 300–318; Ibn Taymiyya, *Majmūʿat al-Rasāʾil wal-masāʾil*, vol. 5, pp. 319–320.

of their actions but only the acquirers of them.[14] The Māturīdīs have a similar approach by suggesting that actions have different aspects (sg. *jiha*), some of which are connected to God's creation and the others to humans' acquisition. Thus, both schools try to propose an alternative view to the absolutist interpretations regarding human agency or predestination.[15]

Addressing mostly the Ashʿarīs, Ibn Taymiyya criticizes the acquisition theory of Sunni theologians and blames it for being quite similar to the Jabrī position, which denies the role of humans in their actions. According to Ibn Taymiyya, although human actions are a part of God's creation, individuals are the genuine agents of their deeds. In other words, God is the ultimate Creator by providing circumstances and offering the power of action; individuals, however, are uniquely responsible for owning the actions by acting freely through their will.[16] But Ibn Taymiyya does not regard the acquisition theory as being sufficient to explain human free will and full responsibility. The theory is both ambiguous and incoherent in opposing rival theories by other schools. Therefore, he says, Muslim scholars regarded three theories, namely Naẓẓām's (d. between 220–230/835–844) "leap" (*ṭafra*), Abū Hāshim al-Jubbāʾī's (d. 320/933) "modes" (*aḥwāl*), and al-Ashʿarī's (d. 324/935) "acquisition" (*kasb*) as the least comprehensible and most peculiar theories in the history of Muslim thought.[17]

Trying to find solutions to the problem, Ibn Taymiyya describes two aspects of divine will. One of them is the creative predestined will, which plans major events in the universe (*al-irāda al-qadariyya al-kawniyya*), and the other the religious moral will, which guides daily

14 For the theory of acquisition see Swartz, Merlin: Acquisition (kasb) in Early Kalām, in: Samuel Miklos Stern, Albert Hourani and Vivian Brown (eds.): *Islamic Philosophy and the Classical Tradition,* Columbia 1972, pp. 355–387; Abrahamov, Binyamin: A Re-examination of al-Ashʿari's Theory of *Kasb* according to *Kitāb al-Lumaʿ*, in: *Journal of the Royal Asiatic Society* 1–2 (1989), pp. 210–221.

15 On details of the Ashʿarī and Māturīdī positions, see al-Ashʿarī, Abū al-Ḥasan: *Kitāb al-Lumaʿ fī al-radd ʿalā ahl al-zaygh wal-bidaʿ*, edited by ʿAbd al-Azīz ʿIzz al-Dīn al-Sayrawān, Beirut 1987, pp. 116–123; al-Māturīdī, Abū Manṣūr: *Kitāb al-Tawḥīd*, edited by Bekir Topaloğlu and Muhammed Aruçi, Ankara 2003, pp. 357–410.

16 Ibn Taymiyya, *Minhāj al-sunna*, vol. 2, pp. 294–302, vol. 3, pp. 13–14, 145–146; Ibn Taymiyya, Taqī al-Dīn: *Darʾ taʿāruḍ al-ʿaql wal-naql*, edited by Muḥammad Rashād Sālim, Riyadh 1979–1983, vol. 1, pp. 81–86.

17 Ibn Taymiyya, *Kitāb al-Nubuwwāt*, pp. 199 and 206; Ibn Taymiyya, *Majmūʿ Fatāwā*, vol. 8, p. 467.

activities of humans (*al-irāda al-dīniyya al-amriyya*). There is a difference between these two aspects of divine will, due to the involvement of human responsibility in the latter one.[18] He therefore criticizes the Ashʿarīs for not paying attention to this crucial difference and for tending toward determination in human actions, almost like the Jabrīs. The Ashʿarī view, he argues, does not propose any proper role for human beings in producing actions at some point in their life.[19]

However, Ibn Taymiyya thinks, that it would be impossible to practice any religious obligation without freedom of action or a free will to act. If human will was not vital in the occurrence of actions, God would not ask individuals to perform according to their capacity, and no difference would be seen between moral and immoral people.[20] Defining the actions as acquisitions of humans, Ibn Taymiyya emphasizes, would limit the power and capacity of humans and would not offer any reason to distinguish between acquiring and doing an action.[21] The ambiguity of the Ashʿarīs about such a difference implies a kind of inclination toward determination in human actions. Moreover, he says, it gives individuals only a symbolic role in their activities, as a result of lacking sufficient authority in their decisions.[22]

With this eclectic approach, Ibn Taymiyya accepts humans' ownership of their actions without denying God's eventual creation and without falling into complex theories, such as of the theory of acquisition. For instance, while he refers to God's creation, he also describes humans as originators (*muḥdith*) of their actions, a term that Sunni theologians often avoided using. The Koran, he says, refers in many verses to various actions directly attributed to humans, and the Muslim community has no doubt about their being the real – not the metaphoric – doers of their actions.[23] Therefore, in Ibn Taymiyya's theory, humans are naturally free in their acts, for God does not force them to do things. Even if they are constrained by other individuals or groups, humans are essentially qualified with free will and under normal cir-

18 Ibn Taymiyya, Taqī al-Dīn: *Majmūʿat al-Rasāʾil al-kubrā*, Cairo 1323/1905–06, vol. 2, pp. 69–71.

19 Idem, *Minhāj al-sunna*, vol. 1, pp. 397–398.

20 Idem, *Majmūʿat al-Rasāʾil al-kubrā*, vol. 1, p. 361. See also Rahman, *Islam*, p. 114.

21 Ibn Taymiyya, *Majmūʿ Fatāwā*, vol. 8, pp. 118–119; Ibn Taymiyya, *Majmūʿat al-Rasāʾil wal-masāʾil*, vol. 5, pp. 315–316.

22 Ibn Taymiyya, *Majmūʿ Fatāwā*, vol. 8, p. 467; Ibn Taymiyya, *Kitāb al-Nubuwwāt*, p. 206.

23 Ibn Taymiyya, *Majmūʿ Fatāwā*, vol. 8, pp. 459–460.

cumstances are able to choose what to do, which makes them responsible for their actions.[24]

Some of his contemporaries claimed that Ibn Taymiyya's solution to the problem actually caused further problems. In their view, attributing actions to humans and connecting them to God's creation would generate a kind of partnership between God and humans. Ibn Taymiyya responded that in such examples various attributions could take place at the same time if the aspects and relations were different. For instance, a person is a child of a parent and at the same time a creature of God. Similarly, a fruit belongs to a tree and is also created by God. Since the relations are not the same in these examples, one cannot observe a partnership between them, he states. He therefore claims the same argument is valid for human actions.[25] Moreover, for him, since humans are created by God, human actions are naturally extensions of divine creation, although they happen of humans' free will. Nevertheless, human actions must depend on their own will, otherwise the actions would not take place.[26]

In the light of these opinions it can be said that Ibn Taymiyya considered human actions as being created by God indirectly. Humans are created with the power of acting, and they perform their actions freely through this given power. Besides, unlike other Sunni theologians, Ibn Taymiyya does not find any difficulty in a person's having the ability (*istiṭāʿa*) to act potentially before the time of his actions. In his view, the *istiṭāʿa* exists both before and during the time of actions.[27] Those who deny the human ability to act before the time of actions do not have any evidence from the authoritative sources. Contrarily, he says, the Koran clearly states that the *istiṭāʿa* was offered to humans for worshipping as a blessing, so theologically there should be no problem in defending its potential existence in advance.[28]

Compared with the acquisition theory, Ibn Taymiyya's approach to solving the problem looks clearer, and in his view it does not create confusion in the mind. Indeed, the aforementioned idea of indirect creation of actions, he suggests, avoids their belonging to God. According

---

24 Ibn Taymiyya, *Majmūʿ Fatāwā*, vol. 8, p. 464.
25 Ibn Taymiyya, *Minhāj al-sunna*, vol. 3, p. 146.
26 Ibn Taymiyya, *Majmūʿ Fatāwā*, vol. 16, pp. 237, 341–342.
27 Ibn Taymiyya, *Majmūʿ Fatāwā*, vol. 18, pp. 172–173. For other Sunni views on *istiṭāʿa*, see al-Ashʿarī, *Kitāb al-Lumaʿ*, pp. 132–136; al-Māturīdī, *Kitāb al-Tawḥīd*, pp. 410–420.
28 Ibn Taymiyya, *Majmūʿ Fatāwā*, vol. 14, pp. 103–104.

to this assumption, the actions can only be objects of God's creation through humans, but they cannot be considered His actions.[29] By this view, Ibn Taymiyya accepts the occurrence of actions through their first causes and denies the attribution of possible evil actions to God, which would cause another theological problem.

It is possible, therefore, to argue that, regarding the issue of divine wisdom and human agency, Ibn Taymiyya moved towards a rational theology more explicitly than early Ḥanbalīs and Ashʿarīs. In addition, he did not strictly follow the views of his school, but instead made combinations out of rival theses. As Gimaret pointed out, he seems to be closer to Māturīdīs, and even more parallel to the Muʿtazilī theologian Abū al-Ḥusayn al-Baṣrī (d. 436/1044).[30] In fact, al-Baṣrī influenced other Sunni theologians, such as ʿAlāʾ al-Dīn al-Usmandī (d. 552/1157), and it would not be strange for him to be one of the sources of Ibn Taymiyya. Nevertheless, al-Juwaynī demonstrated a similar approach in one of his latest treatises, *al-ʿAqīda al-niẓāmiyya*, if not in his earlier works.[31] Fakhr al-Dīn al-Rāzī (d. 606/1209) refers to Juwaynī's diverging view, and suggests that it was originally held by Muslim philosophers and the Muʿtazilī Abū al-Ḥusayn al-Baṣrī.[32]

2. *Fiṭra* as Evidence from the Perspective of Divine Wisdom

The discussions regarding human nature explore mostly the meaning and interpretation of the term *fiṭra*, rather than considering it an argument for belief in God. Muslim thinkers have discussed the term since the early period in various fields, mainly in exegetical, legal, and moral works. Ibn Taymiyya, however, following in the footsteps of some scholars, developed a theological argument in the light of his views on divine wisdom and guidance. In Islamic thought, human nature is

---

29 Ibn Taymiyya, *Majmūʿat al-Rasāʾil wal-masāʾil*, vol. 5, pp. 318–319.

30 See Gimaret, Daniel: Théories de l'acte humain dans l'école hanbalite, in: *Bulletin d'études orientales* 28 (1977), pp. 165–178.

31 Imām al-Ḥarāmayn al-Juwaynī, ʿAbd al-Malik b. Yūsuf: *al-ʿAqīda al-niẓāmiyya*, edited by Aḥmad Ḥijāzī al-Saqqā, Cairo 1979.

32 Al-Rāzī, Fakhr al-Dīn: *Muḥaṣṣal afkār al-mutaqaddimīn wal-mutaʾakhkhirīn min al-ʿulamāʾ wal-ḥukamāʾ wal-mutakallimīn*, edited by Ṭāhā ʿAbd al-Raʾūf Saʿd, Cairo n. d., p. 194.

generally discussed using the Koranic term *fiṭra*.[33] The term is based on the Koranic phrase "the patterns of God upon which He has made mankind" (*fiṭrat allāh allatī faṭara al-nās ʿalayhā*, see 30:30).[34] The term *ṣibghat allāh* (coloring of God) in another verse (2:138) is accepted as another of the Koran's descriptions of human created nature.

Although some scholars interpret the *fiṭra* theologically as "Islam", "religious belief", "original testimony", "neutrality" etc., it is mostly explained as a human quality in its first creation that has the ability to know its creator and inclines toward good manners. It is thus defined as the pure and primary human nature created by God, distinguishing humans from other creatures. Divine wisdom allows humans to have such ability in order to enable them to pursue goodness with their own initiatives. Muḥammad Asad (d. 1992), therefore, renders the term as "natural disposition".[35] Hadith collections also include *riwāyas* regarding inborn human nature. Among them, the famous Hadith saying "all children are born in the *fiṭra*" (*kull mawlūd yūlad ʿalā al-fiṭra*)[36] is also

---

33 The word *fiṭra* comes from its root *f-ṭ-r*, and has various literal meanings, such as "to open", "to divide", "to invent", "to create", and so on. It refers to innate human nature and having a special sort of self-distinctive capacity or ability. See Ibn al-Manẓūr, Jamāl al-Dīn: *Lisān al-ʿarab*, Beirut 2000, vol. 11, pp. 196–198. For a comprehensive study on the concept of *fiṭra* among Muslim thinkers, see Gobillot, Geneviève: *La fiṭra. La conception originelle; ses interprétations et fonctions chez les penseurs musulmans*, Cairo 2000.

34 Various verbs and nouns deriving from the root *f-ṭ-r* occur in the Koran 19 times; the exact word *fiṭra* as cited above occurs only once. In this specific verse (30:30) it says: "And so, set up your face for the true religion, as you incline naturally toward truth in accordance with the *fiṭra* in which God has created humans, there is no change in God's creation […]". It is interpreted as meaning that all types of created beings have their own representative nature with standard qualities. Humans have a specific nature, too. Although traditions differ from society to society, the characters and attributes of human nature are the same in all parts of the world. These common aspects, both abstract and concrete, comprise the basic ontological structure of humans.

35 Asad, Muhammad (transl.): *The Message of the Qur'an*, Bristol 2003, p. 697.

36 For the various versions of the tradition, see al-Bukhārī: *Ṣaḥīḥ*, "Janāʾiz", pp. 80, 93; Muslim: *Ṣaḥīḥ*, "Qadar", 6; Abū Dāwūd: *Sunan*, "al-Sunna", 17; Ibn Ḥanbal, Aḥmad: *Musnad*, Istanbul 1992, vol. 2, pp. 275, 393, 410. Livnat Holtzman gave a paper on this *fiṭra* tradition and its use in the international conference on *Ibn Taymiyya and His Times* at Princeton University. Holtzman, Livnat: Human Choice, Divine Guidance and the fiṭra Tradition. Ibn Taymiyya's and Ibn Qayyim al-Jawziyya's use of Hadīth in Theological Treatises, in: Yossef Rapoport and Shahab Ahmed (eds.): *Ibn Taymiyya and His Times*, Karachi 2010, pp. 247–265.

connected to the original neutral purity of human nature, which may change in different directions during one's lifetime.

In this Koranic approach supported by traditions, each person has a human nature by virtue of being created; it consists of his or her original and distinctive qualities that would direct activities if left unaffected by his or her family or social environment. Thus, all kinds of essential elements that make us human, including the ability to believe, are within the scope of this concept. Humans' instinctual bodily actions, though displaying their nature in some sense, are insufficient if they are not in accordance with inner moral consciousness. The majority of scholars considered this human distinction from other creatures a sign of divine wisdom and benevolence that led them to great material and spiritual achievements.[37] The common point in the discussions is that some thinkers believe happiness can be reached by merely protecting the qualities of human nature and avoiding the effects that may degrade it, even in the absence of education. Ibn Ṭufayl's (d. 581/1185) philosophical novel, *Ḥayy b. Yaqẓān*, tries to demonstrate this positive dimension of human nature.

Most of them, however, did not evaluate human nature as a means of discovering divine wisdom by acknowledging a transcendent existent in God's creation. Even in theological books, the majority of the *mutakallimūn* did not include the human nature argument among their proofs of the existence of God: focusing mainly on the cosmological argument, they paid some attention to the design (*niẓām*) argument, which emphasizes the perfect harmony within the natural world. In the classical period, only a few independent-minded scholars, such as al-Jāḥiẓ (d. 869), Muṭahhar b. Ṭāhir al-Maqdisī (d. 966?), al-Rāghib al-Iṣfahānī (d. early 11th century), and al-Ghazālī (d. 1111), touched upon human nature as an argument for the divine existence, without discussing it in detail. In the later period, Ibn Taymiyya (d. 1328) paid more attention to this argument.

Unlike his fellow Muʿtazilīs, Abū ʿUthmān al-Jāḥiẓ suggests that, for human beings, believing in God is based on natural knowledge rather than argumentative reasoning (*naẓar*). All humans (if not ignorant), he argues, know that God is their creator; they need a prophet to receive His divine message; and they are convinced by this natural knowl-

37 The Koran describes some humans who do not follow their *fiṭra* qualities as "they have hearts but they don't understand with them, they have eyes but they don't see with them, they have ears but they don't hear with them, they are like animals, or even below them!" Koran (7:179).

edge.[38] Muṭahhar al-Maqdisī emphasizes that, despite the differences in their traditions, communities, countries, and views, societies around the world do not differ in having a belief. There is a word for God in all languages, and people usually take refuge in their beliefs when they face dangers.[39] al-Rāghib al-Isfahānī, too, in his division between necessary and rational knowledge, cites the existence of God as self-evident (*badīhī*) knowledge, because all rational beings agree that they were not their own creators. Al-Iṣfahānī considers Abraham's identification of God with a star, the moon, and the sun, mentioned in the Koran (6:76–77), a sign of the human inborn nature to believe in God. That the majority of people pray to God in desperate situations and that most communities observe some sort of belief is further evidence of the inner foundation of believing.[40] In *Iḥyāʾ ʿulūm al-dīn*, al-Ghazālī also clearly indicated that human nature and the examples of the Koran do not require further proofs (*fī fiṭrat al-insān wa-shawāhid al-qurʾān mā yughnī ʿan iqāmat al-burhān*).[41]

Although some Muslim thinkers in the earlier period discussed using human nature as an argument, no one had made it theory yet. In order to build a natural relationship between human inner capacity and divine guidance, Ibn Taymiyya constructed the concept of *fiṭra* as an alternative argument in Islamic theology to the *kalām* cosmological (*ḥudūth*) argument.[42] In classical Islamic theology, the methods of argumentation to prove the existence of God are called *ithbāt al-wājib*, which means proving the existence of the Necessary Being. The exis-

38 See al-Jāḥiẓ, Abū ʿUthmān: *al-Dalāʾil wal-iʿtibār ʿalā al-khalq wal-tadbīr*, Beirut 1988. See also Vajda, George: La connaissance naturelle de Dieu selon al-Ǧāḥiẓ critiqueé par les muʿtazilites, in: *Studia Islamica* 24 (1966), pp. 19–33.

39 Al-Maqdisī, Muṭahhar b. Ṭāhir: *Kitāb al-Badʾ wal-taʾrīkh*, edited by Clément Huart, Baghdad n. d., vol. 1, pp. 58–60.

40 Al-Iṣfahānī, al-Rāghib: *al-Iʿtiqādāt*, edited by Shamran al-ʿAjli, Beirut 1988, pp. 34–38.

41 Al-Ghazālī, Abū Ḥāmid: *Iḥyāʾ ʿulūm al-dīn*, Cairo 1933, vol. 1, pp. 93–94.

42 Henri Laoust refers in a footnote to Ibn Taymiyya's use of *fiṭra* as a proof of the existence of God. He describes the proof as our innate and universal belief in Him (*l'innéisme et l'universalité de notre croyance en lui*). See Laoust, Henri: *Essai sur les doctrines sociales et politiques de Takī-d-dīn Aḥmad Ibn Taimīya, canoniste Ḥanbalite. Né à Ḥarrān en 661/1262, mort à Damas en 728/1328*; thèse pour le doctorat, Cairo 1939, p. 153, n. 1. See also Ssekamanya, Siraje Abdullah: Ibn Taymiyya's Theological Approach Illustrated. On the Essence (*Dhat*) and the Attributes (*Sifat*) of Allah, in: *al-Shajarah* 9 (2004), pp. 43-61, here pp. 50–51; Anjum, Ovamir: *Reason and Politics in Medieval Islamic Thought. The Taymiyyan Moment*, Madison 2008, pp. 267–273.

tence of God is also regarded as the highest level of existence, in contrast to the contingent spheres of other existences. All sort of existences depend on His existence in order to come into being. The Koran cites the existence of God as an undeniable truth and more often emphasizes His unity and unshared authority in order to reject polytheistic beliefs.

In Islamic thought and medieval philosophy in general, thinkers employed various ontological, cosmological, and teleological arguments to prove the existence of God. Among these arguments, the cosmological one is based on the idea of the Prime Mover (*Causa Prima*) of the ancient philosophers, such as Plato and Aristotle, in order to explain motion in the universe. In Islamic intellectual history there is a special emphasis on cosmological arguments, which were applied to Muslim theological thought with their specific terms *ḥudūth* and *imkān*. In addition, teleological forms of arguments were also used under titles such as design (*niẓām*) and providence (*ʿināya*) to explain the universal system. The existence of God, however, is not like any other physical existence, because it eludes direct perception. His existence can only be understood through an acknowledgment of creation and traces of His signs in the world. The employment of these arguments helped to raise the level of the belief from an imitation of others to a serious personal conviction. In addition, the argumentation process aimed at removing doubts about the existence of God that could come to the mind of believers.

Ibn Taymiyya, however, followed an alternative path. He spent his efforts to highlight the sufficiency of human nature and persistently criticize the *ḥudūth* of Muslim theologians. The Koran and the Sunna, Ibn Taymiyya argues, offer a cognitive unity through both knowledge and practice, in order to reach a point of contact with His wise and infinite qualities; the method of the theologians, however, leads only to abstract knowledge.[43] Moreover, the divine message is indicated in a manner that is harmonious with innate human reality, and its proof is direct. The logical instructions of the theologians, on the other hand, use only deductive or analogical reasoning, and therefore their efforts do not convince all aspects of the human being. To put it in his words:

> In the distinction of the Koranic theological method, God commands worship of Him, which provides perfection of the soul and its righteousness. Its aim and end is not limited to mere affirmation of Him, which is the purpose of the *kalām* method. These two [approaches] do not cor-

43 Ibn Taymiyya, *Darʾ taʿāruḍ al-ʿaql wal-naql*, vol. 1, pp. 201–208.

> respond to each other, neither in methods nor in objectives. Indeed the Koranic method indicates to us that it is primordial and approachable, enabling us to reach the specific goal. [In contrast] the other is analogical and distant, allowing us only to reach a type of goal, not the essence. As for the goals, the Koran informs about knowledge and the practice of it. It thus combines the two human faculties of knowledge and practice, which are sensation and motion; intentional perception and reliance; along with oral and practical. As God says, "Worship your Lord." Worship necessarily entails knowledge of Him, having penitence and humility before Him, and impoverishment for Him. This is the goal. The *kalām* method secures only the benefit of affirmation and admission of God's existence.[44]

According to Ibn Taymiyya, the revealed and transmitted sources contain their own rational foundations, which are suitable for the logic of the divine message and satisfy people of different educational backgrounds. They also contain the evidence required to verify the principles of religion and therefore have no need for extraneous theories, whether by theologians or philosophers. For example, rational proofs of the existence of God and of resurrection after death, which are based on observation of the natural world, can easily be derived from some Koranic verses. The theologians use abstract methods to reach a conclusion that normally could have been taken directly from the revealed text. They prove the existence of God in a way that tests human rationality beyond its bounds, speculating by means of a complicated cosmological argument. This theory however, raises difficulties in reconciling the eternity of God with His creation in time. The Muslim Peripatetic philosophers tried to solve the problem by proposing the eternity of the universe in time but not in essence. Ibn Taymiyya completely rejects the eternity of the universe in any form, but also criticizes the theologians for denying any cause or purpose in creation. In his view, God brings things into existence purposefully, through His absolute will and power, as observed in the physical world. Therefore, while rejecting the possibility of eternity for any created being, he accepts the eternity of creation, which does not mean in his opinion an endless chain of causes, but rather the continuity of God's perpetual acting and creating.[45]

---

44 Ibn Taymiyya, *Majmūʿ Fatāwā*, vol. 2, p. 12.

45 Ibn Taymiyya, *Darʾ taʿāruḍ al-ʿaql wal-naql*, vol. 1, pp. 354–367; Ibn Taymiyya, *Majmūʿ Fatāwā*, vol. 18, pp. 222–230. On the differences between Ibn Taymiyya's views on creation and those of the philosophers and theologians, see Hoover,

The *ḥudūth* argument may demonstrate the need for a Creator, Ibn Taymiyya maintains, but it does not prove it in reality. Besides, in the Koran, the existence of God is firmly grounded in the creation of concrete and visible entities (*aʿyān*) by God. The continuous creation of the universe, humans, animals, and other physical beings in a perfect way is there for all to see. It constitutes a more direct proof of the existence of God than theological and philosophical theories.[46] The cosmological argument in fact makes the issue of divine existence more tangled and less grounded in reality.[47] However, the knowledge of God by our inner nature, Ibn Taymiyya suggests, does not require proofs and argumentation to discover His existence. If the person did not know and believe in God prior to the theoretical proofs of the theologians, he would not be able to connect the proof with God. To know God without proof is like knowing a person without knowing his name, or understanding and using things without knowing the rules:[48] "The essence of declaration of belief in God and its confession," he states, "is placed in the hearts of all humans and jinns" (*anna aṣl al-iqrār bil-ṣāniʿ wal-iʿtirāf bihi mustaqirr fī qulūb jamīʿ al-ins wal-jinn*).[49] Ibn Taymiyya gives a specific example to explain his point: those who plan to visit the Kaaba for pilgrimage already know that it exists and may be familiar with some of its attributes through descriptions given by previous visitors and confirmation expressed by guides. Just as people perceive the immediate relation between daylight and the sun or smoke and fire without going into philosophical propositions or logical analogies, a similar relation can be easily set up between created and Creator.[50]

Thus, in Ibn Taymiyya's view, within *fiṭra* the knowledge of truth and human attestation of truth exist, as well as the recognition of false-

---

Jon: Perpetual Creativity on the Perfection of God. Ibn Taymiyya's Hadith Commentary on God's Creation of this World, in: *Journal of Islamic Studies* 15 (2004), pp. 287–329, here pp. 293–295; al-Ālūsī, Ḥusām Muḥyī al-Dīn: *The Problem of Creation in Islamic Thought. Qurʾan, Hadith, Commentaries, and Kalam*, Baghdad 1968, pp. 95–96, 185–186.

46 Ibn Taymiyya, Taqī al-Dīn: *Majmūʿat Tafsīr*, edited by ʿAbd al-Ṣamad Sharaf al-Dīn, Mumbai 1993, pp. 210–212.

47 Ibn Taymiyya, *Darʾ taʿāruḍ al-ʿaql wal-naql*, vol. 1, pp. 38–99; idem, *Majmūʿ Fatāwā*, vol. 3, pp. 303–304. For detailed discussion of the *ḥudūth* argument, see Craig, William Lane: *The Kalām Cosmological Argument,* New York 1979.

48 Ibn Taymiyya, *Majmūʿ Fatāwā*, vol. 1, pp. 48–49.

49 Idem, *Darʾ taʿāruḍ al-ʿaql wal-naql*, vol. 8, p. 482.

50 Idem, *Majmūʿ Fatāwā*, vol. 2, pp. 70–74.

hood and the rejection of it.[51] Every individual is aware of his or her knowledge or lack of it by the *fiṭra*; as such, individuals usually do not contest an issue unless they have knowledge about it. When truth is there and accessible by the mind, the *fiṭra* will naturally accept and feel satisfied with it, but when it is false, it will naturally withdraw from it.[52] This impulse is the natural inclination towards virtue and wisdom. God is the highest truth, and human knowledge about Him is the highest wisdom. Therefore, remembrance (*dhikr*) of Him is the foundation of all goodness, which allows direct contact with His wisdom. By doing *dhikr*, the individual receives spiritual guidance to protect himself or herself from falsehood. When a human individual remembers God, he has knowledge of Him naturally. Reflecting upon Him, however, does not provide the same knowledge, since reflection (*naẓar* or *tafakkur*) depends on using metaphors and comparisons; whereas God is absolutely incomparable to anything and has no equal or similar. Although some may feel satisfied with rational methods, the natural capacity of *fiṭra* differs from reason (*ʿaql*) and does not function through inferential methods. The knowledge of *fiṭra* is simply there, and its source is God's creation (that is why it is attributed to God in the Koran as *fiṭrat allāh*). Thus, Ibn Taymiyya, referring to the Koranic verses (6:91, 22:74, 39:67), argues that *dhikr* pertains to God, and *tafakkur* pertains to the created world, as the human mind will never be able to make an exact estimation of God.[53]

In the modern period, Muslim theologians showed more interest in the *fiṭra* argument than post-Taymiyyan scholars, though with a different terminology. The Syrian Salafi reformist Jamāl al-Dīn al-Qāsimī (d. 1914), the Indian modernist thinker Shiblī Nuʿmānī (d. 1914), and the Ottoman Turkish theologian İzmirli İsmail Hakkı (d. 1946) are the prominent figures who discussed the relation between human nature and belief in God. In his *Dalāʾil al-tawḥīd*, which counts 25 proofs of the existence of God in its first chapter, al-Qāsimī names the first proof *burhān al-fiṭra*. Al-Qāsimī explains that despite its being necessary, he regarded *fiṭra* as a *burhān* (decisive argument), due to its reliability and its being unaffected by doubts and other skeptical views. Quoting al-Iṣfahānī and referring to many Koranic verses, al-Qāsimī

51 Idem, *al-Radd ʿalā al-manṭiqiyyīn*, edited by Syed Sulaiman Nadwi, Bombay 1949, p. 428.

52 Ibn Taymiyya, *al-Radd ʿalā al-manṭiqiyyīn*, p. 381.

53 Madjid, Nurcholis: *Ibn Taymiyya on Kalam and Falsafa*, Ph.D. thesis (The University of Chicago) 1984, pp. 70–72.

emphasizes humans' need to believe, trust, and pray. Like other animals, humans sway between hope and fear, he says, and therefore need a trustworthy being, especially when they are in desperate situations.[54] Shiblī Nuʿmānī, too, quoting philosophers of religion including some Westerners, affirms the role of the human *fiṭra* in believing.[55] İsmail Hakkı, however, emphasizes societies' general tendency to believe and uses "the common belief argument" (*itiqad-i ʿamme delili*) instead of the term *fiṭra* when discussing the same topic.[56] In more recent studies, contemporary scholars continued to examine the issue of human nature and its being an alternative to rational proofs of the existence of God.[57]

As a comparison, it is interesting that in the history of Christian thought some reformist theologians, such as Martin Luther (1483–1546) and Johannes Calvin (1509–1564), emphasized the innate ability of human nature to recognize the divine existence. Luther suggested that God rightly situated beliefs in human hearts and that there was no need for further rational activities and logical deductions in order to prove His existence, since they would not provide additional strength to religious faith.[58] Belief in God, in Luther's approach, was implemented in humankind spiritually, thus negating the need for rational proofs. Similarly, in a chapter entitled "The Knowledge of God Has Been Naturally Implanted in the Minds of Men", Calvin writes:

> There is within the human mind, and indeed by natural instinct, an awareness of divinity. This we take to be beyond controversy. To prevent anyone from taking refuge in the pretence of ignorance, God Himself has implanted in all men a certain understanding of His divine majesty. Ever renewing its memory, He repeatedly sheds fresh drops.[59]

---

54 Al-Qāsimī, Jamāl al-Dīn: *Dalāʾil al-tawḥīd,* Cairo 1986, pp. 23–31.

55 Nuʿmānī, ʿAllāmaʿ Shiblī: *al-Kalām*, Karachi 1979, pp. 158–163.

56 Hakkı, İzmirli İsmail: *Yeni İlm-i Kelam*, Istanbul 1920, vol. 2, pp. 44–45.

57 For some examples, see the works of al-Yasīn, Muḥammad Ḥasan: *Allāh bayna al-fiṭra wal-dalīl*, Beirut 1972; Jawādī ʿĀmulī, Āyat Allāh: *al-ʿAqīda min khilāl al-fiṭra fī al-Qurʾān*, Beirut 1994.

58 Luther, Martin: *Martin Luther's Basic Theological Writings*, edited by Timothy F. Lull, Minneapolis 1989, pp. 13–20. Another comparison between Ibn Taymiyya and Martin Luther is highlighted in the issue of the place of saints in religion. See Olesen, Niels Henrik: Étude comparée des idées d'Ibn Taymiyya (1263–1328) et de Martin Luther (1483–1546) sur le culte des saints, in: *Revue des études islamiques* 50 (1982), pp. 175–206.

59 See Calvin, Johannes: *Institutes of the Christian Religion*, Philadelphia 1975, vol. 1, pp. 43–44.

In fact some modern philosophers including Immanuel Kant also challenged ontological and cosmological arguments for the existence of God; this had a great impact on contemporary discussions in philosophy of religion. Theist thinkers, who are not in favor of using philosophical argumentation methods in matters of faith, suggest that religious texts do not emphasize the issue of evidence, but rather underline the significance of firm conviction of the heart through divine guidance. They point out that philosophical arguments prove the existence of God only as a theoretical conception in the mind and that the logical necessity of His existence that is reached through reasoning may affect the freedom of belief, which is offered by God to everyone.[60] Today, especially, reformed epistemologists strongly defend a view that believing in God is "properly basic" in human beings and does not require proving.[61] Similarities between these views and Ibn Taymiyya's approach are quite remarkable and deserve further studies and comparative analyses.

3. Love of God as a Human Expression of Divine Wisdom

Under the previous headings I focused on Ibn Taymiyya's understanding of divine wisdom, his approach to its reflections on freedom of action in the light of his criticisms of the Muʿtazilīs and Ashʿarīs, and also the innate ability of human nature to comprehend divine wisdom and guidance. Henceforth, I will highlight Ibn Taymiyya's consideration of the love of God as an essential dimension of human nature and its potential to enable one to acknowledge the existence of divine wisdom with greater conviction and efficiency.

In line with his views on divine wisdom and human affinity to belief, Ibn Taymiyya emphasizes that the Koran bases humans' religious belief on true love of and devotion to God. Theologians neglect the

60 For discussions on the topic, see Hick, John: *Arguments for the Existence of God*, London 1970, pp. 101–105. And for the details of the same debate between Richard Swinburne and Dewi Zephaniah Phillips, see Messer, Richard: *Does God's Existence Need Proof?*, Oxford 1993.

61 On this view and various approaches regarding the issue of reason and belief in contemporary discussions in philosophy of religion, see Plantinga, Alvin: Reason and Belief in God, in: Alvin Plantinga and Nicholas Wolterstorff (eds.): *Faith and Rationality*, Notre Dame and London 1991, pp. 16–93.

love of God and the human need for it, he argues, since they mostly focus on theoretical concepts and logical arguments about religion. The Prophets, he says, while conveying messages of God to their communities and calling upon their people to follow the principles of religion, never taught them theoretical and philosophical proofs to strengthen their faith. Instead, they recommended people to adopt a devotional attitude in their life by praying to and worshipping God in order to gain spiritual benefits. The bottom level of the hearts of believers, according to Ibn Taymiyya, always contains the love of God and displays its manifestations quite often.[62]

Ibn Taymiyya also points out the close relationship between belief and action, which provides a connection between the physical and metaphysical worlds. The *mutakallimūn*, who discuss faith in abstract terms, in his view, miss the practical elements, which form a part of religion. Therefore, he argues, it is not a coincidence that religions emphasize worship and obedience to God rather than focusing on theoretical proofs. The roots of religious belief, in Ibn Taymiyya's approach, are acceptance of fundamental principles as well as a strong internal commitment to act according to these principles in daily life. Technical and abstract definitions of faith will not satisfy the expectations of committed believers.[63]

In Ibn Taymiyya's interpretation, believing in God has two elements: confirmation of belief and love of God. The first part is verbal belief and the second is practical belief. Real love motivates the body and creates a unity between it and the soul. Binding belief in God exclusively to confirmation, therefore, would not be satisfactory in terms of its definition; it also needs to include knowledge and love of Him. Believing without love would not reach its perfection; in other words, it needs to refer to inner spiritual words and practices of the heart, as well as reflection in spoken languages and physical practices. In his own words:

> The essence of strength is the strength of the heart that brings love of good and disdain of evil. The believer's strength lies in his heart, while weakness is in his body. The hypocrite, on the other hand, while his strength lies in his body, weakness remains in his heart. Consequently, faith must

62 Ibn Taymiyya, *Majmūʿat Tafsīr*, pp. 269, 277. For Ibn Taymiyya's approach in general Ḥanbalī context, see also Bell, Joseph Norment: *Love Theory in Later Ḥanbalite Islam*, New York 1979.

63 Ibn Taymiyya, *Majmūʿ Fatāwā*, vol. 2, pp. 39–40; Ibn Taymiyya: *Kitāb al-Īmān*, edited by Muḥammad Zabīdī, Beirut 1414/1993, pp. 126–127, 370–371.

> contain these two principles: confirmation of the Truth [God] and love of Him. The first principle is verbal, and the other is practical. Therefore, complete love accompanied with strength requires the movement of the body along with verbal expression. [In addition] outward practice is necessary. As for the ones who consider knowledge and confirmation a requirement for what comes under the title of faith and what is called faith, they are mistaken. On the contrary, it [faith] requires knowledge and love. Knowledge is a prerequisite for loving the beloved, just as life is prerequisite for knowledge. […] But in reality, God deserves by His essence to be loved and worshipped and to love His messenger for His sake. The hearts contain in them a faculty that needs to love and worship Him, just as they contain in them a faculty that requires knowledge and confirmation of Him. Whoever confirms Him and His messenger, but is not a lover of Him and His messenger, is not a believer until it [love of Him and His messenger] exists.[64]

The main element behind a sincere trust in God, Ibn Taymiyya states, is the need of all existence for Him and His protection. The fact of being in need (*iftiqār*) of God is obvious in every thing that exists. For this reason, he says, the Koran highlights the surrendering affinity of existing beings to God, their spiritual testimonies of Him, and special adorations and exaltations by each of them in their own way of expressing. For instance, the breaking forth of springs from the earth, the branching of trees, and the ripening of fruits are examples of such adoration and obedience from various beings. These devotional acts and orderly performances are observed in all species individually and therefore are stronger evidence than theoretical arguments that are proposed by philosophers and theologians for the existence of God.[65]

According to Ibn Taymiyya, by imagining that the divine Being cannot love and be loved due to His transcendence, theologians underestimate the importance of this issue for believers. In counterpoint, Ibn Taymiyya claims that love of God and trust in Him exist in all beings, even in the hearts of unbelievers whose love and trust mostly surfaces in desperate situations; indeed, people sometimes unintentionally find themselves turning toward God or praying to Him. Moreover, one cannot truly worship someone toward whom one does not feel love and respect; therefore, in Ibn Taymiyya's view, denying love of Him would almost be the same as denying Himself.

64 Ibn Taymiyya, *Majmūʿ Fatāwā*, vol. 7, p. 541.

65 Ibn Taymiyya, *Majmūʿ Fatāwā*, vol. 1, pp. 46–47, Ibn Taymiyya, *Darʾ taʿāruḍ al-ʿaql wal-naql*, vol. 3, pp. 265–266.

Thus, in Ibn Taymiyya's approach, love of God (*maḥabbat allāh*) is similarly essential for the believer as knowing and believing in God (*maʿrifat allāh*).[66]

The essence of believing, according to Ibn Taymiyya, is therefore connected to love of God and submission to His path. The Koran's emphasis on the close relationship between belief and good actions and its requirement of sincere dedication in prayers, Ibn Taymiyya suggests, reminds believers of the inner and profound aspects of believing in God. Hence, for Ibn Taymiyya, the denial or rejection of the existence of God is mostly due to a lack of proper love and sufficient knowledge. People are usually not interested in things they do not like, and if they do not care about certain things for a while they begin to deny them. However, if they like something it becomes special and its acknowledgment turns into happiness for them. The essence of belief is a combination of confirmation, which is the language of the heart, and love in submission, which is the action of the heart. Nothing is so close to satisfying human souls as God. Therefore, it is not sufficient to define religious belief only in technical terms by limiting it to mere acceptance without connecting it to love.[67] In understanding the meaning of faith, Ibn Taymiyya continues to distinguish this approach from the methods of the theologians and Sufis with the following words:

> As for the people of knowledge and faith, they combined two matters: knowledgeable confirmation and loving practice. Therefore, their confirmation is based on knowledge and their practice and love is based on knowledge as well. As a result, they are safe from two disasters of the *mutakallimūn* and Sufis that turn people away from the true path.[68]

In this sense, according to Ibn Taymiyya, since it is beyond the sphere of "direct perception" by reason and physical senses, belief is a larger concept than simple confirmation. In order to verify certain judgments concerning physical existences, for example, Ibn Taymiyya asserts that while the term confirmation is employed, the term belief is not; therefore, the existence of God is a matter of belief. The principles that are received through revelation on His unity and qualities, on the other hand, are issues of confirmation. In other words, God is believed in;

66 Ibn Taymiyya, *Majmūʿ Fatāwā*, vol. 16, pp. 343–345; Ibn Taymiyya, *Kitāb al-Nubuwwāt*, pp. 68–69.
67 Ibn Taymiyya, *Majmūʿ Fatāwā*, vol. 2, pp. 39–40.
68 Ibn Taymiyya, *Majmūʿ Fatāwā*, vol. 2, p. 41.

the knowledge He reveals is confirmed. Confirmation, thus, is a logical and epistemological activity; belief is a religious action, which includes confirmation. This means that belief, apart from its admissive dimension, has also a submissive aspect that leads believers to adopt religious responsibilities and to practice them in their daily life. Hence, a simple confirmation alone does not reflect the spirituality, the sensitivity, and the high expectations of believers. For this reason, Ibn Taymiyya does not agree with some theologians who define the term believing as confirmation of heart (*taṣdīq bil-qalb*).[69] He affirms that the perfection of soul would not be complete with only knowing about God, but additionally requires doing good actions, as well as loving God and praising Him.[70]

Belief (*īmān*) and living accordingly (*islām*) are, in Ibn Taymiyya's comparison, like the soul and the body in humans, which do not exist separately on their own. According to this metaphor, belief corresponds with the soul, and practices correspond with the parts of the body; hence the artificial practices of hypocrites (*munāfiq*) represent separating the body from the soul. In a further assessment, Ibn Taymiyya compares religious practices with actions of prayers, and belief with sincerity and compliance during performances.[71]

As shown in the above passages, Ibn Taymiyya intensely uses psychological arguments in his theological discourse to systematize a faith relying on love and spiritual contemplation. Faith for him is beyond mere inner and verbal confirmation, which would be like a technical part of belief. It also has love, which constitutes its real meaning and deeper dimension. This approach resembles the spiritual path of some famous mystics, such as Jalāl al-Dīn al-Rūmī (d. 672/1273) and ʿAbd al-Raḥmān al-Jāmī (d. 898/1492), who put love in the center of belief in God in a sublime sense.[72] According to these thinkers, since God is in possession of the highest beauty, benevolence, and perfection, He deserves the truest and deepest love that maintains devotional belief in Him. God is the only real beloved and the rest of Him is loved as a finite and transitory manifestation. Only love of God, therefore, can exalt the earthly body of humans to the spiritual skies of purification

69 Ibn Taymiyya, *Kitāb al-Īmān*, pp. 126–127, 370–371.
70 Ibn Taymiyya, *al-Radd ʿalā al-manṭiqiyyīn*, pp. 138–140, 145–146.
71 Ibn Taymiyya, *Majmūʿ Fatāwā*, vol. 7, p. 367.
72 For a comprehensive and detailed work on Rumi's philosophy of love, see Chittick, William C.: *The Sufi Path of Love. The Spiritual Teachings of Rumi*, New York 1983, in particular pp. 194–231.

and perfection.[73] Ibn Taymiyya's spirituality, however, is more Koranic than a pure mystical one and is followed by his close student Ibn Qayyim al-Jawziyya, who wrote a book on the love of God (*maḥabbat allāh*).[74] In this monograph, Ibn al-Qayyim states that nothing in the world calms and satisfies the hearts more than divine love.

Conclusion

Theologically, the theory of divine wisdom suggests that purposeful actions by God endow human nature with the ability or tendency to believe in God. Ibn Taymiyya, therefore, openly sided with the defenders of wisdom theory and rejected the Ashʿarī point of a possible limitation of divine omnipotence. As discussed above, Ibn Taymiyya did not hesitate to practice a rational method of theology in this case, despite his belonging to a more traditionalist circle of *aṣḥāb al-ḥadīth* in theology and Ḥanbalism in law. Moreover, he connects human agency to general divine wisdom; the wisdom of God, in his view, actually requires human free choice. In other words, humans having their own actions with their own will is not an obstacle to the authority of God, because humans themselves like other existences are parts of His universal creation.

Ibn Taymiyya regarded human *fiṭra* and its ability to believe as a part of divine wisdom and benevolence, and some Muslim thinkers seem to have employed it in the modern period. It is interesting that this idea was also acknowledged by reformist Christian theologians and has been discussed in the contemporary philosophy of religion. This theory of *fiṭra* may raise further questions, especially in connection with human autonomy and free will;[75] indeed the concept of properly basic belief, which is defended by the reformed epistemologists, brings about new debates because it makes the state of believing a necessary act. Ibn Taymiyya and other Muslim theoreticians of human nature, too, are not very clear in defining the knowledge acquired by *fiṭra* as

73 For a summary of Sufi perception and understanding of divine love, see Valiuddin, Mir: *Love of God. The Sufi Approach*, Lahore 1979.

74 Ibn Qayyim al-Jawziyya, Shams al-Dīn Muḥammad: *Maḥabbat allāh ʿazza wa-jalla*, Damascus and Beirut 2002. See also his *Rawḍat al-muḥibbīn wa-nuzhat al-mushtaqīn*, edited by Sayyid Jamīlī, Beirut 1987.

75 See, for instance, Hallaq, Wael B.: Ibn Taymiyya on the Existence of God, in: *Acta Orientalia* 52 (1991), pp. 52–69, here pp. 58–60.

necessary or dependent on human will. By definition, necessity cannot be a subject of argumentation or proving, and seems to contradict the existence of unbelievers, no matter how few they may be. Rāghib al-Iṣfahānī seems to be aware of this problem and suggests that the denial of divinity by some people is not about its existence *per se*, but about its description, attributes, and unity;[76] many Koranic verses, however, clarify that belief in God is a voluntary action. Besides, the repeated recommendations of the Koran to reflect on the signs of God suggest that human nature needs to be interpreted as a capacity of tendency toward belief, but not a faculty necessitating belief, which may reach toward strict fideism. Furthermore, as an inner ability of human nature, Ibn Taymiyya gives a primary role to the love of God in human discovery and comprehension of divine wisdom by providing a direct relationship between it and His grace and mercy. This, in his view, gives the human being serenity and inner peace.

Consequently, in light of Ibn Taymiyya's general theological thought and the above considerations, human nature needs to be understood as the ability to accept the truth, believe in God, or do good actions, and not the necessity to do so – otherwise there would not be free choice of belief for humans. Ability to have faith through inner nature is like the capacity of human physical organs to see, taste, feel, touch, or hear in normal conditions; similarly, the ability to discern between basic rights and wrongs, and the potentiality for searching for the aim and the source of existence is meaningful only if it is based on human free will and agency.

76 Al-Iṣfahānī, *al-I'tiqādāt*, p. 38.

Debating the Doctrine of *jabr* (Compulsion)

Ibn Qayyim al-Jawziyya Reads Fakhr al-Dīn al-Rāzī*

Livnat Holtzman

Introduction

The doctrine of *jabr* (compulsion) basically states that human actions are created by God, and forced upon human beings, thus defining God as the real agent of human actions. This doctrine was considered heretical by both rationalist and traditionalist thinkers from the inception of *kalāmic* debates.[1] Traditionalist thinkers in particular were required to address the concept of *jabr* because of its proximity to the concept of predetermination (*al-qaḍāʾ wal-qadar*, hence: *qadar*).[2] This major article of faith in the Sunni creed, which states that all human actions are predetermined by God, was perceived by rationalist thinkers (the Muʿtazilīs) as a denial of free will (*ikhtiyār*). This perception led them to describe the traditionalist concept of *qadar* as *jabr* and to apply the derogatory name Jabriyya (sg. Jabrī; upholders of *jabr*) to traditionalist thinkers (mostly the Ḥanbalīs and the Ashʿarīs).

---

* I am grateful to Caterina Bori, Anke von Kügelgen, Jon Hoover, Christopher Melchert, and Abdessamad Belhaj for their valuable comments on prior drafts of this essay. This research was supported by The Israel Science Foundation (grant no. 302/06).

1 For the basic definition of *jabr* in the heresiographical literature, and the discussions on *jabr* in early Kalām, see Watt, W. Montgomery: *Free Will and Predestination in Early Islam*, London 1948, pp. 96–104. In his later works, Watt doubted the existence of thinkers holding Jabrī views, Watt, W. Montgomery: *The Formative Period of Islamic Thought*, Edinburgh 1973, pp. 4–5, 118; Watt, W. Montgomery: D̲j̲abriyya or Mud̲j̲bira, in: *EI²*, vol. 2 (1965), p. 365.

2 I use here *qadar* to denote God's decree and not human freedom. For the problematic use of this term, see Gardet, Louis: al-Ḳaḍāʾ wa-'l-Ḳadar, in: *EI²*, vol. 4 (1978), pp. 365–367.

Traditionalist thinkers reacted to these harsh accusations of heresy by asserting that although human actions are predetermined, they are not forced upon human beings. This assertion was elaborated in different degrees of subtlety and sophistication by traditionalist thinkers primarily to reject the rationalists' claims against the traditionalist concept of *qadar*. The Ashʿarī reaction led to their formulating the theory of *kasb*, which, the Ashʿarīs claimed, was the golden mean between the concept of free will and the concept of *jabr*.[3]

The traditionalist thinkers attempted to disavow any similarity between their concept of *qadar* and the doctrine of *jabr*. However, they could not ignore the substantial resemblance of *jabr* to *qadar*, and more so the possibility that the concept of *jabr* was but an overzealous version deviating from the belief in *qadar*. This possibility is demonstrated by Ibn Taymiyya (d. 728/1328) in the following description of an early debate between the Qadariyya (here the forerunners of the Muʿtazila) and "one of the *muthbita*" (here a Sunni traditionalist scholar). Ibn Taymiyya argues in this passage that the belief in *jabr* emerged as a reaction to early Muʿtazilī attacks on the Sunni belief in *qadar*:

> When the Qadariyya, the deniers of predetermination (*nufāt al-qadar*), first appeared, denying that God leads astray whom He will, and guides whom He will, and that He is the Creator of everything and that human actions are created by Him, people rejected this innovation (*bidʿa*). Therefore, one of them [of the Qadariyya], when debating on this subject, said: "This [the traditionalist doctrine of *qadar*] necessitates that God compels human actions on human beings, and that He assigns them with actions they could not possibly have performed." Thus, one of the *muthbita*[4] who was arguing with them persisted on applying this and said: "Yes,

---

3 Swartz, Merlin: Acquisition (*kasb*) in Early Kalām, in: Samuel M. Stern, Albert Hourani and Vivian Brown (eds.): *Islamic Philosophy and the Classical Tradition. Essays Presented by His Friends and Pupils to Richard Walzer on His Seventieth Birthday*, Columbia 1972, pp. 355–387; Abrahamov, Binyamin: A Re-examination of al-Ashʿarī's Theory of *Kasb* according to *Kitāb al-Lumaʿ*, in: *Journal of the Royal Asiatic Society* 1 (1989), pp. 210–221.

4 Ibn Taymiyya, Taqī al-Dīn Aḥmad: *Darʾ taʿāruḍ al-ʿaql wal-naql aw muwāfaqat ṣaḥīḥ al-manqūl li-ṣarīḥ al-maʿqūl*, ed. by ʿAbd al-Laṭīf ʿAbd al-Raḥmān, Beirut 1417/1997, vol. 1, p. 148. See also in the following edition: *Darʾ taʿāruḍ al-ʿaql wal-naql aw muwāfaqat ṣaḥīḥ al-manqūl li-ṣarīḥ al-maʿqūl*, ed. by Muḥammad Rashād Sālim, Cairo 1979, vol. 1, p. 254. The *muthbita* appear in different sources as *ahl al-ithbāt*. Like Qadariyya and Jabriyya, *ahl al-ithbāt* is used to denote different theological trends. Obviously they are traditionalist Sunni scholars, as al-Ashʿarī himself saw them as his forerunners. Gardet, Louis: ʿIlm al-Kalām, in: *EI*[2], vol. 3 (1971), pp. 1141–1150.

> *jabr* is necessitated, and *jabr* is true (*naʿam, yalzamu al-jabru wal-jabru ḥaqqun*)".[5]

The position taken here by "one of the *muthbita*" is an over enthusiastic application of the Sunni creed, motivated by a desire to attribute to God every existent, human actions included. The prominent traditionalists, such as Abū ʿAmr al-Awzāʿī (d. 157/774) and Aḥmad b. Ḥanbal (d. 241/855) responded to this position by establishing the following rule in order to restrain this overzealous Jabrī doctrine, and at the same time to object to the Qadarī libertarian position: "Whoever says that He (God) compels (*jabara*) is wrong, and whoever states that He does not compel is wrong. Yet, what should be said is: God guides whom He will and leads astray whom He will."[6]

The foundation of this early traditionalist approach of avoiding a debate on *jabr* and concentrating on the linguistic aspect, namely a rejection of the use of the verb *jabara*, is the prohibition to discuss any matter in the domain of theology.[7] However, other early traditionalists contributed several cogent arguments against *jabr*.[8] Later traditionalists, and particularly in the heresiographic literature mainly developed by Ashʿarī scholars, denounced the idea of *jabr* as heresy.[9]

An interesting turning point in the history of the doctrine of *jabr* occurred in the middle of the 12th century, with the emergence of the writings of Fakhr al-Dīn al-Rāzī (d. 606/1209). Within the framework of al-Rāzī's polemics against the Muʿtazila, al-Rāzī provided a rationalized justification for the doctrine of *jabr*, declaring time and again, "affirming the doctrine of *jabr* is inescapable". This, and other sayings

5 Ibn Taymiyya, *Darʾ al-taʿāruḍ*, 1997, vol. 1, p. 148; idem, *Darʾ al-taʿāruḍ*, 1979, vol. 1, p. 254.

6 Idem, *Darʾ al-taʿāruḍ*, 1997, vol. 1, p. 148; idem, *Darʾ al-taʿāruḍ*, 1979, vol. 1, p. 254. See also al-Khallāl, Abū Bakr: *al-Sunna*, ed. by ʿAṭiya al-Zahrānī, Riyadh 1410/1989, vol. 1, p. 550.

7 Abrahamov, Binyamin: *Islamic Theology. Traditionalism and Rationalism*, Edinburgh 1998, pp. 9–10. This reluctance to discuss theology is reflected in Aḥmad b. Ḥanbal's laconic responses to Jabrī sayings, such as "Do not say so!" or "What an evil man is the one who says so!", al-Khallāl, *al-Sunna*, vol. 1, pp. 550.

8 For a survey of the arguments made by the traditionalists al-Zubaydī (d. 149/766) and al-Awzāʿī see Hoover, John: *Ibn Taymiyya's Theodicy of Perpetual Optimism*, Leiden and Boston 2007, pp. 170–171. Ibn Taymiyya's description of the traditionalists' arguments is an accurate rendition from the chapter refuting the Qadariyya, in: Abū Bakr al-Khallāl, *al-Sunna*, vol. 1, pp. 549–557. Ibn Taymiyya, *Darʾ al-taʿāruḍ*, 1997, vol. 1, pp. 66–72; Ibn Taymiyya, *Darʾ al-taʿāruḍ*, pp. 39–42.

9 Watt, *Free Will and Predestination*, pp. 96–104.

in the same vein, shaped al-Rāzī's image as the first and probably the only theologian, whose reputation as a Jabrī is corroborated by his own written declarations. Even so, he never referred to himself as a Jabrī.[10]

Al-Rāzī's rationalized justification of *jabr* is central to the turbulent polemics between Ibn Taymiyya, his disciple, Ibn Qayyim al-Jawziyya (d. 751/1350), and the Ashʿarīs of their times. Following Ibn Taymiyya, Ibn Qayyim al-Jawziyya referred to his Ashʿarī opponents as Jabriyya. One might assume that this agnomen was given to the 14th century Ashʿarīs because of their enthusiastic adoption of al-Rāzī's doctrine of *jabr*, although other explanations for naming the Ashʿarīs thus may be provided.[11] At any rate, al-Rāzī's pro-*jabr* declarations made the cardi-

---

10 Fakhr al-Dīn's sayings on *jabr* are unprecedented and discussed in many researches. Ayman Shihadeh gives useful references to all al-Rāzī's writings, in which these bold Jabrī sayings appear. Shihadeh, Ayman: *The Teleological Ethics of Fakhr al-Dīn al-Rāzī*, Leiden and Boston 2006, p. 37, n. 104–107. As Shihadeh notes, al-Rāzī was very critical towards the early concept of *jabr*, and argued against the views of famous early *kalām* Jabrīs, such as Jahm b. Ṣafwān (executed 128/746), Shihadeh, *The Teleological Ethics*, p. 38. For al-Rāzī's harsh critique against the Jabriyya, see al-Rāzī, Fakhr al-Dīn: *al-Maṭālib al-ʿāliya min al-ʿilm al-ilāhī*, ed. by Aḥmad Ḥijāzī al-Saqā, Beirut 1407/1987, vol. 3, pp. 309–310. Judging from al-Rāzī's own statements against the Jabriyya, Gimaret's assertion, that "Rāzī n'hésite pas à se declarer ǧabrite", (Gimaret, Daniel: *Théories de l'acte humain en théologie musulmane*, Paris 1980, p. 142) is a bit hasty and inaccurate. Hoover also followed Gimaret's assertion. Hoover, *Ibn Taymiyya's Theodicy*, p. 143. The Zaydī scholar Ibn al-Murtaḍā (d. 840/1437) describes al-Rāzī as "one of the Mujbira [syn. of Jabriyya]", Ibn al-Murtaḍā, Aḥmad b. Yaḥyā: *al-Munya wal-amal fī sharḥ al-milal wal-niḥal*, ed. by Muḥammad Jawād Mashkūr, Beirut 1410/1990, p. 209.

11 The identification of the Ashʿarīs as Jabrīs is one of the fundamentals of Ibn Qayyim al-Jawziyya's discourse. See, for example, in Ibn Qayyim al-Jawziyya's long theological treatise in verse, Ibn Qayyim al-Jawziyya: *al-Kāfiya al-shāfiya fī al-intiṣār lil-firqa al-nājiya. Al-Qaṣīda al-nūniyya*, ed. by ʿAbd Allāh b. Muḥammad al-ʿUmayr, Riyadh 1416/1996, pp. 203–205 (verses 2631–2677). Or in Ibn Qayyim al-Jawziyya: *al-Fawāʾid*, ed. by Muṣṭafā b. al-ʿAdawī, al-Mansoura and Farskour-Damietta 1422/2001, pp. 34–35. In the closing paragraph of the epistle entitled *al-Furqān bayna al-ḥaqq wal-bāṭil*, Ibn Taymiyya enfolds the Ashʿariyya with "Jahm b. Ṣafwān and his followers", and adds: "The Ashʿariyya agree with them on *jabr*, however they have a terminological dispute (*nizāʿ lafẓī*) with them in terms of affirming *kasb* and the ability to perform *kasb*." Ibn Taymiyya: *Majmūʿat al-Fatāwā li-shaykh al-islām Taqī al-Dīn Aḥmad ibn Taymiyya al-Ḥarrānī*, ed. by ʿĀmir al-Jazzār and Anwar al-Bāz, Riyadh and al-Mansoura 1419/ 1998, vol. 13, p. 122. See also Hoover's survey on the Jabrīs as Ashʿariyya, Hoover, *Ibn Taymiyya's Theodicy*, pp. 110–111.

nal textual proofs available for Ibn Qayyim al-Jawziyya, and empowered him to refer to his contemporaries the Ashʿarīs as Jabriyya. Still, Ibn Qayyim al-Jawziyya, again following his master, never rejected al-Rāzī's theory of the human act altogether, but adopted the lion's share of al-Rāzī's argumentations, while promoting his theory of the human act. Ibn Taymiyya and Ibn Qayyim al-Jawziyya's theory integrated the concept of free will within the traditionalist teachings on predetermination.

This article deals with Ibn Qayyim al-Jawziyya's critique on the interpretation of his Ashʿarī contemporaries to al-Rāzī's writings on the concept of *jabr*. This theme appears in chapter 19 of Ibn Qayyim al-Jawziyya's magnum opus on predetermination and human choice, *Shifāʾ al-ʿalīl fī masāʾil al-qaḍāʾ wal-qadar wal-ḥikma wal-taʿlīl* (Healing the Person Afflicted with Wrong Concepts about Predetermination, Wisdom and Causality; henceforth *Shifāʾ al-ʿalīl*).[12] Arranged as a debate between a Sunni, holding Ibn Qayyim al-Jawziyya's views and a Jabrī, holding Ashʿarī views, chapter 19 of *Shifāʾ al-ʿalīl* is based on al-Rāzī's discussions on the doctrine of *jabr*. To the best of my knowledge, chapter 19 has not yet been analyzed or even described, thus the link between this text and the writings of al-Rāzī is revealed here for the first time.

Chapter 19 is first and foremost a didactic text, through which Ibn Qayyim al-Jawziyya's unique writing skills are revealed alongside his ambitions to educate and entertain his potential readers. The first part of this article deals with the literary genre of *munāẓara* (debate), on which chapter 19 is modeled. An outline of chapter 19 will be followed by a short discussion of the literary devices used by Ibn Qayyim al-Jawziyya in order to depict a vivid dialogue.

The second part of the article begins with a summary of al-Rāzī's argumentations for *jabr*, and continues with a presentation of these argumentations, as they appear in chapter 19 of *Shifāʾ al-ʿalīl*. The concept of *jabr* in chapter 19 is explored on three levels: the first level gives the basic argumentations for *jabr* in an attempt to simplify the doctrine of *jabr* and convert this doctrine into a standard traditionalist profes-

12 Ibn Qayyim al-Jawziyya, Shams al-Dīn Muḥammad: *Shifāʾ al-ʿalīl fī masāʾil al-qaḍāʾ wal-qadar wal-ḥikma wal-taʿlīl*, ed. by Muḥammad Badr al-Dīn Abū Firās al-Naʿsānī, Cairo 1323/1903. This is a reliable edition, but all the same I provide references here to the more accessible and less reliable Ibn Qayyim al-Jawziyya: *Shifāʾ al-ʿalīl fī masāʾil al-qaḍāʾ wal-qadar wal-ḥikma wal-taʿlīl*, ed. by al-Sayyid Muḥammad al-Sayyid and Saʿīd Maḥmūd, Cairo 1414/1994.

sion of faith. The so-called profession of faith in *jabr* is based entirely on al-Rāzī's teachings, and differs from the early doctrine of *jabr* as recorded in the heresiographic literature. The second level of the discussion deals with al-Rāzī's theory of the human act, from which his pro-*jabr* statements evolve. On the third level, another theme is integrated, that of "obligating what is beyond one's capability" (*taklīf mā lā yuṭāq*). This theme represents the moral and practical implications of the concept of *jabr*. In a way, both debaters offer two possible renderings of al-Rāzī's texts on *jabr*, and the theory of the human act: the Jabrī-Ashʿarī rendering and the Sunni rendering, which is actually Ibn Qayyim al-Jawziyya's rendering. The second part of this article, following the three levels on which the doctrine of *jabr* is explored in chapter 19 of *Shifāʾ al-ʿalīl*, presents the Jabrī-Ashʿarī interpretation of al-Rāzī's texts juxtaposed with the Sunni interpretation.

Unlike other parts of *Shifāʾ al-ʿalīl* copied from Ibn Taymiyya's works,[13] chapter 19 represents Ibn Qayyim al-Jawziyya's original writing. Chapter 19 is abundant in citations from the writings of al-Rāzī, thus raising the question of Ibn Qayyim al-Jawziyya's familiarity with al-Rāzī's thought. Did the Rāziyyan text find its way into *Shifāʾ al-ʿalīl* through a direct delving of Ibn Qayyim al-Jawziyya in the writings of Fakhr al-Dīn al-Rāzī, or through the mediation of Ibn Taymiyya's teachings? This question will be briefly examined in the last part of the article.

1. The Dialogue: Setting, Participants, Outline, and Atmosphere

The polemics between Ibn Qayyim al-Jawziyya and a variety of Ashʿarī and Muʿtazilī thinkers are most vividly reflected in a series of four successive chapters in *Shifāʾ al-ʿalīl*: the last section of chapter 17, chapter 18, chapter 19, and chapter 20. In these chapters, we find a confrontation between Ibn Qayyim al-Jawziyya's views on the theory of the human act and the two opposing theories of the Ashʿarī determin-

---

13 The most conspicuous example is that of chapter 30. See Holtzman, Livnat: Human Choice, Divine Guidance and the *Fiṭra* Tradition. The Use of Ḥadīth in the Theological Treatises by Ibn Taymiyya and Ibn Qayyim al-Jawziyya, in: Yossef Rapoport and Shahab Ahmed (eds.): *Ibn Taymiyya and His Times*, Karachi 2010, pp. 163–188.

ism and the Muʿtazilī libertarian freedom. This quartet of chapters is a didactic manual guiding its reader through the labyrinth of theological debates, and is primarily meant to provide the reader with the proper arguments for defying Ashʿarī and Muʿtazilī views. Among these four chapters, chapters 19 and 20 stand out, because they present the discussion of *jabr* in the form of a debate between a Sunni, representing Ibn Qayyim al-Jawziyya's views, a Jabrī representing Ashʿarī views, and a Qadarī representing Muʿtazilī views.

The title of chapter 19, *Fī dhikr munāẓara jarat bayna jabrī wa-sunnī jamaʿahumā majlis mudhākara* (A Report of a Debate Between a Jabrī and a Sunni Brought Together in a Memorizing Session, hence: chapter 19), provides several details on the event, its setting, participants, and even the atmosphere.

The event is a debate or a theological dispute (*munāẓara* pl. *munāẓarāt*); the participants have no names, but are distinguished by their typical agnomens, Jabrī and Sunni. A tapestry of citations and counter-citations culled from several theological works, the debate serves a didactic purpose of revealing the inventory of Ashʿarī arguments for the doctrine of *jabr*, and confronting the doctrine with Ibn Qayyim al-Jawziyya's refutation of these arguments.[14]

Several examples of *munāẓarāt* in his works testify that Ibn Qayyim al-Jawziyya mastered the art of oral debating both theoretically and practically, and accounts of *munāẓarāt* in which he participated appear in his earlier works.[15] In *Hidāyat al-ḥayārā fī ajwibat al-yahūd wal-naṣārā* (Guiding the Bewildered as for the Ultimate Responses to be Given to the Jews and the Christians), he reports on a debate he had with a Jewish scholar in Egypt.[16] In *Badāʾiʿ al-fawāʾid* (Amazing Ben-

---

14 The first to remark on the didactic purpose in Ibn Qayyim al-Jawziyya's writings is Perho, Irmeli: Man Chooses His Destiny. Ibn Qayyim al-Jawziyya's Views on Predestination, in: *Islam and Christian-Muslim Relations* (12) 2001, pp. 61–70.

15 For *munāẓara* as a literary genre and an actual practice, see Wagner, Ewald: Munāẓara, in: *EI*^{2}, vol. 7 (1993), pp. 565–568; Makdisi, George: *The Rise of Colleges. Institutions of Learning in Islam and the West,* Edinburgh 1981, p. 110. For anecdotes on disputations, see ibid., pp. 135–140. For an interesting example of a 12th century *munāẓara* between the Ḥanbalī scholar Ibn Qudāma (d. 620/1223) and an unknown Damascene Ashʿarī, see Daiber, Hans: The Quran as a "Shibboleth" of Varying Concepts of the Godhead, in: *Israel Oriental Studies* 14 (1994), pp. 249–296.

16 Two *munāẓaras* appear successively in *Hidāyat al-ḥayārā*: one is supposed to be a record of a debate in which Ibn Qayyim al-Jawziyya himself participated. During his stay in Egypt, Ibn Qayyim al-Jawziyya confronted "one of

efits), another fairly early work, Ibn Qayyim al-Jawziyya integrates a report of a dispute he supposedly had with a Samaritan in Nābulus. This report appears in a chapter which discusses the art of debating with a special emphasis on Koranic verses, suitable for use in debates with the unbelievers.[17] In *al-Ṣawāʾiq al-mursala ʿalā al-jahmiyya wal-muʿaṭṭila* (Thunderbolts Directed against the Jahmiyya and the Muʿaṭṭila), a later work most likely composed after *Shifāʾ al-ʿalīl*, he cites a *munāẓara*, the contents of which he heard from ʿAbd Allāh Sharaf al-Dīn Ibn Taymiyya (d. 727/1326–27), his master's brother and a scholar in his own right.[18] None of these *munāẓarāt* equal chapter 19 in *Shifāʾ al-ʿalīl*, neither in richness nor in the complexity of the theological themes.

The *munāẓara* in chapter 19 differs from other *munāẓarāt* described by Ibn Qayyim al-Jawziyya, since it takes place in the course of a session dedicated to the device of memorizing texts (*majlis mudhākara*). Besides the setting of the debate in a *madrasa*, the term *majlis mudhākara* implies that the dispute in chapter 19 is most likely between two students striving to memorize a text and to quiz one another, and not between two mature scholars.[19] The word *majlis* suggests that the two participants sit together while memorizing their texts. Sitting together means that although presented as bitter rivals, the Sunni and the Jabrī, in fact, belong to the same religious trend (both are actually Sunnis), so their ideological differences are not likely to be revealed at first glance. In comparison, the Sunni and the Qadarī arguing in chapter 20 of *Shifāʾ al-ʿalīl* do not sit together but probably conduct their discussion while standing, a clear indication of their belonging to two opposing sides. Actually, they are not allowed to sit together, according to the following prophetic Hadith,

---

the greatest scholars and leaders of the Jews" about the true message of Islam. The other debate is between an anonymous Moroccan scholar and a Jew. Ibn Qayyim al-Jawziyya: *Hidāyat al-ḥayārā fī ajwibat al-yahūd wal-naṣārā*, ed. by Abū ʿAbd al-Raḥmān ʿĀdil b. Saʿd, Cairo n. d., pp. 150–153.

17 Ibn Qayyim al-Jawziyya, Shams al-Dīn Muḥammad: *Badāʾiʿ al-fawāʾid*, ed. by ʿAlī b. Muḥammad al-ʿImrān, Jedda 1424/2003, pp. 1606–1607. For the chapter on the art of debating, see ibid., pp. 1540–1610.

18 Ibn Qayyim al-Jawziyya: *al-Ṣawāʾiq al-mursala ʿalā al-jahmiyya wal-muʿaṭṭila*, ed. by Zakariyyā ʿAlī Yūsuf, n. p. n. d., pp. 42–45. See further details in Bori, Caterina: Ibn Taymiyya. Una vita esemplare; analisi delle fonti classiche della sua biografia, in: *Rivista degli Studi Orientali* 76 (2003), p. 52.

19 For *munāẓara* and *mudhākara* as two important techniques of learning, see Pedersen, Jens and Makdisi, George: Madrasa, in: *EI*², vol. 5 (1984), pp. 1123–1154 (section 6. Courses of instruction and personnel); Makdisi, *The Rise of Colleges*, p. 276.

addressed to the Sunnis: "Do not sit (*lā tujālisū*) in the company of the Qadarīs and do not start a conversation with them."[20]

Although the dialogue is a literary fiction and not an historical record, it is embedded in Ibn Qayyim al-Jawziyya's times, that is the beginning of the 14th century, and not much earlier. The substantial use of al-Rāzī's texts in the debate by both participants, especially by the Jabrī, establishes this assumption.

The debate in chapter 19 comprises nine sections (*faṣl*, pl. *fuṣūl*) of uneven length. Each section (except the fifth and sixth section) begins with a brief statement by the Jabrī. In the first section,[21] the Jabrī professes his faith in *jabr*, while the Sunni rejects *jabr*, seeing it as a dangerous idea. Whereas the Sunni wishes to discuss the dangerous moral implications of the belief in *jabr*, the Jabrī sticks to a theoretical discussion. Using the "preponderance without a preponderator" (*tarjīḥ bi-lā murajjiḥ*) argument, the Jabrī wishes to prove that the belief in *jabr* is unavoidable.[22] The Sunni ignores the Jabrī's argument. He elaborates at length the views of the Muʿtazila on the motives (*dawāʿī*) of the human act, and concludes that the "preponderance without a preponderator" argument does not lead to *jabr*.[23]

In the second section of chapter 19,[24] the Sunni surprisingly recruits a Qadarī. In his only appearance in the dialogue, the Qadarī voluntarily explains to the Jabrī the Muʿtazilī views on motives. The Jabrī claims, that indeed the motive of the human act is the cause of human action (*sabab al-fiʿl*), but because the motive is created by God, the human act as a whole is created by God.[25] To this the Sunni seems to agree. However, he modifies the Jabrī's argument using a new phrase, "a part of a cause" (*juzʾ sabab*).[26] Nevertheless, the apparent momentary agree-

20 The Hadith appears in Abū Dāwūd al-Sijistānī: *Sunan Abī Dāwūd*, ed. by Aḥmad Saʿd ʿAlī, Cairo 1952, vol. 2, p. 224. For traditions in the same vein see Abū Bakr al-Ājurrī: *Kitāb al-Sharīʿa*, Beirut 1421/2000, pp. 197–201.

21 Ibn Qayyim al-Jawziyya, *Shifāʾ al-ʿalīl*, pp. 317–323; Ibn Qayyim al-Jawziyya, *Shifāʾ al-ʿalīl*, 1903, pp. 139–142.

22 Ibn Qayyim al-Jawziyya, *Shifāʾ al-ʿalīl*, p. 319; Ibn Qayyim al-Jawziyya, *Shifāʾ al-ʿalīl*, 1903, p. 140.

23 Ibn Qayyim al-Jawziyya, *Shifāʾ al-ʿalīl*, pp. 321–323; Ibn Qayyim al-Jawziyya, *Shifāʾ al-ʿalīl*, 1903, pp. 140–142.

24 Ibn Qayyim al-Jawziyya, *Shifāʾ al-ʿalīl*, pp. 323–327; Ibn Qayyim al-Jawziyya, *Shifāʾ al-ʿalīl*, 1903, pp. 142–144.

25 Ibn Qayyim al-Jawziyya, *Shifāʾ al-ʿalīl*, p. 324; Ibn Qayyim al-Jawziyya, *Shifāʾ al-ʿalīl*, 1903, p. 143.

26 Ibn Qayyim al-Jawziyya, *Shifāʾ al-ʿalīl*, p. 325; Ibn Qayyim al-Jawziyya, *Shifāʾ al-ʿalīl*, 1903, p. 143.

ment between the two rivals passes away when the Sunni delves into the definition of *jabr*,[27] while insisting on leading the discussion back to the moral implications of this view.[28]

In the third section,[29] the Jabrī succinctly argues against the Muʿtazilī view, which ascribes efficacy to human power. According to the Jabrī, the human act cannot be a *maqdūr* (an outcome of power) of two agents: God and the human being. The Sunni responds with a lengthy description of the views of Ashʿarī and Muʿtazilī scholars, particularly Fakhr al-Dīn al-Rāzī and Abū Ḥusayn al-Baṣrī (d. 436/1044),[30] on the efficacy of human power on the human act. The Sunni concludes this review with his own opinion, according to which the human act is a *maqdūr* of the power of two agents, while applying the phrase *juzʾ sabab*, which he coined earlier.[31]

The fourth section[32] presents the longest argument the Jabrī is allowed to make in this dialogue, which is as follows: had the human being been the effective agent of his actions, he would have known the details of his actions. The Sunni's response, which appears in the fifth and sixth[33] sections, concentrates on the practical aspects of the Jabrī's argument as reflected in the case of a divorce oath taken by a drunkard (*ṭalāq al-sakrān*).[34] Its relevance to the discussion is feeble, as the Sunni

27 Ibn Qayyim al-Jawziyya, *Shifāʾ al-ʿalīl*, pp. 326–327; Ibn Qayyim al-Jawziyya, *Shifāʾ al-ʿalīl*, 1903, p. 144.

28 Ibn Qayyim al-Jawziyya, *Shifāʾ al-ʿalīl*, p. 327; Ibn Qayyim al-Jawziyya, *Shifāʾ al-ʿalīl*, 1903, p. 144.

29 Ibn Qayyim al-Jawziyya, *Shifāʾ al-ʿalīl*, pp. 327–331; Ibn Qayyim al-Jawziyya, *Shifāʾ al-ʿalīl*, 1903, pp. 144–147.

30 For Fakhr al-Dīn's refutation of Abū al-Ḥusayn al-Baṣrī's views, see notes 45, 47 below.

31 Ibn Qayyim al-Jawziyya, *Shifāʾ al-ʿalīl*, pp. 330–331; Ibn Qayyim al-Jawziyya, *Shifāʾ al-ʿalīl*, 1903, pp. 146–147.

32 Ibn Qayyim al-Jawziyya, *Shifāʾ al-ʿalīl*, pp. 331–333; Ibn Qayyim al-Jawziyya, *Shifāʾ al-ʿalīl*, 1903, pp. 147–148.

33 Ibn Qayyim al-Jawziyya, *Shifāʾ al-ʿalīl*, pp. 333–335; Ibn Qayyim al-Jawziyya, *Shifāʾ al-ʿalīl*, 1903, pp. 148–149.

34 Ibn Qayyim al-Jawziyya, *Shifāʾ al-ʿalīl*, pp. 331–333; Ibn Qayyim al-Jawziyya, *Shifāʾ al-ʿalīl*, 1903, pp. 147–148. The theme of *ṭalāq al-sakrān* appears in several of Ibn Qayyim al-Jawziyya's works, see Ibn Qayyim al-Jawziyya: *Āthār al-imām Ibn Qayyim al-Jawziyya wa-mā laḥiqahā min aʿmāl. Ighāthat al-lahfān fī ḥukm ṭalāq al-ghaḍbān*, ed. by ʿAbd al-Raḥmān b. Ḥasan b. Qāʾid, Jedda n. d., vol. 6, pp. 26–28, 41, 64; Ibn Qayyim al-Jawziyya, *Iʿlām al-muwaqqiʿīn ʿan rabb al-ʿālamīn*, ed. by Muḥammad ʿAbd al-Salām Ibrāhīm, Beirut 1414/1993, vol. 4, pp. 38–39; Ibn Qayyim al-Jawziyya, *Zād al-maʿād fī hady khayr al-ʿibād*, Cairo 1425/2004, vol. 4, pp. 23–26.

himself admits, while pointing out that *ṭalāq al-sakrān* is a specific case, which does not apply to the general rule.

In the seventh section,[35] the Jabrī mocks the Muʿtazilī view, according to which apostasy and ignorance are created by the human agent. Is there an intelligent man who wants apostasy and ignorance for himself? He wonders and sums up: the human being commits both apostasy and ignorance, but not out of his own choice and will. The Sunni rejoins that that is indeed the case for many people, who, out of their own stubbornness, evil intentions and hatred, wish for themselves to be ignorant and apostates. Eight Koranic verses, describing the reluctance of the apostates to accept the true message of Islam, corroborate the Sunni's claim.[36]

In the eighth section,[37] a new argument is raised by the Jabrī in order to negate the possibility of the efficacy of human power on the human act: if human power affected the human act, it would affect any created thing. The Sunni refutes this argument easily.

In the ninth and final section,[38] the Jabrī refines the statement in which he started the dialogue: the proof of the existence of a sole Creator negates the possibility of the human being as an agent of his actions. The Jabrī concludes that the "proof from reciprocal hindrance" (*dalīl al-tamānuʿ*) proves his point. The Sunni refuses to accept this argument. He tries to make his point, but the irritated Jabrī refuses to listen. The Jabrī and Sunni merely repeat their previous argumentations. The dialogue concludes with the Sunni's speech of victory, emphasizing his view that the human being is indeed an efficacious agent of his actions.

All in all, the Jabrī makes 15 statements, most of which are relatively short, while the Sunni's answers are longer and more elaborated. Most of the Jabrī's arguments[39] rely on single textual proofs, without disclos-

35 Ibn Qayyim al-Jawziyya, *Shifāʾ al-ʿalīl*, pp. 335–336; Ibn Qayyim al-Jawziyya, *Shifāʾ al-ʿalīl*, 1903, p. 149.

36 Koran (7:146; 41:17; 27:13–14; 29:38; 2:102; 2:90; 3:70–72).

37 Ibn Qayyim al-Jawziyya, *Shifāʾ al-ʿalīl*, p. 337; Ibn Qayyim al-Jawziyya, *Shifāʾ al-ʿalīl*, 1903, pp. 149–150.

38 Ibn Qayyim al-Jawziyya, *Shifāʾ al-ʿalīl*, pp. 337–341; Ibn Qayyim al-Jawziyya, *Shifāʾ al-ʿalīl*, 1903, pp. 150–152.

39 Three of the Jabrī's arguments are fairly long and detailed: his first "preponderance without a preponderator" argument (Ibn Qayyim al-Jawziyya, *Shifāʾ al-ʿalīl*, p. 319; Ibn Qayyim al-Jawziyya, *Shifāʾ al-ʿalīl*, 1903, p. 140), his argument that the human act cannot be a *maqdūr* (an outcome of power) of two agents (Ibn Qayyim al-Jawziyya, *Shifāʾ al-ʿalīl*, pp. 327–328; Ibn Qayyim al-Jawziyya, *Shifāʾ al-ʿalīl*, 1903, pp. 144–145) and his argument on the detailed knowledge

ing their source, and the Jabrī refrains from citing the opinions of leading scholars. In most cases, the Jabrī begins his statements with a new idea without referring to the Sunni's rejoinders.

Although the Jabrī sets the agenda, he discovers soon that the outcome of the debate is beyond his grasp. In two cases, the Jabrī reacts impulsively to the prolonged answers of the Sunni. Close to the beginning of the debate, after the Sunni offers a clear response, the Jabrī frowns: "This answer is worth nothing", while making a minimal effort to address this response.[40] Towards the end of the debate, after the Sunni explains why a certain proof given by the Jabrī is irrelevant to the discussion, the Jabrī looses his temper. "Enough of that subject!" he exclaims.[41] The Jabrī's impulsive responses establish his position as the inferior participant in the debate.

The Jabrī is indeed not a formidable rival for the Sunni, whose wits corroborate his erudition. In the heat of the debate, the Sunni cites the positions of leading Ashʿarī thinkers, such as Abū al-Ḥasan al-Ashʿarī (d. 324/935–936), Fakhr al-Dīn al-Rāzī (referred to in his appellation as *Ibn al-Khaṭīb*), al-Rāzī's disciple Sirāj al-Dīn al-Urmawī (d. 683/1283), Abū Isḥāq al-Isfarāʾīnī (d. 418/1027), Imām al-Ḥaramayn al-Juwaynī (d. 478/1085), and Abū Bakr al-Bāqillānī (d. 403/1013). He also quotes from the teachings of two Muʿtazilī thinkers, Abū al-Ḥusayn al-Baṣrī (d. 436/1044) and al-Malāḥimī al-Khwārazmī (d. 536/1141). As the Sunni's familiarity with the relevant material is beyond doubt, he explains these scholars' viewpoints to the Jabrī. The Jabrī is depicted almost as a layman, mechanically citing the text in front of him, without making the minimal effort to analyze or even understand the material he cites. In contrast to the Jabrī, the erudite Sunni assumes a well-balanced position, and therefore emerges as the superior participant in this debate. Only in one case does the Sunni allow himself to refer specifically to his opponent, when he sarcastically says: "What a remarkable person you are!"[42]

---

of his actions, which the effective agent holds (Ibn Qayyim al-Jawziyya, *Shifāʾ al-ʿalīl*, pp. 331–332; Ibn Qayyim al-Jawziyya, *Shifāʾ al-ʿalīl*, 1903, p. 147).

40 Ibn Qayyim al-Jawziyya, *Shifāʾ al-ʿalīl*, p. 323; Ibn Qayyim al-Jawziyya, *Shifāʾ al-ʿalīl*, 1903, p. 142.

41 Ibn Qayyim al-Jawziyya, *Shifāʾ al-ʿalīl*, p. 338; Ibn Qayyim al-Jawziyya, *Shifāʾ al-ʿalīl*, 1903, p. 150.

42 Ibn Qayyim al-Jawziyya, *Shifāʾ al-ʿalīl*, p. 335; Ibn Qayyim al-Jawziyya, *Shifāʾ al-ʿalīl*, 1903, p. 149.

In an early stage of the debate, the resourceful Sunni even invites a Qadarī passer-by to participate, and the Qadarī voluntarily explains his views on motives to the Jabrī. The Sunni interrupts, and negates the Qadarī's views altogether, thus demonstrating his skills in refuting the arguments of two opponents at the same time.[43]

In the few parts of the text where an apparent connection between the Jabrī's statements and the Sunni's responses exists, we encounter a more natural flow of the dialogue, as found in a face-to-face dispute between two students. For example, after the Jabrī presents his 'preponderance without a preponderator' argument, the Sunni rejoins: "Is this one of the arrows in your quiver? Thank God it does not have a quill feather and an arrowhead! On top of that, your arrow is crooked and cannot fly directly to its target."[44]

In these parts of the text, the author provides the dialogue with a sense of reality by placing typical defamations in the mouth of his protagonists. This sense of reality is interrupted by either the lengthy and tiresome responses of the Sunni, or by the discursive nature of the Jabrī's statements. These text features make chapter 19 a typical didactic piece. Therefore, this chapter cannot be considered a recording or restoration of real life polemics.

2. A Three-Level Debate on *jabr*

Al-Rāzī's argumentations for *jabr*, which form a part of his groundbreaking theory of the human act, appear in several of his works, including his Koran exegesis.[45] Al-Rāzī's theory deals with the way,

---

43 Ibn Qayyim al-Jawziyya, *Shifāʾ al-ʿalīl*, pp. 324–325; Ibn Qayyim al-Jawziyya, *Shifāʾ al-ʿalīl*, 1903, pp. 142–143.

44 Ibn Qayyim al-Jawziyya, *Shifāʾ al-ʿalīl*, p. 319; *Shifāʾ al-ʿalīl*, 1903, p. 140.

45 The relevant texts on *jabr* by al-Rāzī are: al-Rāzī, *al-Maṭālib al-ʿāliya*, vol. 3, p. 73, vol. 8, pp. 11–20, vol. 9, pp. 9–173; idem: *Kitāb al-Arbaʿīn fī uṣūl al-dīn*, ed. by Aḥmad Ḥijāzī al-Saqā, Beirut 1424/2004, pp. 219–27; idem: *Kitāb Maʿālim uṣūl al-dīn*, ed. by Samīḥ Dughaym, Beirut 1992, pp. 61–69; idem: *Muḥaṣṣal afkār al-mutaqaddimīn wal-mutaʾakhkhirīn min al-ʿulamāʾ wal-ḥukamāʾ wal-mutakallimīn*, ed. Samīḥ Dughaym, Beirut 1992, pp. 146–156; idem: *al-Maḥṣūl fī ʿilm uṣūl al-fiqh*, 6 vols., ed. Jābir Fayyāḍ al-ʿAlwānī, Beirut 1412/1992, vol. 2, p. 233. Sherman A. Jackson discussed the "preponderance without a preponderator" argument, as it appears in al-Rāzī, *al-Maḥṣūl*, vol. 1, pp. 126–128; Jackson, Sherman A.: The Alchemy of Domination? Some Asharite Responses to Mutazilite Ethics, in: *International Journal of Middle Eastern Studies* 31

in which the human act comes into being, while concentrating, among other factors, on the efficacy of human power on the human act. This highly theoretical discussion leads him to deal with the psychology of the human being as an agent. The question, whether this agent chooses to act (*mukhtār*) or whether he is compelled to act (*majbūr, muḍṭarr ʿalā afʿālihi*), is central to al-Rāzī's discussions.[46]

The following description of al-Rāzī's position is based mainly on a theological discussion, which appears in the "commands and interdictions" (*al-awāmir wal-nawāhī*) section of al-Rāzī's *fiqh* manual, *al-Maḥṣūl fī ʿilm uṣūl al-fiqh* (What can be Obtained in the Science of the Principles of Jurisprudence; henceforth *al-Maḥṣūl*).[47] This section bears some resemblance to chapter 19, because its format is a theological treatise which refutes adversaries (*al-radd ʿalā*). In this case, the adversary is a libertarian Muʿtazilī. Al-Rāzī toils to convince this adversary of the veracity of his rationalized determinism.

Al-Rāzī's basic assumption is that the voluntary human agent (*mukhtār*) must act, when the motive of the action (*dāʿī, dāʿiya*, pl. *dawāʿī*) combines with the human power (*qudra*). Under the influence of the Muʿtazilī doctrines, al-Rāzī builds his argumentations for *jabr* on the motivations for action. Whereas the Muʿtazilīs claim that the human act depends on the motive for an action, and that the motive derives from the human agent himself, al-Rāzī claims that the occurrence of the human act depends on a motive of an act, and that the motive is created by God. With the existence of this motive, the act

(1999), pp. 185–201. A source which has received the attention of scholars such as Roger Arnaldez, Daniel Gimaret, Wilfred Madelung, and recently Shihadeh and Hoover, is al-Rāzī's interpretation of Koran (2:6–7); al-Rāzī, Fakhr al-Dīn: *Tafsīr al-Fakhr al-Rāzī al-mushtahar bil-tasfīr al-kabīr wa-mafātīḥ al-ghayb*, Beirut 1414/1993, vol. 1, pp. 55–65; Arnaldez, Roger: Apories sur la prédestination et le libre arbitre dans le commentaire de Razi, in: *Mélanges de l'institut dominicain d'études orientales* 6 (1959/1961), pp. 123–126; Madelung, Wilfred: The Late Muʿtazila and Determinism. The Philosophers' Trap, in: Biancamaria Scarcia Amoretti and Lucia Rostagno (eds.): *Yād-Nāma* in Memoria di Alessandro Bausani, Rome 1991, vol. 1 *Islamistica*, pp. 245–257; Gimaret, *Théories de l'acte*, Paris 1980, pp. 140–144; Hoover, *Ibn Taymiyya's Theodicy*, pp. 143–144; Shihadeh, *The Teleological Ethics*, pp. 38–39. The reader might want to consult further texts on *jabr* by al-Rāzī, mentioned in Shihadeh, *The Teleological Ethics*, p. 37, n. 105.

46 Shihadeh, *The Teleological Ethics*, p. 17.

47 Al-Rāzī, *al-Maḥṣūl*, vol. 2, pp. 215–233. *Al-Maḥṣūl* is a fairly early work of al-Rāzī, Shihadeh, *The Teleological Ethics*, p. 7.

must occur. Hence, he concludes, "the compulsion (*jabr*) of the act is necessary".[48]

In order to prove that the motive of the human act indeed comes from God, al-Rāzī uses his "preponderance without a preponderator" argument, as follows: first, al-Rāzī states that the human being is capable of either performing an act or not performing it. Al-Rāzī then argues that since performing the act or not performing it are two equal possibilities as far as the human power is concerned, then a preponderator (*murajjiḥ*) which preponderates one action over the other is needed. In other words, preponderance without a preponderator is impossible. The preponderator cannot come from the human being, again since the human power needs a preponderator to preponderate an action over a non-action. Hence, the preponderator, which is actually the motive to act, comes from God. Al-Rāzī concludes: "Since the human act is dependent on a motive created by God, and since the act must occur when this motive is created, then the compulsion of the act is necessary."[49]

In sum, according to al-Rāzī, the occurrence of human action from the human being is dependent on a motive for an action, which is created by God. Al-Rāzī also declares that this view must be referred to as *jabr*.

Al-Rāzī's rationalized determinism leads him even further, and he expresses a bold view, that "obligating what is above one's capability" (*taklīf mā lā yuṭāq*) is possible. Although this was stated by Ashʿarīs before him,[50] al-Rāzī's views are much more daring, because he identifies the concept of "obligating what is above one's capability" as the upshot of his rationalized concept of *jabr*. In *al-Maḥṣūl* he claims, that while God orders the apostate to believe in Him, He orders him what is impossible, since "faith for the apostate is impossible".[51] In order to

48 Al-Rāzī, *al-Maḥṣūl*, vol. 2, p. 225. For an elaboration of the Muʿtazilī views and al-Rāzī's refutation, see Madelung, The Late Muʿtazila, pp. 245–257; Gardet, Louis: *Les grands problèmes de la théologie musulmane. Dieu et la destinée de l'homme*, Paris 1967, pp. 130–131; Arnaldez, Apories sur la prédestination, pp. 130–131; Gimaret, *Théories de l'acte*, pp. 140–144; Shihadeh, *The Teleological Ethics*, pp. 25–26, 29–39.

49 Al-Rāzī, *al-Maḥṣūl*, vol. 2, p. 228. See Gimaret, *Théories de l'acte*, pp. 140–141.

50 Abrahamov, Binyamin: *al-Ḳāsim b. Ibrāhīm on the Proof of God's Existence*, Leiden 1990, pp. 38–39.

51 Al-Rāzī, *al-Maḥṣūl*, vol. 2, p. 216; see a parallel discussion in Hoover, *Ibn Taymiyya's Theodicy*, pp. 167–169; Shihadeh, *The Teleological Ethics*, pp. 101–105.

prove that, al-Rāzī uses several arguments, among which the "preponderance without a preponderator" argument is conspicuous. Al-Rāzī claims, again, that the occurrence of the human act from the human being depends on a motive (*dāʿiya*), which is created by God. The existence of that motive necessitates human action; hence the belief in *jabr* is necessary. This motive is a preponderator (*murajjiḥ*), preponderating the existence of the act upon its inexistence. Preponderance without a preponderator is impossible. The preponderator is created by God; hence, again, the belief in *jabr* is necessary. Since *jabr* is necessary, all obligations are actually "obligating what is above one's capability".[52]

Turning now to chapter 19, we encounter al-Rāzī's argumentations for *jabr* as cited and interpreted by the Jabrī and the Sunni. In other words, both the Jabrī and the Sunni accurately cite al-Rāzī in the course of their debate. In fact, the Rāziyyan exact wording is the most conspicuous feature of chapter 19. However, in order to simplify the discussion, any reference to parallel statements or passages in al-Rāzī's works will be presented primarily in the footnotes; except in cases in which an emphasis on parallelisms between al-Rāzī's texts and chapter 19 is required.

2.1. First Level: *jabr* as a Profession of Faith

The belief in the unity of God (*tawḥīd*) is the first article in all traditionalist professions of faith.[53] Therefore, the Jabrī's use of the concept of *tawḥīd* in his opening statement actually defines his profession of faith. He claims that the belief in *jabr* is derived from the belief in the unity of God:

> Affirming the doctrine of *jabr* is inescapable, since [it establishes] that the belief in God's unity (*tawḥīd*) is the true faith. Had we not believed in *jabr*, we would have affirmed that another agent, beside God, performs created acts, and that [like God], if he wants, he will perform, and if he does not, he will not. This is pure polytheism (*shirk*), which one can avoid only by declaring his belief in *jabr*.[54]

52 Al-Rāzī, *al-Maḥṣūl*, vol. 2, p. 225.

53 An accessible source for a discussion of Islamic creeds is Watt, W. Montgomery: *Islamic Creeds*, Edinburgh 1994.

54 Ibn Qayyim al-Jawziyya, *Shifāʾ al-ʿalīl*, Jabrī, p. 317; *Shifāʾ al-ʿalīl*, 1903, p. 139. See *al-Maṭālib al-ʿāliya*, vol. 9, pp. 16–17, where al-Rāzī states that there are only two options: either one believes in *jabr* or he denies the existence of the

Although the Jabrī does not define the term *jabr*, here he outlines the first part of the basic rationale of this doctrine: God creates human actions. The Jabrī ignores the second part of this rationale: God compels (*jabara*) the human being to perform these created actions. This avoidance of the basic meaning of *jabr* indicates that the Jabrī's profession of faith is substantially different from the early 8th century formula of *jabr.* Except for the use of the term *jabr*, the Jabrī's opening statement could be in complete accordance with the traditionalist Sunni view. It is however not, because the Sunni view rejects the concept of *jabr*.

The first argument for *jabr* is contained in the Jabrī's profession of faith: in an attempt to avoid polytheism, any attribute of creation is denied from the human being. He does not create his actions; hence he does not really perform them. Affirming that the human being is neither the creator nor the performer of his own actions is, as far as the Jabrī is concerned, the belief in *jabr*.

While presenting the doctrine of *jabr* as a profession of faith, the Jabrī uses two *kalāmic* tools, in order to fortify the basis of his belief in *jabr*. The first tool, the proof from reciprocal hindrance (*dalīl al-tamānuʿ*) is mentioned towards the end of the dialogue, where the Jabrī states that, using the proof from reciprocal hindrance, the human being is not an agent of his actions. [55]

The Jabrī does not identify or explain the proof from reciprocal hindrance, and he does not describe its connection with *jabr* and God's unity (*tawḥīd*). This proof is meant to establish the existence of one God by assuming that two or more equal powers cannot act harmoniously, and are bound to either destroy each other or perform nothing.[56] It fits

---

Creator (*nafy al-ṣāniʿ*). The same view is stated in al-Rāzī's interpretation of Koran (2:7) (*Tafsīr al-Fakhr al-Rāzī*, vol. 1, part 2, p. 59). Here in J. Hoover's translation: "Establishing the Divinity leads necessarily to the view of compulsion (*jabr*)," Hoover, *Ibn Taymiyya's Theodicy*, p. 144. See also Shihadeh, *The Teleological Ethics*, p. 20.

55 Ibn Qayyim al-Jawziyya, *Shifāʾ al-ʿalīl*, p. 337; *Shifāʾ al-ʿalīl*, 1903, p. 150. See al-Rāzī, *Kitāb al-Arbaʿīn*, second proof, p. 214; third proof, p. 217. Both proofs discuss the impossibility of the existence of two gods, without a reference to the human being as a possible creator of his acts.

56 Abrahamov, *Islamic Theology*, pp. 35–36. *Dalīl al-tamānuʿ* is based on two Koranic verses: "Why, were there gods in earth and heaven other than God, they would surely go to ruin", Koran (21:22), and "God has not taken to Himself any son, nor is there any god with Him; for then each god would have taken off that he created and some of them would have risen up over others", Koran

the Jabrī's argument for *jabr*, in the following manner, which is not mentioned by the Jabrī himself: the concept of *jabr* negates the possibility that the human being is a real agent. Had he been a real agent, he would have been considered a creator of his actions. However, the proof from reciprocal hindrance negates the existence of any other creator but God; hence the proof leads to real *tawḥīd*; hence *jabr* leads to *tawḥīd*.

In order to advance his argument for *jabr*, the Jabrī uses another *kalāmic* tool, the *ilzām* (lit. coercion), a method of argumentation which forces the opponent to admit that his argument is absurd.[57] Here the Jabrī provokes his Sunni opponent and supposedly causes him to admit that his opposition to *jabr* leads to the conclusion that the human being is the creator of his actions, a concept which the Sunni himself disagrees with. This provocation ends with a Koranic verse, used here because its first part asserts that God is the sole Creator ("is there any creator…"). The second part of the verse ("There is no god but He") is an assertion of God's unity:

> In the issue of *jabr* I rely on an edge of a sword you cannot escape unless you are forced [to admit the veracity of] *jabr*. This admittance that your argument is absurd (*ilzām*) goes as follows: were the human being an agent, he would have originated (*muḥdith*) his action; hence he would have created (*khāliq*) it. This notion is negated by both Divine law and human reason, as says the Lord: "O men, remember God's blessing upon you; is there any creator, apart from God, who provides for you out of heavens and the earth? There is no god but He: how then are you perverted?"[58]

Both arguments, as presented here by the Jabrī, have their roots in al-Rāzī's writings, however with one conspicuous difference. In *Kitāb al-Arbaʿīn*, when Fakhr al-Dīn al-Rāzī presents *dalīl al-tamānuʿ* in

(23:91). Translation of Koranic verses in this article are taken from Arberry, Arthur J.: *The Koran Interpreted*, Oxford 1962.

57 *Ilzām* is parallel to *argumentum ad hominem*. In its proper variant this argumentation indeed leads the opponent to admit the invalidity of his own opinions, while exploring and inferring conclusions from them. Nevertheless, this argument quite often has abusive and personal variants of merely offending the opponent. Walton, Douglas: Informal Fallacy, in: *The Cambridge Dictionary of Philosophy*, 2nd ed., Cambridge 1999, pp. 432–433; Abrahamov, *Islamic Theology*, p. 27; van Ess, Josef: The Logical Structure of Islamic Theology, in: Gustave E. von Grunebaum (ed.): *Logic in Classical Islamic Culture*, Wiesbaden 1970, pp. 25–26.

58 Ibn Qayyim al-Jawziyya, *Shifāʾ al-ʿalīl*, p. 340; *Shifāʾ al-ʿalīl*, 1903, p. 151. The verse quoted here is Koran (35:3). In his Koran exegesis al-Rāzī does not make a special reference to this verse, al-Rāzī, *Tafsīr al-Fakhr al-Rāzī*, vol. 13, part 26, p. 5.

order to prove the existence of one Creator, and even when he uses *ilzām* in order to lead his Muʿtazilī opponent to admit that only God is an efficacious agent, he does not conclude that his line of argumentation eventually leads to *jabr*.[59] That is precisely the Sunni's comment to the Jabrī in response to the Jabrī's argument, that *dalīl al-tamānuʿ* is connected to *jabr*. The Sunni remarks, that this proof is irrelevant to the discussion, adding that "the most excellent among your later scholars", meaning Fakhr al-Dīn al-Rāzī, used this proof in order to demonstrate that two gods, constantly negating one another, would have prevented each other from creating.[60]

Even the Jabrī's attempt to use *ilzām* does not leave its mark on the Sunni, and he refuses to comply with the Jabrī's demand to admit the veracity of *jabr*. Armed with Koranic verses that indicate that the human being is the agent of his actions,[61] and therefore worthy of reward and punishment accordingly, the Sunni dismisses the Jabrī's *kalāmic* efforts with open contempt, while indicating that addressing this proof is a waste of time:

> We have many such examples in the Koran. Furthermore, the senses indicate so [i. e., that the human being is the agent of his actions]. Therefore, we shall not accept any specious argument (*shubha*) based on [arguments] which are contrary to our proofs. Using this *shubha* is like rejecting necessary proofs, and therefore no attention should be paid to it. A scholar is not obligated to address any *shubha* presented to him, as there is no end to this.[62]

---

59 *Dalīl al-tamānuʿ* is discussed in the 21st question ("which clarifies that the Creator of the world is one"), third proof, *Kitāb al-Arbaʿīn*. There al-Rāzī negates the existence of two gods, when each of them must possess an effective power on all possibilities. In other words, either of the two cannot be more powerful than the other. This leads to three inconceivable possibilities: that both gods create the same thing, that neither gods create, that one of them creates while the other does not. *Kitāb al-Arbaʿīn*, p. 217. The same argument is used by al-Rāzī in the 22nd question ("on the creation of human actions"), third proof, in al-Rāzī, *Kitāb al-Arbaʿīn*. There al-Rāzī refers the readers to *dalīl al-tamānuʿ* in the previous chapter, which helps him to argue that the human being does not have efficacious power. *Kitāb al-Arbaʿīn*, p. 223.

60 Ibn Qayyim al-Jawziyya, *Shifāʾ al-ʿalīl*, p. 338; Ibn Qayyim al-Jawziyya, *Shifāʾ al-ʿalīl*, 1903, p. 150.

61 "And Lot – to him We gave judgment and knowledge; and We delivered him from the city that had been doing deeds of corruption", Koran (21:74); "Are you recompensed but for what you did?" (Koran 27:90); "Every soul shall be paid in full for what it has wrought", Koran (39:70).

62 Ibn Qayyim al-Jawziyya, *Shifāʾ al-ʿalīl*, p. 340; Ibn Qayyim al-Jawziyya, *Shifāʾ al-ʿalīl*, 1903, p. 151.

The Jabrī's attempt to connect *jabr* and *tawḥīd* is refuted by the Sunni several times throughout the dialogue. For example, in the Sunni's second response reflecting Ibn Qayyim al-Jawziyya's own position,[63] the Sunni claims that the belief in *jabr* contradicts both *tawḥīd* and God's justice.[64] This argument is related to the higher level of the discussion on *jabr*, that is, the discussion on the theme "obligating what is beyond one's capability".[65]

While the Sunni totally rejects the doctrine of *jabr* as presented by the Jabrī, he is ready to examine and define the term *jabr*. First, the Sunni indicates that the Jabrī's definition lacks the common meaning of *jabr*, that is, forcing the agent to perform an action against his will.[66] In line with the traditionalist view, the Sunni emphasizes that he is not intimidated by the term *jabr*, but by the harsh deterministic view to which this term indicates. In his response, the Sunni excludes *jabr* as a *kalāmic* term from what he claims to be the basic meaning of the concept of *jabr*:

> *Jabr* is a word laden with meanings. As we have seen before, it can denote either a truth or a lie. If by *jabr* you mean that the human being is forced to perform his actions (*muḍṭarr ʿalā afʿālihi*),[67] and that his movement while climbing the ladder equals his movement while falling from it, then this is a clear contradiction to reason and natural disposition (*fiṭra*). However, if by *jabr* you mean that there is no power and no strength save in God, what you say is true. *Jabr* in that sense is a general phrase and does not indicate specifically [any of the human's actions].[68]

The Sunni's position here is a later modification of the early traditionalist position, categorically rejecting the penetration of innova-

63 On the contradiction between *jabr* and *tawḥīd*, see Ibn Qayyim al-Jawziyya: *Miftāḥ dār al-saʿāda wa-manshūr wilāyat al-ʿilm wal-irāda*, ed. by Sayyid Ibrāhīm and ʿAlī Muḥammad, Cairo 1418/1997, vol. 1, pp. 321–322.

64 Ibn Qayyim al-Jawziyya, *Shifāʾ al-ʿalīl*, p. 319; Ibn Qayyim al-Jawziyya, *Shifāʾ al-ʿalīl*, 1903, p. 140.

65 See below, section 2.3.

66 Ibn Qayyim al-Jawziyya, *Shifāʾ al-ʿalīl*, p. 321; Ibn Qayyim al-Jawziyya, *Shifāʾ al-ʿalīl*, 1903, p. 141.

67 See "The human is compelled under the guise of a voluntary agent" (*al-insān muḍṭarr fī ṣūrat mukhtār*) al-Rāzī, *Maṭālib*, vol. 9, pp. 25, 258. For further references, see Shihadeh, *The Teleological Ethics*, p. 37.

68 Ibn Qayyim al-Jawziyya, *Shifāʾ al-ʿalīl*, p. 326; Ibn Qayyim al-Jawziyya, *Shifāʾ al-ʿalīl*, 1903, p. 144. The Sunni makes a similar statement in *Shifāʾ al-ʿalīl*, p. 320; *Shifāʾ al-ʿalīl*, 1903, p. 140. The rhythm and style of that sentence resembles a sentence quoted by Shihadeh from an unpublished work by al-Rāzī. Shihadeh, *The Teleological Ethics*, p. 38, n. 110.

tive vocabulary and notions into religious discourse.[69] In other words, more than a rejection of the notion of *jabr*, we have here a rejection of the use of the word *jabr* and its derivatives in theological formulae.

2.2. Second Level: *jabr* and the Theory of the Human Act

Amid the second level arguments for *jabr* is a concept shared by the Jabrī and the Sunni, according to which, the components of the human act, that is, the power (*qudra*) to perform an action and the motives (*dāʿī*, pl. *dawāʿī*) of the action, are created by God. From this point forward, the Jabrī will argue that the creation of the human power and the motives of human action eventually lead to the conclusion that the human act is necessary. This concept is the very core of the doctrine of *jabr*. The Sunni will argue that the necessity of human action does not lead to the conclusion that it is forced upon man, as the Jabrī argues, because human actions are the outcome of human choice (*ikhtiyār*).

The Jabrī's reliance on al-Rāzī's discussions of the human act is made explicit when he assumes that the combined existence of the human power (*qudra*) and the motive (*dāʿī*) necessitates human action.[70]

69 This purist approach is well reflected in the following saying, which Ibn Taymiyya attributes to the prominent traditionists as a whole, without stating whose view he is quoting: "They said: The word *jabr* did not originate in the Koran and Sunna. What we have in the Sunna is the word 'creation' (*jabl*) and not the word 'compulsion' (*jabr*)." *Darʾ al-taʿāruḍ*, 1997, vol. 1, pp. 148–149; *Darʾ al-taʿāruḍ*, 1979, vol. 1, p. 255.

70 The Jabrī makes two statements on human power, which are in agreement with al-Rāzī's texts, and with the views of former Ashʿarī thinkers. He claims that human actions are the outcome of divine power and not of human power: Ibn Qayyim al-Jawziyya, *Shifāʾ al-ʿalīl*, pp. 327–328; Ibn Qayyim al-Jawziyya, *Shifāʾ al-ʿalīl*, 1903, pp. 144–145. Towards the end of the dialogue, he claims that human power has no effectiveness over human action, because there cannot be "an object of power" (*maqdūr*) shared between two potent agents: Ibn Qayyim al-Jawziyya, *Shifāʾ al-ʿalīl*, p. 338; Ibn Qayyim al-Jawziyya, *Shifāʾ al-ʿalīl*, 1903, p. 150. Al-Rāzī himself made these claims in *Kitāb al-Arbaʿīn*, the beginning of chapter 22 entitled *khalq al-afʿāl* (the creation of human acts). *Kitāb al-Arbaʿīn*, p. 224, proof no. 4; Shihadeh, *The Teleological Ethics*, pp. 17–19. According to Shihadeh, the centrality of the notion of 'motive' in al-Rāzī's thought reflects his departure from his early Ashʿarī position under the influence of Muʿtazilī thought, ibid., pp. 21, 27. An interesting remark of the Jabrī on human power: "Had the effectiveness of the human power (*taʾthīr qudrat al-ʿabd*) been possible with regard to creation (*ījād*), human power would have been effective with regard to the creation of every existent." In other words, had the human being

Another fundamental assumption of the Jabrī is the impossibility of an infinite regress.[71] While this premise does not require any proof, the premise on the necessity of human actions is thoroughly examined by the Jabrī. These two premises combined are the axis of the Jabrī's set of argumentations for *jabr*:

> We say: when the human power and motivation are obtained, the origination of the action is either necessary or not. If it is necessary, then human action is necessitated (*iḍṭirārī*). That is the essence of *jabr*, because human power and motivation are not originated from the human agent. Were they so, it would have entailed an infinite regress (*tasalsul*), which is quite obvious. Since that is the case, when both of them [i.e. the human power and the motivation] are obtained, the human act becomes necessary (*wājib*). When both of them are not obtained, the human act becomes impossible (*mumtaniʿ*). Thus, *jabr* is by all means necessary.[72]

The necessity of the human act, then, leads the Jabrī once more to assert his belief in *jabr*. But since he is forced to examine this concept throughout the dialogue, the Jabrī focuses his argument for the necessity of the human act on the motive (*dāʿī*) of the human act. The motive, claims the Jabrī, is the cause of human action (*sabab al-fiʿl*), and is created by God.[73] Elsewhere he uses an equivalent term, the preponderator (*murajjiḥ*).

This inconsistent use of both terms in the discourse of the Jabrī is by all means rooted in the works of al-Rāzī himself.[74] The Jabrī seems to use both terms in the same manner: as a major factor which accompanies the human power (*qudra*), and eventually leads towards the production of human action. Following al-Rāzī, the Jabrī defines the motive to act as knowledge:

---

been the creator of his actions, he would have been the creator of every existent. Ibn Qayyim al-Jawziyya, *Shifāʾ al-ʿalīl*, p. 337; Ibn Qayyim al-Jawziyya, *Shifāʾ al-ʿalīl*, 1903, p. 149.

71 Central to *kalāmic* argumentation, the impossibility of an infinite regress is employed by Islamic theologians and philosophers in discussions which argue against the eternity of the world. Hoover, *Ibn Taymiyya's Theodicy*, pp. 77–81. For the basic argument in Plato, see Bradely, Raymond D.: Infinite regress argument, in: Robert Audi (ed.): *The Cambridge Dictionary of Philosophy*, Cambridge 1996, pp. 429–430.

72 Ibn Qayyim al-Jawziyya, *Shifāʾ al-ʿalīl*, p. 319; *Shifāʾ al-ʿalīl*, 1903, p. 140. See al-Rāzī, *al-Maḥṣūl*, vol. 2, p. 225; al-Rāzī, *al-Maṭālib al-ʿāliya*, vol. 9, pp. 13–14; Shihadeh, *The Teleological Ethics*, p. 29.

73 Ibn Qayyim al-Jawziyya, *Shifāʾ al-ʿalīl*, p. 324; *Shifāʾ al-ʿalīl*, 1903, p. 143. See al-Rāzī, *Kitāb al-Arbaʿīn*, p. 225.

74 Shihadeh, *The Teleological Ethics*, pp. 20–22.

> Since the motive (*dāʿī*) is not one of our actions, and it is the knowledge of the potent agent (*ʿilm al-qādir*) that he has an advantage (*maṣlaḥa*) in performing this specific action. Since this is embedded in his nature, with which he was created, and this [knowledge] is the outcome of God's act in him. Since the act is necessary as far as he is concerned, this is precisely the meaning of *jabr*.[75]

Elsewhere, the Jabrī adds inclination (*mayl*) and craving (*shahwa*) to this definition, and demonstrates: "Take the thirsty man, for instance. The motive urges him to drink water, because he knows that there is an advantage in it for him, and because of his craving and inclination for drinking it. These craving and inclination are the act of God."[76]

When the Jabrī wants to prove that the motive of action is created by God, he uses al-Rāzī's famous "preponderance without a preponderator" (*tarjīḥ bi-lā murajjiḥ*) argument.[77] This argument seemingly examines the possibility that with the combination of the human power and the preponderator the origination of the human act is not necessary. Thereafter the argument denies it, and finally concludes that human action is indeed necessary:

> If the origination of human action is not necessary when the human power and motivation are obtained, then the preponderance of an act (*rujḥān al-fiʿl*) over the preponderance of an omission (*rujḥān al-tark*) depends on a preponderator (*murajjiḥ*) or it does not. If it depends on it, then when the preponderator originates, the origination of this action becomes necessary. If it does not, it will entail an infinite regress. But since [the action] is required, it is necessitated, and that is the essence of the belief in *jabr*.[78]

According to the Jabrī, the preponderator comes from a source which is external to the human being. The Jabrī states that the preponderator is created by God, and negates the possibility that it comes from the human being himself. This negation appears several times in the narrative of the Jabrī, and is based on two premises: one, that preponder-

---

75 Ibn Qayyim al-Jawziyya, *Shifāʾ al-ʿalīl*, p. 323; *Shifāʾ al-ʿalīl*, 1903, p. 142. See al-Rāzī, *Kitāb al-Arbaʿīn*, pp. 224–225. The same text appears in Shihadeh, *The Teleological Ethics*, p. 21.

76 Ibn Qayyim al-Jawziyya, *Shifāʾ al-ʿalīl*, p. 323; Ibn Qayyim al-Jawziyya, *Shifāʾ al-ʿalīl*, 1903, p. 142; al-Rāzī, *al-Maṭālib al-ʿāliya*, vol. 9, pp. 28–29; al-Rāzī, *Kitāb al-Arbaʿīn*, pp. 124–125; Shihadeh, *The Teleological Ethics*, pp. 20–23.

77 Shihadeh, *The Teleological Ethics*, p. 20.

78 Ibn Qayyim al-Jawziyya, *Shifāʾ al-ʿalīl*, p. 319; Ibn Qayyim al-Jawziyya, *Shifāʾ al-ʿalīl*, 1903, p. 140. See al-Rāzī, *Kitāb al-Arbaʿīn*, pp. 121–122; Shihadeh, *The Teleological Ethics*, p. 20.

ance without a preponderator (*tarjīḥ bi-lā murajjiḥ*) is impossible, and two, that infinite regress (*tasalsul*) is impossible.[79] The Jabrī's argument goes as follows: to assume that the preponderator comes from a different source other than God leads to an infinite regress, which is impossible. Hence, every preponderator comes from God, and not from the human being. This conclusion, according to the Jabrī, again proves the existence of the Creator (*ithbāt al-ṣāniʿ*),[80] and more so, the veracity of the doctrine of *jabr*: because the preponderator is created by God, the human act is necessitated, "and that is precisely what *jabr* is all about".[81]

The Sunni's responses to the Jabrī's arguments also rely heavily on al-Rāzī's texts. These responses also reveal several points of agreement between the two debaters. The agreement encourages the Sunni to emphasize the difference between his views and that of the Jabrī's. For example, the Sunni seems to agree with the Jabrī's statement that the combined existence of the human power and the motive necessitates human action. However, in order to avoid the Jabrī's conclusion that the necessitation of human action leads to a belief in *jabr*, he adds a reservation, the source of which is absent from the Rāziyyan discourse:

> That the human action is necessary, does not contradict that it is chosen (*mukhtār*) by the [human being], wanted (*murād*) by him, and is the object of his power (*maqdūr*). The action neither is compelled (*mukrah*) nor forced (*majbūr*) upon him.[82]

The way in which the Sunni proves that human action is not forced upon the human being, although it is necessitated with the combination of human power and the motive to act, is interesting. The Sunni compares the action of God, performed through His power and will, with the supposedly compelled action of the human being. He states, that even God's action is necessitated with the combination of power and motive. So, is it possible to conclude that God's acts are forced upon Him?[83] The Sunni uses here an *ilzām* (*argumentum ad homi-*

---

79 Ibn Qayyim al-Jawziyya, *Shifāʾ al-ʿalīl*, pp. 325, 339; Ibn Qayyim al-Jawziyya, *Shifāʾ al-ʿalīl*, 1903, pp. 143, 150. See al-Rāzī, *Kitāb al-Arbaʿīn*, pp. 121–122.

80 Ibn Qayyim al-Jawziyya, *Shifāʾ al-ʿalīl*, p. 325; Ibn Qayyim al-Jawziyya, *Shifāʾ al-ʿalīl*, 1903, p. 143.

81 Ibn Qayyim al-Jawziyya, *Shifāʾ al-ʿalīl*, p. 339; Ibn Qayyim al-Jawziyya, *Shifāʾ al-ʿalīl*, 1903, p. 150.

82 Ibn Qayyim al-Jawziyya, *Shifāʾ al-ʿalīl*, p. 320; Ibn Qayyim al-Jawziyya, *Shifāʾ al-ʿalīl*, 1903, p. 141.

83 Ibn Qayyim al-Jawziyya, *Shifāʾ al-ʿalīl*, p. 320; Ibn Qayyim al-Jawziyya, *Shifāʾ al-ʿalīl*, 1903, p. 141.

nem), which, he declares, he adopted from al-Rāzī. He even gives a fairly accurate citation of that argument from al-Rāzī.[84]

It is through his detailed discussion on the human motivation that the Sunni unfolds his doctrine. At first, the Sunni says, he agrees with the Jabrī that the motive (*dāʿī*) of human action is the cause of the human act (*sabab al-fiʿl*), and is created by God.[85] However, soon enough he clarifies that the motive is not the efficient cause (*muʾaththir*) of the action, nor the *only* cause (*sabab*) of the action, although at the beginning of his response he agrees with the Jabrī on this issue. The Sunni sees the motive, like other factors connected to human action, as a condition (*sharṭ*) or a part of a cause (*juzʾ sabab*) of the action.[86] Reducing the status of the motive from the cause of the action to a partial cause is meant to elevate the weight of human power, human will and more so, human choice in the performance of the human act.[87] According to the Sunni, many factors beyond human control are parts of the cause of action. The fact that all causes are created by God does not mean that the human being is not the agent of his action. In the beginning of his response, the Sunni clarifies this view:

> The motive is created by God in the human being, and it is the cause of action. The action is attributed to its [human] agent, since it was originated from him, and occurred through his power, will and choice. That does not prevent the action from being attributed in general (*bi-ṭarīq al-ʿumūm*) to Him, the Creator and Almighty.[88]

He concludes:

> The power of the human being, his will and motives are but one part of the many parts of the complete cause (*sabab tāmm*), which necessitates the act [...]. Whoever claims that the human being has no effect, some way or the other, on the action, that the existence of his power and will is the same as their inexistence, as far as the action is concerned, arrives at a conclusion which contradicts reason and the senses.[89]

84 Ibn Qayyim al-Jawziyya, *Shifāʾ al-ʿalīl*, p. 320; Ibn Qayyim al-Jawziyya, *Shifāʾ al-ʿalīl*, 1903, p. 141. See al-Rāzī, *al-Maṭālib al-ʿāliya*, vol. 9, p. 15.

85 Ibn Qayyim al-Jawziyya, *Shifāʾ al-ʿalīl*, p. 324; Ibn Qayyim al-Jawziyya, *Shifāʾ al-ʿalīl*, 1903, p. 143. See al-Rāzī, *Kitāb al-Arbaʿīn*, p. 225.

86 Ibn Qayyim al-Jawziyya, *Shifāʾ al-ʿalīl*, pp. 324–325; Ibn Qayyim al-Jawziyya, *Shifāʾ al-ʿalīl*, 1903, p. 143. See al-Rāzī, *al-Maṭālib al-ʿāliya*, vol. 9, p. 257.

87 For the use of the term *ikhtiyār* (choice) in *Shifāʾ al-ʿalīl*, see Holtzman, Human Choice, p. 181.

88 Ibn Qayyim al-Jawziyya, *Shifāʾ al-ʿalīl*, p. 324; Ibn Qayyim al-Jawziyya, *Shifāʾ al-ʿalīl*, 1903, p. 143.

89 Ibn Qayyim al-Jawziyya, *Shifāʾ al-ʿalīl*, p. 325; Ibn Qayyim al-Jawziyya, *Shifāʾ al-ʿalīl*, 1903, p. 143. The part omitted here is a refutation of the Muʿtazilī perception on the efficacy of the human power.

The Sunni gives a statement in the same vein towards the end of the dialogue, but then he uses the term preponderator (*murajjiḥ*) instead of the term motive (*dāʿī*). After declaring that he is satisfied with the Jabrī's "preponderance without a preponderator" argument, and agreeing that there must be a preponderator preponderating the action, the Sunni clarifies that the existence of the preponderator does not negate the existence of human choice.[90]

But does the Sunni equate the terms motive (*dāʿī*) and preponderator (*murajjiḥ*)? According to the Sunni, the motive of human action can indeed be, as the Jabrī claims, knowledge of the benefits which result from the performing a certain action, but it can also be ignorance (*jahl*) and error (*ghalaṭ*), as these also lead a man to perform an action.[91] As for the preponderator (*murajjiḥ*), the Sunni examines the possibility that the *murajjiḥ* is the entire set of inborn faculties in the human being, which include, among others, human will. Hence, like the Muʿtazila claim, the preponderator is the human inborn tendency to act using the human being's own will and choice.[92] This definition, which might have served as a very powerful interface between the traditionalist concept of *fiṭra* (natural disposition) and the Muʿtazilī concept of free will, is ruled out by the Sunni. This definition suggests that once created, the human being acts without the guidance of God. Hence the Sunni immediately retracts to the comfortable point of disagreement with the Muʿtazila, and declares that everything in the human being, including his power, will, and motivation, is created by God.[93]

2.3. Third Level: *jabr* and Obligating What Is Beyond One's Capability

In one of al-Rāzī's most notable declarations he defends the doctrine of "obligating what is beyond one's capability" (*taklīf mā lā yuṭāq*), and

90 Ibn Qayyim al-Jawziyya, *Shifāʾ al-ʿalīl*, p. 339; Ibn Qayyim al-Jawziyya, *Shifāʾ al-ʿalīl*, 1903, p. 151.

91 Ibn Qayyim al-Jawziyya, *Shifāʾ al-ʿalīl*, p. 323; Ibn Qayyim al-Jawziyya, *Shifāʾ al-ʿalīl*, 1903, p. 142. This point is elaborated and serves as an introduction to the brief appearance of the Qadarī participant in the dialogue, *Shifāʾ al-ʿalīl*, pp. 323–324; *Shifāʾ al-ʿalīl*, 1903, pp. 142–143.

92 Ibn Qayyim al-Jawziyya, *Shifāʾ al-ʿalīl*, p. 326; Ibn Qayyim al-Jawziyya, *Shifāʾ al-ʿalīl*, 1903, p. 144.

93 Ibn Qayyim al-Jawziyya, *Shifāʾ al-ʿalīl*, p. 326; Ibn Qayyim al-Jawziyya, *Shifāʾ al-ʿalīl*, 1903, p. 144.

asserts that it is possible that God will command the human being to do what is beyond his capacity.[94] One might expect a similar statement from the Jabrī in chapter 19, however any reference to this statement appears only in the Sunni's responses.

The Sunni, with his keen desire to lead the discussion into the domain of "obligating what is beyond one's capability", actually takes the Muʿtazilī position. He even promises that this theme will be discussed at length later on,[95] but this promise is never fulfilled in this debate. Thus, this theme is never exhausted in chapter 19.

In the beginning of the dialogue, the Sunni accuses the Jabrī that his belief in *jabr* means that all which God obligates the human being to perform is "obligating what is beyond one's capability". The whole system of reward and punishment is superfluous, if the Jabrī's position is accepted:

> [The belief in God's unity] is what [God] has entrusted His messengers with. For the sake of it He brought down His books, incited the human beings to believe, and set reward and punishment. He made laws in order to obtain the [belief in God's unity], and to perfect it. But from what you say, Jabrī, the human being has absolutely no power to obtain it, he cannot affect it, [the belief in God's unity] is not his action. Therefore, obligating him is obligating what is beyond his capability.[96]

Furthermore, the Sunni depicts the belief in *jabr* as absurd: God forbids the human being to perform certain acts, and then punishes him for performing those acts, although he has not actually performed them, as the real agent of those acts is God Himself. In sum, the belief in *jabr* makes laws, orders, and prohibitions, superfluous, as the following examples demonstrate:

> It is you, who declared, that God punishes the human being for not obeying His commands and performing what was prohibited on him. It is as punishing him for failing to fly to the sky and failing to move the mountains and the waters of the oceans […]. It is you, who declared that what God obligates His servants is similar to obligating the blind to write and the chronically ill to fly.[97]

---

94 Al-Rāzī, *al-Maḥṣūl*, vol. 2, p. 215; Shihadeh, *The Teleological Ethics*, pp. 103–104.

95 Ibn Qayyim al-Jawziyya, *Shifāʾ al-ʿalīl*, p. 327; Ibn Qayyim al-Jawziyya, *Shifāʾ al-ʿalīl*, 1903, p. 144.

96 Ibn Qayyim al-Jawziyya, *Shifāʾ al-ʿalīl*, p. 318; Ibn Qayyim al-Jawziyya, *Shifāʾ al-ʿalīl*, 1903, p. 139.

97 Ibn Qayyim al-Jawziyya, *Shifāʾ al-ʿalīl*, p. 318; Ibn Qayyim al-Jawziyya, *Shifāʾ al-ʿalīl*, 1903, p. 139.

The second part of this argument, usually entitled "obligating the incapable" (*taklīf al-ʿājiz*), is that obligating he who has no ability to perform a certain act is of no avail (*ʿabathan*). It is an absurdity to attribute to God an action which is of no avail.[98] The Sunni in the dialogue indeed defines the acts in the passage above as acts which are evidently of no avail (*ʿabath ẓāhir*).[99]

The Sunni's accusations, to which the Jabrī does not respond directly, seem disconnected from the general flow of the dialogue, because the Jabrī never refers to the theme of "obligating what is beyond one's capability". The Sunni's accusations here are therefore addressed to al-Rāzī's position on the same issue. Al-Rāzī, as elaborated before, argues that "obligating what is beyond one's capability" is possible.

In the chapter on "commands and interdictions" in *al-Maḥṣūl*, al-Rāzī presents his adversary's arguments against the possibility of "obligating what is beyond one's capability". The adversary, a libertarian Muʿtazilī, defies al-Rāzī's stand:

> We agree that what you have said proves what you claim [that "obligating what is beyond one's capability" is possible]; however it is contradicted by textual and rational proofs. As for the textual evidence, the Koran states "God charges no soul save to its capacity" (Koran 2:286) and "[He] has laid on you no impediment in your religion" (Koran 22:78). Is there a greater impediment than "obligating what is beyond one's capability"? As for rational evidence [...], it is evident that he, who obligates the blind to vocalize copies of the Quran, or obligates the chronically ill to fly, is considered a fool. God is, of course, exalted above that.[100]

The resemblance between the Muʿtazilī's arguments in *al-Maḥṣūl* and the Sunni's accusations in the debate of chapter 19, is quite evident. That the Sunni takes a Muʿtazilī position is also evident from his frequent use of the term "justice" (*ʿadl*), one of the pillars of the Muʿtazilī doctrines. The Sunni uses this term immediately after the absurd description of obligating the blind to write and the chronically ill to fly, when he states that the doctrine of *jabr* contradicts God's justice.[101]

98 See Ibn Taymiyya's definitions in *Majmūʿat al-Fatāwā*, vol. 10, p. 200 (*al-Tuḥfa al-ʿirāqiyya*); al-Urmawī, Sirāj al-Dīn: *al-Taḥṣīl fī al-maḥṣūl*, ed. by ʿAbd al-Ḥamīd ʿAlī Abū Zayd, Beirut 1408/1988, vol. 2, p. 317.

99 Ibn Qayyim al-Jawziyya, *Shifāʾ al-ʿalīl*, p. 318; *Shifāʾ al-ʿalīl*, 1903, p. 139.

100 Al-Rāzī, *al-Maḥṣūl*, vol. 2, p. 220. The Muʿtazilī adversary presents two more rational proofs, which I have omitted here. See Al-Rāzī, *al-Maṭālib al-ʿāliya*, vol. 3, p. 309 (the fourth proof), vol. 3, p. 310 (the ninth proof) and vol. 3, p. 312 (the sixth and seventh proofs).

101 Ibn Qayyim al-Jawziyya, *Shifāʾ al-ʿalīl*, p. 319; Ibn Qayyim al-Jawziyya, *Shifāʾ al-ʿalīl*, 1903, p. 140.

In *al-Maḥṣūl* al-Rāzī provides a direct rejoinder to the comparison between "obligating what is beyond one's capability' and 'obligating the incapable".[102] Unlike al-Rāzī, the Jabrī in chapter 19 does not address this theme directly, but answers with his "preponderance without a preponderator" argument. This however follows al-Rāzī's response in several sources.[103]

3. A Threefold Cord: Ibn Taymiyya – Fakhr al-Dīn al-Rāzī – Ibn Qayyim al-Jawziyya

In the dialogue, the Jabrī presents a straightforward approach towards al-Rāzī's complex theory of the human act: al-Rāzī's pro-*jabr* declarations are elevated to the rank of a Sunni profession of faith corroborating the concept of God's unity (*tawḥīd*). The kernel of the Jabrī's worldview is the "preponderance without a preponderator" argument, the bottom line of which is that God creates the human act. We do not find in any of the Jabrī's statements a trace of the 8th century formula of God compelling the human being to act. The Jabrī's reliance on al-Rāzī should have led him to state that "obligating what is beyond one's capability" is possible. This, however, is only implied by the accusation which the Sunni addresses to him.

The Sunni in the dialogue offers a different perspective on al-Rāzī's argumentations. This perspective aims at reconciling his theological formulae on the human act with Ibn Qayyim al-Jawziyya's views, while rejecting al-Rāzī's pro-*jabr* declarations in several places. The Sunni rejects *jabr* altogether, and refuses to acknowledge the linkage between *jabr* and *tawḥīd*. However, the rationalized course leading towards al-Rāzī's/the Jabrī's declaration of *jabr*, he embraces willingly. In other words, the Sunni adopts the "preponderance without a preponderator" argument, thus acknowledging that human acts are created by God, but rejects the conclusion that this argument fortifies the concept of *jabr*. In fact, when discussing the "preponderance without

102 Al-Rāzī attacks the Muʿtazilī, as follows: "If by 'of no avail' (*ʿabath*) you mean, that this cannot benefit the human being, why do you not say that this is absurd (*muḥāl*)?" This leads him to a short discussion on the term "absurd", al-Rāzī, *al-Maḥṣūl*, vol. 2, p. 223.

103 In *al-Maḥṣūl*, al-Rāzī does not attack the opponent. In *al-Maṭālib al-ʿāliya*, al-Rāzī first presents his stand, then the adversaries' arguments, to which he does not respond, *al-Maṭālib al-ʿāliya*, vol. 3, pp. 305–315.

a preponderator" argument, the Sunni prefers "complete cause" then "preponderator". Last but not least, the Sunni is concerned with the moral implications of the Jabrī's worldview, thus rejecting completely the possibility of "obligating what is beyond one's capability". This rejection is based on the Sunni's conviction of God's justice.

The entire spectrum of al-Rāzī's views is not revealed in the Jabrī's narrative. The Jabrī consistently emphasizes the creation of the human act by God through a persistent repetition of al-Rāzī's argumentations for *jabr*. Still, al-Rāzī has also expressed a view reconciling between human psychology and his rationalized determinism.

> The [description of] an agent choosing his act (*mukhtār*), as far as we are concerned, is as follows. With the combination of the power and the motive, the act necessitates. Upon this assumption, the human being is truly (*ʿalā sabīl al-ḥaqīqa*) an agent (*fāʿil*), but at the same time his acts are determined by God's predetermination (*qaḍāʾ Allāh wa-qadaruhu*).[104]

The Jabrī in chapter 19 does not make such a statement, however the Sunni does. In fact, this is his goal in the debate: declaring that the human being is truly a voluntary agent, whose acts God creates. In his closing triumphant statement, the Sunni defines the human being as an agent (*fāʿil*). This agent, however, does not create his act independently. The act indeed originates through the combination of the human will and motive, but this combination, as other factors affecting the origination of the act, are but "a part of the cause" (*juzʾ sabab*) of the human act.[105] As these factors are created by God, the human act is indeed created and determined by God.

The Sunni's discourse reflects both Ibn Qayyim al-Jawziyya's position towards al-Rāzī's arguments for *jabr*, and Ibn Qayyim al-Jawziyya's adoption, albeit reserved and selective, of the jewel in the crown of the Rāziyyan discourse: the "preponderance without a preponderator" argument. Ibn Taymiyya preceded Ibn Qayyim al-Jawziyya in this. While adopting al-Rāzī's argument Ibn Taymiyya converted the term "preponderator" into the term "complete cause" (*ʿilla tāmma*).[106] Furthermore, the view that the human being is truly

---

104 Al-Rāzī, *Maʿālim uṣūl al-dīn*, p. 61. See also Hoover, *Ibn Taymiyya's Theodicy*, p. 143. *Maʿālim uṣūl al-dīn* is al-Rāzī's last theological work, Shihadeh, *The Teleological Ethics*, p. 10.

105 Ibn Qayyim al-Jawziyya, *Shifāʾ al-ʿalīl*, pp. 340–341; *Shifāʾ al-ʿalīl*, 1903, p. 151.

106 Ibn Taymiyya, Taqī al-Dīn: *Minhāj al-sunna al-nabawiyya*, ed. by Muḥammad Rashād Sālim, Beirut 1404/1986, vol. 3, pp. 31, 50, 117–119; Ibn Taymiyya,

an agent of his acts, while God creates his acts, is expressed several times by Ibn Taymiyya, as a guiding principle in his theory of the human act.[107] The Sunni's discourse in chapter 19, then, is based on Ibn Taymiyya's teachings.

The influence of Fakhr al-Dīn al-Rāzī on Ibn Taymiyya's theological terminology and argumentations has been discussed in previous researches.[108] Much less, if anything, has been said on the influence of Fakhr al-Dīn al-Rāzī on Ibn Qayyim al-Jawziyya's thought. According to Ibn Taymiyya's biographers, he taught al-Rāzī's theological work, *Kitāb al-Arbaʿīn fī uṣūl al-dīn* (The Book of Forty, on the Principles of Religion), to several students, including Ibn Qayyim al-Jawziyya.[109] The complexities of al-Rāzī's methodology both in the classroom and in his theological writings led Ibn Taymiyya to compose a two-volume commentary on *Kitāb al-Arbaʿīn*, which is unfortunately no longer extant.[110]

As reflected in his theological writings, Ibn Qayyim al-Jawziyya, following Ibn Taymiyya's example and lead, enthusiastically attacked the fundamentals of Ashʿarī *kalām*. Nevertheless, the biographical sources, which are in the case of Ibn Qayyim al-Jawziyya very scarce indeed, specifically indicate that Ibn Qayyim al-Jawziyya received a formal Ashʿarī education, while he himself declares that before meeting his master, he was deeply affected by Ashʿarī *kalām*.[111] In the list

Majmūʿat al-Fatāwā, vol. 8, p. 83 (*Risāla fī al-Amr*). These texts were discussed in length by Gimaret, *Théories de l'acte*; and Hoover, *Ibn Taymiyya's Theodicy*, pp. 146–147.

107 Ibn Taymiyya, *Majmūʿat al-Fatāwā*, vol. 3, p. 99 (*al-ʿAqīda al-wāṣiṭiyya*); Ibn Taymiyya, *Minhāj al-sunna*, vol. 3, pp. 12–13.

108 Laoust, Henri: *Essai sur les doctrines sociales et politiques de Takī-d-dīn Aḥmad Ibn Taimīya, canoniste Ḥanbalite. Né à Ḥarrān en 661/1262, mort à Damas en 728/1328; thèse pour le doctorat*, Cairo 1939, p. 724 (index); Daniel Gimaret: Théories de l'acte humain dans l'école Ḥanbalite, in: *Bulletin d'études orientales* 29 (1977), 156–178; Anawati, George C.: Fakhr al-Dīn al-Rāzī, in: *EI²*, vol. 2 (1965), pp. 751–755; Shihadeh, *The Teleological Ethics*, pp. 36–37, nn. 99, 109, 199; Hoover, *Ibn Taymiyya's Theodicy*, pp. 111–112, 138–139, 141–145, 169–173; in an introduction to the 2004 edition of al-Rāzī's *Kitāb al-Arbaʿīn*, the editor, Aḥmad Ḥijāzī al-Saqā, provides several interesting insights, mainly based on the biographical literature, on Ibn Taymiyya's controversy with al-Rāzī's theological doctrines, al-Rāzī, *Kitāb al-Arbaʿīn*, pp. 5–11.

109 See references in the preface of Fakhr al-Dīn al-Rāzī, *Kitāb al-Arbaʿīn*, p. 6.

110 Hoover, *Ibn Taymiyya's Theodicy*, pp. 9–10 and especially p. 10, n. 21.

111 In his theological treatise in verse, *al-Kāfiya al-shāfiya fī al-intiṣār lil-firqa al-nājiya* (The Sufficient and Healing [*qaṣīda*] about the Victory of *al-Firqa al-Nājiya*), Ibn Qayyim al-Jawziyya describes his enchantment of Ashʿarī *kalām*. Ibn Qayyim al-Jawziyya: *al-Kāfiya al-shāfiya fī al-intiṣār lil-firqa*

of books, which Ibn Qayyim al-Jawziyya read and probably memorized with his teachers, the theological works of Fakhr al-Dīn al-Rāzī, *Muḥaṣṣal afkār al-mutaqaddimīn wal-muta'akhkhirīn* (A Summary of the Opinions of Earlier and Later Scholars) and *Kitāb al-Arbaʿīn*, stand out. Ibn Qayyim al-Jawziyya read portions of these books aloud in front of two teachers: Ṣafī al-Dīn al-Hindī (d. 715/1314–15), the Shāfiʿī kadi of Damascus, and Ibn Taymiyya himself.[112] Ibn Qayyim al-Jawziyya also read with Ibn Taymiyya "a part of *al-Maḥṣūl*".[113]

The exact citations from al-Rāzī's writings, and especially from *al-Maḥṣūl* might indicate that Ibn Qayyim al-Jawziyya was savvy of the Rāziyyan text. *Al-Maḥṣūl* is probably the text which the Sunni and Jabrī are toiling to memorize in the debate in chapter 19. In other words, Ibn Qayyim al-Jawziyya used *al-Maḥṣūl* as the substratum of the dialogue in chapter 19. His former Ashʿarī education helped him formulate the Jabrī's discourse, but it was his joint reading of *al-Maḥṣūl* with Ibn Taymiyya, that directed Ibn Qayyim al-Jawziyya towards the Sunni's discourse, and more so, the Sunni's triumphant closing statement. For Ibn Qayyim al-Jawziyya, as for Ibn Taymiyya before him, Fakhr al-Dīn al-Rāzī played a triple role: as a source of inspiration, a theological authority, and a worthy ideological rival, whose teachings demand rigorous and serious attention.

Conclusion

Chapter 19 in *Shifāʾ al-ʿalīl*, an original piece of Ibn Qayyim al-Jawziyya, offers the author's coherent critique on the Ashʿarī exploitation of al-Rāzī's texts. According to Ibn Qayyim al-Jawziyya, the Ashʿarīs used al-Rāzī in order to promote the heretical doctrine of *jabr*. The Ashʿarī position and its refutation are presented in the guise of a

---

al-nājiya, ed. by ʿAbd Allāh b. Muḥammad al-ʿUmayr, Riyadh 1416/1996, pp. 180–181, verses 2271–2280.

112 Al-Ṣafadī, Ṣalāḥ al-Dīn Khalīl b. Aybak: *al-Wāfī bil-wafayāt*, Istanbul, n.d., vol. 2, pp. 270–273. For further biographical details on Ibn Qayyim al-Jawziyya: Abū Zayd, Bakr b. ʿAbd Allāh: *Ibn Qayyim al-Jawziyya. Ḥayātuhu, āthāruhu, mawāriduhu*, Riyadh 1412/1992; 2nd ed. 1423/2002; Krawietz, Birgit: Ibn Qayyim al-Jawzīyah. His Life and Works, in: *Mamlūk Studies Review* 10 (2006), pp. 19–64; Holtzman, Livnat: Ibn Qayyim al-Jawziyyah, in: Devin J. Stewart and Joseph E. Lowry (eds.): *Essays in Arabic Literary Biography 1350–1850*, Wiesbaden 2009, pp. 202–223.

113 Al-Ṣafadī, *al-Wāfī bil-wafayāt*, vol. 2, p. 196.

debate between a Jabrī and a Sunni. Written from the Sunni's point of view, chapter 19 presents two possible readings of Fakhr al-Dīn al-Rāzī's arguments for *jabr* within his theory of the human act: the standard Ashʿarī reading, manifested in the narrative of the Jabrī, and Ibn Qayyim al-Jawziyya's reading, manifested in the narrative of the Sunni.

As a typical didactic piece, chapter 19 cannot be considered a recording or restoration of real life polemics. However, the chapter demonstrates the acceptance of al-Rāzī's writings in the Damascene scholarly circles of the 14th century. Al-Rāzī's writings were enthusiastically read and discussed by both the Ashʿarīs and the members of the Taymiyyan circle. The Rāziyyan discourse and style which are present in almost every sentence that the Jabrī and the Sunni utter, indeed authentically reflect the real interests of the students of Islamic theology in Mamluk Damascus.

The parallel established in this article between al-Rāzī's *al-Maḥṣūl* and chapter 19 of *Shifāʾ al-ʿalīl* is not based merely on common ideas or identical lines of argumentation. Ibn Qayyim al-Jawziyya placed in his protagonists' mouths exact citations from *al-Maḥṣūl* and other writings of al-Rāzī. Ibn Qayyim al-Jawziyya also shaped his protagonists as striving with the Rāziyyan text and toiling to interpret it. Reading chapter 19 in itself without addressing al-Rāzī's *al-Maḥṣūl* is bound to leave a great deal of the picture in the shadow.

Chapter 19 also reflects Ibn Qayyim al-Jawziyya's theological perception of human actions. Adhering to the viewpoint of Ibn Taymiyya, Ibn Qayyim al-Jawziyya embraced certain arguments from Fakhr al-Dīn al-Rāzī's theory of the human act. In chapter 19, Ibn Qayyim al-Jawziyya, in fact criticizes the Ashʿarīs for not understanding al-Rāzī's nuanced theory. This criticism is made explicit by both the ridiculous presentation of the Jabrī and the Sunni's well-structured interpretation of al-Rāzī's argumentations.

Chapter 19 demonstrates more than a clash between the Ashʿarī theories of the human act and the so-called Sunni doctrine of the human act: this chapter raises the possibility of reconciliation between the Rāziyyan and Taymiyyan-Jawziyyan positions.

Ibn Qayyim al-Jawziyya's Manipulation of Sufi Terms

Fear and Hope

Gino Schallenbergh

Introduction

The medieval Ḥanbalī scholar Ibn Qayyim al-Jawziyya (d. 751/1350) is one of these authors whose work, centuries after his passing away, is still visibly present in the libraries, religious bookshops and pavement bookstalls of the modern Sunni Islamic world. Browsing through the literature on offer in almost any bookstore in Cairo, Damascus or Jakarta, one cannot fail to notice the presence of books such as the *Kitāb al-Rūḥ, Ṭarīq al-hijratayn* and *Madārij al-sālikīn*. A possible explanation for the popularity of his work is that Ibn Qayyim al-Jawziyya addressed the direct religious concerns of the faithful in a style that is accessible to all. He seemed to have been aware that the Muslim community needs concepts and ideas that give due place to the emotions and religious sensations that are felt by the believers. He accepted the Sufi heritage in as far as it did not clash with revealed religion, but tried to elaborate a spiritual language that stays close to Koran and Sunna. Holy scripture held for him the reliable elements that are needed to develop a religious life that keeps God's laws intact and at the same time gives full satisfaction to the spiritual needs of the faithful.

As with the discussions on Ibn Taymiyya's alleged Sufism one can raise the question if Ibn Qayyim al-Jawziyya was a Sufi or identified himself as such. After the publication of George Makdisi's article in 1973 in which he advanced the thesis that Ibn al-Qayyim's master Ibn Taymiyya (d. 728/1328) belonged to the Qādiriyya brotherhood, many similar statements have been made to the effect that Ibn Taymiyya, notwithstanding his virulent attacks on formal Sufism, was a Sufi himself.[1] About

1 Makdisi, George: Ibn Taymīya. A Ṣūfī of the Qādiriya Order, in: *The American Journal of Arabic Studies* 1 (1973), pp. 118–290. We reported some statements on Ibn Taymiyya's pretended Sufism in Schallenbergh, Gino: Intoxication and

his disciple Ibn Qayyim al-Jawziyya Henri Laoust said already earlier that he was "profondement nourri de soufisme".[2] Some comments by Ibn al-Qayyim's contemporaries seem to confirm that impression. Ibn Rajab said that he had knowledge of the terminology of the Sufis (*ʿilm al-sulūk wa-kalām ahl al-taṣawwuf wa-ishārātihim wa-daqāʾiqihim*).[3] We are informed by Ibn al-Ḥajar that "he felt longings and affection for Sufism, not in the way of the radicalising Sufis, but in the way of the pious forefathers" (*lā ʿalā manhaj al-mutaṣawwifa al-ghulāt bal ʿalā ṭarīq al-salaf al-ṣāliḥ*).[4] Conspicuous demonstrations of spiritual emotion in his behaviour seem to plead in favour of his Sufi inclinations. Ibn Kathīr noted that he had a special way in praying which he stretched over a longer period of time than what was usual, although his own partisans had misgivings about this practice and even criticised him openly. Ibn al-Ḥajar speaks of his prolonged prayer and *dhikr*.[5] In the chapter on annihilation (*fanāʾ*) in the *Madārij al-sālikīn* he justifies this way of praying confiding that anyone who is steadfast in his worship does not like to end his prayer (*Idhā dakhala fī al-ṣalāt wadda an lā yakhruja minhā*).[6]

Two works by Ibn Qayyim al-Jawziyya were often presented as authentic Sufi works: the *Ṭarīq al-hijratayn* (The Path of the Two Migrations) and the *Madārij al-sālikīn fī manāzil iyyāka naʿbudu wa iyyāka nastaʿīn* (The Ranks of the Wayfarer Between the Abodes "you do we worship" and "you do we call for help").[7] In his monograph on

Ecstasy. Sufi Terminology in the Work of Ibn Qayyim al-Djawzīya, in: Urban Vermeulen and Jo van Steenbergen (eds.): *Proceedings of the 6th, 7th and 8th Colloquium on the History of Egypt and Syria in the Fatimid, Ayyubid and Mamluk Eras*, Leuven 2005, pp. 459–474.

2 Laoust, Henri: *Les schismes dans l'islam. Introduction à une étude de la religion musulmane,* Paris 1965, p. 273. For the most up-to-date biographical information on Ibn Qayyim al-Jawziyya see Krawietz, Birgit: Ibn Qayyim al-Jawzīyah. His Life and Works, in: *Mamlūk Studies Review* 10 (2006), pp. 19–64, and Holtzman, Livnat: Ibn Qayyim al-Jawziyya, in: Devin Stewart and Joseph Lowry (eds.): *Arabic Literary Biographies*, Wiesbaden 2007, pp. 201–222.

3 Quoted in Krawietz, Ibn Qayyim al-Jawzīyah, p. 22.

4 Ibid., p. 26. The translation of the two quotations is equally adopted from Birgit Krawietz' translation.

5 Ibn Kathīr, Aḥmad al-Dīn Ismāʿīl: *al-Bidāya wal-nihāya*, Cairo 1939, vol. 14, pp. 234–235; and Ibn Ḥajar al-ʿAsqalānī: *al-Durar al-kāmina fī aʿyān al-miʾa al-thāmina*, ed. by M. S. Jād al-Ḥaqq, Cairo 1966, vol. 4, p. 21.

6 Ibn Qayyim al-Jawziyya, Shams al-Dīn Muḥammad: *Madārij al-sālikīn fī manāzil iyyāka naʿbudu wa-iyyāka nastaʿīn*, Beirut n. d., vol. 3, p. 396.

7 Ibn Qayyim al-Jawziyya, Shams al-Dīn Muḥammad: *Ṭarīq al-hijratayn wa-bāb al-saʿādatayn*, Cairo n. d., and Ibn al-Qayyim, *Madārij al-sālikīn*. The text we

Ḥanbalī love theory however, Joseph Bell observed that one should not classify these works too rashly as Sufi texts. He points to the fact that Ibn al-Qayyim himself adapted the terminology of his contemporaries for the sake of clarity. But the real purpose of his exercise, thus Bell, is that;

> Through *Ṭarīq al-hijratayn* and *Madārij al-sālikīn*, works totalling more than fifteen hundred pages in the printed editions, the author has skillfully reproduced model mystical treatises and has manipulated the technical vocabulary of Sufism with the virtuosity of a true master only to expound the conventional message of nomos religion.[8]

After a closer study of the 100 terms listed in the *Madārij al-sālikīn* and Ibn Qayyim al-Jawziyya's treatment of the terms, we have come to the conclusion that Bell's assessment is correct, but on the other hand the spiritual dimension of Ibn al-Qayyim's work cannot be underestimated. It is certainly true that in the greater bulk of the text Ibn Qayyim al-Jawziyya stresses on the precedence of the revealed law over all other considerations. At the same time he was aware that concerns of a more spiritual and religious emotional nature could not be left to the theoretic enquiry and mystical message of the Sufis alone. In fact he tried to modify the terms being used by the mystics and to bring them in line with the rules and ethics of the sharia. Moreover he desired to give expression to his own spiritual feelings in a sometimes more emotional and sensitive way.

Ibn al-Qayyim treated the Sufi terms in a variety of ways. His essential views on Sufism and its translation in popular religion are not much different than Ibn Taymiyya's. He rejected saint cults as a totally unacceptable form of religiosity and fulminated against what he deemed to be the excessive veneration of saints. Like Ibn Taymiyya he defended an ideology that rejected all forms of idolatry. In his attempt to eradicate the ideological premises of associationism (*shirk*) he tried to identify the different types of idol cults. One of his works, the *Ighāthat*

used is the undated Ḥalabī Beirut edition in three volumes. A better edition we did not consult yet is Ibn Qayyim al-Jawziyya: *Madārij al-sālikīn fī manāzil iyyāka naʿbudu wa-iyyāla nastaʿīn*, Damascus 2003. Recently an abridged edition was published; Ibn al-Qayyim: *al-Muhadhdhab min Madārij al-sālikīn*, Beirut 2005.

8 Ibn Taymiyya and Ibn al-Qayyim espoused what Bell calls a "technique of flexibility in religious debate" that enabled them to manipulate the terminology of their adversaries. Bell, Joseph Norment: *Love Theory in Later Ḥanbalite Islam*, New York 1979, p. 92.

al-lahfān min makāyid al-shayṭān (Assistance to the One who Yearns to Escape from Satan's Entrapments)[9] is entirely devoted to all ideologies and creeds that promote consciously or unconsciously polytheism. In this work Ibn Qayyim al-Jawziyya proposes a demonology that discerns one mechanism at work in all cults other than "mainstream" Islam.[10] This mechanism can be explained as satanic plotting. Satan takes advantage of human ignorance and tries to lure away the worshippers from the straight path that leads to God. To this end Satan employs different stratagems. At one time he contaminates the true cult with erroneous ideas or he introduces rituals that give great appeal for the common and the educated alike. Satan corrupts the rituals prescribed by God and substitutes them with practices that are visually more attractive and that soothe the mind, ear and eye. People of learning, on the other hand, are misled by doctrines that are intellectually challenging (philosophy, *kalām*, the Sufi notion of unification with God expressed in monism and others). Sometimes the association with the devil is plain and obvious, in other cults, he explains, the association is far more subtle and difficult to perceive. Ibn Qayyim al-Jawziyya portrayed the history of the polytheistic cults as a process where original pure precepts of religion were deformed, which led ultimately to a new religion or the worshipping of new deities. Sufi saint cults belonged in his opinion to that category.

His probably most important work on Sufism and spirituality in general is the *Madārij al-sālikīn*. It is a commentary on the *Manāzil al-sāʾirīn* (The Abodes of the Spiritual Travellers), composed by the Ḥanbalī Sufi Abū Ismāʿīl al-Anṣārī al-Harawī (d. 481/1089), a work that left a tremendous impact on the development of Sufi thought and that was especially hailed as a valuable contribution to the development of the terminology of the mystic path.[11] Al-Anṣārī al-Harawī's

9 Ibn Qayyim al-Jawziyya, Shams al-Dīn Muḥammad: *Ighāthat al-lahfān min maṣāyid al-shayṭān*, ed. by M. Bayūmī, Cairo 1996.

10 For a brief discussion on Ibn al-Qayyim's "demonology" in the *Ighāthat al-lahfān*, see Perlman, Moshe: Ibn Qayyim and the Devil, in: *Studi orientalistici in onore di Giorgio Levi Della Vida* 2 (1956), pp. 330–337.

11 Serge de Beaurecueil devoted a considerable part of his research to al-Anṣārī's life and works. A series of articles has been published in *Mélanges de l'institut dominicain d'études orientales*. With regard to this article we would like to refer to de Beaurecueil, Serge: Esquisse d'une biographie de Anṣārī, in: *Mélanges de l'institut dominicain d'études orientales* 4 (1957), pp. 95–140, *Mélanges de l'institut dominicain d'études orientales* 5 (1958), pp. 47–113, *Mélanges de l'institut dominicain d'études orientales* 6 (1959), pp. 387–402. Also an article

"Abodes of the Wayfarers" contains hundred essential terms in Sufi doctrine and spirituality in general (for a list of the abodes, see appendix). The *Manāzil al-sāʾirīn* can be stations, spiritual states or so-called halting posts on the road (*mawāqif*). Al-Anṣārī's text proposes a tripartition of the qualities described in the abodes whereby for every abode an ascending classification is made of the common believers, the privileged and the privileged of the privileged. Some of the qualities described in the abodes are shared by the three groups in their totality, while others are only of application to one particular group. The development of the lower ranking groups can find termination in one of the hundred terms. Ibn al-Qayyim's commentary on the *Manāzil* gives an insight in Ibn Qayyim al-Jawziyya's spiritual ideas and is important for a number of reasons. First of all there is Ibn Qayyim al-Jawziyya's identification with and subsequent distancing from the author of the *Manāzil al-sāʾirīn*. He expressed on numerous occasions his admiration for Shaykh al-Anṣārī (among others for the latter's strong condemnation of Ashʿarism in his *Dhamm al-kalām* (Refutation of *kalām*)) but throughout his commentary he criticises al-Harawī al-Anṣārī for the passages in the *Manāzil al-sāʾirīn* that are written in an obscure language, a language that in his opinion is unintelligible for the untrained reader and misleading for the expert.[12] The ambiguity of some definitions of the terms used by al-Anṣārī gave way to monist interpretations and Ibn al-Qayyim betrays in some passages his suspicion that the author of the *Manāzil al-sāʾirīn* himself made this choice deliberately, in which case he warns, serious doubt must be cast on the ideological rectitude of al-Anṣārī. Throughout the *Madārij al-sālikīn* Ibn al-Qayyim refuted on regular intervals parts of the commentary on the *Manāzil*

on the classification of the terms in the *Manāzil al-sāʾirīn* should be mentioned here; de Beaurecueil, Serge: La structure du *Livre des étapes* de Khwaja Abdallah Ansari, in: *Mélanges de l'institut dominicain d'études orientales* 11 (1972), pp. 77–125; and de Beaurecueil, Serge: Le langage imagé du livre des étapes de Khwāja Abdullah Anṣārī, mystique hanbalite du V-e/XI-e s., in: *Bulletin d'études orientales* 30 (1978), pp. 32–44.

12 Ibn Taymiyya was less complacent with al-Harawī's mystical writings and blamed him for his lack of knowledge. For his critique on al-Harawī, see Ibn Taymiyya, Taqī al-Dīn Aḥmad: *Minhāj al-sunna*, ed. by M. Rashād Sālim, Cairo 1989, vol. 5, pp. 340–341. Tāj al-Dīn al-Subkī noted that Ibn Taymiyya rejected the *Manāzil al-sāʾirīn* despite his leaning to al-Anṣārī in other doctrinal matters. Al-Subkī, Tāj al-Dīn ʿAlī: *Ṭabaqāt al-shāfiʿiyya al-kubrā*, ed. by ʿAbd al-Fattāḥ al-Ḥilw and Maḥmūd al-Ṭanāḥī, Cairo 1992, vol. 4, p. 272.

al-sāʾirīn that were written by the monist ʿAfīf al-Dīn al-Tilimsānī (d. 690/1290).[13] In modern research this colourful character is often listed among the mystics that transmitted Ibn ʿArabī's teachings, but Ibn Taymiyya estimated that his doctrine was more radical than Ibn ʿArabī's and that his ideas show indeed more affinity with Ibn Sabʿīn's (d. 669/1269) mysticism.[14] Al-Tilimsānī's comment on the *Manāzil al-sāʾirīn* betrays a strong monist conviction.[15] The author did not dissimulate his ideas, that in this form were not only odious to legal scholars but also inacceptable for mainstream Sufis. In his text al-Tilimsānī referred often to the works of the enigmatic mystic al-Niffarī (d. 366/977), especially the *Kitāb al-Mawāqif*.[16] The *Mawāqif* is written in the template of dialogues with God. Koran quotations however are near to absent and the teachings in the text are presented as Divine speech (*tanazzulāt*) not unlike the speech to prophets (*tanzīl*), which is reserved to advanced mystics. In a way the author of this mystical work makes pretence at reception of Divine inspiration. Al-Tilimsānī read the *Mawāqif* and al-Anṣārī's *Manāzil al-sāʾirīn* as a partly Divinely inspired text as well, but in some cases also as books that provides useful pedagogic information for the instruction of the novice (*murīd*) at hand of his Shaykh. It creates of his commentary a text that is totally different from Ibn Qayyim al-Jawziyya's, although the latter copied freely the parts of al-Tilimsānī's commentary that he deemed innocent. In

---

13 On ʿAfīf al-Dīn al-Tilimsānī see Krenkow, Fritz: al-Tilimsānī, in: *EI²*, vol. 10 (2000), p. 500; and Nwyia, Paul: Une cible d'Ibn Taymiya, le moniste al-Tilimsani, in: *Bulletin d'études orientales* 30 (1978), pp. 127–145.

14 Ibn Taymiyya: *Majmūʿ al-rasāʾil wal-masāʾil*, ed. by Muḥammad Rashīd Riḍā, Beirut 2001, vol. 2, p. 27.

15 We consulted a manuscript conserved in *Dār al-Kutub* in Cairo (Collection Taṣawwuf Ḥalīm 49). There exists a text edition of the *Manāzil al-sāʾirīn* with al-Tilimsānī's commentary attached. Abū Ismaʿīl al-Anṣārī: *Manāzil al-sāʾirīn ilā al-ḥaqq al-mubīn*, ed. by ʿAbd al-Ḥāfiẓ Manṣūr, Tunis 1989.

16 On al-Niffarī see Karamustafa, Ahmet: *Sufism. The Formative Period*, Edinburgh 2007, pp. 284–301; and Knysh, Alexander: *Islamic Mysticism. A Short History*, Leiden 2000, pp. 102–105. Al-Niffarī elaborated at length on the language of the Sufis and he exerted a certain influence on Ibn ʿArabī while his work is prominently present in al-Tilimsānī's writings. On his unusual manipulation of language Ira Lapidus said he invented "a language that condensed human experience with its transcendent reference". Lapidus, Ira M.: *A History of Islamic Societies*, Cambridge 1988, p. 113. Al-Tilimsānī wrote a commentary on the *Mawāqif*; al-Tilimsānī, ʿAfīf al-Dīn Sulaymān: *Sharḥ mawāqif al-Niffarī*, ed. by Jamāl al-Marzūqī, Cairo 1997.

his comments on the chapters that were most likely to suggest a monist reading, Ibn al-Qayyim resisted to the tenets of the monist doctrine and pointed out where al-Anṣārī's incautious formulations left the likes of al-Tilimsānī all opportunity to misuse them for their own designs. At the same time Ibn Qayyim al-Jawziyya directed his critique to the more traditional strands in Sufism and their use of a specific terminology that in his view had little in common with Islamic teachings.[17] It is clear that any remote suggestion of monism was rejected by Ibn al-Qayyim and that partial or absolute unification with the Divine (the second type of monism proposing the total unification of all essence with its Divine source) are unacceptable. In the case of contemplative unification, by which the mystic is subjected to the loss of sensitive awareness in the experience of an ecstatic state, Ibn al-Qayyim seems to hesitate. In many passages of the *Madārij al-sālikīn* he takes a mild position on the experimental phenomenon of ecstatic states. He imputed the loss of conscience in spiritual sensation to the imperfection of the worshipper's soul in moments when he is deeply impressed by a divine truth or when he is visited by a spiritual state (*ḥāl*). With regard to the spiritual states itself, Ibn al-Qayyim did not deny the possibility of its occurrence but in most cases adopts Ibn Taymiyya's observation that the spiritual states are most often not genuine and induced by demons or produced by the troubled state of mind of mystics who deprived themselves of all God-given means that sustain a normal balanced life. What stands above discussion for Ibn al-Qayyim is that loss of conscience and ecstatic states are by no means prerogatives of a mystic elite or markers of a special status. Rather are they signs of weakness and do they indicate an imperfection of the soul. The ecstatic utterances (*shaṭaḥāt*) are treated in the same way; when grotesque religious statements are made in a spiritual state, they are excusable for both Ibn Taymiyya and Ibn al-Qayyim, but only if they are revoked after recovery of the senses.

17 Three such terms that figure high in the *Manāzil al-sāʾirīn* are annihilation (*fanāʾ*), intoxication (*sukr*), ecstasy (*wajd*), see Schallenbergh, Intoxication and Ecstasy, pp. 466–474.

1. Ibn Qayyim al-Jawziyya's Approach to Sufi Terminology

In his treatment of the Sufi terms we discern the following elements in Ibn al-Qayyim's argumentation:

1.1. Relativity of the Path to God

First of all, he challenged the traditional classification of the terms that in Sufism are placed in a detailed mapped out trajectory that serves as a guidebook for spiritual development along the so-called stations and spiritual states on the path to God.[18] Ibn Qayyim al-Jawziyya resisted to the absoluteness with which the stations and states were treated in the Sufi manuals. The moral and religious virtues that find expression in the stations could in his opinion not be dealt with in a rigid system whereby progression on the path brings the itinerant in consecutive stations, ever closer to his goal. In Ibn al-Qayyim's commentary on the Sufi terms there is certainly the possibility of progress in the servant's spirituality. This progression does however not imply that the stations that have been passed would be invalidated by a higher station.[19] The virtues that have been acquired in some stations stay with the servant throughout his journey, Ibn al-Qayyim notes. Love for the Divine, for example, stands on a higher plan than fear and hope, but that does not mean that they are replaced, as is suggested in the monist commentaries.[20]

1.2. Manipulation of Sufi Terms

One of the recurring features in Ibn al-Qayyim's own definitions of the terms is that he explicitly bans all elements that bear a strong mys-

18 On the metaphoric figure of the path and its trajectory, see de Beaurecueil, Khwāja ʿAbdullah Anṣārī, pp. 32–44.

19 Ibn al-Qayyim, *Ṭarīq al-hijratayn*, p. 231.

20 For more information on Ibn Qayyim al-Jawziyya's rejection of the Sufis' linearity of the spiritual path, see Schallenbergh, Gino: Ibn Qayyim al-Jawziyya on Sufi Terminology. The Concept of the Spiritual Path (*ṭarīq*), in: Kristof D'Hulster and Jo Van Steenbergen (eds.): *Continuity and Change in the Realms of Islam. Studies in Honour of Professor Urban Vermeulen*, Leuven 2008, pp. 555–565.

tical sense in the Sufi manuals.[21] Following Ibn Taymiyya's example Ibn Qayyim al-Jawziyya generalised terms that had a specific meaning for Sufis and stripped them of its Sufi connotations.[22] Moreover he elected the words that occur in the Koran and gave them more importance than some of the non-Koranic terms that were introduced in the Sufi manuals. Doing so he retraced these words to the Koranic context. When Ibn Qayyim al-Jawziyya discusses the term *maʿrifa*, for example, a word that is usually translated as gnosis, he tries to give a definition of *ʿārif*, that stays remote from the conventional Sufi understanding. *ʿĀrif*, he explains, is he who knows God, His attributes and His actions and who as a consequence devotes his actions to God with conviction. If the worshipper succeeds in this field, he looses his reprehensible qualities (*awṣāf madhmūma*) and becomes patient in his servitude, even when afflictions befall him. His supplications ascend up to God only and his intentions are unflawed by the incorrect opinions of men inspired by their spiritual states and ecstasies. Such person, thus Ibn Qayyim al-Jawziyya, deserves to be called *ʿārif*, although others received the title by tradition. An important element of knowledge, in Ibn al-Qayyim's use of the word, is that the *ʿārif* is always aware of the absolute dissimilarity (*mubāyana*) between God and men. The *ʿārif* is aware of God's transcendent existence.[23]

1.3. Ibn al-Qayyim's Critique of Sufi Elitism

Ibn Qayyim al-Jawziyya was opposed to Sufis who laid claim to esoteric knowledge pretending thereby to be superior to the *ʿulamāʾ* and other members of the Islamic community. Like Ibn Taymiyya he did not reject the possibility that God gives special knowledge about things to some men and not to others, but in his opinion it is hardly a feature that gives a person more merits than others. As Ibn al-Qayyim sees it

21 Ibn al-Qayyim, *Madārij al-sālikīn*, vol. 3, p. 353.

22 In the opening lines of his letter to al-Manbijī for example, Ibn Taymiyya speaks of *dhawq* and *wajd* in very general terms, and identifies *wajd* as the "finding" (*wujūd*) of faith in the heart, while he describes *dhawq* as the emotionally committed taste of faith. He is silent on the mystic connotation so often attached to these terms. The fact that he wrote these remarks in the introduction of the letter is undoubtedly inspired by the wish to demarcate his own position on such terms from al-Manbijī's. Ibn Taymiyya, *Majmūʿ al-rasāʾil wal-masāʾil*, vol. 1, p. 170.

23 Ibn al-Qayyim, *Madārij al-sālikīn*, vol. 3, p. 356.

esoteric knowledge had been given to unbelievers as well, and he points out the fact that demonstrations of exceptional knowledge occurred rarely in the first centuries of Islam, because of the first believers' firmness and solidity in faith.

On a conceptual level Sufi manuals divided the believers in three groups; the common believers (*ʿāmma*), the privileged or the elite (*khāṣṣa*) and the privileged of the privileged (*khāṣṣat al-khāṣṣa*). For the authors who gave a monist interpretation of Sufi development the spiritual development of the supreme elite leads to existential annihilation, but for most mystics the ultimate goal of their spiritual journey was the mystical contemplation of God. Ibn Qayyim al-Jawziyya rejected this elitist sense of exclusion prevalent among some Sufis in his work *Ṭarīq al-hijratayn*, where he discusses the deficiencies to some abodes advanced by al-Anṣārī but also detracts the ideas of the Andalusian mystic Ibn al-ʿArīf (d. 536/1141) who elaborated on al-Anṣārī's deficiencies in some abodes of the spiritual path.[24] Al-Anṣārī identified a number of deficient abodes, that could in his understanding never be applied to the privileged: will (*irāda*), renunciation (*zuhd*), reliance (*tawakkul*), patience (*ṣabr*), grief (*ḥuzn*), fear (*khawf*), hope (*rajāʾ*), gratitude (*shukr*), love (*maḥabba*) and longing (*shawq*). Ibn al-ʿArīf acknowledged that the Sufi manuals and al-Anṣārī's *Manāzil al-sāʾirīn* were written for different publics, who gather the information that is specific for them. Therefore he decided to compose "The Attractions of Mystical Sessions" (*Maḥāsin al-majālis)* as a work that addresses the needs of the advanced wayfarer on the spiritual path. In his opinion the stations and states that did not introduce love and unification were vulgar, and not worthy to give attention to. He decided to devote all his attention instead to the elite, and made it clear that the deficient stations could not be of no interest to that same elite.[25] Ibn Qayyim

24 In an earlier stage of his life al-Anṣārī composed a short treatise on the deficiencies, the *ʿIlal al-maqāmāt*. For the translated text see de Beaurecueil, Serge: Les déficiences des demeures, in: ʿAbd Allāh al-Anṣārī al-Harawī: *Trois traités spirituels*, Paris 1985, pp. 233–237. See also de Beaurecueil, Serge: Un petit traité de ʿAbdallāh al-Anṣārī sur les deficiences a certaines demeures spirituelles, in: Dominique Sourdel (ed.): *Mélanges Louis Massignon*, Damascus 1957, vol. 1, pp. 154–169.

25 In the introduction of the *Maḥāsin al-majālis* he made clear that the book serves as a guidebook for the novice that helps him overcome the difficulties of the path and at the same time as a work that reinforces the sincerity and realisation of the *murād*. Ibn al-ʿArīf copied al-Anṣārī's deficient stations and added two more: repentance (*tawba*) and intimacy (*uns*). On the life of Ibn al-ʿArīf and

al-Jawziyya agreed only for the term grief (*ḥuzn*) that it does not really belong in a fulfilling religious awareness, referring to the verses in the Koran where mankind is instructed not to grieve. All the other terms are necessary and become even more important when faith grows stronger.[26]

2. Ibn Qayyim al-Jawziyya's Discussion of Fear and Hope

Fear and hope (*khawf* and *rajā*ʾ) belonged to those stations that were perceived by some mystics, the author of the *Manāzil al-sāʾirīn* included, as deficient abodes on the path. In conventional Sufi terminology fear forms an antithetic yet complementary pair with hope, such as other pairs that abound in Sufi terminology and in particular in the *Manāzil al-sāʾirīn* (annihilation-subsistence, constriction-release, union-separation etc.).[27] In the traditional manuals the different aspects and manifestations of fear were discussed. *Khawf*, as explained by the lexicographer Muḥammad al-Sharīf al-Jurjānī (d. 816/1413), is in language the expectation that an undesirable turn of events will take place, or that something desirable stays out.[28] This aspect is also present in religious fear. In the words of Abū al-Qāsim al-Qushayrī (d. 465/1072) fear is a projection of what may be ahead in the future. One is scared about misfortune or calamities that did not take place yet. Fear of God is in its most primitive form the worshipper's mortification at the mere thought of possible punishment in the hereafter.[29] In reverse, God's servant may also fear to be barred entry to paradise. *Rajā*ʾ by contrast is defined by al-Qushayrī as the expectation of the heart for something desirable set in the future. Hope enforces the strength of the believer's heart and guarantees his independent acting that is preserved hencefor-

---

the text of the *Maḥāsin al-majālis*, see M. Acin Palacios' introduction to Ibn al-ʿArīf, Abū al-ʿAbbās: *Maḥāsin al-majālis*, Paris 1939, pp. 13–14. There is an English translation as well, namely Ibn al-ʿArīf, Abū al-ʿAbbās: *The Attractions of Mystical Sessions*, London 1980.

26 Ibn al-Qayyim, *Madārij al-sālikīn*, vol. 3, p. 501; and Ibn al-Qayyim, *Ṭarīq al-hijratayn*, pp. 295–296.

27 De Beaurecueil, La structure du *Livre des étapes*, p. 93.

28 Al-Sharīf al-Jurjānī, Muḥammad: *Kitāb al-Taʿrīfāt*, Beirut 1969, p. 107.

29 Al-Qushayrī, Abū al-Qāsim: *Risāla fī ʿIlm al-taṣawwuf*, Cairo n.d., pp. 198–199.

ward from any distraction. Hope constitutes an important incentive to greater effort in worship.[30] The prospect of a good reward helps the servant to overcome inactivity. Not unlike a child, al-Tilimsānī states, that has been promised candy. In this sense hope alleviates the burden of prescribed religious duties. Another soothing effect of hope translates in the wish to join Paradise and its inhabitants. The hope to find comfort with the *ḥūrīs* (paradise women) in paradise protects the itinerant from the Satan's entrapments (*maṣāʾid al-shayṭān*). His soul is filled with expectant joy when he contemplates the rewards he will receive at the end of his journey.[31] A worshipper known for good works lives with the hope that his works may be accepted, inveterate sinners hope that their sins may be forgiven. Al-Qushayrī makes the observation that it is preferable for the sinner to entertain feelings of fear, rather than hope.[32] In some cases the sensation was classified as a spiritual state rather than a station. Abū Naṣr al-Sarrāj (d. 378/988) for example classifies fear as a spiritual state. In proximity to God (*qurb*), he explains, two spiritual states prevail. In some cases the state of love is dominant, in other cases fear overpowers. God allocates these states to the worshippers guided by His infinite wisdom. When He manifests to the worshipper His power and almightiness He inspires fear. When He shows His generosity and infinite bounty He inspires love.[33] Fear also manifests itself as a physical ailment in the description of the spiritual life of the worshipper. The Yemenite Sufi ʿAbd Allāh b. Asʿad al-Yāfiʿī (d. 768/1367) said that fear originates in the liver. It is a sensation that affects and burns the liver, an organ that is in Galen's anatomy the location from where the veins depart (*aṣl al-ʿurūq*).[34] In Abū Ṭālib al-Makkī's (d. 437/1045) discussion of fear, the sensation can be caused by seven physical dysfunctions depending from its source in the human

30 Al-Tilimsānī, *Sharḥ manāzil al-sāʾirīn*, folio 26.

31 Ibn al-Qayyim, *Madārij al-sālikīn*, vol. 2, p. 55.

32 Al-Qushayrī, *Risāla fī ʿIlm al-taṣawwuf*, pp. 204–205.

33 Al-Sarrāj, ʿAbd Allāh Abū Naṣr: *Kitāb al-Lumaʿ*, ed. by Reynold A. Nicholson, Leiden 1914, pp. 60–61.

34 On Galen's theory on the venal system see the translation by Ḥunayn Ibn Isḥāq (d. 260/873) in Muḥammad S. Sālim (ed.): *al-Ṣināʿa al-ṣaghīra*, Cairo 1988, p. 167; and on the functions of the liver in general see Rodinson, Maxim: Kabid, in: *EI*[2], vol. 4 (1978), pp. 327–333. Al-Yāfiʿī adds that Abū Bakr was so God-fearing that his breath exuded the scent of roast liver; al-Yāfiʿī, ʿAbd Allāh b. Asʿad: *Nashr al-maḥāsin al-ghāliya fī faḍl mashāyikh al-maqāmāt al-ʿāliya*, ed. by Aḥmad Saʿdī, Cairo 2004, vol. 1, p. 281.

body, from where it leads to the heart.[35] When fear is released from the heart itself it affects and consumes the gall bladder with a sometimes fatal outcome for the person being affected. This particular type of fear becomes visible in people who faint. These people, al-Makkī teaches, are of little spiritual value. When fear stemming from the heart affects the brain, reason is impaired and the worshipper gets lost. If a worshipper who experiences this type of fear was in a particular spiritual state, he returns to his previous state and also his station is not preserved. Fear emanating again from the heart, may pierce a lung, which results in loss of digested food and fluids. It wears out the body (as is caused by tuberculosis, sull) and blood dries out. People affected by this fear look hungry and wasted. When fear takes hold of the liver the person falls in a state of enduring depression and sadness. He is deprived of sleep and is awake all night. In al-Makkī's opinion this is the most productive type of fear that brings the person to reflection and meditation. Fear can affect the shoulder-blades (*farāʾiṣ*). The symptoms are trembling and twitching movements of the upper part of the body. In this case as well it affects reason. The entire body is overpowered by it and the agent lacks willpower to move it in the desired way. Fear affects the soul and annihilates personal preference and carnal desire. This is what Abū Ṭālib al-Makkī calls the fear that is most desired by the advanced mystics, it is the fear of the prophets, *ṣiddīqs* and martyrs.

2.1. Awe

Fear occurs in the Koran as a sensation that is designated by nine different words to indicate eschatological fear (*khawf*), anxiety (*khashya*), terror (*rahab* or *ruʿb*), scrupulousness (*waraʿ*), piousness (*taqwā*) etc. Fear however is the overpowering emotion that underlies these types.[36] Mystics tended to prefer anxiety to terror. Al-Qushayrī for example points to the escapism that marks the sensation of terror. In the more elitist approach, embraced among others by the monists, the privileged

---

35 Al-Makkī, Abū Ṭālib: *Qūṭ al-qulūb*, ed. by ʿAbd al-Munʿim al-Ḥifnī, Cairo 1991, vol. 3, pp. 96–97.

36 On the different terms being used in the Koran and their significance see Scott, Alexander: Fear, in: *EI*², vol. 2 (1965), pp. 194–198; and on the semantic shifts of the words that take place within the Koranic context, see Ohlander, Erik S.: Fear of God (*taqwā*) in the Qurʾān. Some Notes on Semantic Shift and Thematic Context, in: *Journal of Semitic Studies* 50 (2005), pp. 137–152.

of the privileged know no fear. The sentiment that was fear in its primitive form, is transformed in awe (*hayba*).[37] Al-Qushayrī explains that the servant struck by the most basic and primitive fear will try to hide or escape, while a servant who shows anxiety seeks to overcome his fear and will move towards God instead. Al-Qushayrī likens fear to a candle that gives light to the heart and enables the servant to decide what is good and what is evil. A person marked by terror will panic and tries to escape. In *khashya* however is a flight to God, because the worshipper enlightened by science knows in which way to act.[38] In Sufi doctrine fear and hope are only stations that need to be developed in stations or spiritual states of more grandeur. In a first movement fear and hope will be transformed to constriction (*qabḍ*) and release (*basṭ*). The advanced mystics are said to have arrived to the stations of awe (*hayba*) and intimacy (*uns*). The spiritual development responds to this model:

khawf → *qabḍ* → *hayba*

rajāʾ → *basṭ* → *uns*

The noblest form of fear is awe, that designates in Sufi handbooks the remainder of the supreme quality of fear, and that is diffidence and humble submission to God, that takes fear on a higher plan. Awe is dismantled of the negative aspects that cling to fear. In this context, fear cannot persist in spiritual progression because it is in the end replaced by security. Awe however is a qualitatively nobler sentiment towards God for the mystics that survives after death in the hereafter. Ibn Qayyim al-Jawziyya accepts the co-existence of fear, anxiety and awe, but he expresses his surprise about the statement that fear, a sensation experienced by the prophets and the angels, would be reduced to a station of the common and replaced by a qualification like awe (*hayba*), a word that was never mentioned in the Koran. He does not deny the virtuousness of awe, but challenges the idea that one abode should dominate another in excellence. And in his desire to stay as close to Koranic terminology as possible, Ibn al-Qayyim prefers to substitute the word

37 Al-Qāshānī, ʿAbd al-Razzāq: *Laṭāʾif al-iʿlām*, Cairo 1995, vol. 1, pp. 456–457. Abū ʿAlī al-Daqāq was probably the first Sufi who classified degrees of fear on the ascending scale of fear, anxiety (*khashya*) and awe (*hayba*). See al-Qushayrī, *Risāla fī ʿIlm al-taṣawwuf*, p. 199; and al-Yāfiʿī, *Nashr al-maḥāsin*, vol. 1, p. 278.

38 Al-Qushayrī suggests even that there is a resemblance in the etymology of terror (*rahab*) and flight (*harab*). Abū al-Qāsim al-Qushayrī, *Risāla fī ʿIlm al-taṣawwuf*, p. 199.

hayba with *ijlāl*, a word that approximates in meaning awe and that is mentioned in the Koran. As for the greater persistence of awe compared to fear and hope, Ibn Qayyim al-Jawziyya agrees that fear dissipates in paradise, while *hayba* remains. But it does not diminish the importance of the abode, he remonstrates, because also other lofty virtues that are essential to the Islamic creed cease to exist in the hereafter. He gives for example jihad that he calls one of the most exalted obligations of Islam, but one that is not perpetuated in the hereafter.[39] As to fear's complementary sensation of hope, on a higher plan in Sufi imagination, hope is present with the masters of spiritual exercise (*arbāb al-riyāḍāt*) in the wish to gain greater knowledge and piety. The masters aspire to leave behind the habits of the carnal soul. This is necessary to arrive to a purified concern and a pure spiritual moment. Doing so, they hope to grasp the meaning of the revealed law to its full extent and at the same time to be protected from even the slightest sign of curiosity for all that procures pleasure. To al-Tilimsānī it entails the purification of the heart in order to activate its receptiveness towards a moment of contemplation. Ibn al-Qayyim connects hope to the desire to understand God's plan behind the formal prescriptions of Divine law.[40]

2.2. Fear, Hope and Mystic Contemplation

Fear in its most basic expression is in general to many mystics a sentiment that belongs to the religiousness of common servants. In the elitist spiritual tripartition the common are outranked by the privileged and on a still higher level by the privileged of the privileged, for whom fear and hope take a different turn. Ibn al-ʿArīf identified fear as the absence of all certainty. Therefore it is in his assessment an abode of the common. The privileged do not have a share in fear because they find sufficient certainty of faith in their desire to mystical contemplation. Therefore Ibn al-ʿArīf indicated that a person immersed in mystic vision goes beyond the abode of fear and enters in the expanse of intimacy (*uns*), because vision brings intimacy, while fear leads at its best to constriction (*qabḍ*), one of the other abodes in the *Manāzil al-sāʾirīn*.[41] Whereas the likes of Ibn al-ʿArīf and in particular the monists went as

39 Ibn al-Qayyim, *Ṭarīq al-hijratayn*, pp. 308–309.

40 Al-Tilimsānī, *Sharḥ manāzil al-sāʾirīn*, folio 26; and Ibn al-Qayyim, *Madārij al-sālikīn*, vol. 2, p. 56.

41 Ibn al-ʿArīf, *Maḥāsin al-majālis*, pp. 39–40.

far as to regard *khawf* as a deficient abode, Ibn Qayyim al-Jawziyya praises *khawf* as one of the most essential qualities of worship and rejects Ibn al-Arīf's indifference to the term. To Ibn al-Qayyim, fear is one of the pillars on which the stations of the itinerants on the path to God are founded. The more a worshipper grows in piety, he sermons, the more his fear will increase, as well as his hope and love for God. Fear becomes in his reading of the *Manāzil al-sāʾirīn* one of the most exalted stations of the path. In his opinion the fear of the so-called privileged should even be more intense, contrary to what Ibn al-ʿArīf and monist interpreters have said, because, thus Ibn al-Qayyim, the elites are in greater need of fear. After all fear and hope are sensations that come forth from the worshipper's firm knowledge of God's retribution in reward and punishment. It is an element which helps the pious servant to maintain a pious and God-fearing life. In addition, he should fear that his return in repentance (*tawba*) would not be accepted. Fear stands in the triangle of fear-hope-love. Fear and hope are in Ibn Qayyim al-Jawziyya's view connected to the works of the believers, while love is connected to the essence and the attributes of God. That is why fear and hope will cease to exist in the hereafter while love continues.[42] On the other hand also traditional Sufi authors have emitted positive remarks on fear. Al-Suhrawardī promotes fear as a station of quality as established by the vast number of Koran quotations and traditions on fear.[43] Fear, al-Qushayrī had said, preserves morality and good conduct. To al-Qāṣānī it entails the purification of the heart to enable its receptiveness towards a moment of contemplation. Al-Qushayrī admits that some mystics prefer hope (*rajāʾ*) to fear, while others believe that by time fear and hope are lifted in temporary states of contemplation.[44] It is again Ibn al-ʿArīf who believes that in mystic contemplation fear is necessarily absent because it obstructs a full contemplative union with God. He tells how a pious man who was flogged a hundred lashes while he was in full contemplation of God showed no sign of fear. The awareness that God was beholding him made him oblivious of the ordeal and he stood the test fearlessly, but when he perceived separation from his Divine vision, he screamed when he was lashed only once.[45] Ibn Qayyim al-Jawziyya is outraged by this

42 Ibn al-Qayyim, *Ṭarīq al-hijratayn*, pp. 297–302.

43 Al-Suhrawardī, Abū Ḥafṣ ʿUmar: *ʿAwārif al-maʿārif*, Cairo n. d., vol. 2, pp. 289–290.

44 Al-Qushayrī, *Risāla fī ʿIlm al-taṣawwuf*, pp. 200–201.

45 Ibn al-ʿArīf, *Maḥāsin al-majālis*, p. 41.

illustration of mystical piety. Ibn al-ʿArīf seems to believe, thus Ibn al-Qayyim, that because of the absence of fear, the pain of the Gnostics turns in pleasure. This would imply that reward and punishment (*waʿd* and *waʿīd*) are interchangeable. Ibn al-ʿArīf had suggested that the elite exchange *waʿd* for *waʿīd*, preferring punishment to reward. As a consequence they indulge in sensing pain, all in line with the mystic conviction that everything sent down by God is in all cases good and benign for the worshippers. Ibn al-Qayyim dismisses this position and he qualifies Ibn alʿArīf's saying as an ecstatic utterance that can only be imputed to his own soul's imperfection (*hādhā min ruʿūnāt al-nafs wa-min al-shaṭaḥāt allatī yajib inkāruhā*) (!).

When such a thing is said in a sane state of mind, Ibn al-Qayyim warns, it is a denial of God's punishment and its description as a terrible ordeal in the Koran, and he cries out: "May God surround these madmen with pain that makes them scream and beg for mercy, and they will discover the stupidity of their allegations." He suspected that this kind of eccentric ideas were inspired by the fatalism and determinism that prevails with some Sufis who believe that all what is God-sent is in all cases good and benign for mankind. Ibn Qayyim al-Jawziyya gives his opinion on determinism in many passages of the *Madārij al-sālikīn*. He noted that Sufis with monist tendencies who believed that one should regard all human deeds as equal since created by God, made the mistake not to distinguish between God's creative will and His prescriptive will.[46] He recognized in Sufi fatalism the hallmarks of the determinist ideology (*jabriyya*) and warned for the resulting nihilism and abolishment of ritual obligations. To Ibn Qayyim al-Jawziyya, these and similar statements are tantamount to heresy or unbelief (*ilḥād*). Even if the mystic pretends to speak about the afflictions and pain suffered in this world, Ibn al-Qayyim adds, he is equally mistaken, because *waʿīd* is not the same as the pain suffered in this world. Ibn Qayyim al-Jawziyya refers to the words of Ibn al-ʿArīf as "drivel" (*hadhayān*). He does not deny however that a person can experience a spiritual state while in pain, which makes

46 Bell, *Love Theory*, p. 179, and on Ibn Taymiyya's doctrine regarding this matter, pp. 61–73. For Ibn al-Qayyim's ideas on determinism see Perho, Irmeli: Man Chooses His Destiny. Ibn Qayyim al-Jawziyya's Views on Predestination, in: *Islam and Christian-Muslim Relations* 12 (2001), pp. 61–70, here p. 68; and for a recent comprehensive and thorough study of Ibn Taymiyya on predestination and God's justice to men see Hoover, Jon: *Ibn Taymiyya's Theodicy of Perpetual Optimism*, Leiden 2007.

him forgetful of the discomfort it causes, although its occasion is rare. In these cases, he explains, intense love for God has overpowered the heart. Afterwards he will return to a natural state and witness pain like anybody else.[47] Al-Tilimsānī on the other hand agrees that the worshipper can very well exist in the conviction that he has more to gain in the pain of separation, sensing that unification is only a pleasure to the carnal soul.[48] To this group belong the mystics who call for the pain of punishment rather than the bliss of paradise. Al-Qāshānī illustrates this sentiment with the verses:[49]

Being tortured in parting
is dearer to me than communion's sweetness
Because in communion I am a servant to the pleasure [of my carnal soul]
and in my parting I am the servant of the Lord.

taʿdhībī maʿa al-hijrāni ʿindī
aḥabbu ilayya min ṭībi al-wiṣāl
li-annī fī al-wiṣāli ʿabdu ḥazzin
wa-fī al-hijrāni ʿabdu al-mawlā

Monists and some mainstream Sufis were equally opposed to the abode of hope, with regard to the advanced Sufi. Hope (*rajāʾ*), al-Anṣārī explained in the *ʿIlal al-maqāmāt*, is the aspiration for something out of reach or the wish to find something lost. It occults the real objective of the spiritual journey.[50] Even in its highest degrees, hope holds for them a great degree of imperfection. Al-Niffarī said on the subject of fear and hope: "Fear is the sign of him who knows his end. Hope is the sign of him who is ignorant of his end."[51] Ibn Qayyim al-Jawziyya is perceptive of this reality and condemns al-Anṣārī in his commentary of the first lines on this chapter.[52] The interpretation that al-Tilimsānī attaches to the text is diametrically opposed to Ibn al-Qayyim's. In al-Tilimsānī's outlook on spirituality, hope is one of the weakest sta-

47 Ibn al-Qayyim, *Ṭarīq al-hijratayn*, pp. 306–307.
48 Al-Tilimsānī, *Sharḥ manāzil al-sāʾirīn*, folio 26b.
49 Al-Qāshānī, *Laṭāʾif al-iʿlām*, vol. 1, p. 483.
50 Al-Anṣārī al-Harawī, *Trois traités spirituels*, pp. 235–236.
51 Al-Niffarī, Muḥammad ʿAbd Allāh: *Kitāb al-Mawāqif*, ed. by Arthur J. Arberry, London 1935, p. 51. This is so, al-Tilimsānī explains, because the hopeful is overpowered by the prospect of felicity. Al-Tilimsānī, *Sharḥ mawāqif al-Niffarī*, p. 328.
52 "The *shaykh al-islām* is very dear to us", he starts, "but dearer still is the truth," Ibn al-Qayyim, *Madārij al-sālikīn*, vol. 2, p. 38.

tions.[53] He seems to be in agreement thus far with al-Anṣārī al-Harawī's own comments on hope. The latter identified it as an act of opposition to God. This vision is supported by al-Tilimsānī who explains that the hope for felicity may be opposed to God's plan. God, he tells, is the owner of all and He only can steer His creation as He wants. Therefore hope can be an audacious act against God's decree.[54] Instead the worshipper should surrender to God's decree and find satisfaction in his fate. Ibn Qayyim al-Jawziyya has identifed the passage in his commentary on the passage as one of al-Anṣārī's ecstatic ravings (*shaṭaḥāt*). Going against al-Anṣārī's assessment our Ḥanbalī author calls it one of the most important abodes, a qualification that it shares with fear (*khawf*) and love (*maḥabba*).[55] He points to the interconnectedness of the three aspects. By nature, he remarks, every person that loves knows what fear and hope is. He hopes to find his beloved, and fears that he may disappear out of his sight.

2.3. Divine Deception

Al-Tilimsāni gave attention to al-Anṣārī's definition of the second degree of fear, a stage of the abode reserved for the privileged who spent time in mystic contemplation. In one of al-Anṣārī's typologies of this abode mention is made of Divine deception (*makr*). *Makr*, the deception created by God to test His servants on the sincerity of their intention and faith, does usually not abstain from mainstream Sufism's terminology. It is a notion that manifests itself in different ways. The fear for *makr* can be every believer's concern to be worried and scared about the day when he gives his last breath. Abū Ṭālib al-Makkī describes the fear of *makr* as the anxiety about the *khawātim al-aʿmāl*, the final culmination to the servant's work. The worshipper lives in fear that eventually he will be confronted by a negative balance or that he will die with a deficient sense of *tawḥīd* or even in plain unbelief due to an incomplete faith that has been flawed overtime be it heretic or alien ideas, by which the intentionality of his faith is diverted from God to a substitute, sometimes without even being aware of this. In this sense Divine deception gives also way to the fear that after a long

53 This is also al-Qāshānī's's conclusion, al-Qashānī, *Laṭāʾif al-iʿlām*, vol. 1, p. 482.
54 Al-Tilimsānī, *Sharḥ manāzil al-sāʾirīn*, folio 25.
55 See Ibn Qayyim al-Jawziyya's list of traditions and Koran quotes that underline the importance of *rajāʾ*, Ibn al-Qayyim, *Madārij al-sālikīn*, vol. 2, pp. 42–43.

life of piousness a last unfortunate sinful action or thought may occur that casts the worshipper in the eternal flames of hell. Being about to die, the worshipper is in the incapacity to repair his works or beliefs and as a result he will die in spiritual torment.[56] But *makr* and the fear thereof occur in other situations as well. The worshipper who is visited by a spiritual state may be afraid that through Divine deception his spiritual state is unreal. That is why, according to al-Qushayrī, even the saints are only rarely completely free of fear. The kind of fear that almost always remains is the fear of God's deception during a spiritual state. Al-Qushayrī illustrates this with the image of a saint who enters a delightful garden and all the birds greet him as a friend of God. For fear of God's deception, al-Qushayrī warns, such miraculous events should be approached with utmost caution.[57] What the *murīd* ought to fear is the deception (*makr*) of the overwhelming wellbeing he experiences in a spiritual awakening that in his belief constitutes an end to his ignorance. In mainstream Sufism this feeling of wellbeing is misleading. But to Ibn Qayyim al-Jawziyya the misconception of many Sufis has more serious consequences. It has to do with the fear of spiritual precariousness and the trickeries that play on the minds of the *murīd*s. It is not a Divine deception that causes error, he observes, but the mystic's proper delusions.[58]

2.4. Fear and Monism

Fear of God and hope for felicity are excluded from the monist project. These sentiments are described as base instincts of worshippers that attempt to avert loss of earthly pleasure and seek to gain felicity in the hereafter. What the mystic wayfarer however should dread

56 Abū Ṭālib al-Makkī explains that three groups in particular can be affected by Divine deception: the people whose ideology was flawed or who were arrogant, those who denied God's miraculous signs and the miracles of His saints (friends), and a third group consisting of three; one who is showing of (*mutaẓāhir*); corrupt (*fāsiq*) and an obstinate addict. All these are faced on the doorstep of death with the revelation of truth (*kashf al-ghiṭāʾ*), but their soul being about to leave its corporal vessel (the point of exit is situated at the level of the throat – *ḥulqūm*), they want to repent but are physically unable to carry it out; al-Makkī, *Qūṭ al-qulūb*, vol. 3, pp. 80–81.

57 Al-Qushayrī, *Risāla fī ʿIlm al-taṣawwuf*, pp. 530–531.

58 "How many", he regrets, "did turn away from God in their quest for spiritual states," Ibn al-Qayyim, *Madārij al-sālikīn,* vol. 1, p. 553.

most, al-Tilimsānī explains, is that God would turn away from him.[59] Selfish fear is futile. In his elitist sense al-Niffarī composed a list of 55 elements of fear where the fear of punishment is totally absent. The aspects he touches relate to the desire of the servant to adopt a proper conduct towards God. Among them we find the fear for sins, hidden unbelief, shortcoming, temporal fears, etc.[60] Contrary to those types of fear, the fear of the common constitutes a loss of tranquillity caused by the believer's contemplation of the prophet's message about reward and punishment. Hope is not treated any differently. Al-Niffarī treats fear as the characteristic of those believers who have knowledge of life after death while those who live in hope are ignorant.[61] In al-Tilimsānī's commentary it is explained by the idea that the hopeful is overpowered by the prospect of felicity.[62] The itinerant however, must go beyond fear and hope develop and steer the process of his spiritual growth; or in al-Niffarī's words: "He is distracted whom thou addresest according to his desire, and he is cut of whom thou addresest according to his fear; but he is united whom thou addressest according to his achievement."[63] Al-Tilimsānī recognises al-Niffarī's observation as a particularly useful guiding principle for the Sufi master when he addresses the novice (*murīd*). It makes no sense, he argues, to support the quest for God based on sentiments of fear (*rahba*) and hope (*raghba*). And he adds that in his actions, the true novice will not be inspired by fear, since there is no sweetness in servitude based on fear.[64]

The prospect of eternal doom and punishment confirms for Ibn al-Qayyim on the other hand, the abode's capital importance. Fear fortifies the spiritual life of the itinerant. Ibn al-Qayyim sums up different forms of fear and ends with a description of the type of fear that brings the spiritual travellers on the true spiritual path.[65] It is the terror felt by the common for impending misfortune that is instilled on them by revelation. At the same time it is the best proof of their faith, indicating here the literal belief in the consequences of reward and punishment. In al-Tilimsānī's design, hope for the privileged of the privileged is the

---

59 Al-Tilimsānī, *Sharḥ manāzil al-sā'irīn*, folio 19a.
60 Al-Niffarī, Muḥammad ʿAbd al-Jabbār: *Kitāb al-Nuṭq wal-ṣamṭ. Nuṣūṣ ṣūfiyya*, ed. by Muḥammad ʿAbbās Qāsim, Amman 2001, pp. 43–44.
61 Al-Niffarī, *Kitāb al-Mawāqif*, p. 51.
62 Al-Tilimsānī, *Sharḥ mawāqif al-Niffarī*, p. 215.
63 Al-Niffarī, *Kitāb al-Mawāqif*, p. 73.
64 Al-Tilimsānī, *Sharḥ mawāqif al-Niffarī*, p. 328.
65 Ibn al-Qayyim, *Madārij al-sālikīn*, vol. 1, pp. 550–551.

hope for unification with God. In the previous stages of spiritual development the itinerant was still preoccupied with the purification of his heart. In the next step, his heart is filled with a hope that resembles a strong feeling of longing, the desire for a prolonged nearness to God. Still, al-Qāshānī argues, this type of hope has the deficiency of separateness and otherness than God. To ʿAfīf al-Dīn al-Tilimsānī as well, the privileged situated in the third and final degree of spiritual development, do not share in any of those sentiments inspired by fear. These mystics, he argues, can not be separated from God who is approaching them of His own volition. They are however marked by a sentiment of awe (*hayba*) for God's magnitude. *Hayba* is a more noble alternative for fear. His sentiment of awe or reverence prevents the privileged from mystic rapture in a moment of contemplative vision and prompts him by consequence to self-control during his spiritual encounter with God. Reverence also instils in him the desire for the direct sensation to see God, comparable, al-Tilimsānī explains, to the state of Moses when he begged God to make Himself manifest.[66]

But Ibn al-Qayyim defends the contemplation of God's beauty in the preservation of subsistence of the lover of God, whose love is intensified, which would not be the case if he was absent of his state.[67] In this balance fear and hope find their place and keep each other in check. Again he underlines the coexistence of fear, hope and love. The heart on its way to God is like a bird, thus Ibn al-Qayyim, his head is love which is supported by the two wings of fear and hope. When head and wing are intact no problem shall arise.[68]

2.5. Constriction and Release

Constriction (*qabḍ*) and release (*basṭ*) are two alternating states that constitute a higher development of fear and hope but that precede awe (*hayba*) and intimacy (*uns*). Constriction and release are represented in the Divine names of "restrictor" (*al-qābiḍ*) and "releaser" (*al-bāsiṭ*).[69] In Sufism some saints are said to live in a permanent state of *qabḍ*

66 Al-Tilimsānī, *Sharḥ manāzil al-sāʾirīn*, folio 19.
67 Ibn al-Qayyim, *Madārij al-sālikīn*, vol. 2, p. 56.
68 Ibid., vol. 1, p. 554.
69 On the qualities of *qabḍ* and *basṭ* in relation to the Divine names, see Gimaret, Daniel: *Les noms divins en Islam. Exégèse lexicographiqe et théologique*, Paris 1988, pp. 333–335.

or *basṭ*. Constriction is for the Gnostic what fear is for the ordinary believer. When God constricts His worshipper, the latter will find it hard and shameful to stand up, take food or speak. When God releases His servant, however, He brings him back to his earthly environment and sets him free to enjoy earthly pleasures. The result is that the worshipper is in a state of elation and joy (*mabsūṭ*). Saints that are in a permanent state of *qabḍ*, usually retreat from society. A Shaykh who undergoes *qabḍ*, al-Sharīf al-Jurjānī explained, is not useful in teaching, the one who lives in *basṭ* bears in him all the required qualifications for this task.[70] Constriction can be described as the sadness of the soul, which is devastated by a particular spiritual sensation (*wārid*). The spiritual wayfarer may already be subject to *qabḍ* in his awareness that the *wārid* painfully underlines his separation from God. It disables him to rejoice in his situation. As long as the spiritual states and Divine manifestations are limited to the personal experience of the worshipper, he is in a state of *qabḍ*. When he manages to transcend this state he arrives to the abode of *basṭ*.[71] According to al-Qushayrī the station of constriction is a follow-up of the station of *khawf*, while expansion is a continuation of *rajāʾ*. The difference in the two sentiments lies in the fact that fear and hope are determined by events to happen in the future, while constriction and release are determined by the immediacy and actuality of the events. They are states that alternate in succession and are usually equal in strength, thus al-Qushayrī, the stronger the constriction is, the stronger also the release that will succeed it. Constriction is a terrifying experience and the origins of the sentiment can not easily be traced. Al-Qushayrī advises the itinerants to give in to the state and surrender to its overpowering force. Than the effect of the state will cease soon and make place for the more blissful state of release.[72] The mystics who claim spiritual realisation (*taḥqīq*) however perceived a deficiency in those alternating states when it comes to the position of the itinerants who attained the end of the journey. The interchangeable nature of these modes prevents by their duality the first steps to unification. Only once the mystic has overcome these spiritual states, that were necessary for his spiritual ascension, he will be enabled to franchise the last step and begin his journey to unification.

---

70 Al-Jurjānī, *Kitāb al-Taʿrīfāt*, p. 178.
71 Al-Qāshānī, *Laṭāʾif al-iʿlām*, vol. 2, p. 227.
72 Al-Qushayrī, *Risāla fī ʿIlm al-taṣawwuf*, p. 121.

In the *Manāzil al-sāʾirīn*, in the abode of *qabḍ* the servant is "seized" by God and belongs to the selected or chosen servants, the so-called *ḍanāʾin*. As al-Harawī indicated, there are three types of the chosen. First of all there is the group God wants to protect, the few people that He severs from their surroundings. He made them go in reclusion (*khalwa*) or made them roam far away from their town (*siyāḥa*). They shun other people's company and are reticent in their contacts with people, as if the inhabitants of this world have nothing in common with them. A second group consists of those saints who live among men but whose spiritual states are dissimulated and unknown to people. To the outward world they appear as common people, but their status with God is sure and their spiritual states sound. For the monist al-Tilimsānī we find in the third group the mystics God has caused to pass away from their formal existence and who stand as a result nearer to God. A sort of annihilation takes place that is not accompanied by feelings of alienation or terror. Al-Tilimsānī tells that God located their ecstatic feelings and spiritual states in their heart so that they have by their innate qualities a better understanding of them.[73]

Ibn Qayyim al-Jawziyya did not adopt the Sufi terminology of *qabḍ* and *basṭ*. First of all, according to him, the verse that was used by al-Anṣārī in the introduction to the station is not appropriate. The passage is *sūrat al-furqān* verse 48: "And then We seize it to Ourselves, drawing it gently" (*thumma qabaḍnāhu ilaynā qabḍan yasīran)*. The direct object of the verb *qabaḍa* refers to the shadow mentioned a verse earlier Ibn al-Qayyim explains and has nothing to do with constriction of men by God.[74] God spoke of the shadow that could be extended or restricted at His will.[75] Ibn Qayyim al-Jawziyya agreed with some of the Sufi definitions of *qabḍ* with regard to the *ḍanāʾin*. If al-Harawī refers to the people for whom God has a special treatment (the so-called *ḍanāʾin*), he says, the author is correct. The *ḍanāʾin* are God's favourites, but Ibn al-Qayyim does not treat them as a mystical elite

73 Al-Tilimsānī, *Sharḥ manāzil al-sāʾirīn*, folio 111.

74 Koran (25:47): "Hast thou not regarded thy Lord, how He has stretched out the Shadow?" Both translations are borrowed from Arthur J. Arberry's interpretation, Arberry, Arthur J.: *The Koran Interpreted*, London 1980, p. 60.

75 Ibn al-Qayyim, *Madārij al-sālikīn*, vol. 3, p. 305. Abū Ṭālib al-Makkī, however, used *qabḍ* and *basṭ* in its Koranic context, with reference to the time of private worship in *wird* from the first prayer until sunrise. The shadow that was cast on the believers who are concentrated in prayer, will be constrained by God in his grip (*qabḍ*), after which he lets the sun shine out (*basṭ*), al-Makkī, *Qūṭ al-qulūb*, vol. 1, p. 40.

but rather as the true believers that stand up in defence of faith in times of corruption after the example of the Biblical prophets.[76] Ibn Qayyim al-Jawziyya observes however that its occurrence in history is rather few. The mystics of our times, he specifies, should not try to see an example in their life. Contrary to the mystics' wish for reclusion and isolation Ibn al-Qayyim recommends all Muslims to pay their duties to society and to become a fully responsible individual in it.[77]

As for release (*basṭ*), the counterpart of constriction, God does not isolate His worshippers in this station from the social world but releases them among people in the created world and makes them act like the common believers. *Basṭ* is similar to the word *ghibṭa*, felicity or beatitude.[78] In Islam, al-Khiḍr, who is said to roam the world and mingle with people, is a figure that epitomises *basṭ*. Elias on the other hand represents *qabḍ*.[79] Usually the states of *qabḍ* and *basṭ* follow each other up in a sequence of alternating moods in the heart of the mystic, but as mentioned above some saints could be in one of each for a longer stretch of time or even on a permanent basis. ʿAbd al-Wahhāb al-Shaʿrānī tells that he saw one of his mentors, Bahāʾ al-Dīn al-Majdhūb always in a state of *basṭ* (that is *mabsūṭ*) because God drew him near (*jadhb*) while he was in a mood of merriness.[80] Al-Ḥasan Ibn Hūd on the contrary was called a Sufi who was in a permanent state of *qabḍ*. He was in the complete inability to rejoice about anything.[81]

God, al-Tilimsanī comments, disperses the servant in this abode in the wider field (*mīdān*) of release (*basṭ*). He is free to roam in a multitude of fields of activity; swaying to the right and to the left as a boy who plays with a ball.[82] There are three types of release, thus al-Tilimsānī. In al-Tilimsānī's description of the first group something of his alleged antinomian leanings rings through. The first group of wayfarers in release, he says, are made to intermingle with people and

---

76 Ibn al-Qayyim, *Madārij al-sālikīn*, vol. 3, pp. 308–309.

77 Ibid, p. 311.

78 As expressed in the tradition, *allāhumma ghabṭan lā habṭan*, which indicates that the believer asks God to prolong sentiments of joy and implores him to be preserved in this joyful state, Ibn Nubāta, Jamāl al-Dīn: *Sarḥ al-ʿuyūn fī Sharḥ Risālat Ibn Zaydūn*, Beirut 1986, p. 383.

79 Al-Qāshānī, *Laṭāʾif al-iʿlām*, vol. 1, p. 444.

80 Al-Shaʿrānī, ʿAbd al-Wahhāb: *al-Ṭabaqāt al-kubrā*, ed. by ʿAbd al-Raḥmān Maḥmūd, Cairo 1993, vol. 2, p. 724.

81 ʿAbd al-Raʾūf al-Munāwī, Zayn al-Dīn: *al-Kawākib al-durriyya fī tarājim al-sāda al-ṣūfiyya*, ed. by Muḥammad Adīb Jādir, Beirut 1999, vol. 3, p. 399.

82 Al-Tilimsānī, *Sharḥ manāzil al-sāʾirīn*, folio 111b.

rejoice in live. They are "released in the field of joy" (*busiṭū fī mīdān al-basṭ*), as al-Anṣārī said. They are allowed to enjoy themselves; to play music, to be in the company of women and to look undisturbed at physical beauty. Other authors as well laid the connection between the state of *basṭ* or *inbisāṭ* and the practice of *samāʿ* (audition).[83] *Samāʿ* is referred to here by al-Tilimsānī as pleasant audition (*samāʿ shahī*). Also other pleasures are allowed for them. A mystic in such a position can bear the theophoric name of *ʿAbd al-Basīṭ*. He is free to enjoy and respond to some calls of the carnal soul, without however transgressing the law.[84] Ibn Qayyim al-Jawziyya protests vehemently against al-Tilimsānī's interpretation, and calls the true field of joy mentioned above, the words of the prophet. The other field proposed by al-Tilimsānī, he sermons, is one that has been opened by Satan, where he plucks the souls of the weak.[85]

The second group has a particular strong vision of the Divine objective. Therefore they are allowed to be dispersed.[86] External signs can not blur their vision. *Basṭ*, for this group, plays the same role for the heart as hope does for the carnal soul, thus al-Qāshānī.[87] But for Ibn Qayyim al-Jawziyya the men who have the best qualifications for this group, are the *ʿulamāʾ*. God has released them to go among people and teach them how to bring their religion to life.[88] The third group consists of the people who function as signposts and guides on the spiritual path for the itinerants. For the Sufis it is the domain of the spiritual masters. They have knowledge about the secrets behind the states of *basṭ* and *qabḍ*, which makes the masters particularly suited for instruction. Ibn Qayyim al-Jawziyya however concludes it is the domain of the prophets only.[89]

83 Al-Suhrawardī, *ʿAwārif al-maʿārif*, vol. 2, pp. 11–12.
84 Al-Qāshānī, ʿAbd al-Razzāq: *Iṣṭilāḥāt al-ṣūfiyya*, ed. by Muḥammad Kamāl Jaʿfar, Cairo 1981, p. 112.
85 Ibn al-Qayyim, *Madārij al-sālikīn*, vol. 3, p. 314.
86 Al-Tilimsānī, *Sharḥ manāzil al-sāʾirīn*, folio 112a.
87 Al-Qāshānī, *Iṣṭilāḥāt al-ṣūfiyya*, p. 37.
88 Ibn al-Qayyim, *Madārij al-sālikīn*, vol. 3, p. 315.
89 Ibid.

Conclusion

Ibn Qayyim al-Jawziyya had tried to incorporate elements of the Sufi lexicon in a broader Islamic spiritual enterprise, that envisaged to instil the values of the sharia in the hearts and minds of the believers, not only as an obligation that is imposed from a transcendent authority, but as elements of a piety that are heartfelt and experienced on a sentimental level as well. In this process he painstakingly shifted through the mass of terms that were employed in al-Anṣārī's *Manāzil al-sā'irīn* and tried to give the words a new sense that stripped the terms of its particular Sufi meaning and reintegrated them in an Islamic lexicon of spirituality that makes sense for all the believers. Throughout the *Madārij al-sālikīn* we see that he employs an overall strategy. In his discussion of the Sufi terminology, Ibn Qayyim al-Jawziyya has done three things. He dismantled the Sufi terms and brought them back to conventional language, where they could serve in the elaboration of an alternative spirituality; he promoted a sense of awareness for the Koranic context of the terms and disqualified the elitist structure of the Sufi path of spiritual self-perfection. First of all, he gave most importance to these words that are found in a Koranic context and he scanned carefully how these words were used in the Sufi lexicon. When he thought that the original meaning of these terms was distorted he did not fail to criticise the Sufi authors. In a second phase, Ibn Qayyim al-Jawziyya dissected the conventional Sufi theories of spiritual progress that were represented by the metaphor of the mystic travel along stations and spiritual states towards God. He learned his disciples that the path to God is common to all believers without distinction. To all likelihood Ibn Qayyim al-Jawziyya saw it as his task to offer an alternative spirituality to Sufism, that is a generalised Sunni spirituality aimed at the internalising of religious precepts and obligations. Ibn Qayyim al-Jawziyya defended a practical doctrine that offers the believers a set of alternative possible works in religious and social life that are all meritorious and necessary in their own right and on their due time; prayer, *dhikr*, pilgrimage, contemplation, etc. It is possibly this practical sense of integrating the religious sentiment in prescribed Sunni devotional practice that makes that Ibn al-Qayyim's works are still so popular today.

Appendix:
Abū Ismāʿīl al-Anṣārī al-Harawī's *Manāzil al-sāʾirīn*

al-bidāyāt **spiritual beginnings**	***al-abwāb*** **gates**	***al-muʿāmalāt*** **works**	***al-akhlāq*** **moral dispositions**	***al-uṣūl*** **principles**
al-yaqẓa awakening	*al-ḥuzn* grief	*al-riʿāya* herding	*al-ṣabr* patience	*al-qaṣd* objective
al-tawba return to God	*al-khawf* fear	*al-murāqaba* watchfulness	*al-riḍā* satisfaction	*al-ʿazm* determination
al-muḥāsaba examination of conscience	*al-ishfāq* compassion	*al-ḥurma* respect for God's law	*al-shukr* gratitude	*al-irāda* will
al-ināba penitence	*al-khushūʿ* humbleness	*al-ikhlāṣ* sincerity	*al-ḥayāʾ* timidity	*al-adab* good conduct
al-tafakkur reflection	*al-ikhbāt* humbling	*al-tahdhīb* rectification	*al-ṣidq* truthfulness	*al-yaqīn* certainty
al-tadhakkur meditation	*al-zuhd* renunciation	*al-istiqāma* rectitude	*al-īthār* preference	*al-uns* intimacy
al-iʿtiṣām adherence	*al-waraʿ* scrupulousness	*al-tawakkul* reliance	*al-khuluq* moral disposition	*al-dhikr* remembrance
al-firār flight	*al-tabattul* dedication	*al-tafwīḍ* entrustment	*al-tawāḍuʿ* humility	*al-faqr* poverty
al-riyāḍa spiritual exercise	*al-rajāʾ* hope	*al-thiqa* trust	*al-futuwwa* chivalry	*al-ghināʾ* sufficiency
al-samāʿ audition	*al-raghba* desire	*al-taslīm* submission	*al-inbisāṭ* naturalness	*al-murād* the wanted

al-awdiya **spiritual valleys**	***al-aḥwāl*** **spiritual states**	***al-wilāyāt*** **sainthood**	***al-ḥaqāʾiq*** **spiritual realities**	***al-nihāyāt*** **spiritual arrival**
al-iḥsān beneficence	*al-maḥabba* love	*al-laḥẓ* spiritual glance	*al-mukāshafa* disclosure	*al-maʿrifa* gnosis
al-ʿilm science	*al-ghīra* jealousy	*al-waqt* spiritual time	*al-mushāhada* contemplation	*al-fanāʾ* annihilation
al-ḥikma wisdom	*al-shawq* longing	*al-ṣafāʾ* purity	*al-muʿāyana* direct vision	*al-baqāʾ* subsistence
al-baṣīra spiritual insight	*al-qalaq* anxiety	*al-surūr* gladness	*al-ḥayāt* life	*al-taḥqīq* spiritual realisation
al-firāsa perspicacity	*al-ʿaṭash* thirst	*al-sirr* secrecy	*al-qabḍ* constriction	*al-talbīs* dissimumation
al-taʿẓīm exaltation	*al-wajd* ecstasy	*al-nafas* breath	*al-basṭ* release	*al-wujūd* finding
al-ilhām inspiration	*al-dahsh* perplexity	*al-ghurba* alienation	*al-sukr* intoxication	*al-tajrīd* abstraction
al-sakīna tranquility	*al-hayamān* bewilderment	*al-gharaq* submersion	*al-ṣaḥw* alertness	*al-tafrīd* singularising
al-ṭumaʾnīna peacefulness	*al-barq* lightning	*al-ghayba* absence	*al-ittiṣāl* connection	*al-jamʿ* union
al-himma drive	*al-dhawq* spiritual taste	*al-tamakkun* stability	*al-infiṣāl* disconnection	*al-tawḥīd* oneness

Section 2:
The Career of Books

Ibn al-Qayyim's *Kitāb al-Rūḥ*

Some Literary Aspects

Y. Tzvi Langermann

1. Preface: An Essay in Progress

This project originally grew out of my interest in some early medieval discussions whose purpose is to distinguish between the two concepts, *nafs* and *rūḥ*.[1] Each of the two terms carries a variety of psychological, medical, and metaphysical or religious meanings; some of the earliest writers in Arabic on science and philosophy, such as Qusṭā b. Lūqā (d. 300/912–913) and Isaac Israeli (d. ca. 343/955), perceived a need to sort matters out in special monographs. I was drawn to Ibn al-Qayyim's *Kitāb al-Rūḥ* because it is a vast repository of information, much of it drawn from early sources. As I studied Ibn al-Qayyim's book more closely, my interests expanded, and some additional topics suggested themselves; one study has already appeared. However, it also became increasingly clearer that there are some basic literary issues that must be dealt with. Though I have no reason to doubt that Ibn al-Qayyim authored the materials that make up the book (as we shall see, some do question its authenticity), I do not believe that Ibn al-Qayyim intended to present this book to his audience in the form in which it now circulates. I am more and more convinced that the book that has been such a resounding success was left unfinished by its author.

Kitāb al-Rūḥ is without doubt Ibn al-Qayyim's most successful book, if we measure success in terms of printings, circulation, and so forth. Birgit Krawietz has called it "a real best-seller" and adds that it "gained him a reputation even in circles opposed to him other

1 See Langermann, Y. Tzvi: David Ibn Shoshan on Spirit and Soul, in: *European Journal of Jewish Studies* 1 (2007), pp. 63–86; idem: Abū al-Faraj Ibn al-Ṭayyib on Spirit and Soul, in: *Le Muséon* 122 (2009), pp. 149–159.

ways."[2] It was first printed in Hyderabad, by the Dā'irat al-maʿārif al-niẓāmiyya, in 1318/1900–1901, then again by that same institution in 1324/1906/07 and 1357/1938–1939. For the purposes of this study I have used the most recent version, put out by Abū ʿAbd al-Raḥmān al-Makkī, and published by Maktabat Nazār Muṣṭafā al-Bāz, Mecca, 1425/2004. I have also consulted the second and third Hyderabad printings, the Cairo printing (Maktabat Naṣīr, 1979), and most of the manuscripts as well.[3]

As far as I know, only two studies on this important book have been published. The very rich article of D.B. Macdonald on the notion of "spirit" in Islam, published in 1931 and cited by Carl Brockelmann in his entry on *Kitāb al-Rūḥ*, devotes a considerable amount of space to the book of Ibn al-Qayyim.[4] Four years later, Francis T. Cooke published a paper devoted entirely to *Kitāb al-Rūḥ*.[5] The two studies differ considerably. Macdonald exploits a great number of sources, ranging from pre-Islamic literature to the Egyptian press of the early twentieth century; his article supplies rich annotations to the secondary literature available at the time. Cooke, by contrast, limits his focus exclusively to *Kitāb al-Rūḥ*, and his study has no footnotes.

On the other hand, both articles share an important common feature: both authors choose to concentrate upon Ibn al-Qayyim because the views he expresses have become dominant in Islam. In other words, whoever wishes to understand what Muslims think about "spirit" had better know what Ibn al-Qayyim says in *Kitāb al-Rūḥ*. Macdonald observes,

> A good statement and study of the position of the corporeal school, which is undoubtedly the fundamental position of orthodox Islam, is to

2 Krawietz, Birgit: Ibn Qayyim al-Jawzīyah. His Life and Works, in: *Mamlūk Studies Review* 10 (2006), pp. 19–64, here p. 34. Langermann, Y. Tzvi: The Naturalization of Science in Ibn Qayyim al-Ǧawziyyah's Kitāb al-Rūḥ, in: Caterina Bori and Livnat Holtzman (eds.): *A Scholar in the Shadow. Essays in the Legal and Theological Thought of Ibn Qayyim al-Ǧawziyyah*, *Oriente Moderno* 15 (2010), pp. 163–180.

3 Ibn Qayyim al-Jawziyya, Shams al-Dīn Muḥammad: *Kitāb al-Rūḥ*, ed. by Abū ʿAbd al-Raḥmān al-Makkī, Mecca 1425/2004.

4 Macdonald, Duncan B.: The Development of the Idea of Spirit in Islam, in: *Acta Orientalia* 9 (1931), pp. 307–351. As the author himself (E.E. Calverley) avers, the entry on *nafs* in the second edition of the *EI* (which incorporates the discussion of *rūḥ* as well) is heavily dependent upon Macdonald.

5 Cooke, Francis T.: Ibn al-Qaiyim's *Kitāb al-Rūḥ*, in: *Moslem World* 25 (1935), pp. 129–144.

> be found in the Kitāb al-Rūḥ of Ibn al-Ḳaiyim al-Djawzīya [...] its influence has not been simply among Ḥanbalites and Wahhābites.[6]

Cooke puts it this way: "Ibn al-Qaiyim's view of *al-rūḥ* and *al-nafs* is important, for it represents the belief of the great majority of Muslims to the present day."[7]

It seems, then, that the concerns of scholarship have come full circle, at least for some, or in some way. Macdonald and Cooke were interested primarily in understanding the contemporary Muslim mind, if I may phrase it that way. Indeed, Macdonald caps his essay with some observations, and impassioned pleas, about the situation in his own day.[8] He opines that the "nexus of ideas and hypotheses" found in the authors covered in his study – some 25 in addition to Ibn al-Qayyim – represent "the creative religious thought of Islam." However, this thought "must fight for its life against western influences in education and general civilization which are specifically non-philosophical or materialistic and mechanical in their philosophy." Moreover, another, even more pernicious element from the West has entered into the fray: "modern spiritism." Macdonald bemoans the fact that Islam, unlike the West, is not endowed with any such "preliminary prejudice against spiritual manifestations as exists with us." Hence the danger that spiritism may latch on to the type of ghost stories found, i. a., in the book of Ibn al-Qayyim, and gain thereby legitimacy among Muslims.

For many decades after the appearance of these two studies, it seems that western scholarship on Islamic thought abandoned the concerns expressed by Macdonald and Cooke; research was motivated by an intrinsic interest in the history and transmission of philosophical, religious, and scientific thought, without any abiding worry about "understanding" Muslims or Islam. In recent years, all that has changed, for better or for worse.

2. Manuscripts and Epitomes

Kitāb al-Rūḥ has never been properly edited. The many printings, as far as I can tell, all derive from the original Hyderabad issue. It is not known which manuscript was used for that version; the manuscripts

6 Macdonald, The Idea of Spirit, p. 318.
7 Cooke, Ibn al-Qaiyim's *Kitāb al-Rūḥ*, p. 129.
8 Macdonald, The Idea of Spirit, p. 349.

known to exist in European and American libraries were almost certainly not consulted. Moreover, *Kitāb al-Rūḥ* has spawned a small satellite literature, mainly in the form of epitomes, and these have not been surveyed. In the following section I present some information about copies that I have seen.

The following manuscript copies of the complete work have come to my attention. The first five are listed by Carl Brockelmann.[9] I have examined, in part or in their entirety, all but the Princeton manuscript:

- Escorial, Derenbourg 1590, dated 798/1395–1396
- Escorial, Derenbourg 1592
- Escorial, Derenbourg 699, dated 920/1514
- London, British Library, India Office Loth 172
- Vienna, Austrian National Library, Cod. Mixt. 186 (= Flügel 1533)
- Leiden, Or. 3001, dated 1204
- Princeton, Yahuda 3866, ff., 194a-302a, Rajab 1058/1648[10]

This list is certainly not complete. The Salafi scholar Mashhūr Salmān owns a manuscript; see below. One would presume that the Hyderabad printing was made from a manuscript found in an Indian library, but I have not been able to learn which.

The earliest dated exemplar is Escorial 1590,[11] which was copied just one generation after Ibn al-Qayyim's demise in 1350, and well before the times of al-Biqāʿī (d. 1480), who, as we shall see, may have authored the preface to the printed version of *Kitāb al-Rūḥ*.

The colophon to the Leiden manuscript indicates that that text has been abbreviated from the twelfth *masʾala* onwards.[12] I have looked at the final few folios of this manuscript, and they display the full text; hence the intention of the colophon remains to be established. Another manuscript at Leiden, Or. 12.055, has, beginning on f. 98b, a treatise entitled *Fī Taḥqīq al-rūḥ*, said to be extracted (*lakhkhaṣtuhu*) from Ibn

9 Brockelmann, Carl: *Geschichte der arabischen Litteratur*, Weimar 1902, vol. 2, p. 106, no. 22.

10 No. 2489 in Mach, Rudolph: *Catalogue of Arabic Manuscripts (Yahuda Section) of the Garrett Collection*, Princeton 1977. Cécile Bonmariage was kind enough to inform me that the shelfmark in Mach is mistakenly given as 3886.

11 Derenbourg, Hartwig: *Les manuscrits arabes de l'Escurial*, Paris 1884, vol. 3, pp. 147–148; for the dating of mansucripts and the interpretation of colophons, I rely throughout on the published manuscript catalogues.

12 See Voorhoeve, Petrus: *Handlist of Arabic Manuscripts in the Library of the University of Leiden*, Leiden 1957, p. 320. I am extremely grateful to Prof. J.J. Witkam for his very generous help with the Leiden manuscripts.

al-Qayyim's *Kitāb al-Rūḥ*. "Extracts" from *Kitāb al-Rūḥ* are found in three other Yahudah manuscripts now at Princeton: 336Y, 38b-43a; 976Y, 147b-163b; 2798Y, 32a-41b. I have no information about these remains of the text.

The opening folios of the India Office manuscript appear to have undergone serious damage since it was described by Otto Loth well over a century ago.[13] The manuscript comprises 331 folios, which obviously contained much more than *Kitāb al-Rūḥ* as we know it. It bears the longish title, *Kitāb fī al-Kalām ʿalā al-rūḥ al-arwāḥ fī taḥqīq aḥwāl mā baʿd al-mawt wal-ākhira wal-barzakh*. Loth of course had no printed version with which to compare his manuscript; nonetheless he indicated the India Office has some materials in addition to Ibn al-Qayyim's book. Loth further observes that "by mistake" only nineteen queries are counted in this manuscript.[14] There certainly was some oversight on the part of the copyist, who gave the seventh query the number five, even though the fifth query had already been correctly numbered earlier on. As we shall see in the following section, the preface in this copy is particularly interesting, though it too is now in a sorry condition.

Several epitomes of *Kitāb al-Rūḥ* are known.[15] A small (eight pages) manuscript found at al-Azhar (no. 302737) and available online[16] contains an epitome of the entire text by one Ismāʿīl b. Muḥammad b. Rakīn. Ibn Rakīn limits himself to the question posed in the title of each of the 21 queries that make up *Kitāb al-Rūḥ*; nearly all of the numerous proof-texts and sources are omitted, as well as the *fuṣūl* that are found in most of the queries and which treat of diverse issues, closely or distantly related to the question posed at the beginning of the *masʾala*. For the most part he is interested in the spirits of the dead, their fate after leaving the body, and the implications for the legal and religious status of the graveyard. Interestingly enough, though, he does devote a good

13 Loth, Otto: *A Catalogue of the Arabic Manuscripts in the Library of the India Office*, London 1877, p. 41.

14 Loth corrects the numbering in the chapter titles that are copied out in his catalogue.

15 Derenbourg, in his description of Escorial 699 (Catalogue, I, pp. 495–496), calls MS Escorial 1591, which is a copy of Ibn al-Qayyim's *Hādī al-arwāḥ*, an abrégé of *Kitāb al-Rūḥ*. This is incorrect. *Hādī al-arwāḥ* covers the whole slate of issues connected to *al-janna*, and it has little if anything to do with the topics covered in *Kitāb al-Rūḥ*.

16 Accessible at www.al-mostafa.com via ahlalhadith.com as m000184.pdf (visited 19.12.2012).

deal of space to the numerous theories displayed in response to the 19th query, which asks, "What is the true reality (*ḥaqīqa*) of the soul (*nafs*)?" This is the most philosophical section of *Kitāb al-Rūḥ*. As we shall see in the next section, there are reports of an abridged version prepared by Burhān al-Dīn al-Biqāʿī.

3. The Preface to *Kitāb al-Rūḥ*

The printed versions of *Kitāb al-Rūḥ* all carry an introduction that is clearly not written by the author, but rather penned by someone else, who observes that the book simply plunges into the topic with a series of queries and replies.[17] *Kitāb al-Rūḥ* clearly stands in need of an introduction, and, therefore, the anonymous prefacer will supply it. Most printings have a note to the passage, indicating that the preface was supplied later by Burhān al-Dīn al-Biqāʿī. The most extensive and penetrating footnote is found in the third Hyderabad printing (1357 A.H.):

> You will learn in the course of this address [to the reader] that is not from the pen of Ibn al-Qayyim. Perhaps it is from the pen of al-Biqāʿī. For in *Kashf al-Ẓunūn*, after mention is made of Ibn al-Qayyim's *Kitāb al-Rūḥ*, are these words: 'It was epitomized by Burhān al-Dīn Ibrāhīm bin ʿUmar al-Biqāʿī, and he called it *Sirr al-rūḥ*. He died in the year 885[/1480–1481]. The incipit is, *al-ḥamd lil-lāh al-muttaṣif bi-ṣifāt al-kamāl*, etc.' It seems as if the author of *Kashf al-Ẓunūn* had some misgivings, so he claimed that al-Biqāʿī epitomized the book of Ibn al-Qayyim.[18] It appears that al-Biqaʿī only supplied the book of Ibn al-Qayyim with this preface. It is as if on his own he called it *Sirr al-rūḥ*, because Ibn al-Qayyim did not give a name to his book. It rather became known as *Kitāb al-Rūḥ*, because it is a book about the meaning of *rūḥ*. This [title] then became widely known. God only knows![19]

The anonymous Hyderabad editor picked up the uncertainty of Ḥājjī Khalīfa, who, so he understands, noticed that the preface is not by Ibn al-Qayyim, and therefore decided that the book that reached us is

17 The web version, available for download at www.al-mostafa.com (accessed April 4, 2010), carries no introduction at all. This has not been scanned from any printing, but rather copied out from one of the printings; I presume that the webmaster(s) decided to dispense with the introduction.

18 Ḥājjī Khalīfa: *Kashf al-ẓunūn*, ed. by Şerefeddin Yaltkaya and Rifat Bilge, 6 vols., Istanbul 1941–1955, vol. 5, p. 85.

19 Ibn Qayyim al-Jawziyya, Shams al-Dīn Muḥammad: Kitāb al-Rūḥ, Hyderabad (India), third printing, 1305 A.H., p. 2.

al-Biqāʿī's epitome, known as *Sirr al-rūḥ* (The Secret of the Soul). The Hyderabad editor disagrees, apparently (he does not tell us) because there are no internal grounds for questioning the authenticity of Ibn al-Qayyim's authorship. Instead he suggests that al-Biqāʿī merely added the preface.

Note also the remarks about the title in this learned footnote: Ibn al-Qayyim gave the book no title. Eventually, it became known as *Kitāb al-Rūḥ* simply because that seemed to the most appropriate title, given the book's contents. *Sirr al-rūḥ* is not an epitome, according to the writer of this erudite note, but rather the title suggested, unsuccessfully as it turns out, by al-Biqāʿī. In fact, as we shall see, Ibn al-Qayyim mentions more than one title because, as we shall claim, parts of the book were originally intended as independent essays.[20]

There are other difficulties as well with the anonymous preface. Its author states that this is the first book devoted to the topic of *rūḥ*, but this seems not to be the case. For example, Ibn al-Qayyim himself cites early on p. 35 a *Kitāb al-Nafs wal-rūḥ* by Abū ʿAbd Allāh al-Ḥāfiẓ.

Of the manuscripts that I have seen, only the copy in Vienna displays the preface found in the printed edition.[21] Two of the Escorial manuscripts, nos. 699 and 1592, as well as the copy found at Leiden, have an introduction written in the first person. It purports to be from the pen of Ibn al-Qayyim himself, for all that I can tell, it indeed is. I publish the Arabic text and an English translation as the final section of this study.

Beyond the standard pious remarks of belief and devotion, Ibn al-Qayyim's preface contains only a citation, interspersed with occasional explanations and expansions, from *Sūrat al-Muʾminūn* (Koran 23:12–14), which describes the formation of the human being. In fact the very same verses are cited, along with much the same commentary, in the introduction to Ibn al-Qayyim's *Tuḥfat al-mawdūd*.[22]

---

20 Nonetheless, the Hyderabad printing carries a very long title, beginning: *Kitāb al-Rūḥ fī al-kalām ʿalā arwāḥ al-amwāt* ... Some manuscripts well have title pages displaying a longish title; in general, we have not paid attention to these in this study.

21 This manuscript has a heavily annotated title page which, however, is quite damaged, and I have not reaped any information from it for the present study. In fact, the Vienna copy has more marginalia and corrections than the others, and for that reason alone it would repay further study.

22 Ibn Qayyim al-Jawziyya, Shams al-Dīn Muḥammad: *Tuḥfat al-mawdūd*, ed. by Muḥammad ʿAlī Abū al-ʿAbbās, Cairo 1988, p. 10.

Why are these verses, and their proper interpretation, so important for Ibn al-Qayyim? I believe that the answer lies in the fourth query of Ibn Ḥanbal's (d. 241/855) *al-Radd ʿalā al-zanādiqa wal-jahmiyya*, a formative text for the Ḥanbalī school.[23] In that query, Ibn Ḥanbal answers the complaint of the heretics that the Koran has a confused, if not self-contradictory, account of the creation of man: in different verses he is said to have been made from earth (*turāb*), clay (*ṭīn*), choicest clay (*sulāla*), mud (*ḥamaʾ*), or dry clay (*ṣalṣāl*). Ibn Ḥanbal replies that the Koran's account is completely consistent; the different materials mentioned refer to different stages in the formation of man, beginning with earth, the fundamental constituent of the human body, and culminating with the drop of sperm (the Koran's *sulāla*), by means of which the human race propagates itself. The polemical edge to this account was probably lost by Ibn al-Qayyim's day. Nonetheless, Ibn al-Qayyim may well have wanted to remind his readers of the consistent and full description of man's creation found in the Koran, much along the lines that the Shaykh of his *madhhab* had established.

Two manuscripts have other texts in lieu of the preface printed in the Hyderabad editions. Escorial 1590 exhibits at the beginning a brief biography (*tarjama*) of Ibn al-Qayyim, taken from an unidentified source. The India Office manuscript has, or should I say had, an extensive preface; in the present state of the manuscript, I cannot say whether it purports to be written by Ibn al-Qayyim himself. The opening page is now torn and damaged, and the photocopies that I received are barely legible. Loth, however, copied out this opening sentence, which differs from any of the other prefaces I have seen:

الحمد لله معزّ من اطاعه ومذلّ من خالف امره وعساه...

> "Praise to God, Who raises in esteem whosoever obeys Him, and humbles whosoever transgresses His command and disobeys Him..."[24]

The end of the preface is legible; I copy out here the final few lines:

فلم يزل صلى الله عليه وسلم مشهرا في ذات الله لا يرده عنه راد صادعا بامره لا يصده عنه صاد حتى طلع فجر الايمان واشرق شمس التوحيد والعرفان وسارت دعوته مسيرة الشمس في الاقطار وبلغ دينه ما بلغ الليل والنهار فصلى الله عليه وعلى آله الطيبين الطاهرين صلوة دائمة بدوام السموات والارضين وسلم وبارك

23 Ibn Ḥanbal's tract has been published several times, and it is available on the web as well. The most widely available version is found in the edition by ʿAlī Sāmī al-Nashshār, Alexandria 1971.

24 Loth, *Catalogue*, p. 41 (see note 13 above)

> He continued – may the prayer of God and peace be upon him – to proclaim the essence of God. No opponent could stop him. [He continued] to execute His order, and no resister could restrainer him, until the dawn of belief rose, and the sun of unicity and gnosis (*ʿirfān*) shone. His call moved along like the sun to the ends of the earth, so that his creed reached what day and night have reached.[25] So may the prayer of God be upon him and his kinsfolk, good and pure, an eternal prayer, as eternal as the heavens and earths, and peace and blessing.[26]

It seems, then, that the preface found in the Hyderabad edition, which so exercised the anonymous editor, is a fluke of whatever manuscript was used for that edition. The Hyderabad printing, unfortunately, gives no information about the manuscript or manuscripts that were utilized. Presumably the manuscript(s) are found in Indian libraries.[27] However, the fact that the same preface reappears in all subsequent printings, rather than the authentic preface by Ibn al-Qayyim, proves that all subsequent printings derive from the Hyderabad version. None of the later "editors" seems to have gone to the trouble of checking manuscripts.

4. The Composite Nature of *Kitāb al-Rūḥ*

In the opening section of this paper I suggested that *Kitāb al-Rūḥ* was left unfinished by Ibn al-Qayyim. It is my opinion that he intended to form the book out of several essays that he had written, suitably edited and sutured together. He did not finish this project, and the *textus receptus* reveals signs of the composite and unpolished state that it was left in. The most important clue to this state of affairs is found in Ibn al-Qayyim's reference, within *Kitāb al-Rūḥ*, to another writing of his, which he calls "our large book on knowing the spirit and the soul" (*kitābunā al-kabīr fī maʿrifat al-rūḥ wal-nafs*). Specifically, he

25 Just like the nycthemeron encompasses the entire earth, so also has Islam spread throughout the world.

26 Ms India Office, Loth, *Catalogue*, 172, f. 3b.

27 This reticence is the usual practice of the Hyderabad printings. See the worthy efforts of Muhsin Mahdi to identify the manuscripts used for a Hyderabad printing of al-Fārābī in his *Alfarabi's Philosophy of Plato and Aristotle*, New York 1962, pp. 152–153. Mahdi was able to establish, with a good deal of probability, that the editors used two manuscripts, one from Rampur and the other from Lucknow.

asserts[28] that he will there provide "more than one hundred proofs" in favour of the view of the Sunna that the spirits that depart from the body are "self-standing entities that rise up and go down, join and disengage, etc.".[29] Scholars have noticed this passage and speculated as to the meaning of the reference.[30] However, as far as I know, no one has realized that the discussion Ibn al-Qayyim refers to there is found in *masʾala* 19 of *Kitāb al-Rūḥ*. One finds in that chapter 100 proofs for the assertion that "humanity" is "a body different in its quiddity from sensible body, [and also] luminous, supernal, etc.". The terminology is of course quite different from that found in the cross-reference, but the idea is very much the same: spirit, soul, the essence of humanity, whatever one wishes to call it, is a substance, a self-standing body, different from earthly bodies, and by no means merely an "accident" (in the Aristotelian sense) of the earthly body. It may also be noticed that, as part of the very long title of the nineteenth query, one finds the following: *Mā Ḥaqīqat al-nafs…wa-hal hiya al-rūḥ am lā?* A question of this sort is appropriate for a work entitled *Fī Maʿrifat al-rūḥ wal-nafs*, and it would fit into the well-established genre of inquiries into the difference (if there is any) between the two terms. Yet this issue is not addressed in the nineteenth query. The twentieth query, however, is devoted entirely to the question, whether soul and spirit are "one thing, or two things, distinct from one another." Whatever Ibn al-Qayyim may have intended to publish as *kitābunā al-kabīr fī maʿrifat al-rūḥ wal-nafs*, large chunks of it appear to have been included in *Kitāb al-Rūḥ*.

The composite nature of *Kitāb al-Rūḥ* may also be seen, perhaps paradoxically, from the recent publication of its final section (*masʾala* 21) as a separate volume by one Abū Ḥudhayfa Ibrāhīm b. Muḥammad.[31] The 21st query discusses the three souls recognized by Muslim tradition (*al-ammāra, lawwāma, muṭmaʾinna*, respectively the commanding, the rebuking, and the serene; see the conspectus below).

28 Ibn Qayyim al-Jawziyya, *Kitāb al-Rūḥ*, p. 44.

29 Ibid., p. 44.

30 A reference in exactly the same words is found in Ibn al-Qayyim's *Miftāḥ dār al-saʿāda*; Abū Zayd takes this to be a reference to our *Kitāb al-Rūḥ* and therefore proof for its authenticity. In his bio-bibliography, item 48 (pp. 258–259), he lists *al-Rūḥ wal-nafs* as a separate work, no copy of which is known, and which Ibn al-Qayyim refers to three times in *Kitāb al-Rūḥ*.

31 Ibn Qayyim al-Jawziyya, Shams al-Dīn Muḥammad: *al-Furūq al-nafsiyya bayn ṣifat al-nafs al-ṭayyiba wal-khabītha*, ed. by Abū Ḥudhayfa Ibrāhīm b. Muḥammad, Ṭantā n. d.

Abū Ḥudhayfa acknowledges that this section was not presented by Ibn al-Qayyim as an independent literary creation. Nonetheless, by publishing this section separately from the rest of the book, he in fact acknowledges that it can stand alone – and perhaps was meant to, at least when Ibn al-Qayyim first wrote it. Abū Ḥudhayfa offers a few short quotations, without comment, in which Ibn al-Qayyim refers to his writings on this subject, including the reference to the "large book" referred to above. His intent seems to be that Ibn al-Qayyim considered writing an independent book, and, if none has reached us, this section of *Kitāb al-Rūḥ* can serve the purpose just as well. As far as I am concerned, the point here is that, as Abū Ḥudhayfa's booklet shows, this section can indeed stand alone as a separate treatise; perhaps, then, that is how it was planned to be by Ibn al-Qayyim.

5. The Authenticity of *Kitāb al-Rūḥ*

The authenticity of *Kitāb al-Rūḥ* has been challenged in recent years, apparently on dogmatic grounds rather than on the basis of any literary or historical qualms. Information about the debate is found mostly on the internet; the relevant websites will be cited in the notes to this section.

The Saudi scholar Bakr Abū Zayd, author of several books on Ibn al-Qayyim, takes up the question of the book's authenticity. He writes:

> Some students have spread the word that *Kitāb al-Rūḥ* of Ibn al-Qayyim is not really by him, or that he wrote it before he came into contact with *shaykh al-islām*, Ibn Taymiyya. This is what some tongues have spread, and this is what has reached [our] ears in various settings and investigations. I have not seen it written down in a book; perhaps something of this has been written down, but it is not easy to get hold of it.[32]

Abū Zayd proceeds to refute both allegations by means of a variety of cross-references to *Kitāb al-Rūḥ* in other writings of Ibn al-Qayyim, numerous citations by later authors, and some stylistic and methodological considerations. Similarly he cites several references to Ibn Taymiyya in *Kitāb al-Rūḥ* for proof that the book was written after Ibn al-Qayyim had met his master.[33]

---

32 Abū Zayd, Bakr: *Ibn Qayyim al-Jawziyya. Ḥayātuhu āthāruhu mawāriduhu*, Riyadh 2002, p. 254; http://saaid.net/Doat/Zugail/61.htm (accessed April 4, 2010).

33 Ibid.

The same question was taken up, and the same affirmative answer given, by Mashhūr Salmān on a Salafi website in April 2005. In order to come to a decision, Salmān studied the book closely, making use also of a manuscript in his possession. He found a cross-reference to *Kitāb al-Rūḥ* in yet another book of Ibn al-Qayyim, *al-Tabyīn fī aqsām al-qurʾān*.[34]

It has been intimated that the late ʿAbd al-Azīz b. ʿAbd Allāh Ibn Bāz, "grand mufti" of the Kingdom of Saudi Arabia, was behind the allegations that the book was not written by Ibn al-Qayyim. I gather as much from the response of a Kuwaiti scholar, Sayyid Yūsuf al-Rifāʿī, a respected jurist (of the Shāfiʿī school), a Sufi leader, and a former government minister, in his "Advice to Our Brothers the Scholars of Najd". In section 47, al-Rifāʿī says,

> You accuse the Muslims who differ with you of being deviant Jahmis or Muʿtazilīs. The truth is, *you are the Jahmiyya* because you agree with them in some of their doctrines and you are the Muʿtazila because you concur with them in denying sainthood and saints as well as their miraculous gifts, the life of the dead, and the arbitration of reason in matters of the unseen in religious issues.

There is a footnote after the phrase, "the life of the dead", which reads: "Hence they deny that Ibn al-Qayyim authored *al-Rūḥ*!"[35] Another website identifies "ʿAbd al-Azīz b. ʿAbd Allāh Ibn Bāz, the late (d. 1999) nescient mufti of the Kingdom of Saudi Arabia, government scholar par excellence, and major innovator whose influence on spreading deviant beliefs is incalculable" as the target of al-Rifāʿī's *Naṣīḥa li-ikhwāninā ʿulamāʾ najd* (Advice to Our Brothers the Scholars of Najd).[36]

---

34 http://www.aqsasalafi.com/vb/showthread.php?p=12052, (accessed April 4, 2010).

35 http://www.rifaieonline.com/advice.htm (accessed April 4, 2010). The "life of the dead", I presume, is a poor English rendering of the revivification of the dead. Jahm's (d. 128/746) role here seems to be very much that of the arch-heretic. Ibn al-Qayyim (Kitāb al-Rūḥ, p. 151), beginning of 17 *masʾala* accuses the *mutakallimūn* who deny that spirit is created of being followers of Jahm; see also the conspectus of that query below. On Jahm and his connection to the early Muʿtazila, see Pines, Shlomo: *Studies in Islamic Atomism*, Jerusalem 1997, appendix A, pp. 142–150.

36 Http://answeringwhabismandsalafism.wordpress.com/2008/01/11/abd-al-aziz-ibn-abd-allah-ibn-baaz-a-concise-guide-to-another-primary-innovator-in-islam/ (accessed April 4, 2010).

I have found one fatwa (all are published online) in which Ibn Bāz takes note of Ibn al-Qayyim's leniency with regard to prayer and Koran recitation at the gravesite. The fatwa[37] addresses the long-standing controversy within Islam whether acts of devotion are permitted in the cemetery. The applicant has heard that Ibn Bāz forbids this, and, moreover, that the mufti has demanded that anyone who allows it should substantiate his view. To this end, the applicant writes to Ibn Bāz that he has found proof in *Kitāb al-Rūḥ*; Ibn Bāz responds that "whatever depends upon the sayings of individuals" carries no weight at all if it contradicts the Koran and the Sunna. Thus, rather than challenging the authenticity of *Kitāb al-Rūḥ*, Ibn Bāz rejects its authority, as he consistently rejects outright the right of anyone to rule against the Koran and the traditional sources of legal authority.

I am not worried about the authenticity of the book (which I see no reason to doubt). On the other hand, the allegations are of interest. Neither Abū Zayd nor Salmān intimates why the authenticity of the book has been called into question. Clearly, Ibn al-Qayyim's endorsement of practices that some groups of Muslims find to be both forbidden and reprehensible furnishes a strong incentive to deny that Ibn al-Qayyim authored *Kitāb al-Rūḥ*. Given Ibn al-Qayyim's very high stature within those same groups, the easiest and most logical course would be to reject the book as a forgery. However, the wide-ranging use of philosophical or scientific idiom that is employed in *Kitāb al-Rūḥ* may just as well have aroused the suspicion of some Salafī students (*ṭullāb*).

6. Conspectus of the Book

We have already observed that the preface found in the various printings is not found in any manuscript that we have seen. However, the basic plan of the book is the same in all the manuscripts, and it indeed conforms to the printings (similarly, spot checks of some passages against manuscripts have not revealed any differences that are worth noting here). *Kitāb al-Rūḥ* is divided into 21 "queries" (*masā'il*) of varying length. Some are subdivided into *fuṣūl* or contain supplementary *fuṣūl* on issues related to the theme of the chapter.

37 Ibid., fatwa no. 4296, Monday, 10 Rabi'a I 1429[/2008].

Here follows a list of the 21 queries, as well as some information about the contents. In order to give the reader a sense of the relative lengths of each section, I put in parentheses the page numbers in the Mecca printing that I have used for this study.

1. Are the dead aware of the visit of the living [to the cemetery] and their greeting, or are they not? (pp. 9–21)
   faṣl: Additional proof from the practice of *talqīn al-mayyit*, "whispering" to the recently buried advice as to how the answer *Nakīr* and *Munkar*.[38]
2. Do the spirits of the dead meet each other, visit each other, and remember each other, or not? (pp. 22–25)
3. Do the spirits of the living meet the spirits of the dead, or not? (pp. 26–39)
4. Does the spirit die, or does death appertain to the body alone? (pp. 40–43)
5. After they [the spirits] depart from the body and become denuded [of matter], by what means are they distinguished one from the other, so that they can be recognized and meet each other? And, after they have become denuded [of matter], do they take the shape of the body that they were once in, garbing themselves in its form; or [if not], then just what is their situation? (pp. 44–46)
6. Does the spirit return to the grave of the departed at the time of the interrogation, or not?[39] (pp. 47–66)
   Several *fuṣūl* take up related issues, especially the correct understanding of the "punishment of the grave" and whether it is corporeal as well.
7. The question is posed: what is our reply to the nonbeliever and heretics who deny the punishment in the grave, its wideness or narrowness;[40] that it is either a pit from among the pits of hell, or a garden from among the gardens of paradise; and that the dead neither sits nor stands in it? (pp. 67–79)

38 *Nakīr* and *Munkar* are the two angels who interrogate the newly departed in the grave.

39 The query refers to the interrogation of the newly departed about his faith, as described in the traditions cited at length by Ibn al-Qayyim.

40 According to Muslim tradition, the grave of the Muslim will be widened (allowing his body to rest in peace), but that of the hypocrite will be so narrowed that his bones will be crushed.

This chapter is divided into ten *fuṣūl*, which function as sub-chapters, each of which is devoted to sequentially numbered issues (*umūr*) related to the question posed. Ibn al-Qayyim knows that much is at stake here. The nonbelievers (*al-malāḥida wal-zanādiqa*), as well as "their brothers", "the folk of invention and misdirection (*ahl al-bid'a wal-ḍalāl*)", i. e. philosophers and philosophically-inclined *mutakallimūn*, challenge all traditions that appear to be irrational. Ibn al-Qayyim addresses this core issue, as well as the specific punishments said to be meted out in the grave.

8. The question is posed: what is the wisdom in not mentioning the punishment of the grave in the Koran, though there is a strong need to know it and to believe in it, in order that one take heed and take care? (pp. 80–81)
9. The question is posed: what are the causes for punishment of those who are in the grave? (pp. 82–84)
10. The causes relieving one of the punishment of the grave. (pp. 85–89)
11. Is the interrogation in the grave [of the departed] universal, applying to Muslims, Hypocrites (*munāfiqūn*), and Deniers, or is it limited to Muslims and Hypocrites? (pp. 90–92)
12. Is the interrogation of *Nakīr* and *Munkar* limited to this nation [of Islam], or does it hold for others as well? (pp. 93–94)
13. Are children examined in the grave? (pp. 95–96)
14. His statement: is the punishment of the grave eternal or delimited? (pp. 97–98)
15. Where do the spirits settle in [the period] between death and the resurrection? Are they in heaven or on earth? Are they in paradise or not? Are they placed within bodies other than those that they had been in, and enjoy or suffer therein, or are they denuded [of body]? (pp. 99–124)
    This is a key question in Islamic theology. Accordingly the chapter is lengthy, and, like the seventh *mas'ala*, it is composed of many *fuṣūl*, each of which usually deals with one of the many opinions that have been expressed in reply to the query.
16. Do the spirits of the dead derive benefit from any effort of the living on [their behalf], or not? (pp. 125–150)
    "The living (*al-aḥyā'*)" refers here to two very distinct groups: it refers to the dead, while they were alive, and it refers as well to those who survive the deceased. In the first instance, the question is this: do the dead derive any benefit from the lasting effects of good works they performed in the course of their lives, e. g., righteous

children? In the second instance, the query once again raises the issue of prayers said for the deceased, or other religious acts that are performed on their behalf. In both cases, Ibn al-Qayyim answers in the affirmative, taking pains to muster the necessary proof texts as well to answer the objections that have been raised. The great bulk of the chapter is concerned with the second instance, raising such particular questions as this: can one dedicate half or quarter of a religious acts for the benefit of the deceased? The *fuṣūl* here function as chapters in a well-constructed essay.

17. Is spirit pre-eternal, or is it generated and created? (pp. 151–163)
    Ibn al-Qayyim asserts that the spirit is created, assigning the doctrine of pre-eternality to assorted deviants and heretics.[41] One *faṣl* displays twelve proofs for its being created; the following one answers the claim that the Koran is unclear or equivocal on this issue; and the last answers the claim the human spirit is divine, hence uncreated.
18. Are the spirits created before the bodies, or are they created only after they [the bodies] are? (pp. 164–182)
    Ibn al-Qayyim leans towards the second alternative, but he far less insistent than he is in the preceding query. The scriptural and traditional evidence are weighed in several *fuṣūl*; the final *faṣl* displays the clinching proof that the spirit is created after the body.
19. What is the true reality (*ḥaqīqa*) of the soul? Is it one of the parts of the body, or one of its accidents, or a body living together with it (*musākin lahu*) lodged within, or is it a non-material (*mujarrad*) substance? Are the commanding (*al-ammāra*) soul, the rebuking (*lawwāma*) soul, and the serene (*muṭma'inna*) soul [all three of them] one single soul that bears these attributes? (pp. 183–221).
    I have already argued that this *mas'ala* comprises an independent treatise that Ibn al-Qayyim refers to in other writings of his as *kitābunā al-kabīr fī ma'rifat al-rūḥ wal-nafs* (our great book on knowing the spirit and the soul). The chapter contains much tradition and evidence for irrational (so we would say) phenomena. However, it is mainly concerned with answering the philosophical questions, especially the materiality or immateriality of spirit (or

41 The Jahmiyya are named here in a long citation from Ibn Taymiyya, who in turn refers to Ibn Ḥanbal's *Radd*. Here again we observe Ibn al-Qayyim and Ibn Taymiyya maintaining a firm and consistent line on a point of doctrine first established by Ibn Ḥanbal in his formative manifesto of Islamic belief. Note also the emphatic assertions in this query that the spirit of Jesus is created.

soul), in a philosophical idiom. Despite the last part of the chapter's title, there is no sustained discussion here of the three traditional "souls" (*al-ammāra*, *lawwāma*, *muṭma'inna*), which form instead the first topic in the 21st *mas'ala*.

20. Are spirit and soul the same thing, or two different things? (pp. 222–224)
This very short chapter takes up the same questions of the very long chapter that precedes it, repeating some of the answers. It is hard to imagine it forming an independent chapter in a well-planned book. Rather, it would seem to be a short essay on the same theme of the 19th *mas'ala*; according to our hypothesis, both would then have been incorporated in the draft of *Kitāb al-Rūḥ*. I presume that Ibn al-Qayyim would have wanted to edit these two essays, so that they would fit together as chapters belonging to a single book.
21. Is the soul one or three? (pp. 225–270) As noted above, this chapter treats of the three souls widely recognized by Muslims. The discussion of the natures of these three souls, all of which have strong religious significance, leads Ibn al-Qayyim to write about the religious mind – for example, the "flashes" (*burūq*) that the faithful can hope for, the tranquillity and certainty of the true believer. The great conflict is between, on the one hand, *al-muṭma'inna*, which is identified with holiness, and, on the other hand, *al-ammāra*, which is associated with damnable thoughts and traits. However, as Ibn al-Qayyim, explains, the Muslim is not aways faced with stark alternatives, one of which is clearly good and the other definitely evil. Instead, one must often face up to two aspects of a certain trait or issue, both of which may appear to be laudable, but one of which is surely wrong. "A single thing has a single form, which is split into laudable and disgraceful things; for example, joy and sorrow, regret and anger, self-respect (*ghayra*) which, if innately strong and fortified by the believer, leads to tranquillity and conceit, (…)" (p. 235). Consequently, most of the chapter consists of a series of *fuṣūl*, each of which begins *wal-farq bayna* and elucidates the difference between a pair of antitheses (not necessarily those listed in the sentence just cited).
Hence the great bulk of this very lengthy chapter is an essay on morals. *Rūḥ* is not discussed here at all; the connection with the theme of the book is by way of the three "souls" and the issue, discussed in earlier chapters, whether soul and spirit are the same thing.

The *masāʾil* fall quite neatly into three groups, and, in fact, they are organized into three parts (*ajzāʾ*) in the earliest manuscript, Escorial 699. Part one, comprising *masāʾil* 1–16, treats of the spirits of the dead, their status and fate, and, in particular, the legitimacy of practices at the graveyard after interment. Part two (*masāʾil* 17–18) delves into the nature of spirit and soul. Part three is made up of the final three *masāʾil*. We have already suggested that the nineteenth *masʾala*, the most "philosophical" of them all, was originally written as an independent treatise. The final *masʾala* is for the most part a treatise on morals. However, it also contains some emphatic passages of religious insight on epistemology, illumination, and, towards the end, some statements on theology as well.

Each *masʾala* is well-organized. Some of the longer ones display a clear internal structure. On the other hand, the *masāʾil* do not cohere well as chapters in a book. In particular, there seems to be a fair amount of repetition.

Appendix: Ibn al-Qayyim's Preface

I have found thus far two nearly identical prefaces, but the differences between them are significant enough of them that I have chosen to publish them separately, rather than producing a single "edition" of the two texts.[42] Only in the Escorial version does the preface begin with *qāla al-shaykh* [...] *Shams al-Dīn* [...] *Ibn al-Qayyim al-Jawziyya*, thus indicating unambiguously that the Ibn al-Qayyim is the author. However, the substantive part of the preface, that is, the section describing the formation of man that I have discussed earlier, is much cleaner in the Leiden manuscript. The Leiden manuscript also hints that the Ibn al-Qayyim answered these queries in response to questions that were posed to him; but this may be a calque on the famous verse of the Koran. Finally, note that the Leiden manuscript alone states clearly that there are 21 queries in the book.

---

42 The preface is found in Escorial 699 as well, but it is badly damaged, and I have not taken it into account here.

A. MS Escorial

بسم الله الرحمن الرحيم
قال الشيخ الامام العالم العلامة الحجة البارع بقية السلف الكرام احد الائمة الاعلام شمس الدين عبد الله محمد بن قيم الجوزية تغمده الله برحمته الحمد لله العلي العظيم الحليم الكريم الغفور الرحيم الحمد لله رب العالمين الرحمان الرحيم مالك يوم الدين خلق الانسان من سلالة من طين ثم جعله نطفة في قرار مكين ثم خلق النطفة علقة سوداء للناظرين ثم خلق العلقة مضغة قطعة لحم بقدر أكلة الماضغين ثم خلق البناء المبين ثم كسا العظام لحما هو لها كالثوب للّابسين ثم انشاه خلقا ءاخر فتبارك الله احسن الخالقين فسبحان من شملت
قدرته كل مقدور وجرت مشيته في خلقه بتصاريف الامور وتفرد بملك السموات والارض يخلق ما يشآء هو الذي يصوركم في الارحام كيف يشآء لا اله الا هو العزيز الحكيم واشهد ان لا اله الا الله وحده لا شريك له الهاجل عن التمثيل والنظير وتعالى عن الشريك والظهير و تقدس عن شبه خلقه فليس كمثله شيء وهو السميع البصير واشهد ان محمدا عبده ورسوله وخيرته من خلقه وامينه على وحيه في حجته على عباده ارسله رحمةة للعالمينوقدرة للعالمين ومحجة للسالكين وحجة على العباد اجمعين فصلى الله وملائكته ورسله عليه وعليه السلام ورحمة الله وبركاته اما بعد فهذه الكتاب مشتمل على مسائل في الروح ومعانيها. اما المسئلة الاولى ...

In the Name of God, the Compassionate, the Merciful;
Said the Shaykh, the *imām*, the learned, the sign, the proof, the skillful, the remnant of the forefathers, the noble, the keenest of the leaders [and of] the eminent, Shams al-Dīn Abū ʿAbd Allāh Muḥammad Ibn Qayyim al-Jawziyya, may God protect him in His mercy. Praise to God, the Sublime, the Great, the Clement, the Noble, the Forgiving, the Merciful; Praise to God, Lord of the Worlds, the Compassionate, the Merciful, Sovereign over Judgment Day;

He created man out of the choicest clay; He then made it into a drop in a firm abode; He then crafted from the drop a clot, black to the beholders; then He made from the clot a lump [of flesh, *muḍgha*], that is, a piece of meat, of the size of a chewable portion [literally, "the size of the food of those who chew", *al-māḍighīn*]; He then created the evident structure; He then covered the bones with flesh, which is like a suit of clothes; then He brought him into being as a different creation. Blessed is God, the best of the creators! Praise to Him, Whose power (*qudra*) prevails over every capability (*maqdūr*), and Whose will pervades His creation in the management of affairs. He is Alone in being sovereign over heavens and earth, creating what He wishes. It is He Who formed you as He wished in the wombs. There is no God other than He, Mighty and Wise! I testify that there is no God other than Allah alone. He has no partner, too noble for any likeness or equivalent. Exalted is He above any partner or assistant, sanctified is He above any comparison to His creation; there is nothing like Him. Now, this book comprises queries about *rūḥ* and its meanings. The first query…

B. MS Leiden

ابسم الله الرحمن الرحيم
الحمد لله العلي العظيم الحليم الكريم الغفور الرحيم الحمد لله رب العالمين الرحمن الرحيم مالك يوم الدين خلق الانسان من سلالة من طين ثم جعله نطفة في قرار مكين ثم خلق النطفة سوداء للناظرين ثم خلق العلقة مضغة وهي قطعة لحم بقدر اكلة الماضغين ثم خلق المضغة عظاما مختلفة المقادير والمنافع اساسا يقوم عليه هذه البنا المتين ثم كسا العظام لحما هو لها كالثوب للابسين ثم انشاه خلقا ءاخر فتبارك الله احسن الخالقين فسبحان من شملت قدرته كل مقدور وجرت مشيته في خلقه بتصاريف الامور وتفرد بملك السموات والارض يخلق ما يشآء هو الذي يصوركم في الارحام كيف يشآء لا اله الا هو العزيز الحكيم واشهد ان لا اله الا الله وحده لا شريك له الآجل عن التمثيل والنظير وتعالى عن الشريك والظهير تقدس عن شبه خلقه فليس كمثله شيء وهو السميع والبصير واشهد ان محمدا عبده ورسوله وخيرته من خلقه وامينه على وحيه في حجته على عباده ارسله رحمة للعالمين ومحجة للسالكين وحجة على العباد اجمعين فصلى الله وملائكته ورسله عليه وعليه السلام ورحمة الله وبركاته. اما بعد فهذه الكتاب مشتمل على احدى وعشرين مسائل في الروح وما يتعلق بها الشيخ الامام العالم العلامة ابو عبد الله محمد ابن قيم الجوزية قدس روحه ونور صريحه وقد سئل عن الروح فقال الحمد لله المسئلة الاولى...

In the Name of God, the Compassionate, the Merciful;
Praise to God, Lord of the Worlds, the Compassionate, the Merciful, Sovereign over Judgment Day; He created man out of the choicest clay; He then made it into a drop in a firm abode; He then made the drop black to the beholders; then He made from the clot a lump of flesh, *muḍgha*, that is, a piece of meat, of the size of a chewable portion [literally, "the size of the food of those who chew (*al-māḍighīn*)"]; He then made from the lump, bones of varying size and utility as a foundation upon which this firm structure will be built; He then covered the bones with flesh, which is like clothing for them; then He brought him into being as a different creation. Blessed is God, the best of the creators! Praise to Him, Whose power (*qudra*) prevails over every capability (*maqdūr*), and Whose will pervades His creation in the management of affairs. He is Alone in being sovereign over heavens and earth, creating what He wishes. It is He Who formed you as He wished in the wombs. There is no God other than He, Mighty and Wise! I testify that there is no God other than Allāh alone. He has no partner, too noble for any likeness or equivalent. Exalted is He above any partner or assis-

tant, Sanctified is He above any comparison to His creation; there is nothing like Him. He is the All-hearing and All-seeing. I testify that Muhammad is His servant and messenger, the best of His creation and the trustee of His revelation, His proof to His servants. He sent him out of compassion for humanity and love for those who travel [in the right path], as proof for all of the servants. May God, His angels and messengers, pray for him; peace be upon him, and the compassion and blessings of God as well. Now then [to our topic:] this book comprises 21 queries about *rūḥ,* its meanings, and what pertains to them. The Shaykh, the *imām*, the learned, the sign, Abū ʿAbd Allāh Muḥammad Ibn Qayyim al-Jawziyya – may his spirit and the light of his tomb be sanctified – was asked about the *rūḥ*. He said, "Praise to God! The first query …"

The Relation of Ibn Taymiyya and Ibn Qayyim al-Jawziyya to the Ḥanbalī School of Law

Christopher Melchert

Ibn Taymiyya and Ibn Qayyim al-Jawziyya were famously adherents of the Ḥanbalī school of law. Abdul Hakim Al-Matroudi has published a book on what the Ḥanbalī school meant to Ibn Taymiyya.[1] My first project here is to determine what Ibn Taymiyya and Ibn Qayyim al-Jawziyya meant to the late-medieval Ḥanbalī school itself, especially as concerns its characteristic rules. My second project is to characterize Ibn al-Qayyim's jurisprudence, especially what the Ḥanbalī school meant to him. Like the other Sunni schools of law (the Ḥanafī, Shāfiʿī, and Mālikī), the Ḥanbalī school was partly an institution for forming jurisprudents. Being Ḥanbalī meant that Ibn Taymiyya and Ibn al-Qayyim had studied under Ḥanbalī teachers who in time had certified them as competent to issue juridical opinions (fatwas) in the Ḥanbalī tradition. In their day, no attention would be paid to opinions from anyone who had not been so certified as competent in one or another of the Ḥanafī, Shāfiʿī, Mālikī, and Ḥanbalī traditions.[2] Those discursive traditions are the second main constitutive element of the Sunni school of laws. The theory of Islamic law that prevailed from at least 1000 C.E. is that God has revealed his will for mankind through the Koran and the word and deed of the Prophet. On some points, God has deigned to make the evidence so clear that no dissent is allowed; e.g. the requirement to perform the ritual prayer five times a day. On most points, God has given us more ambiguous evidence of his will, admitting of multiple legitimate interpretations. Sometimes a school will agree on some point in opposition to all the rest; for example, the

1 Al-Matroudi, Abdul Hakim I.: *The Ḥanbalī School of Law and Ibn Taymiyyah. Culture and Civilization in the Middle East*, London 2006.

2 On the school of law as an institution for forming and certifying jurisprudents, see above all Makdisi, George: *The Rise of Colleges. Institutions of Learning in Islam and the West*, Edinburgh 1981, chapters 1–3, pp. 1–223, esp. pp. 1–9.

Ḥanafiyya (adherents of the Ḥanafī school) raise their hands only at the beginning of the ritual prayer, adherents of the other Sunni schools at multiple other points in the course of it as well. More often, there will be disagreement within the school; for example, at those points of the prayer where one needs to recite the Koran aloud, the Ḥanafiyya disagree whether it suffices to recite loudly enough to hear oneself or only if someone else can hear, too. A full treatment of the rules of Islamic law (a book of many volumes) will normally provide arguments in favour of the rules identified by the author's own school, also review disagreement within that school, sometimes expressing a preference for one or another position but sometimes leaving internal disagreements unresolved. Being Ḥanbalī also meant, then, that Ibn Taymiyya and Ibn al-Qayyim wrote books identifying the range of opinion within the Ḥanbalī school and expressing their preferences.[3]

To judge by how often he is cited in an encyclopaedia of Ḥanbalī opinions from the late fifteenth century, it appears that the Ḥanbalī school after him regarded Ibn Taymiyya as a significant figure but less than some others. Numerous other Ḥanbalī jurisprudents, both earlier and later than he, effectively did more to shape the peculiar range of opinions that defined the school. By contrast, Ibn al-Qayyim attracted little attention from later Ḥanbalī jurisprudents, even with regard to juridical problems that he treated at length with special stress on Ḥanbalī positions. The reason for the difference in their effects on the Ḥanbalī tradition, respectively modest and negligible, seems to be that Ibn Taymiyya made a greater show of respecting the Ḥanbalī discursive tradition, whereas Ibn al-Qayyim too often ignored it in favour of what he took to be the positions of the school's eponym, Aḥmad b. Ḥanbal (d. 241/855).

The chief means I propose to measure the importance of Ibn Taymiyya and Ibn al-Qayyim to the Ḥanbalī school is to count citations of earlier Ḥanābila (adherents of that school) in an encyclopaedia of disagree-

3 For certain and uncertain questions in Islamic law, see Weiss, Bernard G.: *The Spirit of Islamic Law. The Spirit of the Laws*, Athens 1998. For the schools of law as discursive traditions, see Calder, Norman: The Law (in History of Islamic Philosophy), in: Seyyed Hossein Nasr and Oliver Leaman (eds.): *History of Islamic Philosophy*, London 1996, vol. 2, pp. 979–998, and Hallaq, Wael B.: *Authority, Continuity and Change in Islamic Law*, Cambridge 2001, chapter 2; also, for adherence to schools in Damascus a century or two before Ibn Taymiyya and Ibn al-Qayyim, Talmon-Heller, Daniella: Fidelity, Cohesion and Conformity within Madhhabs in Zangid and Ayyubid Syria, in: Peri Bearman, Rudolph Peters and Frank E. Vogel (eds.): *The Islamic School of Law*, Cambridge 2005, pp. 94–116.

ment within the school by ʿAlāʾ al-Dīn ʿAlī b. Sulaymān al-Mardāwī (d. Damascus, 885/1480), *al-Inṣāf fī maʿrifat al-rājiḥ min al-khilāf ʿalā madhhab al-imām Aḥmad ibn Ḥanbal* (Doing Justice Concerning the Knowledge of What Predominates by Way of Disagreement in the School of Aḥmad b. Ḥanbal). This is formally a detailed commentary on Ibn Qudāma al-Maqdisī (d. Damascus, 620/1223), *al-Muqniʿ* (The Convincing).[4] I chose a sample of ten pages per volume (except for the last, of which about a third is given over to other texts), 116 altogether. The more someone is cited, the more important he presumptively was to the evolution of the Ḥanbalī juridical discourse.

Here is a summary of what I found, mainly the twenty-one authorities most often cited, with notes indicating names of books cited and references of first resort for biographical information.

1) Ibn Mufliḥ al-Qāqūnī, Muḥammad (d. Damascus, 763/1362).

256 citations, mostly of *al-Furūʿ* (The Branches). For biographical information, see Laoust, Henri: Le Hanbalisme sous les mamlouks bahrides (658–784/1260–1382), in: *Revue des études islamiques* 28 (1960), pp. 171, at pp. 68–69.

2) Ibn Qudāma, ʿAbd Allāh b. Aḥmad (d. Damascus, 620/1223).

225 citations, of *al-Mughnī* (That Which Relieves of Want), *al-Kāfī* (The Sufficient), etc., often as *al-Muṣannif* (the Author; since he wrote the book on which *al-Inṣāf* is a commentary). For biographical information, see Laoust, Henri: Le Hanbalisme sous le califat de Bagdad (241/855–656/1258), in: *Revue des études islamiques* 27 (1959), pp. 67–128, at pp. 124–125.

4 I use al-Mardāwī, ʿAlāʾ al-Dīn ʿAlī b. Sulaymān: *al-Inṣāf fī maʿrifat al-rājiḥ min al-khilāf ʿalā madhhab al-imām Aḥmad ibn Ḥanbal*, ed. by Muḥammad Ḥāmid al-Fiqī, Cairo 1955–1958, as anonymously reworked and reprinted; Beirut 1419/1998. The edition of Abū ʿAbd Allāh Muḥammad Ḥasan Muḥammad Ḥasan Ismāʿīl al-Shāfiʿī, Beirut 1418/1997, seems to be superior, but not so as to affect my count of citations.

3) Ibn Ḥamdān, Aḥmad (d. Cairo, 695/1295).

192 citations, of *al-Riʿāya al-kubrā* (The Greater Consideration) and *al-ṣughrā* (The Lesser Consideration). For biographical information, see Laoust, Califat, pp. 124–125.

4) Ibn Abī ʿUmar, ʿAbd al-Raḥmān (d. Damascus, 682/1283).

141 citations as *al-Shāriḥ* (the Commentator) or of *al-Sharḥ al-kabīr* (The Great Commentary on Ibn Qudāma, *al-Muqniʿ*). For biographical information, see Laoust, Bahrides, pp. 40–41.

5) Ibn Ḥanbal, Aḥmad (d. Baghdad, 241/855).

135 citations, of which 51 (38 percent) with multiple, contradictory versions (*riwāyāt*) of what Ibn Ḥanbal said. For more on his jurisprudence, see Melchert, Christopher: *Ahmad ibn Hanbal*, Oxford 2006, chapter 3.

6) al-Majd, Majd al-Dīn ʿAbd al-Salām b. ʿAbd Allāh
(d. Harran, 652/1254?).

129 citations, of *al-Muḥarrar* (The Clarifier). For biographical information, see Laoust, Califat, p. 126.

7) al-Qāḍī Abū Yaʿlā b. al-Farrāʾ, Muḥammad b. al-Ḥusayn
(d. Baghdad, 458/1065).

111 citations, of *al-Mujarrad* (The Stripped Down) more than any other work but usually as *al-Qāḍī*. For more biographical information, see Laoust, Califat, pp. 96–98.

8) Abū al-Khaṭṭāb al-Kalwadhānī, Maḥfūẓ b. Aḥmad
(d. Baghdad, 510/1116).

109 citations, of *al-Hidāya* (The Guidance), *al-Intiṣār* (Giving Victory), etc. For biographical information, see Laoust, Califat, pp. 102–103.

9) ʿAbd al-Raḥmān b. Abī al-Qāsim, Basran (d. 684/1285).

95 citations, of *al-Ḥāwī al-ṣaghīr* (The Lesser Comprehensive) and *al-kabīr* (The Greater). For biographical information, see Ibn Rajab, ʿAbd al-Raḥmān b. Aḥmad: *K. al-Dhayl ʿalā ṭabaqāt al-ḥanābila*, ed. by Muḥammad Ḥāmid al-Fiqī, Cairo 1372/1952–53, reprint Beirut n. d., vol. 2, pp. 313–315.

10) Ibn Munajjā, Asʿad (Muḥammad?) (d. Damascus, 606/1209).

86 citations, of *al-Khulāṣa* (The Summary) and *Sharḥ al-Hidāya* (The Commentary on *al-Hidāya*). For biographical information, see Ibn Rajab, *al-Dhayl*, vol. 2, pp. 49–51.

11) Ibn al-Sarī al-Dujaylī, al-Ḥasan (Ḥusayn?) b. Yūsuf, Baghdadī (d. 732/1331).

81 citations, of *al-Wajīz* (The Concise). For biographical information, see Ibn Rajab, *al-Dhayl*, vol. 2, pp. 417–418.

12) ʿIzz al-Dīn al-Maqdisī, Muḥammad b. ʿAlī (d. Damascus, 820/1413).

67 citations, usually of *Naẓm al-mufradāt* (The Versification of *the Peculiar*), also as *shaykhunā* (our Master). For biographical information, see al-ʿUlaymī, ʿAbd al-Raḥmān (d. Jerusalem, 927/1520–1521?): *al-Manhaj al-aḥmad fī tarājim aṣḥāb al-imām Aḥmad* (The Most Praiseworthy Way Concerning the Biographies of the Followers of the Leader Aḥmad), ed. by Riyāḍ ʿAbd al-Ḥamīd Murād, Muḥyī al-Dīn Najīb, Ibrāhīm Ṣāliḥ, Ḥasan Ismāʿīl Muruwwa, Yāsīn Maḥmūd al-Khaṭīb and Walīd Yūsuf al-ʿĀnī, Beirut 1997, vol. 5, p. 203. Also adequate, to my knowledge, is the edition *al-Manhaj al-aḥmad* by Muṣṭafā ʿAbd al-Qādir Aḥmad ʿAṭā, Beirut 1420/1999. Two earlier, two-volume editions by Muḥammad Muḥyī al-Dīn ʿAbd al-Ḥāmid, Cairo 1383/1963 and Beyrut (ʿĀlam al-Kutub) 1403/1983, present only the first half of al-ʿUlaymī's work.

13) al-Sāmarrī, Muḥammad b. ʿAbd Allāh (d. Baghdad, 616/1219).

66 citations, of *al-Mustawʿib* (The Inclusive). For biographical information, see Laoust, Califat, p. 119.

14) Ibn ʿAqīl, ʿAlī (d. Baghdad, 513/1119).

63 citations, of *al-Funūn* (The Varieties), *al-Wāḍiḥ* (The Explainer), *al-Tadhkira* (The Reminder), etc., but usually by name. For biographical information, see Makdisi, George: *Ibn ʿAqīl et la résurgence de l'Islam traditionaliste au XIe siécle (V^e siécle de l'Hégire),* Damascus 1963.

15) Ibn Qāḍī al-Jabal, Aḥmad b. al-Ḥasan (d. Damascus, 771/1370).

53 citations, of *al-Fāʾiq* (The Surpasser). For biographical information, see al-ʿUlaymī, *al-Manhaj al-aḥmad*, vol. 5, pp. 135–137.

16) al-Zarkashī, Muḥammad b. ʿAbd Allāh (d. Cairo, 772/1370?).

47 citations, all by name. For biographical information, see al-ʿUlaymī, *al-Manhaj al-aḥmad*, vol. 5, pp. 137–138.

17) Fakhr al-Dīn b. Taymiyya, Muḥammad b. al-Khaḍir (d. Harran, 622/1225).

41 citations, of *al-Talkhīṣ* (The Summarizing). For biographical information, see Ibn Rajab, *al-Dhayl*, vol. 2, pp. 151–162.

18) Ibn Tamīm al-Ḥarrānī, Muḥammad (d. ca. 675/1276–1277).

39 citations, sometimes of *al-Mukhtaṣar* (The Epitome), but usually by name. For biographical information, see Ibn Rajab, *al-Dhayl*, vol. 2, p. 290.

19) Ibn Taymiyya, Aḥmad b. ʿAbd al-Ḥalīm (d. Damascus, 728/1328).

38 citations, always as *al-Shaykh Taqī al-Dīn*. For biographical information, see Al-Matroudi, *The Ḥanbalī School.*

20) Ibn Rajab, ʿAbd al-Raḥmān b. Aḥmad (d. Damascus, 795/1393).

31 citations, of *al-Qawāʿid al-fiqhiyya* (The Juristic Principles). For biographical information, see al-ʿUlaymī, *al-Manhaj al-aḥmad*, vol. 5, pp. 168–171.

21) al-Ādamī, Aḥmad b. Muḥammad al-Baghdādī (8th/14th?).

31 citations, of *al-Muntakhab* (The Selected), *al-Munawwar* (The Illuminated). For biographical information, see al-ʿUlaymī, *al-Manhaj al-aḥmad*, vol. 5, p. 72.

As for the history of the Ḥanbalī school, the list suggests who were its most important figures, at least as expounders of Ḥanbalī law and from the viewpoint of the later 15th century. There are other ways of getting at who were the most important. Writing in the early twentieth century, Ibn Badrān states that the most important works of the Ḥanbalī school have been three: al-Khiraqī (d. Damascus, 334/945–946), *al-Mukhtaṣar* (The Epitome); ʿAlāʾ al-Dīn al-Mardāwī, *al-Tanqīḥ al-mushbiʿ* (The Satiating Revision); and al-Futūḥī (d. Cairo, 972/1564–65?), *Muntahā al-irādāt* (The Ultimate of Wishes). From this point forward, people devoted themselves to this last and, from laziness and oblivion, abandoned other books. Then along came Mūsā al-Ḥujāwī (d. Cairo, 1051/1641), who wrote *al-Iqnāʿ* (The Convincing). Ḥanbalī writers henceforward depended on these two books, by al-Futūḥī and al-Ḥujāwī.[5] This seems to be a list of leading textbooks for teaching

5 Ibn Badrān, ʿAbd al-Qādir: *al-Madkhal ilā madhhab al-imām Aḥmad b. Ḥanbal* (The Entryway into the School of the Leader Aḥmad b. Ḥanbal), Cairo n.d., p. 221 = ed. by ʿAbd Allāh b. ʿAbd al-Muḥsin al-Turkī, Beirut 1401/1981, pp. 434–435. Khiraqī's *Mukhtaṣar* was the first epitome of Ḥanbalī positions, whose publication provided the nascent Ḥanbalī school with a basis comparable to that provided to the Mālikī school by the epitomes of Ibn ʿAbd al-Ḥakam (d. Old Cairo, 214/829) and Abū Muṣʿab al-Zuhrī (d. Medina, 242/857) and to the Shāfiʿī by the epitomes of al-Buwayṭī (d. Baghdad, 231/846?) and al-Muzanī (d.

purposes. If we are to write a proper history of the Ḥanbalī school, we must consider citations and teaching texts as well as entries in biographical dictionaries.

As for the special purposes of this study, the chief results of my counting citations in al-Mardāwī's *al-Inṣāf* are immediately clear: Ibn Taymiyya appears as a relatively minor figure, less often cited than many other Ḥanbalī jurisprudents, while Ibn al-Qayyim does not even appear among the top 20 (in fact, appears just twice in the sample). It also becomes clear, incidentally, that there has been a considerable break in the tradition between al-Mardāwī's time and ours, for a majority of the books associated with these 21 most-cited jurisprudents have never been printed, so far as I have been able to determine, notwithstanding their importance in the 15th century. Ibn Taymiyya and Ibn al-Qayyim are the most famous 14th-century Ḥanābila today, but other 14th-century Ḥanābila did more to shape the characteristic doctrines of the school.

The reason for Ibn Taymiyya's being seldom cited is not that al-Mardāwī looks down on him. Al-Mardāwī usually names his authorities in series. Here is a typical passage, for example, concerning whom the leader should permit to join the army of jihad:

> He also forbids boys, according to the sound opinion of the school. A number have mentioned this. [The author of] *al-Furūʿ* puts it first. [The authors of] *al-Mughnī*, *al-Kāfī*, *al-Bulghā*, *al-Sharḥ*, *al-Riʿāya al-kubrā*, and others say that he forbids young children (*al-ṭifl*). The Author (*al-muṣannif*) and the Commentator (*al-shāriḥ*) [Ibn Abī ʿUmar] add that it is permissible for him to give permission to whatever boys are strong.[6]

Al-Mardāwī occasionally names Ibn Taymiyya in a series of names like this, but more often quotes him making a special point; for example,

---

Old Cairo, 264/877?). On their significance, see further Melchert, Christopher: The Formation of the Sunnī Schools of Law, in: Wael B. Hallaq (ed.): *The Formation of Islamic Law*, Aldershot 2004, pp. 351–366, at pp. 352–354. For biographical information concerning al-Khiraqī, see Laoust, Califat, p. 84. There is some disagreement over al-Futūḥī's name. Ibn Badrān gives the form *Taqī al-Dīn Aḥmad b. al-Najjār*, whereas Brockelmann indicates rather *Muḥammad b. Aḥmad b. al-Najjār*: Brockelmann, Carl: *Geschichte der arabischen Literatur*, Leiden 1937–1942, vol. 2, p. 447, which see for biographical information. Brockelmann's form is confirmed by Çelebī, Kātib: *Keşf al-zunūn*, ed. by Şerefettin Yaltkaya and Rifat Bilge, Istanbul 1941, 1943, p. 1853. Brockelmann also (more doubtfully) proposes the spelling *Khujāwī*: Brockelmann, *Geschichte der arabischen Litteratur*, suppl., vol. 2, p. 447, which also see for biographical information.

6 Al-Mardāwī, *al-Inṣāf fī maʿrifat al-rājiḥ*, vol. 4, p. 104 (*K. al-Jihād*, *bāb mā yalzamu al-imām wal-jaysh*, after *qawluhu fa-man lā yaṣluḥu lil-ḥarb*).

not long after the passage just quoted, concerning the employment of non-Muslim subjects in positions of authority:

> [Ibn Mufliḥ al-Qāqūnī] says in *al-Furūʿ*, "There are two versions [of what Aḥmad said] concerning this problem. The first is that it is forbidden, which was the choice of our Shaykh [meaning al-Shaykh Taqī al-Dīn] and others as well, for it entails corruption or leads to it. It is more pressing than the question of jihad." The Shaykh Taqī al-Dīn said, "Whoever of them [polytheists] operates a ministry (*dīwān*) for the Muslims has violated the terms of his pact, for it goes against humiliation (*al-ṣaghār*)." [Ibn Ḥamdān] says in *al-Riʿāya* that it is discouraged except when necessary.[7]

Ibn Taymiyya is not the only shaykh quoted as explaining a rule, as here; however, al-Mardāwī seems to quote none other so regularly to explain his preference, nor anyone else so regularly to bring up a ramification not discussed elsewhere. Al-Mardāwī plainly respected Ibn Taymiyya as a significant and original thinker. In a short work, al-Mardāwī even names Ibn Taymiyya as a recent example of *al-mujtahid al-muṭlaq*, someone capable of inferring rules directly from the revealed sources, not bound to adhere to a pre-existing school.[8] However, Al-Matroudi is justified in concluding that al-Mardāwī, although well acquainted with Ibn Taymiyya's views, remained in the end more a reporter of them than an advocate.[9]

As for the apparent insignificance of Ibn Qayyim al-Jawziyya, it might be objected that, although he is little cited in the whole of *al-Inṣāf fī maʿrifat al-rājiḥ*, he may yet appear a leading authority in some specialized parts of the law. The obvious example is the law of non-Muslim subjects, for Ibn al-Qayyim wrote a long (and useful) book on precisely this topic, *Aḥkām ahl al-dhimma* (The Ordinances Concerning the Protected Peoples).[10] I have therefore also counted

7 Ibid., vol. 4, p. 105 (*K. al-Jihād, bāb mā yalzamu al-imām wal-jaysh*, after *qawluhu wa-lā yastaʿīn bi-mushrik*).

8 Al-Mardāwī, ʿAlāʾ al-Dīn ʿAlī b. Sulaymān: *Qāʿida nāfiʿa jāmiʿa li-ṣifat al-riwāyāt al-manqūla ʿan al-imām Aḥmad* (A Beneficial, Comprehensive Principle Concerning the Character of Transmitted Versions of [the Position of] the Leader Aḥmad), appended to idem, *al-Inṣāf fī maʿrifat al-rājiḥ*, vol. 12, pp. 177–218, at p. 191.

9 Al-Matroudi, *The Ḥanbalī School*, pp. 145–150.

10 Ibn Qayyim al-Jawziyya, Shams al-Dīn: *Aḥkām ahl al-dhimma*, ed. by Ṣubḥī al-Ṣāliḥ, n.p. 1381/1961, reprint Beirut 1401/1981. I have looked at two other editions. That of Ṭāhā ʿAbd al-Raʾūf Saʿd, Beirut 1415/1995, is a mere retyping of Ṣubḥī al-Ṣāliḥ's, to be avoided. That of Abū Barāʾ Yūsuf b. Aḥmad al-Bakrī and Abū Aḥmad Shākir b. Tawfīq al-ʿĀrūrī, Dammam and Beirut 1418/1997,

citations in that section of *al-Inṣāf fī maʿrifat al-rājiḥ* that deals with the law of non-Muslim subjects.[11] Here is a list of those authorities whom al-Mardāwī there cites ten times or more:

1) Ibn Ḥamdān, 59 citations.
2) Abū Yaʿlā, 56 citations.
3) Ibn Qudāma, 53 citations.
4) ʿAbd al-Raḥmān, 40 citations.
5) Al-Majd, 34 citations.
6) Aḥmad b. Ḥanbal, 33 citations (with multiple, contradictory versions at 11).
7) Ibn al-Jawzī, ʿAbd al-Raḥmān b. ʿAlī (d. Baghdad, 597/1201), 33 citations.[12]
8) Ibn Abī ʿUmar, 33 citations.
9) Ibn Munajjā, 28 citations.
10) ʿIzz al-Dīn al-Maqdisī, 26 citations.
11) Ibn al-Sarī al-Dujaylī, 22 citations.
12) Abū al-Khaṭṭāb al-Kalwadhānī, 17 citations.
13) Ibn Taymiyya, 15 citations.
14) Al-Sāmarrī, 11 citations.
15) Al-Zarkashī, 10 citations.
16) Al-Ādamī, 10 citations.
17) ʿAlāʾ al-Dīn b. al-Laḥḥām, ʿAlī b. Muḥammad (d. Cairo, 803/1401), 10 citations.[13]

The list is fairly similar to the list of those most cited in *al-Inṣāf fī maʿrifat al-rājiḥ* as a whole. In this section of *al-Inṣāf*, there is just one citation of Ibn al-Qayyim, as author of *Badāʾiʿ al-fawāʾid* (The Astonishing Benefits) and *Aḥkām ahl al-dhimma*. Al-Mardāwī certainly knew of Ibn al-Qayyim's work and singles him out as Ibn Taymiyya's

---

offers many more notes and occasionally a more careful reading of, apparently, the same manuscript source.

11 Al-Mardāwī, *al-Inṣāf fī maʿrifat al-rājiḥ*, vol. 4, pp. 156–186 (*K. al-Jihād, bāb ʿaqd al-dhimma*).

12 Of *al-Mudhhab al-aḥmad* (The Most Praiseworthy Gilt [Book]), and *Masbūk al-dhahab* (The Smeltery of Gold). For biographical information, see Laoust, Califat, pp. 112–116, also Swartz, Merlin: *Ibn al-Jawzī's* Kitāb al-Quṣṣāṣ wal-mudhakkirīn, Beirut 1971, pp. 15–38.

13 Of *Tajrīd al-ʿināya* (The Stripped Attention) and *al-Qawāʾid al-uṣūliyya* (The Originating Principles). For biographical information, see al-ʿUlaymī, *al-Manhaj al-aḥmad*, vol. 5, pp. 190–191.

disciple (*ṣāḥib*), just two others in the larger sample being referred to thus as someone's disciple, Ghulām al-Khallāl (d. 363/974) and Abū al-Khaṭṭāb, disciple to the kadi Abū Yaʿlā. Despite al-Mardāwī's respect for him, he evidently did not think him much help at identifying and elaborating the peculiar rules of the Ḥanbalī school. At the level of identifying rules, even on a section of the law about which he had written a long, specialized book, Ibn al-Qayyim was a fairly minor Ḥanbalī.

My second project is to characterize Ibn al-Qayyim's jurisprudence, especially what the Ḥanbalī school meant to him. As a first essay at identifying its place within the Ḥanbalī tradition, I have randomly chosen and analysed in various ways a sample of seventy items in Ibn al-Qayyim, *Aḥkām ahl al-dhimma*. Among these were 17 examples of Aḥmad's opinion (24 percent), of which only one was a variant version. Eleven items were primarily theological (16 percent), one was historical without obvious legal application, leaving 58 questions of *aḥkām* (ordinances); that is, the classification of actions (83 percent). Eleven items in the sample were supported by Hadith from the Prophet (16 percent), eight by sayings of Companions (eleven percent), four by sayings of Followers (six percent). There was only one example of Hadith criticism. The Shāfiʿī position was cited eight times (eleven percent), the Ḥanafī four (six percent), the Mālikī three (four percent), the Ẓāhiri just once (one percent). Abū ʿUbayd (d. Mecca, 224/838–839?) is quoted six times (nine percent), usually quoting someone else in turn.

Ibn al-Qayyim appears from this to have been something of a Ḥanbalī-fundamentalist. He is a fundamentalist in the sense that he wants to go back to basics, avoiding the complexity of accumulated tradition by reaching behind it; he is a Ḥanbalī-fundamentalist inasmuch as what he goes back to is the opinion of Aḥmad b. Ḥanbal himself.[14] In avoiding the complexity of the tradition, he is similar to today's Salafi primitivists. However, whereas they seek to identify directly prophetic law, before the rise of schools, Ibn al-Qayyim stresses Aḥmad's doc-

---

14 'Fundamentalist' has a particular meaning with regard to 20th-century Protestantism, having been invented by a Protestant faction to designate themselves: Shepard, William: "Fundamentalism" Christian and Islamic, in: *Religion* 17 (1987), pp. 355–378. However, it seems to have some scholarly usefulness when defined not by particular fundamentals but an interest in going past the tradition back to original sources and a tendency to simplify, for which see Marty, Martin E. and Appleby, R. Scott: *Fundamentalisms Observed. Fundamentalism Project 1*, Chicago 1991, introduction, pp. vii–xiii.

trine, before the rise of the Ḥanbalī school but well after the age of the Prophet.

Knowing Aḥmad b. Ḥanbal's doctrine was a complex issue for the tradition, as indicated by the frequency with which it reported multiple versions of what Aḥmad had said. Several collections of Aḥmad's opinions from immediate disciples of his are extant.[15] Contradictions are found among them, the consequence of Ibn Ḥanbal's changing his mind, being misunderstood, or having things put in his mouth that he did not actually say but that the quoter thought he must have said, had someone asked him. However, such contradictions in the earliest record come nowhere near concerning every third question, as in quotations of Ibn Ḥanbal reported by al-Mardāwī.[16] Most of the multiple versions in al-Mardāwī were evidently the consequence of *takhrīj*, attributing to the eponym of the school an opinion not that he was remembered as expressing but that seemed, to the writer, to follow from his principles.[17] Al-Mardāwī himself defines *takhrīj* as the transfer of an assessment from one question to another, similar one, considering them equivalent (*naql ḥukm masʾala ilā mā yushbihuhā wal-taswiya baynahumā fīh*).[18] Ibn Taymiyya describes it as a famous

15 On the *Masāʾil* collections, see Melchert, *Ahmad ibn Hanbal*, chapter 3, pp. 59–81, esp. pp. 68–70. To those cited now add *Masāʾil al-imām Aḥmad b. Ḥanbal wa-Isḥāq b. Rāhawayh*, recension of al-Kawsaj, ed. by Abū al-Ḥusayn Khālid b. Maḥmūd al-Rabāṭ, Wiʿām al-Hawshī and Jumʿa Fatḥī, Riyadh 1425/2004, and *Masāʾil al-imām Aḥmad b. Muḥammad b. Ḥanbal wa-Isḥāq b. Rāhawayh*, recension of Ḥarb b. Ismāʿīl al-Kirmānī, ed. by Nāṣir b. Saʿūd b. ʿAbd Allāh al-Salāma, Riyadh 1425.

16 For a sample of contradictions among the *Masāʾil* collections, see Ibn al-Farrāʾ, Abū Yaʿlā: *al-Masāʾil al-ʿaqdiyya min Kitāb al-Riwāyatayn wal-wajhayn*, ed. by Saʿūd b. ʿAbd al-ʿAzīz al-Khalaf, Riyadh 1419/1999.

17 Al-Mardāwī names three possible bases of a version (*riwāya*): Aḥmad's express declaration (*naṣṣ*), an indirect indication by him of his opinion (*īmāʾ*), and *takhrīj* on the part of adherents of the school: *Qāʿida nāfiʿa*, vol. 12, p. 196. I have not remarked any estimate from him of how many versions were based on each of these, but he certainly seems less naive than the many writers of the present who assume that contradictory quotations are the product of someone's changing his mind, not back projection of opinions from later generations. On *takhrīj* in Islamic legal literature generally, see Hallaq, Wael B.: *Authority, Continuity and Change in Islamic Law*, Cambridge 2001, chapter 2. For examples in the early record of al-Shāfiʿī's opinions, see Melchert, Christopher: The Meaning of *qāla al-Shāfiʿī* in Ninth-Century Sources, in: Montgomery, James E. (ed.): *Abbasid Studies*, Leuven 2004, pp. 277–301.

18 Al-Mardāwī, *al-Inṣāf fī maʿrifat al-rājiḥ*, vol. 1, p. 17; idem, *Qāʿida nāfiʿa*, vol. 12, p. 190.

question among his fellow adherents of the Ḥanbalī school. He considers the authority of an opinion arrived at by *takhrīj* to lie somewhere between that of what Aḥmad said expressly (*al-madhhab al-manṣūṣ*) and something his known position does not manifestly entail.[19] Many reports of alternative versions are quite late; for example (in chronological order), from Abū Yaʿlā, Abū al-Khaṭṭāb, Ibn al-Jawzī, Ibn Munajjā, Sāmarrī, Ibn Abī ʿUmar, ʿAbd al-Raḥmān, Ibn Ḥamdān, and Ibn Taymiyya in the section of al-Mardāwī's *al-Inṣāf fī maʿrifat al-rājiḥ* on *ʿaqd al-dhimma*. These can hardly go back to contradictory quotations in collections of Aḥmad b. Ḥanbal's opinions by his immediate disciples. It is often unclear how Ibn al-Qayyim himself knows what Aḥmad's position was. Even if he relies on a source as early as the *Mukhtaṣar* of al-Khiraqī (d. Damascus, 334/945–946), he risks confusing the tradition with what the *imām* verifiably said; that is, although trying to get behind the tradition to Aḥmad himself, he still has little more than the tradition to tell him what Aḥmad said, and the tradition includes a good deal of back-projection.[20]

To get a sense of how typical Ibn al-Qayyim was of Ḥanbalī jurisprudents, I thought to examine a sample of similar size from Ibn Qudāma, *al-Mughnī*. I found there rather more citations of prophetic Hadith (21 percent of all items), less than half as many citations of Aḥmad b. Ḥanbal's own opinion (eleven percent as opposed to 24), relatively more citations of the Ḥanbalī school's position or the opinions of individual Ḥanābila (14 percent). What we see in al-Mardāwī, Ibn Qudāma, and also al-Mardāwī's favorite source, the *Furūʿ* of Ibn Mufliḥ al-Qāqūnī, is a striking feature of the classical schools of law, mainly insistence on legitimate disagreement (*ikhtilāf*) – something we see much less of in Ibn al-Qayyim, especially disagreement within the Ḥanbalī school. Ibn al-Qayyim does not completely ignore dis-

19 Ibn Taymiyya, Taqī al-Dīn: *al-Qawāʿid al-nūrāniyya al-fiqhiyya*, ed. by Muḥammad Ḥāmid al-Fiqī, Cairo 1370/1951, p. 258.

20 Al-Khiraqī, Abū al-Qāsim: *Mukhtaṣar*, ed. by Muḥammad Zuhayr al-Shāwīsh, Damascus 1378/1958; also published as idem: *al-Matn*, ed. by Abū Ḥudhayfa Ibrāhīm b. Muḥammad, Tanta 1413/1993. Comparison with the extant *Masāʾil* collections of Aḥmad's opinions shows that Khiraqī usually offers a summary of his known position. However, he also often articulates a definite rule where Aḥmad was vague or infers a rule from Aḥmad's known position on other matters. See provisionally Khalid, Anas: *The Mukhtasar of al-Khiraqi*. PhD thesis, New York University 1992, and Hurvitz, Nimrod: The Mukhtaṣar of al-Khiraqī', in: Shaham, Ron (ed.): *Law, Custom, and Statute in the Muslim World*, Leiden 2007, pp. 1–16.

agreement within the school or the complication of multiple versions of Aḥmad's position, but he does bring them up notably less often than mainstream Ḥanbalī writers.[21] His fundamentalism thus manifests itself not only in avoiding the complexity of accumulated tradition by reaching behind it to the opinion of Aḥmad b. Ḥanbal but also in downplaying the difficulty of knowing what Aḥmad actually said.

Why, then, should Ibn Taymiyya have been, if not a major figure in the Ḥanbalī legal tradition, at least a much more prominent one than his disciple Ibn al-Qayyim? As an example of Ibn Taymiyya's legal writing, I have examined two short works, *al-Qawāʿid al-nūrāniyya*, just quoted concerning *takhrīj*, and *al-Masāʾil al-māradīniyya*.[22] It transpires first that Ibn Taymiyya's approach is somewhat closer to Ibn Qudāma's than Ibn al-Qayyim's: the Prophet is cited twice as often as Aḥmad b. Ḥanbal, and Ibn Taymiyya regularly acknowledges alternative versions of Aḥmad's own position. Qualitatively, Ibn Taymiyya much more often describes legitimate disagreement, usually among different schools but also sometimes within the Ḥanbalī school; for example, to observe that the tenth- and eleventh-century ʿUkbaris such as Abū Ḥafṣ and Abū ʿAlī b. Shihāb on the one hand and the Baghdadis such as Abū ʿAbd Allāh b. Ḥāmid and the kadi Abū Yaʿlā on the other disagreed over a certain property transfer.[23] Ibn Taymiyya did not write as a typical Ḥanbalī, and that evidently limited his effect on the elaboration of Ḥanbalī rules. Sometimes he proposes rules completely at odds with the Ḥanbalī tradition; for example, he proposes that Muslims should be allowed to inherit from non-Muslims, lest anyone refrain from converting to Islam for fear of missing an inheritance – an opinion that not even Ibn al-Qayyim

21 E.g., Ibn Qayyim al-Jawziyya, *Aḥkām ahl al-dhimma*, pp. 452–453, where he names five disciples who related three different versions of Aḥmad's position on the question of whether someone may inherit from a Muslim who has converted to Islam some time between the Muslim's death and the division of his property. By contrast, Ibn Qudāma names only two versions of Aḥmad's position on this point: Ibn Qudāma: *al-Mughnī*, ed. by ʿAbd Allāh ʿAbd al-Muḥsin al-Turkī and ʿAbd al-Fattāḥ Muḥammad al-Ḥulw, Cairo 1406–11/1986–90, vol. 9, p. 160.

22 Ibn Taymiyya, Taqī al-Dīn: *al-Masāʾil al-māradīniyya*, ed. by Muḥammad Ḥāmid al-Fiqī, Cairo 1980.

23 Ibn Taymiyya, Taqī al-Dīn: *al-Qawāʿid al-nūrāniyya al-fiqhiyya*, ed. by Muḥammad Ḥāmid al-Fiqī, Cairo 1370/1951, p. 106. On Abū Ḥafṣ al-ʿUkbarī (d. 387/997), see Laoust, Califat, p. 88; on Ibn Shihāb al-ʿUkbarī (d. 428/1037), ibid., p. 98; on Ibn Ḥāmid (d. 403/1012–13), ibid., pp. 93–94.

embraced.[24] Tellingly, though, he sometimes proposes novel opinions but plays down their novelty by referring to unspecified precedents. He wrote at least more traditionally than his disciple Ibn al-Qayyim, with more deference to the discursive tradition, which must partly account for the relatively greater attention that later Ḥanābila paid to Ibn Taymiyya's expositions of the rules.

Conclusion

To sum up, then, it appears that Ibn Taymiyya's disciples (with exceptions, Ibn Mufliḥ and al-Qāqūnī prominent among them) were impatient with the indeterminacy of the tradition. Books like Ibn Qudāma, *al-Mughnī*,[25] Ibn Mufliḥ al-Qāqūnī, *al-Furūʿ*,[26] and al-Mardāwī, *al-Inṣāf*,[27] report a cloud of disagreement on one question after another, not only between the Ḥanbalī school and others but also within the Ḥanbalī school. All of them mention the opinions of other Ḥanābila more often than they do the opinions of Aḥmad b. Ḥanbal himself, along with much disagreement over what Aḥmad said. The God-given rule for each case apparently became impossible to discern with certainty. Somewhat in the fashion of modern Salafi fundamentalists, Ibn Taymiyya's disciples sought a certainty the tradition denied them by going behind it back to original sources: above all to Aḥmad b. Ḥanbal's opinion in the case of Ibn al-Qayyim, to prophetic Hadith in the parallel case of Ibn Kathīr (d. Damascus, 774/1373).[28] A difficulty they faced was for Ibn al-Qayyim to know Aḥmad b. Ḥanbal's opinions, Ibn Kathīr to know what the Prophet had said and done, without depending on the very scholarly tradition they wanted to go behind. (Ibn Kathīr probably faced his problem more frankly, since

24 Al-Mardāwī, *al-Inṣāf fī maʿrifat al-rājiḥ*, vol. 7, p. 259. Many further examples in Al-Matroudi, *The Ḥanbalī School*, chapter 4.

25 Ibn Qudāma, *al-Mughnī* (cited in n. 21).

26 Ibn Mufliḥ al-Qāqūnī: *K. al-Furūʿ*, ed. by ʾAbd al-Laṭīf Muḥammad al-Subkī and ʾAbd al-Sattār Aḥmad Farrāj, Cairo 1379–88/1960–67, reprinted Beirut 1402

27 Al-Mardāwī, *al-Inṣāf fī maʿrifat al-rājiḥ*.

28 For Ibn Kathīr as a fundamentalist bent on simplistically going back to original sources, see Calder, Norman: Tafsīr from Ṭabarī to Ibn Kathīr. Problems in the Description of a Genre; Illustrated with Reference to the Story of Abraham, in: G.R. Hawting and Abdul-Kader A. Shareef (eds.): *Approaches to the Qurʾān*, London 1993, pp. 101–140.

he worked extensively in the field of Hadith and continually discusses the reliability of particular Hadith reports in his Koran commentary; however, his solution was largely to assume that the great ninth-century Hadith collectors had effectively culled the correct versions of what the Prophet had said from the mass of incorrect. The comparable problem for modern Salafiyya is similarly to know what the Prophet said and to interpret the Koran without depending on the very medieval scholarly tradition that they try to go behind when it comes to the schools of law. Like Ibn Kathīr but probably less excusably, they tend to assume that the great ninth-century Hadith collectors, above all al-Bukhārī (d. 256/870), were not men of their time with accordingly limited horizons, similarly to Aḥmad b. Ḥanbal and al-Shāfiʿī (d. 204/820) and their followers, but somehow transcended it, offering us directly what the Prophet said, not just what various later Muslims thought the Prophet must have said.)

As Ibn al-Qayyim largely skipped over the Ḥanbalī tradition between himself and Aḥmad, so the ongoing Ḥanbalī tradition largely, with some justice, ignored him. Ḥanābila of the following centuries paid much more attention to Ibn Taymiyya than to Ibn al-Qayyim in the field of positive law (*furūʿ*). The reason is probably that he seemed more engaged with the tradition, which is to say he seemed to think the same way they did. He did cite previous Ḥanbalī jurisprudents; he propounded original opinions so as to keep them within the spectrum of Ḥanbalī opinion, not so as to make it his evident intention to supersede all earlier Ḥanbalī opinion. However, Ḥanābila of the following centuries paid yet more attention to numerous other Ḥanbalī jurisprudents: men such as Ibn Ḥamdān and Ibn Abī ʿUmar before Ibn Taymiyya, ʿIzz al-Dīn al-Maqdisī and Ibn Qāḍī al-Jabal after him. Insofar as the Ḥanbalī school constituted a peculiar set of answers to juridical problems, Ibn Taymiyya had a significant but limited effect on it. It was when the plundering of *waqf* foundations, the rise of technical education in engineering, medicine, and other fields, mass literacy, and other developments had debilitated the system of schools that Ibn Taymiyya and Ibn al-Qayyim came to the forefront in the 20th century.

Screening Ṣiddīq Ḥasan Khān's Library

The Use of Ḥanbalī Literature in 19th-Century Bhopal[1]

Claudia Preckel

1. The North Indian Landscape in the Late 19th Century

At the end of the 19th century, the reception of Arabic Ḥanbalī literature in India was strongly influenced by the popularization of Ibn Taymiyya's works in certain scholarly circles in the northern part of the Indian subcontinent. The number of translations and books written by authors belonging to the Ḥanbalī school of law (*madhhab*) increased considerably, and quoting Damascene scholars like Ibn Taymiyya (d. 728/1328 A.D.) or Ibn Qayyim al-Jawziyya (d. 751/1350) became a common feature in South Asian Islamic literature.[2] One of those groups responsible for this increase in numbers of Ḥanbalī literature is the Indian Ahl-i Ḥadīth[3] (People of Tradition). This group was a new scholarly Islamic movement that emerged in Northern India in the middle of the 19th cen-

1 This paper is part of my German dissertation: Preckel, Claudia: *Islamische Bildungsnetzwerke und Gelehrtenkultur im Indien des 19. Jahrhunderts. Muḥammad Ṣiddīq Ḥasan Ḫān (st. 1890) und die Entstehung der* Ahl-e ḥadīṯ*-Bewegung in Bhopal*, Ruhr Universität Bochum 2005, http://www-brs.ub.ruhr-uni-bochum.de/netahtml/HSS/Diss/PreckelClaudia/, accessed December 28, 2012.

2 Nizami, Khaliq Ahmad: The Impact of Ibn Taimiyya on South Asia, in: *Journal of Islamic Studies* 1 (1990), pp. 120–149, here pp. 125–134.

3 For the Ahl-i Ḥadīth movement, see Preckel, Claudia: Ahl-i Ḥadīth, in: *EI*[3], vol. 3 (2011), pp. 92–97. For a history of the Ahl-i Ḥadīth from their own perspective, see Riexinger, Martin: *Sanāʾullāh Amritsarī (1868–1948) und die Ahl-i Ḥadis im Punjab unter britischer Herrschaft*, Würzburg 2004; Nawshahrawī, Abū Yaḥyā Imām Khān: *Hindustān mēn Ahl-i ḥadīth kī ʿilmī khidmāt* (The Contribution of Knowledge on the Ahl-i Ḥadīth in India), Lāʾilpūr 1352/1934; idem.: *Tarājim-i ʿulamāʾ-yi ḥadīth-i Hind* (Biographies of Indian Hadith Scholars), New Delhi 1992; Siyālkoṯī, Muḥammad Ibrāhīm Mīr: *Taʾrīkh-i Ahl-i Ḥadīth* (History of the Ahl-i Ḥadīth), New Delhi 1995; Sayf, Muḥammad Aslam: *Taḥrīk-i Ahl-i ḥadīth* (The Ahl-i Ḥadīth Movement), Delhi 1999.

tury. They wanted to imitate the role model of the Prophet Muḥammad, whose sayings and actions were regarded as the greatest authority. Their name also referred to the historical movement of the *ahl al-ḥadīth* (or *aṣḥāb al-ḥadīth*) of the late eighth and early ninth centuries, which likewise claimed that its judgements were based on the prophetic tradition rather than on personal opinion (*ra'y*). The Indian Ahl-i Ḥadīth distinguished themselves from other movements that had also emerged in the course of the 19th century mainly by their interpretation of Islamic law and most visibly by their outward style of prayer. Another aim was to eliminate every custom from the Indian Muslim society that in their eyes was not rooted in the Koran and the Sunna of the Prophet. To the Ahl-i Ḥadīth, certain practices of this community, like venerating Sufis and visiting the shrines of holy men, were *bidaʿ* (sg. *bidʿa*), un-Islamic innovations potentially leading to hell. The Ahl-i Ḥadīth held the view that Indian Islam constant mixing with Hinduism had made it "impure". They specifically criticised the acceptance of Hindu views of purity and impurity, as well as "superstitions" like wearing amulets and charms.[4] According to some Ahl-i Ḥadīth, this would accelerate the approach of the Day of Judgement (*yawm al-qiyāma*).[5] The Ahl-i Ḥadīth did not believe that this process could be stopped and expected the world to end in the Islamic year 1300 (1883/1884). However, they regarded it as their (religious) duty to warn the Muslim community of these upcoming apocalyptic events.

Shortly after the emergence of the Ahl-i Ḥadīth, they took part in fierce debates on the "correct" interpretation of Islam and the sources of Islamic law. Since the Central Asian invasions of India in the 13th

4 In his chapter on *bidʿa* of his work *Ḥujaj al-kirāma fī āthār al-qiyāma* (The Noble Proofs of the Signs of the Last Hour), Bhopal 1874, pp. 309–346, Ṣiddīq Ḥasan Khān criticised Muslims for the construction of separate kitchens outside the main houses, which in his opinion was adopted from Hindu neighbours (p. 317). He also wrote that Muslims should not use cow dung for heating their oven like the Hindus did (p. 316). The Ahl-i Ḥadīth's most important ruling in refuting Hindu concepts of purity and impurity concerned menstruating women: they stressed that these women were allowed to read (pp. 320–321), recite and touch the Koran. Some scholars even encouraged women to perform their prayers in mosques during menstruation. For detailed discussions on menstruating women, women in childbed and concepts of purity, see Preckel, *Islamische Bildungsnetzwerke*, pp. 417–419.

5 See the eschatological books by Muḥammad Ṣiddīq Ḥasan Khān, e.g. *Iqtirāb al-sāʿa* (The Approach of the Last Hour), Kanpur 1301/1883; idem.: *al-Idhāʿa li-mā kāna wa-mā yakūnu bayna yaday al-sāʿa* (The Announcement of What Was and Still Is Attributed to the Last Hour), n.p. n.d., ca. 1980.

century, which were accompanied by an "amalgamation of Islamic and Turkic cultures",[6] the majority of Indian Muslims belonged to the Ḥanafī school of law, whereas the Ahl-i Ḥadīth refused to restrict their legal interpretations to one school of law alone.[7] One of the consequences was that they came into conflict with the Deobandīs, who belonged to the Ḥanafī school of law and were named after the town where they had set up their teaching institution *Dār al-ʿulūm* in 1866.[8] From the late 1880s onwards, the Ahl-i Ḥadīth were also in grim controversies with the so-called Barēlwī movement, founded by Aḥmad Riḍā Khān Barēlwī (d. 1921). Several scholarly disputes (sg. *munāẓara*) took place among the various movements, and sometimes their disputes even led to riots, which the British authorities were hardly able to curb.[9] The members of the Barēlwī movement like the Deobandīs strictly followed the Ḥanafī school of law. They were also initiated into the Sufi order of the Qādiriyya and believed in the miraculous power of the saints and the Prophet Muḥammad. In contrast to that, the Ahl-i Ḥadīth argued that Muḥammad was a human being (*bashar*) who had lived together with other human beings and led an ordinary life with his wives and children. The Ahl-i Ḥadīth often quote the Koranic verse (18:110) in which Muḥammad says, "Say that I am a human being like you are" (*qul innamā anā bashar mithlakum*), in order to underline their view of Muḥammad as a mortal man. And they deny the teachings of the Barēlwīs, who ascribed a "Muḥammadan light" (*nūr muḥammadī*) to Muḥammad and all the prophets before him.[10]

One of the earliest reproaches against the Ahl-i Ḥadīth movement was that it was a mere offshoot of the Arabian Wahhabiyya. Their opponents, mainly the Barēlwīs, were of the opinion that the Ahl-i Ḥadīth were the Indian followers of the Ḥanbalī scholar Muḥammad

6 Malik, Jamal: *Islam in South Asia. A Short History*, Leiden 2008, p. 14.

7 On Islam in India see Basham, Arthur Llewellyn: *The Wonder that was India*, New Delhi 1981, vol. 1; and Robinson, Francis: *Islam and Muslim History in South Asia*, Delhi 2000.

8 For a detailed account of the movement, see Metcalf, Barbara: *Islamic Revival in British India. Deoband, 1860–1900*, Princeton 1982. For recent developments see Haroon, Sana: *Frontier of Faith. Islam in the Indo-Afghan Borderland*, New York 2007, esp. pp. 91–103.

9 Metcalf mentions some examples of disputes between Ahl-i Ḥadīth and Deobandīs in the 1870s and 1880s. See Metcalf, *Islamic Revival*, pp. 275, 286.

10 For a scholarly debate between Ahl-i Ḥadīth and Barēlwīs on this question, see Sahsawānī, Muḥammad Nadhīr: *Munāẓara Aḥmadiyya*, Kanpur 1289/1872, pp. 37–39.

b. ʿAbd al-Wahhāb (d. 1787). This was mainly because the Wahhabis held the same (negative) view of the veneration of saints and Sufis. A second important reproach against the Ahl-i Ḥadīth was that they propagated jihad against the British. The British authorities took up this opinion and used the term "Wahhabi" as a synonym for seditious activities against British rule in 19th-century India.[11] This allegation is not totally unfounded, because there were actually some Ahl-i Ḥadīth who, well into the 20th century, tried to wage jihad from the Afghan border. Whereas the majority of Ahl-i Ḥadīth did not justify a jihad against the British, a small group of them around Wilāyat ʿAlī (d. 1853) and his brothers, ʿInāyat ʿAlī ʿAbd Allāh (d. 1908) and Farḥat Ḥusayn from Ṣādiqpūr, a quarter of Patna, continued their armed struggle. In their *madrasa*, which was one of the first Ahl-i Ḥadīth institutions of higher learning, they taught Hadith, collected money and recruited *mujāhidīn* for their active fight. Although Farḥat Ḥusayn visited Bhopal several times in the early 1860s, he did not succeed in winning the Bēgum or other Bhopalese Muslims for their struggle.[12]

At the end of the 19th century, the local dynasty of Bhopal (r. ca. 1709–1949) in particular was closely associated with such allegedly Wahhabi tendencies. As in other Muslim principalities of India, e.g. Awadh, Rampur or Tonk, the (male) ruler of Bhopal was called Nawwāb. The Arabic word *nawwāb* is the plural of *nāʾib* (deputy). The word "nabob" derives from this term and came to be used for a prince, a deputy or simply a governor. The Nawwāb of the Central Indian Muslim principality of Bhopal[13] – Sayyid Ṣiddīq Ḥasan Khān al-Qannawjī (1832–1890) – is con-

11 In his famous work *Our Indian Muslims, are They Bound in Conscience to Rebel Against the Queen?*, Delhi 1969, the famous British civil servant Sir William W. Hunter (d. 1900) tried to figure out the reasons for the *Mutiny* of 1857 and claimed that the Indian "Wahhabi movement" could be held responsible for it. Hunter further listed "seditious works" written by the "Indian Wahhabis", among which several Ahl-i Ḥadīth works are found (ibid., pp. 34–36). The statement that an "Indian Wahhabi movement" existed and was constantly planning a jihad against the British Government was taken up by Qeyamuddin Ahmad in the work *The Wahhabi Movement in India*, Calcutta 1966, esp. pp. 305–306; Titus, Murray T.: *Indian Islam*, Delhi 1979, p. 186, also called the Ahl-i Ḥadīth the "Indian Wahhabis".

12 Bari, M.A.: A Nineteenth Century Muslim Reform Movement in India, in: George Makdisi (ed.): *Arabic and Islamic Studies in Honor of Hamilton A.R. Gibb*, Leiden 1965, pp. 85–102, here pp. 85–88; Riexinger, *Sanāʾullāh Amritsarī*, pp. 138, 442–448.

13 Bhopal ranked second among the principalities with a Muslim ruler after Hyderabad. The state was renowned neither for its propagation of Islam in all

sidered to have been one of the first and fiercest representatives of the Wahhabi movement in 19th century India. Ṣiddīq Ḥasan Khān was no Nawwāb in his own right, but the husband of the third female Nawwāb Bēgum. In accordance with the example of the British "Prince Consort" Albert (d. 1861), Ṣiddīq Ḥasan Khān was officially called "Nawwāb Consort". Muslim scholarly circles nevertheless always call him "Nawwāb Ṣiddīq Ḥasan Khān" to this day.[14] Dōst Muḥammad Khān (d. 1728), who was of Afghan/Pashtun origin, had already created the Princely State of Bhopal in the 18th century. He was able to break loose from the Mughal power in Delhi[15] and to establish a ruling class of Pashtuns as independent rulers. From 1818 onwards, the Nawwābs co-operated with the British

administrative fields, nor for its close co-operation with the British authorities. As Bhopal belonged to the "Central India Agency", it also played a strategic role for British troops. Bhopal belonged to the "First Class States", which meant that the ruler could enact his own legislation and that he dealt directly with the Government of India and not the governor of any adjacent province. Only in questions of death sentences, the marriage of the heir apparent or in succession matters, did the British authorities have the right to intervene. In 1901, the number of inhabitants was 720,000 and the state reached an area of ca. 7,000 square miles, which can be compared to Wales. Although the ruling family was Muslim, the majority of the population was Hindu (73 percent). It was only in the capital Bhopal (city) that the Muslim community constituted more than 70 percent of the local population. See Preckel, Claudia: Bhopāl, in: *EI*³, vol. 3 (2011), pp. 123–132. Bhopal was merged into the Indian Union in 1949. In 1956 the territory was dissolved into the newly founded state Madhya Pradesh, whose capital became the city of Bhopal. The city became known to the world through the Bhopal disaster in 1984, when the Union Carbide plant leaked 40 tons of toxic gas into the atmosphere. The death toll is estimated between 3,000 and 20,000 people. This event is often mentioned as the world's worst industrial disaster.

14 For a biography, see Khān, Zafar ul-Islām: Nawwāb Sayyid Ṣiddīḳ Ḥasan Khān, in: *EI*², vol. 7 (1993), pp. 1048–1050, here p. 1049. Saeedullah published an English Ph.D. on Ṣiddīq Ḥasan Khān: *The Life and Works of Muhammad Siddiq Hasan Khan, Nawab of Bhopal (1248–1307/1832–1890)*, Lahore 1973. Two Arabic books on Ṣiddīq Ḥasan Khān (by Indian Muslims), namely Luqmān, Akhtar J.: *al-Sayyid Ṣiddīq Ḥasan al-Qannawjī*, Riyadh 1996; and Nadwī, Muḥammad: *al-Amīr Sayyid Ṣiddīq Ḥasan Khān*, Beirut 1999. In Urdu there is Ḥāmid, Raḍiyya: *Nawwāb Sayyid Ṣiddīq Ḥasan Khān*, Delhi 1983. All these works rely on the biography that Sayyid Ṣiddīq Ḥasan Khān's son wrote on his father, ʿAlī Ḥasan Khān: *Maʾāthir-i Ṣiddīqī. Sīrat-i Walājāhī*, Lucknow 1924.

15 For the Mughals in Delhi, see e.g. Alam, Muzaffar: *The Crisis of Empire in Mughal North India*, Delhi 1986; Blake, Stephen: *Shahjahanabad. The Sovereign City of Mughal India 1639–1739*, Cambridge 1991. Gupta, Narayani: *Delhi Between Two Empires. 1803–1931. Society, Government and Urban Growth*, Delhi 1981.

and were therefore able to secure their own territories. In the 19th century, no male heir was born to the ruling dynasty. The state was therefore ruled for almost a century by four generations of female rulers, the Bēgums.[16] Their rule is marked by many Islamic educational, economic and administrative reforms, which gained the full support of the British. The third Bēgum, Shāh Jahān (r. 1868–1901), made the Ahl-i Ḥadīth doctrine a kind of state religion. Widowed at an early age, she married Ṣiddīq Ḥasan Khān in 1871. From that time on, the Ahl-i Ḥadīth and especially Ṣiddīq Ḥasan Khān enjoyed the full financial and institutional support of the ruler.

Ṣiddīq Ḥasan Khān was one of the most central figures of the early Ahl-i Ḥadīth networks and a strong supporter of the teachings of Ibn Taymiyya in South Asia.[17] He is also said to have adopted Muḥammad b. ʿAbd al-Wahhāb's strict, sometimes "puritan" interpretation of Islam, which is an essential pillar of the Saudi Arabian state today.[18] One of the reasons Ṣiddīq Ḥasan Khān's opponents called him a "Wahhabi" was that he relied on the same sources as Muḥammad b. ʿAbd

---

16 The Urdu word Bēgum means a lady or queen. It was also used for the female members of the Mughal elite. The female rulers of Bhopal intended to express a certain continuity from Mughal rule by choosing the title Bēgum in combination with names like Shāh Jahān. Qudsiyya Bēgum (r. 1819–37) was the first female ruler able to set aside the claims of her male family members. It was only during her reign that the British authorities had objections to a female Muslim ruler. She had to hand over power to her son-in-law, who according to British accounts lacked abilities as a ruler. Thus, the British installed Qudsiyya's daughter Sikander Bēgum on the throne (*masnad*). Her period of reign (1844–68) is regarded as the "Golden Age" of Bhopal. Sikander never appeared veiled in public and gave herself the image of an Amazon. This marked a significant difference from the reign of her daughter Shāh Jahān Bēgum (r. 1868–1901), who was always veiled especially after her marriage to Ṣiddīq Ḥasan Khān. Sikander's second marriage caused a rift between herself as the ruler and her only surviving daughter, Sulṭān Jahān Bēgum (r. 1901–26). Sulṭān Jahān gave birth to three sons, and abdicated in favour of her youngest son Nawwāb Ḥamīdullāh Khān in 1926. This ended a remarkable period of female rule in Muslim India. For the rule of the Bēgums, see Preckel, Claudia: *Begums of Bhopal*, New Delhi 2000; Khan, Shaharyar Muhammad: *Begums of Bhopal*, London 2000; Chishtī, Wahhāj al-Dīn: *Bēgamāt-i Bhōpāl* (The Begamat of Bhopal), Karachi 1981. For an account of Sulṭān Jahān's reign and Ṣiddīq Ḥasan Khān's dynastic ambitions, see Lambert-Hurley, Siobhan: *Muslim Women, Reform and Princely Patronage. Nawab Sultan Jahan Begam of Bhopal*, London 2007, esp. pp. 37–41.

17 Nizami, The Impact of Ibn Taimiyya, p. 139.

18 For general information on the Wahhabis, see Steinberg, Guido: *Religion und Staat in Saudi-Arabien*, Würzburg 2002; Commins, David: *The Wahhabi Mission and Saudi Arabia*, London 2006; Peskes, Esther: *Muḥammad b. ʿAbdalwahhāb im Widerstreit*, Stuttgart 1993.

al-Wahhāb did: both scholars drew inspiration from the famous 14th-century Ḥanbalī reformers Taqī al-Dīn Ibn Taymiyya and Ibn Qayyim al-Jawziyya. This claim by critics of the Ahl-i Ḥadīth is underlined by more recent Saudi Arabian scholars who mention either Ṣiddīq Ḥasan Khān or other Ahl-i Ḥadīth members among prominent supporters of the Arabian Wahhabiyya.[19]

This article analyses whether Ṣiddīq Ḥasan Khān and his scholarly movement, the Ahl-i Ḥadīth, were deeply and directly influenced by the Arabian Wahhabiyya or whether it was their reliance on the aforementioned Damascene reformers Ibn Taymiyya and Ibn al-Qayyim that gave this movement a strong Wahhabi flavour:

i. This very first part deals with reception of the Ahl-i Ḥadīth movement among the Muslim community in India. The use of Ibn Taymiyya and other Ḥanbalī authors was widely regarded as proof of the Ahl-i Ḥadīth's linkage with the Saudi Arabian Wahhabiyya.
ii. Part two highlights influences of a decisive predecessor movement, the Ṭarīqa-yi Muḥammadiyya, that had a strong impact on the shaping of the Ahl-i Ḥadīth.
iii. Part three focuses on the latter's Yemen connection.
iv. Part four depicts the rise of Ṣiddīq Ḥasan Khān to power in the North Indian Muslim principality Bhopal.
v. In the fifth part, attention is given to the question of the kinds of books Ḥanbalī authors read, how they worked with and commented on them in 19th-century Bhopal. The genres of traditional Islamic science from which these works were mainly taken will also be analysed.

Overall, the following study is based on the list of books that Ṣiddīq Ḥasan Khān claimed to have bought for his personal library. He listed these 603 books in his work *Silsilat al-ʿasjad fī dhikr mashāʾikh al-sanad* (The Golden Chain Commemorating the Shaykhs of the Line of Transmission).[20] The books he mentioned belong to various disciplines of Islamic science and were written in Arabic, Persian or Urdu. Ṣiddīq

19 See Āl al-Shaykh, ʿAbd al-Raḥmān b. ʿAbd al-Laṭīf: *Mashāhīr ʿulamāʾ Najd wa-ghayrihim*, Riyadh 1394/1974, p. 451; and al-Salafī, Abū al-Mukarram ʿAbd al-Jalīl: *Daʿwat al-imām Muḥammad b. ʿAbd al-Wahhāb fī shibh al-qārra al-hindiyya*, Riyadh 1413/1993.

20 Ṣiddīq Ḥasan Khān, Muḥammad: *Silsilat al-ʿasjad fī dhikr mashāʾikh al-sanad*, Bhopal 1293/1876.

Ḥasan Khān explicitly noted every book, whether he bought a printed copy or a manuscript. He also mentioned the place of publication. Thus, it is easy to assess which books the Nawwāb possessed. After Ṣiddīq Ḥasan Khān's death in 1890, his sons transferred the complete library from Bhopal to Lucknow, where it is kept in a room of its own. So far, only parts of the library could be compared to the list in *Silsilat al-ʿasjad*, which, however, gives a detailed account of Ḥanbalī literature in 19th-century India.

2. Ṣiddīq Ḥasan Khān's Ascent to Power and Indian Influences

Sayyid Ṣiddīq Ḥasan Khān, the most famous of the Ahl-i Ḥadīth founders and its most prominent figurehead, was born into a family with a strong Sunni reformist orientation. His father Sayyid Awlād Ḥasan Khān (d. 1837)[21] had converted from Shiism to Sunnism and later became a supporter of the reformist movement of Sayyid Aḥmad Barēlwī and Shāh Muḥammad Ismāʿīl "Shahīd" (both martyred in 1831).[22] The latter movement, commonly known as the Ṭarīqa-yi

21 For a biography of Sayyid Awlād Ḥasan as a supporter of the Ṭarīqa-yi Muḥammadiyya, see Nawshahrawī, Abū Yaḥyā Imām: *Tarājim-i ʿulamāʾ-i ḥadīth-i Hind*, Lahore 1992, pp. 277–311.

22 The two leaders shared a reformist orientation before they started their so-called jihad. They belonged to the inner circle of students of the family of the famous reformer Shāh Walī Allāh Dihlawī (d. 1762, see below). In 1816, they started a journey through the cities of Benares, Lucknow, Rampur and Bareilly, preaching and teaching. In common accounts of the movement, Sayyid Aḥmad and Muḥammad Ismāʿīl are reported to have met some Afghan scholars in Rampur, who told them about the atrocities of the Sikhs against the Muslims in the Sikh-dominated areas of the Punjab. Hearing about this, Sayyid Aḥmad and Muḥammad Ismāʿīl decided to call for a jihad. First they travelled to Mecca, where their idea for a jihad is reported to have received further impetus through contacts to Arabian Wahhabi scholars. After their return to India, they started another preaching and missionary tour throughout India, where they received financial and military support. Finally, 7,000 fighters calling themselves *mujāhidūn* set out for military actions against the Sikh. They had to go to Afghanistan first and later reached Peshawar through the Khyber Pass. After initial military successes in Akora (1826) and other cities of the Punjab, their troops were defeated in Balakot in 1832. Sayyid Aḥmad and Muḥammad Ismāʿīl were both killed, but their corpses were never found. This nourished the theories that Sayyid Aḥmad might have been the *mahdī* (the rightly guided one) who

Muḥammadiyya[23] (The Muḥammadan Path), undertook several military actions against the Sikh occupation of the Punjab. Later, the Indian nationalist movement perceived their fight against the Sikhs as a fight against the British colonial power. Many Indian Muslims interpreted the activities of the Ṭarīqa-yi Muḥammadiyya as harbingers of the Great Revolt ("Mutiny") of 1857.[24] The degree to which the reformative Ḥanbalī thinking of late medieval Damascus scholars influenced the Ṭarīqa-yi Muḥammadiyya remains to be analysed.

2.1. The Role of Shāh Walī Allāh Dihlawī and the Ṭarīqa-yi Muḥammadiyya

The Ṭarīqa-yi Muḥammadiyya leadership network consisted of a network of family members and disciples of the famous reformer and Hadith scholar Shāh Walī Allāh Dihlawī (d. 1762).[25] His *madrasa*,

vanished into the unseen (*ghayb*). For an Urdu biography, see Mehr, Ghulām Rasūl: *Sayyid Aḥmad Shahīd*, Lahore n.d; ʿAbd al-Ḥafīẓ, Chawharī: *Taʿārif-i Jamāʿat-i mujāhidīn*. Lahore n.d. For a biography in Arabic, see Nadwī, Abū al-Ḥasan ʿAlī: *Sīrat Sayyid Aḥmad Shahīd*, Lucknow 1986. Abū al-Ḥasan ʿAlī Nadwī (d. 1999), Rector of the Islamic university of the *Nadwat ul-ʿUlamāʾ* in Lucknow (Uttar Pradesh), claimed to have both family and scholarly relations to Sayyid Aḥmad. On him, see also n. 65. All the Urdu biographic accounts mentioned are rather hagiographic.

23 On the role of the Ṭarīqa-yi Muḥammadiyya movement, see Pearson, Harlan O.: *Islamic Reform and Revival in Nineteenth-century India*, New Delhi 2008.

24 The "Mutiny" of 1857 is often regarded as a forerunner of the struggle for independence against the British. Following a common explanation, the "Mutiny" was a rebellion of native soldiers of the East India Company, called sepoys (from Persian: *sipāhī*, soldier). After rumours spread that the rifles and cartridges of the East India Company were greased with lard (pig fat), Hindu and Muslim soldiers started riots. The fights, which concentrated mainly on the plain of the Ganges, lasted for several months. The city of Lucknow was besieged by mutineers, and the British had to abandon the Residency, which was ultimately destroyed. In her book on 19th-century Delhi, Pernau gave several interpretations by Indian Muslims of the "Mutiny", see Pernau, Margrit: *Bürger mit Turban*, Göttingen 2008, pp. 185–193.

25 Like almost all reformist movements in Indian Islam, the Ahl-i Ḥadīth regard Shāh Walī Allāh as a forefather of their movement, they even called him "the proof of God on earth" (*ḥujjat allāh fī al-arḍ*). For a biography of him from the Ahl-i Ḥadīth perspective, see Nawshahrawī, *Tarājim*, pp. 135–154; Siyālkoṭī, *Taʾrīkh-i Ahl-i ḥadīth*, pp. 411–416; Sayf, *Taḥrīk-i Ahl-i ḥadīth*, pp. 181–209; Ṣiddīq Ḥasan Khān, *Abjad al-ʿulūm*, Lahore 1403/1983, here vol. 3, pp. 241–244. For biographies on Shāh Walī Allāh, see Jalbani, Ghulam Husain: *Teachings*

named *Madrasa-yi Raḥīmiyya*[26] in the South of the Jama Masjid in Delhi, became a meeting place for people who cherished a reformist orientation in the interpretation of Islam. Concerning the reception of Ḥanbalī literature in India, Shāh Walī Allāh had come across works of Ibn Taymiyya and Ibn al-Qayyim during his pilgrimage to Mecca and Medina. In the wake of his stay in the Hijaz, Shāh Walī Allāh had met Abū Ṭāhir al-Kurdī al-Madanī (d. 1733).[27] Shāh Walī Allāh studied Hadith with him and was also initiated into the Naqshbandiyya order. Later the Ahl-i Ḥadīth considered Abū Ṭāhir to be a fierce defender of Ibn Taymiyya.[28] For example, the likewise famous Salafi Khayr al-Dīn al-Ālūsī (d. 1899) of Baghdad wrote on al-Kūrānī:

> He was a Salafī who used to be a defender of shaykh al-islām Ibn Taymiyya by refuting the terminology of the Sufis, who apparently aimed at incarnation (*ḥulūl*), unification (*ittiḥād*) or consubstantiality (*laʾīna*) of the human soul with God.[29]

---

of Shāh Walīyullāh of Delhi, Lahore 1967; Baljon, Johannes M. Simon: *Religion and Thought of Shāh Walī Allāh Dihlawī. 1703–62*, Leiden 1986.

26 Named after Shāh Walī Allāh's father ʿAbd al-Raḥīm (d. 1718). For a biography of ʿAbd al-Raḥīm, see Ḥasanī, ʿAbd al-Ḥayy: *Nuzhat al-khawāṭir wa-bahjat al-masāmiʿ wal-nawāẓir*, Hyderabad 1402/1981, here part 6, p. 146.

27 Abū Ṭāhir was the son of the famous scholar Ibrāhīm al-Kurānī (d. 1690), who became extremely influential for networks of scholars in South East Asia. On Kūrānī, see Ṣiddīq Ḥasan Khān, *Abjad al-ʿulūm*, part 3, p. 167; Nafi, Basheer: Taṣawwuf and Reform in Pre-Modern Islamic Culture. In Search of Ibrāhīm al-Kurānī, in: *Die Welt des Islams* 42 (2002), pp. 307–355. On Abū Ṭāhir, see Ṣiddīq Ḥasan Khān, *Abjad al-ʿulūm*, part 3, pp. 168–169. He was a renowned scholar of the Shāfiʿī school of law.

28 Sayf, *Taḥrīk-i Ahl-i ḥadīth*, p. 193.

29 Al-Ālūsī, Nuʿmān Khayr al-Dīn: *Jalā al-ʿaynayn fī muḥākamat al-Aḥmadayn* (Clearance of the Eyes on Trying the Two Aḥmads), Cairo 1980, defending Ibn Taymiyya against his opponents, quoted by Sayf, *Taḥrīk-i Ahl-i ḥadīth*, p. 193. Al-Ālūsī and Ṣiddīq Ḥasan Khān never met personally, but they exchanged several letters in which they provided each other with licences to teach (*ijāzāt*) several works on Hadith (on such licences, see Vayda, George: Idjāza, in *EI*², vol. 3 (1971), pp. 1020–1030). Further, Nuʿmān Khayr al-Dīn was allegedly very fond of Ṣiddīq Ḥasan's publications in general. He asked the Nawwāb to spend money to publish the *tafsīr* of his – al-Ālūsī's – father Abū al-Thanā Shihāb al-Dīn (d. 1854). Ṣiddīq Ḥasan Khān indeed financed publication of this work, titled *Rūḥ al-maʿānī* (The Soul of Meaning), in India. Later, he also paid for the publication of Nuʿmān Khayr al-Dīn's *Jalā al-ʿaynayn* in Cairo. Some copies of the *Jalā al-ʿaynayn* contain the letters between Nuʿmān Khayr al-Dīn and Ṣiddīq Ḥasan Khān. The most important of these was a fatwa that al-Ālūsī had requested from Ṣiddīq Ḥasan Khān concerning the "binding the heart" (*rābiṭa*) between a Sufi master and his disciple (*murīd*) of the Naqshbandiyya. Ṣiddīq

This quotation of al-Ālūsī, which the Ahl-i Ḥadīth often mention, implies that Abū Ṭāhir shared his father's critical views of Sufism and thereby constructed a line of continuity of thought from Ibn Taymiyya to Shāh Walī Allāh and the Ahl-i Ḥadīth. Abū Ṭāhir's is also said to have introduced Shāh Walī Allāh to the literature of Ibn Taymiyya. It may have been under his influence that Shāh Walī Allāh brought some manuscripts of Ibn Taymiyya's works to India, where they were later extensively commented upon. After his Hajj in 1731, Shāh Walī Allāh is said to have developed an opposition to some Sufi practices and to the intermingling of Hindu ceremonies with Muslim rituals. But one of his most important teachings was the focus on the traditional transmitted sciences (*manqūlāt*) in the *Madrasa-yi Raḥīmiyya* in Delhi. The curriculum of this *madrasa* changed significantly after Shāh Walī Allāh inherited the post of director (*mudīr*) from his father. From that time (ca. 1733) onwards, disciplines like the recitation and interpretation of the Koran, Hadith or Islamic jurisprudence were more often taught than disciplines associated with philosophy (*falsafa*) or logic (*manṭiq*). In his major work, *Ḥujjat Allāh al-bāligha* (The Conclusive Argument from God),[30] Shāh Walī Allāh stressed the importance of Hadith studies, which he considered the most important discipline of all. He considered exact knowledge of relevant Hadith was indispensable for the scholar because he was convinced that the disciplines of Hadith and *fiqh* were interwoven. Regarding Shāh Walī Allāh's attitudes on Islamic jurisprudence, he clearly claimed "making [judgements] according to the ḥadīth" (*ʿamal bil-ḥadīth*).[31] He thought that only the most reliable

Ḥasan Khān, although himself initiatied into the Naqshbandiyya-Mujaddidiyya, answered that this concept was an "unlawful innovation" in Islam. For this fatwa, see Meier, Fritz: *Zwei Abhandlungen über die Naqschbandiyya*, Stuttgart 1994, p. 228; the Arabic text is given in Ṣiddīq Ḥasan Khān, Muḥammad: *al-Tāj al-mukallal min jawāhir maʾāthir al-ṭirāz al-ākhir wal-awwal*, 2nd ed., Bombay 1383/1963, pp. 515–516. For the contact between Ṣiddīq Ḥasan Khān and Nuʿmān Khayr al-Dīn, see al-Atharī, Muḥammad Bahjat: *Aʿlām al-ʿIrāq*, Cairo 1345/1926; and Nafi, Basheer M.: Salafism Revived. Nuʿmān al-Ālūsī and the Trial of Two Ahmads, in: *Die Welt des Islams* 49 (2009), pp. 49–97. For the further relations of the Ālūsīs to Bhopalese scholars, see Preckel, *Islamische Bildungsnetzwerke*, pp. 229–237.

30 Al-Dihlawī, Shāh Walī Allāh: *Ḥujjat Allāh al-bāligha*, Cairo 1977, here part 1, pp. 147–152 (*bāb al-farq bayna ahl al-ḥadīth wa-ahl al-raʾy*). English translation by Hermansen, Marcia K.: *The Conclusive Argument from God*, Leiden 1995.

31 In his paper on the methodology of *aṣḥāb al-ḥadīth* (adherents of Hadith), Basheer M. Nafi differentiates between those *aṣḥāb al-ḥadīth* who apply

collections of Hadith should be taken as sources for decisions in law. This relativised the positions of the four schools of law (*madhāhib*, sg. *madhhab*), because the text of the Hadith itself was regarded to be "more authentic". Shāh Walī Allāh did not criticise adherence to one school of law in general, but the "blind following of one particular school of law" (*taqlīd*), especially in cases in which the opinion of one school of law contradicted the Hadith. He further warned against a certain fanaticism in following one particular school (*taʿaṣṣub fī al-madhhab*), since all schools of law could be regarded as equal. Shāh Walī Allāh's critical position against *taqlīd* was further developed by the Ṭarīqa-yi Muḥammadiyya and later by the Ahl-i Ḥadīth. The focus on Hadith was promulgated in the *Madrasa-yi Raḥīmiyya*, where Shāh Walī Allāh, his sons, grandsons, nephews and other family members taught. The members of the Ṭarīqa-yi Muḥammadiyya acquired teaching licenses (*ijāzāt*) in Hadith from Shāh Walī Allāh's family members, were often initiated into Naqshbandī Sufism and had studied works on the relevance of the independent legal reasoning (*ijtihād*) from Yemen. Students of this profile linked with each other and formed new networks that later became the Ahl-i Ḥadīth.

2.2. Ḥasan Khān's Hadith-Teacher ʿAbd al-Ḥaqq Banārsī

Ṣiddīq Ḥasan's father Sayyid Awlād Ḥasan Khān had been deeply influenced by the Ṭarīqa-yi Muḥammadiyya. He died in 1837, when Ṣiddīq Ḥasan was a child of only five years. Some of his father's friends decided to take care of young Ṣiddīq Ḥasan's education, and thus he travelled to the Northern Indian cities Kanpur, Rampur and Delhi. In Delhi, he studied with some Hadith experts, for example with the sons and grandsons of Shāh Walī Allāh in the *Madrasa-yi Raḥīmiyya*. He is also said to have met the most renowned Hadith scholar of his time, Nadhīr Ḥusayn Dihlawī (d. 1902),[32] who became one of the

---

the method of *ʿamal bil-ḥadīth* to back their legal decisions and the mere *muḥaddithūn* who analyse the corpus of the Hadith concerning the chain of transmission (*sanad*) and text (*matn*). See Nafi, Basheer: A Teacher of Ibn ʿAbd al-Wahhāb. Muḥammad Ḥayāt al-Sindī and the Revival of *aṣḥāb al-ḥadīth's* Methodology, in: *Islamic Law and Society* 13 (2006), pp. 208–241, here pp. 208–209.

32 Although Nadhīr Ḥusayn is one of the founding figures of the Ahl-i Ḥadīth, so far no extensive biography has been written on him in a European language.

central figures of the Ahl-i Ḥadīth network. Almost all major late 19th- and early 20th-century Ahl-i Ḥadīth scholars studied under him, which earned him the appellation *shaykh al-kull* ("teacher of all"). Ṣiddīq Ḥasan Khān met another person who was extremely influential in shaping the teachings of the Ahl-i Ḥadīth: ʿAbd al-Ḥaqq Banārsī (d. 1870),[33] who became Ṣiddīq Ḥasan's Hadith teacher in Delhi. ʿAbd al-Ḥaqq also wrote the first Indian treatise against blindly following juridical opinions (*taqlīd*), calling instead to search for juridical proofs only in the Koran and the Sunna of the Prophet. These ideas, which went beyond Shāh Walī Allāh's understanding of *ijtihād*[34] within one school of law, were the foundation for the later Ahl-i Ḥadīth. ʿAbd al-Ḥaqq had been a member of the Ṭarīqa-yi Muḥammadiyya before he became a follower of the Ahl-i Ḥadīth. In 1821, he went to Mecca and Medina with Sayyid Aḥmad Barēlwī's pilgrimage group. Unlike the other members of this group, ʿAbd al-Ḥaqq decided to stay behind in the Hijaz. Later he travelled to the Yemenite capital, Sanaa, where he met and studied with Muḥammad b. ʿAlī al-Shawkānī (d. 1834). ʿAbd al-Ḥaqq Banārsī later became the first man in India to teach al-Shawkānī's works (and, as will be demonstrated in the course of this article, thus indirectly also Ibn Taymiyya's). When Ṣiddīq Ḥasan met ʿAbd al-Ḥaqq, the latter was already a renowned teacher of Hadith and of works against *taqlīd*.

2.3. The Intellectual Precursor Shāh Muḥammad Ismāʿīl

One of Shāh Walī Allāh's grandsons, Shāh Muḥammad Ismāʿīl (1779–1832), gained special importance for the later movement of the Ahl-i Ḥadīth. Muḥammad Ismāʿīl, who might be considered its intellectual precursor, compiled among others, three Persian and Urdu works in which he explained the theories and teachings of the Ṭarīqa-yi Muḥammadiyya. The first book is called *Taqwiyat al-īmān* (Strength-

For short biographies in Urdu, see Nawshahrawī, *Tarājim*, pp. 135–154; Sayf, *Taḥrīk-i Ahl-i ḥadīth*, pp. 323–330. For an extensive, quite hagiographic Urdu biography, see Bihārī, Faḍl-i Ḥusayn: *al-Ḥayāt baʿd al-mamāt*, Delhi 1908, various reprints.

33 For a biography, see Nawshahrawī, *Tarājim*, pp. 280–282; Sayf, *Taḥrīk-i Ahl-i ḥadīth*, pp. 391–392.

34 He wrote the treatise *al-Durr al-farīd fi-manʿ al-taqlīd* (The Precious Pearls About the Prohibition of *taqlīd*), or simply *Radd al-taqlīd* (Against *taqlīd*).

ening of the Faith),[35] the second *al-Ṣirāṭ al-mustaqīm* (The Straight Path)[36] and the third *Yak rūzī* (One Dayer). All these works called on the believer to keep to the principle of the unity of God (*tawḥīd*) and to abstain from all kinds of polytheism (*shirk*). In the *Taqwiyat al-īmān*, in particular, Shāh Muḥammad Ismāʿīl described the different forms of polytheism (*shirk*) and their bad effects on the Islamic community of India. The leaders of the Ṭarīqa-yi Muḥammadiyya also tried to restrict all kinds of "un-Islamic practices" (*bidaʿ*) in the Muslim community in India. In their eyes, the veneration of saints and Sufis and pilgrimages to their graves, in particular, evoked the criticism of the Ṭarīqa-yi Muḥammadiyya. They argued that the members of the Sufi brotherhoods showed undue devotion to the saints, whereas respect and veneration were reserved to God. Only God had ultimate knowledge of the hidden things, like details of Doomsday, the time of people's death and the characteristics of a child in its mother's womb.

Muḥammad Ismāʿīl further criticised that some Indians (whose ancestors might have converted to Islam only some generations before) still adhered to Hindu practices. Some of them even venerated Hindu gods and goddesses like Kali,[37] considered stones or trees to be holy places or asked for the opinions of astrologers or soothsayers before making important decisions. According to Muḥammad Ismāʿīl, all these practices had to be eradicated from Muslim society. The strict adherence to *tawḥīd* was considered the only way out of the crisis afflicting the Muslim society of India. As mentioned earlier, the Ṭarīqa-yi Muḥammadiyya (like some Ahl-i Ḥadīth after them) believed that the end of the world was to come at the end of the 14th Islamic century, i.e. around year 1882/83. The movement also cherished certain ideas of mahdism. The belief in the expected "rightly guided one" (*mahdī*) as one of the major signs of the Day of Judgement was common not only in Shiite movements, but also in several Sunni groups like the Ṭariqa-yi Muḥammadiyya and the Ahl-i ḥadīth. They

35 Dihlawī, Shāh Ismāʿīl Shahīd: *Taqwiyat al-īmān*, English translation, Delhi 1998, and Arabic/English, Riyadh 1995.

36 Colvin, John Russell: Notice on the Peculiar Tenets Held by the Followers of Syed Ahmed, Taken Chiefly from the Sirát-úl-Mústaqím, a Principal Treatise of that Sect, Written by Moulaví Mahommed Ismaíl, in: *Journal of the Asiatic Society of Bengal* 1 (1832), pp. 479–498.

37 Kali, "the black one", is one of the most important goddesses in Hinduism. She is normally portrayed as a mother goddess with a fearsome appearance, i.e. with her sword in one hand and the head of a demon in the other, her face and breasts covered with blood.

believed that the *mahdī* would join the "promised messiah" (*al-masīḥ al-mawʿūd*), who is commonly identified as Jesus (ʿĪsā), in his fight against the "Anti-Christ" (*dajjāl*). After the victory over the *dajjāl*, the *masīḥ* would establish a "kingdom of justice" that would last for one thousand years. After that, people would be sent to paradise or hell.[38] The Ṭarīqa-yi Muḥammadiyya considered Sayyid Aḥmad to be not only a "renewer of the faith" (*mujaddid*), but also the "rightly guided one" (*mahdī*). In the eyes of the Ṭarīqa-yi Muḥamadiyya, the fact that Sayyid Aḥmad's dead body could not be found after the battle of Balakot in 1832[39] was a proof that he was the *mahdī*. The Ahl-i Ḥadīth also believed that the Day of Judgement was approaching and that Sayyid Aḥmad and Muḥammad Ismāʿīl were *mujaddidūn*. Ṣiddīq Ḥasan considered himself a renewer of the faith of the 14th century.[40] According to common Sunni belief, there is a "*mujaddid* at the head of each century".[41] Hence, the Nawwāb claimed to be the „*mujaddid* of the 13th century", interpreting the Arabic word for head (*ra's*) as the "end". Undoubtedly, Ṣiddīq Ḥasan took the teachings about the *mujaddid* from the works of al-Shawkānī, who himself had claimed to be a *mujaddid*.[42] Ibn Taymiyya was not on Ṣiddīq Ḥasan's list, but the latter mentioned no *mujaddid* between the seventh and eleventh century at all, although he stated that there must have been at least one *mujaddid* in each century.[43]

Today's nationalist view of Indian Muslim history, in particular, constructs an intellectual continuity between Ibn Taymiyya, Muḥammad b. ʿAbd al-Wahhāb, the Ṭarīqa-yi Muḥammadiyya and the Ahl-i Ḥadīth.[44] For example, the preface of Shāh Muḥammad Ismāʿīl's

38 See Madelung, Wilfried: Mahdī, in: *EI²*, vol. 5 (1985), pp. 1230–1231.

39 On the battle of Balakot, see Pearson, *Islamic Reform and Revival*, pp. 41–44; and Ahmad, *The Wahhabi Movement*, pp. 55–65.

40 See Ṣiddīq Ḥasan Khān, *Iqtirāb al-sāʿa*, pp. 116–118.

41 On this subject, see Landau-Tesseron, Ella: The Cyclical Reform. A Study of the Mujaddid Tradition, in: *Studia Islamica* 79 (1989), pp. 79–119. This theory was supported by the famous Hadith "God will send for his umma, at the head of each century, one who will renew for it its religion" (*inna allāh yabʿathu ʿalā ra's kull mi'at sana man yujaddidu lahā dīnahā*), see Abū Da'ūd, *Sunan Abī Da'ūd*, vol. 2, *Kitāb al-malāḥim*.

42 Haykel, *Revival and Reform*, p. 194.

43 For this complete list of *mujaddidūn*, see Preckel, *Islamische Bildungsnetzwerke*, pp. 432–433.

44 On this phenomenon in India, see Hartung, Jan-Peter: *Viele Wege und ein Ziel. Leben und Wirken von Sayyid Abū al-Ḥasan ʿAlī al-Ḥasan Nadwī (1914–1999)*, Würzburg 2004, p. 216–217.

Taqwiyat al-īmān, which was translated into Urdu in 1833–34 but seems to have been written ten years earlier, states:

> The services which he [Muḥammad Ismāʿīl] has rendered for the reformation of Ummah and his undertaking the task of Da'wah [the mission of propagating Islam]; especially after the previous works of Shaikhul-Islam Ibn Taimiyah and Muhammad bin Abdul Wahhab, are absolutely unforgettable and shall always be cherished in our minds.[45]

Although in general Muḥammad Ismāʿīl himself makes no direct references to specific writings of Ibn Taymiyya, far more obvious is the appreciation of Ibn Taymiyya through another strand of transmission, the works of the Yemenite scholar Muḥammad b. ʿAlī al-Shawkānī.[46] Ṣiddīq Ḥasan Khān in his work *al-Idrāk li-takhrīj aḥādīth radd al-ishrāk* (Grasping the Interpretation of Hadith in the Negation of Polytheism),[47] which comment on Muḥammad Ismāʿīl's works and make some references to Ibn Taymiyya, also without mentioning bibliographic details.[48] Here, it is obvious that Ṣiddīq Ḥasan Khān had become familiar with some of Ibn Taymiyya's thoughts through the Ṭarīqa-yi Muḥammadiyya. Especially during their pilgrimage to the Hijaz in 1821, the leaders and members of the Ṭarīqa-yi Muḥammadiyya might have studied some of Ibn Taymiyya's writings. It is possible that they also came across the works of Muḥammad b. ʿAbd al-Wahhāb, although this is not explicitly stated. Hence, the influences to which Ṣiddīq Ḥasan Khān was exposed in India were already decisively shaped by reform ideas from the Arab world, notably but in no way exclusively from the Arabian Peninsula.

---

45 Mujahid, Abdul-Malik: Publishers Note, in: Shah Ismail Shaheed *Taqwiyat al-īmān* Riyadh: Dar-us-Salam Publ., 1995, p. 9.

46 Following Muḥammad Ismāʿīl's work *Radd al-ishrāk*, which is a collection of his own and Sayyid Aḥmad's sermons, Ṣiddīq Ḥasan conceived the following kinds of polytheism: polytheism in knowledge (*shirk fī al-ʿilm*), polytheism in the field of authority (*shirk fī al-taṣarruf*), polytheism in worship (*shirk fī al-ʿibāda*) and polytheism in blind following (*shirk fī al-taqlīd*).

47 Kanpur 1873.

48 See also Saeedullah, *Life and Works*, pp. 109–111, here p. 110.

3. Central Impact of the Yemen Connection

Around the mid-19th century, Ṣiddīq Ḥasan Khān got to know two brothers in Bhopal[49] who originally came from Ḥudayda in Yemen: Ḥusayn Ibn Muḥsin[50] (d. 1910) and Zayn al-ʿĀbidīn Ibn Muḥsin (d. 1880).[51] Their family had met the ruler of Bhopal, Sikander Bēgum, and her entourage, when the Bēgum performed her pilgrimage to Mecca (*ḥajj*) in 1863–1864.[52] Some family members had accompanied the Indians on their Hajj, and the Bēgum later also asked Zayn al-ʿĀbidīn to come to Bhopal. He followed her invitation and became the state kadi. His younger brother Ḥusayn joined him later in India[53] and gained fame as a teacher of Hadith. The Yemenite brothers brought a new impetus of Islamic reformism to Bhopal, namely the works of the

49 There are contradictions in the chronology of events in the history of this Arab family and Ṣiddīq Ḥasan Khān's autobiographical accounts that could not be clarified. It is still questionable whether Ḥusayn Ibn Muḥsin had already come to Bhopal at the time Ṣiddīq Ḥasan Khān arrived there in 1854.

50 For a short biography, see Ṣiddīq Ḥasan Khān, *Abjad al-ʿulūm*, part 3, pp. 211–213; Sayf, *Taḥrīk-i Ahl-i ḥadīth*, pp. 642–645. I am deeply indebted to Ḥusayn b. Muḥsin's descendant Rāfiʿ ʿArab (Bhopal), who is also a prominent member of the Ahl-i Ḥadīth in India, for writing down his family history in Urdu for me.

51 On him, see the family history mentioned above. In contrast to his brother Ḥusayn, Zayn never became a prominent supporter of the Ahl-i Ḥadīth and never wrote any books in its favour. Also important is that the Yemenite brothers were a link between Ṣiddīq Ḥasan Khān and prominent Yemenite Hadith scholars, like the families of the al-Ahdāl and al-Mizjājī from Zabīd, and also to the Idrīsī tradition of Aḥmad b. Idrīs (d. 1837). On them, see Voll, John O.: Linking Groups in the Networks of Eighteenth-century Revivalist Scholars. The Mizjaji Family in Yemen, in: Nehemia Levtzion and John O. Voll (eds.): *Eighteenth-century Renewal and Reform in Islam*, Syracuse 1992, pp. 69–92, here pp. 79–80; Radtke, Bernd: *The Exoteric Aḥmad Ibn Idrīs. A Sufi's Critique of the Madhāhib and the Wahhābīs*, Leiden 2000. For these connections, which are beyond the scope of this paper, see also Reichmuth, Stefan: *The World of Murtaḍā al-Zabīdī (1732–91). Studies on the Life, Networks and Writings of an Islamic Humanist Scholar of the 18th Century*, Cambridge 2009, pp. 22–25, 107–109, 152–158 (al-Ahdal family) and pp. 21–25, 220, 230, 282 (al-Mizjājī family); Preckel, *Islamische Bildungsnetzwerke*, pp. 127–130.

52 For an account of her pilgrimage, see Bēgum, Sikander: *A Pilgrimage to Mecca*, Calcutta 1906, new edition by Siobhan Lambert-Hurley, Bloomington 2008.

53 The reason for Ḥusayn's final migration to India was a dispute with the Ottoman authorities of Ḥudayda on the taxation of pearls. After Ḥusayn had even been imprisoned and tortured, he finally followed his brother to Bhopal.

Yemenite scholar Muḥammad b. ʿAlī al-Shawkānī.[54] Zayn al-ʿĀbidīn and his brother had been students of al-Shawkānī's son Aḥmad (d. 1864?). Al-Shawkānī was a Zaydī Shii,[55] but he used many Sunni sources – especially in the fields of *fiqh* and Hadith.[56] He refused to take radical Shii positions, like slandering the companions or favouring the *ahl al-bayt*. This was in accordance with those Zaydī ideas that the Shāfiʿī population of the Yemen regarded as having tendencies toward "Sunnitisation". Recent Zaydī scholars even held al-Shawkānī responsible for dismantling the Zaydiyya by introducing Salafi or even Wahhabi thoughts into the Yemen.[57] Al-Shawkānī was the Chief Judge (*qāḍī al-quḍāt*) of the Imamate of Yemen. Besides his career as a judge, he gained great popularity even among Sunni scholars because of his criticism of *taqlīd* in legal matters. In contrast to those modernists who consider *ijtihād* to be "free reasoning", al-Shawkānī wanted a fatwa (legal judgement) to be in accordance with the Koran and the Sunna of the Prophet. He even claimed the necessity of *ijtihād* for the layman (*ʿāmmī*). Shawkānī's position was deeply rooted in the school of the Ẓāhirīs, especially in the works of the Andalusian scholar Ibn Ḥazm (d. 1046). Ṣiddīq Ḥasan Khān – like al-Shawkānī before him – also fully approved and even admired the Ẓāhirīs,[58] who denied the legitimacy of legal decisions based on analogy (*qiyās*), consensus (*ijmāʿ*) and

---

54 For a biography, see Haykel, Bernard: *Revival and Reform in Islam. The Legacy of Muhammad al-Shawkānī*, Cambridge 2003; al-Amri, Husayn Ibn-Abdullah: *The Yemen in the 18th and 19th Centuries. A Political and Intellectual History*, London 1985; Ibn ʿAbbās al-Wājih, ʿAbd al-Salām: *Aʿlām al-muʾallifīn al-Zaydiyya* (Leading Authors of the Zaydiyya), Sanaa 1420/1999, pp. 958–978. Ṣiddīq Ḥasan Khān stressed the important role of al-Shawkānī for his own works in *Abjad al-ʿulūm*, part 3, pp. 194–211 and *al-Tāj al-mukallal*, pp. 443–456.

55 Recent scholars of the Ahl-i Ḥadīth strictly deny that al-Shawkānī was a Zaydī Shii, but maintain that he belonged to the Sunni Shāfiʿī school of law. Personal communication by the author with Ahl-i Ḥadīth members and students at the *Nadwat ul-ʿulamāʾ* in Delhi and Lucknow in 2001.

56 Haykel, *Revival and Reform*, pp. 109–110.

57 On tensions between the Zaydiyya and the Salafis/Wahhabis in the 20th/21st century, see the paper by vom Bruck, Gabriele: Regimes of Piety Revisited. Zaydī Political Moralities in Republican Yemen, in: *Die Welt des Islams* 50 (2010), pp. 185–223.

58 Ignaz Goldziher's famous book *Die Zahiriten* was first published in Leipzig in 1884 and was much later translated into English as Goldziher, Ignaz: *The Ẓāhirīs. Their Doctrine and Their History. A Contribution to the History of Islamic Theology*, Leiden 2007. For a biography of Ibn Ḥazm from the Ahl-i Ḥadīth perspective, see Sayf, *Taḥrīk-i Ahl-i ḥadīth*, p. 79.

blind acceptance of other scholars' opinions (*taqlīd*) and who held their main proponent Ibn Ḥazm in special esteem. Like Ibn Ḥazm and al-Shawkānī, Ṣiddīq Ḥasan Khān denied the legacy of those decisions based on the *taqlīd*, which was regarded as "full of *ra'y*", i. e. free reasoning. No consistent opinion on scholarly consensus (*ijmāʿ*) can be traced in Ṣiddīq Ḥasan Khān's works. In some works, he stated that the *ijmāʿ* was that of the companions of the Prophet (*ṣaḥāba*), whereas in others he wrote that only the *ijmāʿ* of the four rightly guided caliphs (*al-khulafāʾ al-rāshidūn*) could be regarded as valid. Like the Ẓāhirīs, Ṣiddīq Ḥasan Khān considered the *ijmāʿ* of all religious scholars of the epochs after Muḥammad to be invalid, because this *ijmāʿ* was "based on *taqlīd*". He regarded this form of *ijmāʿ* as forbidden, whereas a consensus of the early *mujtahidūn* was valid. Further, the *ijmāʿ* of some scholars of a certain region or a certain time could not be regarded as binding, because other scholars might decide otherwise. Ultimately, there was no proof (*dalīl*) in these decisions.[59] Ṣiddīq Ḥasan Khān's positive views can be easily assessed in his biographies of Ibn Ḥazm.[60] However, his greatest admiration was for al-Shawkānī himself, whom he regarded as an "unrestricted mujtahid" (*mujtahid muṭlaq*) and one of the most important renewers of the faith (*mujaddidūn*) ever. Ṣiddīq Ḥasan stated in his works that his personal aim was to spread al-Shawkānī's works and ideas throughout India and beyond in order to popularize them. He wrote in *al-Tāj al-mukallal* that it was the result of his own activities to spread al-Shawkānī's works through his own writings in Arabic and Persian language. He stressed: "They will arrive in all places of the world, near and far."[61]

59 For Ṣiddīq Ḥasan's different positions on the *ijmāʿ*, see Saeedullah, *Life and Works*, pp. 97–98; Preckel, *Islamische Bildungsnetzwerke*, pp. 331–334; on today's Ahl-i Ḥadīth view of Ibn Ḥazm, see for example Sayf, *Taḥrīk-i Ahl-i ḥadīth*, pp. 79–80.

60 Ṣiddīq Ḥasan Khān, *Abjad al-ʿulūm*, part 3, pp. 148–149; for a short biography of Ibn Ḥazm, see Sayf, *Taḥrīk-i Ahl-i ḥadīth*, p. 79. It is also no coincidence that some of Ṣiddīq Ḥasan Khān's works have been reprinted by the publishing house Dār Ibn Ḥazm, Beirut, since the year 2000.

61 Ṣiddīq Ḥasan Khān, *al-Tāj al-mukallal*, p. 50.

4. Ṣiddīq Ḥasan's Rise to Power and Subsequent Fall

During the first years of his stay in Bhopal from 1854–1856, Ṣiddīq Ḥasan was not yet in a position to promote his religious views or to support any reformist ideas. It was only due to the adherence of the Prime Minister Jamāl ul-Dīn Khān to the Ṭarīqa-yi Muḥammadiyya that Ṣiddīq Ḥasan received the post of a scribe (Urdu: *munshī*). One year later, he was forced to leave Bhopal, following a dispute with the Ḥanafī Second Prime Minister about the legitimacy of smoking the water pipe (*ḥuqqa*).[62]

However, the Bēgum of Bhopal personally invited Ṣiddīq Ḥasan to return to Bhopal and offered him a new job. He arrived in Bhopal for the second time in 1859. Only a few months later, Ṣiddīq Ḥasan married Dhākiyya Bēgum, one of the daughters of Prime Minister Jamāl al-Dīn Khān. The couple had three children. This marriage brought Ṣiddīq Ḥasan into closer contact with the Bēgum and her family. In 1865, he decided to leave Bhopal again and to perform the pilgrimage to Mecca. From the beginning of this journey, Ṣiddīq Ḥasan started collecting, buying and copying books that were not available in India.[63] Here, Ibn Taymiyya's *al-Siyāsa al-sharʿiyya*[64] (Governance According to God's Law) is worth mentioning. Ṣiddīq Ḥasan was able to get a manuscript of the work, which he kept in his private library. This work is of interest, because it is widely regarded as a foundation for running a state with an Islamic trademark according to the laws of the Sharia.[65] This book seems to foreshadow the theoretical framework for Ṣiddīq

62 See Khan, Zafar ul-Islam: Nawwāb Sayyid Ṣiddīḳ Ḥasan Khān, in: *EI*², vol. 7 (1993), pp. 1048–1049, here p. 1048, where he states about Ṣiddīq Ḥasan that the Nawwāb was against the use of tobacco and coffee.

63 For a detailed account of his Hajj and the books he studied during his journey, see Ṣiddīq Ḥasan Khān, Muḥammad: *Riḥlat al-Ṣiddīq ilā bayt Allāh al-ʿatīq* (Ṣiddīq's Journey to the Noble House of God), Lucknow 1289/1872. For instance, he bought some books by Muḥammad b. ʿAlī al-Shawkānī, namely *Irshād al-fuḥūl fī ʿilm al-uṣūl*, *Nayl al-awṭār* and *Fatḥ al-qadīr fī uṣūl al-tafsīr*. We are further informed that Ṣiddīq Ḥasan Khān combated seasickness by reading and copying Ibn Qudāma al-Maqdisī's (d. 1283) work *al-Ṣārim al-mubkī*. See Saeedullah, *Life and Works*, pp. 43–44.

64 The complete title being *al-Siyāsa al-sharʿiyya fī iṣlāḥ al-rāʿī wal-raʿiyya* (Governance According to God's Law in Reforming Both the Ruler and his Flock). For an annotated French translation, see Ibn Taymiyya, *Le Traité de droit public d'Ibn Taimīya*. translated by Henri Laoust, Damascus 1952.

65 On this issue, see the article by Abdessamad Belhaj in the present volume.

Ḥasan's future career as a Nawwāb and his efforts to transform Bhopal into a state broadly governed by Islamic principles. It is further said to have reinforced the reception of Ibn Taymiyya in India.[66]

Shortly after his return to Bhopal in 1871, Ṣiddīq Ḥasan married a second time: his second wife was the widowed ruler of Bhopal, Shāh Jahān Bēgum (d. 1901, r. 1868–1901). From that time on, Ṣiddīq Ḥasan had an almost free hand in propagating the ideas and teachings of the Ahl-i Ḥadīth. Two things are interesting: first, Ṣiddīq Ḥasan did not officially divorce his first wife. Second, one of the teachings of the Ahl-i Ḥadīth was that widows should be allowed to remarry.[67] They claimed that the practice of forbidding widows to remarry was rooted in Hinduism and not in Islam. Therefore, Muslim women should be encouraged to remarry after divorce or the death of their husbands. Indeed, in the South Asian context, widows of all non-Hindu religions are allowed to remarry, but it is socially not accepted. The Hindu Widow's Marriage Act of 1856 regulated the allowance of remarriage – but widows thereby lost their limited interest in their husband's estate. According to more recent studies, "in the opinion of 20.08 per cent Hindu widows, 8.33 per cent Muslim widows and non-Christian widows remarriage is against religion".[68] In the 19th century, belief in the prohibition of widow remarriage might have been even more deeply rooted in the Muslim community. Since the mid-19th century, Muslim reformist movements propagated allowing widow remarriage. The Ṭarīqa-i Muḥammadiyya, for example, had started their campaign to allow widow remarriage in the North Western Frontier Provinces.[69]

66 See von Kügelgen, Anke: Ibn Taimiyyas Kritik an der aristotelischen Logik, in: Dominik Perler and Ulrich Rudolph (eds.): *Logik und Theologie. Das Organon im arabischen und lateinischen Mittelalter*, Leiden and Boston 2005, pp. 167–226, see p. 172. Wael B. Hallaq reports that the manuscript of this key treatise was kept in the Āṣafiyya Library, Hyderabad. In contrast to this, it has been stated that it was in the private collection of the Zaydī Imams, from whence Ṣiddīq Ḥasan brought it to India. See Hallaq, Wael B.: *Ibn Taymiyya Against the Greek Logicians*, Oxford 1993, p. lv.

67 Preckel, Claudia: Interpretations of Widow Remarriage and Divorce. Shah Jahan Bēgum's (d. 1901) *Tahdhib an-Niswan* and the *Ahl-e Hadith* Movement in 19th-century Bhopal, in: *Pakistan Journal of Women's Studies* 11 (2004), pp. 41–51, here pp. 44–45; see also several certificates of marriage and divorce in the edited volume by Imtiaz Ahmad (ed.): *Divorce and Remarriage Among Muslims in India*, New Delhi 2003.

68 See Kitchlu, T. N.: *Widows in India*, New Delhi 1993, pp. 67–68.

69 Shāh Muḥammad Ismāʿīl seems to have pleaded for the forced remarriage of women. This might have been to win the support of the local Pashtuns, who

In Bhopal, the second marriage of the Bēgum in 1871 did not remain undisputed. Shāh Jahān Bēgum's own daughter Sulṭān Jahān Bēgum was one of her stepfather's fiercest opponents and often declared him to be a Wahhabi who forced her mother to be in *purda*, the Indian (Muslim) version of veiling.[70] The official documents of that time and the daughter's memoirs make it clear that she was against her mother's marriage for dynastic reasons. Nevertheless, Ṣiddīq Ḥasan remained Nawwāb until 1885, when he was accused of instigating Indian Muslims against the British. The British deprived him of all his titles and sentenced him to house arrest in his palace Nūr Maḥall, where he lived until his death in 1890. He was not allowed to see his wife Shāh Jahān Bēgum during the day, but could spend the night with her in her palace, the Tāj Maḥall.[71] After Ṣiddīq Ḥasan was forced to give up his titles, his personal networks were also destroyed. He was not able to keep up his contacts with publishers in Cairo or Istanbul, and the publication of his works ended. It was only with the emergence of the Salafiyya that some of his Arabic works were reprinted in Beirut. The majority of his books in Persian and Urdu, however, have not been reprinted. One of the main reasons might be that other persons in the Ahl-i Ḥadīth[72] became more influential within the movement. The fact that other scholars of the Ahl-i Ḥadīth from Bhopal, like Ḥusayn b.

---

practiced the remarriage of widows to the deceased husband's younger brother. Here, tensions between the Ḥanafī law, the Pashtuns' "code of honour", the Pashtūnwalī, and the reformers' interpretation of Islam become obvious. See Colvin, Notice of the Peculiar Tracts, p. 493.

70 At the end of the 19th century, India (especially Bhopal) was the scene of fierce controversies about the system of *purda* (literally Urdu for "curtain"). The *purda* system not only meant wearing a veil, but also implied the segregation of women in separate parts of the household, the *zenāna*. Although Sulṭān Jahān Bēgum severely criticised her mother for wearing purda, she herself was a fierce supporter of the *purda* system. Pictures of her public appearance show her completely veiled in a burqa (in light colours) including a face veil. In 1922, she even published a book titled *Hijab, or Why Purda is Necessary*, Calcutta 1922. However, she abandoned the *purda* system after her abdication in 1926, four years before her death. Her argument was that the veil was no longer necessary for her because of her age. For more discussions on the issue of the veil in the 19th century, see Minault, Gail: *Secluded Scholars. Women's Education and Muslim Social Reform in Colonial India*, Delhi 1999.

71 Saeedullah, *Life and Works*, p. 73 (quoting ʿAlī Ḥasan Khān, *Maʾāthir-i Ṣiddīqī*, vol. 3, pp. 169–173) and personal communication with Ṣiddīq Ḥasan's descendent Ali Hasan Mujeeb, Bhopal 2001.

72 I. e. Thanāʾallāh Amritsārī, see the article by Martin Riexinger in this volume.

Muḥsin and Muḥammad Bashīr Sahsawānī, were still able to publish their books indicates that Ṣiddīq Ḥasan Khān's deposition was rooted in a conflict within the ruling family.

5. Ṣiddīq Ḥasan's Patterns of Translation, Abridgement and Distribution of Manuscripts and Books

After he had married Shāh Jahān Bēgum in 1871, Ṣiddīq Ḥasan Khān actively started to buy books and manuscripts from Arab countries. For this purpose, he sent his book agents to the most important cities of the Islamic world, for example Cairo, Istanbul, Mecca and Medina.[73] Their duty was to gather writings by certain Arab authors like Ibn Taymiyya, Jalāl al-Dīn al-Suyūṭī (d. 1505), ʿAlī al-Qārī (d. 1606) and al-Shawkānī. In Bhopal, the books were copied, translated into Persian or Urdu, abridged or commentated. Some of them were simply translated and distributed in Bhopal under Ṣiddīq Ḥasan's name. It might be assumed that this strategy was carried out with the full approval of Ṣiddīq Ḥasan. Ṣiddīq Ḥasan probably did not work on the manuscripts himself, since he conducted his official duties as the Nawwāb. It is unrealistic to assume that he wrote his almost 300 works all by himself. The system of patronage at that time also supported the publication of books under the name of the ruler. It must have been a great honour for a scribe to see a work that he had translated or commentated published under the Nawwāb's name. At the courts of the princely states, the role of the scribes who wrote the manuscripts (in most cases in Persian) and prepared the textbooks should not be underestimated. Especially in Bhopal, where four printing presses existed, the scribes held important positions.[74] Ṣiddīq Ḥasan showed great confidence in the staff of the publishing houses in Bhopal. Thus, he also appointed some of them his "agents" (Arabic/Urdu: *nāʾib*) and sent them abroad to buy or copy Arabic manuscripts for him. Scribes even functioned as intermediates between the indigenous (Muslim) elite and the colonial power, because they often served as private secretaries of members

73 Other cities visited by his agents included Alexandria, Aden, Tunis, Bombay (Mumbai) and Delhi. For a complete list of his visits, see Luqmān, *al-Sayyid Ṣiddīq Ḥasan al-Qannawjī*, pp. 58–59.

74 For the role of scribes in South Asia, see Pollock, Sheldon I.: *Literary Cultures in History. Reconstructions from South Asia,* Berkeley 2003, esp. pp. 163–165 et passim.

of the British administration.[75] One of Ṣiddīq Ḥasan's "agents" was Dhū al-Fiqār Aḥmad Bhøpālī (d. 1922),[76] who was also linked to the Yemenite tradition of al-Shawkānī. He worked as a corrector in the local printing presses and wrote several books supporting the Ahl-i Ḥadīth. His major work was a continuation of Ṣiddīq Ḥasan's Koranic exegesis, *Tarjumān al-Qur'ān* (Interpreter of the Koran), which was published in 17 volumes. Whereas volume one to six and 16 to 17 were clearly written by Ṣiddīq Ḥasan himself, volume 14 and 15 were published under Dhū al-Fiqār's name. According to some of the prefaces and eulogies (*taqārīẓ*) in the books, Dhū al-Fiqār also copied and corrected several of Ṣiddīq Ḥasan's works.[77] Many of the books brought to Bhopal by the "agents" were freely distributed in the local *madrasas*. Following al-Shawkānī, it was Ṣiddīq Ḥasan's aim to educate independent legal scholars and to propagate the idea of *ijtihād* as conceptualised by the Ahl-i Ḥadīth. Here, Ṣiddīq Ḥasan relied on al-Shawkānī's book *Adab al-ṭalab* (Refinement for the Quest of Knowledge).[78]

Some years after his marriage to Shāh Jahān Bēgum in 1871, Ṣiddīq Ḥasan published his work *Silsilat al-ʿasjad fī dhikr mashā'ikh al-sanad* in Bhopal. This was also based on a book written by al-Shawkānī, his *Itḥāf al-dafātir* (Presenting of the Register). Here, again, al-Shawkānī listed all the books he recommended for the education of independent legal scholars. In *Silsilat al-ʿasjad*, Ṣiddīq Ḥasan gave a detailed chain of transmission, linking him personally to the Prophet Muḥammad[79] reinforcing his authority and the authentic transmission of the disciplines

75 Unfortunately, the sources do not tell us very much about Ṣiddīq Ḥasan's contacts to the British administration and his abilities in speaking or writing English.

76 For a biography, see Ḥasanī, *Nuzhat al-khawāṭir*, vol. 8, p. 140.

77 Ṣiddiq Ḥasan Khān, Muḥammad: *Qurrat al-a'yān wa-masarrāt al-ādhān fī ma'āthir al-malik al-jalīl al-Nawwāb Muḥammad Ṣiddīq Ḥasan Khān* (Consolation of the Eyes and Pleasures of the Ears in the Works of the Exalted King, the Nawwāb Ṣiddīq Ḥasan Khān), Constantinople 1298/1881, p. 100.

78 Al-Shawkānī, Muḥammad b. ʿAlī: *Adab al-ṭalab wa-muntahā al-arab* (Refinement for the Quest of Knowledge and the Ultimate Goal), Sanaa 1419/1998, pp. 195–204. This book was later abridged and commentated by ʿAbd al-Ṣamad Peshāwārī's (d. 1880) as *Ṭalab al-arab min Adab al-ṭalab* (Reaching out for the Goal to Refine the Quest for Knowledge), Bhopal 1878. Peshāwārī was formerly a fierce supporter of the Ḥanafī *madhhab*. When he heard about the Hadith studies in Bhopal, he travelled there from his hometown, Peshawar. He worked for several printing projects in Bhopal until his death.

79 Ṣiddiq Ḥasan Khān, Muḥammad: *Silsilat al-asjad fī dhikr mashā'ikh al-sanad*, Bhopal: 1293/ 1876, pp. 2–8.

he identified, he studied and of which he possessed several books. Like almost all *ʿulamāʾ* in the Indian context, Ṣiddīq Ḥasan Khān had studied the important languages of Muslim Indian culture of his time: Arabic, Persian and Urdu. Therefore, his library contained works in all these languages:

Koran reading and recitation, interpretation of the Koran (*tafsīr*), principles of Koran interpretation (*uṣūl-i tafsīr*), tradition literature (*ḥadīth*), principles of the study of Hadith (*uṣūl-i ḥadīth*), names of the transmitters of Hadith (*asmāʾ al-rijāl*), classified biographies of famous Muslims (*ṭabaqāt*), life stories of the Prophet Muḥammad (*sīrat*), Islamic law according to the rulings of the Koran (*fiqh al-qurʾān*), Islamic law according to the rulings of the Hadith (*fiqh al-ḥadīth*), dogmatic theology (*ʿaqāʾid*), speculative theology (*kalām*), Islamic law (*fiqh*), inheritance law (*farāʾiḍ*), methodology and principles of Islamic jurisprudence (*uṣūl-i fiqh*), Arabic language (*lugha*), principles of (Arabic) language (*uṣūl-i lughat*), morphology (*ṣarf*), syntax (*naḥw*), literature (*adab*), explanation of meanings and the science of style (*maʿānī wa-bayān*), prosody and rhyme (*ʿurūḍ wa-qāfiya*), logic (*manṭiq*), philosophy (*ḥikma*), astronomy (*hayʾa*), religious ethics (*akhlāq*), sufism (*taṣawwuf*), preaching (*mawāʿiẓ*), knowledge of eschatology (*ʿilm al-ākhira*), works refuting *taqlīd* (*radd al-taqlīd*), Persian (*fārsī*) and history (*taʾrīkh*).

All in all, Ṣiddīq Ḥasan Khān enumerated 603 books to have all of them collected in the various disciplines mentioned above. Some of these were printed, others were manuscripts or autographs. He claimed to have all of them in his private library.[80] Many of these books were printed in Arabic countries or in Istanbul, but he also possessed many manuscripts. It is fair to assume that the majority of Ṣiddīq Ḥasan Khān's works dealt with the disciplines of Hadith and other transmitted sciences (*manqūlāt*). He listed more than 150 works on Hadith and related sciences alone, which is more than 25 percent. A closer look at the Nawwāb's library shows that Ṣiddīq Ḥasan Khān possessed not a single monograph by a Wahhabi author, neither by Muḥammad b. ʿAbd al-Wahhāb nor by his supporters. It can be assumed, however, that Ṣiddīq Ḥasan Khān knew the *Kitāb al-Tawḥīd*, but he never explicitly quoted from it. The book circulated in reformist circles throughout India these days, and was also printed there from 1889 onwards. The book was first published in India in 1874, and then several times

80 Ibid., pp. 65–66.

more already during Ṣiddīq Ḥasan's lifetime. As will be discussed later, other Bhopalese scholars of the Ahl-i Ḥadīth certainly knew the *Kitāb al-Tawḥīd*, since their own works referred to it. Thus it is quite improbable that Ṣiddīq Ḥasan Khān simply ignored the book. In his work *al-Dīn al-khāliṣ*[81] he referred to the idea of *tawḥīd* and gave a refutation of polytheism (*shirk*). The lines of argumentation were similar to those of the *Kitāb al-Tawḥīd*. Some authors do not consider the Nawwāb to be the author of this book because of several contradictions in content.

5.1. The Yemen Background of Ṣiddīq Ḥasan Khān's Library

A large percentage of the books in Ṣiddīq Ḥasan's library were by scholars from Yemen. The majority of the 112 books written by Yemeni authors (42 monographs) were composed by Muḥammad b. ʿAlī al-Shawkānī (d. 1834). 24 books were written by Muḥammad b. Ismāʿīl al-Amīr (d. 1769),[82] and Muḥammad Ibrāhīm al-Wazīr (d. 1436)[83] was the author of seven books. These scholars were the intellectual predecessors of al-Shawkānī, as both of them were defenders of *ijtihād* and argued their legal decisions based on the Koran and Hadith. They were also renowned for their knowledge of Hadith and their fight against "un-Islamic" practices. Especially the Yemenite commentaries on the famous Hadith work *Bulūgh al-marām*[84] by the Shāfiʿī scholar Ibn Ḥajar al-ʿAsqalānī (d. 1149) drew the special attention of the Ahl-i Ḥadīth. They claimed that this work was of special importance because Ibn Ḥajar quoted all the important collections of Hadith and also listed the traditions promulgated by the founders of the four

81 Ṣiddīq Ḥasan Khān, Muḥammad: *al-Dīn al-khāliṣ* (The True Religion), Cairo 1959.

82 Al-Wajīh, *Aʿlām al-muʾallifīn al-Zaydiyya*, pp. 863–873; Ṣiddīq Ḥasan Khān, *Abjad al-ʿulūm*, part 3, pp. 184–185; idem, *al-Tāj al-mukallal*, pp. 414–416. In his biography, Ṣiddīq Ḥasan Khān considers him an "independent *mujtahid*".

83 Al-Wajīh, *Aʿlām al-muʾallifīn al-Zaydiyya*, pp. 932–934; Ṣiddīq Ḥasan Khān, *Tāj al-mukallal*, pp. 340–342; he also came across Muḥammad b. ʿAlī al-Shawkānī's famous biographical work *al-Badr al-ṭāliʿ*, vol. 1, part 2, Cairo 1929, pp. 81, which tried to give a proof that the chain of independent *mujtahidīn* remained unbroken in Islamic history.

84 Full title *Bulūgh al-marām fī adillat aḥādīth al-aḥkām* (Reaching the Objective Concerning Traditions for Legal Opinions), see Brockelmann, Carl: *Geschichte der arabischen Litteratur*, 2nd ed., Leiden 1943–49, here vol. 2, p. 69.

schools of law, of whom Aḥmad b. Ḥanbal was regarded as the greatest authority. The Ahl-i Ḥadīth further claim that this work was free of statements by "authors of speculative theology" (*mutakallimūn*). The aforementioned Muḥammad b. Ismāʿīl al-Amīr commented on Ibn Ḥajar al-ʿAsqalānī's *Bulūgh al-marām* with his *Subul al-salām* (Paths of Peace) and a rhymed version called *Manẓūmat Bulūgh al-marām*. Ṣiddīq Ḥasan addressed these works by al-ʿAsqalānī and Muḥammad b. Ismāʿīl al-Amīr with three commentaries, namely *Misk al-khitām* (The Final Seal), *al-Rawḍ al-bassām* (The Smiling Gardens) and *Fatḥ al-ʿallām sharḥ Bulūgh al-marām* (Explanation of the Understanding of the *Bulūgh al-marām*). This shows that the early generation of the Ahl-i Ḥadīth regarded these Yemenite authors, i.e. al-Amīr al-Yamanī and Ibrāhīm al-Wazīr, as the first representatives of their movement.

The fight against *bidaʿ* was the aim of a Khorasanian author whose books can also be found in Ṣiddīq Ḥasan Khān's library: ʿAlī al-Qārī (d. 1606). Born in Herat (Afghanistan), al-Qārī travelled widely and became one of the most prolific teachers and writers on Hadith in 17th-century Mecca.[85] It is astonishing that Ṣiddīq Ḥasan owned 35 works in 18 books written by someone like him who was also known for his strict adherence of the Ḥanafī school of law. But a close look at al-Qārī's works shows that he often differs from the Ḥanafī mainstream: for example on the question of raising one's hands during the ritual prayer (*rafʿ al-yadayn*), al-Qārī took the position of the Meccan Shāfiʿīs of his time, which was later to become the argumentation of the Ahl-i Ḥadīth.[86] There were further several congruencies between the teachings of the Ahl-i Ḥadīth and al-Qārī, e.g. in the critical assessment of the works of the famous mystic Ibn ʿArabī (d. 1240)[87] or in their hostile

---

85 Only recently have Western scholars become aware of the role of al-Qārī, see Franke, Patrick: *Mullā ʿAlī al-Qārī. Textproduktion und Gedankenwelt eines mekkanischen Religionsgelehrten der islamischen Jahrtausendwende*, (forthcoming).

86 It is worth mentioning that though belonging to the Zaydiyya al-Shawkānī held several dogmatic positions that were also found in the Sunni schools of law. Here, the Shāfiʿī school of law was of great importance in that the Zaydī Shiis and the Shafiʿī scholars of Yemen were exchanging teaching licenses (*ijāzāt*). Here, the scholarly families like the Ahdal family, who later became important for the Ahl-i Ḥadīth, were leading experts of the Hadith and Shafiʿī traditions. Some of the Ahl-i Ḥadīth I met in India even denied the fact that al-Shawkānī was a Zaydī and maintained that he was a Shāfiʿī instead.

87 Al-Qārī, ʿAlī: *al-Wujūdiyya fī nayl masāʾil al-shuhūdiyya* (The Philosophy of Existence on the Acquaintance of the Question of the Philosophy of Direct

attitude towards the Shia.[88] Also, both al-Qārī and the Ahl-i Ḥadīth were objected to the celebration of the Prophet Muḥammad's birthday (*mawlid al-nabī*).[89] In several works, Ṣiddīq Ḥasan quoted Ibn Taymiyya indirectly through al-Qārī. Whereas the majority of Indian scholars do not mention al-Qārī and his influence on Indian Islam up to the 19th century, Abū Ḥasan ʿAlī Nadwī (d. 1999) stressed al-Qārī's importance for the reception of Ibn Taymiyya:

> Then, Mullā 'Ali Qāri b. Sultān Muhammad (d. 1014/1605) suddenly appeared on the scene who went to Hijaz for the study of the hadīth under some reputed scholar [...] His probity and courage led him to defend Shaikh-ul-Islām Ibn Taimiyah and to boldly affirm that the Shaikh-ul-Islām was a savant with a pious soul who should be reckoned among the saints of Islam.[90]

Testimony); Brockelmann, *Geschichte der Arabischen Litteratur*, vol. 2, p. 395, in Ṣiddīq Ḥasan's library no. 87. In this work, al-Qārī criticizes Ibn ʿArabī and his monistic interpretations of *waḥdat al-wujūd* and calls it – like Ibn Taymiyya befor him – *Ittiḥādiyya* (Believers in the Union/Unity). This refutation of the theories of Ibn ʿArabī is extremely relevant in the Indian context. In India, the Sufi orders of the Chishtiyya and the Suhrawārdiyya are very common. Both of them are recipients of Ibn ʿArabī's works. The origin of the Ahl-i ḥadīth, on the other hand, can be seen in the Naqshbandiyya, which spread critical works against Ibn ʿArabī and *waḥdat al-wujūd*. On al-Qārī and Ibn ʿArabī further see Knysh, Alexander: *Ibn ʿArabī in the Later Islamic Tradition. The Making of a Polemical Image in Medieval Islam*, Albany 1999, pp. 164, 392. Some Ahl-i Ḥadīth even refer to Ibn ʿArabī in legal matters. Even Ṣiddīq Ḥasan Khān held the view that Ibn ʿArabī followed Ibn Ḥazm in his insistance on *ijtihād* and the limitation of the the *ijmāʿ* to that of the *ṣaḥāba*. See Preckel, *Islamische Bildungsnetzwerke*, p. 332 and Riexinger, *Sanāʾullāh Amritsarī*, p. 149, and idem: Legalist Sufis and Sufi Legalists in British India, in: Alfonso Carmona (ed.): *El Sufismo y las Normas del Islam. Trabajados del IV Congreso Internacional des Estudios Jurídicos Islámicos. Derecho y Sufismo*, Murcia 2006, pp. 409–420.

88 Al-Qārī, ʿAlī: *Shiyam al-ʿawāriḍ fī dhamm al-Rawāfiḍ* (The Noble Character Against the Shia); see Brockelmann, *Geschichte der arabischen Litteratur*, vol. 2, p. 395, no. 40, Ṣiddīq Ḥasan's library no. 87.

89 Ṣiddīq Ḥasan Khān, *Ḥujaj al-kirāma,* pp. 232–233, quoting Ibn Taymiyya through al-Qārī. Here, he focuses on al-Qārī's books on the prohibition of *mawlid* celebrations, *al-Mawrid al-rabawī fī al-mawlid al-nabawī*, which, however, was not in Ṣiddīq Ḥasan's library.

90 Nadwi, Abul Hasan Ali: *Saviours of Islamic Spirit*, Lucknow 1993 (1st English ed.), p. 125, here vol. 4, *Hakim-ul-Islam Shah Waliullah*, p. 125. Nadwi, who was head of the famous Muslim institution and Islamic university of *Nadwat al-ʿulamāʾ*, Lucknow, is regarded as one of the most prolific Islamic scholars of 20th-century India and often co-operated with Saudi scholars in the Muslim World League (*Rābiṭat al-ʿālam al-islāmī*). He was one of the founding figures of

In the same work, Nadwī suggests that there was a "successive chain of reformers and revivalists from Shaikh ul-Islam Ibn Taimiyah to Hakīm-ul-Islām Shāh Waliullah" and from Shāh Walī Allāh down to the Ahl-i Ḥadīth. Indeed, there is a transmission of Ḥanbalī literature that was prevalent in certain scholarly circles. Scholars belonging to these networks increasingly produced literature containing Ḥanbalī ideas or referring to Hadith texts from Ḥanbalī collections or from collections that were composed by some cherished individual representatives of other schools of law. These networks often used the same (Ḥanbalī and Hadith) books. Sometimes, as in the case of the Ahl-i Ḥadīth, the scholarly networks even became institutionalised in new *madrasas* and organisations. Scholars with a strong focus on Hadith studies who were critical of *taqlīd* founded their own religious schools (Arab. pl. *madāris*). In these *madrasas*, students shared their teacher's attitude that all transmitted sciences (*manqūlāt*) were important. Clearly, the greatest number of teaching permits were issued in the field of Hadith, linking the Indian strands of transmission with the Yemenite ones. Thus, the number of Hadith teachers and students grew constantly. Likewise, many new schools that can be called *Ahl-i ḥadīth madāris* were established, most of them in Delhi, Benares or Bhopal.

We have some information on Ṣiddīq Ḥasan's teaching permits. Here we can see two lines of transmission of Ḥanbalī literature relevant for the early Ahl-i Ḥadīth:[91]

i. The Indian strand of transmission beginning with Abū Ṭāhir Shāh Walī Allāh; scholars of the *Madrasa-yi Raḥīmiyya* in Delhi; Shāh Walī Allāh's grandson Muḥammad Ismāʿīl Shahīd; Ṣiddīq Ḥasan Khān's father, Sayyid Awlād Ḥasan, up to Ṣiddīq Ḥasan Khān.
ii. The Arab/Yemenite strand of transmission from the scholars Muḥammad al-Amīr al-Yamanī; Muḥammad al-Shawkānī; his

---

this famous international organization. Nadwi's personal networks also link him to Ṣiddīq Ḥasan Khān and Ḥasan Khān's sons Sayyid Nūr al-Ḥasan Khān and ʿAlī Ḥasan Khān. After their father's death, they settled in Lucknow (in a palace that is called "Bhopal House" to the present day) and held important positions at the *Nadwat al-ʿulamāʾ*. They donated Ṣiddīq Ḥasan's library to the Shibli Library in the Nadwa in Lucknow, where it is preserved to this day. For more intersections between Nadwi's networks, those of the Wahhabiyya, and the Ahl-i Ḥadīth, see Hartung, *Viele Wege und ein Ziel*, pp. 337–360. For a general account of the *Nadwat al-ʿulamāʾ*, see Malik, Jamal: *Islamische Gelehrtenkultur in Nordindien. Entwicklungsgeschichte und Tendenzen am Beispiel von Lucknow*, Leiden 1997.

91 Ṣiddīq Ḥasan Khān, *Silsilat al-ʿasjad*, pp. 2–88.

students, notably Nāṣir al-Ḥāzimī, ʿAbd al-Ḥaqq Banārsī, ʿAbd al-Qayyūm Buḍhānawī and Ḥusayn b. Muḥsin al-Yamanī (living in Bhopal) finally to Ṣiddīq Ḥasan Khān.

Ṣiddīq Ḥasan considered the second one of these, the Yemenite connection, the most important. This is shown by the fact that he asked his teacher Ḥusayn b. Muḥsin to write down his chain of transmission (*isnād*) and thus could easily link himself with the Yemenite scholars. The documents of these chains of transmission and of Ḥusayn's teaching license are still kept in Lucknow.[92]

5.2. Ṣiddīq Ḥasan Khān and Al-Shawkānī's *Nayl al-awṭār*

Ṣiddīq Ḥasan Khān's writings hint at his sources of inspiration. In his book *al-Maqāla al-fasīḥa* (The Pure Speech), Ṣiddīq Ḥasan stressed that he received his inspiration from "*Aḥāmid wa-Maḥāmid*", i.e. from some Aḥmads and Muḥammads. In his work on Ṣiddīq Ḥasan Khān, Saeedullah provides a list of who those people were: [Taqı al-Dīn] Aḥmad Ibn Taymiyya, Aḥmad Shāh Walī Allāh, Aḥmad Barēlwī, Muḥammad b. ʿAlī al-Shawkānī, Muḥammad Ismāʿīl "Shahīd" (d. 1832) and Muḥammad al-Amīr al-Yamanī (d. 1769).[93] Indeed, works by all these authors are found in Ṣiddīq Ḥasan's own oeuvre.

Ṣiddīq Ḥasan's own compositions focus strongly on al-Shawkānī's writings. Ṣiddīq Ḥasan considered al-Shawkānī's method of basing legal decisions on the corpus of Hadith as the right one. Thus, he drew much inspiration from al-Shawkānī's major work *Nayl al-awṭār sharḥ Muntaqā al-akhbār min aḥādīth Sayyid al-Akhyār* (Fulfilment of Wishes, Commentary on Selection of Messages from the Sayings of the Lord of the Virtuous Ones, i. e. the Prophet), which Ṣiddīq Ḥasan considered his most important source of inspiration. *Muntaqā al-akhbār*[94] had been written by ʿAbd al-Salām Ibn Taymiyya (d. 1254), who was the grandfather of the more famous Taqī al-Dīn Ibn Taymiyya and also a Ḥanbalī scholar. His *Muntaqā al-akhbār* belongs to a certain

92 Al-Anṣārī, Ḥusayn b. Muḥsin: *Asānīd al-Shaykh Ḥusayn Ibn Muḥsin*, manuscript, Lucknow, Maulana Shibli Library, Nadwat ul-ʿUlama, *radīf* 607. See idem: *al-Ijāza li-Sayyid Ṣiddīq Ḥasan Khān*, manuscript, Lucknow, Maulana Shibli Library, Nadwat ul-ʿUlama, addition to *radīf* 401.

93 Quoted by Saeedullah, *Life and Works*, p. 36.

94 Brockelmann, *Geschichte der arabischen Litteratur*, vol. 1, p. 399, suppl. 1, p. 6.

category of Hadith, namely classified (*muṣannaf*) Hadith works. This means that this Hadith material is arranged in accordance with certain topics. These works thereby made it easier to find relevant Hadith material for the process of issuing a fatwa. The pious juridically relevant reports compiled in such a collection are called *aḥādīth al-aḥkām*. In Bhopal, ʿAbd al-Salām Ibn Taymiyya's *Muntaqā al-akhbār* was the most popular collection of jurisprudential traditions. It contained the traditions relevant to Islamic law that are contained in the six major collections of Hadith (*al-ummahāt al-sitta* or *al-kutub al-sitta*).[95] ʿAbd al-Salām Ibn Taymiyya mostly chose the traditions taken from the collections of al-Bukhārī or Aḥmad b. Ḥanbal (the latter's Hadith collection does not belong to "the six books"). Ṣiddīq Ḥasan Khān, however, preferred al-Shawkānī's *Nayl al-awṭār*, because al-Shawkānī was more able to differentiate between sound traditions and dubious ones. *Nayl al-awṭār* and other commentaries became very popular teaching materials, especially in Yemen and in India.[96] Ṣiddīq Ḥasan considered the *Nayl al-awṭār* so important that he gave an account of a dream in which al-Shawkānī granted him and Ṣiddīq Ḥasan teaching permits for this work. In his *al-Tāj al-mukallal* he wrote that he received a "direct" permission without any other persons/teachers in the chain of transmission (*bi-lā wāṣita*).[97] The dream thus provides considerable authentification. It is also a proof of blessing (*tabarruk*) for the dreamer. Ṣiddīq Ḥasan repeatedly saw not only al-Shawkānī in his dreams for a period of more than three years, but also the Prophet Muḥammad, who told him to perform his pilgrimage to Mecca. It is noteworthy that the Ahl-i Ḥadīth did not criticize these dreams, although they did not believe in the miraculous power of the dead. The reason for their acceptance might be the widespread role of dreams in Islam.[98] Obviously Ṣiddīq Ḥasan Khān wanted to establish a direct link to

95 These works are *al-Jāmiʿ al-ṣaḥīḥ* by Abū ʿAbd Allāh Muḥammad al-Bukhārī; *Ṣaḥīḥ Muslim* by Abū al-Ḥusayn Muslim b. Ḥajjāj; *Jāmiʿ Tirmidhī* by Abū ʿĪsā Muḥammad al-Tirmidhī; *Sunan Ibn Māja* by Ibn Māja al-Qazwīnī; *Sunan Nasāʾī* by ʿAbd al-Raḥmān al-Nasāʾī and *Sunan Abī Daʾūd* by Abū Daʾūd al-Sijistānī.

96 Al-Amri, The Yemen in the 18th and 19th Centuries, p. 174.

97 Ṣiddīq Ḥasan Khān, *al-Tāj al-mukallal*, pp. 449–450.

98 On the role of dreams in Islam, see Jedrej, Marian Charles and Shaw, Rosalind (eds.): *Dreaming, Religion, and Society in Africa*, Leiden 1993 and Hermansen, Marcia K.: Dreams and Dreaming in Islam, in: Kelly Bulkeley (ed.): *Dreams. A Reader in the Religious, Cultural and Psychological Dimensions of Dreaming*, New York 2001, pp. 73–110; Bulkeley, Kelly: *Dreaming in the World Religions*, New York 2008; on Islam see pp. 192–199, on "dream *ijāzāt*" see p. 199.

al-Shawkānī either in his personal network or in his chain of transmission. It was not sufficient for him to be "the pupil of al-Shawkānī's pupils", he also wanted a direct link to al-Shawkānī.

6. Topical Influences by Ibn Taymiyya and Ibn al-Qayyim

Searching for strictly Ḥanbalī writings in Ṣiddīq Ḥasan's library of more than 600 works, we can identify at least 28 monographs, mainly those by Ibn Taymiyya and Ibn al-Qayyim. It has been shown how Ṣiddīq Ḥasan's personal networks – including his educational ones – have had a significant influence on the Indian reception of Ibn Taymiyya's oeuvre. The following topical influences of Ibn Taymiyya and Ibn al-Qayyim on Ṣiddīq Ḥasan Khān are the most important: (i) Sunni creed in theology, (ii) insistence on *ijtihād* and rejection of *taqlīd*, (iii) critique of instant divorce, (iv) un-Islamic novelties and apocalyptic fear, (v) critique of polytheism, (vi) the veneration of graves.

6.1. Sunni Creed in Theology

All in all, 17 students from what is today Saudi Arabia – most of them from the central highland region of Najd – are reported to have studied from the late 1870s to 1900 with Indian Ahl-i Ḥadīth scholars, mainly in Delhi, Bombay and Bhopal. Not until the 1920s were discussions about the legitimacy of studies in foreign countries begun. Wahhabi scholars issued several fatwas claiming that it was not permissible to study "in the lands of the polytheists" (*mushrikūn*).[99] Interestingly in this context, the Wahhabis regarded primarily the Ottoman lands as a place of the *mushrikūn* – and not India, where the Muslims had only a minority status. With the beginning of Saudi Arabia as a nation state, the Wahhabiyya also had the resources to set up new universities, printing presses and possibilities to finance education. Since then, Indian students have been travelling to Saudi Arabia. Ahl-i Ḥadīth members used to study at the Islamic University in Medina. Whereas at the end of the 19th century, the Indians could exert considerable influence on the Najdīs, it is the other way round today. Since the 1930s, the Ahl-i Ḥadīth, although still against *taqlīd* and adherence to only a single

99 Steinberg, *Religion und Staat*, pp. 163–165 et passim.

school of law, have often relied on fatwas from Saudi-Arabian scholars, who are adherents of the Ḥanbalī school of law. A close look at these Saudi scholars who are now quoted by Ahl-i Ḥadīth scholars shows that they often refer to Ibn Taymiyya.[100]

Ibn Taymiyya was eager to spread his interpretation not only of Muslim law but also of what he considered the "real Sunni creed". Some of his works contain the expression "dogmatics" (*ʿaqīda*) and are written in response to the request of petitioners from a certain city, for example, for two Syrian towns, *al-ʿAqīda al-ḥamawiyya al-kubrā* (The Great Creed of Hama), *al-ʿAqīda al-tadmuriyya* (The Creed of Palmyra) and, for an Iraqi town on the Tigris, *al-ʿAqīda al-wāsiṭiyya* (The Creed of Wasit). These late medieval writings later became relevant for the instruction of the Arabian Wahhabiyya as well as the Ahl-i Ḥadīth. Ṣiddīq Ḥasan owned several manuscripts and printed copies of all three works.

6.1.1. Ibn Taymiyya's ʿAqīda wāsiṭiyya

Among the three *ʿaqīda* works mentioned, *al-ʿAqīda al-wāsiṭiyya*,[101] was especially widely used for the purpose of instruction. The main reason for this is that it was relatively easy to understand. Its composi-

100 For example, the book by the famous Salafi Nāṣir al-Dīn al-Albānī (d. 1999): *The Prayer as Offered by Allah's Messenger* (*Kitāb Ṣifāt ṣalāṭ al-nabī*), *translated from Arabic into English by the Ahl-i Ḥadīth scholar A. Q. Naqvi*, published by the Maktaba-yi Tarjumān, Delhi 2002, is full of quotations of Ibn al-Qayyim and Ibn Taymiyya (e.g. pp. 124, 127, 129). In his introduction, Naqvi compared al-Albānī to Ibn Taymiyya, because both of them "were thrown behind the prison bars". The maybe most visible network link between the Ahl-i Ḥadīth and the Wahhabiyya was that created by Masʿūd ʿĀlam Nadwī (d. 1954), who wrote a famous book on the founder of the Wahhabiyya. The book has been re-published since its first publication in the 1940s; Nadwī, Masʿūd ʿĀlam: *Ibn ʿAbd al-Wahhāb, Muḥammad. Ek maẓlūm awr bad-nām muṣliḥ* (A Wrongfully Treated and Defamed Reformer), Lahore n.d. The book was also translated into English by Muhammad Rafiq Khan and published under the title *Mohammad Bin Abdul Wahhab. A Slandered Reformer*, Benraris 1982. The book contains numerous quotations from Ibn Taymiyya, e.g. pp. 11, 95, 98 and in the bibliography.

101 For a short introduction and an English translation, see Swartz, Merlin: A Seventh-century (A.H.) Sunni Creed. The *ʿAqīda wāsiṭiyya* of Ibn Taymīya, in: *Humaniora Islamica* 1 (1973), pp. 91–131. A French translation was made by Henri Laoust, see Ibn Taymiyya: *La profession de foi d'Ibn Taymiyya. Texte, traduction et commentaire de la Wāsiṭiyya*, Paris 1986.

tion and style of language were not as complex as in the other *ʿaqīda* treatises mentioned before. It also differs from other monographs of the same category in that it observes the principle of *wasaṭ*, "the golden mean". Ibn Taymiyya applied this principle of *wasaṭ* notably in his explanation of the attributes of God (*ṣifāt allāh*). Here, Ibn Taymiyya stressed that neither anthropomorphism nor the negation of the divine attributes was the correct way to deal with this subject. Another important aspect of the *ʿAqīda wāsiṭiyya* was the growing sectarianism of the Muslim community (*umma*) and the existence of various sects and groups aberrant from the straight path of Sunni Islam. It is also worth mentioning that *al-ʿAqīda al-wāsiṭiyya* did not contain any hints or references to the Ḥanbalī school of law. This confirms Ibn Taymiyya's claim to speak generally for Sunni Islam as *al-firqa al-nājiya*, the group of Muslims who are saved from hellfire. Because of its selection of subjects, Ibn Taymiyya's *ʿAqīda wāsiṭiyya* was of special interest for the Arabian Wahhabiyya. Being quite short, it has represented an ideal medium for instruction, also for the Ahl-i Ḥadīth. Ṣiddīq Ḥasan especially supported Ibn Taymiyya's views on the endangered umma and his criticism that groups, like certain Sufis and the Shia, were sectarians.

6.1.2. *Al-ʿAqīda al-ḥamawiyya al-kubrā*

A close look at the groups Ibn Taymiyya refuted in his works shows that his opponents resemble those of the Ahl-i Ḥadīth: one of Ibn Taymiyya's main aims in *al-ʿAqīda al-ḥamawiyya al-kubrā* was to criticise the scholars of rationally inspired theology (*kalām*), the *mutakallimūn*. In several of his own works, Ṣiddīq Ḥasan[102] declared that he did not want *kalām* and logic (*manṭiq*) to be included in Islamic curricula because *kalām* "was full of speculation" introduced by scholars of "Greek philosophy".[103] In his view, the works of Aristotle and Plato had been completely misunderstood by Muslim, especially Iranian philosophers. The consequence was that the principle of the unity of God (*tawḥīd*) was constantly violated.[104] Because of all these aberrations and innovations (Pers. *mulḥida o-mubtadiʿa*), the teaching of *kalām* was not necessary (Pers. *ghayr-i ḍarūrī*). Another concern of

102 E.g. Ṣiddīq Ḥasan Khān, *Abjad al-ʿulūm*, part 2, p. 452.
103 On this topic, see also the article by Anke von Kügelgen in the present volume.
104 Ṣiddīq Ḥasan Khān, *Abjad al-ʿulūm*, part 2, p. 452 and Sayf, *Taḥrīk-i Ahl-i ḥadīth*, p. 198.

al-ʿAqīda al-ḥamawiyya al-kubrā taken up by Ṣiddīq Ḥasan was Ibn Taymiyya's criticism of the Ashʿariyya, although Ṣiddīq Ḥasan did not follow Ibn Taymiyya on this point. The reason may have been that the Ashʿarīs were often associated with the Shāfiʿī school of law, to which the Bhopal Yemenites' fatwas showed a leaning. Al-Shawkānī likewise displayed a certain affinity to the Shāfiʿī school of law. The Māturīdiyya, on the other hand, was traditionally associated with the Ḥanafī school of law, which constituted the main opponent of the Ahl-i Ḥadīth. In the eyes of the Ahl-i Ḥadīth, the optimal position was that of the Ḥanbalīs, who declined any kind of interpretive speculation (*taʾwīl*) about God's characteristics. In *Ḥujaj al-kirāma*,[105] Ṣiddīq Ḥasan wrote that he took a close look at the differences between the Māturīdiyya, Ashʿariyya and Ḥanbaliyya. He claims to have realized that there were only three or four differences between the Ashʿariyya and Ḥanbaliyya – but without naming them in detail. These were merely "practical" divergences (*khilāf-i taṭbīq*) and differences in terminology (*nizāʿ-yi lafẓī*), which were of minor importance.[106] Ṣiddīq Ḥasan did not mention the Māturīdiyya in this specific context, and he did not possess a single work by a Māturīdī. In this regard, he did not follow the recommendations of al-Shawkānī, who had instructed future *mujtahids* to study books from every school of *kalām* because each of them would be able to refute the works of one's opponents.[107]

6.1.3. *Najdī Wahhābīs' Reactions to Ibn al-Qayyim's* Nūniyya

The Ahl-i Ḥadīth used to study another *ʿaqīda* work that was considered much more complicated than the others and that was also controversially discussed, *al-Kāfiya al-shāfiya fī al-intiṣār al-firqa al-nājiya* (The Sufficient and Salutary Concerning the Triumph of the Rescued Group)[108] by Ibn Qayyim al-Jawziyya. This work, which is composed as a poem, rhyming on the Arabic letter N (*nūn*), has also become known as the *Nūniyya*. It discusses some attributes of God and refutes

105 Ṣiddīq Ḥasan Khān, *Ḥujaj al-kirāma*, p. 122.

106 Ibid., pp. 122–123, chapter on the "truth about the Ashʿariyya". He strictly avoids the discussion on the divergences between Ashʿariyya and Ḥanbaliyya, but it becomes clear that he favoured a kind of synthesis between those positions. For similar statements see Riexinger, *Sanāʾullāh Amritsarī*, pp. 153–154.

107 Haykel, *Revival and Reform*, p. 125.

108 Brockelmannn, *Geschichte der arabischen Litteratur*, vol. 2, p. 106.

the idea of the unity of being (*waḥdat al-wujūd*) of Ibn ʿArabī (d. 1240). Even scholars who spoke Arabic as their mother tongue seemed to have difficulties understanding the *Nūniyya*.[109] Nevertheless, the Indian scholar Ṣiddīq Ḥasan Khān was requested to write a commentary on the *Nūniyya*. The man who asked him to do so was Ḥamad b. ʿAtīq (d. 1884) from al-Aflāj in the Najd. Ḥamad b. ʿAtīq belonged to one of the most prolific scholarly families of the Najd, the Āl al-ʿAtīq, who had been closely connected to the Wahhabiyya.[110] In his letter[111] (written ca. 1880), Ḥamad b. ʿAtīq praised Ṣiddīq Ḥasan Khān for his role as one of the leading scholars of his time. He stressed that the times were hard for strict believers of Islam. He complained that sound knowledge on Islam had vanished and that crime, corruption and polytheism were prevalent even in the heartlands of Islam. Only the continuous efforts of persons like the Nawwāb of Bhopal preserved honesty on earth. He added that Muslims should be glad God had sent someone like Ṣiddīq Ḥasan to guarantee the proper guidance for all believers. After these initial lines, Ḥamad b. ʿAtīq changed the tone of his letter and began to criticise Ṣiddīq Ḥasan Khān for some "mistakes" in his *Tafsīr Fatḥ al-bayān*.[112] He added that this might be because "Ṣiddīq Ḥasan did not have the time to correct the manuscript."[113] For whatever reasons Ḥamad claimed that Ṣiddīq Ḥasan's *tafsīr* contained too many unfounded speculations, his main criticism was that Ṣiddīq Ḥasan used inappropriate human characteristics to describe God, e.g. he ascribed mercy (*raḥma*) to God, which Ḥamad b. ʿAtīq considered a human characteristic. The second point of criticism was Ṣiddīq Ḥasan's interpretation of the Koranic verses referring to God sitting on the throne (*thumma istawāʾ ʿalā ʿarsh*), for example (Koran 10:3), meaning "then he (God) sat down on his throne". There was no discussion between Ṣiddīq Ḥasan[114] and the Najdis about the question whether *istiwāʾ*

109 Steinberg, *Religion und Staat*, pp. 90–91. On the *Nūniyya*, see also the article by Livnat Holtzman in this volume.

110 Steinberg, *Religion und Staat*, pp. 119, 203–206.

111 The text of the letter can be found in Āl al-Shaykh, ʿAbd al-Raḥmān b. ʿAbd al-Laṭīf: *Mashāhīr ʿulamāʾ Najd wa-ghayrihim*, Riyadh 1394/1974, pp. 245–253.

112 Ṣiddīq Ḥasan Khān, Muḥammad: *Fatḥ al-bayān fī maqāṣid al-qurʾān*, Bulāq 1884–85.

113 Āl al-Shaykh, *Mashāhīr ʿulamāʾ Najd*, p. 247.

114 Ṣiddīq Ḥasan Khān wrote his *Iḥtiwāʾ fī masʾalat al-istiwāʾ* (Contents on the Question of God Sitting on His Throne), Lahore 1294/1874. It was not available to me.

should be interpreted other than "sitting on the throne". God's attributes must be characterised as they were described in the Koran, they had to be accepted without any qualification (*bi-lā kayf*). In accordance with Ibn Taymiyya and following Aḥmad b. Ḥanbal, scholars of the Wahhabiyya further interpret that *istiwāʾ* is not identical with *istīlāʾ* (capture or seizure) or *qahr* (force or power), but simply means "sitting". The Wahhabiyya keeps up the view that "the quality of the *istiwāʾ* is unknown, the belief in it is obligatory, and questioning its nature is a *bidʿa*".[115] Ḥamad b. ʿAtīq criticised that Ṣiddīq Ḥasan interpreted the word *thumma* in Koran (10:3) as "and then" because this would mean that time was relevant to God. Instead, he said that *thumma* in this case was not a sign for a certain order, but a simple conjunction.[116] Thus, Ṣiddīq Ḥasan should interpret it as simply "and" (*wa*). After eliminating these mistakes, Ṣiddīq Ḥasan's Koran interpretation would be in accordance with famous scholars like Ibn Taymiyya or Ibn Ḥanbal. They had stated that in describing God, the only permissible terms are those already used by God himself or by his Prophet Muḥammad. Continuing his letter, Ḥamad b. ʿAtīq complained about the hard circumstances of the times they were living in. He described the difficulties scholars from the Najd faced in acquiring literature and books. Indeed, there was a considerable lack of scholarly literature in 19th-century Najd. There was also a lack of qualified teachers. So Ḥamad b. ʿAtīq asked Ṣiddīq Ḥasan whether he would accept his son Saʿd (1862–1930) as a student of Hadith. If Ṣiddīq Ḥasan accepted, Saʿd could start his journey to Bhopal within a short time. Indeed, Saʿd b. Ḥamad travelled to India in 1881. In his letters to his family, he com-

115 For a detailed view on this question see Ibn Bāz, ʿAbd al-ʿAzīz: *Bayān* of the *Madhhab ahl al-sunna fī al-istiwāʾ* (Explanation of the People of the Sunna's Teachings of the *istiwāʾ*), in: *Majallat al-Buḥūth al-Islāmiyya* 8 (1403/1983), pp. 169–172.

116 The interpretation of this Koranic verse also caused the famous Ahl-i Ḥadīth scholar Thanāʾullāh Amritsarī problems within his own movement. In addition to his position on the *istiwāʾ* the scholars of the famous Ghaznawī family, who had a dense commercial network in today's Saudi Arabia, referred to his denial of certain Koranic miracles and his neglect of the exegetical traditions to bolster their claim that he was a heretic. For this controversy, see Riexinger, *Sanāʾullāh Amritsarī*, pp. 338–417; idem: How Favourable is Puritan Islam to Modernity? A Case Study on the Ahl-i Hadis in British India, in: Gwilym Beckerlegge (ed.): *Colonialism, Modernity and Religious Identities. Religious Reform Movements in South Asia*, New Delhi and New York 2008, pp. 147–165.

plained about the difficulties and obstacles on his journey.[117] Later, he seemed to have changed his mind and gave very positive accounts of his studies in India and his teachers. After his return to Saudi Arabia, Saʿd b. Ḥamad b. ʿAtīq became kadi of Riyadh. He issued many fatwas against the "cult at the graves", in which he frequently quoted Ṣiddīq Ḥasan Khān. This might also be why his letters and fatwas were even translated into Urdu.[118]

Nevertheless, Ṣiddīq Ḥasan Khān did not write any commentary on the *Nūniyya*. One of his network partners, Aḥmad b. ʿĪsā (d. 1909),[119] a renowned bookseller and defender of the Wahhabiyya, undertook this task. Aḥmad Ibn ʿĪsā was Ṣiddīq Ḥasan Khān's agent (*wakīl*) in Mecca. They were not teacher and student nor did they ever meet personally. Aḥmad had been only responsible for buying and selling books. After Ṣiddīq Ḥasan's deposition, their network relationship ended.

6.2. Insistence on *ijtihād* and Rejection of *taqlīd*

As demonstrated, Ṣiddīq Ḥasan's study of Yemenite literature deeply influenced him and modified his legal views and religious outlook. Whereas he had formerly drawn much inspiration from Indian reformist authors like Muḥammad Ḥayāt al-Sindī (d. 1750),[120] Shāh Walī Allāh Dihlawī, and Thanāʾullāh Pānīpatī (d. 1810),[121] this immediately changed after his contact with Arab scholars during his pilgrimage to Mecca. The three Indian authors favoured by him had been educated in the tradition of the Ḥanafī school of law, but later in their lives came

117 Ismāʿīl b. Saʿd b. Ḥamad b. ʿAtīq: "Muqaddima" (Introduction) to Ibn ʿAtīq, al-Shaykh Saʿd b. Ḥamad: *al-Majmūʿ* (The Beneficial Collection of Letters and Fatwas of Shaykh Saʿd b. Ḥamad b. ʿAtīq), Riyadh 1415/1995.

118 Published in Lahore (Ibn Taymiyya Akāḍēmī) 1976.

119 Āl al-Shaykh, *Mashāhīr ʿulamāʾ al-Najd*, pp. 260–264.

120 On him, see Voll, John O.: Muḥammad Ḥayyā al-Sindī and Muḥammad Ibn ʿAbd al-Wahhāb. An Analysis of an Intellectual Group in 18th-century Medina, in: *Bulletin of the School of Oriental and African Studies* 38 (1975), pp. 32–39.

121 Thanāʾullāh Pānīpatī was a pupil of Shāh Walī Allāh. The Ahl-i Ḥadīth consider him a critic of the *taqlīd*. Consequently, his biography can be found in several collections of Ahl-i Ḥadīth members, see e.g. Sayf, *Taḥrīk-i Ahl-i ḥadīth*, pp. 178–180. For an English biography and assessment of this works see Alvi, Sajida: Qāẓī Sanāʾ Allāh Pānīpatī. An Eighteenth-Century *ṣufī ʿālim*; a Study of his Writings in their Sociopolitical Context, in: Wael B. Hallaq and Donald Little (eds.): *Islamic Studies Presented to Charles J. Adams*, Leiden 1991, pp. 11–26.

into contact with other influences, mostly during their pilgrimage to Mecca. Nevertheless, all of them remained supporters of the Ḥanafī school of law. Hence, the Ahl-i Ḥadīth acknowledged only them as their intellectual predecessors. This is mainly because of their interest in the study of Hadith though they cannot be considered as Ahl-i Ḥadīth in the narrow sense of this word, simply because they lived before the institutionalisation of the Ahl-i Ḥadīth in 1912. They never officially announced to have left the Ḥanafī school of law, and their interpretation of the *ijtihād*.

Muḥammad Ḥayāt al-Sindī, for example, never claimed to have left the Ḥanafī *madhhab*, but insisted on "finding a legal decision according to Hadith", called *ʿamal bil-ḥadīth* in Urdu. In contrast to him, Shāh Walī Allāh, who also claimed to have never left the Ḥanafī school of law, but gave different views on *ijtihād/taqlīd* in his numerous works. In his Arabic work *ʿIqd al-jīd fī aḥkām al-ijtihād wal-taqlīd* (The Necklace about the Rulings of the *ijtihād* and *taqlīd*),[122] Shāh Walī Allāh stressed the necessesity of the four schools of law, especially for the layman. Every Muslim needed guidance, and the fatwas of the mufti should likewise be the layman's guide. Every Muslim and especially the scholars should try to learn about the traditions. The exact transmission of the Hadith is of utmost importance. Therefore, there should be a close link between the disciplines of *fiqh* and Hadith, and the *ʿamal bil-ḥadīth* should be performed in each legal decision. In this point the Ahl-i Ḥadīth followed Shāh Walī Allāh. In his work *Ḥujjat Allāh al-bāligha*,[123] Shāh Walī Allāh further stated that the *ijtihād* is not a necessity in all times and for all Muslims, meaning that it is a duty which is fulfilled when parts of the umma do accomplish it (*farḍ kifāya*).[124] This meant that Shāh Walī Allāh held the qualified scholars to be responsible for the *ijtihād*. Following the famous Shāfiʿī schol-

122 Dihlawī, Shāh Walī Allāh: *ʿIqd al-jīd fī aḥkām al-ijtihād wal-taqlīd*, Bombay 1306/1889 (see Brockelmann, *Geschichte der arabischen Litteratur*, suppl. 2, p. 615). For this book see the partial translation by Rahbar, Mohammad Daud: Shah Waliullah and Ijtihad, in: *Muslim World* 45 (1955), pp. 346–358.

123 This paragraph is a summary of Dihlawī, Shāh Walī Allāh: *Ḥujjat Allāh al-bāligha*, part 1–2 (see Brockelmann, *Geschichte der arabischen Litteratur*, vol. 2, p. 418), suppl. 2, p. 615, especially part I, pp. 144–146 (chapter on the reasons for the differences of the schools of law) and pp. 147–152 (chapter on the difference between the *ahl al-ḥadīth* and the *ahl al-raʾy*). For several important quotations see Sayf, *Taḥrīk-i Ahl-i ḥadīth*, pp. 108, 197–199, 200–202.

124 For Shāh Walī Allāh's interpretation of this see Nadwi, *Saviours of Islamic Spirit*, vol. 4, pp. 42–43.

ar al-Nawawī, Shāh Walī Allāh developed four stages of the rank of *mujtahidūn*.[125] In contrast to Shāh Walī Allāh, scholars of the Ahl-i Ḥadīth considered the *ijtihād fī al-madhhab* to be a form of *taqlīd* and not acceptable. Following al-Shawkānī, they propagated the *ijtihād* for the layman. Although the Ahl-i Ḥadīth divergated in some points from the scholars mentioned above, they still consider them as their forefathers or first adherents.

The reception of the writings of al-Shawkānī meant a shift in the curricula of Indian Muslims. In India, works from the Yemenite tradition were not considered important before the late 19th century. Al-Shawkānī's insistence on *ijtihād* clearly challenged the dominant Ḥanafī concept of authority in interpreting the sources of law. Thus, the topic became also relevant for patronage by Muslim rulers. The question of following schools of law grew in significance during the disputes about the origins of the Ahl-i Ḥadīth. In 1881 and later in 1884/1885, Ṣiddīq Ḥasan was accused of being a staunch Wahhabi who wanted to instigate a jihad against the British in India and beyond. He was deprived of all his titles and personal influence, because the power of members of the Ahl-i Ḥadīth in the state administration was clearly restricted. When all these accusations against him became known to the public (even in London), Ṣiddīq Ḥasan Khān wrote a book titled *Tarjumān al-wahhābiyya* (Interpreter of the Wahhabiyya), in which he explained the history of the word Wahhabi in India. He further denied being a Wahhabi, because the Wahhabis "followed the school of Aḥmad b. Ḥanbal, whereas the Ahl-i Ḥadīth did not practice *taqlīd*".[126] Although Ibn Taymiyya is often regarded as a *muqallid* of the Ḥanbalī school of law, Ṣiddīq Ḥasan clearly states that he regards him as a renewer of the faith (*mujaddid*) and an "absolute *mujtahid*"

125 Shāh Walī Allāh listed the "independent absolute *mujtahid*" (*mujtahid muṭlaq mustaqill*). This rank was only to be given to the founders of the schools of law. After them the "affiliated absolute *mujtahid* " (*mujtahid muṭlaq muntasib*) and the *mujtahid al-fatwā* followed. According to Shāh Walī Allāh, those *mujtahids* are able to issue a fatwa, because they know the important texts of their own schools of law. For al-Nawawī see Calder, Norman: Al-Nawawi's Typology of *muftīs* and its Significance for a General Theory of Islamic Law, in: *Islamic Law and Society* 3 (1996), pp. 137–164. For the debates between the Ahl-i Ḥadīth and their opponents on this subject see Preckel, *Islamische Bildungsnetzwerke*, pp. 327–342.

126 Ṣiddīq Ḥasan stated that Muḥammad b. ʿAbd al-Wahhāb himself was a *muqallid* of Ibn Taymiyya. See Ṣiddīq Ḥasan Khān, Muḥammad: *Tarjumān al-Wahhābiyya*, Benares 1898, pp. 29–30.

(*mujtahid muṭlaq*). Benjamin Jokisch has shown in some detail that Ibn Taymiyya indeed practised *ijtihād*.[127] This made Ibn Taymiyya a scholar attractive to the Ahl-i Ḥadīth. Today's Ahl-i Ḥadīth have active contacts and exchange with scholars from Saudi Arabia who are adherents of the Ḥanbalī school of law.

The rejection of *taqlīd* and the method of deducting legal decisions from Hadiths (*al-ʿamal bil-ḥadīth*) became the most important issue for the further development of the Ahl-i Ḥadīth movement in general. However, the direct employment of Ḥanbalī works did not play an important role in this regard. Instead, mainly al-Shawkānī's works were translated or commentated: Ṣiddīq Ḥasan's Arabic work *al-Iqlīd li-adillat al-ijtihād wal-taqlīd* (The Key to the Proofs for *ijtihād* and *taqlīd*) is an abridgement of and commentary on al-Shawkānī's *al-Tashkīk ʿalā al-tafkīk* (Casting Doubts about *al-Tafkīk*).[128] His Hadith work *al-Fatḥ al-mughīth bi-fiqh al-ḥadīth* (The Helpful Victory in the Science of Hadith) is an Urdu translation of al-Shawkānī's *al-Durar al-bahiyya fī al-masāʾil al-fiqhiyya* (The Shining Pearls of the Questions of Islamic Law).[129] In his Arabic work *al-Rawḍa al-nadiyya* (The Lush Meadow), Ṣiddīq Ḥasan Khān commented extensively on *al-Durar al-bahiyya* again and stressed that he regarded it as al-Shawkānī's most important work in the discipline of *fiqh*. Further, his Arabic work *Ḥuṣūl al-maʾmūl min ʿilm al-uṣūl* (Attainment of the Hoped for in the Discipline of the Principles of Law) is a commentary upon and an abridgement of al-Shawkānī's *Irshād al-fuḥūl ilā taḥqīq al-ḥaqq min ʿilm al-uṣūl*[130] (Guidance of Mankind to the Verification of the Truth in the Science of Principles of Law) and *Fatḥ al-bayān fī al-maqāṣid al-Qurʾān* (Victory of Clearness on the Higher Objectives of the Koran) are in large parts a commentary on and an Urdu translation of al-Shawkānī's *Fatḥ al-qadīr fī uṣūl al-tafsīr* (Victory of the Almighty on the Principles of Koranic Exegesis). Thus, al-Shawkānī's influence on the Ahl-i Ḥadīth was extremely prevalent in these works on *uṣūl al-fiqh*, which discuss *ijtihād* and *taqlīd*. The main differences

---

127 Jokisch, Benjamin: *Ijtihād* in Ibn Taymiyya's *fatāwā*, in: Robert Gleave and Eugenia Kermeli (eds.): *Islamic Law. Theory and Practice*, London and New York 1997, pp. 119–137, here pp. 120, 129.

128 Brockelmann, *Geschichte der arabischen Litteratur*, suppl. 2, p. 819. It might be supposed that *Tafkīk* is the title of a book, but this could not be clarified. See ibid., vol. 2, p. 433 with insufficient bibliographical hints.

129 Ibid., suppl. 2, p. 818.

130 Ibid.

between the Ahl-i Ḥadīth and the Ḥanafīs are in this field of Islamic law.

Two juridical topics, the outward style of ritual prayer and triple divorce, played a major role in public debates. The Ahl-i Ḥadīth supported the style of prayer that they considered the "Prophet's prayer". They stressed the "raising of the hands" (*rafʿ al-yadayn*), in which the believer raises his hands to his ears at the beginning of the prayer, praises Allāh (*takbīrat al-iḥrām*), while bowing down (*rukūʿ*), raising his head and after bowing down. According to the Ahl-i Ḥadīth, this was the exact method of the Prophet; the Mālikīs, Ḥanbalīs and Shāfiʿīs prayed in this way. The Ḥanafīs, on the other hand, promoted raising the hands only at the beginning of the prayer.[131] As Maribel Fierro has shown, the discussion of the "correct" style of prayer dated back to fifth-/tenth-century Andalus, where the Mālikīs discussed the *rafʿ al-yadayn* within their own school of law.[132] In the English translation of al-Albānī's book on the prophet's prayer, the translator/commentator A.Q. Naqvi mentioned the Mālikīs practice of the *rafʿ al-yadayn*.[133] The Mālikīs also debated the question of *sadl*,[134] which is holding one's hands at one's sides instead of folding them over the navel or lifting them (*rafʿ al-yadayn*). Another question was where to cross the hands during prayer: below the navel (as the Ḥanafīs did) or on the chest (as the Ahl-i Ḥadīth did). The third problem was whether to speak the amen (*āmīn*) aloud (*bil-jahr*) or silently (*khāfī*). The Ahl-i Ḥadīth claimed that at least ten traditions supported the amen aloud.[135] The

---

131 The necessity of the *rafʿ al-yadayn* is stressed to the present day. Specifically on this issue, see Allāhābādī, Raḥmat Allāh Rabbānī: *Masʾalat rafʿ al-yadayn maʿ āmīn bil-jahr*, Delhi 1983.

132 Fierro, Maribel: La polémique à propos de rafʿ al-yadain fī l-ṣalāt dans al-Andalus, in: *Studia Islamica* 65 (1987), pp. 69–90, here esp. pp. 73–80. Fierro does not claim that the dispute had originated there, instead she refers to Kufa and Medina (ibid., pp. 77–79). In fact already the early Ḥanafīs in Iraq and Transoxania rejected the *rafʿ al-yadayn* and occasionally even persecuted those who practised it, i.e. the *ahl al-ḥadīth*. See also van Ess, Josef: *Theologie und Gesellschaft im 2. und 3. Jahrhundert Hidschra*, vol. 2, Berlin 1991, pp. 533–535, 566.

133 Al-Albānī, *The Prayer*, pp. 51, 122.

134 Dutton, Yasin: *ʿAmal* v. *ḥadīth* in Islamic Law. The Case of *sadl al-yadayn* (Holding One's Hands by One's Sides) When Doing the Prayer, in: *Islamic Law and Society* 3 (1996), pp. 13–40, here pp. 29–33.

135 For the Ahl-i Ḥadīth point of view on all three questions, see al-Anṣārī, Ḥusayn b. Muḥsin: *Nūr al-ʿayn min fatāwā Shaykh Ḥusayn*, Lucknow [?] 1339/1921, pp. 148–152.

reason for these debates was the question of authenticity and to demonstrate one's familiarity with the life, practice and utterings of the Prophet. The discussion often even resulted in riots in several Indian cities, as the Ḥanafīs dispelled the Ahl-i Ḥadīth from their mosques.[136] The Ahl-i Ḥadīth therefore started to build new mosques throughout North India and from the 1870s onwards claimed that Ahl-i Ḥadīth members should not pray behind a Ḥanafī *imam*.[137] Moreover, the Ahl-i Ḥadīth demanded that men and women should bend their hands on the chest or at the height of their navels (*nāf ūpar*), whereas the Ḥanafīs said that only men should do so. Further debates between the Ahl-i Ḥadīth and the Deobandīs arose on the question about the legitimacy of the Friday prayer (*jumʿa*). The Ḥanafīs claim that *jumʿa* could only be held in towns with a congregational mosque (*masjid-i jāmiʿ*). The Ahl-i Ḥadīth claimed that Friday prayers should be held even in villages with a small Muslim population. They kept the view that the number of believers in such a prayer was not fixed in Islamic traditions, and thus the *jumʿa* can be regarded as valid with e. g. three or four believers. Another question that arose between the Ahl-i Ḥadīth and the Ḥanafīs was that of the language of the sermon during the *jumʿa*, called *khuṭba*. Whereas the Ḥanafīs said that a *khuṭba* should only be held in Arabic, the Ahl-i Ḥadīth accept sermons either in Arabic, Persian or Urdu.

6.3. Triple Divorce

The second controversy between Ahl-i Ḥadīth and the Ḥanafīs (again including especially the Deobandīs) concerned divorce.[138] It is cor-

---

136 Metcalf, *Islamic Revival*, p. 152; see also Riexinger, *Sanāʾullāh Amritsarī*, pp. 165–167.

137 Ibid., pp. 275, 282.

138 On this subject in general, see Rapoport, Yossef: Ibn Taymiyya on Divorce Oaths, in: Michael Winter and Amalia Levanoni (eds.): *The Mamluks in Egyptian and Syrian Politics and Society*, Leiden and Boston 2004, pp. 191–217; and idem: *Marriage, Money and Divorce in Medieval Islamic Society*, Cambridge 2005; El Azhary Sonbol, Amira: *Women, the Family, and Divorce Laws in Islam*, Syracuse 1996. On India, see Ahmad, Furqan: *Triple talaq. An Analytical Study*, New Delhi 1994; Ahmad, Furqan and Ali, Firasat: *Divorce in Mohammedan Law. The Law of "Triple Divorce"*, New Delhi 1988; and the volume by Ahmad, Imtiaz (ed.): *Divorce and Remarriage Among Muslims in India*, New Delhi 2003.

rect that, according to Koran and Sunna, divorce is permitted, but not pleasing to Allah. Islamic law distinguishes between divorce in accordance to the Sunna (*ṭalāq-i sunnat*) and the *ṭalāq-i bidʿat*, meaning "divorce that is an unlawful innovation to Islam". There are two types of permissible *ṭalāq-i sunnat*: the "best divorce" (*ṭalāq-i aḥsan*) means that the husband pronounces the formula "you are free" (*anti ṭāliq*) once. After the period of waiting (*ʿidda*), which lasts for three menstrual cycles (*qurūʾ*), the husband decides whether to revoke the divorce, in which case the marriage is still valid.

The second type of *ṭalāq-i sunnat* is the "the approved divorce" (*ṭalāq-i ḥasan*). The husband pronounces the formula of *ṭalāq* once during a period of purity (*ṭuhr*) of his wife. The period of waiting (*ʿidda*) starts, and no sexual intercourse is allowed. Most scholars agree that the period in this case lasts only one month. If the husband does not want to take back his decision, and the woman is in the state of purity, the process starts again. Until the end of the third *ʿidda* is over, the divorce is revocable. After the third pronouncement of *ṭalāq* the divorce is valid and the woman has to leave the husband's home. If the husband seeks reconciliation, a new marriage ceremony (*nikāḥ*) has to be performed, including the payment of a dowry (*mahr*).

The Ahl-i Ḥadīth[139] support both forms of the *ṭalāq-i sunnat*, but oppose the irregular *ṭalāq-i bidʿat*.[140] For this latter form of *ṭalāq*, the husband pronounces "*ṭalāq*, *ṭalāq*, *ṭalāq*", which counts as three announcements. This means that the marriage has become invalid and the woman immediately has to leave the husband's home. If the husband wants his wife back, remarriage is not easy. First the woman has to marry another man who then repudiates her (so called *muḥallil*). After that she can marry her first husband for the second time. This form of *ṭalāq* is practiced by the Ḥanafīs, who argue that the *ṭalāq* formula spoken once counts as three – even if the husband is joking or drunk. In India, the Ahl-i Ḥadīth are the only community beside the

139 On the Bhopalese point of view, formulated by Shāh Jahān Bēgum, see Preckel, Interpretations of Widow Remarriage, pp. 41–51.

140 Ṣiddīq Ḥasan Khān, Muḥammad: *Ḥusn al-uswa bi-mā thabata min rasūlihi fī al-niswa* (Excellence of the Good Example Concerning What is Confirmed from God's Messenger about Women), Constantinople 1301/1884, pp. 18–19; Ḥusayn b. Muḥsin commented extensively on this subject in his collections of fatwas, such as *Nūr al-ʿayn*; see the table of contents of vol. 2, which is an appendix to the table of contents of vol. 1. Vol. 2 was not available to me. A modern book on this subject: Pīrzāda, Shams: *Ikaṯṯhī tīn ṭalāqīṅ* (Collections on the Triple *ṭalāq*), Bombay 1997.

Shia who deny the legitimacy of the triple *ṭalāq*. Until the present day, the All India Muslim Personal Law Board does not accept this stance, and declares the triple *ṭalāq* to be "the Sunni" ruling. The question of divorce, sustenance after divorce and temporal marriages remain relevant questions discussed in a secular, multi-religious India.[141] Protecting women's status was not the only reasons for the rejection of the triple *ṭalāq*. Another surely was to break with the Ḥanafī traditions to prove one's own authenticity and familiarity with the Sunna of the Prophet. On the other hand, the Ahl-i Ḥadīth wanted to win the support of women and mothers, whom they regarded as responsible for the education of coming generations. The growing number of books on marriage, family and education and especially the support of the ruling Bēgum of Bhopal reinforced the position of the Ahl-i Ḥadīth. The Ahl-i Ḥadīth scholars in 19th-century Bhopal successfully enforced their rejection of the triple *ṭalāq*. They even influenced some Wahhabi scholars who travelled to India to study Hadith. In the beginning, the Wahhabis used to base their fatwas on divorce on the Ḥanbalī school of law in general, which mostly supports the "three counts as three" ruling.[142] However, after some Wahhabi scholars returned from their journeys to India, they started issuing fatwas in favour of the "three counts as one ruling". For example, ʿAbd al-ʿAzīz b. Ḥamad Ibn ʿAtīq issued a fatwa in which he explicitly supported Ibn Taymiyya's rulings against a solution "three counts as one", i. e. he declared such a divorce invalid. Up to the early 20th century, this ruling against rapid divorce did not win wider support in Saudi Arabia. It was only ʿAbd al-ʿAzīz b. Ḥamad's most famous pupil, the Grand Mufti of Saudi Arabia ʿAbd al-ʿAzīz Ibn Bāz (d. 1999),[143] who further popularised the rejection of the triple *ṭalāq* in Saudi Arabia.

---

141 For some controversies on Muslim Personal Law see Hartung, *Viele Wege und ein Ziel*, pp. 170–181.

142 On the Ḥanbalī school of law see Laoust, Henri: *Essai sur les doctrines sociales et politiques de Takī-d-dīn Aḥmad Ibn Taimīya, canoniste Ḥanbalite: Né à Ḥarrān en 661/1262, mort à Damas en 728/1328; thèse pour le doctorat*, Cairo 1939, pp. 430–432; Al-Matroudi, Abdul Hakim I.: *The Ḥanbalī School of Law and Ibn Taymiyyah. Conflict or Conciliation*, London 2006, pp. 171–185; on the Wahhabiyya see Vogel, Frank: *Islamic Law and Legal System. Studies of Saudi Arabia*, Ann Arbor 1997, pp. 5–11; Steinberg, *Religion und Staat*, pp. 310–312.

143 On Ibn Bāz, see ʿAbd al-ʿAzīz Asad (ed.): *Mawsūʿat imām al-muslimīn fī al-qarn al-ʿishrīn samāḥat al-shaykh al-ʿAllāma ʿAbd al-ʿAzīz b. ʿAbd Allāh Ibn*

In the discussion on triple *ṭalāq*, the Ahl-i Ḥadīth opinion became very influential in their networks. It seems that they even exerted an influence on scholars from Najd. After their studies in India, Wahhabi scholars from Najd started adopting Ibn Taymiyya's works, fatwas and treatises on Islamic law, which had not been available to them before. In their time, Ibn Taymiyya and Ibn al-Qayyim had faced fierce opposition to and much criticism of their related divorce fatwas. And today, fatwas issued by Saudi scholars like Ibn Bāz[144] and Ibn ʿUthaymīn (d. 2001) are regularly published in India and thus further spread the legal methods and specific decisions of Ibn Taymiyya and Ibn al-Qayyim.[145]

6.4. Un-Islamic Novelties and Apocalyptic Fear

According to the Ahl-i Ḥadīth, a great variety of un-Islamic novelties (sg. *bidʿa*, pl. *bidaʿ*) characterised 19th-century Indian Muslim society and beyond. They perceived *bidaʿ* as aberrations of "true Islamic belief", which will automatically "lead to hell".[146] The Ahl-i Ḥadīth

Bāz (The Encyclopaedia of the Imam of the Muslims in the 20th Century, Shaykh al-ʿAllāma ʿAbd al-ʿAzīz b. ʿAbd Allāh Ibn Bāz), Beirut 2007.

144 See a collection of speeches and sermons by Ibn Bāz (on cassette), compiled by Abū Khadīja ʿAbd al-Wāḥid Salafī, Birmingham 2004. The name Salafī as well as the place of publication (Birmingham is the European headquarter of the Ahl-i ḥadīth) supports the view that it is an Ahl-i Ḥadīth publication.

145 See Luqmān al-Salafī, Muḥammad (ed.): *Fatāwā barāy-i khawātīn-i Islām* (Fatwas on the Women of Islam), Delhi n.d., where Ibn Bāz and Ibn ʿUthaymīn are among those extensively quoted.

146 In his works, Ṣiddīq Ḥasan Khān often quotes a famous Hadith: "The worst thing are these novelties (*muḥdathāt*), every novelty is an innovation (*bidʿa*), every innovation is an aberration (*kullu bidʿa ḍalāla*), and every aberration leads to hell-fire." Whereas the first part of this Hadith can partly be found in several collections of authentic Hadith (Ṣaḥīḥ Muslim, *Kitāb al-ṣalāt*, no. 1885; and Sunan Abī Da'ūd, *Kitāb al-Sunna*, no. 4590), the last part "and every aberration is in (hell)fire" (*kullu ḍalāla fī al-nār*) is of dubious authenticity. It cannot be traced in those collections of Hadith which the Ahl-i Ḥadīth normally regard as authentic. Although Ṣiddīq Ḥasan was frequently quoting this Hadith, he supported technological progress and innovations in Bhopal and India in general. He wrote that he admired the introduction of a postal system (*intiẓām-i ḍāk*) throughout India by the British, steam ships and electricity (Ṣiddīq Ḥasan Khān, *Ḥujaj al-kirāma*, pp. 219–220). This shows that the Ahl-i Ḥadīth were favourable to at least some technologies and justified their use. For Islamic literature on *bidʿa*, further see Fierro, Maribel: The Treatises

propagated that the Muslim community had begun to decline in general, including morally, culturally, and economically, with the death of the Prophet Muḥammad and that this would continue to the end of the world. Ṣiddīq Ḥasan even went so far as to predict "the great hour" (*al-sāʿa al-kubrā*)[147] for the beginning of the Muslim year 1300 (1882/1883). The approach of the Hour was *the* central subject of 17 books written by Ṣiddīq Ḥasan. In these books he focused on the signs that portended the approaching end of the world. These signs could be categorised as major, middle or small. For example, the appearance of the "the rightly guided one" (*al-mahdī*), the promised messiah (*al-masīḥ al-mawʿūd*) or the Anti-Christ (*al-dajjāl*)[148] definitely belonged to the major signs. For the Ahl-i Ḥadīth, the *mahdī* and the *masīḥ* are two different persons, whereas the members of the Aḥmadiyya movement consider their founder, Ghulām Aḥmad (d. 1908), to be both in one person. The Yemenite scholar Ḥusayn

against Innovations (*Kutub al-bidʿa*), in: *Der Islam* 69 (1992), pp. 204–246; Lohlker, Rüdiger: „Unstatthafte Neuerungen" oder das Feld der religiösen Diskussion im Islam, in: *Zeitschrift der Deutschen Morgenländischen Gesellschaft* 149 (1999), pp. 221–244. For the discussion on *bidʿa* in the South Asian context, see Masud, Muhammad Khalid: The Definition of *bid'a* in the South Asian *fatāwā* Literature, in: *Annales Islamologiques* 27 (1993), pp. 55–75. It is noteworthy that technical innovations (e.g. the printing press) are not generally considered unlawful innovations.

147 See Rubin, Uri: Sāʿa, in: *EI*[1], vol. 8 (1995), pp. 656–658.

148 On the *mahdī* see Madelung, Wilfried: al-Mahdī, in: *EI*[2], vol. 5 (1986), pp. 1230–1238; on the messias see Bosworth, Clifford Edmund: al-Masīḥ, in: *EI*[2], vol. 6 (1991), p. 726. On the *dajjāl* see Abel, Armand: al-Dadjdjāl, in: *EI*[2], vol. 2 (1960–65), pp. 76–77. The *dajjāl* (the great deceiver) is said to have the Arabic word k-f-r (*kufr*) on his forehead, meaning disbelief. It is important to note that the Ahl-i Ḥadīth never considered the British to be the *dajjāl*, whereas the Sudanese Mahdists believed the colonial power to be identical with the *dajjāl*. See Boddy, Janice Patricia: *Civilizing Women. British Crusades in Colonial Sudan*, Princeton 2007, p. 55. It is further important to say that Ṣiddīq Ḥasan Khān did not acknowledge the Sudanese *mahdī's* claims, although the British stated otherwise. See Preckel, *Islamische Bildungsnetzwerke*, pp. 383–385. Since 2008, the "best selling book 2008 from Bangladesh" (cover page) by Mohammed Bayazeed Khan Panni is flourishing throughout Asia and beyond and can be downloaded from the internet in several languages. As it can be seen from the title, the author identifies the "Judeo-Christan 'Civilizaton'" as the *dajjāl*. See Bayazeed Khan Panni, Mohammed: *Dajjal. The Judeo-Christan 'Civilization'*, translated from Bangla by Ummut Tijah Makhduma Panni, Dhaka 2008.

Ibn Muḥsin wrote a refutation of this view,[149] in which he drew on the works of al-Shawkānī and his theories on the renewal (*tajdīd*) and the end of the world. Like Ṣiddīq Ḥasan after him, al-Shawkānī had described the emergence of a renewer (*mujaddid*) in every century since the death of the Prophet Muḥammad. The existence of *mujaddidūn* was necessary because of the sinfulness of the Muslim community after they lost their guidance through Muḥammad. The spread of numerous *bidaʿ* was a consequence.

This increase of *bidaʿ* was one of the small and middle signs of the Hour. In his work *Ḥujaj al-kirāma fī āthār al-qiyāma* (The Noble Proofs of the Signs of the Last Hour), Ṣiddīq Ḥasan listed dozens of *bidaʿ* that he thought were prevalent in every field of life of Indian Muslims. For example, he listed several festivals and festivities, in which he saw a corruption of the true Islamic belief. To him, preparing sweets in the name of the dead and taking them to the graves was a kind of polytheism (*shirk*). Celebrating Muslim festivals with fireworks or other costly things was also *bidaʿ*. Such festivals could be regarded as waste of money, which the Prophet Muḥammad would have condemned. But even worse than this was to celebrate the festivals of other religious communities. Thus, the celebration of Christmas was a "scandalous" act for a Muslim. Ṣiddīq Ḥasan added other smaller *bidaʿ* as indicators of decadence, e.g. playing chess,[150] hanging up portraits of people in houses, selling puppies and alcohol and female forms of immodesty (talking to men who are not relatives, visiting houses of friends, being on the streets for festivities, not caring about purity regulations[151] and superstition. Here, Ṣiddīq Ḥasan

149 Al-Anṣārī, Ḥusayn Ibn Muḥsin: *al-Fatḥ al-rabbānī al-radd ʿalā al-Qādiyānī* (The Divine Victory Against the Qādiyānīs), Delhi 1309/1892. The main purpose of Ḥusayn b. Muḥsin's book was to proof that the promised messias and Jesus (ʿĪsā b. Maryam) was one person. For a detailed analysis of this book see Preckel, *Islamische Bildungsnetzwerke*, pp. 397–406. For Jesus' role in the Islamic tradition see Anawati, Georges Chehata: ʿĪsā, in: *EI*², vol. 4 (1978), pp. 81–86.

150 Here, Ṣiddīq Ḥasan quoted Ibn Taymiyya's *Risāla fī Ḥukm al-shaṭranj* (Writing on the Rulings on Chess), which he possessed in his library; see Ṣiddīq Ḥasan Khān, *Silsilat al-ʿasjad*, p. 94, no. 361.

151 The Ahl-i Ḥadīth shocked their Ḥanafī opponents by claiming that women were allowed to read, to quote and even to touch the Koran during their menstruation. Some Ahl-i Ḥadīth even propagated that such women could perform ritual prayers, since the restrictions concerned only fasting, performing the Hajj and sexual intercourse. Ṣiddīq Ḥasan Khān denied the necessity of the separation of women during the menstruation (*iʿtizāl-i zann dār ḥālat-i ḥayḍ*);

Khān was convinced that women were more susceptible to commit *bid'a* than men were, as the examples of *bid'a* concerning immodesty showed). Ṣiddīq Ḥasan reminded the Muslim community that the general process of the end of the world could not be completely stopped and that it was only a question of time when it would occur. He said that he himself wanted to warn the people, so that the process might be slowed down.[152] A close look at his works shows that Ṣiddīq Ḥasan considered himself a "renewer of the faith", a *mujaddid*.

In his works, Ṣiddīq Ḥasan supported also the Yemenite author Ibrāhīm al-Wazīr's and al-Shawkānī's claims to be renewers. The works of Ibn Taymiyya and other Ḥanbalīs were not relevant to Ṣiddīq Ḥasan in respect to the end of time. Again, he extensively quoted authors from the Yemenite tradition. Following these Yemenite authors, Ṣiddīq Ḥasan was one of the few Indian scholars of the Ahl-i Ḥadīth interested in apocalyptic theories. After the advent of the Islamic year 1300, the interest of the Ahl-i Ḥadīth in eschatological subjects decreased, but never completely disappeared. For example, in 2003, the Ahl-i Ḥadīth publishing house Markazī Jam'iyyat-i Ahl-i Ḥadīth-i Hind published an Urdu translation of Yūsuf al-Wābil's famous Arabic work *Ashrāṭ al-sā'a* (The Signs of the Hour).[153] Ḥanbalī scholars, on the other hand, were of great importance for Ṣiddīq Ḥasan's list of *bida'*. For some

---

see Ṣiddīq Ḥasan Khān, *Ḥujaj al-kirāma*, p. 227. The more recent Ahl-i Ḥadīth scholar Abū al-Barakāt Aḥmadī did not explicitely forbid reciting, reading and touching the Koran during the menstruation, but also did not allow it. See Aḥmadī, Abū al-Barakāt: *Fatāwā-yi Ahl-i ḥadīth al-ma'rūf bihi Fatāwā Barakatiyya*, Delhi 1992, p. 301. See also Riexinger, *Sanā'ullāh Amritsarī*, pp. 162–163. In *Ḥujaj al-kirāma*, Ṣiddīq Ḥasan did not refer to these claims. He only stressed that it was forbidden for women to visit the public bath (*ḥammām*) during menstruation. Here, he might have known of Ibn Taymiyya's *Risāla fī Ḥukm ḥammām al-nisā'* (Treatise on the Rulings Concerning Public Baths for Women), which was part of his library. See Ṣiddīq Ḥasan Khān, *Silsilat al-'asjad*, p. 94, no. 363.

152 Ṣiddīq Ḥasan Khān, Muḥammad: *Iqtirāb al-sā'a* (Approaching of the Hour), n.p. n.d., pp. 221–222. None of his works contains an explicit statement on how the process of the apocalypse could be stopped. According Ṣiddīq Ḥasan Khān, following authors like al-Barzanjī, the process of the apocalypse followed a process, which was fixed by Allah and is unstoppable. For an overview of Muslim apocalyptic theories see Cook, David: *Studies in Muslim Apocalyptic*, Princeton 2002. For a detailed account of the Sunni view of the apocalypse according to the Indian sources see Preckel, *Islamische Bildungsnetzwerke*, pp. 370–391.

153 Al-Wābil (d. 2001), who was born in Indonesia, studied and lived in Medina for a long time. See al-Wābil, Yūsuf b. 'Abd Allāh b. Yūsuf: *Qiyāmat kī*

bidaʿ, he added that his source was Ibn Taymiyya or Ibn Qayyim al-Jawziyya, but without mentioning any exact title.[154] Of relevance in this regard, however, ist the *Kitāb Iqtidāʾ al-ṣirāṭ al-mustaqīm fī mukhālafat aṣḥāb al-jaḥīm* (Following the Straight Path Against the Proprietors of Hell).[155] This book was especially famous for its arguments against celebrations on the Prophet's birthday (*mawlid*) and many other customs, which the author and the Ahl-i Ḥadīth both regarded as *bidʿa*.[156] So it is definitely no coincidence that one of the most popular works of Indian reformist literature is also called *al-ṣirāt al-mustaqīm*.[157]

Another work by Taqī al-Dīn Ibn Taymiyya was *Risāla fī Bayān al-amr bil-maʿrūf wa-nahy ʿan al-munkar* (Treatise on the Explanation of Commanding Good and Forbidding Evil). This formula refers to a Koranic command (3:104) to "command the good and to fight evil". Later on, the institution of "verification" or "balance" (*ḥisba*)[158] was

---

nishāniyān (Signs of the Hour), translated by Muḥammad Muqīm b. Ḥāmid ʿAlī Fayḍī, Delhi 2003.

154 Ṣiddīq Ḥasan Khān, *al-Idhāʿa*, p. 109.

155 Idem, *Silsilat al-ʿasjad*, p. 84, no. 249. Memon, Muhammad Umar: *Ibn Taimiyya's Struggle Against Popular Religion. With an Annotated Translation of the* Kitāb iqtidāʾ al-ṣirāṭ al-mustaqīm fī mukhālafat aṣḥāb al-jaḥīm, The Hague 1976.

156 Ṣiddīq Ḥasan Khān considered the celebration of the *mawlid* as "waste of money" (*isrāf*). For the Ahl-i Ḥadtīh's teachings concerning the *mawlid*, see Preckel, *Islamische Bildungsnetzwerke*, pp. 462–464. For general debates on the celebration of the *mawlid* see Kaptein, Nico J. G.: *Muhammad's Birthday Festival. Early History in the Central Muslim Lands and the Development in the Muslim West until the 10th/16th Century*, Leiden 1993; Holmes Katz, Marion: *The Birth of the Prophet Muhammad*, Leiden 2007, p. 14–15 et passim; Nagel, Tilman: *Allahs Liebling*, München 2008, p. 153–158 et passim.

157 See the chapter on the Ṭarīqa-i Muḥammadiyya. Clearly, the title is an allusion to the first sura of the Koran, the *fātiḥa*, which, according to the Ahl-i Ḥadīth is an important part of the prayer. They were even of the opinion that "there is no prayer without the *fātiḥa*" (*lā ṣalāṭ illā bil-fātiḥa*). Ṣiddīq Ḥasan Khān wrote a *tafsīr* of the *fātiḥa*, which is available as an unpublished manuscript from his private library in Lucknow.

158 For the translation of Ibn Taymiyya's work on the *ḥisba*, *al-Ḥisba fī al-Islām* (The *ḥisba* in Islam), see Ibn Taymiyya, Taqī al-Dīn: Traité sur la Ḥisba/ *al-ḥisba fī al-islām aw waẓīfat al-ḥukūma al-islāmiyya*, translated by Henri Laoust, in: *Revue des études islamique* 52 (1984), pp. 17–208; Ibn Taymiyya, Taqī al-Dīn: *Public Duties in Islam. The Institution of the Ḥisba*, translated by Muhtar Holland, Leicester 1982; for more on the *ḥisba* in general and at several courts, see Vikør, Knut S.: *Between God and the Sultan. A History of Islamic Law*, London 2005, pp. 195–198; on the institution of the muḥtasib see

created, which should guarantee public order, justice in society and an effective economy by controlling the markets. The market inspector (*muḥtasib*) had to observe the traders and the correctness of weights and scales. But this institution also included a strong moral instance. The Wahhabiyya extended *al-amr bil-maʿrūf wa-nahy ʿan al-munkar* to call for every Muslim's commitment to observe his duties. The local authorities also had to control the regularity of praying, the prohibition of smoking and gambling and other things.[159] The Ahl-i Ḥadīth, however, were not equally successful in practicing *al-amr bil-maʿrūf wa-nahy ʿan al-munkar* in Bhopal. According to some sources, Ṣiddīq Ḥasan tried to prohibit drinking wine, but he was not successful in this.[160] Additionally, he instituted the office of the *muḥtasib* to ensure the control of weights and measures, especially for those practitioners of the Unani Medicine (*ṭibb-i yūnānī*) and vendors of medicines and herbs.[161] Another important issue was the control of the mosques. During Sikander Bēgum's reign, rulings were issued concerning the behaviour of the believers in the local mosques: for example, it was prohibited to sleep in the mosque, and beggars were forbidden to enter the

---

Shayzari, Abd al-Rahman b. Nasr: *The Book of the Islamic Market Inspector. Nihayat al-rutba fi talab al-hisba*, transl. by R. Paul Buckley, Oxford 1999.

159 Steinberg, *Religion und Staat*, pp. 397–422; on Ibn Taymiyya's advocacy of intervention, see Cook, Michael A.: *Commanding Right and Forbidding Wrong in Islamic Thought*, Cambridge 2000, pp. 151–158, on the Ḥanbalīs of Najd, see pp. 165–195.

160 ʿAlī Ḥasan Khān, *Maʾāthir-i Ṣiddīqī*, part 3, p. 93; Luqmān, Akhtar J.: *al-Sayyid Ṣiddīq Ḥasan al-Qannawjī*, Riyadh 1996, p. 68.

161 The Unani medicine, meaning "Greek medicine", is a traditional medicine which is based on the four humours (blood, yellow and black bile, and phlegm). It is widely practiced in South Asia and in countries with a South Asian diaspora. One of the most important sources of Unani Medicine is the work *al-Qānūn fī al-ṭibb* (Canon of Medicine) by Ibn Sīnā (d. ca. 1037). Since the times of the Mughals, Unani Medicine is associated with the Muslim culture in India, although it is also influenced by Ayurveda, traditional Indian medical traditions and "Western" medicine. Since the colonial times, Unani Medicine developed as a kind of "national medicine" in India. The Bēgums of Bhopal have always been strong supporters of Unani Medicine. For this see the author's project "Medical Knowledge and Plural Culture. The Graeco-Islamic Medicine (*tibb-i yūnānī*, Unani Medicine) and its representation in South Asia" at the Ruhr-University Bochum (http://www.darstellung.rub.de/preckel.html). See also Attewell, Guy: *Refiguring Unani tibb. Plural Healing in Late Colonial India*, New Delhi (Orient Longman) 2007; Alavi, Seema: *Islam and Healing. Loss and Recovery of an Indo-Muslim Medical Tradition; 1600–1900*, New York 2008.

buildings.[162] These rulings were kept during Ṣiddīq Ḥasan's period of rule, but not expanded. Thus, the elimination of *bidaʿ* was an important element of the Ahl-i Ḥadīth's teachings, but it never had the practical consequences that it had in the Wahhabi state. Ṣiddīq Ḥasan remained in India more a warner than a fierce enforcer.

6.5. Insistence on *tawḥīd* as Opposed to *shirk*

The genre of dogmatic creed was one of the most important elements of Ṣiddīq Ḥasan Khān's library. It contained twelve books of Ibn Taimiyya in this group, the majority of which was on the insistence on *tawḥīd*. In this regard, they followed the line of Ibn Taymiyya. For instance in *al-Qāʿida fī al-tawḥīd wa-ikhlāṣ* (The Base of the Unity of God and Purity), Ibn Taymiyya emphasised the role of *tawḥīd* and described it in detail. He clearly differentiated between the "the oneness of the lordship of God" (*tawḥīd al-rubūbiyya*) and the *tawḥīd al-ulūhiyya*, which is also called the "the oneness of God in worshipping him" (*tawḥīd al-ʿibāda*). The first kind of *tawḥīd* means that only God can be regarded as Lord of all creation. God is the creator and sustainer of all creatures on earth. The second category of *tawḥīd* means that only God is entitled and worthy to be worshipped. Ṣiddīq Ḥasan Khān later took up Ibn Taymiyya's concepts of *tawḥīd al-rubūbiyya* and *tawḥīd al-ʿibāda*, especially in his work *al-Dīn al-khāliṣ* (The Pure Religion).[163] Interestingly, the first part of this work is partly identical to Muḥammad Ismāʿīl's *Taqwiyat al-īmān*. In this part, Ṣiddīq Ḥasan describes the different forms of *shirk*, which became evident in the worship of God. Here, he criticizes people who ask soothsayers, astrologers or oracles about their future, because knowledge of the future is God's alone. He also considered the making of pictures and statues to be *shirk*, since it is comparable to the veneration of stones and rocks. The Ahl-i Ḥadīth also believed that people who performed *shirk* in all fields of life were a constant danger to the *tawḥīd*. Thus, they held it to be necessary to purify the religion by insisting on *tawḥīd*. This concept of the "sincere devotion to *tawḥīd*" (*ikhlāṣ al-tawḥīd*) was adopted

---

162 ʿUbayd Allāh Khān, Sulṭān Jahān Bēgum: *Ḥayāt-i Sikanderī* (Life of Sikander), Bhopal (Shāh Jahānī) 1921, pp. 144–146.
163 Ṣiddīq Ḥasan Khān, *al-Dīn al-khāliṣ*, pp. 236–240.

from al-Shawkānī, who had incorporated Ibn Taymiyya's most important teachings in his own works.

Al-Shawkānī wrote extensively on the subject of *ikhlāṣ al-tawḥīd* in his *Kitāb al-Durr al-naḍīḍ fī ikhlāṣ kalimat al-tawḥīd* (The Book of the Well-Strung Pearls on the Sincere Devotion to the Word of the Unity of God).[164] The book focuses on condemning the practice of veneration of dead saints at their graves (*qubūr*). To al-Shawkānī (following Ibn Taymiyya), this practice was a form of polytheism (*shirk*). He accused the "believers in the dead" (*qubūriyyūn*, *muqabbirūn*) of constantly violating the principles of purifying the *tawḥīd* by worshipping someone other than God. He explained that the dead lived in the world between this world (*dunyā*) and the other world (*al-ākhira*), which is called *barzakh* ("barrier" or "separation"), in the sense of limbo.[165] According to Ibn Taymiyya, al-Shawkānī and the Ahl-i Ḥadith, the dead cannot hear the prayers and requests for intercession of the living while in the *barzakh*. So it is of no avail to ask them for help in worldly or other matters. According to al-Shawkānī, it was also useless – and even forbidden – to pray to the Prophet Muḥammad for aid on the Day of Judgement (*yawm al-qiyāma*). This was because the knowledge of the unseen (*ʿilm al-ghayb*) is God's alone. Devotion to *tawḥīd* was one of the central subjects of the Ahl-i Ḥadīth. Ṣiddīq Ḥasan Khān wrote three treatises on *tawḥīd*: the Persian work *Murād al-murīd fī ikhlāṣ al-tawḥīd* (Desire of the Disciple of Devotion to the Oneness of God), the Urdu work *Diʿāyat al-īmān ilā tawḥīd al-raḥmān* (Call to the Right Belief in the Oneness of God) and the Urdu work *Ikhlāṣ al-tawḥīd lil-ḥamīd al-majīd* (Dedication to the Oneness of God for the Praiseworthy and Glorious).[166] These writings were not available to the author of this article, so it remains to be checked whether they are compilations or abridgements of al-Shawkānī's works, which might contain many more quotations from Ibn Taymiyya.

6.6. Veneration of Graves

In Bhopal, it was not Ṣiddīq Ḥasan Khān alone who was concerned about the veneration of (dead) saints in India and beyond and about vis-

164 Haykel, *Revival and Reform*, pp. 127–129.

165 On this, see the article by Y. Tzvi Langermann in the present volume.

166 All three works have not been printed. Information on them were only given by Nawshahrawī, *Tarājim*, pp. 251, 253, 254.

its to the grave of the Prophet in Medina. Another prominent member of the Ahl-i Ḥadīth, Muḥammad Bashīr Sahsawānī (d. 1908), became famous for criticising these customs.[167] He was born around 1839 in the traditional quarter (*qaṣba*)[168] of Sahsawān, district Badayun (today Uttar Pradesh). His first studies comprised disciplines like logic, the Arabic language, philosophy and medicine. His contacts to Sahsawān's leading Ahl-i Ḥadīth scholar Amīr Ḥasan Sahsawānī (d. 1874)[169] made him one of the fiercest and most controversial figures of the movement. Before Muḥammad Bashīr Sahsawānī came to Bhopal, he travelled throughout India (e.g. Bihar and Assam), where he constantly sharpened his rhetorical abilities and his knowledge as a preacher. He became known to a wider public after entering a debate with ʿAbd al-Ḥayy Lakhnawī Farangī Maḥallī (d. 1887)[170] on the subjects of visiting the Prophet's grave and the unity of God (*tawḥīd*). ʿAbd al-Ḥayy and Ṣiddīq Ḥasan Khān had debated the issue of *ijtihād* and *taqlīd* before.[171] This might be why Ṣiddīq Ḥasan had invited Muḥammad Bashīr Sahsawānī to come to Bhopal. In Bhopal, Muḥammad Bashīr was offered a position in the financial administration. He later worked as controller of the entire educational system of the principality. After a short while, he resigned from his post and started to teach Hadith and *tafsīr* and regularly preach in several local mosques. His controversial style of preaching and his religious outlook led to various pub-

167 For a biography, see Ḥasanī, *Nuzhat al-khawāṭir*, vol. 8, p. 415; Sayf, *Taḥrīk-i Ahl-i ḥadīth*, pp. 379–382. Muḥammad Bashīr was among the Indians mentioned in *Mashahīr ʿulamāʾ Najd*, pp. 472–477.

168 The *qaṣbas* in India were often located along important trading routes. Following South Asian Muslim historiography, they were often founded by Sufis, who were actively involved in Islamic mission and conversion to Islam. On the reaction of the population of the *qaṣbas*, mostly consisting of Islamic teachers or scholars, to the British rule see Malik, *Islamische Gelehrtenkultur*, pp. 105–125 (chapter on the *qaṣba* as a "place of Islamic tradition"). On Muslim culture in Indian *qaṣbas* of Awadh see Hasan, Mushirul: *From Pluralism to Seperatism. Qasbas in Colonial Awadh*, New Delhi (Oxford University Press) 2004.

169 For a biography, see Ḥasanī, *Nuzhat al-khawāṭir*, vol. 7, p. 79; Nawshahrawī, *Tarājim*, pp. 239–241. Sahsawānī and Ṣiddīq Ḥasan shared a network of teachers of Hadith.

170 Ḥasanī, *Nuzhat al-khawāṭir*, vol. 8, pp. 234–237. On his role as one of the leading Ḥanafī scholars of the 19th century, see Robinson, Francis: *'Ulama of Farangi Mahall*, Delhi (Permanent Black) 2001, pp. 121–125, 151.

171 Ṣiddīq Ḥasan wrote *Shifāʾ al-ʿayy ʿan mā awradahu al-Shaykh ʿAbd al-Ḥayy*. ʿAbd al-Ḥayy Ḥasanī refuted Ṣiddīq Ḥasan's book with his own *Ibrāz al-ghayy al-wāqiʿ fī shifāʾ al-ʿayy*.

lic debates (*munāẓara*) with almost all the other religious movements of his time.

Muḥammad Bashīr Sahsawānī wrote a refutation of the theories of the Shāfiʿī Meccan mufti Aḥmad Zaynī Daḥlān (d. 1886)[172] called *Ṣiyānat al-insān ʿan waswasat Shaykh Daḥlān* (Preserving the People from the Evil Suggestions of Shaykh Daḥlān). Daḥlān had gained prominence in the whole Islamic world by attacking the Wahhabiyya for their "fanaticism" concerning the veneration of Sufis and their destruction of several tombs – even of some Companions of the Prophet – in Mecca and Medina. Daḥlān's *Fitnat al-Wahhābiyya* (Dangerous Temptation of the Wahhabiyya) and his *al-Durar al-saniyya fī al-radd ʿalā al-Wahhābiyya* (The Shining Pearls against the Wahhabiyya) criticised the Wahhabiyya for declaring their fellow Muslims to be infidels (*kuffār*, sg. *kāfir*). He also accused the Wahhabiyya of extremism (*ghuluww*) for killing their (Muslim) opponents.[173] Muḥammad Bashīr Sahsawānī started an exchange of letters (and even whole books) with Aḥmad Zaynī Daḥlān. The subjects of these works were the veneration of the saints and the correct behaviour when visiting the grave of the Prophet Muḥammad during the Hajj. The controversy was conducted very harshly and ended only when Aḥmad Zaynī Daḥlān died in 1887. Muḥammad Bashīr's wrote and published *Ṣiyānat al-insān* in Bhopal in 1890; it contained the material of several letters and books mentioned above. The third edition from 1958 deserves great interest, because it was published in Cairo (by al-Maṭbaʿa al-Salafiyya) and contains a foreword by the famous Salafī Muḥammad Rashīd Riḍā (d. 1935).[174] Rashīd Riḍā had travelled to India in 1912 and had delivered two speeches in the *Nadwat ul-ʿulamāʾ* in Lucknow.[175] On this

---

172 On Aḥmad Zaynī Daḥlān see Freitag, Ulrike: Der Orientalist und der Mufti. Kulturkontakt im Mekka des 19. Jahrhunderts, in: *Die Welt des Islam* 43 (2003), pp. 37–60.

173 Steinberg, *Religion und Staat*, p. 105.

174 On the Arab Salafiyya, see e.g. Weismann, Itzchak: *Taste of Modernity. Sufism, Salafiyya, and Arabism in late Ottoman Damascus*, Leiden 2001; Commins, David D.: *Islamic Reform. Politics and Social Change in Late Ottoman Syria*, Oxford 1990. On Rashīd Riḍā see Ende, Werner: Rashīd Riḍā, Muḥammad, in: *EI*², vol. 8, pp. 446–448 and Jomier, Jacques: al-Manār, in: *EI*², vol. 6, pp. 360–361.

175 On his journey to India, see Rashīd Riḍā, Muḥammad: Riḥlat ṣāḥib *al-Manār* ilā al-Hind (Journey of the Owner of *al-Manār* to India), in: *al-Manār* 15 (1315/1898–9), pp. 225–226, 331–333, 799; and ibid., in: *al-Manār* 16 (1316/1899–1900), pp. 18, 104, 396.

occasion, he had met several influential Ahl-i Ḥadīth scholars. As we know from some articles in his journal *al-Manār*, Rashīd Riḍā was fully aware of such discussions and debates in India.

In *Ṣiyānat al-insān*, Muḥammad Bashīr Sahsawānī extensively quoted Ibn Taymiyya, but without indicating specific works.[176] According to Muḥammad Bashīr, Ibn Taymiyya had correctly explained how a Muslim should behave when visiting the grave of the Prophet in the Mosque of the Prophet in Medina, namely that the believer should not hope that the Prophet would intercede between human beings and God before the Day of Judgement. Like Ibn Taymiyya, Muḥammad Bashīr even denied that the Prophet Muḥammad himself was alive (*ḥayy*) in his grave.[177] Until the Day of Judgement, the Prophet "lived" a life in the *barzakh*. Muḥammad Bashīr (like Ibn Taymiyya before him) stressed that the Prophet was definitely separated from life on earth and therefore could not hear the prayers of the believers. As a consequence, he was not able to intercede for human beings until the Day of Judgement. Asking for the fulfilment of earthly wishes was therefore forbidden. It was even not recommended to ask for Muḥammad's intercession (*tawassul*) on the Day of Judgement. When visiting Muḥammad's grave, one should also avoid touching, rubbing or kissing the walls of the grave. Nor is it permitted to perform any kind of prayer at the grave – since only Allah is worthy of worship. Instead, the believer should speak out a simple greeting, namely an *al-salām ʿalaykum* (Peace be upon you) when entering the Mosque of the Prophet in Medina. The Ahl-i Ḥadīth tried to follow all these rules and regulations. It is reported that some did not visit Muḥammad's grave after having finished the Hajj. Some of them, by way of precaution, even did not perform the "minor pilgrimage" (*ʿumra*) which is often carried out in conjunction with the Hajj.[178]

176 It might be assumed that Muḥammad Bashīr used Ibn Taymiyya's *Kitāb al-Ḥajj wal-ʿumra* (Book of the Greater and Smaller Pilgrimage to Mecca), which was available to him from Ṣiddīq Ḥasan's private library.

177 On the question of Muḥammad being alive in his grave, see Meier, Fritz: Eine Auferstehung Muḥammads bei Suyūṭī, in: *Der Islam* 62 (1985), pp. 20–58.

178 In his *Nuzhat al-khawāṭir*, ʿAbd al-Ḥayy Ḥasanī often describes persons with *ḥajja wa-zāra* (he performed the pilgrimage and visited the Prophet's grave). Several biographies of Ahl-i Ḥadīth contain only a *ḥajja*. The most prominent of these was Muḥammad Bashīr Sahsawānī.

Conclusion

Ṣiddīq Ḥasan's career and the personal networks he was able to establish have been analysed here in some detail. The degree to which he was (not) reading and quoting Ḥanbalī scholars should also be clear through the number of selected manuscripts and books he owned in his private library in Bhopal. A major part of these works were printed in the cities to which Ṣiddīq Ḥasan had sent one of his *wakīls*. Ṣiddīq Ḥasan was definitely influenced by Ibn Taymiyya and to a minor degree by Ibn Qayyim al-Jawziyya. He quoted them mainly in the fields of *tawḥīd* and the elimination of *bidaʿ*. Often he did not mention the exact source, hence it may be assumed that he sometimes did not quote from these references directly, but through the works of al-Shawkānī or another author of the Yemenite tradition. Ṣiddīq Ḥasan wanted to establish a direct network with this Yemenite tradition of al-Shawkānī and his pupils. Like al-Shawkānī, Ṣiddīq Ḥasan Khān described himself as an independent *mujtahid*, which in his eyes additionally qualified him to govern the state of Bhopal. By the means of *ijtihād*, the Ahl-i Ḥadīth challenged the prevalent positions in the widespread Ḥanafī school of law and gave religious life in Bhopal a new outlook, for instance in the style of prayer. Practising *ijtihād* in interpreting the holy sources, they extended the religious discourse on the "authenticity" and "truthfulness" of the religious texts. Several newly emerged groups were debating about the "real Islam" and the ideal of the Prophet Muḥammad. This polarised and separated Muslim groups or other religious communities who were regarded either as *bidʿatīs* (people who commit religious innovations) or even *mushrikūn* (polytheists), on the one hand, and the Ahl-i Ḥadīth on the other. In the multi-religious settings of the former with a variety of religious cults and even shared use of holy places, debates on *bidaʿ* developed into a medium of self-identification and separation. Such controversies even led to harsh verbal and physical attacks, which had to be ended by the British authorities.[179]

---

179 For example, an "oral debate" (*munāẓara lisāniyya*) took place in Delhi between members of the Ahl-i Ḥadīth and the Aḥmadiyya in 1902. Muḥammad Bashīr Sahsawānī heavily attacked the Aḥmadīs on the question of the *mujaddid.* British authorities ended this debate before open revolts started. In 1870, another *munāẓara* between Ahl-i Ḥadīth and the members of the Ahl-i sunnat wa-jamāʿat took place in Punjabi town of Shaikhupura. The different viewpoints were written down by the Ahl-i Ḥadīth Muḥammad Nadhīr Sahsawānī (d. 1882) who published the book *Munāẓara Aḥmadiyya* in Kanpur 1289/1871.

The personal networks of Ahl-i Ḥadīth members became a topic of the Muslim discourse of those days: while the Ahl-i ḥadīth's opponents accused them of sedition and fanaticism, some scholars of the movement, like Muḥammad Bashīr Sahsawānī, did not care about this and supported the Wahhabi's claims about *tawḥīd*.

The connection with Wahhabi circles that some modern Ahl-i Ḥadīth aspired to was not yet a reality in Ṣiddīq Ḥasan's lifetime and developed only some decades later. The Ahl-i Ḥadīth and the Wahhabis share a common interest in their curricula, but this does not automatically imply that the Ahl-i Ḥadīth are "Indian Wahhabis". Although Ṣiddīq Ḥasan placed a considerable number of Ḥanbalī books in his library – he is neither a "staunch Ḥanbalī" nor a "committed Wahhabi". The lack of Wahhabi literature in the narrow sense in Ṣiddīq Ḥasan's library is quite astonishing. His publishing and manuscript-purchasing strategies provide no evidence for the reproach that he was "a staunch Wahhabi". Hence, the most important influence must be somewhere else. His literary contributions, however, paved the way for the spread of Ḥanbalī thoughts on the Indian subcontinent. The most interesting aspect of Ṣiddīq Ḥasan's reception of Ḥanbalī books is that he introduced the Yemenite tradition of Hadith studies to India and thus (indirectly) propagated works of Ibn Taymiyya and other important Ḥanbalī scholars. But this gradually reduced the importance of the earlier Ahl-i Ḥadīth's focus on al-Shawkānī and the role of the descendants of Ḥusayn b. Muḥsin in Bhopal, for the movement at the end of the 20th century, so that the erroneous impression of a direct Wahhabi-Ahl-i Ḥadīth alliance could take centre stage. In India the works of the early scholars of the Ahl-i Ḥadīth are almost completely neglected. However, Ṣiddīq Ḥasan's Arabic titles are often reprinted in Salafi publishing houses of Beirut or Riyadh. By this means, Ṣiddīq Ḥasan's aim to popularize al-Shawkānī's books, became achieved. This also means that Ḥanbalī literature reaches an Arabic readership through the reception of an Indian author of the 19th-century.

The book is preserved in the Central Library/Bhopal until the present day. Also see Preckel, *Islamische Bildungsnetzwerke*, pp. 510–526.

Ibn Qayyim al-Jawziyya in the "Lands Below the Wind"[1]

An Ideological Father of Radicalism or a Popular Sufi Master?

Syamsuddin Arif

The recent upsurge of the so-called radicalism[2] in predominantly Muslim-populated regions of Southeast Asia like Indonesia and Malaysia, has been attributed to, among other things, the influence of Salafi thought going back to the two prominent Ḥanbalīs Ibn Taymiyya (d. 728/1328) and his closest disciple Ibn Qayyim al-Jawziyya (d. 751/1350), as interpreted and promulgated later by Muḥammad b. ʿAbd al-Wahhāb

1 The Malay nomenclature *negeri bawah angin* is borrowed from Persian *zīr-bād*, meaning literally "below the wind", i.e., *leeward*, which has acquired a specific meaning among seafaring folk who used it to designate the countries east of India. The islands "above the wind" were probably Ceylon, the Maldives, Socotra, etc., whereas those situated "below the wind" were Malacca, Sumatra, Tenasserim, Bengal, Martaban, and Pegu. See Yule, Sir Henry: *Hobson-Jobson. A Glossary of Colloquial Anglo-Indian Words and Phrases, and of Kindred Terms, Etymological, Historical, Geographical and Discursive*, ed. by William Crooke, London 1903, s.v. *Zirbad*, s.v. "zirbad". See Clifford, Hugh and Swettenham, Frank A.: *A Dictionary of the Malay Language*, Taiping 1894, vol. 1, p. 63, cited in Azra, Azyumardi: *Jaringan Ulama Nusantara*, Bandung 1995, p. 183, n. 70.

2 Western observers and political analysts use both categories – "radical Islamism" and "Islamic radicalism" – to refer to the ideology that allegedly calls for radical transformation of society and politics by whatever means into an absolute theocracy. See Barton, Greg: *Jemaah Islamiyah. Radical Islamism in Indonesia*, Sydney 2004, p. 28; and van Bruinessen, Martin: Genealogies of Islamic Radicalism in Post-Suharto Indonesia, in: *South East Asia Research* 10 (2002), pp. 117–154, here pp. 117–118. See Center for Strategic and International Studies: *Currents and Crosscurrents of Radical Islamism. A Report of the CSIS Transatlantic Dialogue on Terrorism*, April 2006, Washington 2006, p. 15; Desker, Barry and Ramakrishna, Kumar: Forging an Indirect Strategy in Southeast Asia, in: *The Washington Quarterly* 25 (2002), pp. 161–176, esp. p. 163. The author would like to thank the Research Management Center of IIUM.

(d. 1206/1792), the founder of the Saudi-based Wahhabi movement.[3] This article argues that while it is true that the intellectual relationship established through multipurpose pilgrimage to the heartland of Islam has never lost its significance,[4] the political implications of this connection seem to be overestimated. As will be shown by the following survey, although the number of writings by and on Ibn Qayyim al-Jawziyya in the Malay-Indonesian language is strikingly considerable, the nature and extent of their impact in the religious life and thought of people have yet to be seen. Hence, to construe a link between them and the emergence of radicalism in the "Lands below the Wind" would be too hasty a conclusion. To begin with, a historical overview on the coming of Islam and the intellectual role it plays in this region is given here to provide a general framework for the discussion that follows.

1. Islamic Literature in the Malay World: An Overview

Although the coming of Islam to the Malay-Indonesian archipelago – i.e., the vast area now covering southern Thailand, Malaysia, Indonesia, Brunei and the southern Philippines – was sometimes dated as early as the seventh century,[5] the new faith did not gain a foothold in

3 For example, van Bruinessen, while recognizing that for most political observers all inter-ethnic and inter-religious violence which occurred in Indonesia in the past few years was provoked by power struggles between rival elite factions, or deliberately fomented by certain factions with the aim of destabilizing the current government, nonetheless asserts that "[t]he roots of most present Muslim radical groups in Indonesia can be traced to two relatively 'indigenous' Muslim political movements, the Darul Islam movement and the Masyumi party, and to a number of more recent *transnational Islamic networks*" (my emphasis). See van Bruinessen, Genealogies of Islamic Radicalism, pp. 117–118; Sivan, Emmanuel: *Radical Islam. Medieval Theology and Modern Politics*, New Haven 1990; and Miller, Judith: The Challenge of Radical Islam, in: *Foreign Affairs* 72 (1993), pp. 47–56.

4 The important role of pilgrimage in intellectual network-building among South East Asian Muslims is made clear in Vredenbregt, Jacob: The Haddj. Some of Its Features and Function in Indonesia, in: *Bijdraagen tot de Taal-, Land- en Volkenkunde de Koninlijke Institut* 118 (1962), pp. 91–154; Husson, Lawrence: Indonesians in Saudi Arabia. Worship and Work, in: *Studia Islamika* (Jakarta) 4 (1997), pp. 109–135; Azyumardi, Azra: *The Origins of Islamic Reformism in Southeast Asia*, Leiden 2004, pp. 8–11.

5 Al-Attas, Syed Muhammad al Naquib: Indonesia, in: *EI*[2], vol. 3 (1971), pp. 1218–1221; see idem: *Preliminary Statement on a General Theory of the Islamization of the Malay-Indonesian Archipelago*, Kuala Lumpur 1969.

the area until late in the 13th century with the emergence of a Muslim kingdom in Aceh, in northeast Sumatra.[6] There has been much discussion of the chronology, provenance and modality of the Islamization process.[7] Scholars generally agree, however, (i) that Islam reached the region via international maritime trade routes, which had existed since antiquity,[8] (ii) that its subsequent spread in various parts of the archipelago was gradual and peaceful,[9] by persuasion and not by force or sword, and (iii) that the wandering Sufi teachers, particularly from the 13th century on, played a crucial role in effecting mass conversion of the local population to Islam.[10]

The process of Islamization was to give rise to a new body of Malay Islamic literature. Gradually, the pre-existing, Hindu-Buddhist literature was adapted and in some cases even recast to meet the demands of the new religion, as evident in the Malay *hikayat* and Javanese *serat* genres. New terms and concepts mirroring the Islamic worldview, mostly from Arabic and Persian, were adopted, and old terms were

6 Among the earliest historical accounts of the presence of Islam in the region is that of Marco Polo, who on his way back to Venice made a stop at Perlak on the north coast of Sumatra in 1292 and noted that the people there had been converted by "Saracen merchants" (see Polo, Marco: *The Travel of Marco Polo*, transl. by Aldo Ricci, London 1950, p. 282). This was confirmed by Ibn Baṭṭūṭa, who visited the kingdom in 1345 (see Ibn Baṭṭūṭa, Abū ʿAbd Allāh Muḥammad: *Riḥlat Ibn Baṭṭūṭa*, Beirut 1960, p. 618). See Winstedt, Richard O.: The Advent of Muhammadanism in the Malay Peninsula and Archipelago, in: *Journal of the Straits Branch of the Royal Asiatic Society* 77 (1917), pp. 171–175, here p. 171; and Djajadiningrat, P. A. Hoesein: Islam in Indonesia, in: Kenneth W. Morgan (ed.): *Islam. The Straight Path; Islam Interpreted by Muslims*, New York 1958, pp. 375–402.

7 Azra, *Jaringan Ulama*, pp. 24–36.

8 See Hourani, George F.: *Arab Seafaring in the Indian Ocean in Ancient and Early Medieval Times*, Princeton 1995.

9 Arnold, Thomas W.: *The Preaching of Islam*, London 1935 (repr. Lahore 1979), p. 12. See Johns, Anthony H.: From Coastal Settlement to Islamic School and City. Islamization in Sumatra, the Malay Peninsula and Java, in: *Hamdard Islamicus* 4 (1981), pp. 3–28, here p. 5.

10 See Johns, Anthony H.: Sufism as a Category in Indonesian Literature and History, in: *Journal of Southeast Asian History* 2 (1961), pp. 10–23, here p. 15; Ibn Bakar, Osman: Sufism in the Malay-Indonesian World, in: Seyyed Hossein Nasr (ed.): *Islamic Spirituality. Manifestations*, London 1991, pp. 259–263; and Azra, Azyumardi: Opposition to Sufism in the East Indies in the Seventeenth and Eighteenth Centuries, in: Frederick de Jong and Bernd Radtke (eds.): *Islamic Mysticism Contested. Thirteen Centuries of Controversies and Polemics*, Leiden 1999, pp. 665–686, here p. 665.

given new meanings, e. g. lord or god (*tuhan*), worship (*sembah-yang*), fasting (*puasa*) – to mention but a few. Yet the literary output of this early phase of Islamization, which continued until the 16th century, was not confined to tales and chronicles.[11] Rather, it covered a wide range of genres, from law and theology to ethics and morality. It is to be noted that by the 16th century the Malay language had become a lingua franca in the archipelago.[12]

By the latter part of the 16th and throughout the 17th centuries, mystico-theological literature of remarkable profundity was flourishing. Some of the best examples of such works, written in Malay but using the Arabic script,[13] are those of the poet Ḥamza Fanṣūrī, who lived during the reign of Sulṭān ʿAlāʾ al-Dīn Riʿāyat Shāh (r. 1589–1604) of Aceh. Ḥamza Fanṣūrī belonged to the Qādiriyya order and drew upon the mystical doctrines of Muḥyī al-Dīn Ibn ʿArabī (d. 1240), ʿAbd al-Raḥmān al-Jāmī (d. 1492) and ʿAbd al-Karīm al-Jīlī (d. 1428).[14]

Another important scholar was Shams al-Dīn al-Sumatranī (d. 1630), who enjoyed the patronage of Sultan Iskandar Muda (r. 1607–1636) and served as the *shaykh al-islām* of Aceh.[15] Al-Sumatranī is said to be the one responsible for the popularization of the doctrine of "seven grades of Being" (*martabat tujuh*) based on the teaching of the Indian Sufi scholar al-Burhānpūrī (d. 1620), whose work *al-Tuḥfa al-mursala*

11 An excellent survey is given by Winstedt, Richard: A History of Classical Malay Literature, in: *Journal of Malaysian Branch of the Royal Asiatic Society* 31 (1958), pp. 1–261, esp. pp. 61–63, "From Hinduism to Islam"; reprint: Singapore 1961.

12 Kratz, E. Ulrich: Malay as Lingua Franca. A Historical Survey, in: *Malay Literature* 12 (1999), pp. 46–57; Awang, Omar: The Major Arabic Sources which Determined the Structure of Islamic Thought in the Malay Archipelago Before the Nineteenth Century A.D. in the Field of Law, Theology and Sufism, in: Lutpi Ibrahim (ed.): *Islamika. Esei-esei Sempena Abad ke-15 Hijrah*, Kuala Lumpur 1981, pp. 80–85.

13 Now it is generally known as *Kitab Jawi* or *Kitab Kuning*. See Bin Ngah, Mohd Nor: *Kitab Jawi. Islamic Thought of the Malay Muslim Scholars*, Singapore 1983; Matheson, Virginia and Hooker, Michael B.: Jawi Literature in Patani. The Maintenance of an Islamic Tradition, in: *Journal of the Malaysian Branch of the Royal Asiatic Society* 60/61 (1988), pp. 1–86; van Bruinessen, Martin: Kitab Kuning. Books in Arabic Script Used in the Pesantren-Milieu, in: *Bijdragen van het Koninklijk Instituut voor de Taal-, Land- en Volkenkunde* 146 (1990), pp. 249–250.

14 For his life and legacy, see al-Attas, Seyd Muhammad al Naquib: *The Mysticism of Ḥamzah Fanṣūrī*, Kuala Lumpur 1970.

15 See van Niewenhuijze, Christoffel A. O.: *Samsu'l-Din van Pasai*, Leiden 1945; and Johns, Anthony H.: *Nur al-Daqa'iq* by Shams al-Din of Pasai, in: *Journal of the Royal Asiatic Society* 85 (1953), pp. 137–151.

ilā al-nabī (The Gift Sent to the Prophet) was well-received and was even translated into Javanese.[16]

Scholarly discussions about mystico-philosophical matters ensued and soon developed into polemics during the reign of Sultan Iskandar II (r. 1637–1641), when he appointed Nūr al-Dīn al-Rānīrī (d. 1666), an Indian scholar of Arab descent, as the chief kadi of Aceh. Al-Rānīrī attacked the Wujūdiyya Sufism of his predecessors in his numerous writings, such as the *Ḥujjat al-ṣiddīq li-dafʿ al-zindīq* (Authority of the Righteous to Ward off the Freethinkers), *Jawāhir al-ʿulūm fī kashf al-maʿlūm* (The Essences of the Sciences Regarding the Revealing of What is Known) and *al-Tibyān fī maʿrifat al-adyān* (Exposition of Knowledge on the Religions). He regarded the Sufi teachings of Ḥamza Fanṣūrī and Shams al-Dīn al-Sumatranī as heretic and had their books burned and their followers punished to death.[17] Al-Rānīrī also wrote *al-Ṣirāṭ al-mustaqīm* (The Straight Path), a compendium on law, the *Hidāyat al-ḥabīb* (Guidance for the Beloved) and the celebrated *Bustān al-salāṭīn* (Garden of the Rulers), all in the Malay language but using Arabic script.

After al-Ranīrī's return to India, the outstanding figure to appear on the scene was ʿAbd al-Ra'ūf al-Sinkilī (d. 1693), a native of Aceh who lived during the reign of Sultana Tāj al-ʿĀlam Ḥafiyyat al-Dīn Shāh (r. 1641–1675). Having spent long years studying with a range of prominent scholars on the Arabian Peninsula, including Aḥmad al-Qushāshī (d. 1660), the then chief of the Shaṭṭāriyya order, as well as under his successor Ibrāhīm al-Kūrānī (d. 1690)[18] in Medina, ʿAbd al-Ra'ūf became the first Malay scholar to write a full rendering and commentary on the Koran, titled *Tarjumān al-mustafīd* (Translator of the Concluded), drawing mainly on the *Tafsīr al-Jalālayn* (Koran Commentary of the two Jalāls), i.e. of the Arab scholars al-Maḥallī (d. 864/1459) and al-Suyūṭī (d. 911/1515), the *Anwār al-tanzīl* (Lights of the Revelation) of al-Bayḍāwī (d. ca. 716/1316) and *Lubāb al-ta'wīl* (Kernels of Explanation) of al-Khāzin (d. 741/1459).[19] Equally worthy

16 For details, see Johns, Anthony H.: *The Gift Addressed to the Spirit of the Prophet*, Canberra 1965.

17 A full account is given by al-Attas, Syed Muhammad al Naquib: *Rānīrī and the Wujūdiyyah of 17th-Century Acheh*, Singapore 1966; and idem: *A Commentary on the Ḥujjat al-Ṣiddīq of Nūr al-Dīn al-Rānīrī*, Kuala Lumpur 1986.

18 On Ibrāhīm al-Kūrānī see the article by Claudia Preckel in this volume.

19 Riddell, Peter G.: The Sources of ʿAbd al-Ra'ūf's *Tarjumān al-Mustafīd*, in: *Journal of Malaysian Branch of the Royal Asiatic Society* 57 (1984), pp. 113–118.

of note is Shaykh Yūsuf al-Maqassarī (d. 1111/1699), a famous scholar-warrior who led the Banten war against the Dutch and was later banished by the latter first to Ceylon (Sri Lanka) and then to Capetown, South Africa, where he breathed his last. Al-Maqassarī wrote mainly in Arabic but also in Buginese, his mother tongue.[20]

The coming of Europeans to the archipelago in the 16th century was to have paradoxical consequences. On the one hand, it weakened the nascent Muslim sultanates, diminished their suzerainty and even brought them into armed clash with one another – e.g. the civil wars that broke out between Sultan Ageng Tirtayasa of Banten and his son (Sultan Haji), Sultan Hasanuddin of Macassar versus Aru Palakka of Bone and Sultan Agung of Mataram against Trunajaya. Yet, on the other hand, the challenge posed by the European colonial powers also engendered awareness among the Malays that as Muslims they belonged to one and the same umma.[21] Thus, for instance, following the Portuguese capture of Malacca in 1511, the Sultans of Aceh, who already had contacts with Muslim India and Arabia, sought an alliance with the Ottoman Turks against the Portuguese.[22] No wonder during the famous, long-fought war (1873–1904) against the Dutch, the Acehnese received military support from the Ottomans. Islam became a unifying force in resisting the colonial powers and in checking their proselytizing efforts.

The 18th century witnessed the emergence of the puritanical movement in Arabia under the leadership of Muḥammad b. ʿAbd al-Wahhāb (1703–1787). Inspired by the Ḥanbalī Ibn Taymiyya (d. 728/1328), Muḥammad b. ʿAbd al-Wahhāb sought to purge the Muslim society of all its heretical beliefs and ritual innovations. In his call for reform and return to the fundamental doctrines and practices of Islam, he was supported by the Saudi ruler of Najd, who gathered the Arabian tribal forces to oppose the Ottoman rule. The movement, dubbed Wah-

---

On his relations with the scholars of Medina, see Johns, Anthony H.: Friends in Grace. Ibrāhīm al-Kūrānī and ʿAbd al-Raʾūf al-Singkelī, in: Udin, Saifuddin (ed.): *Spectrum. Essays Presented to Sutan Takdir Alisjahbana*, Jakarta 1978.

20 On his life and works, see Galigo, Andi Syamsul Bahri: *Pemikiran Tasauf Syeikh Abu Mahasin Yusuf al-Taj*, Kuala Lumpur 2004.

21 See Laffan, Michael F.: *Islamic Nationhood and Colonial Indonesia. The Umma Below the Winds*, London and New York 2003.

22 Seljuq, Affan: Relations Between the Ottoman Empire and the Muslim Kingdoms in the Malay-Indonesian Archipelago, in: *Der Islam* 57 (1980), pp. 301–310, here pp. 302–304.

habism by its adversaries,[23] soon fecundated vigorous counterparts in the Malay world. The so-called Padri movement (1807–1832) in West Sumatra is a case in point. Initiated by three returning pilgrims by the name of Haji Miskin, Haji Piobang and Haji Sumanik, it set itself against the local elite, which it regarded as compromising with non-Islamic beliefs and customs.[24]

On the scholarly level, the neo-Sufi reform movement was championed, among others, by ʿAbd al-Samad al-Falimbānī (d. ca. 1789), who wrote many important works, including a Malay translation of al-Ghazālī's *Iḥyāʾ ʿulūm al-dīn* (Revival of the Religious Sciences) titled *Siyar al-sālikīn* (Ways of the Wayfarers), which advocated a "moderate" kind of Sufism in contrast to the monistic or pantheistic one of the previous era. Al-Falimbānī was also famous for his "radical" treatise, the *Naṣīḥat al-muslimīn wa-tadhkirat al-muʾminīn fī faḍāʾil al-jihād fī sabīl allāh wa-karāmāt al-mujāhidīn* (Sincere Advise for the Muslims and Reminder of the Faithful Concerning the Holy Struggle on the Path of God and the Noble Deeds/Miracles of those who Strive for God), in which he encouraged the local Muslims to fight against infidel European colonials.[25]

In the 19th century, the religious-intellectual link between the Malay world and the Middle East was further consolidated, as was evident from the growing number of Muslims who travelled from the archipelago to the Middle East and stayed there to study for years. Some of them even succeeded in making a bright scholarly career in Mecca, e.g. Muḥammad Nawawī al-Jāwī (1813–1897) of Banten, West Java; Muḥammad Maḥfūẓ (1842–1919) of Termas, Central Java; and Aḥmad Khaṭīb (1852–1916) of Minangkabau, Sumatra. The latter is known to have influenced generations of Jawi (Malay) students, contributing to

23 One of its staunch opponents was no less a figure than Shaykh Aḥmad Zaynī Daḥlān (d. 1304/1886/87), the then Grand Mufti of Mecca, who wrote a polemical treatise *al-Durar al-saniyya fī al-radd ʿalā al-wahhābiyya*, which later was refuted by his contemporary Shaykh Muḥammad Bashīr al-Sahsawānī of India in a book titled *Ṣiyānat al-insān ʿan waswasat al-shaykh Daḥlān*, foreword by Muḥammad Rashīd Riḍā, 5th ed., n. p. 1395/1975. The article by Claudia Preckel in this volume also deals with al-Sahsawānī.

24 See Dobbin, Christine: *Islamic Revivalism in a Changing Peasant Economy. Central Sumatra, 1784–1847*, London 1983.

25 Mansurnoor, Iik Arifin: Muslims in Modern Southeast Asia. Radicalism in Historical Perspectives, in: *Taiwan Journal of Southeast Asian Studies* 2 (2005), pp. 3–54, here pp. 16–17.

the spread of moderate Sufism and "fuelling" anti-colonialism in his home country.[26]

Apart from the influence of Wahhabism, the Malay world around this time also began to be acquainted with the moderate reform ideas of Jamāl al-Dīn al-Afghānī (1838–1897), Muḥammad ʿAbduh (1849–1905) and Muḥammad Rashīd Riḍā (1865–1935). Letters were sent by Malays to the editors of *al-Manār* in Egypt, asking for fatwas concerning legal matters, theological problems, as well as current political issues such as patriotism and nationalism.[27] Meanwhile, the number of students from Indonesia who came to study at al-Azhar University continued to increase significantly.[28]

The influence of Egyptian reformism in the Malay world was reflected most clearly in the Muhammadiyyah, a social movement founded by Kiyai Haji Aḥmad Daḥlān in 1912 in Yogyakarta, Central Java, whose primary aim was to deliver the local Muslim community from backwardness and to purify their religion from superstitions, traditional accretions and deviant mysticism, not by violent means but through education and economic activities. Two other organizations followed in suite, namely: the Irsyād (*Jamʿiyyat al-iṣlāḥ wal-irshād al-islāmiyya*) and the Persatuan Islam (PERSIS), founded in 1915 and 1923 respectively.[29] Members of these three institutions not only campaigned against syncretism and mysticism, but also rejected blind dogmatism (*taqlīd*) in favor of independent thinking (*ijtihād*)

26 For the dynamics around the life of Indonesian students in Mecca in the 19th century, see Hurgronje, C. Snouck: *Mekka in the Latter Part of the 19th Century. Daily Life, Customs and Learning of the Moslims of the East-India-Archipelago*, Leiden 1970.

27 Johns, Anthony H.: Islam in Southeast Asia, in: Mircea Eliade (ed.): *The Encyclopedia of Religion*, New York 1987, vol. 7, pp. 410–411; Bluhm-Warn, Jutta: Al-Manar and Ahmad Soorkattie, in: Peter G. Riddell and Tony Street (eds.): *Islam. Essays on Scripture, Thought and Society*, Leiden 1997, pp. 295–308. See Kaptein, Nico: Meccan Fatwas from the End of the Nineteenth Century on Indonesian Affairs, in: *Studia Islamika* 2 (1995), pp. 141–160.

28 On al-Azhar as the centre of religious learning for Indonesians, see Abaza, Mona: *Indonesian Students in Cairo. Islamic Education, Perceptions and Exchanges*, Paris 1994.

29 Literature on the 20th-century reform movements abounds: Peacock, James L.: *Purifying the Faith. The Muḥammadiyyah Movement in Indonesian Islam*, Menlo Park 1978; Bisri, Affandi: *Shaikh Aḥmad al-Shurkātī. His Role in the al-Irshād Movement*, unpublished M.A. thesis, Montreal (McGill University) 1976; see Noer, Deliar: *The Modernist Muslim Movement in Indonesia, 1900–1942*, Singapore 1973.

and rationally justified preference (*ittibāʿ*). These movements were met with resistance from the Nahdlatul Ulama (NU), a rather conservative organization founded in 1926 with the aim of defending traditionalism and of reaffirming the necessity to be attached to one of the four major Sunni (i.e. Ḥanafī, Mālikī, Shāfiʿī or Ḥanbalī) schools of law and to encourage participation in one of the "recognized Sufi orders" (*ṭuruq muʿtabara*).[30]

After World War II, which marked the end of the colonial era and the rise of the nation states of Indonesia, Malaysia, Singapore and Brunei – that is, from 1945 on, Malay Islamic literature received a fresh impetus from prolific scholars such as Ahmad Hassan, T.M. Hasbi al-Shiddiqy and Hamka (Haji ʿAbdul Malik Karīm Amrullāh), each of whom wrote a full commentary on the Koran in Malay – i.e. the *Tafsīr al-Furqān*, *Tafsīr al-Nūr* and *Tafsīr al-Azhar* respectively. It is to be noted that most of the literary production during this new era reflected the growing interest of the Muslim population in learning the "true" Islam directly from its primary sources. Hence, in addition to Koranic exegesis, there soon appeared a complete rendering into Malay of the six canonical Hadith collections of al-Bukhārī, Muslim, Abū Dāwūd, al-Dārimī, al-Nasāʾī, Ibn Māja and al-Tirmidhī. A great deal of *fiqh* works were also translated, such as the *Bulūgh al-marām* of Ibn Ḥajar al-ʿAsqalānī (d. 1449), the *Subul al-salām* of al-Ṣanʿānī, the *Nayl al-awṭār* of al-Shawkānī (1760–1834) and the modern *Fiqh al-sunna* of Sayyid Sābiq (d. 2000) – to mention but a few.

In the political arena, however, the tension between the so-called *Abangan* (nominal, syncretic) and the *Santri* (Sharia-oriented, committed) Muslims continued unabated. There was a heated debate over whether Indonesia should be an Islamic or a secular state. Eventually, however, the secular-nationalists won the parliament and Islam was declared but one of the five official religions of the nation, besides Protestantism, Catholicism, Hinduism and Buddhism.[31]

30 See Chumaidy, A. Farichin: *The Jamʿiyyah Nahdlatul ʿUlama. Its Rise and Early Development (1926–1945)*, unpublished M.A. thesis, Montreal (McGill University) 1976; and Fealy, Greg: *Ulama and Politics in Indonesia. A History of Nahdlatul Ulama (1952–1967)*, Ph.D. thesis, Victoria (Monash University) 1988.

31 See Anshari, Endang Saifuddin: *The Jakarta Charter of June 1945. A History of the Gentlemen's Agreement Between the Islamic and the Secular Nationalists in Modern Indonesia*, M.A. thesis (McGill University), Montreal 1976. See Boland, Bernard Johan: *The Struggle of Islam in Modern Indonesia*, The Hague 1971, pp. 45–54.

Three decades later, following the so-called Islamic "resurgence" or "revival," exemplified in such historic events as the 1979 Iranian Revolution, Pakistan's Islamization program (1977–79) launched by President Zia-ul Haqq (d. 1988) and the assassination of the Egyptian President Anwar Sadat in October 1981, Muslims in Indonesia and Malaysia were becoming more assertive about their commitment to the faith,[32] in spite of all kinds of restraint imposed by their oppressive regimes. The establishment of Islamic universities, Islamic banks, Islamic insurance companies etc. represented this revivalist trend. It is during this period that the writings of "revolutionary" thinkers were introduced to Malaysia and Indonesia. Works of varying length written by authors such as Ibn Taymiyya, Sayyid Quṭb, Abū al-Ḥasan al-Nadwī, Abū al-Aʿlā al-Mawdūdī, ʿAlī Sharīʿatī, Seyyed Hossein Nasr, Fazlur Rahman, Yūsuf al-Qaraḍāwī and others began to pervade Indonesia, causing a remarkable increase in religious fervour and giving impetus to political activism, especially among university students.[33]

2. Literature of Ibn Qayyim al-Jawziyya

Few medieval Arabic authors enjoy as much popularity and credibility among Indonesian Muslim readership today as Ibn Qayyim al-Jawziyya.[34] A visit to any Islamic bookstore in the country confirms this fact. Quite a number of his works in Indonesian rank among the bestsellers and have therefore gone through several editions. This is

---

32 See Nash, Manning: Islamic Resurgence in Malaysia and Indonesia, in: Martin E. Marty and Scott E. Appleby (eds.): *Fundamentalism Observed*, Chicago and London 1991, pp. 691–739.

33 A good survey of contemporary Islamic publications in Indonesia is given in Watson, C. William: Islamic Books and Their Publishers. Notes on the Contemporary Indonesian Scene, in: *Journal of Islamic Studies* 16 (2005), pp. 177–210.

34 On his life and works, see Brockelmann, Carl: *Geschichte der arabischen Litteratur*, Leiden 1949, vol. 2, pp. 127–129; Laoust, Henri: Ibn Ḳayyim al-Djawziyya, in: *EI²*, vol. 3 (1971), pp. 821–822; ʿAbd al-Salām, ʿAbd al-ʿAẓīm: *Ibn Qayyim al-Jawziyya*, Kuwait 1984; Abū Zayd, Bakr b. ʿAbd Allāh: *Ibn Qayyim al-Jawziyya. Ḥayātuhu, āthāruhu, mawāriduhu*, Riyadh 1400/1980; al-Baqarī, Aḥmad Maḥmūd Māhir: *Ibn Qayyim al-Jawziyya. Min āthārihi al-ʿilmiyya*, Beirut 1404/1984 and Alexandria 1407/1987; Apaydın, H. Yunus: İbn Kayyim el-Cevziyye, in: *İslām Ansiklopedisi*, Istanbul 1999, vol. 20, pp. 109–123; and Krawietz, Birgit: Ibn Qayyim al-Jawzīyah. His Life and Works, in: *Mamlūk Studies Review* 10 (2006), pp. 19–64.

a recent phenomenon, however. For unlike al-Ghazālī, al-Qushayrī, al-Nawawī and al-Suyūṭī, whose works have been used in traditional schools (*pesantren*) for a long time, Ibn al-Qayyim was not a familiar name to most Southeast Asian Muslims until the late 1980s and early 1990s. It was only during the last decade that interest in Ibn al-Qayyim emerged and grew especially among university students and urban Muslims, as can be seen from the numerous translations of Ibn al-Qayyim's works and quite a number of scholarly studies on him. Some observers have associated this development with the mushrooming of Salafi groups in recent years. A steadily growing number of talented preachers (sg. *dāʿī*) who received their training in Saudi Arabia or Saudi-sponsored institutions such as Lembaga Ilmu Pengetahuan Islam dan Bahasa Arab (Institute of Islamic and Arabic Studies, LIPIA), formerly known as Lembaga Pengajaran Bahasa Arab (Institute of Arabic Teaching, LPBA), which began its operations in 1981, is believed to have played a major role in spreading Salafism in Indonesia. While the exact extent of their influence cannot be assessed, graduates of Saudi universities and their affiliated institutions have indeed contributed a lot in the dissemination of Ḥanbalism in Indonesia and in popularizing the works of Ibn Taymiyya (d. 1328), Ibn Qayyim al-Jawziyya (d. 1350), in addition to the writings of contemporary scholars such as Shaykh ʿAbd Allāh b. Bāz (d. 1999), Nāṣir al-Dīn al-Albānī (d. 1999), Muḥammad b. Ṣāliḥ al-ʿUthaymīn (d. 2001) and Ṣāliḥ al-Fawzān.[35]

A second factor contributing to the wide acceptance of Ibn al-Qayyim's works, most of which deal with Sufism based on the Koran and Sunna, is the innate disposition of the Malays (Indonesians) towards mysticism. Indeed, as pointed out by scholars, it is evident that in the Malay world as in India since the earliest times Sufism, both orthodox and heretical, appealed most to the population. This holds true even today, where heretical, pantheistic mysticism continued to exist

35 As recently pointed out by Watson, Islamic Books and Their Publishers, p. 187: "One impetus behind these ventures into translation was the initiatives taken by young students returning to Indonesia after study in Pakistan and the Middle East. Inspired by what they read or heard about while abroad, they returned with boxes of books which they suggested to publishers should be translated. Very often publishers take up these suggestions, working on the principle that what has proved popular elsewhere will find a market in Indonesia. Thus, for example, the works of one of the contemporary post-ikhwān al-muslimīn figures, Yūsuf al-Qaraḍāwī, have proved to be very popular at one end of the political spectrum; at the liberal end, Fazlur Rahman's work has found enthusiastic supporters among the younger generation of progressive intellectuals."

despite the fact that orthodox Sufism – also known as "tasauf modern" (Hamka), "neo-Sufism" (Rahman), or "urban Sufism" (*Sufi kota)* – is becoming more popular and has attracted many followers among the educated middle class, who now look to religion and preachers for guidance and practical tips on how to attain spiritual happiness.[36] Gradually, the writings of Ibn al-Qayyim and the like become alternative to older treatises on Sufism. Many now compare Ibn al-Qayyim to al-Ghazālī since both helped to uncover and clarify the orthodox roots of Islam's interior dimension, explaining the way to God with insistence upon the main sources of orthodoxy: Koran, Sunna and the practice of the first two generations of Muslims.

Last but not least, even though Ibn al-Qayyim was deeply influenced by Ibn Taymiyya and likewise engaged in polemics against heretical groups such as the Jahmiyya, Jabriyya and Qadariyya, he was more ready than his teacher to be lenient and amiable to those with whom he differed. In refuting the views of his opponents, Ibn al-Qayyim refrained from using offensive words and preferred instead a sober tone typical of a spiritual teacher. Ibn al-Qayyim managed to talk to the heart, combining verses and tradition with logical persuasion and stylistic finesse. It is this sympathetic approach that makes his writings more popular and fascinating. Lastly, one finds in him flashes of linguistic genius, pious spiritual insights and the answer to the most vital questions of life, soul, happiness, the afterlife etc.

In order to illustrate and map this recent interest in Ibn al-Qayyim as an eminent scholar especially of Sufism, I provide in what follows a list and a brief description of published as well as unpublished works by and on Ibn al-Qayyim, mostly in Indonesia but also in Malaysia and Singapore classifying them in three categories: full translation, partial translation (of excerpt or abridgement) and studies on his texts. Such an account enables us to trace important patterns of perception and preference.

36 For an interesting discussion about "urban Sufism" in Indonesia, see Howell, Julia Day: Sufism and the Indonesian Islamic Revival, in: *The Journal of Asian Studies* 60 (2001), pp. 701–729. See Sila, Muhammad Adlin: *Tasawuf Perkotaan. Kasus Pusat Kajian Tasawuf (PKT) Tazkiyah Sejati Jakarta*, Jakarta 2000.

2.1. Works by Ibn al-Qayyim in Full Translation

2.1.1. The Soul (al-Rūḥ)

This is no doubt Ibn al-Qayyim's most popular work.[37] It was rendered into the Malay-Indonesian language for the first time by Jamaluddin Kafie as *Masalah Ruh* (The Question of the Soul) and published in Surabaya, Indonesia by Bina Ilmu in 1980. It was reprinted the following year by Pena Mas, Johor Bahru, Malaysia. However, it was apparently based on the abridged text *Sirr al-rūḥ* written by Burhān al-Dīn Ibrāhīm b. ʿUmar al-Biqāʿī (d. 885). A second Malay edition was prepared by Syed Ahmad Semait and published in 1990 by the Pustaka Nasional of Singapore with the title *Roh. Satu Analisa tentang Roh-roh Orang Mati dan Orang Hidup* (The Soul. An Analytical Exposition on the Souls of the Living and the Dead). It was reprinted in 2000. There is even a third translation by Kathur Suhardi, published in 1999 by Pustaka al-Kautsar, Jakarta. A comparison between the three versions shows no significant difference apart from minor stylistic improvement and printing quality. All of them were best seller, however. The book attempts to answer various questions concerning the human soul, its nature, origin, destiny, power, predicaments and related issues such as the nature of dream and death, the difference between the soul of the living and that of the dead human being, about punishment in the grave and what will happen to the soul in the afterlife.

2.1.2. A Guide for the Soul to the Land of Joy (Ḥādī al-arwāḥ ilā bilād al-afrāḥ)

There are three Indonesian versions of this important treatise. The first of these, *Tentang Roh. Perjalanan bersama Roh di Alam Lain* (On the Soul and its Journey to the Other World) was completed by Abu Abdillah Almansur and H. Effendi Zarkasyi and published in 1988 by Gema Insani Press, Jakarta. A second translation by Fadhli Bahri was published in 2000 by Dārul Falāḥ, Jakarta, with the title *Tamasya ke Syurga* (Trip to Paradise). The latter, running to over five hundred pages, comprises 69 chapters. It discusses the reality of Paradise, the

37 The article by Tzvi Langerman in this volume discusses Ibn al-Qayyim's *Kitāb al-Rūḥ* in detail.

question whether or not it has been created and whether there is any difference between the Paradise in which Adam and Eve used to live and that which the rest of humankind will later occupy. Also covered are the issues of who will be granted and denied entrance to Paradise, the different gates and classes therein, the various names of Paradise and all sorts of wonderful experiences awaiting its inhabitants.

2.1.3. On the Maladies of the Heart (Risāla fī Amrāḍ al-qulūb)

Based on the 1395/1975 critical edition by Muḥammad Ḥāmid al-Fiqī (Dār al-Ṭayyibah, Riyadh), this work was translated into Indonesian by Fadhli Bahri with the title *Keajaiban Hati* (Wonders of the Heart) and published by Pustaka Azzam, Jakarta in 1999. But this is not the only one available; other translations include *Noktah-noktah Dosa. Terapi Penyakit Hati* (Spots of Sin. Healing the Illness of the Heart) by Kathur Suhardi (Darul Falah, Jakarta, 2000) and *Terapi Penyakit Hati* by Salim Bazemool (Qisthi Press, Jakarta, 2005). A closer look into the book reveals a striking fact: there is no difference between this book and the *Ighāthat al-lahfān* in terms of its content, leaving aside the title wording. Both books discuss the three spiritual states of the heart, i. e. the causes of its health, misery and happiness.

2.1.4. Enlightening Minds Concerning the Prayer and Invoking Blessings on [the Prophet Muḥammad] Who is the Best of Human Kind (Jalā᾽ al-afhām fī faḍl al-ṣalāh ʿalā khayr al-anām)

The Indonesian version of this epistle titled *Shalawat Nabī SAW* was published in 1997 also by Pustaka Azzam. Its translator, Ibn Ibrahim (apparently a sobriquet), rendered not only the whole text but also the editor's preface and the introduction, which comprises a bio-bibliography of Ibn al-Qayyim as well as a review of related literature. Consequently the book becomes more than 600 pages long, divided into five chapters: (i) analysis of various authentic as well as less authentic Hadiths on the importance prayer for the Prophet as reported by over 50 Companions; (ii) detailed explanation of the meaning of each phrase such as *allāhumma* and a review of different opinions concerning the inclusion of the Prophet's wives, relatives and descendants in the prayer; (iii) general guidelines about how to make prayer for the

Prophet; (iv) the best time, place and/or occasion to utter it; and finally (v) the benefits of such prayer.

2.1.5. Secrets of Prayer (Asrār al-ṣalāt)

There are two editions of this work in Indonesian: the first one, titled *Lezatnya Shalat* (The Sweetness of Prayer) is published by Dārul Falāḥ, Jakarta, in 2004 and another titled *Rahasia Dibalik Shalat* (The Secrets behind Prayer) by Pustaka Azzam, Jakarta. The latter has already been printed more than eight times since it came out in January 2000. It is based on *Kitāb al-Ṣalāh wa-ḥukm tārikihā* (The Book of Prayer and what Should be Done with who Fails to Perform it), a text that was edited by Muḥammad Niẓām al-Dīn al-Fātiḥ, published in Medina by Maktabat Dār al-Turāth in 1412/1992. In the preface, the translators (Amir Hamzah Fachruddin and Kamaluddin Saʿdiatulharamain) explain what has driven them to render the book into their mother tongue: "We believe it is part of our responsibility as scholars to share with others the knowledge that God has given us. But we also do this to teach and remind ourselves." The book addresses legal and technical issues pertaining to prayer, explicating numerous sayings of the Prophet about the punishment for those who miss the daily and weekly prayers. However, the two different Indonesian renderings of the title avoid the harshness of the Arabic original.

2.1.6. Implements for the Patient and Provisions for the Grateful (ʿUddat al-ṣābirīn wa-dhakhīrat al-shākirīn)

The Indonesian version of this treatise is made available by three publishers with three different titles: *Sabar Perisai Seorang Mukmin* (Patience (*Ṣabr*) The Shield of the Believers) by Pustaka Azzam, Jakarta, 2000, *Kemuliaan Sabar dan Keagungan Syukur* (The Highest and the Most Excellent of all Virtues. *Ṣabr* and *Shukr*) by Mitra Pustaka, and *Indahnya Sabar. Bekal Sabar Agar Tak Pernah Habis* (The Beauty of *Ṣabr* (Patience). Tips to Maintain the Degree of *Ṣabr*) by Maghfirah Pustaka. It seemed to sell so well that it was printed twice within six months. In the preface to the book, the publisher explains to the reader its continuous relevance: everyone in this transient life is confronted by many problems, which they often regard as fortune (*niʿma*) but also sometimes disaster (*muṣība*). But both of these can be perceived as nothing but a test (*ibtilāʾ*) by God so as to distinguish the faithful from the faithless, the true believers from the false ones. In this book Ibn al-Qayyim makes clear the meaning and nature of *ṣabr*, its kinds and degrees and the positive impacts it will have on a person. Worth-quoting is Ibn al-Qayyim's statement of his purpose:

> This is a book to benefit kings and princes, the wealthy and the indigent, the Sufis and scholars; a [book meant] to inspire the sedentary to set out, accompany the wayfarer on the path and inform the one travelling towards the ultimate Destination.[38]

2.1.7. The Travellers' Stages Between "Thee alone we worship and in Thee alone we seek help" (Madārij al-sālikīn bayna manāzil iyyāka naʿbudu wa iyyāka nastaʿīn)

This major work has been rendered into Indonesian by Aunur Rafiq Shaleh and published in several volumes by Robbani Press Jakarta in 1998–2000 with the following title *Madarijus Salikin. Jenjang Spiritual Para Penempuh Jalan Ruhani*. A second translation appeared in 2000. Published by Risalah Gusti in Surabaya, it was jointly prepared by Abdul Aziz Mustafa, Maghfur Wachid and Muhammad Luqman Hakiem and titled *Mahabbatullah Tangga Menuju Cinta Allah. Wacana Imam Ibnul Qayyim al-Jauziyah*. Pustaka al-Kautsar Jakarta published a third one titled *Madarijus Salikin. Pendakian Menuju Allah* in one volume comprising three parts. Aside from these, the Malay-speaking public may also enjoy the reflections of Shaykh Ṣalāḥ Shādī titled *Menggapai Manisnya Iman. Butir-butir Ma'rifatullah Ibnu Qayyim al-Jawziyyah* (Tasting the Sweetness of Faith. Jewels of Knowledge About God Presented by Ibn al-Qayyim). The translation was done by Marsuni Sasaky, published in Jakarta (Pustaka Azzam) 1420/2000, on the basis of *Taʾammulāt fī Kitāb Madārij al-Sālikīn li-Ibn al-Qayyim al-Jawziyyah*, Kuwait (Sharikat al-Shuʿāʾ) 1405/1985. Written when he was still in jail due to his association with the Muslim Brotherhood of Egypt, Shādī's is a fascinating book to read, split into four chapters: (i) the nature of virtue (*akhlāq*); (ii) the meaning of devotion (*ikhlāṣ*); (iii) interest-free human relations; and (iv) self-management and control.

38 See *ʿUddat al-ṣābirīn*, Cairo 1993, p. 11.

2.1.8. *The Heavy Shower of Good Utterances* (al-Wābil al-ṣayyib min al-kalim al-ṭayyib)

One of Ibn al-Qayyim's bestsellers, the Malay-Indonesian version of this treatise is titled *Zikir Cahaya Kehidupan* (Remembrance of God as Illumination in Life). Based on the excerpt titled *Fawāʾid al-Dhikr*, the task of rendering it from Arabic was done by Abdul Hayyie al-Kattani and his team members, and was published in 2002 by Gema Insani Press, Jakarta. Due to its brevity and portability, the book sold very well, having gone through over five editions within two years. It consists of 80 chapters dealing with the various benefits of remembrance (*dhikr*), the guidelines and proper method of doing it and elucidation of related matters. The value of this treatise is explained by Ibn al-Qayyim in his other work: "In our book *al-Wābil al-ṣayyib wa-rāfiʿ al-kalim al-ṭayyib* we have already mentioned nearly one hundred benefits of remembrance of God, its secrets, advantages and its sweet fruits."

2.1.9. *Path of the Two Migrations and Gate to the Two Joys* (Ṭarīq al-hijratayn wa-bāb al-saʿādatayn)

This work has been translated as *Bekal Hijrah Menuju Allāh* (Provision for the Journey to God), published by Gema Insani Press, Jakarta, 2002) and *Hijrah Paripurna Menuju Allāh dan Rasūlnya* (A Perfect Journey to God and His Messenger), published variously by Pustaka Azzam, Jakarta. It is based on the 1979 Cairo edition covering wide-ranging topics from the meaning of ontological need and contingency (*faqr*), servitude (*taʿabbud*), benefit (*manfaʿa*) and harm (*maḍarra*) in relation to God's decree (*al-qaḍāʾ wal-qadar*), to forbearance (*ṣabr*) and longing (*shawq*) for God.

2.1.10. *The Sufficient Answer to the One Who Seeks a Cure* (al-Jawāb al-kāfī li-man saʾala ʿan al-dawāʾ al-shāfī)

This work is also known as *al-Dāʾ wal-dawāʾ* (The Malady and the Remedy). Translated as *Siraman Rohani Bagi Yang Mendambakan Ketenangan Hati* (A Spiritual Shower for Those Who Need Spiritual Tranquility) by Arief B. Iskandar, the book was published in 2000 by

Pustaka Lentera, Jakarta. It outlines the importance of invocation (*duʿāʾ*) and remembrance (*dhikr*) of God and spells out the consequences of sins (*al-maʿāṣī*). According to Ibn al-Qayyim, diseases of the soul such as anxiety, stress and depression can be cured through remembrance of God. Referring to the Hadith transmitted by Abū Yaʿlā, Ibn ʿAdī and al-Ḥākim, he explains that invocation is the most effective means of psycho-therapy; it is the "enemy" of spiritual illness - repressing it and removing it, or at least preventing its occurrence; "It is the weapon of the believer, the pillar of the religion and the light of the heaven and earth", quoting another Hadith reported by al-Ḥākim.

2.1.11. *The Garden of Lovers and the Promenade of Those Who Yearn* (Rawḍat al-muḥibbīn wa-nuzhat al-mushtāqīn)

This bestselling work was rendered into Indonesian by Kathur Suhardi and published by Al Baz in 1997 with the title *Taman Orang-orang Cinta dan Rindu.* It also appeared in 1996 as *Taman Orang-orang Jatuh Cinta dan Memendam Rindu* from Darul Falah, Jakarta. A third edition, titled *Taman Orang-orang Jatuh Cinta dan Rekreasi Orang-orang Dimabuk Rindu* was published in 2006 by the Bandung-based Irsyad Baitus Salam. As Ibn al-Qayyim himself stated in the introduction, the aim of the book was to assist believers in properly subordinating all secondary, profane affections to the supreme, sacred love owed to God. In his view, love (*maḥabba*) is both the means and final cause of creation as well as the soul's way to beatitude. Needless to say, Ibn al-Qayyim always cited the sayings of the Prophet and other religious authorities before concluding with selections of verses in support of his opinions.

2.1.12. *God's Beautiful Names* (Sharḥ Asmāʾ Allāh al-ḥusnā)

Published by Pustaka al-Kautsar, Jakarta, as *Asmāʾ-ul Ḥusnā – Nama-nama Indah Allah* (The Beautiful Names of God). The translation is based on the Arabic text edited by Yūsuf ʿAlī and Ayman ʿAbd al-Razzāq Shawwā, Beirut (Dār al-Kalim al-Ṭayyib) 1998. The Malay-Indonesian edition includes the translation of the editorial preface. The ten chapters of the book spell out the etymology and significance of the 99 Divine Names.

2.1.13. Gift for the Beloved on the Rules Pertaining to New Born Babies (Tuḥfat al-mawdūd bi-aḥkām al-mawlūd)

This epistle has been published by Pustaka at-Tibyan Jakarta under the title *Kado Sang Bayi* (The Baby's Present). In this book we find Ibn al-Qayyim's explanation about what the Muslim parents should do to their new-born babies. This includes uttering the call to prayer (*adhān*) and *iqāma* (call for prayer) in the baby's right and left ear respectively; doing *taḥnīk*, i. e. putting sweet things in the mouth of the baby and invoking Allah to bless the newly born baby; slaughtering a sheep (*ʿaqīqa*), shaving the child's head and anointing it with saffron and giving the child a good name – the latter preferably on the seventh day. Ibn al-Qayyim regards this *ʿaqīqa* as a means by which the child is brought close to Allah soon after he comes into this world, since it is a ransom that would enable him or her to intercede for the parents in the Afterlife. Also recommended by Ibn al-Qayyim is circumcision (*khitān*) which signifies natural purity (*sunan al-fiṭra*).

2.1.14. Cure for the Sick (Shifāʾ al-ʿalīl fī masāʾil al-qaḍāʾ wal-qadar wal-ḥikma wa-taʿlīl)

Published by Pustaka Azzam, Jakarta, it has been translated under the title *Qadha dan Qadar* (On Divine Ordinance and Predestination). It was apparently based on the text printed in 1407/1987 by Dār al-Kutub al-ʿIlmiyya, Beirut. The treatise was basically written in order to refute two major heresies: the so-called *qadariyya* (belief in man's free will) and its opposite, i. e. fatalism (*jabriyya*). The issues addressed include whether one's felicity or misery in the afterlife are predetermined or not, the difference between predetermination (*qaḍāʾ*) and causality (*qadar*), the meaning of guidance (*hudā*) and aberrance (*ḍalāl*), human effort (*kasb*) in relation to God's domination (*jabr*). Equally interesting is the imaginary debate Ibn al-Qayyim relayed between the two opposing camps. In his views, the fatalists' thesis is untenable because it would render meaningless the sending of the prophets, and would defeat the purpose of reward and punishment in the hereafter.

2.1.15. *Informing Those in Charge About the Master of the Two Worlds* (Iʿlām al-muwaqqiʿīn ʿan rabb al-ʿālamīn)

The translation of this important work into Indonesian was done by Kamaluddin Sa'diyatulharamain and Asep Saefullah. Titled *Panduan Hukum Islam,* it was published in four volumes by Pustaka Azzam, Jakarta in 2000. A section of this book on the question of *taqlīd* has been published separately as *Risāla fī al-Taqlīd*, ed. by Muḥammad Ḥusaynī ʿAfīfī, Beirut (al-Maktab al-Islāmī) 1405/1985. The Malay-Indonesian version of this excerpt was prepared by Kathur Suhardi and published by Dārul Falāḥ, Jakarta in 1421/2000. In the preface, the editor informs the reader about the effort he made to correct mistakes found in the previously printed texts, besides tracing the numerous Koran and Hadith references to their sources, clarifying technical terms as well as unfamiliar or ambiguous words and pointing out the possible basis of every legal ruling cited therein. A new table of content is supplied: (i) What is *taqlīd*? How and why it is different from *ittibāʿ*; (ii) The four Imams were against *taqlīd*; (iii) An imaginary debate between those who practice *taqlīd* and those who oppose it.

2.2. Ibn al-Qayyim's Works in Partial Translation

2.2.1. *Prophetic Medicine* (al-Ṭibb al-nabawī)

This text is part of the book *Zād al-maʿād fī hady khayr al-ʿibād* (Provisions for the Afterlife on the Teachings of the Best of All People). There are more than four editions of this work in Malay-Indonesian: the first one, titled *Panduan Rawatan Perubatan Berdasarkan al-Qurʾān dan al-Sunnah* (A Guide for Medical Treatment from the Holy Koran and the Prophetic Tradition), was translated by Rozali Md. Isa and published by Thinker's Library, Selangor, Malaysia, 1996. A second one, *Sistem Perubatan Nabi* (The Prophet's Medical System) was published by Albaz Publisher, Selangor, Malaysia, 2000. The other two appeared in Indonesia, titled *Kiat Sehat ala Rasulullah SAW. Cara Hidup Sehat Rasulullah dan Sahabat* (Tips for Health from the Prophet. How to Lead a Healthy Life as the Prophet and his Companions Used to Do) and *Metode Pengobatan Nabi* (The Method of Prophetic Medicine), that were published by the Jakarta-based Najla Press and Griya Ilmu respectively. In this book Ibn al-Qayyim advocated the medical practices of the Prophet and those mentioned in the Koran in preference to the medical theories assimilated from the Greeks, thereby providing a guide to medical therapy that was in conformity with the Islamic principles. The therapy recommended included diet and simple drugs, especially honey, bloodletting and cautery, but no surgery. Other topics included fevers, leprosy, plague, poisonous bites, protection from night-flying insects, protection against the evil eye, rules of coitus, theories of embryology and anatomy, the proper conduct of physicians and the treatment of minor illnesses such as headaches, nosebleeds, cough, colic and sciatica. The use of wine and soporific as medicaments was strictly prohibited. In addition, Ibn al-Qayyim provided numerous prayers and pious invocations to be used by the devout patient, with designs for the occasional amulet and talisman.

2.2.2. Physiognomy (al-Firāsa)

This small text, which is part of the work *al-Ṭuruq al-ḥukmiyya fī al-siyāsa al-sharʿiyya* (The Ways of Governance in Accordance with the Revealed Law) was translated into Indonesian by A. H. Ba'adillah and published as *Firasat* by Pustaka Azzam Jakarta in 2000. The basis for it was the text edited by Ṣalāḥ Aḥmad al-Sāmarrāʾī and published in 1986 by al-Maktaba al-Waṭaniyyah, Baghdad. The editor informs us that he has collated the manuscript with the printed text edited by Muḥammad Ḥāmid al-Fiqī. In spite of its somewhat misleading title, the book in fact deals with intuition as one of the valid methods in settling legal disputes – what we today call law of evidence governing the use of testimony (oral or written) and other kinds of proof in a judicial proceeding.

2.2.3. A Guide for the Soul to the Land of Joy (Ḥādī al-arwāḥ ilā bilād al-afrāḥ)

The abridged version of this monograph with annotations by Leila Mabrūk was published in 1988 by Pustaka al-Kautsar, Jakarta, bearing the title *Tentang Roh. Perjalanan bersama Roh di Alam Lain*. The book like its complete, original version is an answer to all questions one might pose about the eternal life in Paradise, what will be provided for and experienced by its inhabitants.

2.2.4. Rescuing the Afflicted from Satan's Snares (Ighāthat al-lahfān min maṣā'id al-Shayṭān)

The Indonesian version of this work, titled *Manajemen Kalbu – Melumpuhkan Senjata Syetan* (Breaking the Weapon of Satan) was prepared by Ainul Haris Umar Arifin Thayib and published by Dārul Falāḥ, Jakarta in 2000. It is the translation of an abridgement of the original written by ʿAlī b. Ḥasan b. ʿAlī b. ʿAbd al-Ḥamīd, namely: *Mawārid al-amān al-muntaqā min Ighāthat al-lahfān min maṣā'id al-shayṭān*, Riyadh (Dār Ibn al-Jawzī), 1411/1991. The Indonesian editor proudly mentioned his personal acquaintance with the author of the abridgement, who happened to be a student to the celebrated Shaykh Nāṣir al-Dīn al-Albānī. Close 500 pages long, the book is organized into 13 chapters, with each being sub-divided into several sections. It begins with a discussion about three different conditions of the heart – the healthy, the sick and the dead one. Analytical explanation of various causes of spiritual illness, paralysis and death is given in the subsequent chapters. Also discussed are the method and the means recommended by Ibn al-Qayyim to remedy the situation and restore one's spiritual health. The remaining chapters talk about all kinds of tricks and weapons that demons normally use against humans, including of course Ibn al-Qayyim's practical tips to overcome them.

2.2.5. On the Virtues and Vices of the Soul (al-Furūq al-nafīsa bayna ṣifāt al-nafs al-ṭayyiba wal-khabītha)

According to its editor, Abū Ḥudhayfa Ibrāhīm b. Muḥammad, this is an excerpt from Ibn Qayyim's celebrated *Kitāb al-Rūḥ*, namely the section dealing with the three aspects of human soul: at peace (*muṭma'inna*), blaming (*lawwāma*) and urging evil (*ammāra bil-sū'*). It has been translated by Abu Aḥmad Najieh as *Etika Kesucian. Wacana Penyucian Jiwa, Entitas Sikap Hidup Muslim* (The Ethics of Purity. How to Purify the Soul which is the Essential Aspect of a Muslim's Life), and was published in 1998 by Risalah Gusti, Surabaya.

2.2.6. *Provision for the Appointed Day from the Teachings of God's Best Servant* (Zād al-maʿād fī hady khayr al-ʿibād)

A complete translation of this work was published in 1999 by Pustaka al-Kautsar, Jakarta. The publisher tells the reader that this book is a must reading for every Muslim who is bound to follow the Prophet's way of life. Ibn al-Qayyim's book provides the readers with everything they need to know about the Prophet – his genealogy, his personal traits and habits, his way of dealing with people of all walks of life, his legal rulings and his military expeditions. The original text used is that published in 1420/1999 by Dār al-Taqwā, Beirut.

2.2.7. *The Key to the Abode of Happiness and the Decree of the Sovereignty of Knowledge and Will* (Miftāḥ dār al-saʿāda wa-manshūr wilāyat al-ʿilm wal-irāda)

The Indonesian version of this treatise, titled *Buah Ilmu* (Fruit of Knowledge) was published by Pustaka Azzam, Jakarta in 1420/1990. It was based on the excerpt published by Abū al-Ḥārith al-Ḥalabī al-Atharī as *al-ʿIlm* (Knowledge) in Riyadh, 1412/1992.[39] Also available is another partial translation done by Kathur Suhardi and published by Pustaka al-Kautsar, Jakarta in 1988 with a slightly different title: *Mendulang Faidah dari Lautan Ilmu* (Drawing Benefits from the Ocean of Knowledge). The latter is based on the text edited by ʿAlī b. Ḥasan al-Ḥalabī al-Atharī titled *Fawāʾid al-fawāʾid*, Damascus (Dār Ibn al-Jawzī) 1417/1997. It was a great fortune for us, says the Indonesian publisher in the preface, to have a scholar of outstanding quality like Ibn Taymiyya who produced no less a figure than Ibn Qayyim al-Jawziyya. The book is divided into 14 sections: (i) on *ʿaqīda* and *tawḥīd*-related notions such as sincerity (*ikhlāṣ*), servitude (*ʿubūdiyya*), trust and reliance on God (*tawakkul*); (ii) on the Holy Koran and interpretation of selected chapters and verses; (iii) lessons from the Prophetic Hadith on the significance of fear of God (*taqwā*) and the necessity of abiding by the Sunna; (iv) admonition that failure to do what God commands is much more serious than failure to avoid what He forbids; (v) on the types of knowledge and the knowledgeable; (vi) the psychology of human soul; (vii) on faith and infidelity, their

39 This is corresponding to vol. 1, pp. 219–542 of the original text, Cairo 1323–25/1905–07.

nature and characteristics; (viii) the problem of sins and disobedience; (ix) on the spiritual journey to God; (x) on the subtleties of the heart; (xi) on the life of some pious personalities; (xii) various issues pertaining to human nature; (xiii) solution to the riddle about good and evil, angel and Satan, what is *ḥalāl* and what is *ḥarām*, obedience and disobedience; and (xiv) short notes on God's decree (*taqdīr*), moral maxims and proverbs.

2.3. Studies on Ibn al-Qayyim

2.3.1. Harun, Nasrun: Ijtihad Ibn Qayyim al-Jauziyyah dalam Konteks Perubahan Sosial (*Ibn Qayyim al-Jawziyya's* ijtihād *within the Context of Social Change*)[40]

The author attempts to shed light on the dialectical relation between jurisprudence and the changing situations of society with special reference to Ibn al-Qayyim's critical attitude towards "total reliance on authority" (*taqlīd*), "dogmatic fanaticism" (*taʿaṣṣub*) and independent legal judgement (*ijtihad*). We are told that although he adhered to the Ḥanbalī legal thought, Ibn al-Qayyim did not always agree with Ibn Ḥanbal's views. Hence one might call him a *mujtahid muntasib* – that is, a qualified scholar who was capable of arriving at an independent, sometimes also different legal opinion while still following the methodological principles of his school. The author further notes that Ibn al-Qayyim did not accept juristic preference (*istiḥsān*) as a valid method of legal inference, dismissing it as a blameworthy kind of reasoning (*al-ra'y al-madhmūm*). However, since Ibn al-Qayyim did acknowledge the validity of analogical reasoning (*qiyās*), the author concludes that the issue was less substantial than terminological – i. e. what Ibn al-Qayyim rejected was the term *istiḥsān* (which was a later invention), and not the practice of solving a legal problem by means of reasoning when explicit statement (*naṣṣ*) could nowhere be found. The author seemed fascinated by the principle that legal opinions change and vary at different times, places, circumstances, aims and customs (*taghayyur al-fatāwī wa-ikhtilāfuhā bi-ḥasab ikhtilāf al-azmina wal-amkina wal-aḥwāl wal-niyyāt wal-ʿawā'id*) which he claimed is central to Ibn al-Qayyim's legal thought and useful for present-day Muslims.

40 Ph. D. thesis (Institut Agama Islam Negeri (IAIN), Syarif Hidayatullah University), Jakarta 1997.

2.3.2. Ibn Nizar, Tamar Jaya: Pemikiran Kalām Ibn Qayyim al-Jauziyyah (*The Theological Thought* (kalām) *of Ibn Qayyim al-Jawziyya*)[41]

The chief aim of this analytical study of Ibn al-Qayyim's theological writings is to expose his stance on issues such as human reason versus revelation, the attributes of God, free-will and predestination and the problem of *taʾwīl.* According to the author, Ibn al-Qayyim preferred the method of rapprochement (*al-jamʿ*) when the sacred text seems to contradict reason. God's acts are concomitants of His attributes, and His attributes are concomitants of His essence. All this must be accepted as it is, without implying anthropomorphism nor making allegorical interpretation. Ibn al-Qayyim distinguished two kinds of volition with respect to God, one pertaining to nature (*irāda kawniyya*), the other to one's relationship to God's religion (*irāda dīniyya*). God's justice should be understood in connection with His wisdom (*ḥikma*) for His creatures' benefit (*maṣlaḥa*). Man is granted freedom to choose and act within the constraint of and in accordance with God's rule (*sunnat allāh*). Ibn al-Qayyim believed in the eternality of Paradise but he denied the eternality of the Hell.[42] The author finally observed that Ibn al-Qayyim's approach to theological issues differed from most Sunni *mutakallimūn* in several respects. He was able to provide logical arguments in support of his theses while at the same time holding fast to the revealed text and tradition.

2.3.3. Ibrahim, Mohammad: Konsep Tauhid dan Sifat-sifat Allah Menurut Ibn Qayyim al-Jawziyya (*The Concept of* tawḥīd *and the Divine Attributes According to Ibn Qayyim al-Jawziyya*)[43]

This study consists of six chapters, including a general introduction, a bio-bibliography and a conclusion. The main discussion is found in chapter four, where Ibn al-Qayyim's distinction between *tawḥīd al-ʿilm* and *al-tawḥīd al-qaṣdī al-irādī* and their negation are elucidated. The subsequent chapter deals with Ibn al-Qayyim's views on

41 Ph. D. thesis (IAIN, Syarif Hidayatullah University), Jakarta 1999.

42 On the question of hellfire and its eternality see the article by Jon Hoover in this volume.

43 M. A. thesis (Academy of Islamic Studies, University of Malaya), Kuala Lumpur 1999.

the Divine attributes (*ṣifāt*). We are told that Ibn al-Qayyim's position is similar to that of his teacher Ibn Taymiyya: to affirm God's attributes as stated by the Revelation without questioning (*bi-lā kayf*) and without falling into anthropomorphism, and therefore rejecting deism (*taʿṭīl*) of any kind. The conclusion underscores several important points, stating that Ibn al-Qayyim is a true reformer (*mujaddid*) in theology who devoted his life to the cause of rectifying errors and eradicating confusion among the Muslims; that while he built his views on the basis of Koran and Sunna, Ibn al-Qayyim did use rational arguments to support his theses; therefore, it is not groundless to say that Ibn al-Qayyim belongs to the Ahl al-Sunna scholars who follow in the footsteps of the first generations of pious Muslims (*al-salaf al-ṣāliḥ*).

2.3.4. Saiful Anam, Ahmad: Kriteria Kesahihan Hadis menurut Ibn Qayyim al-Jawziyya (*Ibn Qayyim al-Jawziyya's Criteria for Determining the Authenticity of Hadith*)[44]

Focusing on Ibn al-Qayyim's *Kitāb al-Manār al-munīf fī al-ṣaḥīḥ wal-ḍaʿīf*, this study sought to expose the criteria used by Ibn al-Qayyim in ascertaining whether or not a Prophetic tradition is authentic and valid. It was found that in Ibn al-Qayyim's view the reliability of the transmitters (*sanad*) does not always guarantee the validity of the reported content (*matn*). According to Ibn al-Qayyim, so we are told, five conditions must be met in order for a Hadith to be authentic: (i) it must be transmitted by trustworthy authorities; (ii) it must be free from any defect (*ʿilla*); (iii) it must be free from aberrations (*shudhūdh*); (iv) it must be free from opposition (*nakāra*) and finally (v) there should be no conflict or contradiction between its transmitters. The author applied these five criteria against a dozen Hadiths which he randomly picked from Ibn al-Qayyim's *al-Manār al-munīf*. The finding was not surprising: Ibn al-Qayyim's judgement of the Hadiths in question seems to be consistent with the criteria of authenticity which he upholds. The author concluded by stating that generally speaking, Ibn al-Qayyim's methodology was quite moderate – that is, neither strict nor loose, whilst conforming as he was to the standard procedure of the *muḥaddithūn*.

44 Ph. D. thesis (IAIN, Syarif Hidayatullah University), Jakarta 1997.

2.3.5. *Abdillah, Mujiyono:* Dialektika Hukum Islam dan Perubahan Sosial. Sebuah Refleksi sosiologis atas pemikiran Ibn Qayyim al-Jauziyyah (*Dialectical [Relationship] between Islamic Law and Social Change. A Sociological Reflection on Ibn Qayyim al-Jawziyya's Legal Thought*)[45]

Based on the author's dissertation, this book attempts to explore the alleged flexibility principle that Ibn al-Qayyim adopted in his legal theory: that legal rulings vary according to the changing circumstances. The first two chapters sketch the general theoretical framework where the author's erroneous assumptions are laid down: that Islamic law is the intellectual product of Muslim scholars and jurists; that Islamic law went through a gradual development and is therefore subject to change and never final; and that social change will inevitably affect and even dictate the further development of Islamic law. It is clear that the author has confused the Sharia with jurisprudence (*fiqh*); he failed to distinguish the legal dicta (*naṣṣ*) from the personal opinion (*fatwā*) reflecting the intellectual effort (*ijtihād*) of the jurists (*fuqahā*ʾ). In short, Abdillah mistook Ibn al-Qayyim's orthodox stance for a liberal attitude according to which the ends would justify the means, and the Divine law must obey the society. After giving a biographical overview in chapter three, the author proceeds to elaborate on what he claims to be Ibn al-Qayyim's theory of legal transformation which he discusses in sociological terms.

2.3.6. *Yusof, Ahmad Ikbal b. Mohammad:* Ibn Qayyim's Critique of Philosophical Sufism. The Refutation of al-Tilimsānī's Version of Waḥdat al-Wujūd[46]

This work presents a comparative textual analysis of Ibn al-Qayyim's Kitāb *Madārij al-sālikīn* and al-Tilimsānī's *Sharḥ Manāzil al-sāʾirīn ilā al-ḥaqq al-mubīn*, each of which being an extended commentary on a short treatise written by the celebrated Ḥanbalī Sufi al-Harawī (d. 481/1089). Special attention was given to the concept of "mystical witnessing" (*mushāhada*) in order to highlight the opposing views of Ibn al-Qayyim vis-à-vis al-Tilimsānī on the question of ontic unity

45 Surakarta 2003.
46 M. A. thesis (International Islamic University Malaysia), Kuala Lumpur 2004.

(*waḥdat al-wujūd*). The author observed that Ibn al-Qayyim held an uncompromising, critical stance towards the so-called philosophical Sufism (*al-taṣawwuf al-falsafī*) just as his master Ibn Taymiyyah did. In his conclusion the author proposed that *waḥdat al-shuhūd* should be adopted instead of *waḥdat al-wujūd* and that Sufism should be guided and based on the Prophetic tradition rather than philosophy.

2.3.7. Ismail, Masthurah: Analisis Terhadap Pandangan Ibn Qayyim al-Jawziyya mengenai Hak Beragama Orang bukan Islam di dalam Negara Islam. Kajian dalam Aḥkām ahl al-Dhimmah (*Ibn Qayyim al-Jawziyya's Views on the Rights of Non-Muslim Citizens in an Islamic State. An Analytical Study of His Aḥkām ahl al-dhimma*)[47]

This important work brings into focus the views of Ibn al-Qayyim on the religious rights of non-Muslims as expressed quite in detail in a compilation of his writings titled *Aḥkām ahl al-dhimmah*. The author claims that Ibn al-Qayyim's views concerning non-Muslims do not diverge markedly from those established by other scholars. This is so, she says, because they used a common methodology. The only difference on the issue is to be found in their understanding and application of *maṣlaḥa*. The author concludes that according to Ibn al-Qayyim, the religious rights of the non-Muslim citizens must be protected by the state – not unconditionally, of course, but rather with the provisions described by the jurists.

2.3.8. Mohd Yusof, Mohd Izwan: Metodologi Ibn Qayyim al-Jawziyya dalam Kitāb *al-Amthāl fī al-qur'ān* (*Ibn Qayyim al-Jawziyya's Interpretive Methodology in His* al-Amthāl fī al-qur'ān)[48]

This dissertation details the exegetical methodology of Ibn al-Qayyim as reflected in his book *al-Amthāl fī al-qur'ān*. The author begins with a discussion about the method Ibn al-Qayyim applied in composing the book. According to the author, Ibn al-Qayyim did not invent any new method of interpretation; rather, he stuck to the traditional one

47 M.A. thesis (Academy of Islamic Studies, University of Malaya), Kuala Lumpur 2007.
48 M.A. thesis (Academy of Islamic Studies, University of Malaya), Kuala Lumpur 2007.

commonly used by the classical *mufassirūn* before him. That is to say, he interpreted the similes found in the Koran by referring to other verses and the Prophetic Hadith as well as to the statements going back to the Companions (*ṣaḥāba*). Nevertheless, Ibn al-Qayyim did in a few cases manage to come up with his own understanding of the verses in question, so we are told.

Conclusion

One of the results of the Islamization process that has been going on since the 13th century in the Malay-Indonesian archipelago is the radical change in the *Weltanschauung* of the people. As al-Attas rightly pointed out, following the conversion of the "body" which represented the first phase of the process (from 1200–1400 CE), the Malay-Indonesian Muslims gradually came to understand the fundamental concepts constituting the worldview of Islam such as *tawḥīd* and *nubuwwa*, albeit in the opaque sense, still influenced by the old *Weltanschauung*. In the third phase (from 1700 CE onwards) the Islamization process was boosted by the cultural influences of the Western colonials who bolstered the scientific-rationalistic spirit whose philosophical foundations were laid earlier by Islam.[49] Consequently by the late 19th and 20th centuries, Islam became so entrenched in the souls of the people that many would consider Islam as an essential part of their ethnic identity; hence being Malay, Acehnese, Sundanese, Banjarese, Buginese, Madurese was identical to being Muslim, just as being European would imply being Christian. It should be noted, however, that throughout these centuries up to the present day the overwhelming majority of the population of the Malay-Indonesian archipelago was dominated by Shāfiʿīs and Ashʿarīs. Lay people would consider those who do not belong to these groups to be deviating from the straight path. There might have been some Shiites in Sumatra and other parts of the region but they have left few traces. The same holds true for Wahhabism and associated doctrines like that of Ibn Taymiyya which have always met resistance from people.

As regards Ibn al-Qayyim, it is may be concluded from the foregoing survey that his influence is quite evident not only in the popu-

49 See al-Attas, Syed Muhammad al Naquib: *Islam and Secularism*, Kuala Lumpur 1978, pp. 161–162.

lar literature on Sufism but also in the academic works dealing with theology and law. The continuous reprinting of his translated works in the Malay-speaking world is indeed one of many signs of an unfading attention to his thought. Besides the impact of the reform movements such as the Muhammadiyah, Nahḍat al-ʿUlamāʾ and Persatuan Islam, it was the young people returning from the Middle East that have been playing a crucial role in popularizing Ibn al-Qayyim's works on spirituality, ethics, law and theology. Although the translation is generally quite legible and faithful to the original, the fact that numerous mistakes abound and no effort was made to collate the text and annotate it is a clear indication that these were in most cases done for commercial rather than scholarly aims.

Coming back to the issue of radicalism touched upon at the outset, we have seen that historical evidence points out to the fact that Salafi ideas were brought to the Malay world long before the works of Ibn Taymiyya, Ibn Qayyim al-Jawziyya and others were made available to the Malay-Indonesian speakers. If there were any link between Salafism and radicalism as some have suggested, it is more likely to be chronological than causal. That is to say, it would be *post hoc, ergo propter hoc* to attribute the booming of radicalism to the plethora of such authors. One should look into a bundle of factors which are primarily political, economic or psychological in nature to better explain such annoying phenomenon.

Section 3: Philosophy

The Poison of Philosophy

Ibn Taymiyya's Struggle For and Against Reason[1]

Anke von Kügelgen

Ibn Taymiyya (d. 728/1328) lived in a period in which the claim of the priority of reason/intellect (*ʿaql*) over religious tradition (*naql*) in the case of their contradiction was prevailing in scholarly circles reading and commenting on philosophical texts in Iran, Iraq, Syria, Egypt and the Maghreb. Representatives of these circles were scholars with different intellectual interests and opinions, such as Fakhr al-Dīn al-Rāzī (d. 606/1209), Athīr al-Dīn al-Abharī (d. 663/1264), Ibn Sabʿīn (d. 668 or 669/1269–71), Naṣīr al-Dīn al-Ṭūsī (d. 672/1274) and Najm al-Dīn al-Kātibī (d. 657/1276), who saw Aristotelian logic as a neutral and infallible instrument of reason,[2] in fact, al-Abharī's[3] summary of logic

1 I would like to thank Caterina Bori, Kurt Flasch, Dimitri Gutas, Jon Hoover, Birgit Krawietz and Georges Tamer for their very helpful comments on drafts of this paper. It benefited as well from the careful readings of some parts by Stephan Reichmuth and Jan-Peter Hartung and supportive criticisms of the participants at the Workshop "Neo-Hanbalism Reconsidered: The Impact of Ibn Taymiyya and Ibn Qayyim al-Jawziyya". Moreover I am much obliged to Kata Moser who proofread several versions of the article, adjusted the transliteration and helped me in preparing the bibliography, and express my gratitude also to Florian Zemmin for his assistance with the last text editing. The composing deadline was spring 2008. All publications after that date were not taken into account except the contributions of Caterina Bori, Livnat Holtzmann, Sait Özervarli and Yossef Rapoport to *Ibn Taymiyya and His Times*, ed. by Yossef Rapoport and Shahab Ahmed in 2010, and Caterina Bori's contribution to *The Mamlūk Studies Review* 13 (2009), with which the authors or editors kindly provided me when they were still in press.

2 Street, Tony: Arabic Logic, in: Peter Adamson and Richard C. Taylor (eds.): *The Cambridge Companion to Arabic Philosophy*, Cambridge 2005, pp. 572–579; see also below, chapters 2 and 5.

3 Atademir, Hamdi R.: Porphyrios ve Ebherî'nin Isagoci'leri, in: *Ankara Üniversitesi Dil ve Tarih-Coğrafya Fakültesi Dergisi* 6 (1948), p. 468 (according to Gutas, Dimitri: Aspects of Literary Form and Genre in Arabic Logical Works, in:

(*Īsāghūjī*) and al-Kātibī's[4] treatise on some logical questions (*al-Risāla al-Shamsiyya*) respectively were to become the most often-copied and annotated handbooks. Another common feature was the adoption of philosophical terminology, categories and concepts in their own writings.[5] The extent of adoption differed, however, from scholar to scholar. Philosophical notions were thus often modified and harmonized with theological and mystical dogmata.[6] Ibn Taymiyya was not only well-familiar with their works,[7] but was also in direct or indirect touch with several of their pupils, among them Naṣr al-Dīn al-Manbijī (d. 719/1319–20), a powerful Sufi Shaykh who propagated the doctrines of mystical union according to the teachings of Ibn al-ʿArabī (d. 638/1240) and Ibn Sabʿīn and provoked Ibn Taymiyya's banishment from Damascus in 1305 and his subsequent imprisonment in Egypt.[8] In the penultimate decade of his life, Ibn Taymiyya took up his pen

---

Charles Burnett (ed.): *Glosses and Commentaries on Aristotelian Logical Texts. The Syriac, Arabic and Medieval Latin Traditions*, London 1993, p. 63, n. 161); Gutas, Dimitri: The Study of Arabic Philosophy in the Twentieth Century. An Essay on the Historiography of Arabic Philosophy, in: *British Journal of Middle Eastern Studies* 29 (2002), pp. 5–25, here 15–16; İzgi, Cevat: *Osmanlı Medreselerinde İlim*, Istanbul 1997, vol. 1, pp. 164, 168–174.

4 Street, Arabic Logic, pp. 247, 252–256.

5 Gutas, The Study of Arabic Philosophy, pp. 6–7, 13, 15–17 et passim; on p. 7 he presents an "outline of Arabic Philosophy (IX–XVIIIc.)" in which he shows that philosophy was vivid during the whole period, with different types of "Avicennism" as the dominant directions; Gutas, Dimitri: The Heritage of Avicenna. The Golden Age of Arabic Philosophy, 1000–ca. 1350, in: Jules Janssens and Daniel de Smet (eds.): *Avicenna and His Heritage. Acts of the International Colloquium, Leuven – Louvain-la-Neuve, September 8–11, 1999*, Leuven 2002, pp. 82–97, here 89–97.

6 Griffel, Frank: *Apostasie und Toleranz im Islam. Die Entwicklung zu al-Ghazālīs Urteil gegen die Philosophie und die Reaktionen der Philosophen*, Leiden, Boston and Cologne 2000, pp. 341–353.

7 See Ibn Taymiyya: *Darʾ taʿāruḍ al-ʿaql wal-naql*, ed. by Muḥammad Rashād Sālim, Riyadh 1399–1400/1979–1980, "Fihris al-aʿlām", s. v.; and below, chapters 9–11.

8 Laoust, Henri: *Essai sur les doctrines sociales et politiques de Takī-d-dīn Aḥmad Ibn Taimīya, canoniste Ḥanbalite. Né à Ḥarrān en 661/1262, mort à Damas en 728/1328; thèse pour le doctorat*, Cairo 1939, pp. 128–132; Bori, Caterina: Ibn Taymiyya. Una vita esemplare; analisi delle fonti classiche della sua biografia, in: *Rivista degli Studi Orientali* 76 (2003), pp. 131–132. While in custody in Alexandria in 1309/1310 he met several disciples of the Maghrebian philosophical, mystical and juridical schools; see Laoust, Henri: La biographie d'Ibn Taymīya d'après Ibn Kathīr, in: *Bulletin d'études orientales* 9 (1942), pp. 115–162, here 144–146; Laoust, Henri: L'influence d'Ibn Taymiyya, in: Alford T. Welch and Pierre Cachia (eds.): *Islam. Past Influence and Present Challenge*, New York 1979, pp. 15–33, here p. 16.

against those "heretics" and wrote two voluminous refutations of logic and rationalism, namely *al-Radd ʿalā al-manṭiqiyyīn* (The Refutation of the Logicians) and *Darʾ taʿāruḍ al-ʿaql wal-naql* (Averting the Conflict between Reason and Tradition). These two interlinked works have, until now, only been scarcely studied. They constitute one of the most thorough – and certainly the harshest and most comprehensive – critique of logic and philosophy and certainly the harshest and most comprehensive one in the realm of Islam.

Yet, as every intense preoccupation leaves its traces on the preoccupied, the arguments and tenets Ibn Taymiyya so deeply studied and vigorously dismissed left positive imprints on his thought. The present article examines some of these imprints and aims to challenge further the still-widespread view of Ibn Taymiyya as a rigorous fideist and anti-rational theologian, not only in Wahhabi circles.[9] In recent years this view has been seriously questioned especially by Yahya Michot[10] and by Jon Hoover.[11] My research mainly draws on different sources than the ones used by them and thus elucidates Ibn Taymiyya's rationality and his vote for "clear reason" from another perspective. In the few studies devoted to *al-Radd ʿalā al-manṭiqiyyīn*, mine included, Ibn Taymiyya's position has been presented so far as one of a "nominalist" and/or an "empirist" and thus as a fervent rejection of the rationalist deductions and universal propositions gained from experience. Further investigation led me, however, to a more differentiated view.

9 See the studies mentioned by Krawietz, Birgit: Ibn Taymiyya. Vater des islamischen Fundamentalismus? Zur westlichen Rezeption eines mittelalterlichen Schariatsgelehrten, in: Manuel Atienza, Enrico Pattaro, Martin Schulte, Boris Topornin and Dieter Wyduckel (eds.): *Theorie des Rechts und der Gesellschaft. Festschrift für Werner Krawietz zum 70. Geburtstag*, Berlin 2003, and by Hoover, Jon: *Ibn Taymiyya's Theodicy of Perpetual Optimism*, Leiden and Boston 2007, pp. 19–20.

10 Yahya Michot reveals in almost all of his translations and studies of Ibn Taymiyya's works the rationality of his arguments (for an almost complete bibliography with the possibility to download many writings see www.muslimphilosophy.com/it/index.html, accessed April 3, 2008).

11 Hoover, Jon: Perpetual Creativity in the Perfection of God. Ibn Taymiyya's Hadith Commentary on God's Creation of this World, in: *Journal of Islamic Studies* 15 (2004), pp. 287–329; Hoover, *Ibn Taymiyya's Theodicy* (it includes – in a revised form – two articles that had been published in the *Theological Review of the Near East School of Theology* in 2006). The monograph was published when I was preparing the final draft of this article. Therefore, in the sections where I deal with subjects he treated, I include his findings in the course of my presentation and not at the beginning.

For a better assessment of the value of Ibn Taymiyya's critiques, I shall in the first part briefly place them in the context of other Muslim refutations of logic and philosophy and shortly present the two works and their main addressees. Part two focuses on Ibn Taymiyya's distinction between the rationalists' and the "clear" reason and traces peripatetic tenets in his own theory of knowledge and interlinked ontological assumptions. The two parts are connected, but can be read seperatedly.

1. Greek Poison

The enemies of philosophy (*falsafa/ḥikma falsafiyya*) regarded their practitioners, the *falāsifa*, as followers of the Greek unbelievers, as heretics and as "freethinkers" who reflected on what is inconceivable to the senses and immediate understanding without recourse to the divine revelation. The Muslim philosophers themselves, like al-Fārābī (d. 339/950), Ibn Sīnā (d. 428/1037), and Ibn Rushd (d. 595/1198) – all of whom Ibn Taymiyya extensively criticizes – philosophized mainly on the ground of a corpus of Greek wisdom with the conviction that it led to true happiness. They paraphrased, commented upon, modified, criticized or harmonized the writings of Aristotle and Plato especially, being persuaded that – because they relied on sound reasoning – they basically represented the ultimate truth.[12] In their view, mankind had gained an infallible instrument to reach truth with the logic (*al-manṭiq*) Aristotle and his disciples had elaborated and systemized and declared as the propaedeutics of philosophy. So, in the theoretical sciences, especially in metaphysics, i.e. the field of knowledge which rose the greatest suspicion, their instrument of reasoning was the demonstrative, apodictic syllogism (*burhān/qiyās burhānī*) which was based on indubitable premises.[13]

12 Arnaldez, Roger: Falsafa, in: *EI*², vol. 2 (1991), pp. 769–775; Arnaldez, Roger: Falāsifa, in: *EI*², vol. 2 (1991), pp. 764–767; Endress, Gerhard: Die wissenschaftliche Literatur, in: Wolfdietrich Fischer (ed.): *Grundriss der Arabischen Philologie*, Wiesbaden 1992, suppl., vol. 3, pp. 25–57.

13 See for instance al-Fārābī, Abū Naṣr: *Risāla fī al-ʿAql*, ed. by Maurice Bouyges, Beirut 1938, pp. 7.9–9.3, 11.10–12.3; idem: *al-Manṭiq ʿind al-Farābī*, ed., intr., and comm. by Rafīq al-ʿAjam, Beirut 1985–1986, vol. 1 (*Naṣṣ al-tawṭiʾa*), p. 57.2–9; idem: *Iḥṣāʾ al-ʿulūm*, ed. by Angel González Palencia, Madrid 1932, pp. 23–24; and Ibn Rushd who in substance embraces al-Fārābī's view: Ibn Rushd: *Kitāb Faṣl al-maqāl with Its Appendix (ḍamīma) and an Extract from Kitāb al-Kashf ʿan manāhij al-adilla*, ed. by George F. Hourani, Leiden 1959, pp. 2, 17, 19–21,

Yet they did not dismiss divine revelation, but confirmed its truth and its social necessity.[14]

Among those who condemned *falsafa* as such or were suspicious of the main metaphysical tenets, only few stood against it with a deep knowledge of the rejected concepts. None of the latter, however, remained untouched by what he refuted. Ibn Taymiyya was not exempt from that rule. The historian and well renowned Shāfiʿī scholar Shams al-Dīn al-Dhahabī (d. 748/1348) had attended some of Ibn Taymiyya's courses and expressed both positive and negative impressions of his character and knowledge in several of his writings.[15] In a letter, he addressed him with the following accusation:

> By God, we have become the laughing stock of creation! How long will you dig up intricate philosophical blasphemies for us to refute with our brains? You have repeatedly swallowed the poison of the philosophers

24.2–8 (the pagination refers to the one of Mueller given by Hourani at the margin); van den Bergh, Simon: *Averroes' Tahafut Al-Tahafut (The Incoherence of the Incoherence)*, Cambridge 1987 (reprints, London 1954 and 1969), pp. 409.1–410.1 et passim; Averroès: *Tafsīr mā baʿd al-ṭabīʿa*, ed. by Maurice Bouyges, Beirut 1967–1973, vol. 1, p. 192.1–5 et passim; see Galston, Miriam: al-Fārābī on Aristotle's Theory of Demonstration, in: Parviz Morewedge (ed.): *Islamic Philosophy and Mysticism*, Delmar and New York 1981, pp. 23–34. Ibn Sīnā also holds the Aristotelian apodictic syllogism to be *the* method of verification (Ibn Sīnā, Abū ʿAlī: *al-Ishārāt wal-tanbīhāt, maʿa sharḥ Naṣīr al-Dīn al-Ṭūsī*, ed. by Sulaymān Dunyā, Cairo 1971, vol. 1, p. 460; Avicenna: *Remarks and Admonitions*, part 1: *Logic*, transl. by Shams Constantine Inati, Toronto 1984, p. 148; Gutas, Dimitri: *Avicenna and the Aristotelian Tradition. Introduction to Reading Avicenna's Philosophical Works*, Leiden 1988, pp. 311–318), and states that the middle term can be acquired spontanously through "intuition" (*ḥads*) (Gutas, Dimitri: *Avicenna and the Aristotelian Tradition*, pp. 159–176; Endress, Gerhard: The Defense of Reason. The Plea for Philosophy in the Religious Community, in: *Zeitschrift für Geschichte der arabisch-islamischen Wissenschaften* 6 (1990), pp. 1–49, here p. 32).

14 See for instance al-Fārābī, Abū Naṣr: *Mabādiʾ ārāʾ ahl al-madīna al-fāḍila. Al-Farabi on the Perfect State; a Revised Text with Introduction, Translation and Commentary by Richard Walzer*, Oxford 1985, pp. 276–285; Ibn Sīnā: *Ithbāt al-nubuwwāt* (Proof of Prophecies), ed. by Michael E. Marmura, Beirut 1968; Ibn Rushd, *Kitāb Faṣl al-maqāl*; Endress, The Defense of Reason, pp. 20–23, 30–33.

15 See Bori, *Ibn Taymiyya*, s.v. Ḏahabī (al-); idem: A New Source for the Biography of Ibn Taymiyya, in: *Bulletin of the School of Oriental and African Studies* 67 (2004), pp. 324, 326–328, 331–348; idem: Ibn Taymiyya *wa-Jamāʿatuhu*. Authority, Conflict and Consensus in Ibn Taymiyya's Milieu, in: Shahab Ahmad and Yossef Rapoport (eds.): *Ibn Taymiyya and His Times*, Karachi 2010, pp. 23–52.

and their works; the body becomes addicted to the frequent use of poison so that it is secreted, by God, in the very bones.[16]

The authenticity of al-Dhahabī's authorship was for some time doubted, but can be now regarded as proven.[17] The accusation against Ibn Taymiyya is corroborated by a statement of the Ḥanbalī traditionist (*muḥaddith*) and biographer Ibn Rajab (d. 795/1393) saying that some of Ibn Taymiyya's learnt and pious admirers "disapproved of his preoccupation with (*tawaghghul maʿa*) the *kalām* theologians and the philosophers".[18]

---

16 *Wal-lāhi qad ṣirnā ḍuḥka fī al-wujūd fa-ilā kam tanbush daqāʾiq al-kufriyyāt al-falsafiyya li-narudda ʿalayhā bi-ʿuqūlinā. Yā rajul qad balaʿta sumūm al-falāsifa wa-muṣannafātihim marrāt, wa-bi-kathrat istiʿmāl al-sumūm yudmin ʿalayhā al-jism wa-takmun wal-lāhi fī al-badan*, al-Dhahabī, Shams al-Dīn: *al-Naṣīḥa al-dhahabiyya li-Ibn Taymiyya*, ed. by Muḥammad Zāhid al-Kawtharī, Damascus 1347/1928–1929, p. 33; I follow the translation of Little, Donald P.: Did Ibn Taymiyya Have a Screw Loose?, in: *Studia Islamica* 41 (1975), pp. 93–111, here p. 101; also hinted at by Michot, Yahya: Vanités intellectuelles… L'impasse des rationalismes selon le *Rejet de la contradiction* d'Ibn Taymiyyah, in: *Oriente Moderno* 19 (2001), pp. 597–617, here p. 600, n. 10.

17 Doubts were uttered by Laoust (*Essai sur les doctrines sociales et politiques*, p. 484) and two Pakistani scholars (Little, Did Ibn Taymiyya Have a Screw Loose?, p. 102), but Donald Little (ibid., pp. 100–105) and especially Caterina Bori (Ibn Taymiyya, pp. 142–148) have provided strong evidences for al-Dhahabī's authorship. Bori, furthermore, indicates possible personal reasons for the polemical tone of his letter (ibid., pp. 144–148).

18 Ibn Rajab Zayn al-Dīn, Abū al-Faraj: *Dhayl ʿalā ṭabaqāt al-ḥanābila*, part 4 (part 2), Beirut n. d. (based on the print of Maṭbaʿat al-Sunna al-Muḥammadiyya 1372/1953), p. 394 (biography n. 495); cited already by Michot, Yahya: A Mamlūk Theologian's Commentary on Avicenna's *Risāla aḍḥawiyya* Being a Translation of a Part of the *Darʾ taʿāruḍ al-ʿaql wal-naql* of Ibn Taymiyya, with Introduction, Annotation, and Appendices, in: *Journal of Islamic Studies* 14 (2003), pp. 149–203, here p. 166, n. 39. Ibn Taymiyya's deep knowledge of *kalām* theology and philosophy was considered by several of his biographers as outstanding to such a degree that he excelled over the best in the respective disciplines and was able to counter them and to disclose their weaknesses (Ibn Rajab, *Dhayl ʿalā ṭabaqāt al-ḥanābila*, p. 388, his praise includes Ibn Taymiyya's knowledge of arithmetics and algebra; al-Karmī, Marʿī b. Yūsuf: *al-Kawākib al-durriyya fī manāqib al-mujtahid Ibn Taymiyya*, ed. by Najm ʿAbd al-Raḥmān Khalaf, Beirut 1406/1986, pp. 62, 66 (quotations from al-Dhahabī)). For a thorough analysis of the dissent towards Ibn Taymiyya from within the Ḥanbalī and traditionalist community in general and Ibn Rajab in particular, see the study of Caterina Bori: Ibn Taymiyya *wa-Jamāʿatuhu* under the heading "Voices of Internal Dissent – Ḥanbalīs".

Research on Ibn Taymiyya in the last decades has revealed striking similarities between some of his tenets and those of other philosophers. Special attention has been paid to affinities between Ibn Rushd and Ibn Taymiyya in respect to their concepts of causality[19] and of the creation of the world.[20] Also mentioned are their common rejection of Aristotle's scientific method and the use of terms like *qidam* (eternity) or *ḥudūth* (origination) in the sphere of religion; and in general, their attempt to clearly separate religion from philosophy.[21] With respect to theodicy, several remarkable common features between Ibn Sīnā's and

---

19 Al-Ṣughayyir points also to a correspondence of Ibn Taymiyya's and Ibn Rushd's theory of causality (Mawāqif "rushdiyya" li-Taqī al-Dīn Ibn Taymiyya? Mulāḥaẓāt awwaliyya, in: al-Ṭāhir Waʿzīz (ed.): *Dirāsāt maghribiyya. Muhdāt ilā al-mufakkir al-maghribī Muḥammad ʿAzīz al-Ḥabbābī* (*Lahbabi*), ed. by al-Ṭāhir Waʿzīz, Casablanca 1987, pp. 176–177, refering to Ibn Taymiyya, Taqī al-Dīn Aḥmad: *Kitāb al-Nubuwwāt*, Cairo 1346/1927–1928, p. 219 and idem: *al-Radd ʿalā al-manṭiqiyyīn*, ed. by ʿAbd al-Ṣamad Sharaf al-Dīn al-Kutubī, Bombay 1368/1949, p. 270). Harās considers the Damascene even "strongly influenced" by the Andalusian (Harās, Muḥammad Khalīl: *Bāʿith al-nahḍa al-islāmiyya. Ibn Taymiyya al-salafī; naqduhu li-masālik al-mutakallimın wal-falāsifa fī al-ilāhiyyāt*, Beirut 1984, p. 168, refering to Ibn Taymiyya's *Minhāj al-sunna* and his *Majmūʿat al-Rasāʾil al-kubrā*, Cairo 1323/1905. See below, chapter 11.2.

20 ʿAbd al-Majīd al-Ṣughayyir and Jon Hoover have shown that Ibn Taymiyya's theory of God's "perpetual creativity" disclose a great similarity to Ibn Rushd's theory of continuous creation from eternity; Hoover, Perpetual Creativity, especially pp. 290, 295. Ibn Taymiyya does, however, not refer to Ibn Rushd in regard to that theory (ibid., p. 295). A very simple explanation for it would be that he was not aware of it, since he apparently did not know *Faṣl al-maqāl* and he might have been not in the possession of the whole *Tahāfut al-Tahāfut*. Still, an exhaustive study of Ibn Taymiyya's position towards Ibn Rushd, taking Ibn Taymiyya's main purposes into account, might reveal other reasons. It is noteworthy that Ibn Rushd's theory of continuous creation, developed from the Koran, enjoys much more attention among Arab intellectuals in the 20th century than the theory of eternity he exposes in his commentaries on Aristotle (von Kügelgen, Anke: *Averroes und die arabische Moderne. Ansätze zu einer Neubegründung des Rationalismus im Islam*. Leiden 1994, pp. 385–398) and that these intellectuals are obviously not aware of Ibn Taymiyya's very similar theory.

21 Von Kügelgen, Anke: Dialogpartner im Widerspruch. Ibn Rushd und Ibn Taymīya über die "Einheit der Wahrheit", in: Rüdiger Arnzen and Jörn Thielmann (eds.): *Words, Texts and Concepts Cruising the Mediterranean Sea. Studies on the Sources, Contents and Influences of Islamic Civilization and Arabic Philosophy and Science Dedicated to Gerhard Endress on His Sixty-fifth Birthday*, Leuven 2004, pp. 455–481, here 474–475.

Ibn Taymiyya's theories have been disclosed.[22] How far Ibn Taymiyya borrowed these or other tenets from the philosophers cannot be answered with certainty. The high degree of similarity, however, suggests that Ibn Taymiyya was at least inspired by his enemies, although he never openly adopts their tenets and always embeds them in broader theories that do not correspond with the philosopher's views of man, God and the universe. The present paper will identify a few striking resemblances between Ibn Taymiyya and the philosophers, especially in regard to key epistemological concepts.

2. The Status of Logic up to Ibn Taymiyya's Times

With his rebuttal of logic, Ibn Taymiyya deviated from the mainstream of Muslim theologians.[23] After al-Ghazālī's (d. 505/1111) skillfull pleading for the innocence of logic and its successful introduction into *kalām* theology,[24] many Muslim "speculative theologians" (*mutakallimūn*)

22 Hoover, *Ibn Taymiyya's Theodicy*, pp. 70–72 et passim. Husâm Muhî Eldin al-Alousî describes Ibn Taymiyya's thinking as a melange of "elements of theological origin, elements derived from Ibn Sīnā, and elements attributable to Abū Barakāt al-Baghdādī" (al-Alousî, Husâm Muhî Eldîn: *The Problem of Creation in Islamic Thought. Qur'an, Hadith, Commentaries, and Kalam*, Baghdad 1968 (Ph.D. thesis, Cambridge University 1965), p. 262; see Hoover, Perpetual Creativity, pp. 289–290.

23 For an excellent overview of the state of the study of Peripatetic logic in the Islamic world and an exposition of the main changes regarding Aristotelian logic upto 1300, see Street, Arabic Logic.

24 Similar attempts by other scholars, like the one of the Andalusian Ibn Ḥazm (383/993–456/1064) were less successful (Brunschvig, Robert: Pour ou contre la logique grecque chez les théologiens juristes de l'Islām. Ibn Ḥazm, al-Ghazālī, Ibn Taymiyya, in: *Etudes d'Islamologie*, Paris 1979, pp. 303–327, here 304–313; Chejne, Anwar G.: Ibn Ḥazm of Cordova on Logic, in: *The Journal of the American Oriental Society* 104 (1984), pp. 52–72; Yāfūt, Sālim: *Ibn Ḥazm wal-fikr al-falsafī bil-maghrib wal-andalus*, Casablanca 1986, especially pp. 200–227). Recently, Cornelia Schöck has shown that major elements of Aristotelian logic have been discussed and used for Koran exegesis by *mutakallimūn* already before the eleventh century (Schöck, Cornelia: *Koranexegese, Grammatik und Logik. Zum Verhältnis von arabischer und aristotelischer Urteils-, Konsequenz- und Schlusslehre*, Leiden and Boston 2006). For a new assessment of al-Ghazālī's attitude towards Aristotelian logic and his own use of it, see Rudolph, Ulrich: Die Neubewertung der Logik durch al-Ġazālī, in: Dominik Perler and Ulrich Rudolph (eds.): *Logik und Theologie. Das Organon im arabischen und lateinischen Mittelalter*, Leiden and Boston 2005, pp. 73–97.

had praised logic, on the contrary, as an excellent, infallible instrument of reason with no relation to the objects of knowledge. As such, it was a useful tool for understanding scripture. The majority of *kalām* theologians from the twelfth century onwards denounced only philosophy or parts of philosophy (see below).[25] Ibn Taymiyya – and after him, Ibn Khaldūn (d. 808/1406) – makes the use of logic in theology the essential mark of distinction between the *kalām* theologians, labeling those who rely on logic the "later" ones (*al-muta'akhkhirūn*) and those who don't the "earlier" ones (*al-mutaqaddimūn; al-aqdamūn*).[26] Apparently from the late 13th century on, logic became a subject that was taught at the *madrasa*.[27] Even Ibn al-Jawzī (d. 597/1200), one of the harshest critics of metaphysics before Ibn Taymiyya, admits that the Greek philosophers "possessed attainments in mechanics, logic, and natural science, and by their sagacity they discovered hidden things."[28] Neverthe-

25 For an overview of the scarce material concerning early Muslim critiques of logic, see al-Nashshār, ʿAlī Sāmī: *Manāhij al-baḥth ʿind mufakkirī al-islām wa-naqd al-muslimīn lil-manṭiq al-arisṭuṭālīsī*, Cairo 1978, and Hallaq, Wael B.: *Ibn Taymiyya Against the Greek Logicians*, Oxford 1993, pp. xlii–xlvii.

26 Ibn Taymiyya, *al-Radd*, p. 31; al-Suyūṭī, Jalāl al-Dīn: Jahd al-qarīḥa fī tajrīd al-naṣīḥa, see idem: *Ṣawn al-manṭiq wal-kalām ʿan fann al-manṭiq wal-kalām wa-yalīhī Mukhtaṣar al-Suyūṭī li-kitāb naṣīḥat ahl al-īmān fī al-radd ʿalā manṭiq al-yūnān li-Taqī al-Dīn Ibn Taymiyya. Jahd al-qarīḥa fī tajrīd al-naṣīḥa*, ed. by ʿAlī Sāmī al-Nashshār, Cairo 1366/1947, pp. 208–209; Hallaq, *Ibn Taymiyya*, p. 15; Ibn Taymiyya, *Darʾ taʿāruḍ*, vol. 1, p. 250; vol. 3, pp. 96, 277, 287, 334; vol. 4, p. 84 et passim; Ibn Khaldūn: *Muqaddimat Ibn Khaldūn. Prolégomènes d'Ebn-Khaldoun; texte arabe publié d'après les manuscrits de la Bibliothèque Impériale par M. Quatremère*, Beirut 1970 (reprint of Paris 1858), vol. 3, pp. 41, 113; Ibn Khaldūn: *The Muqaddimah. An Introduction to History*, transl. by Franz Rosenthal, New York 1974, vol. 3, pp. 52, 143; Gardet, Louis and Anawati, Georges C.: *Introduction à la théologie musulmane. Essai de théologie comparée*, Paris 1948, pp. 72–74.

27 Street, Arabic Logic, pp. 524, 579–582; idem: Logic, in: Peter Adamson and Richard C. Taylor (eds.): *The Cambridge Companion to Arabic Philosophy*, Cambridge 2005, pp. 572–579, here p. 249. His statement seems convincing in view of the many logical treatises that were written from that period on and in regard to the "institutionalization" of logic in higher education in the Ottoman Empire (see ch. 5), but an historical overview of the books and subjects taught at the *madrasas* throughout the Islamic world is still missing. See also below, n. 80.

28 Ibn al-Jawzī, Abū al-Faraj ʿAbd al-Raḥmān: *Talbīs Iblīs*, ed. by Khayr al-Dīn ʿAlī, Beirut n.d., p. 58; Ibn al-Jawzī: *The Devil's Delusion*, transl. by D.S. Margoliouth, in: *Islamic Culture* 9 (1935), pp. 1–21, here p. 19. For Ibn al-Jawzī's rejection of analogy in *fiqh* see *Talbīs Iblīs*, pp. 130–132; Ibn al-Jawzī: *The Devil's Delusion*, transl. by D.S. Margoliouth, in: *Islamic Culture* 10 (1936), pp. 20–39, here 29–31.

less, like his schoolfellow, Ibn al-Jawzī accused "the philosophers" of unbelief because of their metaphysical tenets that contradict religious dogmas[29] and is notorious for his active persecution of philosophers of his time.[30] In contrast to Ibn Taymiyya, however, he does not consider logic to be Satan misleading the philosophers, but the use of reason in the sphere of the metaphysical world. The divine world is, for this Ḥanbalī, still a realm that is beyond the scope of reason.[31] Therefore, obviously, Ibn al-Jawzī makes no attempt to prove the untenability of their tenets. Not all Ḥanbalīs prior to Ibn Taymiyya, however, shared Ibn al-Jawzī's fideistic attitude. Ibn ʿAqīl (d. 513/1119), for instance, viewed the relation between revelation and reason in a different way. After his abjuration of the Muʿtazilī teaching and "other innovators'" teachings he had adopted in his youth and whom Ibn Taymiyya then much respected for his adherence to "the pure *sunna*",[32] he holds that "reason conforms with revelation, and nothing in revelation contradicts reason." This conviction is based on the view that it is reason that conceives God's existence and leads men to live according to His commands.[33] Ibn ʿAqīl thus opens the sphere of reason for the Ḥanbalīs;

---

29 Ibn al-Jawzī, *Talbīs Iblīs*, pp. 55–59; idem, *The Devil's Delusion* (1935), pp. 15–20.

30 Laoust, Henri: Le Hanbalisme sous le califat de Bagdad (241/855–656/1258), in: *Revue des études islamiques* 1 (1959), pp. 67–128, here 112–115; Hartmann, Angelika: *an-Nāṣir li-Dīn Allāh (1180–1225). Politik, Religion, Kultur in der späten ʿAbbāsidenzeit*, Berlin and New York 1975, p. 258.

31 See above, n. 28 and 29.

32 Ibn Taymiyya, Taqī al-Dīn Aḥmad: *Naqḍ al-manṭiq*, ed. by Muḥammad b. ʿAbd al-Razzāq Ḥamza, Sulaymān b. ʿAbd al-Raḥmān al-Ṣanīʿ and Muḥammad Ḥāmid al-Fīq, Cairo 1370/1951, p. 135; Makdisi, George: *Ibn ʿAqīl et la résurgence de l'Islam traditionaliste au XIe siècle* (*Ve siècle de l'Hégire*), Damascus 1963, pp. 508–509; idem: *Ibn ʿAqīl. Religion and Culture in Classical Islam*, Edinburgh 1997, pp. 48–49. For his abjuration see Makdisi, *Ibn ʿAqīl et la résurgence*, pp. 424–441.

33 Ibn ʿAqīl, Abū al-Wafā: *al-Taʿlīqāt al-musammāt "Kitāb al-Funūn"*, ed. by George Makdisi, Beirut 1970–1971, vol. 2, p. 509 *inna al-ʿaql muṭābiq lil-sharʿ, wa-innahu lā yaridu al-sharʿ illā bi-mā yuwāfiqu al-ʿaql*. This and other of Ibn ʿAqīl's opinions about reason were scrutinized by Makdisi, *Ibn ʿAqīl*, pp. 92–99 (I follow his translation, p. 97). With another Ḥanbalī, Ibn Qudāma (541/1146–620/1223), who like Ibn Taymiyya severely condemned *kalām* theology, logic met in jurisprudence a strong Ḥanbalī advocate (Hallaq, Wael B.: Logic. Formal Arguments and Formalization of Arguments in Sunnī Jurisprudence, in: *Arabica* 37 (1990), pp. 315–358, here 322–327; Makdisi, *Ibn ʿAqīl*, pp. 47–48. Hallaq exposes the strong impact of Aristotelian and Stoic logic on several eminent jurists as "successors" of al-Ghazālī and Ibn Qudāma, like, among others, the

still, he is not reflecting on logic and its consistency and seems to have taken the "soundness" of reason and reasoning for granted.

3. The Fatwa of Ibn al-Ṣalāḥ

The probably most frequently quoted condemnation of logic belongs to the Shāfiʿī jurist and well renowned Hadith scholar Ibn al-Ṣalāḥ al-Shahrazūrī (d. 643/1245) and is inseparably linked to the condemnation of philosophy. In his youth, Ibn al-Ṣalāḥ had studied logic in Mosul, but – according to Ibn Khallikān (d. 681/1282) – had to give it up, because he was obviously unable to grasp it.[34] Ibn al-Ṣalāḥ then reversed course and launched a fatwa against philosophy and against logic as the preparation for it, stating that philosophy was "the foundation of folly, the cause of all confusion, all errors and all heresy. The person who occupies himself with it becomes colorblind to the beauties of religious law, supported as it is by brilliant proofs" (*al-ḥujaj al-ẓāhira wal-barāhīn al-bāhira*).[35] In another fatwa, Ibn Sīnā

Shāfiʿī jurist Sayf al-Dīn al-Āmidī (d. 631/1233) and the Malikite jurist Jamāl al-Dīn Ibn al-Ḥājib (570/1174–646/1249)).

34 Ibn Khallikān: *Kitāb Wafayāt al-aʿyān. Biographical Dictionary; transl. from the Arabic by Mac Guckin de Slane*, Beirut 1970, vol. 3, p. 470 (within the biography of Abū al-Fatḥ Kamāl al-Dīn); Ibn Khallikān: *Wafayāt al-aʿyān*, ed. by Iḥsān ʿAbbās, n. p. n. d., vol. 5, p. 314; Goldziher, Ignaz: Stellung der alten islamischen Orthodoxie zu den antiken Wissenschaften, in: Joseph Desomogyi (ed.): *Ignaz Goldziher. Gesammelte Schriften*, Hildesheim 1970 (first publ. in 1916), vol. 5, pp. 357–400, here p. 389; Ignaz Goldziher: The Attitude of Orthodox Islam Toward the "Ancient Sciences", in: Merlin L. Swartz (ed.): *Studies on Islam*, New York and Oxford 1981, pp. 204–205. Ibn Khallikān (608/1211–681/1282) further reports that he was taught logic "secretly" by Abū al-Fatḥ Kamāl al-Dīn, who warned him that the public "consider those who apply to this branch of knowledge as holding pernicious opinions on religious matters" (Ibn Khallikān, *Kitāb Wafayāt al-aʿyān*, transl. by de Slane, vol. 3, p. 470; ed. by ʿAbbās, vol. 5, p. 314). This statement implies that logic was not accepted outside certain scholarly circles and somehow contradicted what has been said in chapter two. The solution to this problem might lie in that Ibn Khallikān was not a very reliable biographer, as Dimitri Gutas has shown in regard to his accounts on al-Fārābī (Gutas, Dimitri: Fārābī, Abū Naṣr i. Biography, in: Ehsan Yarshater (ed.): *Encyclopedia Iranica*, vol. 9, New York 1999, pp. 208–213.).

35 Ibn al-Ṣalāḥ: *Fatāwā Ibn al-Ṣalāḥ fī al-tafsīr wal-ḥadīth wal-uṣūl wal-fiqh*, ed. by ʿAbd al-Muʿṭī Amīn Qalʿajī, Cairo 1403/1983, p. 70; I cite the translation of Goldziher, which relies on a slightly shorter version, Goldziher, The Attitude of Orthodox Islam, p. 205.

(d. 428/1037) is explicitly called a "devil of the human devils" and the study of his work is prohibited.[36] Ibn al-Ṣalāḥ prohibits logic for three reasons: first, because "the means of access to something bad"[37] must itself be bad; second, because

> preoccupation with the study and teaching of logic has not been permitted by the Lawgiver, nor has it been suggested by his Companions or the generation that followed him, nor by the learned imams, the pious ancestors, nor by the leaders or pillars of the Islamic community whose example is followed;[38]

and third, because "God has made it dispensable for those who have common sense (*kull ṣaḥīḥ al-dhihn*), and it is even more dispensible for the specialists in the speculative branches of jurisprudence."[39] Ibn al-Ṣalāḥ ends his famous fatwa with the conclusion that people who devote themselves to philosophy (and logic) shall be executed if they (continue to) refuse Islam.[40]

Ibn al-Ṣalāḥ's argumentation differs from the abovementioned by referring to "the common sense"[41] and to the "clear arguments and brilliant proofs"[42] of the sharia itself and, not least, by its explicit death threat. Ibn al-Ṣalāḥ is not known for having refuted logic and philosophy other than by the cited arguments, and although his fatwa probably fueled the persecution of those in touch with these sciences and was often referred to, even in introductions to logic, it failed to erase logic from the education of the "later" *kalām* theologians.[43] Therefore, Ibn Taymiyya might have felt obligated to deeply penetrate into their methods and subjects, in order to refute them from within by demonstrating their internal incoherences.

---

36 Ibn al-Ṣalāḥ, *Fatāwā*, pp. 69–70. The fatwas are not dated and the *mustaftī*(s) are not known.

37 Ibn al-Ṣalāḥ, *Fatāwā*, p. 71; Goldziher, The Attitude of Orthodox Islam, p. 205.

38 Ibid.

39 Ibn al-Ṣalāḥ, *Fatāwā*, p. 71; Goldziher, The Attitude of Orthodox Islam, p. 206.

40 Ibn al-Ṣalāḥ, *Fatāwā*, pp. 71–72; I follow Goldziher's translation, The Attitude of Orthodox Islam, p. 206. For a comparison of Ibn al-Ṣalāḥ's position with that of al-Ghazālī, see Griffel, *Apostasie*, pp. 354–357.

41 Ibn al-Ṣalaḥ, *Fatāwā*, p. 71; Goldziher, The Attitude of Orthodox Islam, p. 206.

42 Ibn al-Ṣalaḥ, *Fatāwā*, p. 70; Goldziher, The Attitude of Orthodox Islam, p. 205.

43 Goldziher, Stellung der alten islamischen Orthodoxie, pp. 393–396; idem, The Attitude of Orthodox Islam, pp. 206–209, al-Nashshār, *Manāhij al-baḥth*, pp. 226–227; Endress, Die wissenschaftliche Literatur, vol. 3, pp. 56–57.

4. Ibn Taymiyya's Writings Against Logic

In his refutations of logic, Ibn Taymiyya refers to previous opponents of logic in a rather general way by pointing to the fact that "the Muslim religious scholars and the leaders of religion" slandered and forbade Greek logic.[44] He mentions only a few by name, mainly the theologian Ḥasan b. Mūsā al-Nawbakhtī (d. between 300/912 and 310/922),[45] the grammarian Abū Saʿīd al-Sīrāfī (d. 368/979),[46] and Ibn al-Ṣalāḥ.[47]

For Ibn Taymiyya, logic (*manṭiq*) is not the propaedeutics of philosophy and as such a harmless and useful instrument, but in fact the core of philosophy. When he speaks of "logic" or "Greek logic" (*manṭiq al-yunān*), he has in mind Aristotelian logic.[48] He considers it the source of many other evils, leading astray theologians and Sufis and contaminating areas of knowledge that had initially been untainted by that human invention, that "conventional balance (established by) one individual".[49] In fact, since Aristotle's death, Aristotelian logic had turned into "Peripatetic" logic with the many additions and amendments that were introduced to the original Aristotelian texts by their various commentators, not least in Arabic. In *Darʾ taʿāruḍ al-ʿaql wal-naql* which Ibn Taymiyya composed in the same period as his main refutation of logic, he refers extensively to Ibn Sīnā's logical work

44 Ibn Taymiyya, *Naqḍ al-manṭiq*, p. 156 (*ʿulamāʾ al-muslimīn wa-aʾimmat al-dīn*).

45 Ibn Taymiyya, *al-Radd*, pp. 331, 337–339; al-Suyūṭī, *Jahd al-qarīḥa*, pp. 325–236; Hallaq, *Ibn Taymiyya*, pp. 154–155, xlii–xliii.

46 Ibn Taymiyya, *al-Radd*, p. 178; al-Suyūṭi, *Jahd al-qarīḥa*, p. 276; Hallaq, *Ibn Taymiyya*, pp. 100, xlii–xliii. For the famous debate on logic between the grammarian Abū Saʿīd al-Sīrāfī and the logician Abū Bishr Mattā (d. 328/940), see Endress, Gerhard: Grammatik und Logik. Arabische Philologie und griechische Philosophie im Widerstreit, in: Burkhard Mojsisch (ed.): *Sprachphilosophie in Antike und Mittelalter*, Amsterdam 1986, pp. 163–299.

47 Ibn Taymiyya, *Naqḍ al-manṭiq*, p. 156. He does not explicitly refer to Ibn al-Ṣalāḥ's fatwa, but instead to the rumours about the latter's militant attitude towards the theologian and jurist Abū al-Ḥasan al-Āmidī (d. 631/1233).

48 Most explicit is his statement "Greek logic was formulated by Aristotle three hundred years before Christ." Hallaq, *Ibn Taymiyya*, p. 162; al-Suyūṭī, *Jahd al-qarīḥa*, p. 333; Ibn Taymiyya, *al-Radd*, pp. 26, 373; similar is a statement in: Ibn Taymiyya, *Naqḍ al-manṭiq*, p. 185.

49 "Rational knowledges are known by the instruments of understanding bestowed by God to man; they do not rely on a conventional balance (established by) one individual" (*fa-inna al-ʿulūm al-ʿaqliyya tuʿlamu bi-mā faṭara allāh ʿalayhi banī Ādam min asbāb al-idrāk, lā taqifu ʿalā mīzān waḍʿī li-shakhṣ muʿayyan*; Ibn Taymiyya, *al-Radd*, p. 26).

al-Ishārāt wal-tanbīhāt[50] and calls it the "*muṣḥaf* [Koran copy] of these heretical philosophers."[51] He probably also drew his knowledge of logic from Abū al-Barakāt (d. after 560/1164–5), to whose *al-Muʿtabar fī al-ḥikma* and other writings he refers in several passages of *Darʾ taʿāruḍ al-ʿaql wal-naql.*[52] To trace all the sources from which Ibn Taymiyya gained his knowledge on logic, let alone to compare his understanding and exposition of them with the original, is a task far beyond the present study.

Ibn Taymiyya's major refutation of logic is *al-Radd ʿalā al-manṭiqiyyīn* (The Refutation of the Logicians), which is also known as *Naṣīḥat ahl al-īmān fī al-radd ʿalā manṭiq al-yūnān* (Advice to the People of Faith to Refute Greek Logic).[53] Ibn Taymiyya starts this major refutation by asserting that he always knew that "Greek logic is neither needed by the intelligent nor of any use to the dullard", but that he had first considered its propositions true and then discovered the falseness of some of them (*ṭāʾifa min qaḍāyāhu*), whereupon he took up his pen against it.[54] Of this work, only one manuscript has come down to us; it bears many glosses by Ibn Taymiyya himself.[55] Ibn Taymiyya started its composition in 1309/1310 while he was held

50 Ibn Taymiyya, *Darʾ taʿāruḍ*, vol. 11, "Fihris asmāʾ al-kutub," s. v.; "al-Ishārāt wal-tanbīhāt," s. v.; see also chapter 11.1.

51 Ibn Taymiyya, *Darʾ taʿāruḍ*, vol. 6, p. 19. At two points, in relation to ontology and epistemology, he also hints to *al-Shifāʾ* (vol. 1, p. 288, vol. 6, pp. 47–48; see also chapter 11.1). His distinction between *taṣawwur* (conception) and *taṣdīq* (judgement to which one assents) is a further indication that his main source for Peripatetic logic was Ibn Sīnā and those who followed his line in logic. Concerning this distinction, see Street, Arabic Logic, pp. 540–542. Al-Ghazālī, obviously in the footsteps of Ibn Sīnā, also explicitly and sharply distinguishes between *taṣawwur* and *taṣdīq* (Rudolph, Die Neubewertung der Logik, p. 76). Although Ibn Taymiyya does not mention one of al-Ghazālī's logical treatises in his two major refutations, he seems at least to have known *al-Qisṭās al-mustaqīm* (see below, n. 270).

52 Ibn Taymiyya, *Darʾ taʿāruḍ*, vol. 11, "Fihris al-aʿlām," s. v.; "Fihris asmāʾ al-kutub," s. v.

53 The second title is mentioned by al-Suyūṭī (al-Suyūṭī, *Jahd al-qarīḥa*, p. 201; Hallaq, *Ibn Taymiyya*, p. 3).

54 Ibn Taymiyya, *al-Radd*, p. 3; al-Suyūṭī, *Jahd al-qarīḥa*, p. 202; Hallaq, *Ibn Taymiyya*, pp. 3–4. (I follow his translation). The Shāfiʿī jurist Muḥammad b. ʿAbd Allāh b. Aḥmad al-Hakkārī al-Salṭī (d. 786/1384) reproduces in his summary of Ibn Taymiyya's major rebuttal of rationalism (see chapter 7) a biting poem against logic that he attributes to the young Ibn Taymiyya (see Ibn Taymiyya, *Darʾ taʿāruḍ*, introduction, pp. 63–64).

55 For the history of this manuscript, see Ibn Taymiyya, *al-Radd*, pp. *zāʾ-mīm*.

in custody in Alexandria, but apparently completed it only after his major refutation of the rationalists *Darʾ taʿāruḍ al-ʿaql wal-naql* (see chapter 7).[56] While imprisoned in Alexandria, he was visited by some scholars whose plea for logic and philosophy triggered his vehement impugnment.[57] He tries to demonstrate that – contrary to what many Muslim scholars of his time believed – logic is not a universal and infallible guide to truth shared by all mankind, but simply a matter of convention between some people, and in addition, a completely useless instrument of the intellect, especially in metaphysical matters.

Ibn Taymiyya criticizes some essential principles of definition and deduction from various points of view, although not very systematically and with many repetitions and digressions.[58] Some of what might be understood as a digression in fact constitutes an explication of his own epistemology. His style is sometimes polemical, but mostly technical, trying to refute his enemies by arguments. Most of his counter-arguments had already been stated by Greek or Muslim thinkers,[59] but as Wael B. Hallaq states, Ibn Taymiyya's critique "represents not so much

---

56 At the beginning of *al-Radd*, he states that he wrote down what he had to comment upon logic at that time after a visit of one of his philosophising visitors and that he followed it through in several sessions afterwards (Ibn Taymiyya, *al-Radd*, p. 3; al-Suyūṭī, *Jahd al-qarīḥa*, p. 202; Hallaq, *Ibn Taymiyya*, p. 4). This statement implies that he started the work in 1309/10. Ibn Taymiyya mentions *Darʾ taʿāruḍ al-ʿaql wal-naql* at least three times in *al-Radd ʿalā al-manṭiqiyyīn* (Ibn Taymiyya, *al-Radd*, pp. 253 (this hint is missing in al-Suyūṭī's abridgement), 323 (al-Suyūṭī, *Jahd al-qarīḥa*, p. 322; Hallaq, *Ibn Taymiyya*, p. 150) and 373 (this hint is missing in al-Suyūṭī's abridgement)). So he seems to have finished it only four to eight years after his custody, since *Darʾ taʿāruḍ al-ʿaql wal-naql* is thought to have been written between 713/1313–1314 and 717/1317–1318 (see below, n. 103). If the dates are rightly assumed, this would either imply that Ibn Taymiyya worked on the two refutations simultaneously or that he inserted the two hints to *Darʾ taʿāruḍ al-ʿaql wal-naql* as additional glosses. Against the latter assumption speaks the short treatment of the estimative propositions (*wahmiyyāt*) in *al-Radd ʿalā al-manṭiqiyyīn* with the reference to "another work," where he expounded upon the subject. *Darʾ taʿāruḍ al-ʿaql wal-naql* contains long passages discussing the *wahmiyyāt* and thus is most probably the work Ibn Taymiyya refers to (see below, chapter 11.1).

57 Ibn Taymiyya, *al-Radd*, pp. 3–4; al-Suyūṭī, *Jahd al-qarīḥa*, p. 202; Hallaq, *Ibn Taymiyya*, p. 4; Laoust, La Biographie d'Ibn Taymīya, pp. 144–146; idem, L'influence d'Ibn-Taymiyya, in: Alford T. Welch and Pierre Cachia (eds.): *Islam. Past Influence and Present Challenge*, New York 1979, pp. 15–33, here p. 16.

58 For a concise summary of his critique, see Hallaq, *Ibn Taymiyya*, pp. xiv–xxxiv.

59 Al-Nashshār, *Manāhij al-baḥth*, pp. 149–159; Hallaq, *Ibn Taymiyya*, pp. xxxix–xlviii.

the culmination of a tradition of anti-logical discourse as an ingenious and creative selection of already existing but disparate arguments".[60] *Al-Radd ʿalā al-manṭiqiyyīn* was printed for the first time in 1949 in Bombay with a foreword by Sayyid Sulaymān Nadwī (d. 1953), a former commissioner of teaching at the Islamic Academy (*Dār al-ʿulūm*) of *Nadwat al-ʿulamāʾ* in Lucknow.[61] A much shortened, but very concise abridgment of it by al-Suyūṭī (see chapter 5) was masterfully translated into English by Wael B. Hallaq and prefaced with a substantial introduction.[62] Detailed studies of specific aspects of the original, its summary, or his minor rejections of logic are still rather few.[63]

60 Hallaq, *Ibn Taymiyya*, p. xlvii.

61 It was printed a second time in Cairo in 1977 by ʿAbd al-Sattār Naṣṣār and ʿImād Khafājī. For further information on Sayyid Sulaymān Nadwī, see Hartung, Jan-Peter: *Viele Wege und ein Ziel. Leben und Wirken von Sayyid Abū l-Ḥasan ʿAlī al-Ḥasanī Nadwī (1914–1999)*, Würzburg 2004, index, "Nadwī, Sayyid Sulaymān," s.v. (he regrets the absence of a biography of that eminent scholar, pp. 87–88, n. 178).

62 Hallaq, *Ibn Taymiyya*.

63 Haque, Sirajul: Ibn Taimīyyah. A Life and Works, in: Mian Mohammad Sharif (ed.): *A History of Muslim Philosophy. With Short Accounts of Other Disciplines and the Modern Renaissance in Muslim Lands*, 2 vols., Wiesbaden 1963–1966, vol. 2, pp. 796–819, here 805–812; Qadir, Chaudhry A.: An Early Islamic Critique of Aristotelian Logic. Ibn Taymiyyah, in: *International Philosophical Quarterly* 8 (1968), pp. 498–512; Fakhry, Majid: *A History of Islamic Philosophy*, New York and London 1970, pp. 350–353; al-ʿAbd, ʿAbd al-Laṭīf Muḥammad: *al-Tafkīr al-manṭiqī bayna al-manhaj al-qadīm wal-manhaj al-jadīd*, Cairo 1977, pp. 43–51; al-Nashshār, *Manāhij al-baḥth*, pp. 146–219; Brunschvig, Pour ou contre la logique grecque; Madjid, Nurcholis: *Ibn Taymiyya on Kalām and Falsafa. A Problem of Reason and Revelation in Islam*, unpublished PhD thesis, University of Chicago 1984; Heer, Nicholas: Ibn Taymiyah's Empiricism, in: Farhad Kazemi and Robert D. McChesney (eds.): *A Way Prepared. Essays on Islamic Culture in Honor of Richard Bayly Winder*, New York and London 1988, pp. 109–115; Özervarlı, M. Sait: İbn Teymiyye. İtikadî Görüşleri, in: Tufan Buzpınar and Tayyar Altıkulaç (eds.): *Türkiye Diyanet Vakfı İslâm Ansiklopedisi*, vol. 20, İstanbul 1999, pp. 409–411; von Kügelgen, Anke: Ibn Taymīyas Kritik an der aristotelischen Logik und sein Gegenentwurf, in: Dominik Perler and Ulrich Rudolph (eds.): *Logik und Theologie. Das Organon im arabischen und lateinischen Mittelalter*, Leiden and Boston 2005, pp. 167–225. See also Nadwī, Sayyid Abū al-Ḥasan ʿAlī: Naqd al-falsafa wal-manṭiq wa-ʿilm al-kalām wa-tarjīḥ uslūb al-kitāb wal-sunna, transl. into Arabic by Saʿīd al-Aʿẓamī al-Nadwī, in: *Majallat al-Baʿth al-Islāmī* 18 (1973), pp. 49–63; idem: *Taʾrīkh daʿwa wa-ʿazīma*, Lucknow 1419/1998, vol. 2, especially pp. 219–258; for these references I thank Jan-Peter Hartung who published a comprehensive study on that scholar in 2004. See Nizami, Khaliq Ahmad: The Impact of Ibn Taimiyya on South Asia, in: *Journal of Islamic Studies* 1 (1990), pp. 120–149, here p. 144.

Ibn Taymiyya wrote also minor refutations of logic. The main one that has come down to us is *Naqḍ al-manṭiq* (The Demolition/Contradiction of Logic) and is seemingly also transmitted in only one manuscript.[64] It was probably written before *al-Radd ʿalā al-manṭiqiyyīn*[65] and constitutes an answer to a request for a formal legal opinion as to whether it is right or wrong to regard logic as a collective duty (*farḍ kifāya*).[66] In content, it resembles the major refutation because of its concentration on definition and methods of deduction. However, his argumentation is less lucid and detailed, being instead more polemical. Besides these two refutations of logic, Ibn Taymiyya wrote several short treatises or chapters dealing with specific aspects of logic; the longest one is entitled *Fī Ḍabṭ kulliyyāt al-manṭiq wal-khalal fīhi* (On the Formation of Universals in Logic and its Defect).[67]

---

64 See also next footnote. The editors mention no further manuscript and Carl Brockelmann (*Geschichte der arabischen Litteratur*, Leiden 1898–1949) does not have it in his list of Ibn Taymiyya's writings. It was edited twice (see the footnote after next).

65 In *al-Radd ʿalā al-manṭiqiyyīn* Ibn Taymiyya mentions that he had earlier written something against logic when he became aware of its falseness (p. 3); see, however, below, n. 67. See also Hallaq, who points out his change in position concerning the intramental character of mathematical principles (Ibn Taymiyya, p. xxxi); see chapter 10.1. In the present article I shall rely on *al-Radd ʿalā al-manṭiqiyyīn* as the main source.

66 The first edition (Cairo 1951) comprises far more than a critique of logic: Ibn Taymiyya discusses and criticizes many teachings and methods of Muslim theological, mystical and philosophical schools; only on the last 67 pages (pp. 155–210), does he come to Aristotelian logic. The part concerning logic is included in *Majmūʿat al-Fatāwā li-shaykh al-islām Taqī al-Dīn Aḥmad b. Taymiyya al-Ḥarrānī*, al-mujallad 9, ed. by ʿAmīr al-Jazzār and Anwār al-Bāz, Mansoura and Cairo 1421/2001, vol. 5, pp. 7–46, the first part in *Majmūʿat al-Fatāwā li-shaykh al-islām Ibn Taymiyya*, al-mujallad 4, ed. by ʿAbd al-Raḥmān b. Muḥammad b. Qāsim and Muḥammad b. ʿAbd al-Raḥmān, Cairo s.d. (reprint of the Riyadh edition 1381–1386/1961–1967), vol. 2, pp. 7–115; see Jon Hoover, who indicates the pages for Ibn Qāsim's edition (*Ibn Taymiyya's Theodicy*, p. 241).

67 Ibn Taymiyya, *Majmūʿat al-Fatāwā*, al-mujallad 9, vol. 5, pp. 137–153 (-170). Ibn Taymiyya mentions in *Naqḍ al-manṭiq* that he had already laid down a summary of Greek logic and some of its errors and misleading concepts (p. 184). It is unlikely that he meant his extensive wor *al-Radd ʿalā al-manṭiqiyyīn*. The oldest and most comprehensive biography of Ibn Taymiyya, the one by Abū ʿAbd Allāh Muḥammad b. Aḥmad b. ʿAbd al-Hādī, mentions that Ibn Taymiyya wrote two refutations of logic besides *al-Radd ʿalā al-manṭiq* (according to al-Nashshār's foreword to al-Suyūṭī, *Ṣawn al-manṭiq*, p. *zāʾ*). Ibn Taymiyya's disciple Ibn Qayyim al-Jawziyya refers only to two works by his master against logic, a big and a small one (*Miftāḥ dār al-saʿāda wa-manshūr wilāyat al-ʿilm*

5. The Impact of Ibn Taymiyya's Refutation of Logic via al-Suyūṭī

In the 15th century, the encyclopedist and Shāfiʿī jurist al-Suyūṭī (d. 911/1505) abridged Ibn Taymiyya's *al-Radd ʿalā al-manṭiqiyyīn* (*naṣīḥa*) to about a fourth of its size, but kept the wording of the original. He removed many of the repetitions and digressions, whereby he reduced the text mainly to the critique, at the cost of some interesting parts of Ibn Taymiyya's epistemology.[68] It is entitled *Kitāb Jahd al-qarīḥa fī tajrīd al-naṣīḥa* and was edited with al-Suyūṭī's *Ṣawn al-manṭiq wal-kalām ʿan fann al-manṭiq wal-kalām*,[69] which probably represents the most comprehensive compilation of Muslim refutations of logic until the 20th century.[70] Al-Suyūṭī mentions having obtained a copy of *al-Radd ʿalā al-manṭiqiyyīn* only after 20 years of searching.[71] Although al-Suyūṭī's abridgement is extant in but two manuscripts, it seems to have been more widespread than its model.[72] In his autobiography al-Suyūṭī mentions Ibn al-Ṣalāḥ's fatwa as the main reason he gave up the study of logic.[73] However, as a major motivation for his compila-

---

wal-irāda, ed. by Maḥmūd Ḥasan Rabīʿ, Cairo 1358/1939, p. 172; see, however, al-Nashshār, foreword to al-Suyūṭī, *Ṣawn al-manṭiq*, pp. *zāʾ-ḥāʾ*).

68 Unless the manuscript al-Suyūṭī possessed was defective, with great likelihood he intentionally omitted the chapter on causality (see below, chapter 11.2) and the whole ninth consideration on widespread (*mashhūrāt*) and estimative (*wahmiyyāt*) propositions, which Ibn Taymiyya, unlike the logicians, grants the possibility of generating certainty (Ibn Taymiyya, *al-Radd*, pp. 396–437; Hallaq, *Ibn Taymiyya*, p. 167, n. 307.1; see below, chapter 11.1).

69 Al-Suyūṭī, *Ṣawn al-manṭiq*, pp. 1–2, 201–343. Since 1947 al-Suyūṭī's summary has been edited several times: as a reprint of al-Nashshār's edition in Beirut 1981; with amendments by Suʿād ʿAbd al-Rāziq in Cairo 1970 (see Hallaq, *Ibn Taymiyya*, p. lvi) and in Ibn Taymiyya's *Majmūʿat al-Fatāwā* (vol. 5, part 9, pp. 47–136 without mentioning al-Suyūṭī's name; see Hallaq, *Ibn Taymiyya*, pp. lv–lvi).

70 Al-Nashshār, foreword to al-Suyūṭī, *Ṣawn al-manṭiq*, pp. *alif-ḥāʾ*; al-Nashshār, *Manāhij al-baḥth*, p. 224.

71 Al-Suyūṭī, *Ṣawn al-manṭiq*, pp. 1–2.

72 Hallaq, *Ibn Taymiyya*, p. lv. It is also known under the title *Mukhtaṣar al-Suyūṭī li-Kitāb Naṣīḥat ahl al-īmān fī al-radd ʿalā manṭiq al-yūnān*. For the main editions and their shortcomings, see Hallaq's translation (Hallaq, *Ibn Taymiyya*, pp. lv–lvii).

73 *Jalāl al-Dīn al-Suyūṭī*, vol. 2: *al-Taḥadduth bi-niʿmat Allāh*, ed. by Elizabeth M. Sartain, Cambridge 1975, p. 241; Sartain, Elizabeth M.: *Jalāl al-Dīn al-Suyūṭī*, vol. 1: *Biography and Background*, Cambridge 1975, p. 32; Goldziher already hinted at it (Stellung der alten islamischen Orthodoxie, pp. 394–395; idem, The Attitude of Orthodox Islam, p. 208). Al-Suyūṭi mentions neither *Jahd al-qarīḥa* nor *Ṣawn al-manṭiq* in his autobiography; instead, he refers to a refutation of

tion, he mentions his annoyance at seeing many of those who deal with logic justifying themselves by pointing to the weakness of arguments by which Ibn al-Ṣalāḥ had forbidden it.[74] Therefore, al-Suyūṭī feels obliged to show that the four "founders" of the law schools and other eminent righteous forefathers forbade innovation (*bidʿa*) and speculative theology (*ʿilm al-kalām*). He argues that since logic represents an innovation, they had clearly forbidden it.[75] Al-Suyūṭī repeats the claim that logic was forbidden by the main religious scholars in an apparently far-reaching fatwa entitled *al-Qawl al-mushriq fī taḥrīm al-ishtighāl bil-manṭiq* (The Illuminating Statement about the Prohibition of the Study of Logic), enumerating nearly 50 persons whom he classifies by juridical schools.[76] Therein, he declares logic to be

> a harmful (*khabīth)* and reprehensible (*madhmūm*) discipline, the study of which is forbidden, being partly based on the theory of the primary matter (*hayūlā*), which is unbelief leading to philosophy and heresy (*zandaqa*) and bearing no religious nor worldly fruit whatsoever.[77]

His few further arguments against logic are very simplistic, reducing it to a science whose proofs are based on universals and consequently have no extramental existence. He only mentions inference by signs or indicators as an alternative (see chapter twelve).[78] Thus, al-Suyūṭī's rejections take into account only some points of Ibn Taymiyya's sophisticated critique and leave his epistemological considerations completely aside.

There seems to have been no further elaborate refutation of logic based on Ibn Taymiyya's works or on al-Suyūṭī's compilation of Ibn Taymiyya's *al-Radd ʿalā al-manṭiqiyyīn*.[79] The reason might be that any

---

logic that he likewise titles *al-Ghayth al-mughriq fī taḥrīm al-manṭiq* (Sartain, *Jalāl al-Dīn al-Suyūṭī*, vol. 2, p. 241) or *al-Qawl al-mushriq fī taḥrīm al-ishtighāl bil-manṭiq* (ibid., p. 114; al-Suyūṭī, *Ṣawn al-manṭiq*, p. 1); edited in al-Suyūṭī, Jalāl al-Dīn: *al-Ḥāwī lil-fatāwā fī al-fiqh wa-ʿulūm al-tafsīr wal-ḥadīth wal-uṣūl wal-naḥw wal-iʿrāb wa-sāʾir al-funūn*, Beirut 1395/1975, vol. 1, pp. 255–257.

74 Al-Suyūṭī, *Ṣawn al-manṭiq*, p. 2.

75 Ibid., pp. 14–190.

76 Al-Suyūṭī, *al-Qawl al-mushriq*, pp. 255–257. See also below, n. 165.

77 Al-Suyūṭī, *al-Qawl al-mushriq*, p. 255.

78 Ibid., p. 256.

79 ʿAlī al-Wardī regards Ibn Khaldūn's (732/1332–808/1406) critique of logic (Ibn Khaldūn, *Muqaddima*, pp. 209–220; see Mahdi, Muhsin: *Ibn Khaldūn's Philosophy of History. A Study in the Philosophic Foundation of the Science of Culture*, London 1957, pp. 100–112) as having been influenced by Ibn Taymiyya

doubts regarding logic had vanished among influential scholars, so that the study of logic became obligatory in many *madrasas* (i.e. in Muslim higher schools that prepared their students for religious posts), at least in the Ottoman Empire.[80] In addition, renowned religious scholars composed commentaries on logic and compiled logical handbooks well into the 19th century. Al-Suyūṭī's refutations, though, remained a point of reference for supporters of logic, such as the Maghrebian scholars al-Maghīlī (d. 909/1503–1504 or 910/1505–1506) and al-Ḥasan al-Yūsī (d. 1102/1691),[81] and for its opponents, like the eminent encyclopedic scholar Murtaḍā al-Zabīdī (d. 1205/1791).[82] Al-Zabīdī accepted logic as a means to defend Islamic dogmas against those who tainted it, but was deeply disturbed by what he saw as its obvious "side effects" – namely the vicious conviction that only logic brings perfection, which, in his eyes, had led to an increasing neglect and ignorance of the words and deeds of the prophet and his companions.[83] He was, of course, aware of the high esteem in which logic was held, and he opposed, in a quite balanced manner, refutations of logic from al-Dhahabī, Ibn

(*Muqaddima*, p. 48). A thorough comparison might be a challenging question of research.

80 For the "institutionalization" of logic in higher education, see for instance the programs of Ottoman madrasas, İzgi, Cevat: *Osmanlı Medreselerinde İlim*, vol. 1, pp. 163–183 et passim; El-Rouayheb, Khaled: Was there a Revival of Logical Studies in Eighteenth-Century Egypt?, in: *Die Welt des Islams* 45 (2005), pp. 1–19, here 5–6 (in regard to the Azhar in the 18th and 19th century). For defences of logic in later centuries, see above, n. 43.

81 Al-Zabīdī quotes a passage from al-Maghīlī's verse polemic addressed to al-Suyūṭī and another from al-Yūsī's *Ḥāshiya ʿalā al-kubrā* (i.e., al-Sanūsī's (d. 895/1490) *al-ʿAqīda al-kubrā*; I am indepted to Stefan Reichmuth for the solution of this abbreviation) in which they refute al-Suyūṭī's rejection of logic in *al-Ḥāwī lil-fatāwā*, i.e., in his *al-Qawl al-mushriq* (*Kitāb Itḥāf al-sāda al-muttaqīn bi-sharḥ asrār Iḥyāʾ ʿulūm al-dīn* (*wa-bi-hāmish Kitāb al-Imlāʾ ʿan ishkālāt al-Iḥyāʾ lil-Ghazālī*), Beirut n.d. after 1970 (reprint of Egypt 1311/1894), vol. 1, pp. 177–179, 182–183; see also above or *al-Qawl al-mushriq* (ibid., p. 114; al-Suyūṭī, *Ṣawn al-manṭiq*, p. 1); edited in al-Suyūṭī, *al-Ḥāwī lil-fatāwā*). Khaled El-Rouayheb has revealed the important contributions of al-Yūsī and other Maghrebian scholars in the field of logic from the 14th Century onwards (Was there a Revival, pp. 5, 7–14; idem: Opening the Gate of Verification. The Forgotten Arab-Islamic Florescence of the 17th Century, in: *International Journal of Middle East Studies* 38 (2006), pp. 263–281, here 269–271).

82 Concerning this scholar, see the monograph by Reichmuth, Stefan: *The World of Murtaḍā al-Zabīdī (1732–1791). Studies on the Life, Networks and Writings of an Islamic Humanist Scholar of the 18th Century*, [Cambridge] 2009.

83 Al-Zabīdī, *Kitāb Itḥāf al-sāda*, vol. 1, pp. 179–180.

Qayyim al-Jawziyya (d. 751/1350), al-Suyūṭī, and others to justifications of logic from Taqī al-Dīn al-Subkī (d. 756/1355) and the aforementioned Maghrebian scholars al-Maghīlī and al-Ḥasan al-Yūsī.[84] Al-Zabīdī supports al-Suyūṭī, repeating the latter's judgments in *al-Qawl al-mushriq fī taḥrīm al-ishtighāl bil-manṭiq*, namely that logic is harmful, reprehensible, of no use to the dogma of God's unity, and a cause of great harm to the heart.[85] Al-Zabīdī refers to Ibn Taymiyya as the last who devoted himself to illuminating "[logic's] wrongness and inconsistency,"[86] but cites only one sentence from him, indirectly, i.e., as transmitted by ʿAlī al-Qārī (d. 1016/1607): "I do not think that God – He is mighty and sublime – overlooks (that deed of) al-Maʾmūn. He certainly will punish him for what he has brought into the [Muslim] community by translating that science from Greek into Arabic."[87] The history of the impact of Ibn Taymiyya's refutations of logic still waits to be written. It remains to be studied whether they were mainly received via the popularizer al-Suyūṭī, as seems to be the case, judging from the aforementioned examples, or whether they had a direct influence or other popularizers.

6. Forerunners of Ibn Taymiyya in Rejecting *falsafa*

As to the refutation and anathematization of *falsafa*, Ibn Taymiyya had far more "concurrence" regarding elaborate rejections.[88] Before he

84 Ibid., pp. 176–184. The whole chapter has been recently scrutinized by El-Rouayheb, Was there a Revival, especially pp. 2–14. See also below, n. 165. Stefan Reichmuth thoroughly studied al-Zabīdī's whole commentary on al-Ghazālī's *Iḥyāʾ ʿulūm al-dīn* (*The World of Murtaḍā al-Zabīdī*, ch. 5).

85 Al-Zabīdī, *Kitāb Itḥāf al-sāda*, vol. 1, pp. 180–181. Al-Zabīdī tries to support this view also with a statement by al-Ghazālī (ibid., pp. 183–184). El-Rouayheb has shown, however, that his quotation was taken out of context and thus neglects the fact that al-Ghazālī considered logic a neutral, harmless science in regard to religion (Was there a Revival, p. 4). Noticeably, al-Suyūṭī also claims that al-Ghazālī became hostile to logic at the end of his life (*al-Qawl al-mushriq*, p. 255).

86 *Mā aẓunn Allāh ʿazza wa-jalla yaghfulu ʿalā al-Maʾmūn wa-lā budd an yuʿāqibahu bi-mā adkhala ʿalā al-umma min naql hādhā al-ʿilm min al-yūnāniyya ilā al-ʿarabiyya*, al-Zabīdī, *Kitāb Itḥāf al-sāda*, vol. 1, p. 176. On al-Qārī see the article by Claudia Preckel in this volume.

87 Al-Zabīdī, *Kitāb Itḥāf al-sāda*, vol. 1, p. 176.

88 For a diachronic, though in its generalisation outdated survey of the rejection of Greek philosophy in general, see Goldziher, Stellung der alten islamischen

entered the scene, Abū Ḥāmid al-Ghazālī had already refuted major subjects of the *falāsifa* in several of his writings. He seriously challenged the coherence of their theories and concepts in *Tahāfut al-falāsifa* on the basis of reasoning. As a result of his own experience, he tried to prove the harm of philosophy to the soul of the individual and to the unity of the community in his spiritual autobiography *al-Munqidh min al-ḍalāl* and presented a Sufi-inspired alternative that he considered the "right way" to truth and blissfulness in his *Iḥyāʾ ʿulūm al-dīn* and other writings.[89] Tāj al-Dīn al-Shahrastānī (d. 548/1153), a contemporary of al-Ghazālī whose refutation, however, he does not mention,[90] tried to show the inconsistency of Ibn Sīnā's main metaphysical tenets in several writings, such as the survey of different religions, philosophies, and Muslim sects *Kitāb al-Milal wal-niḥal*, the comparatistic theological work *Kitāb Nihāyat al-aqdām fī ʿilm al-kalām*, and treatises solely devoted to the critique of Ibn Sīnā.[91] Some decades later, Fakhr al-Dīn al-Rāzī (d. 606/1209), who considered al-Ghazālī and al-Shahrastānī to

---

Orthodoxie, pp. 357–400; for the translation, see idem, The Attitude of Orthodox Islam, pp. 185–215. See Dimitri Gutas' critique: *Greek Thought, Arabic Culture. The Graeco-Arabic Translation Movement in Baghdad and Early ʿAbbāsid Society* (*2nd–4th/8th–10th Centuries*), London and New York 1998, pp. 166–175.

89 These works and al-Ghazālī's refutations of and attitudes against philosophy are well studied; for references see Daiber, Hans: *Bibliography of Islamic Philosophy*, Leiden 1999, vol. 1 and vol. 2, s. v. "Ghazzālī". Al-Ghazālī was evidently not the first to refute philosophy in a detailed manner. Al-Ashʿarī (260/873–874–324/935–936), for instance, wrote a book *Fī al-Radd ʿalā al-falāsifa* in which he argued against teachings that might contradict God's creative power; unfortunately however, this book has not come down to us (McCarthy, Richard Joseph: *The Theology of al-Ashʿarī. The Arabic Texts of al-Ashʿarī's Kitāb al-Lumaʿ and Risālat Istiḥsān al-khawḍ fī ʿilm al-kalām; with briefly annotated translations, and appendices containing material pertinent to the study of al-Ashʿarī*, Beirut 1953, p. 225, n. 70).

90 Al-Shahrastānī, Muḥammad: *Struggling with the Philosopher. A Refutation of Avicenna's Metaphysics*; A new Arabic edition and English translation of Muḥammad b. ʿAbd al-Karīm b. Aḥmad al-Shahrastānī's *Kitāb al-Muṣāraʿa* by Wilferd Madelung and Toby Mayer, London and New York 2001, pp. 8–9.

91 The currently best known of these separate treatises is *Kitāb al-Muṣāraʿa* (see al-Shahrastānī, *Struggling with the Philosopher*). Concerning references to the other works and his critique of Ibn Sīnā, see Monnot, Guy: al-Shahrastānī, in: *EI²*, vol. 9 (1997), pp. 214–216; Daiber, *Bibliography of Islamic Philosophy*, vol. 1 and vol. 2, s. v. *Shahrastānī*; and Steigerwald, Diane: *La pensée philosophique et théologique de Shahrastānī* (*m. 548/1153*), Laval 1997.

be only mediocre thinkers,[92] thoroughly criticized – with purely rationalistic arguments – many metaphysical and physical tenets of prior *kalām* theologians and *falāsifa* (especially Ibn Sīnā) in several of his works. He does this in his commentary and his summary of Ibn Sīnā's *Kitāb al-Ishārāt wal-tanbīhāt*, for instance, and in his main theological and philosophical book *al-Mabāḥith al-mashriqiyya fī ʿilm al-ilāhiyyāt wal-ṭabīʿiyyāt*.[93] These three authors were clearly influenced by what they refuted, by consciously or unconsciously adopting philosophical concepts or using their opponents' arguments while rejecting them. Al-Shahrastānī and al-Rāzī, especially, were confronted with the reproach that their teachings were deeply tainted with philosophy, and apparently al-Rāzī even had to fear for his life.[94] It was not easy to reject this charge in either case, since – in contrast to al-Ghazālī – they did not charge the philosophers with unbelief, and while al-Shahrastānī adopted Ismāʿīlī tenets in some of his writings,[95] al-Rāzī followed and developed several of Ibn Sīnā's and other philosopher's theses.[96] In fact, both expressed many of their ideas in philosophical terms. Al-Ghazālī was regarded with suspicion in traditionalist circles, not least by Ibn Taymiyya,[97] and there is no doubt that al-Ghazālī remained influenced by philosophy even after his disillusion about its leading to truth.

92 Kraus, Paul: Les "Controverses" de Fakhr al-Dīn Rāzī, in: *Bulletin de l'Institut d'Égypte* 19 (1937), pp. 187–214, here 204–212.

93 At the end of his treatise *Iʿtiqādāt firaq al-muslimīn wal-mushrikīn wa-maʿahu baḥth fī al-ṣūfiyya wal-firaq al-islāmiyya li-Muṣṭafā Bek ʿAbd al-Rāzī*, ed. by ʿAlī Sāmī al-Nashshār, Cairo 1356/1938, pp. 91–92, Fakhr al-Dīn al-Rāzī enumerates nine writings he reckons as his refutations of the *falāsifa*, some of which seem not to have survived. These and other of his works are nowadays less studied than those of al-Ghazālī and al-Shahrastānī; see Arnaldez, Roger: L'oeuvre de Fakhr al-Dīn al-Rāzī. Commentateur du Coran et philosophe, in: *Cahiers de Civilisation Médiévale Xe-XIIe siècles* 3 (1960), pp. 307–323; Anawati, George C.: Fakhr al-Dīn al-Rāzī, in: *EI*^{2}, vol. 2 (1991), pp. 751–755; Gutas, The Heritage of Avicenna, p. 89.

94 See al-Shahrastānī, *Struggling with the Philosopher*, pp. 2, 6; al-Rāzī, *Iʿtiqādāt firaq al-muslimīn wal-mushrikīn*, p. 189.

95 Al-Shahrastānī, *Struggling with the Philosopher*, pp. 1–16 et passim.

96 Arnaldez, L'oeuvre de Fakhr al-Dīn al-Rāzī, pp. 316–318; Kraus, Les "Controverses", pp. 190, 203–205.

97 For Ibn Taymiyya's critique of al-Ghazālī, see Ibn Taymiyya, *Darʾ taʿāruḍ al-ʿaql*, vol. 11, s. v. "al-Ghazālī". See also below, chapter 8.

Besides these highly rationalistic rejections and discussions of *falsafa*,[98] there were also long and harsh refutations and anathematizations that mainly argued on the basis of the Koran and the Sunna. Especially successful were the attacks by a contemporary of al-Rāzī, Shihāb al-Dīn Abū Ḥafṣ ʿUmar al-Suhrawardī (d. 632/1234), the so-called founder of the Sufi brotherhood al-Suhrawardiyya. His books *Idālat al-ʿiyān* and *Kashf al-faḍāʾiḥ al-yūnāniyya wa-rashf al-naṣāʾiḥ al-īmāniyya* (or *Rashf al-naṣāʾiḥ al-īmāniyya wa-kashf al-faḍāʾiḥ al-yūnāniyya*), which demonstrate his utilization of the Ismāʿīlī arguments of al-Shahrastānī in addition to the Koran and the Sunna,[99] were utilized by the ʿAbbāsid rulership to persecute scholars interested in *falsafa*.[100] *Kashf al-faḍāʾiḥ al-yūnāniyya wa-rashf al-naṣāʾiḥ al-īmāniyya* was translated into Persian under the Muẓaffarid Shāh Shujāʿ (d. 786/1384) and his clique, who were also outspoken enemies of all kinds of rationalism.[101]

7. Ibn Taymiyya's *Opus Magnum* Against Rationalism

In his major rejection of rationalism, Ibn Taymiyya takes into account al-Ghazālī's, al-Shahrastānī's, and al-Rāzī's refutations of *falsafa*. He harshly criticizes, however, his forerunners for having given preference to reason in cases where it conflicts with the religious tradition

98 Probably still more common at that time were short and banal, pseudo-rationalistic refutations like Zakariyyā al-Qazwīnī's (600/1203–682/1283) *Fī al-Radd ʿalā l-falāsifa* (a chapter of his *Mufīd al-ʿulūm wa-mubīd al-humūm*, ed. by Muḥammad ʿAbd al-Qādir ʿAṭā', Beirut n. d., around 1985, pp. 86–87; the work is often attributed to Jamāl al-Dīn Abū Bakr al-Khwārazmī).

99 Hartmann, Angelika: Ismāʿīlitische Theologie bei sunnitischen ʿulamāʾ des Mittelalters?, in: Ludwig Hagemann and Ernst Pulsfort (eds.): *"Ihr alle aber seid Brüder". Festschrift für A. Th. Khoury zum 60. Geburtstag*, Würzburg and Altenberge 1990, pp. 190–206, here 201–203; Hartmann, Angelika: al-Suhrawardī, Shihāb al-Dīn Abū Ḥafṣ ʿUmar, in: *EI*², vol. 9 (1997), pp. 780–781.

100 Hartmann, *an-Nāṣir li-dīn Allāh*, pp. 34–36, 250–260.

101 The translator was a well known jurist of his region, Muʿīn al-Dīn Yazdī (d. 789/1387). He freely intermingled his own opinions in the text and left several passages out. In his rejection of *falsafa* and of all those who even touched it, he is no less fervent than al-Suhrawardī. (Hartmann, Angelika: Eine orthodoxe Polemik gegen Philosophen und Freidenker – eine zeitgenössische Schrift gegen Ḥāfiẓ? – Muʿīn ud-Dīn Yazdī und sein "Tarǧama-yi rašf an-naṣāʾiḥ", in: *Der Islam* 56 (1979), pp. 274–293; idem, al-Suhrawardī, p. 781; idem: Muʿīn al-Dīn Yazdī, in: *EI*², vol. 7 (1993), pp. 480–481).

(*al-naql/al-sharʿ*), holding that they thereby missed the right path to truth.[102] His vigorous and eminent rebuttal of all schools and individuals adopting that rule was most probably written between 713/1313–1314 and 717/1317–1318,[103] i.e., some years after Ibn Taymiyya had started his work on *al-Radd ʿalā al-manṭiqiyyīn*. This work is known under several titles. Ibn Taymiyya himself refers to it mostly as *Darʾ taʿāruḍ al-ʿaql wal-naql*, but other titles of this work, like *Bayān muwāfaqat al-ʿaql al-ṣarīḥ lil-naql al-ṣaḥīḥ* express more precisely Ibn Taymiyya's intention to prove the congruity of "clear reason" with sound religious tradition.[104] No complete copy of *Darʾ taʿāruḍ al-ʿaql wal-naql* has come down to us. Large or small parts of it are preserved in less than ten manuscripts; by collating them, Muḥammad Rashād Sālim reconstructed the work as a whole. Only four of the manuscripts are dated; the oldest one dates from 737–738/1336–1338,[105] one either

102 Ibn Taymiyya, *Darʾ taʿāruḍ al-ʿaql*, vol. 1, pp. 5–6; vol. 9, pp. 66–68 (among many other instances, see vol. 11, "Fahāris al-aʿlām"). Ibn Taymiyya is well aware of al-Ghazālī's different stages and ways of searching for the truth, but rejects them all (*Darʾ taʿāruḍ al-ʿaql*, vol. 1, pp. 162–163). For Ibn Taymiyya's borrowing of arguments from his forerunners, see below.

103 Ibn Taymiyya, *Darʾ taʿāruḍ al-ʿaql*, vol. 1, introduction, p. 9.

104 Ibid., introduction, p. 6. (I follow the English translation by Michot, A Mamlūk Theologian's Commentary, p. 156). Other titles are *al-Jamʿ bayna al-maʿqūl wal-manqūl* and further slight variations (Ibn Taymiyya, *Darʾ taʿāruḍ al-ʿaql*, vol. 1, introduction, pp. 5–7). Under the heading *Bayān muwāfaqat ṣarīḥ al-maʿqūl li-ṣaḥīḥ al-manqūl*, the first third of it had already been published – based on one single manuscript with many amendations by the editors – in Cairo 1321–1322/1903–1905 at the margins of Ibn Taymiyya's *Minhāj al-sunna al-nabawiyya fī naqḍ kalām al-shīʿa wal-qadariyya* (the origin of the manuscript of *Bayān* is not indicated and the scarcity of copies lamented, see Ibn Taymiyya, *Darʾ taʿāruḍ al-ʿaql*, p. 69); there exist several reprints of this edition (for the exact correspondence of pages, see Hoover, *Ibn Taymiyya's Theodicy*, p. 240). In a second edition of *Minhāj al-sunna* in Cairo 1370/1950–1951 (reprint: Beirut 1985), Muḥammad Muḥyī al-Dīn ʿAbd al-Ḥamīd and Muḥammad Ḥāmid al-Fiqī edited a manuscript of *Muwāfaqat ṣaḥīḥ al-manqūl li-ṣarīḥ al-maʿqūl* from Medina that is now lost (Ibn Taymiyya, *Darʾ taʿāruḍ al-ʿaql*, introduction, pp. 69–70). In 1987, ʿAbd al-Laṭīf ʿAbd al-Raḥmān published *Darʾ taʿāruḍ al-ʿaql wal-naql aw-Muwāfaqat ṣaḥīḥ al-manqūl li-ṣarīḥ al-maʿqūl* in five volumes without any hint either of his manuscript basis or to Sālim's edition; annotations are limited to Hadith references and names of people and there are no indices; I therefore do not refer to it. In fact, the congruity of clear reason and sound religious tradition is a subject that Ibn Taymiyya upholds and treats in many of his writings, see Hoover, *Ibn Taymiyya's Theodicy*, p. 20, n. 7.

105 Ibn Taymiyya, *Darʾ taʿāruḍ al-ʿaql*, vol. 1, pp. 48–55.

from the early 17th or late 19th century[106] and two from the turn of the 19th to the 20th century.[107]

The work is divided into 44 arguments, all of which echo its *leitmotif*, the refutation of the precedence of *ratio* over scripture in case of their divergence. Binyamin Abrahamov has concisely summarized them, and only some major points shall be mentioned. Ibn Taymiyya questions the assumption that reason is the basis of tradition or of the knowledge of its soundness; pointing to the numberless disagreements about dogmas that are based on so-called rational proofs, he maintains that multiply-transmitted reports constitute a necessary knowledge, qualifies his adversaries' use of the Arabic language as improper, and distinguishes in the Koran and the Sunna between orally transmitted (*samʿī*) and rational (*ʿaqlī*) proofs.[108] As shall be shown, Ibn Taymiyya eventually aims to show that "clear reason" cannot contradict the sound religious tradition, thereby dismissing his adversaries' use and understanding of reason.

The appearance of his *leitmotif* is always the beginning of a long and vigorous attack on the metaphysical positions of philosophers and *kalām* theologians. He therein displays a tremendous first-hand knowledge not only of his forerunners' refutations of *falsafa* among the *kalām* theologians, but also of the works of the most prominent Muslim philosophers, like al-Fārābī, Ibn Sīnā and Ibn Rushd.[109] This

---

106 Ibid., p. 45.

107 Ibid., pp. 33, 37.

108 Abrahamov, Binyamin: Ibn Taymiyya on the Agreement of Reason with Tradition, in: *The Muslim World* 82 (1992), pp. 256–272. Nicholas Heer directly confronted Ibn Taymiyya's arguments with those of *kalām* theologians: The Priority of Reason in the Interpretation of Scripture. Ibn Taymiyyah and the Mutakallimun, in: Mustansir Mir (ed.): *Literary Heritage of Classical Islam. Arabic and Islamic Studies in Honor of James A. Bellamy*, Princeton 1993, pp. 181–195. Yahya Michot translated and commented upon the ninth of the 44 arguments (Michot, Vanités intellectuelles, pp. 597–617). Some of them are reproduced in a programmatic manner by the Moroccan Islamist Muḥammad Yatīm (b. 1956) (Yatīm, Muḥammad: Ibn Taymiyya wa-masʾalat al-ʿaql wal-naql, in: *al-Furqān* 3 (1407/1987), pp. 16–24.) Ibn Taymiyya's distinction between rational and transmitted within the Koran and the Sunna has been recently studied by Sait Özervarli: The Qurʾānic Rational Theology of Ibn Taymiyya and His Criticism of the Mutakallimūn, in: Yossef Rapoport and Shahab Ahmed (eds.): *Ibn Taymiyya and His Times*, Karachi 2010; I am grateful to Yossef Rapoport for providing me with the article in press.

109 Laoust, *Essai sur les doctrines sociales et politiques*, pp. 84–86; Hallaq, *Ibn Taymiyya*, p. xlv; see *Darʾ taʿāruḍ al-ʿaql*, vol. 11, "Fihris al-aʿlām" and "Fihris

knowledge has led him to declare their writings to be bare of any guidance or restoration of the soul. They serve only one useful purpose, namely to provide arguments to refute each other.[110] Indeed, Ibn Taymiyya frequently uses a critique of one rationalist against another and seldom fails to immediately reject the respective counter-argument in turn.[111] Moreover, he states that their works occasionally served him as a source for the history of specific schools and theories, which they doubtless did.[112] He deconstructs most of the theories about God, His messengers, and the invisible world that were known at his time and often confronts them with his own views. Although his tone is at times very polemical, his questions and critiques are mostly of considerable depth and pertinence. In consistency with his view that the application of logic is the main reason for their false dogmas, he repeatedly criticizes in *Darʾ taʿāruḍ al-ʿaql wal-naql* their methods of gaining definitions and deductions. Thus, this work completes *al-Radd ʿalā al-manṭiqiyyīn*, where he in turn blames several metaphysical theories and their logical foundations. As a matter of fact, both refutations have much in common and supplement each other. They deserve to be studied in a thorough comparative work. The basis for such an immense task, however, is not yet laid. Researchers on Ibn Taymiyya's huge *Darʾ taʿāruḍ al-ʿaql wal-naql* have so far only picked

---

asmāʾ al-kutub", s. v., and below, chapters 10 and 11.1. Ibn Taymiyya can probably be considered with Yahya Michot as "the most important reader of *falāsifa* after Faḫr al-Dīn al-Rāzī in the sunnite world" (Michot, Vanités intellectuelles, p. 599). The fact that Ibn Taymiyya so extensively quotes passages from the main Peripatetics shows, of course, that he wanted to rely on first-hand, not second-hand sources. In addition, this seems to contradict the view that the works of these philosophers ceased to be studied from the turn of the twelfth century on, although there were times and places for which that view holds true (Griffel, *Apostasie*, p. 353). Still, Ibn Taymiyya's library remains to be reconstructed, in order to be able to judge the degree to which Ibn Taymiyya relied on the original works and not on citations of them in later writings.

110 Ibn Taymiyya, *Darʾ taʿāruḍ al-ʿaql*, vol. 9, p. 67.

111 Several times, for instance, Ibn Taymiyya agrees with Ibn Rushd's critique of some of Ibn Sīnā's tenets (*Darʾ taʿāruḍ al-ʿaql*, vol. 6, p. 245; vol. 8, pp. 174–175, 181; vol. 9, p. 116 et passim). See also al-Ṭablāwī, M. S.: *Mawqif Ibn Taymiyya min falsafat Ibn Rushd fī al-ʿaqīda wa-fī ʿilm al-kalām wal-falsafa*, Cairo 1409/1989; al-Ṣughayyir, Mawāqif, pp. 169–172, 175–180; Michot, A Mamlūk Theologian's Commentary, pp. 170–172.

112 See, for instance, Ibn Taymiyya, *Darʾ taʿāruḍ al-ʿaql*, vol. 6, pp. 212, 245; vol. 8, pp. 174, 198.

up a few of the subjects he touched therein[113] – and this is true of the present study, as well.

8. The Reception of Ibn Taymiyya's Repudiation of Rationalism

In Ḥanbalī circles, *Darʾ taʿāruḍ al-ʿaql wal-naql* was regarded as an *opus magnum* and often referred to, but the real scope of its impact is still unknown.[114] Ibn Qayyim al-Jawziyya (d. 751/1350), for instance, reproduces several of Ibn Taymiyya's lines of reasoning in his works, not least the core of Ibn Taymiyya's arguments against the precedence of *ratio* over scripture in his *al-Ṣawāʾiq al-mursala*, arranging them in an independent way and adding his own arguments.[115] Muḥammad b.

113 Ibn Taymiyya's rejection of *falsafa* in general is treated by Nurcholis Madjid (*Ibn Taymiyya on Kalām and Falsafa*) and touched upon by Thomas Michel (Ibn Taymiyya's Critique of Falsafa, in: *Hamdard Islamicus* 6 (1983), pp. 3–14). His rebuttal of specific metaphysical and theological subjects and arguments are dealt with quite extensively by Muḥammad Khalīl Harās, *Bāʿith al-nahḍa al-islāmiyya*; al-Ṣughayyir, Mawāqif "rushdiyya" li-Taqī al-Dīn Ibn Taymiyya, pp. 164–182; M. S. al-Ṭablāwī, *Mawqif Ibn Taymiyya min falsafat Ibn Rushd*; Michot, A Mamlūk Theologian's Commentary, pp. 149–203; Michot, Jean R.: *Ibn Taymiyya. Lettre à Abû l-Fidâʾ; traduction de l'arabe, présentation, notes et lexique*, Louvain-La-Neuve 1994; Çağrıcı, Mustafa: İbn Teymiyye'nin bakışıyla Gazzâlî-Ibn Rüşd tartışması, in: *İslam Tetkikleri Dergisi* (*Review of Islamic Studies*) 9 (1995), pp. 77–126; Özervarlı, *İbn Teymiyye*, pp. 405–413; Marcotte, Roxanne D.: Ibn Taymiyya et sa critique des produits de la faculté d'estimation (Wahmiyyāt) dans le *Darʾ taʿāruḍ al-ʿaql wa al-naql*, in: *Luqmān* 18 (2002), pp. 43–58, I am indebted to Jon Hoover for knowledge of this study; von Kügelgen, Dialogpartner im Widerspruch, pp. 455–481; Özervarli, The Qurʾānic Rational Theology of Ibn Taymiyya. See also above, n. 63.

114 Ibn Taymiyya, *Darʾ taʿāruḍ al-ʿaql*, vol. 1, pp. 4–6; [Ibn Murrī, Shihāb al-Dīn:]: Athāra min al-taʾrīkh, in: *al-Manār* 10 (1325/1907), pp. 616–621 (especially p. 617; see below, n. 118).

115 Ibn Qayyim al-Jawziyya: *al-Ṣawāʾiq al-mursala ʿalā al-jahmiyya wal-muʿaṭṭila*, ed. by ʿAlī b. Muḥammad al-Dakhīl Allāh, Riyadh 1408/1987–1988, vol. 3–4, pp. 796–1538. I am grateful to Livnat Holtzman for having drawn my attention to Ibn Qayyim al-Jawziyya's reference in this work to Ibn Taymiyya's *Darʾ taʿāruḍ al-ʿaql wal-naql* and for having provided me with a copy of the respective pages in Muḥammad b. al-Mawṣilī's *Mukhtaṣar* (see next note). She recently pointed out that Ibn Qayyim al-Jawziyya inserted Ibn Taymiyya's long discussion of the Hadith concerning *Fiṭra* (*Darʾ taʿāruḍ al-ʿaql*, vol. 8, pp. 365–468) in his *Shifāʾ al-ʿalīl* (Holtzman, Livnat: Human Choice and the *Fiṭra* Tradition. Some Remarks on the Later Ḥanbalī Use of *Ḥadīth* in Theo-

al-Mawṣilī (d. 774/1372–1373) included some of them in his *Mukhtaṣar al-ṣawāʾiq al-mursala*.[116] Beyond the Ḥanbalī circles, less is known about the impact of *Darʾ taʿāruḍ al-ʿaql wal-naql*. The Shāfiʿī jurist Muḥammad b. ʿAbd Allāh b. Aḥmad al-Hakkārī al-Salṭī (d. 786/1384) abridged it into two volumes in 773/1371 on the basis of a six-volume manuscript,[117] which he claims was partly an autograph.[118] It is an open question whether al-Hakkārī's abridgement fostered a dissemination of that work. Some of its contents, at least, seem to have been discussed.

---

logical Treatises, in: Yossef Rapoport and Ahmed Shahab (eds.): *Ibn Taymiyya and His Times*, Karachi 2010, pp. 163–188).

116 Ibn al-Mawṣilī, Muḥammad: *Mukhtaṣar al-Ṣawāʾiq al-mursala ʿalā al-jahmiyya wal-muʿaṭṭila li-Ibn Qayyim al-Jawziyya*, ed. by al-Ḥasan b. ʿAbd al-Raḥmān al-ʿAlawī, Riyadh 1425/2004, vol. 1, pp. 246–364, vol. 2, pp. 365–544 (pdf file at http://www.archive.org/details/ muktsr_swaik_mursla, last accessed April 4, 2008). Ibn Qayyim al-Jawziyya's *al-Ṣawāʾiq al-mursala* of which only the first half has come down to us and the abridgement of the entire work by al-Mawṣilī deserve a thorough study. One aspect of it, namely Ibn Qayyim al-Jawziyya's discussion of the fire's duration has recently been scrutinized by Jon Hoover: Islamic Universalism. Ibn Qayyim al-Jawziyya's Salafī Deliberations on the Duration of Hell-Fire, in: *The Muslim World* 1 (2009), pp. 181–201.

117 Muḥammad Rashād Sālim refers to al-Hakkārī's *Mukhtaṣar* in his introduction to *Darʾ taʿāruḍ al-ʿaql* (vol. 1, pp. 60–64) and uses it for his collation. Apparently, only one copy of it is known. Al-Hakkārī states that he has summarized it, because of "the many strange citations" from "strange books", but to have fully preserved Ibn Taymiyya's intentions (Ibn Taymiyya, *Darʾ taʿāruḍ*, vol. 1, p. 62).

118 According to a letter from the Ḥanbalī scholar Shihāb al-Dīn Ibn Murrī al-Baʿlbakī, one of Ibn Taymiyya's pupils, which he addressed to other followers of his master, the autograph was soon "severely disrupted." He also states that the complete copy of it that he himself used to possess was scattered, and he urges them to bring all parts together. Ibn Murrī refers to the work as *al-Radd ʿalā ʿaqāʾid al-falāsifa*. Thanks to Caterina Bori, I was able to trace the origin of the letter, which I knew only from Rashīd Riḍā's reprint in the journal *al-Manār* 10 (1325/1907), pp. 616–621 under the heading *Athāra min al-taʾrīkh*, here p. 617. She was kind enough to provide me with her forthcoming study on the methods and difficulties of collecting Ibn Taymiyya's works after his death, in which she presents the same paragraph as an example. According to her well founded assumption, the letter was written between 728 and 731 (1327–1331); it was published by M. ʿA. Shams and ʿA. b. Muḥammad al-ʿImrān (*al-Jāmiʿ li-sīrat Shaykh al-Islām Ibn Taymiyya*, Mecca 1420/1999, pp. 97–104, see: Bori, Caterina: The Collection and Edition of Ibn Taymiyya's Works. Concerns of a Disciple, in: *The Mamlūk Studies Review* 13 (2009), pp. 1–21. I thank Caterina Bori for having provided me with the article while still in press.

The prominent Shāfiʿī jurist and preacher Taj al-Dīn Abū Naṣr ʿAbd al-Wahhāb al-Subkī (d. 771/1370), for instance, apparently accuses Ibn Taymiyya and others of having unwarrantedly denounced al-Ghazālī and al-Rāzī – this although al-Subkī was in no way a friend of Greek rationalism; however, he only allowed the study of logic and philosophy for the purpose of refuting them, and even in this case limited it to those whose high degree of knowledge of the Koran, the Sunna, and jurisprudence had been unshakably rooted in their hearts.[119]

The fact that Ibn Taymiyya rejected not only *falsafa*, but also logic, the "later" *kalām* theology, and other schools of thought may have kept his substantial rebuttal from becoming an important point of reference. *Falsafa* in the sense of an adherence to the teachings of Plato, Aristotle, their Greek commentators, and their Muslim followers and thus the claim to reason about the human, the divine, and the universe independently from revelation was instead predominantly rejected with reference to al-Ghazālī and sometimes with reference to al-Rāzī and to al-Suhrawardī.[120] Thus, it was the arguments of al-Ghazālī's *Tahāfut al-falāsifa* that, in the second half of the 15th century, Mehmet II ordered weighed against those of the philosophers.[121] Again, it is *Tahāfut al-falāsifa* that the well-known bibliographer and historiographer, the Ottoman state employee Ḥājjī Khalīfa (Kātib

119 Al-Subkī, Tāj al-Dīn Abū Naṣr ʿAbd al-Wahhāb: *Kitāb Muʿīd al-niʿam wa-mubīd al-niqam. The Restorer of Favours and the Restrainer of Chastisements,* ed. by David W. Myhrman, London 1968, pp. 110–112; he does not explicitly mention Ibn Taymiyya's name, but in all likelihood refers to him. See al-Nashshār, *Manāhij al-baḥth,* p. 225; Tāj al-Dīn's father, Taqī al-Dīn al-Subkī, was an explicit enemy of Ibn Taymiyya and wrote several tracts against juridical and theological tenets of Ibn Taymiyya and his followers, see Bori, *Ibn Taymiyya*, pp. 155–169; al-Subkī, Tāj al-Dīn Abū Naṣr ʿAbd al-Wahhāb: Tâj Eddîn Es-Subkî's Muʿîd en-niʿam wa mubîd en-niqam. Über die moralischen Pflichten der verschiedenen islamischen Bevölkerungsklassen, mit Kürzungen aus dem Arabischen übersetzt von Oskar Rescher, in: idem: *Gesammelte Schriften*, sect. II, vol. 2, Osnabrück 1980 (reprint, Constantinople 1925), pp. 71–74.

120 Hartmann, Angelika: Bemerkungen zu Handschriften ʿUmar as-Suhrawardīs, echten und vermeintlichen Autographen, in: *Der Islam* 60 (1983), pp. 112–142, here p. 117; idem, Hartmann, *al-Nāṣir li-dīn Allāh*, p. 36; see also above, n. 95.

121 Ḥājjī Khalīfa (Kātib Çelebi): *Kashf al-ẓunūn ʿan asāmī al-kutub wal-funūn*, ed. by Şerefeddin Yaltakaya and K. Rifat Bilge, vol. 1, Istanbul 1941, p. 513; Ṭāshköprü-Zāda: *al-Shaqāʾiq al-nuʿmāniyya fī ʿulamāʾ al-daula al-ʿuthmāniyya*, ed. by Aḥmad Ṣubḥī Furāt, Istanbul 1985, pp. 98–99; Türker, Mubahat: *Üç Tehâfüt Bakımından Felsefe ve Din Münasebeti*, Ankara 1956, pp. 56–61.

Çelebi, d. 1067/1657), qualifies as a book that one ought to know.[122] *Darʾ al-taʿāruḍ*, in contrast, is simply characterized as "volumes" (*mujalladāt*) of the Shaykh Ibn Taymiyya.[123] Prominent scholars of the 18th century, such as Muḥammad al-Sājaqlī (Sacaqlı-zāde, d. around 1145/1733)[124] and Murtaḍā al-Zabīdī (d. 1205/1791)[125] still refer to al-Ghazālī when denouncing *falsafa*. However, the history of the fate of Ibn Taymiyya's refutations of the rationalists remains to be written.

20th-century apologists for Islam regard Ibn Taymiyya as a "philosopher," especially on the basis of *al-Radd ʿalā al-manṭiqiyyīn* and *Darʾ taʿāruḍ al-ʿaql wal-naql*.[126] Here, "philosophy" is no longer understood as taking Greek thought to be the ultimate truth.[127] Al-Sayyid Sulaymān al-Nadwī (d. 1953), sees in Ibn Taymiyya a forerunner of David Hume (d. 1776) and John Stuart Mill (d. 1873),[128] whereas the

---

122 Ḥājjī Khalīfa, *Kashf al-ẓunūn*, vol. 1, p. 512; his exposition of al-Ghazālī's book is long in comparison with the usual size of his summaries in *Kashf al-ẓunūn*.

123 Ibid., vol. 1, p. 730.

124 Reichmuth, Stefan: Bildungskanon und Bildungsreform aus der Sicht eines islamischen Gelehrten der anatolischen Provinz: Muḥammad al-Sājaqlī (Saçaqlı-zāde, gest. um 1145/1733) und sein *Tartīb al-ʿulūm*, in: Rüdiger Arnzen and Jörn Thielmann (eds.): *Words, Texts and Concepts Cruising the Mediterranean Sea. Studies on the Sources, Contents and Influences of Islamic Civilization and Arabic Philosophy and Science Dedicated to Gerhard Endress on His Sixty-fifth Birthday*, Leuven 2004, pp. 498–500, 511–516.

125 Al-Zabīdī, Murtaḍā: *Kitāb Itḥāf al-sāda al-muttaqīn bi-sharḥ asrār Iḥyāʾ ʿulūm al-dīn (wa-bi-hāmish Kitāb al-Imlāʾ ʿan ishkālāt al-Iḥyāʾ lil-Ghazālī)*, Beirut n.d. (after 1970; reprint of Egypt 1311/1894), vol. 1, pp. 170–185; see also above, chapter 5.

126 It is noteworthy that on the Website www.muslimphilosophy.com (as accessed on January 11, 2007), Ibn Taymiyya figures prominently among "al-Ghazali, Ibn Sina, Ibn Rushd, al-Kindi, al-Farabi and Muhammad Iqbal"; the Website hosts also the online e-Journal *Journal of Islamic Philosophy*.

127 ʿAlī al-Wardī explicitly says this in his lectures on Ibn Khaldūn, *Muqaddima li-dirāsat al-manṭiq al-ijtimāʿī. Manṭiq Ibn Khaldūn fī ḍawʾ ḥaḍāratihi wa-shakhṣiyyatihi; muḥāḍarāt*, Cairo 1962, pp. 222–223. In a sense of philosophy that encompasses "every rational attempt to interpret the universe and man's place in it", he qualifies Ibn Taymiyya as one of the "great philosophical personalities in Islam" (ibid., pp. 57, 228).

128 Ibn Taymiyya, *al-Radd*, preface, pp. *fāʾ*, *qāf*. Similarily, he states in an English article: "In reality he (Ibn Taymiyya) was the first founder of Mill's system of logic and the forerunner of Hume's philosophy." (Nadvi, Syed Sulaiman: Muslims and Greek Schools of Philosophy, in: *Islamic Culture* 1 (1927), pp. 85–91, here p. 89; cited also in his foreword to Ibn Taymiyya, *al-Radd*, p. *rāʾ*). Other authors have also outlined similarities between his critique and the British

Moroccan scholar Muḥammad Yatīm (b. 1956) praises him as "one of the most eminent philosophers of our history" for having created an "Islamic theory of knowledge."[129] The Egyptian professor of Islamic philosophy ʿAbd al-Qādir Maḥmūd labels Ibn Taymiyya's critique a "philosophical revolution,"[130] and his compatriot Muḥammad ʿAmāra characterizes him as "the philosopher of the salafiyya."[131] The term "philosophy" obviously has different meanings for them, but seems to have lost the former connotations of "unbelief" and "heresy" although they clearly agree with Ibn Taymiyya in his critique of the *falāsifa*.

9. The Addressees of Ibn Taymiyya's Critique of Logic and Rationalism

9.1. *Falāsifa* and *mutafalsifa*

Ibn Taymiyya himself would, without a doubt, have vigorously objected to being called a philosopher. In his view, philosophy (*falsafa*) taught heresy and contaminated almost every Muslim school of thought, causing Muslims to trivialize God's message and His messengers seriously – the exception being the followers of the "pious forefathers" (*al-salaf al-ṣāliḥ*), among whom he counted himself. Logic was, in his eyes, the main cause of false teaching about metaphysics: all theories about the divine world (*al-ilāhiyyāt*) entirely or partly based on philosophy inevitably led people astray. Ibn Taymiyya asserted that not only the teachings of the Greek philosophers, their Muslim followers,[132] and the

Empiricist's theories of cognition. Seen in the wider theoretical and ideological frame of the respective thinkers, their concepts of universals, particulars, and definitions, however, have fundamentally different purposes (see von Kügelgen, Ibn Taymīyas Kritik, pp. 215–218). Furthermore, Ibn Taymiyya's own epistemological assumptions deviate considerably from his critique (see below, chapters 11.2 and 11.3).

129 Yatīm, Ibn Taymiyya, pp. 18 (2nd column), 17 (1st column), 24, n. 6.

130 Maḥmūd, ʿAbd al-Qādir: *al-Fikr al-islāmī wal-falsafāt al-muʿāriḍa fī al-qadīm wal-ḥadīth*, Cairo 1986, pp. 350–355.

131 ʿAmāra, Muḥammad: Faylasūf al-salafiyya, in: *al-Miṣriyyūn* (Oct. 25, 2007), online: www.almesryoon.com. I owe this information to Lutz Rogler.

132 He refers to Aristotle, Plato, Alexander of Aphrodisias, Proklus, Themistius, Plotin, al-Fārābī, Ibn Sīnā, and Ibn Rushd, among others. For them and

"later" *kalām* theologians,[133] but also those of Shiites,[134] theosophists,[135] mystics,[136] and other sects relied on false premises and inferences far removed from truth.

Ibn Taymiyya therefore undertakes to deconstruct logic first. He states in *al-Radd ʿalā al-manṭiqiyyīn* that he initially intended to write a refutation of the *mutafalsifa*'s metaphysics, but had realized "that much in their views on (the basis of metaphysics (*ilāhiyyāt*) and) logic is the source of their errors in metaphysics" and thus engaged in the rebuttal of the logicians.[137] He sometimes, as in this case, uses the term *mutafalsifa*, literally "pseudo-philosophers," as a general denomination for all those he criticizes.[138] Wael B. Hallaq has convincingly argued that Ibn Taymiyya does not distinguish between the semantic use of *falāsifa* and *mutafalsifa*, since for Ibn Taymiyya "philosophy *qua* philosophy is erroneous, and those who make it their business to study it are pseudo-scholars," no matter how they are called.[139]

---

the references in the following four notes, see the entries in the indices: Ibn Taymiyya, *Darʾ taʿāruḍ al-ʿaql*, vol. 11, "Fihris al-aʿlām", and "Fihris al-firaq wal-ṭawāʾif wal-qabʾil"; and Hallaq, *Ibn Taymiyya*.

133 He differentiates several groups within the *Ashʿariyya*, the *Muʿtazila*, the *Jahmiyya*, and the *Qadariyya*, among others, and often refers to specific persons.

134 He sometimes subsumes them under *al-Shīʿa* or *al-Rāfiḍa*, among others, sometimes alluding to leading proponents of Shiite subgroups.

135 His favorite addressee of critique among them is al-Suhrawardī al-Maqtūl (d. 587/1191).

136 Ibn Taymiyya especially criticizes Ibn al-ʿArabī (560/1165–638/1240) and his school.

137 Ibn Taymiyya, *al-Radd*, p. 4. Al-Suyūṭī either omitted some words of the original (here in brackets) or his copy of *al-Radd ʿalā al-manṭiqiyyīn* differed from the edited one (*Jahd al-qarīḥa*, p. 202; Hallaq, *Ibn Taymiyya*, p. 4). Ibn Taymiyya seems, however, to have completed his refutation of the rationalist's metaphysics before the rebuttal of logic (see above, chapters 4 and 7).

138 Ibn Taymiyya, *al-Radd*, p. 3; al-Suyūṭī, *Jahd al-qarīḥa*, p. 202; Hallaq, *Ibn Taymiyya*, p. 4; see also the following note.

139 Hallaq, *Ibn Taymiyya*, p. 4, nn. 3–4 (with many references also to other writings of Ibn Taymiyya). He thereby disproved Michel (Ibn Taymiyya's Critique of Falsafa, p. 4); Hoover came to the same conclusion (*Ibn Taymiyya's Theodicy*, p. 31, n. 41). See also Ibn Taymiyya, *Darʾ taʿāruḍ al-ʿaql*, vol. 11, "Fihris al-firaq wal-ṭawāʾif wal-qabāʾil", s. v. *al-falāsifa=ahl al-falsafa=al-mutafalsifa*.

9.2. The Attitude Towards the Prophets' Veracity as a Criterion of Distinction

In *al-Radd ʿalā al-manṭiqiyyīn* and *Darʾ taʿāruḍ al-ʿaql wal-naql*, Ibn Taymiyya attacks the same strains of thought and circles of people, even though in *Darʾ taʿāruḍ al-ʿaql wal-naql* he addresses many more thinkers personally. Ibn Taymiyya often refers to the different schools of thought using the categories established at his time, but draws an unusual line of distinction between them. He distinguishes among the many persons and groups he considers as having gone astray in accordance with their approach to revelation. On the highest level, he discerns two general approaches, I: *ṭarīqat al-tabdīl* (the method of alteration) and II: *ṭarīqat al-tajhīl* (the method of stultification). The approach to revelation that Ibn Taymiyya regards as characteristic of the second category (II) is the conviction that the prophets and those who follow them were either without knowledge about the meaning of God's words or knew it but concealed it from the people, thus making people ignorant. Some of these thinkers hold that the real meaning of scripture, which no one knows but God, is exactly the opposite of its outward meaning; others would say that it has to be understood in accordance with its outward meaning, but nevertheless they interpret in a way that contradicts it.[140] Ibn Taymiyya does not attribute these attitudes to any specific group, but – as an example of the latter position – mentions the Ḥanbalī scholar Abū Yaʿlā b. al-Farrāʾ (380/990–458/1066).[141] The conjecture is thus not far that Ibn Taymiyya counted also other schoolfellows as belonging to this category.

He instead subsumes the main addressees of *Darʾ taʿāruḍ al-ʿaql wal-naql* under the first approach, "the method of alteration" (I). He subdivides this category into the method of *ahl al-wahm wal-takhyīl* (the people of delusion and suggestion) and the method of *ahl al-taḥrīf wal-taʾwīl* (the people of distortion and interpretation).[142] "The people of delusion and suggestion" (I. 1) are those who profess that some

140 Ibn Taymiyya, *Darʾ taʿāruḍ al-ʿaql*, vol. 1, pp. 8–19, here 15–19. A part of this section has been translated by Michot, *Ibn Taymiyya*, pp. 26–27. M. Sait Özervarli has summarized some key points of the classifications (Özervarlı, *İbn Teymiyye*, pp. 409–410).

141 Ibn Taymiyya mentions that Ibn ʿAqīl (see above, chapter 2) blamed him for precisely this reason (*Darʾ taʿāruḍ al-ʿaql*, vol. 1, p. 16).

142 The whole section, of which I give but a short summary, has been translated by Michot, *Lettre à Abū l-Fidāʾ*, pp. 21–26.

things about which the prophets received revelation – such as God, the Day of Judgment, the afterlife, and bodily resurrection – do not correspond to the truth, but have to be believed by the common people for their welfare. Among these he counts Sevener Shiites (*al-Bāṭiniyya kal-malāḥida al-ismāʿīliyya wa-aṣḥāb rasāʾil ikhwān al-ṣafāʾ*), al-Fārābī (d. 339/950), Ibn Sīnā, al-Suhrawardī al-Maqtūl (d. 587/1191), Ibn Rushd (d. 595/1198) and "the heretic Sufis who left the path of their forerunners among the Sunnis", like Ibn al-ʿArabī (d. 638/1240), Ibn Sabʿīn (d. 669/1270), Ibn Ṭufayl (d. 581/1185), "and many others."[143] He considers all of them *bāṭinīs* – that is, "esotericists" – since they distinguish between the outward meaning of the revelation (*ẓāhir*), as it is to be understood by the common people, and its inward meaning (*bāṭin*) that is preserved for themselves.[144] Nevertheless, he distinguishes among them in regard to their positioning of the prophets above or beneath outstanding scholars. He cites Ibn Sīnā as an example of those who propagate that the prophets have more knowledge than the philosophers, since they know how to address the common people and to disguise the truth for their sake. As examples of those who hold that the prophets are inferior, he mentions Ibn (al-)ʿArabī as holding that the Sufi masters excel them and al-Fārābī and Mubashshir b. Fātik (fifth/eleventh century) as proclaiming that the philosophers have a better knowledge of the truth than the prophets.[145]

The second group, "the people of distortion and interpretation" (I. 2), he characterizes as people who believe that the words of the prophets represent the truth but at the same time are convinced that truth is what reason tells us. As such, these people attempt to inter-

143 Ibn Taymiyya, *Darʾ taʿāruḍ al-ʿaql*, vol. 1, pp. 8–11.

144 Ibid., vol. 6, p. 237 (here, he speaks of *Bāṭiniyyat al-falāsifa*); for applications of the term to other groups, see *Darʾ taʿāruḍ al-ʿaql*, vol. 11, s.v. *Bāṭiniyya* and its composita.

145 Ibn Taymiyya, *Darʾ taʿāruḍ al-ʿaql*, vol. 1, pp. 9–10. See Ibn Taymiyya, *Darʾ taʿāruḍ al-ʿaql*, vol. 5, pp. 359–363. Concerning al-Fārābī's theory about the position and the duties of the prophets and the philosopher king, which Ibn Taymiyya alters, see al-Fārābī, *On the Perfect State*, pp. 221–227, 421–423; see, however, Michot, who approves of Ibn Taymiyya's reading (*Lettre à Abū l-Fidāʾ*, p. 23). Mubashshir b. Fātik is especially known for a collection of wisdom of ancient Greek sages (Rosenthal, Franz: al-Mubashshir b. Fātik, in: *EI*², vol. 7 (1993), pp. 282–283). As to Ibn ʿArabī's comprehension of prophecy and the "perfect man", which Ibn Taymiyya also distorts, see Chodkiewicz, Michel: *Le sceau des saints. Prophétie et sainteté dans la doctrine d'Ibn Arabî*, Paris 1986.

pret the words of the prophets in accordance with their own opinions. Thus, under the pretense of explaining the intentions of the prophets and by misusing language, they often say the opposite of what is revealed. Among them Ibn Taymiyya counts "many *kalām* theologians and others," naming "the Muʿtazila, the Kullābiyya, the Sālimiyya, the Karrāmiyya and the (Twelver) Shia."[146]

Ibn Taymiyya's leading criterion of distinction among the different thinkers is in fact their attitude towards the veracity of the prophet,[147] and – on first glance – not their epistemology, as one might expect in regard to the main aim of *Darʾ taʿāruḍ al-ʿaql wal-naql*. Ibn Taymiyya obviously regarded "veracity" (*ṣidq*) as the most important attribute of the prophet, as Shahab Ahmed has shown with the example of Ibn Taymiyya's interpretation of the so-called Satanic verses.[148] In fact, however, the criterion of veracity is closely linked to Ibn Taymiyya's concept of cognition, since he regards the messages of the prophets as being in full congruity with "clear reason" and as bearing reasonable proofs themselves and teaching rational methods (see below chapters 10.2, 11–12). It is not astonishing that his general judgment about "the people of delusion and suggestion" (I. 1), i.e., about those who either impute that the prophets lie or are less knowledgeable than certain groups of wise men (the philosophers or the Sufi masters), is markedly stern. He repeatedly calls them heretics (*malāḥida*),[149] classifies

146 Ibn Taymiyya, *Darʾ taʿāruḍ al-ʿaql*, vol. 1, pp. 8, 12–13. For the schools mentioned by Ibn Taymiyya, see the respective entries in the 1st and 2nd edition of *The Encyclopaedia of Islam* (Kullābīya s.v. Ibn Kullāb; according to Ibn Ḥazm, he belonged to the Ashʿariyya; Ibn Taymiyya, *Darʾ taʿāruḍ al-ʿaql*, vol. 1, p. 13, n. 2; Ibn Taymiyya calls him a predecessor of al-Ashʿarī (after Michot, *Ibn Taymiyya*, p. 25, n. 4)).

147 There is a striking resemblance between Ibn Taymiyya's classification and a typology of one of Ibn Taymiyya's main enemies, namely Ibn ʿArabī, who in his *al-Futūḥāt al-makkiyya* classifies people in six groups with respect to their belief in the veracity of the prophets. Jon Hoover, to whose monograph I owe my knowledge of Ibn al-ʿArabī's typology (*Ibn Taymiyya's Theodicy*, pp. 46–47), referred to Ibn al-ʿArabī's typology to point to still another similarity between the two thinkers. It would be worthwile to study both typologies in a comparative way.

148 Ahmed, Shahab: Ibn Taymiyyah and the Satanic Verses, in: *Studia Islamica* 87 (1988), pp. 67–124, esp. pp. 100–105; see also Hoover, *Ibn Taymiyya's Theodicy*, p. 44.

149 Ibn Taymiyya, *Darʾ taʿāruḍ al-ʿaql*, vol. 8, pp. 242–243; vol. 9, p. 123; vol. 10, p. 270. *Mulḥid* (pl. *malāḥida*) is difficult to render in another language, because of its use in the senses of "deviator, apostate, heretic, atheist" (Madelung, Wil-

them as disbelievers, sometimes on the same level as the Christians and Jews – since they believe in some part of the Sharia and disbelieve in other parts of it[150] – or sometimes even classifies them as inferior to the Christians and Jews,[151] predicting that their future residence will be hell.[152] Yet "the people of distortion and interpretation" (I. 2), namely the majority of the *kalām* theologians and the Twelver Shiites,

ferd: Mulḥid, in: *EI*², vol. 7 (1993), p. 546). Ibn Taymiyya denies that the philosophers have proven God to be the *Creator* of the world (see below, n. 152) and thereby that they have found what he considers the only valuable proof of God. Ibn Taymiyya's denial could thus be interpreted as a case of "ascription of atheism," although the philosophers themselves are far from professing atheism. I owe the distinction between "attributed atheism" and "professed atheism" to Kurt Flasch (Attributionsatheismus in Boccaccios Decameron VI 9: Guido Cavalcanti, in: Friedrich Niewöhner and Olaf Pluta (eds.): *Atheismus im Mittelalter und in der Renaissance*, Wiesbaden 1999, pp. 115–127, here 115–116).

150 Ibn Taymiyya in his famous fatwa against the Mongols (*Majmūʿat al-Fatāwā*, al-mujallad 28, Cairo, vol. 14, part 28, p. 285; also in: al-ʿAẓma, ʿAzīz: *Ibn Taymiyya*, Beirut 2000, p. 99); see Ibn Taymiyya, *Darʾ taʿāruḍ al-ʿaql*, where he also counts the *mutakallimūn* among them (vol. 1, pp. 134–137, 177–178).

151 Ibn Taymiyya, *al-Radd*, p. 133. Michel cites a similar statement of Ibn Taymiyya's *Risāla fī Lafẓ al-sunna fī al-Qurʾān* (Ibn Taymiyya's Critique of Falsafa, pp. 4, 13, n. 3).

152 Ibn Taymiyya, *Darʾ taʿāruḍ al-ʿaql*, vol. 1, pp. 371–372. The tenet that Ibn Taymiyya ascribes to "the people of delusion and suggestion" corresponds to what was officially condemned by the Church in Medieval Europe as the "two contradictory truths," a religious and a philosophical, which were mainly attributed to the so-called Averroists, i. e., true and falsely alleged followers of Ibn Rushd. Ibn Taymiyya was, of course, not aware of the uproar the "double truth theory" caused in Europe, but also takes Ibn Rushd as one of his main targets to fight it, though proceeding from the latter's theologico-philosophical treatises and not his commentaries on Aristotle (see von Kügelgen, Dialogpartner). His fight against the "double truth" and philosophy, and Aristotelism as the worst of the philosophical theories (Ibn Taymiyya, *al-Radd*, pp. 395–396; idem, *Darʾ taʿāruḍ al-ʿaql*, vol. 1, pp. 151–152; vol. 8, pp. 181, 186, 189, 233; vol. 9, pp. 398–399 et passim), however, did not hinder Ibn Taymiyya from respecting Ibn Rushd as a thinker. Thus, he characterizes Ibn Rushd as one of the most intelligent philosophers (*ḥudhdhāq al-falāsifa*) (Ibn Taymiyya, *Darʾ taʿāruḍ al-ʿaql*, vol. 10, p. 317; he does not call the philosophers by name, but from the context it is obvious that he counts Ibn Rushd among them; see vol. 3, p. 413; vol. 8, p. 181; vol. 9, pp. 69, 332–333). In a tract concerning the philosophers' proof of God as the first cause, he qualifies Ibn Rushd as "the nearest of them [the philosophers] to Islam" (*Majmūʿat al-Fatāwā*, al-mujallad 17, Cairo, vol. 9, p. 163; Hoover, Perpetual Creativity, p. 295). There and elsewhere, however, Ibn Taymiyya severely criticizes that Ibn Rushd only proves God as a condition (*sharṭ*) for the existence of the world, but not as its *Creator*

despite their belief that the prophets have come up with the truth, are also accused of heresy (*ilḥād*),[153] not least because of his conviction that a distortion of some parts of the revelation leads to a distortion of the whole.[154] Although Ibn Taymiyya rejects most of their theories, his judgment about them is, generally, slightly milder than his verdict on the theories of "the people of delusion and suggestion" (I.1).[155] He characterizes the theories of the latter, i. e., of the *falāsifa*, the Ismāʿīlīs, the theosophists (mainly the *ishrāqī* philosophers), and the intellectualistic mystics (mainly the "pantheists") as even less reasonable and more inconsistent.[156] So, for instance, he vehemently denies that God created the intellect as the first and noblest creature,[157] a conception that was transmitted as a saying of the prophet Muhammad and was widely acknowledged in mystical and theosophical circles.[158] No less harsh is his rebuttal of Neoplatonic and Peripatetic notions of supralunar intellects (see chapter 11c) and the philosophical concepts of human reason. Some of Ibn Taymiyya's main arguments against the latter will be considered in the next chapters that deal with his own concepts of perception and cognition.

(*Darʾ taʿāruḍ al-ʿaql*, vol. 8, pp. 216–219; vol. 9, pp. 82–84; for a short analysis, see von Kügelgen, Dialogpartner, pp. 470–472).

153 Ibn Taymiyya, *Darʾ taʿāruḍ al-ʿaql*, vol. 5, p. 363; vol. 10, p. 270.

154 Ibid., vol. 1, pp. 134–137, 177–178.

155 Ibid., vol. 3, pp. 425, 431, 437; vol. 9, pp. 70–71, 334, 371–373; vol. 10, pp. 223, 228–229 et passim.

156 Ibid., vol. 3, pp. 417–418, 431; vol 9, pp. 111, 354–355; vol. 10, pp. 223, 228–229 et passim.

157 Ibn Taymiyya, *al-Radd*, pp. 275–278; Ibn Taymiyya: *Kitāb Tafsīr sūrat al-ikhlāṣ*, ed. by al-Sayyid Muḥammad Badr al-Dīn al-Naʿsānī al-Ḥalabī, Cairo 1323/1905, pp. 58–59; see al-Alousī corrects Goldziher's presentation of Ibn Taymiyya's view (*The Problem of Creation*, p. 71).

158 Goldziher, Ignaz: Neuplatonische und gnostische Elemente im Ḥadīṯ, in: Joseph Desomogyi (ed.): *Gesammelte Schriften*, Hildesheim 1970 (reprint), vol. 5, pp. 108–114; al-Alousī mentions further possible sources for the Hadith and more instances where it is quoted (*The Problem of Creation*, pp. 69–73). For instance, it is cited and extensively commented upon by ʿUmar al-Suhrawardī in his refutation of the philosophers *Kashf al-faḍāʾiḥ al-yūnāniyya wa-rashf al-naṣāʾiḥ al-īmāniyya* (p. 162–168; Hartmann, Angelika: Kosmogonie und Seelenlehre bei ʿUmar as-Suhrawardī (st. 632/1234), in: Dieter Bellmann (ed.): *Gedenkschrift Wolfgang Reuschel, Akten des III. Arabistischen Kolloquiums, Leipzig, 21.-22. November 1991*, Stuttgart 1994, pp. 139–151; she hints to further treatments of the subject: idem, Eine orthodoxe Polemik, pp. 286–287).

10. Glimpses into Ibn Taymiyya's Critique of Logic in Connection with His Epistemology

10.1. The Particular and the Universal: Ibn Taymiyya's Nominalistic Attitude

There is one point Ibn Taymiyya and the philosophers seem to agree upon, namely that God is the necessary *existent*, the highest of all existent beings.[159] Yet, this impression is wrong; Ibn Taymiyya, on the contrary, insists upon disclosing that, in fact, the philosophers are incapable of proving that God is an *external existent* and thus are completely missing the essential knowledge through which the soul reaches perfection.[160] The cause of this failure, fatal since it results in heresy, is their instrument of reasoning, i.e., logic. As Ibn Taymiyya claims their method of deduction – namely, that a sound categorical syllogism has to consist of two premises, and that at least one of them has to be universal – is one of the main faults in their proofs of God's existence: [161]

> As for the Necessary Existent, blessed and exalted may He be, the syllogism does not prove what is characteristic of Him; rather, it proves a universal matter common to Him as well as to others. According to the logicians, what is proven by categorical syllogism is nothing but a universal, common matter having no bearing upon the Necessary Existent, the Lord of beings, may He be glorified and exalted. Therefore, their demonstration does not lead them to any knowledge of a matter which must be constant – whether it belongs to the Necessary Existent or to possible beings.[162]

God's existence, as Ibn Taymiyya clearly states, has to be particular (*muʿayyan*), because otherwise God would not be unique.[163] Moreover,

---

159 Ibn Taymiyya, *al-Radd*, p. 125; al-Suyūṭī, *Jahd al-qarīḥa*, p. 237; Hallaq, *Ibn Taymiyya*, p. 54.

160 Ibn Taymiyya, *al-Radd*, pp. 131–150 et passim; al-Suyūṭī, *Jahd al-qarīḥa*, pp. 236–251; Hallaq, *Ibn Taymiyya*, pp. 52–71.

161 Ibn Taymiyya, *al-Radd*, p. 107; al-Suyūṭī, *Jahd al-qarīḥa*, pp. 221–222; Hallaq, *Ibn Taymiyya*, p. 34, n. 46.

162 Al-Suyūṭī, *Jahd al-qarīḥa*, p. 251; Hallaq, *Ibn Taymiyya*, p. 71 (I follow his translation); Ibn Taymiyya, *al-Radd*, p. 150.

163 Ibn Taymiyya, *al-Radd*, pp. 125, 150; al-Suyūṭī, *Jahd al-qarīḥa*, pp. 237–238, 251; Hallaq, *Ibn Taymiyya*, pp. 54, 71; Ibn Taymiyya, *Darʾ taʿāruḍ al-ʿaql*, vol. 8, pp. 466–467; see also below, chapter 11.1. For a thorough analysis of this argument and Ibn Taymiyya's own proof of God's existence, see: Hallaq,

Ibn Taymiyya repeatedly states in his direct critique that universals exist solely intramentally (*post res*) and have no correlate whatsoever in the extramental world, the world of particulars[164] – a tenet that met opposition.[165] Hence, he vigorously argues against "radical" and "moderate realism" disclosing thereby a plain "nominalism" that he infers from the Koran.[166]

"Nominalism" and "radical" or "moderate realism" are terms that the historians of the "dispute on universals" in Latin scholasticism use to classify the different viewpoints on the existence and mode of the universals, such as genus or species. These terms are not without pitfalls in Latin scholasticism, since, as Alain de Libera has convincingly shown, the manner of understanding and looking at universals and particulars differs from author to author and cannot be understood solely from their respective epistemologies.[167] These terms have to be used all the more carefully in a context like the history of ideas in the Islamic world, where there was apparently no broader "dispute on universals." I would like, however, to argue that the concepts commonly associated with "nominalism" and "realism" existed[168] and that Ibn Taymiyya's statements on the "reality" of the universals fit to a certain extent into that dispute. My presentation is but a preliminary approach and I use these terms for lack of better alternatives. Further

Wael B.: Ibn Taymiyya on the Existence of God, in: *Acta Orientalia* 52 (1991), pp. 49–69. As to Ibn Taymiyya's rejection of Ibn Rushd's "Koranic proofs" of God's existence, see von Kügelgen, Dialogpartner, pp. 470–472.

164 Ibn Taymiyya, *al-Radd*, pp. 9–10, 64–67; significantly shortened in: al-Suyūṭī, *Jahd al-qarīḥa*, p. 215; Hallaq, *Ibn Taymiyya*, pp. 24–25; Ibn Taymiyya, *Darʾ taʿāruḍ al-ʿaql*, vol. 6, pp. 26–28; vol. 8, pp. 219–220.

165 The Moroccan scholar and *homme de belles lettres* al-Yūsī (see above, chapter 5) vehemently rejects the tenet of a solely intramental existence of universals. If someone accepts as knowledge only the extramental particulars perceivable by the senses, he has to reject all sciences, since "he does not know any juridical, theological, grammatical, or other rule (*qānūnan*)" and thus "only knows the Scripture and the Sunna" (al-Zabīdī, *Kitāb Itḥāf al-sāda*, vol. 1, p. 178). Al-Yūsī draws these inevitable consequences from al-Suyūṭī's *al-Qawl al-mushriq fī taḥrīm al-ishtighāl bil-manṭiq*, where the latter definitively severely simplified Ibn Taymiyya's concepts of universals and particulars (see chapters 5, 10.1 and 11.2–3).

166 See von Kügelgen, Ibn Taymiyyas Kritik, pp. 181–183, 206–209; see also Hoover, *Ibn Taymiyya's Theodicy*, p. 52.

167 De Libera, Alain: *La querelle des universaux de Platon à la fin du Moyen Age*, Paris 1996.

168 Von Kügelgen, Ibn Taymiyyas Kritik, pp. 219–220.

studies might develop more appropriate designations and markers of distinction.

Ibn Taymiyya's rejection of the existence of universals outside the mind, be it *ante res* as quiddities, for instance the species "horse," what would correspond to "radical realism," or *in rebus* as part of the particulars (*mawjūda fī al-aʿyān*),[169] what one might call "moderate realism," for example the assumption that two men share *in reality* features of the concept "human being,"[170] allows and leads him to dismiss his enemies' key concepts in metaphysical matters. There are, however, major parts of human knowledge about particulars where he himself, sometimes implicitly, sometimes explicitly, adheres to "moderate realism" and thus contradicts his absolute negation of it (see chapters 11.2–3).

On the basis of his rebuttal of the existence of extramental universals, be it *ante res* or *in rebus*, Ibn Taymiyya refutes much more than what would have been subsumed under "universals" in Medieval Europe. His concept of "universals" encompasses the Muʿtazilī and in part Shiite concept of the "nonexistent,"[171] the Platonic forms, the Aristotelian primary matter, the extramental existence of "duration" and "place," among other things,[172] and last but not least, the categories, "the essences of the species, the genera and the remaining universals" (*māhiyyāt al-anwāʿ wal-ajnās wa-sāʾir al-kulliyyāt*).[173]

Now we will examine Ibn Taymiyya's denial of the possibility of encompassing in a definition the "essence," the "reality" of a thing.

---

169 Ibn Taymiyya, *al-Radd*, p. 64 (not reproduced in al-Suyūṭī's *Jahd al-qarīḥa*).

170 Ibn Taymiyya, *Darʾ taʿāruḍ al-ʿaql*, vol. 6, pp. 26–27. He states that "we know with necessity that this individual man has nothing in himself from the other individual man, rather each of them is distinguished by his essence and his attributes (*mukhtaṣṣ bi-dhātihi wa-ṣifātihi*) and they have nothing in common whatsoever that is fixed outside [the mind]; therefore one of the two may exist while the other is inexistent and conversely and one may die while the other is alive and conversely." This statement is part of a critique Ibn Taymiyya launches against the element of universality with which Ibn Sīnā has invested the estimative propositions (see Marcotte, *Ibn Taymiyya et sa critique*, pp. 50–51). In *al-Radd* (pp. 9–10), Ibn Taymiyya claims that what the philosophers call the "essence" (*māhiyya*) of a thing would exist only intramentally and everyone would conceive it a little differently.

171 Ibn Taymiyya, *al-Radd*, p. 66. See also Hallaq, *Ibn Taymiyya*, p. xxiv–xxvii (see Knysh, Alexander D.: *Ibn ʿArabī in the Later Islamic Tradition. The Making of a Polemical Image in Medieval Islam*, Albany 1999, pp. 100–111).

172 Ibn Taymiyya, *al-Radd*, p. 66; al-Suyūṭī, *Jahd al-qarīḥa*, p. 215; Hallaq, *Ibn Taymiyya*, pp. 24–25.

173 Ibn Taymiyya, *al-Radd*, 64.

What he rebuts is thus the "real definition" *(ḥadd ḥaqīqī)* of the logicians by which they claim to grasp the "essence" of a thing[174] and thus its genus, species, and difference. One of his examples is their common definition of man as a "rational animal," maintaining that "rational" constitutes the difference *(faṣl)* marking the species.[175] He argues that the definition could just be "laughing animal,"[176] "laughing" being characterized by the logicians only as a proprium (*khāṣṣa*).[177] In addition, "rational" would not, as the philosophers claim, constitute a distinguishing essential attribute of a single species, because, as philosophers themselves hold, "rationality" characterizes angels and the supralunar intellects as well.[178] Ibn Taymiyya also points to the circularity of the "real definition".[179] With these examples, Ibn Taymiyya wants to demonstrate the conventional character or the relativity of "real definitions" and that, contrary to what the philosophers claim, they cannot grasp the "essence" or "reality" of a species or a genus.[180] Therefore, Ibn Taymiyya sees the "real definition" as

174 Robinson, Richard: *Definition*, Oxford 2003 (reprint), pp. 153–155.

175 Ibn Taymiyya, *al-Radd*, pp. 8, 70 et passim; al-Suyūṭī, *Jahd al-qarīḥa*, pp. 204, 216; Hallaq, *Ibn Taymiyya*, pp. 7, n. 9, 26, n. 35. Porphyrius (Einleitung in die Kategorien, in: Aristoteles: *Organon*, transl. and with notes by Eugen Rolfes, Hamburg 1974, p. 3 (3b)) adds "mortal" and philosophers and later *kalām* theologians follow him in that (Ibn Sīnā, *al-Ishārāt wal-tanbīhāt*, vol. 1, p. 207; Avicenna, *Remarks and Admonitions*, p. 71). Ibn Taymiyya opposes that "mortal" is an attribute of every living being, let alone that man's life in the hereafter is eternal (*al-Radd*, pp. 57–57).

176 Ibn Taymiyya, *al-Radd*, p. 67. See for instance Ibn Sīnā, *al-Ishārāt wal-tanbīhāt*, vol. 1, pp. 210–212; Avicenna, *Remarks and Admonitions*, pp. 72–73.

177 It is noteworthy that the Moroccan scholar al-Ḥasan al-Yūsī who defended logic against al-Suyūṭī's repudiation (see above, chapter 5 and n. 165), wrote a treatise entirely devoted to the distinction between the *differentia specifica* and the *proprium*, entitled *al-Qawl al-faṣl fī al-farq bayna al-khāṣṣa wal-faṣl* (El-Rouayheb, Was there a Revival, pp. 12–13; this seems not to have been edited yet).

178 Ibn Taymiyya, *al-Radd*, p. 58. See van Ess, Josef: *Die Erkenntnislehre des Aḍudaddīn al-Īcī. Übersetzung und Kommentar des ersten Buches seiner Mawaqif*, Wiesbaden 1966, p. 371.

179 Ibn Taymiyya, *al-Radd*, pp. 73–76, 10–11, 39–40, 59, 79–80; (much shortened al-Suyūṭī, *Jahd al-qarīḥa*, pp. 205, 211, 217; Hallaq, *Ibn Taymiyya*, pp. 9–10, 18, 29).

180 It is obvious from these examples that Ibn Taymiyya was not interested in the questions the logicians dealt with when they established the differences between "difference" and "proprium", or correlating ones between "essential" (*bil-dhāt*) and "accidental" (*bil-ʿaraḍ*) or "essential" (*dhātī*) and "descriptive" (*waṣfī*) with Aristotle's modal syllogistic as their starting point. "Laugh-

"a wrong way in itself and distraction" (*ʿayn al-ḍalāl wal-iḍlāl*),[181] a waste of time that distracts from what benefits the soul,[182] and a corrupter of reason.[183]

Yet Ibn Taymiyya does not deny the usefulness of establishing concepts by inferring common features of particulars and thereby creating definitions. Thus, he explicitly accepts various types of nominal definitions, most of which are word-thing definitions.[184] He even admits their usefulness for the sciences, but he insists on their being a convention that several people have agreed upon: "Whoever reads the books of grammar, medicine, or other sciences has to know what the respective specialists mean by those terms and phrases."[185] However, the existing variety of definitions even within one field of knowledge, for instance the more than 20 definitions of "noun" in grammar and of "analogy" in jurisprudence proves for him that definitions are not the indispensable basis for understanding and forming judgments.[186]

Ibn Taymiyya expresses his conviction that man is incapable of formulating absolutely certain universal propositions, denying men the capacity to ever observe all particulars. Thus, he regards universals won by abstraction as fallible. As one example, he quotes the universal statement "animals move their lower jaws when they eat, for we have observed them and found them to do so" and falsifies it by the observation "that crocodiles move their upper jaws".[187] He thereby takes an

---

ing" had to be "accidental" or "descriptive," because otherwise the statement "every laughing being is necessarily a human" must, according to Aristotle's rules of necessary propositions, also be true when converted into the proposition "some humans are *necessarily* laughing," which is wrong (on this, see the penetrating exposition of Street, Arabic Logic, pp. 256–261).

181 Ibn Taymiyya, *al-Radd*, p. 75; al-Suyūṭī, *Jahd al-qarīḥa*, p. 217; Hallaq, *Ibn Taymiyya*, p. 28, n. 37. Concering the Koranic terminology of *ḍalāl* and *iḍlāl* see Rahbar, Daud: *God of Justice. A Study in the Ethical Doctrine of the Qurʾān*, Leiden 1960, pp. 86–90, 349–354; Izutsu, Toshihiko: *The Structure of Ethical Terms in the Koran. A Study in Semantics*, Tokyo 1959, pp. 196–199, 201–204.

182 Ibn Taymiyya, *al-Radd*, p. 31; al-Suyūṭī, *Jahd al-qarīḥa*, p. 208; Hallaq, *Ibn Taymiyya*, pp. 14–15, n. 20.

183 Ibn Taymiyya, *al-Radd*, p. 32.

184 Von Kügelgen, Ibn Taymīyas Kritik, pp. 187–204.

185 Ibn Taymiyya, *al-Radd*, p. 49.

186 Ibid., pp. 8, 26; al-Suyūṭī, *Jahd al-qarīḥa*, p. 204; Hallaq, *Ibn Taymiyya*, pp. 7–8.

187 Ibn Taymiyya, *al-Radd*, pp. 159–160.; al-Suyūṭī, *Jahd al-qarīḥa*, p. 259; Hallaq, *Ibn Taymiyya*, pp. 79–80, n. 119 (I follow his translation).

example that Ibn Sīnā, for instance, uses to discredit induction as a way of inference that can lead to certainty.[188]

Yet, although Ibn Taymiyya himself makes no explicit categorization, one can distinguish in *al-Radd ʿalā al-manṭiqiyyīn* three categories of universals that Ibn Taymiyya holds to be absolutely true.[189] One consists of the axioms, i. e., the primary arithmetic, geometric, and logical principles, such as one being half of two, the total being more than the part, or the incompatibility of contraries.[190] Ibn Taymiyya considers them in *Naqḍ al-manṭiq* as *a priori* knowledge and in *al-Radd ʿalā al-manṭiqiyyīn* as gained by the observation of one single particular.[191]

The conviction that all concepts, including the rational axioms, are inferred through sense perceptions, which is in fact one of the cornerstones of Empiricism, had already been upheld in Islamic realms since the tenth century, by, among others, the renowned Shii theologian Naṣīr al-Dīn al-Ṭūsī (597/1201–672/1274), with whose writings Ibn Taymiyya was quite familiar.[192] Although he regarded these principles as certain, Ibn Taymiyya does not rank this knowledge and the sciences based upon them as something especially precious. He asserts their validity, refers to mathematics as the most valid (*aṣaḥḥ*) of the rational sciences,[193] and even admits in one place that it can help the soul to become "accustomed to sound knowledge, to valid and truthful propositions, as well as to valid syllogisms" and "to utter the truth

188 Ibn Sīnā, *al-Ishārāt wal-tanbīhāt*, vol. 1, pp. 367–368; Avicenna, *Remarks and Admonitions*, p. 129.

189 Wael B. Hallaq already pointed out two of the categories, the "universal statements embodied in the revealed texts" and the primary principles (Hallaq, *Ibn Taymiyya*, pp. 30–31).

190 Ibn Taymiyya, *al-Radd*, pp. 108–109. See ibid., pp. 133–134; al-Suyūṭī, *Jahd al-qarīḥa*, pp. 238–239; Hallaq, *Ibn Taymiyya*, p. 56.

191 Ibn Taymiyya, *Naqḍ al-manṭiq*, p. 202; idem, *al-Radd*, pp. 108–109, 316; al-Suyūṭī, *Jahd al-qarīḥa*, pp. 222–223, 317; Hallaq, *Ibn Taymiyya*, pp. 36–37, 145–146. For Ibn Taymiyya's obvious difficulty to explain men's apprehension of the so-called self-evident principles and their being certain in spite of being universal, see Hallaq, *Ibn Taymiyya*, p. xxxi-xxxii and below, chapters 11.2–3.

192 Van Ess, *Die Erkenntnislehre*, pp. 188–189. That Ibn Taymiyya was well acquainted with the teachings of Naṣīr al-Dīn al-Ṭūsī is obvious (Ibn Taymiyya, *al-Radd*, pp. 15, 149; al-Suyūṭī, *Jahd al-qarīḥa*, pp. 207, 250; Hallaq, *Ibn Taymiyya*, pp. 13, n. 18; 70 , n. 103; Ibn Taymiyya, *Darʾ taʿāruḍ al-ʿaql*, vol. 11 "Fihris al-aʿlām", s. v. *Ṭūsī*. See also Laoust, *Essai sur les doctrines sociales et politiques*, p. 97.)

193 Ibn Taymiyya, *Darʾ taʿāruḍ al-ʿaql*, vol. I, p. 158; transl. by Michot, Vanités intellectuelles, p. 606.

in order to utilize it in the knowledge of that which is higher than mathematics".[194] Nevertheless, mathematics do not gain his profound respect; in fact, he places it below the natural sciences, because he regards it as being restricted to the intramental world and without use for the main aim of the human being: the knowledge of God and the perfection and salvation of the soul.[195]

The other category of universals that Ibn Taymiyya judges infallible is religious commands and prohibitions, such as "the two universal statements" (*qaḍiyyatān kulliyyatān*) of the Prophet Muḥammad: "Every inebriant is an alcoholic beverage, and every alcoholic beverage is prohibited."[196]

Thus Ibn Taymiyya accepts these two kinds of universals as certain, i.e., the revealed truths that, as a matter of fact, concern mostly the moral sphere, and the so-called self-evident first principles that involve some basic aspects of the extramental world. Still, there is a third category of universals that, on the level of his epistemology, contradicts his denial of universals *in rebus*, namely the universal propositions that are related to the "empirical matters" and that attribute essences and causal efficiencies to things (see chapter 11.2).

10.2. The "Uncontaminated" Reason (*ṣarīḥ al-ʿaql*)

Ibn Taymiyya's great scepticism toward universals won by inference and referring to the physical and the metaphysical world, however, is

194 Ibn Taymiyya, *al-Radd*, p. 136; al-Suyūṭī, *Jahd al-qarīḥa*, p. 240; Hallaq, *Ibn Taymiyya*, p. 58.

195 Ibn Taymiyya, *al-Radd*, pp. 133–134; al-Suyūṭī, *Jahd al-qarīḥa*, p. 238; Hallaq, *Ibn Taymiyya*, pp. 55–56. Ibn Taymiyya admits arithmetic to be a necessary science for the shares of inheritance, "but it is not a science that is sought for its own sake, nor does the soul reach perfection by means of it." (Ibn Taymiyya, *al-Radd*, pp. 136–137; al-Suyūṭī, *Jahd al-qarīḥa*, p. 241; Hallaq, *Ibn Taymiyya*, p. 59). For Ibn Taymiyya's validation of astronomy see Michot, Vanités intellectuelles, p. 605; Michot, Yahya J.: Ibn Taymiyya on Astrology. Annotated Translation of Three Fatwas, in: *Journal of Islamic Studies* 11 (2000), pp. 147–208.

196 Ibn Taymiyya, *al-Radd*, pp. 110–112, 299, 355–357; al-Suyūṭī, *Jahd al-qarīḥa*, pp. 225, 328–328; Hallaq, *Ibn Taymiyya*, pp. 38–39, n. 52, 157, n. 287–288 Ibn Taymiyya refers to the Hadith transmitted by Muslim (*kullu muskirin khamrun wa-kullu muskirin ḥarāmun*) (Muslim b. al-Ḥajjāj al-Qushayrī: *Ṣaḥīḥ Muslim*, Liechtenstein 2000, vol. 2 (*Kitāb al-Ashriba*) *bāb* 7 (pp. 875–877, here p. 877); Wensinck, Arent Jan: *Concordance et indices de la tradition musulmane*, Leiden 1936–1988, vol. 2 (1943), p. 79).

not a result of serious doubts about man's rational capacity. On the contrary, Ibn Taymiyya is convinced that man can reach true knowledge of particulars, and this conviction is the key to his affirmation that "clear reason" (*ṣarīḥ al-ʿaql*) congrues with sound religious tradition (*ṣaḥīḥ al-naql*).[197] He thus posits a faculty of true reasoning shared by all healthy human beings.[198] Ibn Taymiyya nowhere systematically exposes his own epistemology or explains what he categorizes under "clear reason," and this subject has not yet been exhaustively studied.[199] The following presentation is but an attempt to shed new light on some of its main features.

From Ibn Taymiyya's repeated comparison of *ṣarīḥ al-ʿaql* with the reasoning of his enemies, it is apparent that he sees his enemies' reason as contaminated by logic in most of its elements. Therefore, I render *ṣarīḥ al-ʿaql* as "uncontaminated reason." To translate it as "common sense," as is often done, is somewhat misleading, because it suggests a restriction of reason to what *everyone* is able to grasp and excludes what one *usually* would consider as a knowledge gained through inference or, in the terms of the theologians and philosophers, as an acquired (*muktasab*) knowledge. For Ibn Taymiyya, however, the spectrum of what a person endowed with sound reason might understand immediately is broader than "common sense," and the range of knowledge he considers necessary (*ḍarūrī*) in the sense of certain is wide. His view is based on two main epistemological assumptions, that of an inborn intelligence (*fiṭra*) whose soundness differs from individual to individual and that of two modes of knowledge.

---

197 Concerning the criteria and methodology Ibn Taymiyya uses to assess the soundness of reports from the prophet Muḥammad and his companions, see Ahmed: Ibn Taymiyyah and the Satanic Verses, pp. 78–86.

198 Abrahamov, in a footnote, already pointed out the similarity between the philosophers and Ibn Taymiyya in asserting "one kind of true reasoning" (Ibn Taymiyya, p. 272, n. 102). Yet, he wondered about this, since he understood Ibn Taymiyya's acceptance of reason as solely bound to revelation. In a later work, however, Abrahamov corrected his view, stating that Ibn Taymiyya apparently "also maintains the independent status of rational proofs" (*Islamic Theology, Traditionalism and Rationalism*, Edinburgh 1998, p. 51); see Hoover, to whom I owe the information on Abrahamov's change of view (*Ibn Taymiyya's Theodicy*, p. 30).

199 The case is similar to Ibn Taymiyya's assertion of God's existence, which he obviously considered so evident that his proofs have to be sought mainly in his refutations (Hallaq, Ibn Taymiyya on the Existence of God).

For Ibn Taymiyya, *fiṭra* has different connotations and is never described as such in his two refutations.[200] In the context of his discussions on the different ways of cognition, he clearly uses it in the universalistic sense of "innate intelligence" every human being is bestowed with by God. He holds that "rational knowledge is based upon sound and healthy natural intelligence"[201] and that as long as the innate intelligence is sound, it will not be affected by either a change of faith (*iʿtiqād*) or by passions.[202] In his refutations of the logicians, he mostly presents *fiṭra* as not being comprised *a priori* knowledge, but as being activated through the inner and outer organs of perception.[203] Sound *fiṭra* could

200 Several aspects are shown by Nurcholis Madjid, *Ibn Taymiyya on Kalām and Falsafa*, pp. 65–77; Hoover describes some of these various connotations mainly on the basis of other works of Ibn Taymiyya: *Ibn Taymiyya's Theodicy*, pp. 39–44. For Ibn Taymiyya's use of *fiṭra* in the sense of an inborn monotheism, see Hallaq, Ibn Taymiyya on the Existence of God, pp. 55–66, and as a cornerstone in regard to assert the freedom of choice, Holtzman, Human choice. For other universalistic and exclusivistic interpretations of *fiṭra* in Muslim theology and philosophy, see Josef van Ess: *Zwischen Ḥadīṯ und Theologie. Studien zum Entstehen prädestinatianischer Überlieferung*, Berlin and New York 1975, pp. 101–114 and Gobillot, Geneviève: *La fiṭra. La conception originelle; ses interprétations et fonctions chez les penseurs Musulmans = Cahier des Annales Islamologiques* 18 (2000).

201 *Mabnā al-ʿaql ʿalā ṣiḥḥat al-fiṭra wa-salāmatihā* (Ibn Taymiyya, *al-Radd*, p. 323; al-Suyūṭī, *Jahd al-qarīḥa*, p. 321; Hallaq, *Ibn Taymiyya*, p. 150, I follow his translation).

202 Ibn Taymiyya, *Darʾ taʿāruḍ al-ʿaql*, vol. 1, p. 168. Ibn Taymiyya makes this statement in the context of asserting that clear, "uncontaminated" reason cannot contradict the scripture. For a French translation of the whole chapter (ninth aspect of the 44 aspects concerning the refutation of the rationalists' claim of the priority of reason over revelation), see Michot, Vanités intellectuelles, pp. 615–616.

203 Ibn Taymiyya, *Naqḍ al-manṭiq*, p. 194; idem, *al-Radd*, pp. 316, 108–109; Hallaq, Ibn Taymiyya on the Existence of God, p. 58. Elsewhere in *Naqḍ al-manṭiq*, however, Ibn Taymiyya presents the self-evident first principles as directly bestowed by God upon the souls at the beginning (p. 202, Hallaq, *Ibn Taymiyya*, p. xxxi); a passage in *al-Radd* might be interpreted in the same vein (pp. 302–303). Ibn Taymiyya's terms are ambivalent about knowledge of God's existence; an expression such as that the *fiṭra* testifies *(shahidat)* to it suggests *a posteriori* knowledge (*Darʾ taʿāruḍ al-ʿaql*, vol. 3, p. 129), whereas the expression of its "being rooted" (*markūz*) in the *fiṭra* (ibid., vol. 3, p. 72) suggests *a priori* knowledge. In his *Risāla fī al-Kalām ʿalā al-fiṭra*, Ibn Taymiyya develops a concept of *fiṭra* that does not depend on the senses (idem, in: *Majmūʿat al-rasāʾil al-kubrā, al-juzʾ al-thānī*, Beirut 1972, pp. 345, 348 et passim; French translation: Gobillot, Geneviève: L'Épitre du discours sur la fiṭra (*Risāla fī-l-kalām ʿalā-l-fiṭra*) de Taqī-l-Dīn Aḥmad Ibn Taymīyya (661/1262–728/1328).

be described, then, as the predisposition and the faculty to correctly and immediately grasp true knowledge and to reject false knowledge. It enables man to apprehend the existence of God,[204] to distinguish the useful from the harmful[205] and the true from the untrue,[206] to know the causal efficiencies of things (see chapter 11.2), or to form sound concepts and judgments (see chapter 10.1, 11.2).[207]

Ibn Taymiyya admits, however, that there are great differences between people concerning the soundness of their innate intelligence and their organs of perceptions. Ibn Taymiyya connects these differences with the common distinction between two modes of knowledge: necessary (*ḍarūrī*) or evident (*badīhī*) knowledge, on the one hand, and acquired (*kasbī/muktasab*) or speculative (*naẓarī*) knowledge, on the other.[208] The first is regarded as immediate and "certain" (*yaqīnī*) and the latter as inferred and only "probable" (*ẓannī*). Ibn Taymiyya maintains this distinction for concepts (*taṣawwurāt*) and judgments (*taṣdīqāt*).[209] It is most likely that Ibn Taymiyya considered evident knowledge to be clear and "uncontaminated." Still, in his view the evident or speculative character of a concept or a judgment does not depend on the subject matter, but on the soundness of the innate intel-

---

Présentation et traduction annotée, in: *Annales Islamologiques* 20 (1984), pp. 29–53, here 31, 49, 52–53 et passim). See Hallaq, Ibn Taymiyya on the Existence of God, pp. 65–66.

204 Ibid.; Madjid, *Ibn Taymiyya on Kalām and Falsafa*, pp. 71–72. In *Darʾ taʿāruḍ al-ʿaql* he claims that the *fiṭra* understanding that God is above the world is shared by old and young and by every people, be they Muslims, Jews, Christians or polytheists (vol. 6, p. 12); see also above, n. 203.

205 Ibn Taymiyya, *al-Radd*, p. 428–430; Madjid, *Ibn Taymiyya on Kalām and Falsafa*, pp. 65–69.

206 For instance, Ibn Taymiyya, *al-Radd*, p. 71; al-Suyūṭī, *Jahd al-qarīḥa*, p. 216; Hallaq, *Ibn Taymiyya*, pp. 26–27; Ibn Taymiyya, *Darʾ taʿāruḍ al-ʿaql*, vol. 9, p. 366.

207 See Hoover, who studied other writings of Ibn Taymiyya and came to similar conclusions in regard to Ibn Taymiyya's understanding of *ʿaql* (*Ibn Taymiyya's Theodicy*, pp. 32–34), states that it is difficult "to pinpoint the exact relationship" between Ibn Taymiyya's concepts of *ʿaql* and *fiṭra* (ibid., p. 39).

208 For the development of this distinction, see van Ess, *Die Erkenntnislehre*, pp. 114–128; Marmura, Michael E.: Ghazali's Attitude to the Secular Sciences and Logic, in: George F. Hourani (ed.): *Essays on Islamic Philosophy and Science*, Albany 1975, pp. 104, 110, n. 13.

209 Ibn Taymiyya, *al-Radd*, pp. 11, 13–14, 88–91; (al-Suyūṭī severely shortened Ibn Taymiyya's explanation: *Jahd al-qarīḥa*, pp. 205–206, 219–220; Hallaq, *Ibn Taymiyya*, pp. 10–12, 31–32); see also chapter 11.3.

ligence and the senses. He regards them as belonging to "the relative, relational matters" (*min al-umūr al-nisbiyya al-iḍāfiyya*):[210]

> It is well known that people vary in mental aptitude more than they do in physical strength. The quickness and quality of one man's perception may be much greater than that of another. Such a man would then form a complete concept of the two terms so as to reveal through that complete concept the necessary attributes which would not be evident to those who cannot form such a concept. That in some propositions certain people need the middle, which is the indicant, while others do not, is an obvious matter. For many people the proposition may be sensory (*ḥiṣṣiyya*), empirical (*mujarraba*), demonstrative (*burhāniyya*), or multiply transmitted (*mutawātira*), while for others it may be known by means of investigation and inference.[211]

In this statement Ibn Taymiyya plainly expresses his conviction that the mental aptitudes of people differ. He holds that for some people there is no need to form a definition or a syllogism or an analogy in order to comprehend a concept or a judgment. Being evident knowledge, concepts and judgments thus become necessary and certain. He clearly states that sense perception, experience, demonstration,[212] and multiply transmitted reports provide immediate and therefore evident, certain (*yaqīnī*) knowledge.[213] In fact, Ibn Taymiyya also counts

---

210 Ibn Taymiyya, *al-Radd*, p. 13; al-Suyūṭī, *Jahd al-qarīḥa*, p. 205; Hallaq, *Ibn Taymiyya*, p. 11.

211 Ibn Taymiyya, *al-Radd*, p. 91; al-Suyūṭī, *Jahd al-qarīḥa*, pp. 219–220; Hallaq, *Ibn Taymiyya*, p. 32 (I follow his translation; the additions in angular brackets are mine.).

212 Ibn Taymiyya does not explain what he means in this context by *burhān*. It could well be the first figure of categorical syllogism, which he considers to be spontaneously apprehensible (see chapter 11.3) or "the rational, demonstrative inferences mentioned in the Koran" (see chapter 12).

213 It is noteworthy that ʿAbd al-Qāhir al-Baghdādī (d. 429/1037–1038) exposes in his *Uṣūl al-dīn* that "deduction" (*istidlāl bil-ʿaql*), "experience and common practice" (*al-tajārub wal-ʿādāt*), "divine commands" (*al-sharʿ*), and "inspiration" (*ilhām*); "e. g. the taste for poetry, the knowledge of metre, the composition of melodies" (Wensinck, Arent Jan: *The Muslim Creed. Its Genesis and Historical Development*, London 1965, p. 259) may belong to the primary, necessary kind of knowledge, if God gives that knowledge directly to the heart (al-Baghdādī, Abū Manṣūr ʿAbd al-Qāhir al-Tamīmī: *Kitāb Uṣūl al-dīn*, Beirut 1401/1981 (reprint, Istanbul 1346/1928), pp. 14–15; Wensinck, *The Muslim Creed*, pp. 259–260). Yet Ibn Taymiyya considerably deviates from him in several respects, adopting a terminology and tenets that evoke the epistemology of philosophers and "later" *kalām* theologians.

estimative propositions (*wahmiyyāt*) and widespread propositions (*mashhūrāt*) among the premises that can lead to certainty.[214] Ibn Taymiyya explains these different ways to gain knowledge in *al-Radd ʿalā al-manṭiqiyyīn* and *Darʾ taʿāruḍ al-ʿaql wal-naql* and thereby uses several distinct philosophical terms and concepts.

11. Traces of the Rationalists' "Poison" in Ibn Taymiyya's Theory of Knowledge

11.1. Perception of the Senses, Estimations, Multiply Transmitted Reports, and Widespread Propositions

In accordance with early and also "later" *kalām* theologians and philosophers, Ibn Taymiyya divides the perceptions of the senses between those that can form immediate concepts of the outside world, such as "taste," "color," "odor" and "bodies that possess these attributes," on the one hand, and those that can form immediate concepts of one's own physical and psychological states, like "hunger," "satiety," "love," "hate," "joy," and "sadness."[215]

He further makes a distinction between individual sense perceptions and those apprehensions shared by all or some people, such as the sight of the sun and the moon or the sight of a local mountain or mosque.[216] According to his statement in *al-Radd ʿalā al-manṭiqiyyīn*, the sense perceptions include the apprehension of the primary arithmetic, geometric, and logical principles (see chapter 10.1). Ibn Taymiyya does not discuss the question of "errors of the senses" or false judgments about right perceptions.[217]

214 Ibn Taymiyya, *al-Radd*, pp. 206, 396–437. This chapter is not summarized by al-Suyūṭī (Hallaq, *Ibn Taymiyya*, p. 167, n. 307.1).

215 Ibn Taymiyya, *al-Radd*, pp. 11 (in respect to the inner senses, he speaks also of "feelings," *mashāʿir*), 55–56, 92, 96. Here he states that, of the five powers, sight and hearing are the basis for the knowledge that separates man from animal; shortened or omitted by al-Suyūṭī, *Jahd al-qarīḥa*, p. 205; Hallaq, *Ibn Taymiyya*, p. 10; Ibn Taymiyya, *Darʾ taʿāruḍ al-ʿaql*, vol. 6, p. 108. Concerning the development of the classification of sense perceptions in *kalām* and *falsafa*, see van Ess, *Die Erkenntnislehre*, pp. 164–166.

216 Ibn Taymiyya, *al-Radd*, p. 92; Hallaq, *Ibn Taymiyya*, pp. 32–33 n. 43.4.

217 This question was much disputed by several of the authors Ibn Taymiyya had read. Aristotle's view that the senses cannot err, but that the judgment rea-

He does not disqualify sense perceptions, especially those perceived by the spirit (*rūḥ*), that are not shared by everyone present at one place, e.g., seeing and hearing jinns or angels, or the perceptions that will occur only after death; indeed, he counts these perceptions of the hidden existences (*mawjūdāt ghāʾiba*) as certain knowledge (*yaqīniyyāt*) and identifies them with the estimations (*wahmiyyāt*) that "Ibn Sīnā and philosophers of his kind" reckoned as false. Ibn Taymiyya thereby refutes the tenet that these perceptions are but in the soul of the person who senses them and wants to assert the concrete existence of "hidden" existences in the sensible world, on the one hand, and the bodily sensible torments and blessings in the hereafter, on the other.[218] However, Ibn Sīnā's denial of the certainty of estimations that Ibn Taymiyya quotes to support his rebuttal does not touch upon jinns or angels, but apparently concerns illusions that Ibn Taymiyya himself also refutes.[219] Thus, Ibn Taymiyya rejects as corrupt estimative propositions (*qaḍāyā al-wahm al-fāsid*), propositions that affirm the existence of what exists neither inside nor outside the world.[220] He furthermore admits that Ibn Sīnā affirms the existence of true estimative propositions and, appar-

---

son forms about the perception might be wrong, was falsely transmitted by al-Rāzī, for instance van Ess, *Die Erkenntnislehre*, pp. 174–177.

218 Ibn Taymiyya, *Darʾ taʿāruḍ al-ʿaql*, vol. 6, pp. 109–111. In *al-Radd ʿalā al-manṭiqiyyīn*, Ibn Taymiyya does not expound his views on estimations. He asserts that he has already refuted at length the logicians' exclusion of the estimative propositions from the premises leading to certainty and that he has shown that they belong to the class of knowledge that innate intelligence can grasp immediately (*al-Radd*, pp. 206, 396; al-Suyūṭī, *Jahd al-qarīḥa*, p. 294; Hallaq, *Ibn Taymiyya*, pp. 120–121). He most probably was referring to his statements in *Darʾ taʿāruḍ al-ʿaql wal-naql* (vol. 6 et passim; see vol. 11 s.v.). Ibn Sīnā expounded his theory of the survival of the soul and his denial of the bodily resurrection in *al-Risāla al-Aḍḥawiyya fī amr al-maʿād*, ed. by Sulaymān Dunyā, Cairo 1368/1949; see Ibn Taymiyya's critique of Ibn Sīnā's hermeneutical approach in this tract, which he also presents in *Darʾ taʿāruḍ al-ʿaql* (Michot, A Mamlūk Theologian's Commentary).

219 Ibn Taymiyya (*Darʾ taʿāruḍ al-ʿaql*, vol. 6, p. 101–111; see pp. 20–22) comments upon Ibn Sīnā's rather confusing passage on the estimative propositions in *al-Ishārāt wal-tanbīhāt* (vol. 1, pp. 353–355; see Inati's translation and explanation (Avicenna, *Remarks and Admonitions*, part 1, pp. 123–124). It is not the passage in which Ibn Taymiyya quotes Ibn Sīnā with a sharp difference about the wording in manuscripts that were known to the editor of *al-Ishārāt wal-tanbīhāt*, namely Sulaymān Dunyā (Marcotte, Ibn Taymiyya et sa critique, pp. 51–53). Roxanne D. Marcotte has shown that Ibn Taymiyya repeatedly misrepresented tenets of Ibn Sīnā in order to refute them (ibid., pp. 53–58).

220 Ibn Taymiyya, *Darʾ taʿāruḍ al-ʿaql*, vol. 6, p. 106.

ently, only disagrees with their denomination. Ibn Sīnā explains a true estimation as a knowledge that is not won by the senses, but triggered by a perceptible particular, such as a sheep's fear of a wolf without ever having seen one before.[221] Ibn Taymiyya calls this instinctive faculty simply "inner faculty" (*quwwa bāṭina*), "reason" (*ʿaql*), or "uncontaminated reason," and regards the estimative propositions as being certain in the innate intelligence (*fiṭra*) and natural disposition (*jibla*).[222]

The multiply transmitted reports (*mutawātirāt*) are defined by Ibn Taymiyya as relying on the apprehension of particulars through sight or hearing, i.e., through immediate knowledge.[223] This knowledge, such as the knowledge of the existence of Mecca or of the prophets Moses, Jesus, and Muḥammad, reaches most people, but may miss those living in very remote places.[224] Not only "earlier" *kalām* theologians, but also the *falāsifa* and the "later" *kalām* theologians consider multiply transmitted reports to be certain.[225]

---

221 Ibn Sīnā, Abū ʿAlī: *Avicenna's* De Anima *(Arabic Text). Being the Psychological Part of* Kitāb al-Shifāʾ, ed. by Fazlur Rahman, London, New York and Toronto 1959, pp. 45, 184; Ibn Sīnā, *al-Ishārāt wal-tanbīhāt*, p. 354 (Ibn Sīnā: Livre des directives et remarques (*Kitāb al-Ishārāt wa l-tanbīhāt*), traduction avec introduction et notes par Amélie M. Goichon, Beyrut and Paris 1951, p. 317); Ibn Taymiyya, *Darʾ taʿāruḍ al-ʿaql*, vol. 6, p. 22 (he quotes here the passage from *al-Ishārāt,* but cites and discusses later on (*Darʾ taʿāruḍ al-ʿaql*, vol. 6, pp. 47–55) parts of Ibn Sīnā's theory of the estimative faculty (*al-quwwa al-wahmiyya*) from *al-Shifāʾ* (*De Anima*, especially pp. 167, 168–169). Some main stages in the development of the judgments about estimative propositions in Muslim theology and philosophy are mentioned by van Ess, *Die Erkenntnislehre*, pp. 398–399.

222 Ibn Taymiyya, *Darʾ taʿāruḍ al-ʿaql*, vol. 6, pp. 50–55, 105–106.

223 Ibn Taymiyya, *al-Radd*, p. 302.

224 Ibid., p. 92; al-Suyūṭī was either working with another wording of *al-Radd ʿalā al-manṭiqiyyīn* or else himself added that "the miracles of the prophets are known through multiple transmission" and that the negation of the reliability of the *mutawātirāt* leads to "heresy and unbelief" (*Jahd al-qarīḥa*, p. 220; Hallaq, *Ibn Taymiyya*, p. 32). In two passages in the edited manuscript of *al-Radd ʿalā al-manṭiqiyyīn* (which contains marginals in Ibn Taymiyya's handwriting), Ibn Taymiyya mentions miracles in the context of empirical matters and says he has treated them elsewhere (*al-Radd*, pp. 300–301; see his *Kitāb al-Nubuwwāt*). Al-Suyūṭī does not mention these hints (see *Jahd al-qarīḥa*, p. 315; Hallaq, *Ibn Taymiyya*, p. 143). Shahab Ahmed has shown that Ibn Taymiyya had a broader understanding of *tawātur* transmissions of prophetic sayings than the majority of the jurists (Ibn Taymiyyah and the Satanic Verses, pp. 84–85).

225 See, for instance, Ibn Sīnā, *al-Ishārāt wal-tanbīhāt*, vol. 1, p. 349; Avicenna, *Remarks and Admonitions*, p. 121; al-Ghazālī, Abū Ḥāmid: *Miḥakk al-naẓar*,

In contrast, the *falāsifa* and some "later" *kalām* theologians more or less doubt the certainty of the widespread propositions (*mashhūrāt*).[226] Ibn Taymiyya therefore tries to show that their distinction between axioms (*awwaliyyāt*) and widespread propositions is arbitrary.[227] He further shows that man by himself (*al-insān min nafsihi*) finds justice, sincerity, and knowledge more delightful than tyranny, falsehood, and ignorance and adduces arguments to prove that a judgment, such as "justice is good and tyranny is deplorable,"[228] can be grasped immediately and is thus certain.[229]

So one might already say that, in principle, Ibn Taymiyya regarded a broader spectrum of propositions as certain than the philosophers did.

---

ed. by Rafīq al-ʿAjam, Beirut 1994, p. 105; see Rudolph, Die Neubewertung der Logik, p. 79; van Ess, *Die Erkenntnislehre*, p. 398. For ʿAbd al-Qāhir al-Baghdādī, the *mutawātirāt* already included geographical and historical knowledge (al-Baghdādī, *Kitāb Uṣūl al-dīn*, pp. 11–12; Wensinck, *The Muslim Creed*, p. 257).

226 See, for instance, Ibn Sīnā, *al-Ishārāt wal-tanbīhāt*, vol. 1, pp. 342, 350–353; Avicenna, *Remarks and Admonitions*, pp. 119, 122–123. Ibn Taymiyya mainly refers to al-Rāzī's commentary on this work of Ibn Sīnā.

227 Ibn Taymiyya, *al-Radd*, pp. 396–420.

228 Ibid., p. 423; see the following note.

229 Ibid., pp. 420–437. Hallaq summarized some of his arguments (*Ibn Taymiyya*, p. 167, n. 307.1); see van Ess, *Die Erkenntnislehre*, p. 400, for the discussion in philosophical and theological circles in general. They certainly deserve a thorough comparative study, not least with other of Ibn Taymiyya's own writings. In a tract published in a collection of Ibn Taymiyya's formal legal opinions, he expounds a theory of ethics comprising three levels: "rational" (*ʿaqlī*), "confessional" (*millī*) and "legal" (*sharʿī*) (Ibn Taymiyya, *Majmūʿat al-Fatāwā*, al-mujallad 20, Cairo 1421/2001, vol. 10, pp. 37–43; transl. by Michot, Yahya J.: Textes spirituels d'Ibn Taymiyya. XIV. Raison, confession, loi. Une typologie musulmane du religieux, in: *Le Musulman* 27 (1996), pp. 24–29, here 24, 26–28). The "rational" level encompasses the basis of ethics, "that what all sons of Adam bestowed with reason agree upon, whether they were given a scripture (*lahum ṣilat kitāb*) or not" (*Majmūʿat al-Fatāwā*, al-mujallad 20, Cairo, vol. 10, p. 40). As one example among others, he mentions "justice," though admitting that its application depends on the concrete situation (ibid., p. 69). See also Hoover, *Ibn Taymiyya's Theodicy*, p. 42.

11.2. Empirical Matters and Natural Efficient Causation: Ibn Taymiyya as a "Moderate Realist"

Ibn Taymiyya's great concern with empirical matters (*mujarrabāt*) certainly has to be seen against the background of the treacherous ground he entered with this subject, namely the question whether or not natural efficient causation exists. Ibn Taymiyya affirms its existence and speaks even of "universal propositions." It is in this part of his theory of knowledge that he explicitly and implicitly confirms an essential tenet of Peripatetic epistemology, namely man's capability to grasp the essences of things, i. e., the universals *in rebus*. He starts by explaining that

> the generality of people has experienced that drinking water brings quenching and that decapitation brings death and that a strong blow causes (*yūjib*) pain. The knowledge of this universal proposition (*hādhihi al-qaḍiyya al-kulliyya*) is empirical (*tajrībī*). The sense apprehends one particular quenching and the death of one particular person and the pain of one particular person. The universal proposition that the same would occur to everyone who would be treated similarly is not known by sense, but by what is composed by sense and reason, and the sense here is not the hearing.[230]

Reading this paragraph, one is reminded of Ibn Taymiyya's rigorous denial of the possibility of establishing true universal propositions by abstraction through the observation of particulars, because no one is able to observe all particulars (see chapter 10.1). It looks like a plain contradiction and so does the consequence of this part of the Peripatetic epistemology on the ontological level. Ibn Taymiyya continues his explanation of empirical matters as follows:

> Those who do not affirm the causes (*al-asbāb wal-ʿilal*) among the *kalām* theologians, like al-Jahm [b. Ṣafwān] and those who agree with him in this, like Abū al-Ḥasan [al-Ashʿarī] and his followers, take the known [relation between two things] as a connection of one thing to the other [which is due] solely to the volition of the Mighty and Willing, without one being the cause (*sababan*) of the other or generating (*muwallidan*) it. Instead, the majority of the intelligent people (*al-ʿuqalāʾ*) among the Muslims and non-Muslims, the Sunnites among the *kalām* theologians, the jurists, the traditionists and the Sufis, and the non-Sunnites among

230 Ibn Taymiyya, *al-Radd*, pp. 92–93. Ibn Taymiyya's whole elaboration on empirical matters is missing in al-Suyūṭī's summary.

> the Muʿtazilīs and others, affirm the causes (*al-asbāb*) and say: 'As the connection (*iqtirān*) [between two things] is known as one to the other, so it is known that there is in the fire a power (*quwwa*) that necessitates (*yaqtaḍī*) burning, and in water a power that necessitates refreshment. Likewise there is in the eye a power that necessitates sight and in the tongue a power that necessitates taste.' And they affirm the nature (*al-ṭabīʿa*) that is called *al-gharīza* (the implanted disposition), *al-naḥīza* (the natural disposition), *al-khulq* (the innate peculiarity), *al-ʿāda* (the habit), and [that is given] other similar names.[231]

Ibn Taymiyya leaves no doubt that he adheres to the conviction of "the majority of intelligent people."[232] He thereby explicitly admits one of the key theories of the Peripatetics, the theory of natural efficient causation, which, in contrast to his assertion, was far from having been adopted by "the majority" to which he refers.[233] Seen in this light, his

---

231 Ibn Taymiyya, *al-Radd*, p. 94 (The additions in angular brackets are mine); see Ibn Taymiyya, *Darʾ taʿāruḍ al-ʿaql*, vol. 9, pp. 339–342. In one passage, in relation to the regular movements of the sun and the moon, Ibn Taymiyya explicitly speaks of God's custom (*ʿāda*), Ibn Taymiyya, *al-Radd*, p. 272.

232 Ibn Taymiyya confirms this in addition by several Koranic verses (2:164; 7:57; 50:9), *al-Radd*, p. 270; see the very similar argumentation in Ibn Taymiyya's major fatwa on astrology, where he explicitly states that God sets "radiance and burning in the fire, purification and irrigation in the water, and the other similar blessings that He mentions in His Book" and harshly rebuts those *kalām* theologians who say "that God does these affairs with (*ʿind*) and not by (*bi-*) them" (Michot, Ibn Taymiyya on Astrology, pp. 155–156) and validates it also in *Minhāj al-sunna* and *al-ʿAqīda al-tadmuriyya* (Hoover, *Ibn Taymiyya's Theodicy*, pp. 147, 157–159). Henry Laoust pointed to the "Aristotelian spirit" of Ibn Taymiyya "en s'efforçant de 'raisonner comme raisonne la nature' et de pénétrer le secret des choses" (*Essai sur les doctrines sociales et politiques*, pp. 167, 244–254). He refers to one of Ibn Taymiyya's juridical tracts where he speaks of the "essence", the "quiddity" of the thing (*māhiyyat al-shayʾ*) (Ibn Taymiyya, Kitāb al-Samāʿ wal-raqṣ, in: idem, *Majmūʿat al-rasāʾil al-kubrā*, Cairo, vol. 2, p. 293). On the basis of several of Ibn Taymiyya's writings, Nurcholis Madjid also showed that Ibn Taymiyya was no occasionalist. His main interest, however, lies not in the logical implications, but in the differences in metaphysics between Ibn Taymiyya and his opponents (*Ibn Taymiyya on Kalām and Falsafa*, pp. 142–181). For the genesis and devolopment of occasionalism in Islam, see Ulrich Rudolph and Dominik Perler: *Occasionalismus. Theorien der Kausalität im arabisch-islamischen und im europäischen Denken*, Göttingen 2000, pp. 23–124.

233 Ibn Taymiyya himself admits that "there are people who reject the forces [*al-quwā* and the natures [*ṭabāʾiʿ*], as is the case with Abū al-Ḥasan [al-Ashʿarī] and those who followed him, among the companions of Mālik, al-Shāfiʿī, Aḥmad [b. Ḥanbal] and others" (Ibn Taymiyya, Fatwā on Human Reason in:

denial of the Aristotelian "real definition" (*ḥadd ḥaqīqī*) that is held to grasp the "essence" of a thing (see chapter 10.1) gains a new dimension.[234] Ibn Taymiyya obviously negates neither that a particular thing, a species, or a genus has a natural disposition peculiar to it – like the philosophers, he too calls these dispositions *ḥaqāʾiq* ("true natures", "essences")[235] and *māhiyya* (sg., "essence")[236] – nor that man's knowledge about them is certain. Ibn Taymiyya, thus, seems to accept the very substance of the Peripatetic theory of causality, namely the natural necessity of cause and effect inherent in the essence of things.

Coming back to Ibn Taymiyya's assertion that "empirical matters" are comprehended as universal propositions, we must uncover whether he distinguishes his claim from those of his enemies. He himself produces that confrontation:

> It is known that through the senses universal and general matters cannot be perceived. Sensory matters do not lend themselves to universal and general propositions which can serve as premises in apodictic demonstration (*al-burhān al-yaqīnī*). In their (the logicians') example 'Fire burns', etc., they do not know for certain the universality of this proposition. All they rely on is experiment (*tajriba*) and custom (*ʿāda*), which are of the same kind as analogy. If the universality of the proposition is known

---

Majmūʿat al-Fatāwā, Cairo, vol. 5, part 9, p. 153; Michot, Ibn Taymiyya on Astrology, pp. 155–156, n. 34 (I follow his translation, the Arabic terms in angular brackets are my additions)). In fact, the Muʿtazilīs negated the secondary, intermediary causes, assuming that God governs the world all by himself (Wolfson, Harry Austryn: *The Philosophy of the Kalam*, Cambridge and London 1976, pp. 520–543). This denial, however, concerns only the world, i.e., nature, as long as man does not intervene. In regard to man's acting in the world, most of them upheld an efficient causal relation between the act and the result, a theory they usually called *tawallud* (van Ess, Josef: *Theologie und Gesellschaft im 2. und 3. Jahrhundert Hidschra. Eine Geschichte des religiösen Denkens im frühen Islam*, Berlin and New York 1991–1997, vol. 3, pp. 116–117, 250, 423; vol. 4, pp. 139, 475, 487, see also Index s.v. *tawallud*). See also below, n. 250.

234 For the role of causality in the Aristotelian theory of definition and demonstration, see, for instance, Madkour, Ibrahim: *L'organon d'Aristote dans le monde arabe, ses traductions, son étude et ses applications*, Paris 1969, pp. 125–127 (with further references).

235 Ibn Taymiyya, *al-Radd*, pp. 26, 299; al-Suyūṭī, *Jahd al-qarīḥa*, p. 314; Hallaq, *Ibn Taymiyya*, p. 142 (he translates *al-ḥaqāʾiq al-mawjūda fī al-khārij* only as "extramental reality").

236 See above, n. 232; Henry Laoust holds that Ibn Taymiyya's logical terminology is largely taken from al-Ghazālī (*Essai sur les doctrines sociales et politiques*, p. 84).

> on the basis of the fact that fire possesses a power (*quwwa*) to burn, then the knowledge that every fire necessarily possesses this power is a universal judgment as well. Someone may argue: 'The stuff of fire (*al-ṣūra al-nāriyya*) must include this power, and whatever lacks this power is not fire.' Though this statement may be true, it does not conclusively ascertain that all things possessing this power will burn everything they encounter, albeit this is usually the case. (The burning ability of fire) is the object of analogy (*qiyās al-tamthīl*), categorical syllogism (*qiyās al-shumūl*),[237] custom, and imperfect induction – that is, if we grant them this. But how could this be the case when it is known that fire does not burn salamander stone, hyacinth, and objects coated with manufactured material? I do not know of any universal proposition that is based on sense perception which cannot be refuted, though universal propositions are not sensory. A sensory proposition would be of the type '*This* fire burns', since only particular things are perceived through the senses.[238]

In this paragraph of his "Refutation of the Logicians," Ibn Taymiyya appears less apodictic in asserting the causal efficiencies of things. His remark, however, that perhaps not everything will burn when it comes in contact with fire does not at all deny "burning" as the natural disposition of fire, but only states that there are things that have the natural disposition not to be consumed by fire. In fact, Ibn Taymiyya and the Peripatetic logicians agree on this. He himself admits it by asserting that one can also reach this truth by categorical syllogism.

In the frame of Ibn Taymiyya's discussion of man's will (*irāda*), which serves him also as a proof of God's existence, he again appears as a "moderate realist" as far as causality is concerned. He also accepts the Aristotelian tenet of the impossibility of an infinite regress in regard to final and efficient causes. After having established that every soul, i.e., every living being, has feeling (*shuʿūr*) and will, he distinguishes between the thing that is wanted because of something else (*murād li-ghayrihi*) and the one that is wanted for itself (*murād li-nafsihi/li-dhātihi*). To the former belongs food, for instance. It is wanted

---

237 *Qiyās al-shumūl* is an unusual term for the categorical syllogism and perhaps coined by Ibn Taymiyya himself, Hallaq, *Ibn Taymiyya*, p. xiv. The common one is *qiyās iqtirānī* or *qiyās ḥamalī*. R. Brunschvig assumes that Ibn Taymiyya wants to underline the claim that it encompasses the universal (Pour ou contre la logique grecque, p. 324).

238 Al-Suyūṭī, *Jahd al-qarīḥa*, pp. 314–315; Hallaq, *Ibn Taymiyya*, pp. 142–143. (I follow his translation; the Arabic terms in angular brackets are my additions); Ibn Taymiyya, *al-Radd*, p. 300 (the end of the paragraph is a little longer and the wording differs slightly).

because of its genus (*murād jinsahu*), namely the dispelling of hunger. Not everything, Ibn Taymiyya argues, can be wanted for something else, since that would lead to "an infinite regress of formal causes, and that is as impossible as an infinite regress of efficient causes, nay the more so."[239] Hence, there has to be something wanted and loved for itself and not as a genus and "this cannot be anything but a particular" (*lā yakūnu illā muʿayyanan*), and this particular is God. While God does not share anything with something or someone else, the other particulars have common, universal features. The universal feature, however, does not exist separately, but as a particular *in rebus* (*al-kullī lā wujūda lahu fī al-aʿyān illā muʿayyanan*).[240] Ibn Taymiyya could hardly have expressed more clearly in terminology and as a concept the congruity between the Peripatetics and himself.

Natural causality is a tenet Ibn Taymiyya upholds also in other writings, indeed, in a great number of his works, as Jon Hoover has recently shown in his eminent monograph on Ibn Taymiyya's concept of theodicy.[241] Hoover convincingly argues that this constitutes one side of the coin of Ibn Taymiyya's theodicy, that of the "human perspective." The other side is the "divine perspective," from which creation looks different, fully displaying God's omnipotence. Likewise, Ibn Taymiyya views human acts as a result of man's own will, power, and free choice, on the one hand, and as bound to God's will, on the other hand.[242] Hoover therefore regards Ibn Taymiyya's approach as "compatibilism."[243] To ensure "the responsibility of humans for their destiny," Ibn Taymiyya presents the visible world from the "human perspective" as organized in accordance with secondary causality that looks "natural."[244] Yet Ibn Taymiyya views secondary causality as instrumental from the "divine perspective." Though things behave in accordance with the causes God created, everything depends solely on His will. He is perpetually creating and willing from eternity for

239 *Tasalsul fī al-ʿilal al-ghāʾiyya wa-huwa mumtaniʿ ka-imtināʿ al-tasalsul fī al-ʿilal al-fāʿiliyya bal awlā*, Ibn Taymiyya, *Darʾ taʿāruḍ al-ʿaql*, vol. 8, p. 465; see Ibn Taymiyya, *al-Radd*, pp. 147–148; al-Suyūṭī, *Jahd al-qarīḥa*, pp. 249–250; Hallaq, *Ibn Taymiyya*, pp. 68–70.

240 Ibn Taymiyya, *Darʾ taʿāruḍ al-ʿaql*, vol. 8, pp. 464–467.

241 Hoover, *Ibn Taymiyya's Theodicy*, pp. 133–134, 147, 156–165 et passim (see index, s. v. *cause*).

242 Ibid., pp. 136–156, 173–176 et passim (see index, s. v. *act*).

243 Ibid., pp. 154, 173 et passim (see index, s. v. *compatibilism*).

244 Ibid., p. 163.

wise purposes.[245] If God does not will something to happen that would result from a cause or a combination of causes He created, He does not perfect the combination of causes and conditions or He creates an impediment.[246] However, God does not alter the order He has fixed for the things, because otherwise He would undermine His own all-embracing wise purpose. Thus, He cannot create "contraries simultaneously in one place, and He cannot create a son before his father."[247] God's wise purpose, thus, entails that his creatures follow a fixed order and are bestowed with specific powers. The essences He bestowed things with, for instance His bestowal on fire of the power to burn, are their necessary concomitants and aren't lost when God does not will them to "act" or to "react," but are rendered ineffective by impediments God creates.

On the epistemological level – as far as the way to knowledge of causes and effects is concerned – Ibn Taymiyya does not deviate from the Peripatetic method. He also tries to grasp the universals that are shared by similar particulars. Even on the ontological level, there is a great similarity, since Ibn Taymiyya does not deny the existence of fixed essences and a fixed order of causes and effects. Furthermore, philosophers also hold that an effect depends on numerous conditions, i.e., other causes besides the main efficient cause, and can be hindered by impediments.[248] Ibn Taymiyya's harsh rebuttal of the existence of universals *in rebus* can, therefore, be motivated only by the great difference between the philosophers' and his own metaphysical theories. Whereas the philosophers conceive God as an inactive first cause and

---

245 Ibid., pp. 80–95. The Tunesian Islamist Rāshid al-Ghannūshī came to a similar conclusion in his study of Ibn Taymiyya's notion of predestination and free will, mainly on the basis of *Majmūʿ al-fatāwā* (without indicating neither the "title" of the writing nor the volume), *al-Ḥasana wal-saʾya* and *Risālat fī al-Iḥtijāj bil-qadar*. He interprets Ibn Taymiyya as viewing "God's will as an active part in the divine order" creating by the causes He Himself bestowed his creatures with (*al-Qadar ʿind Ibn Taymiyya*, London 1999, pp. 87, 91–92). I am grateful to Lutz Rogler for having provided me with a copy of this work.

246 Hoover, *Ibn Taymiyya's Theodicy*, pp. 160–162.

247 Ibn Taymiyya, *Minhāj al-sunna*, vol. 3, p. 103–104, here rendered in the concise wording of Hoover (*Ibn Taymiyya's Theodicy*, p. 133).

248 See, for instance, Ibn Sīnā, *al-Shifāʾ, al-Ilāhiyyāt*, ed. by Ibrāhīm Madkūr, al-Ab Qanawātī and Saʿīd Zāyid, Cairo 1380/1960, vol. 1, p. 180; Marmura, Michael E.: The Metaphysics of Efficient Causality in Avicenna (Ibn Sina), in: idem (ed.): *Islamic Theology and Philosophy. Studies in Honor of George F. Hourani*, Albany 1984, pp. pp. 172–187, here 181–182.

the secondary causes as acting on their own,[249] Ibn Taymiyya views God, as Hoover has shown, as perpetually creating the secondary causes and their effects or impediments in compliance with His wise purpose.

In one passage of *al-Radd ʿalā al-manṭiqiyyīn* concerning evil, this view is also very explicit. Ibn Taymiyya maintains that, when He knotted the causes of evil (*inʿiqād asbāb al-sharr*), God instructed the prophet Muḥammad which pious acts, such as prayers, repentance, or almsgiving, could repel its effect (*mūjab*).[250] Thus, an evil cause can be prevented from producing its evil effect due to the nature with which God bestowed the evil cause, but the actual connection between the causes and their effects, for instance an invocation of God that provokes the repelling of the enemy, depends on God's will and power.[251]

---

249 For a concise summary of these metaphysical holdings of the philosophers, see Fakhry, *Islamic Philosophy*, pp. 136–142, 158–166, 320–325; for a thorough analysis of the implied theories and their discussions, see Davidson, Herbert A.: *Proofs for Eternity, Creation and the Existence of God in Medieval Islamic and Jewish Philosophy*, New York and Oxford 1987.

250 In his *Risālat al-Wāsiṭa bayna al-khalq wal-ḥaqq*, Ibn Taymiyya also upholds that God is the one who creates causes and effects and counts invocation among the causes decreed by Him (Michot, Yahya J.: Ibn Taymiyya. Les intermédiaires entre dieu et l'homme (*Risâlat al-wâsiṭa bayna l-khalq wa l-ḥaqq*). traduction française suivie de "Le Shaykh de l'Islam Ibn Taymiyya; chronique d'une vie de théologien militant", in: *Le Musulman* Numéro hors-série de la revue (1417/1996), pp. 1–27, here p. 8; I am indebted to the author for this reference).

251 Ibn Taymiyya, *al-Radd*, pp. 271–272. Noticeably, Ibn Taymiyya here in no way tries to confront the *falāsifa*, but instead even cites a statement of Ptolemy concerning the influence of prayer on the stars as evidence (Ibn Taymiyya, *al-Radd*, p. 272; I did not verify whether the citation is from Ptolemy; it could be from his authentic astrological handbook or the apocryphal one (see Endress, Die wissenschaftliche Literatur, vol. 3, p. 105)). In *Minhāj al-sunna* Ibn Taymiyya explains God's wise purpose behind seemingly bad things as leading to "invocation, humility, repentance … and softening of the heart" (Hoover, *Ibn Taymiyya's Theodicy*, p. 132). The same author has now thoroughly studied Ibn Taymiyya's view of the origin of evil (*Ibn Taymiyya's Theodicy*, pp. 177–210).

11.3. Induction, Categorical Syllogism and Analogy: The Rational Balance in the Koran

Ibn Taymiyya treats his comparison between induction, analogy, syllogism, and other methods without reference to his views of causality. In consistency with his high esteem for particulars and his proof that it is impossible to observe every single particular of a genus in regard to the essence or property they share, he affirms that analogy and induction are not inferior to categorical syllogism as the philosophers claim.[252] He repeatedly tries to show that all concepts and judgments – be they reached by induction, analogy, syllogism, or other methods – are formed on the basis of particulars and not of universals.[253] He challenges the logicians' assertion that induction (*istiqrāʾ*) leads from particular to universal:

> As far as induction is concerned, it is certain if it is complete, in which case you will have reached a judgment about the common factor (*al-qadr al-mushtarak*) on the basis of what you have found in all the particulars. But this is neither an inference proceeding from particular to universal nor is it one proceeding from specific to general; rather, it is an inference that proceeds from one particular to another particular concomitant with it. For the existence of a judgment concerning each and every particular that falls under a universal necessitates that the judgment be concomitant with that universal.[254]

Ibn Taymiyya does not see induction as a way to reach certainty; elsewhere, he even adduces the same proof of this as Ibn Sīnā does (see chapter 10.1). His argumentation therefore seems to be in congruence with his nominalistic attitude of denying the existing of universals *ante res* and *in rebus* (see chapter 10.1). However, seen in the light of his theory of causality and his comparison between analogy and categorical syllogism (see chapter 11.2–3), his statement that induction is an

252 See, for instance, Ibn Sīnā, *al-Ishārāt wal-tanbīhāt*, vol. 1, pp. 365–370; Avicenna, *Remarks and Admonitions*, pp. 129–130; see also Hallaq, *Ibn Taymiyya*, pp. 114, n. 190.1, 117, n. 197.1.

253 Ibn Taymiyya, *al-Radd*, (especially concise) pp. 300–303 (in fact, he treats that subject until the end of the book); slightly shortened by al-Suyūṭī, *Jahd al-qarīḥa*, pp. 314–316; Hallaq, *Ibn Taymiyya*, pp. 142–145.

254 Ibn Taymiyya, *al-Radd*, p. 201; al-Suyūṭī, *Jahd al-qarīḥa*, p. 290; Hallaq, *Ibn Taymiyya*, pp. 115–116. (I follow his translation except for the first sentence, where I want to stress Ibn Taymiyya's focus on the "common factor"; Hallaq renders *al-qadr al-mushtarak* here as "the entire class").

inference from one particular to another that, if it could be completed, would reveal their common factor, might be understood as an acceptance of the existence of universals *in rebus*.

Ibn Taymiyya lays much more stress on a comparison between the first figure of categorical syllogism (as it appears in Aristotelian syllogistics)[255] and analogy, the main method in Islamic jurisprudence. He wants to disprove the rationalists' assertion that, because of its inference from a particular to a particular, analogy is inferior to syllogism and that the latter alone can lead to certainty.[256] In fact, he asserts that the two methods can be converted into each other.[257] Al-Fārābī had already shown the possibility of transforming an analogy into a categorical syllogism and al-Ghazālī demonstrated it once again.[258] However, both of them and more explicitly Ibn Sīnā, probably Ibn Taymiyya's main source of Peripatetic logic, held syllogism in higher esteem.[259]

Analogy (*qiyās al-taʿlīl* or *al-tamthīl*), by Ibn Taymiyya's times, was already much advanced in comparison with the time of Aristotle and his Greek commentators.[260] Ibn Taymiyya mainly uses the *qiyās*

---

255 Ibn Taymiyya, *al-Radd*, p. 6.

256 See, for instance, Ibn Sīnā, *al-Ishārāt wal-tanbīhāt*, vol. 1, pp. 368–369; Avicenna, *Remarks and Admonitions*, pp. 129–130; see also Hallaq, *Ibn Taymiyya*, pp. 114 n. 190.1, 117 n. 197.1.

257 Ibn Taymiyya, *al-Radd*, pp. 116 (*qiyās al-tamthīl wa-qiyās al-shumūl sawāʾ*), 121, 299, 351–364; al-Suyūṭī, *Jahd al-qarīḥa*, pp. 230, 234, 314, 328–331; Hallaq, *Ibn Taymiyya*, pp. 44–45, 50, 142, 156–159.

258 *Kitāb al-Qiyās*, in: al-Fārābī, *al-Manṭiq*, vol. 2, pp. 11–64, here p. 54–55. He already uses the example of the prohibition of *khamr*; idem, Kitāb al-Qiyās al-ṣaghīr, in: ibid., pp. 65–93, here p. 68; Street, Arabic Logic, p. 539; for a detailed analysis of al-Farābī 's arguments and his critique of analogy, see Schöck, Cornelia: *Koranexegese, Grammatik und Logik. Zum Verhältnis von arabischer und aristotelischer Urteils-, Konsequenz- und Schlusslehre*, Leiden and Boston 2006, pp. 342–372; van Ess pointed out that al-Fārābī dismissed the method of *ṭard* and *ʿaks* (*Die Erkenntnislehre*, p. 391); al-Ghazālī: *Kitāb al-Mustaṣfā min ʿilm al-uṣūl, bi-sharḥ Muḥibb Allāh b. ʿAbd al-Shakūr (al-Bihārī)*, Cairo, Bulaq 1322–1324/1904–1906, pp. 38–39; al-Ghazālī: *Miʿyār al-ʿilm fī fann al-manṭiq*, Beirut 1983, pp. 98–100, 109, see 123–124; Marmura, Ghazali's Attitude, pp. 105, 110, n. 14, 17; Heer, Ibn Taymiyah's Empiricism, p. 113; Rudolph, Die Neubewertung der Logik, pp. 77–79.

259 Ibn Sīnā equates analogy with the Aristotelian *parádeigma* (*tamthīl*) and considers it valable only for dialectical, not for demonstrative proofs (van Ess, *Die Erkenntnislehre*, p. 392); see the previous note.

260 For other forms of analogical inferences in jurisprudence, see Hallaq, *Ibn Taymiyya*, p. 44, n. 59.1; Bernand, M.: Ḳiyās, in: *EI*², vol. 5 (1986), pp. 238–

al-taʿlīl (causational inference), and its subdivisions, the co-extensive analogy (*qiyās al-ṭard*) und the co-exclusive analogy (*qiyās al-ʿaks*).[261] Although he does not restrict its use to juridical questions in his refutations of logic and the rationalists, he nevertheless exemplifies it with a well-known case of co-extensive analogy from jurisprudence, which he presents at the same time as a piece of evidence of the possibility of converting it into the first figure of categorical syllogism. It is the example of the inference from the revealed prohibition of wine from grapes (*khamr al-ʿinab*) to wine from other fruits (*nabīdh*).[262] The inference relies on their common factor (*al-qadr al-mushtarak*), i. e., their intoxicating nature, which constitutes the *ratio legis* (*ʿilla*, *manāṭ*, *jāmiʿ*) in an analogy or the middle term (*ḥadd awsaṭ*) in a syllogism.[263] It can easily be given the form of a syllogism: "All inebriants are forbidden, wine from fruits other than grapes is an inebriant. Therefore,

---

242; see van Ess, *Die Erkenntnislehre*, pp. 382–394, for a summary of the devolopment of analogy in *kalām* theology.

261 Ibn Taymiyya, *al-Radd*, p. 371; al-Suyūṭī, *Jahd al-qarīḥa*, p. 332; Hallaq, *Ibn Taymiyya*, p. 161; Ibn Taymiyya, Taqī al-Dīn Aḥmad: Risālat al-Qiyās, in: *Risālatān fī Maʿnā al-qiyās li-shaykhay al-islām Ibn Taymiyya wa-Ibn al Qayyim*, ed. by ʿAbd al-Fattāḥ Maḥmūd ʿUmar, ʿAmmān 1407/1987, pp. 11–89, here p. 14; Haqq, Sirajul: Ibn-Taimiyya's Conception of Analogy and Consensus, in: *Islamic Culture* 17 (1943), pp. 77–87; Jokisch, Benjamin: *Islamisches Recht in Theorie und Praxis. Analyse einiger kaufrechtlicher Fatwas von Taqī'd-Dīn Aḥmad b. Taymiyya*, Berlin 1996; Madjid, *Ibn Taymiyya on Kalām and Falsafa*, pp. 106–111; Al-Matroudi, Abdul Hakim I.: *The Ḥanbalī School of Law and Ibn Taymiyyah. Conflict or Conciliation*, London and New York 2006, pp. 72–74; Rapoport, Yossef: Ibn Taymiyya's Radical Legal Thought. Rationalism, Pluralism and the Primacy of Intention, in: Yossef Rapoport and Shahab Ahmed (eds.): *Ibn Taymiyya and His Times*, Karachi 2010 (he elaborates on *qiyās* and other juridical methods of Ibn Taymiyya, such as *istiḥsān* and the judgment according to *maṣlaḥa* and mentions further studies on Ibn Taymiyya's legal thought; I thank him for providing me with his article when it was in press).

262 In one passage in *al-Radd* (p. 116; al-Suyūṭī, *Jahd al-qarīḥa*, pp. 230–231; Hallaq, *Ibn Taymiyya*, pp. 44–45), Ibn Taymiyya does not explain *nabīdh*; elsewhere, however, he does, subsuming in it the wine made from the grains (*ḥubūb*) of wheat (*ḥinṭa*), barley (*shaʿīr*), rice (*ruzz*), or other things (*al-Radd*, p. 372; in al-Suyūṭī's abridgement, this clarification is missing; here he compares simply *khamr* [without the specification *al-ʿinab*] with *nabīdh*). For the usage of this inference in other of Ibn Taymiyya's writings, see Hoover, *Ibn Taymiyya's Theodicy*, p. 57–58, n. 146. See also above, chapter 10.1.

263 Ibn Taymiyya uses the four terms (*al-Radd*, pp. 116, 212, 372; al-Suyūṭī, *Jahd al-qarīḥa*, pp. 230, 300, 333, Hallaq, *Ibn Taymiyya*, pp. 45, 127, 162); see below, n. 274.

wine from fruits other than grapes is forbidden."[264] This is exactly the example al-Ghazālī had already used.[265]

This rival seems to have inspired Ibn Taymiyya also in view of his interpretation of the balance spoken of in the Koran.[266] Still, whereas al-Ghazālī declared that logic, i.e., syllogistics in general, was that balance, Ibn Taymiyya warns in one place against understanding the balance as Greek logic[267] and states in another that it is "not limited to Greek logic."[268] This second, more moderate attitude is probably due to the fact that he himself explicitly identifies the balance with the inference (*qiyās*) itself, "be it the juridical (*al-sharʿī*) or the rational (*al-ʿaqlī*) one,"[269] that is with juridical analogy and syllogism. In another instance, he calls the balance the "common factor," the "universal quality in the mind" analogy, to which categorical syllogism and immediate insight can lead.[270] He thereby again appears as a "moder-

264 Ibn Taymiyya, *al-Radd*, p. 116 (al-Suyūṭī, *Jahd al-qarīḥa*, pp. 230–231; Hallaq, *Ibn Taymiyya*, pp. 44–45; Heer, Ibn Taymiyah's Empiricism, p. 111; Ibn Taymiyya does not explicitly mention the conclusion; in the conclusion of my article "Ibn Taymīyyas Kritik", p. 211, I erroneously wrote "Trauben-Wein" instead of "Nabīdh-Wein"); see also above, n. 262. The co-exclusive inference would be to find a case where wine is inebriant, but not forbidden or where wine is not inebriant but forbidden (van Ess, *Die Erkenntnislehre*, p. 384).

265 Al-Ghazālī, *Kitāb al-Mustaṣfā*, pp. 38–39.

266 Al-Ghazālī dedicated a whole book to the proof that God taught man the main rules of syllogism in the Koran. See Rudolph, Die Neubewertung der Logik, pp. 86–88. For a partial translation into English, see al-Ghazālī: *Deliverance from Error. An Annotated Translation of "al-Munqidh min al-ḍalāl" and Other Relevant Works of al-Ghazālī*, transl. by Richard Joseph McCarthy, Louisville 1980, Appendix III *al-Qisṭās al-mustaqīm* ("the Correct Balance"), pp. 245–283. The title of the book *al-Qisṭās al-mustaqīm* explicitly refers to the Koranic verse (17:35), where God urges man to give full measure and to weigh with the just balance.

267 Ibn Taymiyya, *al-Radd*, p. 373; al-Suyūṭī, *Jahd al-qarīḥa*, p. 333; Hallaq, *Ibn Taymiyya*, p. 162.

268 Ibn Taymiyya, *al-Radd*, p. 383; al-Suyūṭī, *Jahd al-qarīḥa*, p. 335; Hallaq, *Ibn Taymiyya*, p. 164.

269 Ibn Taymiyya, *al-Radd*, p. 373; it is not included in al-Suyūṭī's abridgement.

270 Ibn Taymiyya refers to two other verses of the Koran, namely 42:17 and 42:25, where God says that He sent down the scripture and the balance (*al-mīzān*) (*al-Radd*, p. 371; al-Suyūṭī, *Jahd al-qarīḥa*, p. 332; Hallaq, *Ibn Taymiyya*, p. 161; Madjid, *Ibn Taymiyya on Kalām and Falsafa*, p. 108 (he inadvertently referred to *al-Radd*, pp. 271–273, instead of pp. 371–373)). Ibn Taymiyya does not mention al-Ghazālī's work, but it is likely that he had the latter's interpretation of the balance in mind – firstly because of its usual interpretation as "justice," as he himself states, and secondly because he warns against under-

ate realist" and not a "nominalist." The following quotations support these assumptions:

> One of the greatest attributes of the intellect is the apprehension of similitude and difference. Once the intellect conceives of two similar things, it knows that they are alike, and thus it applies the same judgement to both of them, such as, for example when it observes two pools of water, two piles of soil, or two portions of air. The intellect thus applies a universal judgement (*ḥukm kullī*) to the common factor.[271]

Ibn Taymiyya then states in the course of his explanation of the co-extensive and the co-exclusive analogy:

> God said that He sent down the Balance just as He revealed the Book, so that people may uphold equity (*qisṭ*). The means by which similar qualities and measures are known belongs to the Balance. And so does that by which differences among different things are known.[272]

As an example, he mentions the prohibition of grape wine and what resembles it in respect to the reason for the prohibition[273] and concludes that

> the common factor – namely, the middle term[274] – is the Balance[275] which God has revealed into our hearts so that we may weigh one (thing) and treat it as the other. By so doing we will not draw a distinction between two similar things. Valid inference (*al-qiyās al-ṣaḥīḥ*) thus stems from

---

standing the balance as being Greek logic or at least as being limited to Greek logic.

271 Ibn Taymiyya, *al-Radd*, p. 371; al-Suyūṭī, *Jahd al-qarīḥa*, p. 332; Hallaq, *Ibn Taymiyya*, p. 160. The Arabic expressions in angular brackets in this and the following quotations are mine. Otherwise I follow Hallaq's translation.

272 Ibn Taymiyya, *al-Radd*, p. 371; al-Suyūṭī, *Jahd al-qarīḥa*, pp. 332–333; Hallaq, *Ibn Taymiyya*, pp. 161–162.

273 Al-Suyūṭī abridged the passage concerning the prohibition (see above, n. 262).

274 Hallaq, *Ibn Taymiyya*, p. 162, translates *al-ʿilla* here as "middle term", and Ibn Taymiyya definitively uses it also in that sense (see Ibn Taymiyya, *al-Radd*, p. 364; al-Suyūṭī, *Jahd al-qarīḥa*, p. 331; Hallaq, *Ibn Taymiyya*, p. 159) and not only in the sense of *ratio legis*. In this case, he obviously uses it in both senses.

275 He repeats this identification a little later in even more explicit terms: "The Balance is the sound inference (*al-aqyisa al-ṣaḥīḥa*) that encompasses equating two similar things and differentiating between two dissimilar things, whether the form of that inference is a categorical syllogism or an analogy. But the forms of analogy are the source, and they are more perfect [than the syllogism]. The balance is the common factor, namely the middle term (*jāmiʿ*)." (Ibn Taymiyya, *al-Radd*, p. 383; al-Suyūṭī, *Jahd al-qarīḥa*, p. 335; Hallaq, *Ibn Taymiyya*, p. 164).

> the justice God has commanded. He who knows the universal without knowing the particular will have possession of the Balance only. The purpose of the Balance is to weigh those matters existing extramentally, for if it were not for their particulars the universals would not be considered (*fal-kulliyyāt law lā juzʾiyyātuhā al-muʿayyanāt*[276] *lam yakun bihā iʿtibār*) – just as without the weighable objects the Balance would be needless. There is no doubt that if a weighable object is weighed against another object by means of the Balance – which is the common, universal quality in the mind (*al-waṣf al-mushtarak al-kullī*[277] *fī al-ʿaql*) – such weighing will be more perfect than that in which any of the individual particulars present in the mind is weighed in the absence of another.[278]

Ibn Taymiyya thus leaves no doubt that he considers the common factors to be the intramental universals. Besides their intramental existence, the common factors must, however, also have an extramental existence in the particulars, otherwise reason would be unable to grasp them. And Ibn Taymiyya clearly admits this here by speaking of "the universals' particulars."

Thus, Ibn Taymiyya reveals himself again as a "moderate realist." Like the Peripatetics, he also shares the conviction that the certainty of the conclusion is not dependent on the form, but on the premises, i. e., the subject matter.[279]

Nevertheless, Ibn Taymiyya tries to overcome the logicians by declaring their most cherished judgment, the first figure of the categorical syllogism, to be superfluous inasmuch as it would be conceivable by innate intelligence (*fiṭra*) and thus be immediate knowledge.[280] Despite the fact that rendering the first figure of the categorical syllogism as superfluous would render analogy superfluous as well – since the common factor can, in his view, be grasped without inference by

---

276 Al-Suyūṭī has *al-muʿayyana* (*Jahd al-qarīḥa*, p. 333).

277 Al-Suyūṭī has *al-kullī al-mushtarak* (ibid., p. 333).

278 Ibn Taymiyya, *al-Radd*, p. 372; al-Suyūṭī, *Jahd al-qarīḥa*, p. 333; Hallaq, *Ibn Taymiyya*, p. 162.

279 Ibn Taymiyya, *al-Radd*, pp. 116, 121; al-Suyūṭī, *Jahd al-qarīḥa*, pp. 230, 234; Hallaq, *Ibn Taymiyya*, pp. 44–45, n. 60, 50, n. 67. See, for instance, Ibn Sīnā, *al-Ishārāt wal-tanbīhāt*, vol. 1, pp. 460–472; Avicenna, *Remarks and Admonitions*, pp. 148–151; al-Ghazālī, *Miʿyār al-ʿilm*, pp. 180–181.

280 Ibn Taymiyya, *al-Radd*, pp. 297 (*al-fiṭra tuṣawwiru al-qiyās al-ṣaḥīḥ min ghayr taʿlīm*; he is speaking here of the first figure syllogism), 167, 200, 293–294; al-Suyūṭī, *Jahd al-qarīḥa*, pp. 314, 266, 289, 313; Hallaq, *Ibn Taymiyya*, pp. 141–142, n. 254, 88, n. 136, 114, n. 189, 141, n. 253.

people with good mental conditions[281] – he again forces an open door. One of his main opponents in logic, Ibn Sīnā, also held that the middle term of a syllogism, i.e., what is usually apprehended through an act of inference, can be an immediate knowledge. Ibn Sīnā calls the mental power that is able to spontaneously grasp the middle term at some instance *fiṭra* and at another *ḥads* ("intuition").[282] In addition, he considers it a kind of infallible understanding and thus superior to reflection, which can err,[283] a view that Ibn Taymiyya, again, advocates.[284] In fact, by the 13th century, *ḥads* and the *ḥadsiyyāt* had gained many supporters, although *ḥads* seems not to have been "a tool of scientific investigation that is to be honed and applied in order to solve problems, but rather a way of explaining, *post facto*, how a thinker hit upon the solution to a difficult problem."[285]

Ibn Taymiyya, too, regards *ḥads* as a means of apprehension providing evident, certain knowledge. He seems, however, to prefer not to count it as another kind of perception, and he apparently nowhere identifies it *expressis verbis* with *fiṭra*. Instead, he classes the *ḥadsiyyāt* as an experience, admitting that one might say that empirical matters relate "to the *very acts* of the experiencers," whereas the *ḥadsiyyāt* relate to experiences that are out of the reach of one's own acts, such

281 Ibn Taymiyya, *al-Radd*, pp. 373–374; al-Suyūṭī, *Jahd al-qarīḥa*, p. 330; Hallaq, *Ibn Taymiyya*, p. 159; see also above, chapter 10.2.

282 Dimitri Gutas has translated and scrutinized Ibn Sīnā's many statements on *ḥads*, which all amount to equating the knowledge of the immediate grasping of the middle terms with *ḥads* ("intuition"), be it in "an infinitesimally short period of time" or "all at once" (*Avicenna and the Aristotelian Tradition*, pp. 159–176, esp. 163, 165); see Langermann who assumes that the slight difference in time did not concern the advocates of that way of understanding (Langermann, Tzvi: Ibn Kammūna and the "New Wisdom" of the Thirteenth Century, in: *Arabic Sciences and Philosophy* 15 (2005), pp. 277–327, 288–289, 292). For Ibn Sīnā's identification of *ḥads* with *fiṭra*, see Gutas, *Avicenna and the Aristotelian Tradition*, p. 170 and Gobillot, *La conception originelle*, pp. 128–129).

283 Ibn Sīnā, *De Anima*, p. 250; Davidson, Herbert A.: *Alfarabi, Avicenna, and Averroes on Intellect. Their Cosmologies, Theories of the Active Intellect, and Theories of Human Intellect*, New York and Oxford 1992, pp. 101–102; Langermann, Ibn Kammūna, p. 288.

284 It is questionable, however, whether Ibn Taymiyya would have agreed to count this immediate understanding among the "powers of prophethood" and to regard it as a "sacred power (*quwwa qudsiyya*) that is the highest rank of human powers", as Ibn Sīnā does (*De Anima*, p. 250).

285 Langermann, Ibn Kammūna, p. 296.

as the connection between the sun and the shapes of the moon.[286] Ibn Taymiyya, in fact, not did reduce *fiṭra* to "intuition" (*ḥads*) in the sense of the immediate grasping of the middle term. As a broader concept of "innate intelligence," it bears for him the meaning of "immediate insight"[287] into knowledge in general, be it scientific or religious.

There are, however, fundamental differences between Ibn Taymiyya's apprehension of analogy and categorical syllogism and their understanding by his enemies, some of which are mentioned in the following. Most followers of al-Fārābī and Ibn Sīnā regarded the celestial, active intellect (*al-ʿaql al-faʿʿāl*) as the "giver of the forms" (*wāhib al-ṣuwar*) to all matters in the sublunar world and a communicator of principal, abstract thoughts to the human mind.[288] For Ibn Sīnā, it is also the provider of the middle term and the conclusions to the human mind by *ḥads*.[289] Ibn Taymiyya, by contrast, vigorously rejects the whole theory of the celestial intellects and of the active intellect as the creator of sublunary forms and of the universal knowledge in the mind.[290] Furthermore, whereas for the Peripatetics the middle term in the categorical syllogism has to be an essential attribute, for Ibn Taymiyya this is not a necessary condition. Although his critique of the real definition does not lead him to the conclusion that particular

286 Ibn Taymiyya, *al-Radd*, pp. 93, 302 (very similar and clearer in idem, *Naqḍ al-manṭiq*, p. 202); al-Suyūṭī, *Jahd al-qarīḥa*, p. 316; Hallaq, *Ibn Taymiyya*, p. 144 (I do not follow Hallaq in his translation of *al-ḥadsiyyāt takūn ʿan afʿālihim* as "the former are *about* their acts", but understand it as "the intuitions are out of the reach of their [the experiencers'] acts," because of Ibn Taymiyya's explanation in *al-Radd* on p. 302). The example of the explanation of the moon's light seems to have been often the single concrete example of intuitive scientific knowledge cited by the advocates of *ḥads* (Langermann, Ibn Kammūna, pp. 287, 289, 291). For a relation between *ḥads* and experience, see Langermann, Ibn Kammūna, pp. 296–299.

287 I was inspired to choose "insight" as a translation by Davidson's (*Alfarabi*, p. 99) and Langermann's (Ibn Kammūna, p. 288, n. 31) preference for it as an English equivalent for *ḥads*.

288 Davidson, Herbert A.: Alfarabi and Avicenna on the Active Intellect, in: *Viator* 3 (1972) 109–178; idem, *Alfarabi*, see index, s. v. *active intellect*.

289 Davidson, *Alfarabi*, pp. 100–102.

290 Ibn Taymiyya, *al-Radd*, pp. 102–106, 115; much shortened in: al-Suyūṭī, *Jahd al-qarīḥa*, pp. 220–221, 229; Hallaq, *Ibn Taymiyya*, pp. 33, 43. He rebuts the theory of the originating power of the celestial spheres also in other writings, such as his tract about the philosopher's proof of God as the first cause, *Majmūʿat al-Fatāwā*, al-mujallad 17, Cairo, vol. 9, pp. 158–163 (see Madjid, *Ibn Taymiyya on Kalām and Falsafa*, pp. 158–181; Hoover, *Ibn Taymiyya's Theodicy*, p. 160).

things have no essences that make them belong to a species or genus (see chapters 10.1, 11.2), he also accepts attributes as common factors, which a Peripatetic would regard as accidental. This is a natural result of the equation of syllogism and analogy. The juridical analogy in particular often has premises given by a Koranic verse or a saying of the prophet Muḥammad, which Peripatetic logicians would not classify as essential attributes. Thus, jurists often take the faculty of upsetting good behavior as the *ratio legis* for the prohibition of alcoholic drinks other than grape wine, and Ibn Taymiyya does not deny but supports this;[291] upsetting good behavior is an attribute that might compromise many other things besides alcohol.

In further contrast to the logicians, Ibn Taymiyya held analogy in higher esteem than syllogism. He argues that in analogy there is always an original case of a particular, which makes it easier for the mind to understand the common universal.[292]

Another eminent disparity lies in the fact that Muslim philosophers regard syllogism as *the* way to establish God's existence, whereas Ibn Taymiyya denies to both kinds of inferences, syllogism and analogy, the ability to establish the knowledge of God and the prophecy (*ithbāt al-ʿilm bil-ṣāniʿ wal-nubuwwāt*) and acknowledges it only to inferences by signs or the *a fortiori* argument (see chapter 12).[293]

Still, for Ibn Taymiyya, the weakness of analogy and syllogism does not diminish their value. Ibn Taymiyya is convinced that "an authoritative wording of the prophets cannot be in conflict with a sound inference (*qiyās ṣaḥīḥ*), be it a juridical or a rational one."[294] Where there

291 Ibn Taymiyya also mentions it as a *ratio legis* (*al-Radd*, p. 372; al-Suyūṭī, *Jahd al-qarīḥa*, p. 333; Hallaq, *Ibn Taymiyya*, p. 162); see Bernand, Ḳiyās, p. 241.

292 Ibn Taymiyya, *al-Radd*, p. 364; al-Suyūṭī, *Jahd al-qarīḥa*, p. 331; Hallaq, *Ibn Taymiyya*, p. 159.

293 Ibn Taymiyya, *al-Radd*, p. 356; al-Suyūṭī, *Jahd al-qarīḥa*, p. 329; Hallaq, *Ibn Taymiyya*, pp. 157–158. Ibn Taymiyya argues similarly in his *Risālat al-Qiyās* (p. 50) when he blames the philosophers and *kalām* theologians for their drawing of analogies between matters, such as the necessity of God and the necessity of the creatures, which, in fact, "impose the outmost difference." I share Jon Hoover's interpretation of this passage that "in matters of theological doctrine, Ibn Taymiyya argues that the juristic analogy is always invalid because it brings God and creatures into a relationship of direct comparison" (*Ibn Taymiyya's Theodicy*, p. 57).

294 *Fa-lā yakhtalifu naṣṣ thābit ʿan al-rasūl wa-qiyās ṣaḥīḥ – lā qiyās sharʿī* [analogy] *wa-lā ʿaqlī* [syllogism] (Ibn Taymiyya, *al-Radd*, p. 373; it is not included in al-Suyūṭī's abridgement); see his *Risālat al-Qiyās*, where he also states that what is in the Sharia cannot contradict the sound inference (p. 14); for further

seems to be a contradiction, there are three possibilities on the side of the wording (*naṣṣ*): either the indicant established on the basis of the wording is corrupt, or the wording itself is not authoritative, or the indicant is not in conformity with what it is meant to indicate. On the side of the inference, one or all of the premises can be corrupt. Ibn Taymiyya here explicitly refers to his *Darʾ taʿāruḍ al-ʿaql wal-naql*.[295]

In fact, in order to save theology from philosophical inferences that are based on the common factor, Ibn Taymiyya would not have needed to deny the universals *in rebus*. He could have simply argued that syllogism is not fit for the investigation of God, just as juridical analogy is not fit for it, since God has no like and cannot be placed on an equal footing with other particulars. The reason for Ibn Taymiyya's rejection of syllogistic logic therefore seems to lie in his holistic view of the basis and consequences of Peripatetic reasoning.

12. Methods of Inferences Adopted from the Early *kalām* Theologians

There are other methods of inference that Ibn Taymiyya indeed adopts from the early *kalām* theologians.[296] He presents them as an ostensible challenge to the Peripatetic logicians, who restrict the methods of inference to syllogism, induction, and analogy[297] and who see these as

references, see Rapoport, Ibn Taymiyya's Radical Legal Thought, ch. Legal Theory. Correct Analogy and Qurʾānic Rationalism.

295 Ibn Taymiyya, *al-Radd*, p. 373 (the passage is not included in al-Suyūṭī's abridgement); see his slightly less differentiated position in the *Risālat al-Qiyās* (p. 14, translated and commented upon by Rapoport, Ibn Taymiyya's Radical Legal Thought, chapter: Legal Theory. Correct Analogy and Qurʾānic Rationalism, n. 261.)

296 They ressemble methods from Stoic logic. For parallels between the logic of the early *kalām* theologians and the stoics, see van Ess, Josef: The Logical Structure of Islamic Theology, in: Gustave Edmund von Grunebaum (ed.): *Logic in Classical Islamic Culture. First Giorgio Levi della Vida Biennial Conference; May 12, 1967*, Los Angeles, Wiesbaden 1970, pp. 21–50, here p. 27. Still, it is unclear whether Stoic logic and philosophy has been appropriated by Muslim theologians, see Gutas, Dimitri: Pre-Plotinian Philosophy in Arabic (other than Platonism and Aristotelianism). A Review of the Sources, in: *Aufstieg und Niedergang der Römischen Welt* 36 (1994), pp. 4939–4973, 4959–4962.

297 Ibn Taymiyya, *al-Radd*, p. 162; al-Suyūṭī, *Jahd al-qarīḥa*, pp. 261–262; Hallaq, *Ibn Taymiyya*, p. 83, n. 126. See for instance Ibn Sīnā, *al-Ishārāt wal-tanbīhāt*, vol. 1, pp. 365–369; Avicenna, *Remarks and Admonitions*, pp. 129–130.

the sole methods to prove God's existence. Ibn Taymiyya blames them for not taking into account inference by signs or indicators, wherein the existence of one particular entails the absence of the other and vice versa.[298] Ibn Taymiyya calls it "God's method of proof through signs" (*istidlāluhu taʿālā bil-āyāt*),[299] and considers it an immediate – that is a *fiṭrī* knowledge – insofar as the signs indicate the existence of one Creator.[300] He cites the examples that the existence of daylight indicates the rising of the sun (an inference which he supports also by God's signs in the Koran)[301] and that the rising of one star indicates the setting of another.[302] Here again, Ibn Taymiyya implicitly assumes that God has created a stable order of nature. He explains that this kind of inference could be understood either as that from a particular to a particular ("that from a particular rising of the sun there is a particular daylight") or as "an inference that proceeds from universal to universal" ("that from the genus of daylight there follows the genus of the rising of the sun").[303] By speaking of a "genus of daylight" and of the genus as a universal, Ibn Taymiyya is once again accepting what he otherwise so vehemently rejects.

The other kind of inference, which he blames his enemies for neglecting, is the *a fortiori* argument (*qiyās al-awlā*; *via eminentiae*), which was used, as Ibn Taymiyya emphasizes, by the early Muslims (*salaf*).[304] He also calls it "the method of the prophets" (*ṭarīqat al-anbiyāʾ*) and holds that "the rational, demonstrative inferences mentioned in the Koran" (*al-aqyisa al-ʿaqliyya al-burhāniyya al-madhkūra fī al-Qurʾān*) are of this kind.[305] In fact, this kind of inference is restricted to establish that God "has no like, and He

298 Ibn Taymiyya, *al-Radd*, pp. 163–165; shortened: al-Suyūṭī, *Jahd al-qarīḥa*, pp. 262–264; Hallaq, *Ibn Taymiyya*, pp. 84–85, n. 128–131.
299 Ibn Taymiyya, *al-Radd*, p. 151; al-Suyūṭī, *Jahd al-qarīḥa*, p. 252; Hallaq, *Ibn Taymiyya*, p. 71, n. 107.
300 Hallaq, Ibn Taymiyya on the Existence of God, pp. 58–60.
301 Koran (17:12); Ibn Taymiyya, *al-Radd*, p. 151; al-Suyūṭī, *Jahd al-qarīḥa*, p. 252; Hallaq, *Ibn Taymiyya*, p. 71.
302 Ibn Taymiyya, *al-Radd*, 163–165; shortened: al-Suyūṭī, *Jahd al-qarīḥa*, pp. 262–264; Hallaq, *Ibn Taymiyya*, pp. 84–85, n. 128–131.
303 Ibn Taymiyya, *al-Radd*, p. 163; al-Suyūṭī, *Jahd al-qarīḥa*, p. 262; Hallaq, *Ibn Taymiyya*, p. 84.
304 Ibn Taymiyya, *al-Radd*, p. 154; al-Suyūṭī, *Jahd al-qarīḥa*, p. 255; Hallaq, *Ibn Taymiyya*, p. 74, n. 111. *A fortiori* arguments were used, for instance, by Ibn Ḥanbal (Hoover, *Ibn Taymiyya's Theodicy*, pp. 59–60, n. 150).
305 Ibn Taymiyya, *al-Radd*, pp. 150, 157; al-Suyūṭī, *Jahd al-qarīḥa*, p. 252; Hallaq, *Ibn Taymiyya*, pp. 71–72, n. 106–107.

cannot be subsumed under a universal whose instances are equal; the unblemished perfection affirmed of others is, *a fortiori*, affirmed of Him."[306] Jon Hoover has shown that Ibn Taymiyya uses the *a fortiori* extensively to prove God's wisdom and justice and thereby often draws inferences from human characteristics to display what applies all the more to God.[307] Obviously, in Ibn Taymiyya's eyes "the *a fortiori* argument preserves the unlikeness between God and creatures, which univocal use of analogy and syllogism fails to respect."[308] Ibn Taymiyya, thus, displays here a nominalistic attitude suggesting that "there is no longer any similarity between the referents of identical names when they are particularized in the Creator and the creature apart from the very names themselves."[309] Both of these two methods – the inference by sign and the *a fortiori* argument – reveal that Ibn Taymiyya conceives the Koran as bearing in itself rational proofs drawn from or concerned with the *ontological* sphere. Analogy included (see chapter 11), Ibn Taymiyya thus identifies three methods of inference mentioned in the Koran.

In fact, as has already been demonstrated several times, Ibn Taymiyya gives priority to scripture if it conflicts with reason.[310] His arguments rest on the presumption that "reason has proved the truth of scripture and the necessity of accepting that which the messenger has related."[311] Therefore, it cannot be given priority, because that would contradict its own verdict of the truth of scripture. However, when Ibn Taymiyya asserts that "the message brought by the apostle conforms with sound

---

306 Ibn Taymiyya, *al-Radd*, pp. 150, 154–157, 350–351; shortened: al-Suyūṭī, *Jahd al-qarīḥa*, pp. 252, 255; Hallaq, *Ibn Taymiyya*, pp. 71, 74–75.

307 Hoover, *Ibn Taymiyya's Theodicy*, pp. 56–62, 130–135, 156 et passim (see index, s. v. *highest similitude*).

308 Ibid., p. 62. See Wael B. Hallaq, who distinguishes between analogy and the *a fortiori* argument, arguing that in the latter case, in contrast to analogy, the similarity is no prerequisite and that "the *a fortiori* argument is asyllogistic, and has virtually nothing to do with the category of analogical inferences" (Hallaq, Wael B.: *A History of Islamic Legal Theories. An Introduction to Sunnī* uṣūl al-fiqh, Cambridge 1997, p. 99)

309 Hoover, *Ibn Taymiyya's Theodicy*, p. 51.

310 Heer, The Priority of Reason, pp. 190–191.

311 *Al-ʿaql qad dalla ʿalā ṣiḥḥat al-samʿ wa-wujūb qubūl mā akhbara bihi al-rasūl ṣallā Allāh ʿalayhi wa-sallam*, Ibn Taymiyya, *Darʾ taʿāruḍ al-ʿaql*, vol. 1, p. 170; Heer, The Priority of Reason, pp. 190–191. (I follow his translation). See Michot, *Lettre à Abū l-Fidāʾ*, pp. 18, 57–58; Hoover, *Ibn Taymiyya's Theodicy*, pp. 30–32.

tradition and uncontaminated reason,"[312] he does not limit reason to the teachings of the Koran and the soundly transmitted deeds and utterances of Muḥammad and his companions. "Uncontaminated" reason can lead man to truths independently from revelation, as has been shown in the last chapters. Still, revealed truths remain the touchstone. Scripture can correct errors, i.e., conclusions that reason has falsely considered true. Scripture is thus the ultimate measure of truth.

Conclusion

Ibn Taymiyya's critique of the rationalists, on the one hand, and his own epistemology, on the other, have to be seen against the background of the philosophical terminology, categories, and concepts which dominated wide realms of knowledge at his time. Many eminent *kalām* theologians and Sufis had accepted Peripatetic logic as *the* rational method to reach truth. Each of them, however, rejected philosophical metaphysical tenets that they saw in conflict with essential religious dogmas. Nonetheless, their own theories were more or less markedly imprinted by philosophy. Ibn Taymiyya did not escape this rule. As our glimpses into his struggle for and against reason have shown, intense preoccupation with the writings of the rationalists left distinct imprints on his terminology and on a key concept of his epistemology and ontology. Al-Dhahabī's somewhat polemical statement about Ibn Taymiyya's addiction to the poison of the philosophers was not completely ill-founded.

On the other hand, Ibn Taymiyya himself regarded logic and philosophy as a great danger, i.e., as a kind of poison that corrupts reason and distracts from what benefits the soul. He would certainly have vigorously disputed any influence of the philosophers and the late *kalām* theologians on his own doctrines, let alone being called a philosopher. In his two closely interlinked works, *al-Radd ʿalā al-manṭiqiyyīn* and *Darʾ taʿāruḍ al-ʿaql wal-naql*, he harshly criticizes the philosophers' ways of reasoning and concept of reason in general, dismissing the claim that Peripatetic logic is the sole and universal means to truth.

Although he decisively denies its universality, his struggle against logic does not lead him to negate the existence of a universal canon

312 *Al-Qawl alladhī jāʾa bihi al-rasūl wa-huwa al-muwāfiq li-ṣaḥīḥ al-manqūl wa-ṣarīḥ al-ʿuqūl*, Ibn Taymiyya, *Darʾ taʿāruḍ al-ʿaql*, vol. 9, p. 67.

of true understanding. Instead, he posits a faculty of true reasoning shared by all healthy human beings, the "clear reason" that is uncontaminated by Peripatetic logic, and he asserts the complete congruence of its knowledge with that of "sound religious tradition." Ibn Taymiyya gives no systematic account of his concept of "clear reason" and his epistemology in general, but his many statements concerning the immediate ways to true knowledge and the methods of cognition and inferences he considers capable of producing true knowledge allow a rather precise idea of it. If my understanding of some of the main features of Ibn Taymiyya's epistemology is right, the "uncontaminated reason" comprises more than mere "common sense." Indeed, Ibn Taymiyya diverges much less from some major Peripatetic epistemological principles and interlinked ontological assumptions than he often pretends to do, especially in the case of his overall denial of an extramental existence of the universals.

Yet Ibn Taymiyya himself states at the very beginning of his "Refutation of the Logicians" – right after his declaration that logic is superfluous – that he first considered the propositions of logic as true and then discovered the falseness of "some of them," thereby clearly stating that he holds others to be true, and he frankly admits it in regard to the form of the first figure of categorical syllogism. Other points of congruity, however, are not mentioned. Among the main ways that provide immediate, i.e., certain, evident knowledge, Ibn Taymiyya counts sense perceptions, experiences, multiply transmitted reports, and widespread propositions. By including widespread propositions among immediate knowledge, he regarded a broader spectrum of knowledge as certain than that regarded by the philosophers and some "later" *kalām* theologians.

But the remaining congruity is great. Ibn Taymiyya's belief in the truth of sense perception was, in principle, shared by friend and foe, although his conviction that concepts are formed directly by the senses was rather uncommon. In addition, Ibn Taymiyya left open some questions that were much disputed, namely how to conceive "errors of the senses" or false judgments about right perceptions. The distinction Ibn Taymiyya adopts between necessary knowledge and acquired knowledge had been made already in the early times of Muslim theology and was also held by the *falāsifa*. He is, however, closer to the "later" *kalām* theologians and the philosophers in asserting that certain knowledge is provided not only by sense apprehensions and multiply transmitted reports, but also by experience. He shares the conviction that some people are able to form concepts and judgments by immediate insight, i.e., without cogitation. The most striking congruity between Ibn Taymiyya's teaching and the theories of the philosophers, however, is the tenet of an extramental existence of the universals in the particulars and man's principal capacity to gain a true concept of them. This adherence to "moderate realism" stands in sharp contrast to his nominalistic attitude of denying any extramental existence of universals whatsoever in the course of his direct rejection of the real definition and the rules of syllogistic logic.

The "moderate realism" he reveals while explaining the causality of empirical matters and the common factor (*ratio legis*/middle term) on which the judgments of the juridical analogy and the philosophical syllogism are built rests on two main assumptions he shares with the Peripatetics. The first assumption is that there are similar particulars that are bestowed with powers or essences that are specific to their genus or species; and second, that their powers to "act" or "react" can be hindered by impediments.

On the basis of other writings of Ibn Taymiyya, Jon Hoover has convincingly shown that Ibn Taymiyya tried to give man the responsibility for his destiny without denying God's omnipotence. Causality thus looks "natural" from the "human perspective" while it is "instrumental" from the "divine perspective." God can, if He wills, hinder a cause from producing its effect by creating an impediment, or He can neglect to perfect the combination of causes needed for the effect. Still, in view of His all-embracing wise purpose, He will not change the order and natures He fixed for His creatures. Against this background of "compatibilism," Ibn Taymiyya's denial of the existence of universals *in rebus* gains no plausibility. That a cause can be hindered from producing its effect by an impediment or an imperfect combination of causes is not alien to the philosophers' view of causality. The difference lies in the explanation of such an impediment, and on this level, there is doubtless a huge gap between Ibn Taymiyya's and the philosophers' view of God and the universe.

The denial of the existence of universals *in rebus* also gains no plausibility if one takes into account Ibn Taymiyya's doctrine that God has no like. Since analogy and syllogism are built on the parity of the subjects of their propositions, he excludes analogy and syllogism as means to prove God's existence or to make statements about Him and thus takes a nominalistic attitude. He assumes, however, that God's creatures are not unique in kind, i.e., that they share common attributes, the universals *in rebus*, and that they can, therefore, be placed on an equal footing. Thus, it would have been enough to reject the rationalists' use of syllogism in the realm of theology.

His apologetic rebuttal of a key tenet of the Peripatetics that he himself adheres to is probably due to a holistic view that takes into account the foundations and the consequences of Peripatetic reasoning. It is thus comprehensible that he refers to the Koran as the authoritative source of the rational methods he himself counts among the demonstrative inferences, dismissing Peripatetic logic as a balance established by but one individual. In his two refutations, he expounds three kinds of such rational inferences that he considers capable of leading to true knowledge within and beyond the scope of revelation: 1) the inference by signs, 2) the *a fortiori* argument, and 3) the inference based on the "common factor," i.e., analogy and the first figure of the categorical syllogism. His equation of the last inference with the balance that God revealed to the hearts of men and spoke of in the Koran is reminiscent of al-Ghazālī's "correct balance". Yet whereas the latter identified this balance with Peripatetic syllogistics in general, Ibn Taymiyya warns against understanding it as such or at least underlines that it is "not limited to Greek logic," a statement that might reflect his acknowledgement of the search for the middle term. At any rate, the knowledge reached by these three kinds of inferences has an unmistakable corrective in the sound religious tradition, for God will not contradict himself. Outside the scope of revelation, there is no such absolute measure for true reasoning.

Seen as a whole, the philosophical elements in his own epistemology and the interlinked ontological theory should certainly not be overestimated. Ibn Taymiyya did not take over whole theories as such, but only tenets of his opponents that were functional for his own vision of God, man, and the universe. In regard to the deconstruction of the arguments of his rivals, Ibn Taymiyya is adroit. The fact that, in spite of their acuity, his refutations were apparently not much appreciated and transmitted outside the Ḥanbalī circles until the turn of the 19th to the 20th century is probably due to his extremist tendency to refute every theory and to offend everyone whom he considered guilty of not following his own, right path. Thereby, he discredited a wide range of theological, philosophical, and mystical reasoning about the divine world in his time and for many centuries to come.

The Curse of Philosophy

Ibn Taymiyya as a Philosopher in Contemporary Islamic Thought

Georges Tamer

Arabic philosophy, or *falsafa*, was born out of the translation of Greek and Syriac works of logic, philosophy and other sciences to meet the intellectual and practical challenges facing Muslims in Abbasid society. In the realm of Arabic, it flourished as a uniquely Muslim hybrid creatively integrating the intellectual traditions of Plato, Ptolemy and Aristotle. Though these thinkers were foreign and ancient, their reliance on sound reasoning established their reputation – especially that of Aristotle – as representatives of the highest truth to be attained by human intellectual endeavor.[1] In some cases, rational judgments might even be more esteemed than revealed knowledge; al-Fārābī (d. 339/950), for instance, did not consider religion to be the ultimate foundation unconditionally necessary for the existence of the virtuous city (*al-madīna al-fāḍila*), but rather viewed philosophy (*ḥikma*, also meaning "wisdom", itself the basis for wise leadership) as essential for the perfect society's survival.[2] Similarly, Ibn Rushd (d. 595/1198) granted authority to philosophers – whom he describes as those well established in knowledge – to interpret Koranic statements as metaphorical if seeming to contradict reason. In doing so, Ibn Rushd endorsed a method for establishing harmony between reason and religion on the

1 Maimonides, who ascribes to Aristotle perfect knowledge in regards to the sublunar world, adequately represents this pertinent view in the pre-modern period of Arabic philosophy; knowledge of the supralunar world, on the other hand, is reserved for the prophets: *Dalālat al-ḥāʾirīn*, edited by Ḥussayn Atay, Cairo n. d., part 2, chapter 22, pp. 342–343. English: Maimonides, Moses: *The Guide of the Perplexed*, translated by Shlomo Pines, Chicago 1963, pp. 319–320.

2 Al-Fārābī, Abū Naṣr: *Al-Farabi on the Perfect State. Abū Naṣr al-Fārābī's Mabādiʾ ārāʾ ahl al-madīna al-fāḍila, edited with introduction, translation and commentary by Richard Walzer*, Oxford 1985, chapter 15, § 14, p. 252.

ground of rationality. Rationality becomes, thus, the criterion for the soundness of the scripture.[3]

A counterpoint to this lineage existed in *kalām* and *fiqh*, with scholars such as Ibn Ḥanbal (d. 241/855)[4] and al-Ashʿarī (d. 324/936)[5] emphasizing the supremacy of revealed truth. This line of Islamic thought gained momentum in the twelfth century with the vast work of al-Ghazālī (d. 505/1111), whose rationalistic arguments against the *falāsifa* were seen as a staggering blow to philosophy, even though al-Ghazālī substantially included logic in the field of *fiqh*.[6] After al-Ghazālī, al-Shahrastāni (d. 548/1153)[7] and Fakhr al-Dīn al-Rāzī (d. 606/1209)[8] utilized rational arguments to attack *falsafa* from vari-

3 Ibn Rushd (Averroes): *Kitāb Faṣl al-maqāl with Its Appendix (Ḍamīma) and an Extract from Kitāb al-Kashf ʿan manāhiǧ al-adilla*, Arabic text edited by George F. Hourani, Leiden 1959, pp. 13–15.

4 On his position: Laoust, Henri: Aḥmad b. Ḥanbal, in: *EI*², vol. 1 (1960), pp. 272–277; Melchert, Christopher: *Ahmad ibn Hanbal*, Oxford 2006.

5 See Watt, W. Montgomery: al-As̲h̲ʿarī, Abu'l-Ḥasan, ʿAlī b. Ismāʿīl, in: *EI*², vol. 1 (1960), p. 694; McCarthy, Richard C.: *The Theology of al-Ashʿarī. The Arabic Texts of al-Ashʿarī's Kitāb al-Lumaʿ and Risālat Istiḥsān al-khawḍ fī ʿilm al-kalām, with briefly annotated translations, and appendices containing material pertinent to the study of al-Ashʿarī*, Beirut 1953.

6 Al-Ghazālī's views on rationality in relation to religion have been subject of intensive study; for his position in general, see Frank, Richard: *Al-Ghazālī and the Ashʿarite School*, Durham 1994; Ormsby, Eric: *Ghazali: The Revival of Islam*, Oxford 2008; Griffel, Frank: *Al-Ghazālī's Philosophical Theology*, Oxford 2009. Most recently: Girdner, Scott Michael: *Reasoning with Revelation. The Significance of the Koranic Contextualization of Philosophy in al-Ghazālī's* Mishkāt al-Anwār (the Niche of Lights), unpublished dissertation, Boston University 2010. See also the special issues of *The Muslim World* 101, 4 (October 2011) and 102, 1 (January 2012) on the occasion of al-Ghazālī's 900th anniversary with important contributions on several aspects of his work, and the forthcoming conference proceedings *Islam and Rationality. The Impact of al-Ghazālī*, vol. 1, edited by Georges Tamer and vol. 2, edited by Frank Griffel.

7 See Monnot, Guy: al-S̲h̲ahrastānī, in: *EI*², vol. 9 (1997), pp. 214–216. Al-Shahrastānī's position is best exposed in the treatise: al-Shahrastānī, Muḥammad b. ʿAbd al-Karīm: *Kitāb Muṣāraʿat al-falāsifa*, edited by Suhayr Muḥammad Mukhtār, Cairo 1976/1396; *Struggling with the Philosopher. A Refutation of Avicenna's Metaphysics;* a new Arabic edition and English translation of Moḥammed b. ʿAbd al-Karīm b. Aḥmad al-Shahrastānī's *Kitāb al-Muṣāraʿa* by Wilferd Madelung and Toby Mayer, London and New York 2001.

8 See Anawati, Georges: Fakhr al-Dīn al-Rāzī, in: *EI*², vol. 2 (1965), pp. 751–755. Al-Rāzī's main philosophical and theological work in particular contains his critical views on philosophy: al-Rāzī, Fakhr al-Dīn: *Kitāb al-Mabāḥith al-mashriqiyya fī ʿilm al-ilāhiyyāt wal-ṭabīʿiyyāt*, edited by Muḥammad al-Muʿtaṣim bi-llāh al-Baghdādī, Beirut 1990.

ous perspectives. Later, Ibn Taymiyya (d. 728/1328) delivered a ferocious attack against the Greek philosophers and their Muslim followers; this was articulated in his substantial critique of logic, *al-Radd ʿalā al-manṭiqiyyīn*,[9] as well as in his voluminous work *Darʾ taʿāruḍ al-ʿaql wal-naql* (Averting the Conflict between Reason and Religious Tradition)[10]. Ibn Taymiyya's diatribe is possibly the fiercest assault on *falsafa* in the intellectual history of Islam: criticizing his predecessors among theologians and theorists of jurisprudence for their laxity in refuting both logic and the basic metaphysical ideas of Greek and Muslim philosophers, Ibn Taymiyya upholds the utter supremacy of the Koran and the Sunna of the Prophet. These, he asserts, are the exclusive gates to correct knowledge.

Interestingly, however, authors seeking to renounce philosophy were ensnared by the very methods they sought to refute; al-Ghazālī, for instance, was viewed with suspicion among traditionalists for his speculative leanings and for his infusion of logic into *fiqh*; furthermore, he was roundly condemned for simultaneously employing and being inextricably entangled with the very philosophical methods he sought to disprove.[11] Ibn Taymiyya, likewise, found himself criticized for his simultaneous rejection and absorption of philosophical principles. Though he railed against philosophers and repudiated the exalted position of their science, the Shāfiʿī scholar and historian Shams al-Dīn al-Dhahabī (d. 748/1348), in a famous statement, excoriates Ibn Taymiyya for having "repeatedly swallowed the poison of the philosophers and their works" (*qad balaʿta sumūm al-falāsifa wa-muṣannafātihim marrāt*). As a result, Ibn Taymiyya's body had become addicted to the frequent use of poison so that it was secreted in the very bones; through this route, his speech had likewise been corrupted.[12] Through an organic, recip-

---

9 See below, footnote 20.

10 *Darʾ taʿāruḍ al-ʿaql wal-naql*, edited by Muḥammad Rashād Sālim, Riyadh 1399–1403/1979–1983. Both works, *al-Radd* and *Darʾ*, need to be subjected to comparative study in order to uncover their relationship and how they complement each other.

11 Paradigmatic for the traditionalist critique against al-Ghazālī is Ibn Taymiyya's famous dictum: *Wa-qad ankara aʾimmat al-dīn ʿalā Abī Ḥāmid hādhā fī kutubih, wa-qālū maraḍuhu al-shifāʾ, yaʿnī Shifāʾ Ibn Sīnā fī al-falsafa* (The religious leaders blamed Abū Ḥāmid for that what is in his books. They said: he is sick, and his sickness is "the healing", meaning by this Ibn Sīnā's book *The Healing* in philosophy), *Majmūʿ fatāwā Ibn Taymiyya*, Riyadh 1416/1995, vol. 10, p. 552.

12 For this, see Anke von Kügelgen's valuable contribution in the present volume, especially n. 16.

rocal process which they, perhaps, had not consciously perceived, the enemies of *falsafa* had become philosophers themselves.

In confirmation of this, contemporary Muslim authors have not hesitated to appoint Ibn Taymiyya – with not a little irony – to the philosophical field. Identifying him, especially in regards to his comprehensive view, as a true philosopher, they describe him as equal to or even superseding the most famous medieval Muslim philosophers. Indeed, for these authors, Ibn Taymiyya is considered an "unequal genius" who entered "the bewitched house of philosophy" without being harmed; he is "a great philosopher" whose refutation of Aristotle's logic is the foundation of John Stuart Mill's logic and David Hume's philosophy.[13] A more recent author even attributes to Ibn Taymiyya "unique philosophical views" capable of opening new horizons for Arabic-Islamic studies.[14] In a programmatic statement, the Egyptian Islamist Muḥammad ʿAmāra grants Ibn Taymiyya the title of "the philosopher and sage of Salafism" (*faylasūf al-salafiyya wa-ḥakīmuhā*), whose rationalism is a paradigm to be adopted in modern Islamic thought.[15]

Indeed, *Shaykh al-Islām* Ibn Taymiyya – who has often been criticized for his radical attitude against philosophy and his harsh critique of dialectical theology and Sufism; whose ideas play a fundamental role in Saudi Wahhabism;[16] who is accused of being the "father of Islamic fundamentalism";[17] and whose words have been even used by Muslims to justify terroristic activities;[18] – receives, despite all of this, a flat-

13 Nadvi, Syed Sulaiman: Muslims and Greek Schools of Philosophy, in: *Islamic Culture* 1 (1927), pp. 85–91, here p. 89.

14 ʿAbd al-Rāziq, Muṣṭafā: *Khamsa min aʿlām al-fikr al-islāmī*, Cairo n. d., p. 123.

15 ʿAmāra, Muḥammad: Faylasūf al-salafiyya, in: *Shabakat al-difāʿ ʿan al-sunna* (http://www.dd-sunnah.net/forum/showthread.php?t=67742, accessed May 3, 2009).

16 Laoust, Henri: *Essai sur les doctrines sociales et politiques de Takī-d-dīn Aḥmad b. Taimīya*, Cairo 1939, pp. 506–540. See Steinberg, Guido: *Religion und Staat in Saudi-Arabien. Die wahhabitischen Gelehrten 1902–1953*, Würzburg 2002, pp. 87–103, 337–341 et passim.

17 This cliché is discussed in Krawietz, Birgit: Ibn Taymiyya, Vater des islamischen Fundamentalismus? Zur westlichen Rezeption eines mittelalterlichen Schariatsgelehrten, in: Manuel Atienza, Enrico Pattaro, Martin Schulte, Boris Topornin and Dieter Wyduckel (eds.): *Theorie des Rechts und der Gesellschaft. Festschrift für Werner Krawietz*, Berlin 2003, pp. 39–62.

18 See Jansen, Johannes J. G.: The Creed of Sadat's Assassins. The Contents of "The Forgotten Duty" Analyzed, in: *Die Welt des Islams* 25 (1985), pp. 1–30; idem: *The Neglected Duty. The Creed of Sadat's Assassins and Islamic Resur-*

tering portrait in the works of contemporary Muslim authors. These authors depict him as a unique Muslim philosopher who alone knew how to destroy the house of Greek logic and metaphysics and how to erect, in its place, a house of genuine Islamic philosophy. According to this view, Ibn Taymiyya digested the "poison of philosophy" – yet, his brilliant mind turned the poison into honey. This very honey, extracted from the hive of his writings, can accordingly nourish a new era of modern Islamic philosophy. That Ibn Taymiyya himself, no doubt, would have taken umbrage at this sort of labeling of his work demonstrates how rich in irony the history of ideas can actually be!

In this study, I will present the main features of Ibn Taymiyya's 'philosophical identity' as they appear in works of contemporary Muslim authors. The first section (1) includes Ibn Taymiyya's refutation of Aristotle's formal logic as presented by three characteristic Muslim scholars. The second section (2) is dedicated to Ibn Taymiyya as an Averroist. The third section (3) deals with his renewal of philosophy in Islam through the establishment of Islamic metaphysics. The fourth section (4) presents Ibn Taymiyya as an original representative of philosophical nominalism. In the final section (5), I will discuss the present views with a special focus on the concept of philosophy that emerges from proclaiming Ibn Taymiyya a philosopher. I will conclude by reviewing the symptomatic value, for the situation of contemporary Islamic thought, of celebrating Ibn Taymiyya as a philosopher.[19]

---

gence in the Middle East, New York 1986; Sivan, Emmanuel: Ibn Taymiyya. Father of the Islamic Revolution; Medieval Theology & Modern Politics, in: *Encounter* 60 (1983), pp. 41–50; idem, *Radical Islam. Medieval Theology and Modern Politics*, New Haven 1985, pp. 96–107, 124 et passim. Most bluntly of all, the members of al-Qāʿida and other radical Islamic groups are called Ibn Taymiyya's children in Daniel Benjamin and Steven Simon: *Age of Sacred Terror*, New York 2002, pp. 38–94.

19 In clear difference to the positions presented in this study, Yahya Michot, a prominent scholar of Ibn Taymiyya, identifies him as a "classical Islamic" thinker, "theologian and mufti" and "a great spiritual master of the *via media*, the middle way that is at the heart of traditional Islam" (*Ibn Taymiyya (d. 728/1328). Against Extremisms*; *Texts translated, annotated and introduced by Yahya M. Michot, with a foreword by Bruce B. Lawrence*, Ozoir-la-Ferrière 2012, pp. xx–xxi). Some of the texts included in the manuscript are posted in French translation on the website muslimphilosophy.com as "Textes Spirituels d'Ibn Taymiyya." I wish to thank Prof. Michot for generously making his manuscript available to me prior to its publication.

In the present study, I am not primarily interested in Ibn Taymiyya but rather in the way contemporary Muslim authors view him as a philosopher, utiliz-

1. Ibn Taymiyya's Philosophical Critique of Aristotelian Logic

Central to Ibn Taymiyya's ferocious defense of Islam by means of reason is his refutation of Aristotelian logic, which he clearly considered the foundation of the metaphysical system developed by the Greeks. For Ibn Taymiyya, this metaphysical system, which the philosophers of Islam had adopted, was in full disagreement with the Islamic worldview.[20] His critical assessment of Greek logic bears, thus, important implications for both his general attitude towards philosophy and his orientation towards certain schools of Islamic theology.[21] As such, contemporary Muslim authors who deal with this subject cannot explicitly claim the identity of a philosopher for Ibn Taymiyya *per se*. In presenting how he utilized philosophical terminology to fight the logicians with their own weapons, however, these authors connect his critique to possible sources in the Greek philosophical tradition as well as to later European critics of logic. By doing so, these authors apparently grant Ibn Taymiyya space among the philosophers without attributing to him a clear philosophical identity.

---

ing his ideas in contemporary Islamic discourses intending a revival of Islamic philosophy with Ibn Taymiyya as its patron, As such, I will defer from dealing directly with his texts. References to the sources used by contemporary authors treated in this study will, however, be made when necessary.

20 His critique reached its highest point in *Naṣīḥat ahl al-imān fī al-radd ʿalā manṭiq al-yūnān*, better known as *al-Radd ʿalā al-manṭiqiyyīn*, edited by ʿAbd al-Ṣamad Sharaf al-Dīn al-Kutubī, reviewed by Muḥammad Ṭalḥa Bilāl Minyār, with an introduction by al-Sayyid Sulaymān al-Nadwī, Beirut 1426/2005. This new edition is identical with the first edition of the book by al-Kutubī published in Bombay 1368/1949. The page numbers of the first edition are given on the page margins in the new edition and will be mentioned in the present study following page numbers according to the new edition. Another edition of the book, done by ʿAbd al-Sattār al-Nashshār and ʿImād Khafājī, was published in Cairo 1977. This extensive volume was abridged by Jalāl al-Dīn al-Suyūṭī (849/1445–911/1505) as *Jahd al-qarīḥa fī tajrīd al-naṣīḥa*, edited by ʿAlī Sāmī al-Nashshār, Cairo 1947, and edited by Suʿād ʿAbd al-Rāziq and ʿAlī Sāmī al-Nashshār, Cairo 1970. It also is part of vol. 9 of *Majmūʿ fatāwā shaykh al-islām Aḥmad Ibn Taymiyya*, edited by ʿAbd Allāh b. Qāsim, Rabat 1961. An English translation of the abridged book is: *Ibn Taymiyya Against Greek Logicians. Translated with Introduction and Notes by Wael B. Hallaq*, Oxford 1993.

21 See Ibn Taymiyya, *al-Radd*, p. 46/4. The number preceding the backslash is the page number in the new edition, the number following the backslash refers to the first edition of the book. See above n. 20.

How do contemporary Muslim authors locate Ibn Taymiyya's critique of Aristotle's logic? Three examples should prove instructive; in one example, ʿAlī Sāmī al-Nashshār[22] – an Egyptian professor of philosophy who deals with this subject during the course of his attempt to present a specifically Islamic methodology – follows the structure of *al-Radd ʿalā al-manṭiqiyyīn* and presents Ibn Taymiyya's critique of the Aristotelian definition,[23] logical proposition[24] and syllogism.[25] Each critical section is divided into a subversive part, in which Ibn Taymiyya encounters the Aristotelian arguments, and a constructive part, in which he develops his alternatives.[26] The Iranian scholar Muṣṭafā Ṭabāṭabāʾī, for his part, delivers a concise presentation of Ibn Taymiyya's arguments.[27] In another case, C. A. Qadir's article published in the *International Philosophical Quarterly* is obviously less interested in discussing Ibn Taymiyya's arguments than in presenting him as a pioneer of modern critique of Aristotelian logic.[28]

---

22 Al-Nashshār, ʿAlī Sāmī: *Manāhij al-baḥth ʿinda mufakkirī al-islām*, 4th ed., Cairo 1978.

23 Al-Nashshār, *Manāhij*, pp. 149–163. Ibn Taymiyya refers to the definition, as introduced by Aristotle and adopted by medieval Muslim philosophers and, since the eleventh century, by the *kalām*-theologians as well. See Kennedy-Day, Kiki: *Books of Definition in Islamic Philosophy. The Limits of Words*, London and New York 2003; Gutas, Dimitri: The Logic of Theology (*kalām*) in Avicenna, in: Dominik Perler and Ulrich Rudolph (eds.): *Logik und Theologie. Das* Organon *im arabischen und im lateinischen Mittelalter*, Leiden and Boston 2005, pp. 59–72; van Ess, Josef: The Logical Structure of Islamic Theology, in: Gustave E. von Grunebaum (ed.): *Logic in Classical Islamic Culture,* Wiesbaden 1970, pp. 21–50.

24 Al-Nashshār, *Manāhij*, pp. 164–179.

25 Ibid., pp. 180–219.

26 Al-Nashshār's discussion of Ibn Taymiyya's refutation of Aristotle's logic is taken into account in von Kügelgen, Anke: Ibn Taymīyas Kritik an der aristotelischen Logik und sein Gegenentwurf, in: Dominik Perler and Ulrich Rudolph (eds.): *Logik und Theologie. Das* Organon *im arabischen und lateinischen Mittelalter*, Leiden and Boston 2005, pp. 167–225, here pp. 177–179.

27 Ṭabāṭabāʾī, Muṣṭafā: *al-Mufakkirūn al-muslimūn fī muwājahat al-manṭiq al-yūnānī*, translated into Arabic by ʿAbd al-Raḥīm M. al-Balūshī, Beirut 1990.

28 Qadir, Chaudry Abdul: An Early Islamic Critic of Aristotelian Logic. Ibn Taymiyyah, in: *International Philosophical Quarterly* 8 (1968), pp. 498–512. Despite its strong arguments, the article contains remarkably few references to Ibn Taymiyya's works; as such, the author's assertions are somewhat suspect in regards to their textual foundation. In regards to Ibn Taymiyya as a pioneer, the conservative Moroccan author and political activist Muḥammad Yatīm ascribes to Ibn Taymiyya the foundation of an "Islamic logic" (*manṭiq islāmī*) and an "Islamic epistemological method" (*manhaj al-maʿrifa al-Islāmī*); Yatīm, Muḥammad: Ibn Taymiyya wa-masʾalat al-ʿaql wal-naql, in: *al-Furqān* 3:8 (1407/1987), pp. 16–24, here 17–18.

To begin, it is certainly worth noting that al-Nashshār, the first author, in a tone which can be considered representative of Islamic traditionalism, calls the transmission of Greek logic into Islamic culture a comprehensive "conspiracy" initiated by the Umayyads, encouraged by the Byzantines, and secretly carried out by converted Manicheans, Zoroastrians, and oriental Christians. Their goal, for al-Nashshār, was to contaminate pure Islamic thought; their strategy was to translate works of Greek logic into Arabic and, therewith, to destroy Islam from within.[29] Consequently, he asserts that Greek logic, intrinsically related as it is to Greek language, has been always alien to Arabic-Islamic culture.[30] Al-Nashshār identifies Stoic elements in Ibn Taymiyya's critique of Aristotelian logic that are analogously alien to Islam.[31] An important source of Ibn Taymiyya's critique can furthermore be found in the writings of Sextus Empiricus[32] as well as in the writings of Greek Skeptics and Sophists.[33]

Even so, Ibn Taymiyya delivered the most substantial critique of Aristotelian logic from an Islamic point of view. Utilizing "philosophical language",[34] he brought the Islamic critique of Aristotelian logic

29 Al-Nashshār, *Manāhij*, pp. 5–7 et passim. According to al-Nashshār, ʿAbd Allāh b. al-Muqaffaʿ – or rather his son Muḥammad – belongs to the earliest group of the conspirators, as he presumably prepared the first Arabic translation of certain books of Aristotle's logic: ibid., pp. 21, 169. See Gabrieli, Francesco: Ibn al-Muḳaffaʿ, in: *EI²*, vol. 3 (1971), pp. 883–885.

30 Al-Nashshār, *Manāhij*, p. 29. Despite a dramatic plot, al-Nashshār's argument is actually an old one popular among Muslim critics of logic, as the famous debate which took place in 938 between the grammarian Abū Saʿīd al-Sīrāfī (d. 368/979) and the Christian logician Abū Bishr Mattā ibn Yūnus (d. 328/940) clearly documents. The text of the debate is in al-Tawḥīdī, Abū Ḥayyān: *Kitāb al-Imtāʿ wal-muʾānasa*, edited by Aḥmad Amīn and Aḥmad al-Zayn, Beirut n. d., part 1, pp. 107–128. English translation: Margoliouth, David Samuel: The Discussion Between Abū Bishr Mattā and Abū Saʿīd al-Sīrāfī on the Merits of Logic and Grammar, in: *Journal of the Royal Asiatic Society NS*, 37 (1905), pp. 79–129. See Endreß, Gerhard: Grammatik und Logik. Arabische Philologie und griechische Philosophie im Widerstreit, in: Burkhard Mojsisch (ed.): *Sprachphilosophie in Antike und Mittelalter*, Amsterdam 1986, pp. 163–299, including a German translation of the debate, pp. 235–270, and of a text by Mattā's student Yaḥyā ibn ʿAdī (363/974) on the difference between logic and grammar, pp. 271–296; Kühn, Wilfried: Die Rehabilitierung der Sprache durch den arabischen Philologen as-Sīrāfī, in: Burkhard Mojsisch (ed.): *Sprachphilosophie in Antike und Mittelalter*, pp. 301–402, offers an analytical study of al-Sīrāfī's arguments.

31 Al-Nashshār, *Manāhij*, pp. 152, 175.

32 Ibid., p. 170.

33 Ibid., p. 159.

34 Ibid., p. 168.

to its summit in a unique attempt to establish a uniquely Islamic logic.[35] In the view of the Muslim authors who dealt with this topic, Ibn Taymiyya undertakes the task without falling like al-Ghazālī into the trap of philosophy. Ultimately derived from the sacred texts of Islam, i.e. the Koran and Sunna, Ibn Taymiyya's alternatives to Aristotelian logic confirm, thus, the jurists' judgment that whoever studies logic is a heretic (*man tamanṭaq tazandaq*).[36]

The core of Ibn Taymiyya's critique of Aristotle's logic is his denial of the logicians' claim that the "true definition" (*al-ḥadd al-ḥaqīqī*) is the only way to conceptually capture the quiddity of an existent (*taṣawwur al-māhiyya*).[37] Such a definition consists essentially of two elements: 1) the essential attributes which are common (*al-dhātiyya al-mushtaraka*) between the existent and other existents of the same genus (*jins*); and 2) the attributes which are common between the existent and its species (*nawʿ*) and which distinguish a specific existent from other existents (*al-dhātiyya al-mumayyiza*), i.e. the difference (*al-faṣl*).[38] He furthermore argues that such a definition is either impossible or extremely difficult to develop, which makes definitions actually useless for the perception of truth.[39] For him, existents are too complicated to be conceptually captured through such insufficient and superficial logical constructions; natural beings should, rather, be investigated rationally and empirically. This is, actually, what Muslim scholars after Ibn Taymiyya failed to do, according to critical contemporary Muslim authors.[40] However, Ibn Taymiyya considers the definition useful in distinguishing the *definiendum* from other similar things. Definitions, thus, essentially resemble names; they do not lead to the conception of existents, but merely serve as "reminders".[41] Ibn Taymiyya is, thus, a nominalist.[42]

---

35 Ibid., p. 148.

36 Ibid., p. 169.

37 Ibn Taymiyya, *al-Radd*, p. 46/5. See Aristotle: *Topica et Sophistici Elenchi*, edited by Sir William David Ross, Oxford 1979, p. 5.

38 Ibn Taymiyya, *al-Radd*, p. 47/5.

39 Ṭabaṭabāʾī, *al-Mufakkirūn*, p. 94; Ibn Taymiyya, *al-Radd*, p. 50/9.

40 ʿAbd al-Rāziq, *Khamsa*, p. 125; Tabatabāʾī, *al-Mufakkirūn*, p. 98.

41 Ṭabaṭabāʾī, *al-Mufakkirūn*, 98; Ibn Taymiyya, *al-Radd*, p. 84/43. Ibn Taymiyya's views continue the tradition of Arab grammarians; see von Kügelgen, Ibn Taymīyas Kritik an der aristotelischen Logik, pp. 187–188.

42 Qadir, An Early Islamic Critic, pp. 499–501. See the concise discussion of this subject in von Kügelgen, Ibn Taymīyas Kritik an der aristotelischen Logik, pp. 187–192.

Ṭabaṭabāʾī develops his own reaction. Rejecting Ibn Taymiyya's plea for the unity of the quiddity and the existence of an existent,[43] Ṭabaṭabāʾī maintains the cognitive separation of both categories and argues that the external existence of a certain existent is not identical with its identity or specific characteristics, as far as these can be cognitively captured.[44] Ṭabaṭabāʾī shares, however, Ibn Taymiyya's view that existence in the real world is prior to the perception of the quiddity and that logical universals do not exist in reality outside the cognitive sphere.[45] As such, only that which is "partial and particular" (*juzʾī muʿayyan*) exists in the real world of existence.[46] Indeed, Ibn Taymiyya believes that universals (*al-qaḍāyā al-kulliya*) are constructed through a cognitive process of abstraction from particular existents.[47]

Ṭabaṭabāʾī further discusses Ibn Taymiyya's statement that everything that can be known by means of syllogism can be known without it,[48] rejecting, thus, syllogism as a source of new knowledge and demoting it to a mere way of "remembrance and repetition of knowledge" (*al-tadhakkur wa-takrār al-maʿrifa*).[49] Ibn Taymiyya replaced syllogism with analogy (*tamthīl*), which Muslim jurists employed as a way to develop similar judgments regarding two similar objects, rejecting the logicians' view that analogy produces only assumptions.[50]

Comparing the critique of Aristotelian logic by Muslim thinkers – such as, for example, al-Fārābī, Ibn Sīnā, al-Ghazālī, Ibn Rushd and Ibn Taymiyya – with its critique by European philosophers like Roger Bacon, Francis Bacon, Descartes and John Locke, both Ṭabaṭabāʾī and Qadir, in their turn, emphasize the excellence of these Muslim critics who preceded – and in some ways exceeded – their counterparts in uncovering the shortcomings of Aristotle's logical system.[51] Ibn Taymiyya's achievements in this field occupy much of

43 Ibn Taymiyya, *al-Radd*, 107/65: *fa-wujūd al-shayʾ fī al-khārij ʿayn māhiyyatihi fī al-khārij*. See von Kügelgen, Ibn Taymīyas Kritik an der aristotelischen Logik, pp. 181–182.

44 Ṭabaṭabāʾī, *al-Mufakkirūn*, pp. 99–100.

45 Ibid., pp. 101–103; Ibn Taymiyya, *al-Radd*, p. 113/71.

46 Ṭabaṭabāʾī, *al-Mufakkirūn*, p. 105; Ibn Taymiyya, *al-Radd*, p. 126/84.

47 Ibn Taymiyya, *al-Radd*, pp. 101/59, 123–124/82–83.

48 Ṭabaṭabāʾī, *al-Mufakkirūn*, p. 111; Ibn Taymiyya, *al-Radd*, pp. 384–385/339–340.

49 Ṭabaṭabāʾī, *al-Mufakkirūn*, p. 109.

50 Ibid., pp. 113–115; Ibn Taymiyya, *al-Radd*, pp. 156/115–117, 161–162/120–121, 399–401/354–356.

51 Ṭabaṭabāʾī, *al-Mufakkirūn*, pp. 126–148.

Ṭabaṭabāʾī's presentation of this topic: compared with Francis Bacon (1561–1626)[52], Ibn Taymiyya argues "in clear scientific language" that a judgment achieved through syllogistic evidence is correct if the premises are proven to be correct; this can only be done through empirical investigation prior to establishing the form of syllogism. In this regard, Ṭabaṭabāʾī notes that Ibn Taymiyya uses analogy to ascribe a decisive role to practical experience in developing philosophical judgments. For Ibn Taymiyya – and thus for Ṭabaṭabāʾī – empirical knowledge results from "both sense and reason" (*al-ḥiss wal-ʿaql kilāhumā maʿan*); Ibn Taymiyya's favorite examples come from medicine and jurisprudence, both disciplines in which theory and practice are intrinsically interconnected.[53] Furthermore, his methodological doubt regarding the value of Aristotelian logic for the achievement of rational knowledge precedes the critique made by John Locke (1632–1704),[54] and the readers of Ibn Taymiyya's critique of Aristotelian logic would find the same arguments and nominal interpretation of the definition[55] brought by John Stuart Mill (1806–1873)[56] five centuries later. Finally, Ibn Taymiyya's nominal definition predates Bertrand Russell's (1872–1970) critique of Aristotle and can even answer some of his questions.[57]

In conclusion to this section, it is relevant to point out that Ibn Taymiyya's refutation of logic has been connected, so al-Nashshār, to ancient philosophers who raised doubt concerning the epistemological value of Aristotle's logic. Nevertheless, it seems nearly impossible to establish any concrete link between Ibn Taymiyya and Sextus Empiricus or any of the Skeptics, as their writings were, as far as known, never

52 Bacon, Francis: *Novum Organon/The New Organon*, edited by Lisa Jardine and Michael Silverthorne, Cambridge and New York 2000.

53 Ṭabaṭabāʾī, *al-Mufakkirūn*, pp. 130–131; Ibn Taymiyya, *al-Radd*, pp. 437–438/393–394.

54 Ṭabaṭabāʾī, *al-Mufakkirūn*, pp. 135–138. See Locke, John: *An Essay Concerning Human Understanding. Collated and Annotated with Biographical, Critical and Historical Prolegomena by Alexander Campbell Fraser*, New York 1959, especially book 4, chapter 17.

55 Ṭabaṭabāʾī, *al-Mufakkirūn*, pp. 145–147. Al-Nashshār, *Manāhij*, pp. 162, 170, 178, is also interested in showing similarities between Ibn Taymiyya's and Mill's critique of Aristotle's logic.

56 Mill, John Stuart: *A System of Logic*, New York 1919.

57 Al-Nashshār, *Manāhij*, p. 162; Qadir, An Early Islamic Critic, pp. 499–501. Further similar statements are referred to in von Kügelgen, Ibn Taymīyas Kritik an der aristotelischen Logik, pp. 215–217.

translated into Arabic.[58] At best, isolated skeptical thoughts could have indirectly reached the Abbasid society.[59] This, of course, does not mean that Islamic civilization did not know situations "that independently may have given rise to intellectual developments that were similar, or at least receptive, to Stoic, Sceptic, and other ideas".[60]

Beyond this, the explicit claim – very often pronounced by contemporary Muslim scholars – that Ibn Taymiyya was a nominalist and empiricist who foreshadowed British empiricism appears groundless by a comparative study of the sources. Of course, striking similarities between Ibn Taymiyya's views and teachings of British empiricists can be identified; the equivalence of analogy and syllogism exists in Mill and Locke; Mill and Hume emphasize the role of induction and analogy, based on empirical experience and sensual perception, for knowledge; Mill and Locke even consider the axioms of mathematics and logic derived from particulars.[61] Other similarities are captured by Ṭabaṭabāʾī; Anke von Kügelgen indicates even more.[62] These parallels, nevertheless, seem limited in regards to their function within the philosophical system of each one of these thinkers: Francis Bacon places the empirical methods for obtaining knowledge in the service of technology;[63] Locke and Hume consider knowledge primarily to be

58 See Hallaq, *Ibn Taymiyya Against the Greek Logicians*, p. xli. See ibid., pp. xxxix–xxxx; Gutas, Dimitri: Pre-Plotinian Philosophy in Arabic (Other than Platonism and Aristotelianism). A Review of the Sources, in: Wolfgang Haase (ed.): *Aufstieg und Niedergang der Römischen Welt*, vol. II. 36.1, Berlin and New York 1994, pp. 4939–4973, here 4943.

59 Van Ess, Josef: Skepticism in Islamic Religious Thought, in: Charles Malik (ed.): *God and Man in Contemporary Islamic Thought*, Beirut 1972, pp. 83–98, especially pp. 84, 86–87. [The article was first published in *Al-Abhath* 21 (1968), pp. 1–18].

60 Gutas, Pre-Plotinian Philosophy in Arabic, p. 4948. See his critique of proponents of a "hidden tradition" of transmitting Greek philosophical ideas into Arabic, ibid., pp. 4944–4949, and his rejection of the views in van Ess, Skepticism in Islamic Religious Thought, in: Charles Malik (ed.): *God and Man in Contemporary Islamic Thought*, p. 94. See on the influences of Stoic ideas in Islam: Jadaane, Fehmi: *L'influence du stoicisme sur la pensé musulmane*, Beirut 1968.

61 This topic has been investigated by Nicholas Heer: Ibn Taymiyah's Empiricism, in: Farhad Kazemi and Robert Duncan McChesney (eds.): *A Way Prepared. Essays on Islamic Culture in Honor of Richard Bayly Winder*, New York and London 1988, pp. 109–115.

62 Von Kügelgen, Ibn Taymīyas Kritik an der aristotelischen Logik, pp. 216–217.

63 Milton, John R.: Bacon, Francis, in: Craig, Edward (ed.): *Routledge Encyclopedia of Philosophy*, London 1998, 2003, http://www.rep.routledge.com/article/DA002SECT1, accessed February 06, 2012.

a psychological process;[64] Mill ascribes to natural sciences the ability to explain everything that happens in the world.[65] In deep contrast to these cosmetic similarities, for Ibn Taymiyya the object of knowledge is the real existent in the external world; each and every thing has its specific quiddity which can be captured only through sensual perception. Abstraction can only produce vulnerable individual knowledge.[66] Ibn Taymiyya's basic empiricist approach is not a vehicle for the development of natural science and technology, but serves a religious agenda based on his conviction that the knowledge of essence, as such, is both naturally possible for God and completely impossible for humans. Finally, acknowledging sacred writings as the ultimate source of secure knowledge, Ibn Taymiyya takes a course which European empiricists could simply never share.

2. Ibn Taymiyya's Averroistic Attitudes

In Islam, Ibn Rushd (Averroes) and Ibn Taymiyya represent two contrary fields of knowledge with antithetical approaches to the relationship between religion and rationality: Ibn Rushd established his philosophy on Aristotle's works, on which he diligently commented; truth, for Ibn Rushd, was strictly apodictic. On the other hand, Ibn Taymiyya, as it has been made clear in the previous section, rejected Aristotelian logic; for him, truth was what is clearly attested by the Koran or the Hadith. In addition to their difference in method and position, their legacies took remarkably different paths: Ibn Rushd's works, in their Hebrew and Latin translations, fertilized rational discourses in Europe through the 19th century, almost until the time they were rediscovered by Arab intellectuals in the Eastern Mediterranean.[67] Ibn

64 Copleston, Frederick S.J.: *A History of Philosophy*, vol. 5: *Hobbes to Hume*, London 1959, pp. 108–109, 263–264.

65 Copleston, Frederick S.J.: *Modern Philosophy. Empiricism, Idealism, and Pragmatism in Britain and America*, London 1959, pp. 50–92; see von Kügelgen, Ibn Taymīyas Kritik an der aristotelischen Logik, p. 217.

66 This view is shared by von Kügelgen, Ibn Taymīyas Kritik an der aristotelischen Logik, p. 218.

67 See Niewöhner, Friedrich and Sturlese, Loris (eds.): *Averroismus im Mittelalter und in der Renaissance*, Zurich 1994; von Kügelgen, Anke: *Averroes und die arabische Moderne. Ansätze zu einer Neubegründung des Rationalismus im Islam*, Leiden 1994; Tamer, Georges: Averroism, in: *EI*³, http://static.ribo.brill.

Taymiyya, as discussed above, has become – not incidentally – perhaps the most influential author in Muslim conservative circles.

In several of his writings, Ibn Taymiyya spared no critique of Ibn Rushd.[68] Despite fundamental discrepancies, however, both thinkers seem to agree on one thing: namely, the unity of truth, which is accessible to human beings through divine revelation and by means of rationality equivalently.[69] Arguing against the prevailing view that Ibn Rushd's influence is to be sought in late Medieval and Renaissance Europe rather than in the Islamic world, the Moroccan scholar ʿAbd al-Majīd al-Ṣaghīr presents Averroistic positions in Ibn Taymiyya's work to demonstrate aspects of Ibn Rushd's legacy in the pre-modern Islamic context.[70] His study serves also as a response to the alleged epistemological break, proclaimed by none less than Muḥammad ʿĀbid al-Jābirī, between intellectual discourses in the Islamic East and the Islamic West.[71] In the following, al-Ṣaghīr's views will be presented.

First, al-Ṣaghīr makes clear that Ibn Taymiyya shares a basic methodological principle with Ibn Rushd: the ultimate agreement between reason and religion. For Ibn Taymiyya, clear reason necessarily agrees with true tradition transmitted through the Koran and the authentic statements of the prophet. In stating, therefore, that the purpose of the Koran is identical with the purpose of pure rational demonstration, Ibn Taymiyya actually adds nothing new to Ibn Rushd's teachings.[72]

According to al-Ṣaghīr, both thinkers respectively developed their critique of Muslim philosophers and *kalām*-theologians based on

---

semcs.net/entries/encyclopaedia-of-islam-3/averroism-COM_24253, accessed April 10, 2011.

68 Saʿd, al-Ṭablāwī Maḥmūd: *Mawqif Ibn Taymiyya min falsafat Ibn Rushd fī al-ʿaqīda wa-ʿilm al-kalām wal-falsafa*, Cairo 1409/1989, provides a thorough presentation of Ibn Taymiyya's critical attitude towards Ibn Rushd's major theological and philosophical views.

69 See on this topic von Kügelgen, Anke: Dialogpartner im Widerspruch. Ibn Rushd und Ibn Taymīya über die "Einheit der Wahrheit", in: Rüdiger Arnzen and Jörn Thielmann (eds.): *Words, Texts and Concepts Cruising the Mediterranean Sea. Studies on the Sources, Contents and Influences of Islamic Civilization and Arabic Philosophy and Science; Dedicated to Gerhard Endress on His Sixty-fifth Birthday*, Leuven 2004, pp. 455–481.

70 Al-Ṣaghīr, ʿAbd al-Majīd: Mawāqif "rushdiyya" li-Taqī al-Dīn Ibn Taymiyya?, in: *Dirāsāt Maghribiyya muhdāt ilā al-mufakkir al-Maghribī Muḥammad ʿAzīz al-Ḥabbābī*, Casablanca 1987², pp. 164–182.

71 He articulates this view in several works. See e.g. al-Jābirī, Muḥammad ʿĀbid: *Naḥnu wal-turāth*, Beirut 1993⁶, pp. 49–50, 212.

72 Al-Ṣaghīr, Mawāqif, p. 166.

their shared conviction that reason and revelation stood in fundamental agreement. Ibn Taymiyya's "critical project" (*al-mashrūʿ al-naqdī*) resulted from a comprehensive vision similar to that of his predecessor: Muslim theologians were to be criticized because they did not distinguish between "clear reason" (*al-ʿaql al-ṣarīḥ*) on the one hand and corrupt dialectic and syllogism on the other. While "clear reason" was desirable, Greek logic could only lead them astray from the very Koran and Hadith they claimed to be defending. As a result of the theologians' adoption of the corrupt methods of the philosophers, so al-Ṣaghīr, Ibn Taymiyya took to calling them "the Harranian Sabians" (*al-ṣābiʾa al-ḥarrāniyya*), accusing them of corrupting the original philosophy of Aristotle.[73]

Al-Ṣaghīr acknowledges the differing outcomes of both Ibn Rushd's and Ibn Taymiyya's critical projects in regards to the relation between religion and philosophy. He states, nevertheless, that Ibn Taymiyya's critique of Islamic philosophy in the East (*al-mashriq*) actually "enriches and supports" Ibn Rushd's critique. Due to his intellectual environment, Ibn Taymiyya was well acquainted with the "Eastern ideas" under which influence this philosophy deviated from its Aristotelian origins; his critique of *kalām*-theology is, thus, an extension of Ibn Rushd's critique of the Ashʿarī school and particularly of al-Ghazālī.[74] Furthermore, al-Ṣaghīr points out that both personalities, although living under different social and political circumstances, shared a strong desire to reject established theological traditions and to both challenge and transform the predominant intellectual situation in which they respectively flourished. Ibn Taymiyya fought rigorously for the political and dogmatic unity of the *umma*, a goal which had been formulated by Ibn Tūmart (d. 524/1130). This was also the aim of Ibn Rushd.[75]

Discussing specific Averroistic ideas in Ibn Taymiyya's works, al-Ṣaghīr highlights the following:

---

73 Ibid., p. 167. On Harran and its famous school of philosophy, which had a considerable impact on Arabic philosophy, see Fehérvári, G.: Ḥarrān, in: *EI*², vol. 3 (1971), pp. 227–230; Chwolsohn, Daniel: *Die Ssabier und der Ssabismus*, St. Petersburg 1856; Lewy, Hans: *Chaldean Oracles and Theurgy*, Paris 1978; Theurgus, Iulianus: *The Chaldean Oracles. Text, translation and commentary by Ruth Majercik*, Leiden 1989.

74 Al-Ṣaghīr, Mawāqif, pp. 167–168.

75 Ibid., p. 168. A possible influence of Ibn Tūmart on Ibn Taymiyya is contested by Al-Matroudi, Abdul Hakim I.: *The Ḥanbalī School of Law and Ibn Taymiyya. Conflict or Conciliation*, London and New York 2006, p. 18.

1. Like Ibn Rushd, Ibn Taymiyya was aware of the need to criticize the syllogism of the *kalām*-theologians and fundamental notions related to it: indeed, the arguments the *kalām*-theologians used to prove God's existence were based on thinking that the invisible could be held as analogous to the visible (*qiyās al-ghā'ib 'alā al-shāhid*). This inductive view, Ibn Taymiyya and Ibn Rushd point out, radically differs from the deductive method used in the Koran.[76]

2. Ibn Taymiyya and Ibn Rushd share a negative attitude towards the theologians' rejection of God's corporeal attributes. For both of them, these arguments empty the divinity of any attributes (*ta'ṭīl*) whatsoever. They differ, however, in the way they deal with Koranic anthropomorphisms: Ibn Taymiyya advocates, in the name of both reason and scripture, a literal reading of such passages; Ibn Rushd strongly argues for their allegorical interpretation. Nevertheless, they again seem to be on the same line; in the name of both the Koran and rationality, they defend the theological teaching about God's spatiality – i. e., His "being somewhere" (*al-jiha*) – against the Ash'arīs.[77]

3. Ibn Taymiyya follows Ibn Rushd in rejecting the theological arguments for the createdness of the world; their response to the most controversial question in Islamic philosophy is, therefore, the same.[78] By stating that the createdness of the world was made possible without reason (*al-tarjīḥ bilā sabab*), the *kalām*-theologians not only opposed rationality, but moreover supported the Dahrīs and those who argued for the eternity of the world.[79] Though both philosophers and the theologians brought arguments to assert a maker (*al-ṣāni'*) for the world, Ibn Taymiyya, similar to Ibn Rushd, dismissed these assertions as useless and confusing, emphasizing thereby the proof of predestination (*dalīl al-'ināya*). This proof, in a simple, understandable way, presented

76 Al-Ṣaghīr, Mawāqif, p. 169. Regarding this, see Ibn Rushd: *al-Kashf 'an manāhij al-adilla fī 'aqā'id al-milla*, edited by Muṣṭafā Ḥanafī and Muḥammad 'Ābid al-Jābirī, Beirut 1998, pp. 100–102; Ibn Taymiyya, *Dar'*, edited by Sālim, vol. 3, pp. 389–438; vol. 8, pp. 136–251; vol. 9, pp. 68–105.

77 Al-Ṣaghīr, Mawāqif, pp. 175–176. See Ibn Rushd, *al-Kashf*, pp. 138–142, 145–148; Ibn Taymiyya, *Dar'*, edited by Sālim, vol. 6, pp. 212–249; vol. 9, pp. 105–132, 334–400; vol. 10, pp. 147–157, 197–317. See von Kügelgen, Dialogpartner, pp. 462–470.

78 See Al-Alousī, Husām Muhī Eldīn: *The Problem of Creation in Islamic Thought*, Baghdad 1968.

79 Al-Ṣaghīr, Mawāqif, p. 170. On the Dahrīs see Goldziher, Ignaz and Goichon, Amélie Marie: Dahriyya, in: *EI*², vol. 2 (1965), pp. 95–97; Shaki, Mansour: Dahrī I (In Middle Persian Literature), in: *Encyclopedia Iranica*, vol. 6, p. 587b.

God's care for the world and, thus, His continuous creating activity.[80] Wielding the same verses against the *kalām*-theologians, Ibn Taymiyya points out that the Koran does not teach creation out of nothing[81]; like Ibn Rushd, he refutes the theological principle that "whatever is not free of caused beings is itself caused" (*mā lā yakhlū min ḥawādith fa-huwa ḥādith*), declaring it invalid according to both reason and the Koran. In nearly Ibn Rushd's own words Ibn Taymiyya states that the "truth does not contradict itself" (*al-ḥaqq lā yatanāqaḍ*).[82]

Ibn Taymiyya, in a position close to Ibn Rushd's, as al-Ṣaghīr states, asserts that the Koran and Hadith do not include any statement supporting the theologians' view that the contingent existents came into being at a precise instant (*al-ḥawādith lahā ibtidāʾ*); indeed, this would imply that God's activity began at a certain point in time. This, however, does not mean that the world is eternal, as the philosophers argued: for, believing in God's eternal creating activity does not mean accepting that the world is eternal; agency (*al-fāʿiliyya*) precedes action just as the agent precedes the act. Ibn Taymiyya refers, in this regard, to the same Koranic verses used by Ibn Rushd in a similar context and interprets them in an astonishingly similar way.[83] Al-Ṣaghīr concludes that a "unity of mind" (*wiḥdat al-rūḥ*) must exist between Ibn Taymiyya and Ibn Rushd, who both use the same arguments to obtain the same results. Yet, it must be noted that despite this basic agreement, each thinker treats the Koranic text differently: Ibn Rushd, on the one hand, draws it closer to Aristotle's position, making demonstration the highest criterion of truth and asserting that the interpreted scripture necessarily must agree with demonstration. Ibn Taymiyya, on the other hand, strictly holds the view that the literal text of the Koran is valid and does not need interpretation.[84]

4. Ibn Taymiyya and Ibn Rushd deal also similarly with the theological question of causality. Criticizing the Ashʿarīs' rejection of other causes than God, they both assert with similar arguments that accept-

80 Regarding this, see von Kügelgen, Dialogpartner, pp. 470–472 with references to relevant passages in Ibn Rushd's and Ibn Taymiyya's oeuvre.

81 Al-Ṣaghīr, Mawāqif, pp. 170–171. See, for instance, Koran (41:11).

82 Al-Ṣaghīr, Mawāqif, p. 172. See Ibn Rushd, *Faṣl*, p. 13; Ibn Taymiyya, *Minhāj al-sunna al-nabawiyya fī naqḍ kalām al-shīʿa al-qadariyya*, edited by Muḥammad Rashād Sālim, Riyadh n. d., vol. 1, p. 300.

83 Al-Ṣaghīr, Mawāqif, pp. 173–175. Ibn Rushd, *al-Kashf*, pp. 171–172; idem, *Faṣl*, p. 21.

84 Al-Ṣaghīr, Mawāqif, p. 175.

ing natural causality is a requirement of both reason and the Koranic belief in God's wisdom as well. To deny the impact of causes is inconceivable for both of them, inasmuch as such a denial would render God's wisdom and knowledge useless.[85]

5. Both Ibn Rushd and Ibn Taymiyya agree, furthermore, that the endeavor to harmonize *kalām* and *falsafa* failed on both sides. For Ibn Taymiyya, those theologians who attempted to bring theological and philosophical arguments to a synthesis defaulted into error and contradiction. Al-Ghazālī is a favorite target of critique from both thinkers, who accuse him of using contradictory rhetorical statements (which he claimed to be demonstrative) and of being inconsistent with his position. They likewise agree to criticize Ibn Sīnā; Ibn Taymiyya interestingly traces Ibn Sīnā's erroneous ideas back to the "deviated (*munḥarifa*) Harranian Sabiasm", a heritage he similarly imputes to al-Fārābī.[86] It is mainly Ibn Sīnā's attempt to provide proof for the existence of God that draws both Ibn Rushd's and Ibn Taymiyya's ire; after all, Ibn Sīnā differentiated between two kinds of existence: the necessary (*al-wājib*) and the possible (*al-mumkin*), in order to describe the heavens as both eternal and possible.[87]

6. Al-Ṣaghīr points out that, in the context of his critique of Ibn Sīnā, Ibn Taymiyya admits Ibn Rushd's closeness to Aristotle, acknowledging that the Andalusian philosopher surpassed his Greek master in his explanation of the movement of the heavenly spheres.[88] Additionally, Ibn Taymiyya's critical advance against the Muslim philosophers of the East resembles that of Ibn Rushd, originating as it did from similar principles. One of the reasons for the agreement is, according to al-Ṣaghīr, the "traditionalist character" (*al-ṭābiʿ al-salafī*) of Ibn Rushd's approach in discussing theological questions, especially in his philosophical-theological writings *Tahāfut al-Tahāfut*, *Faṣl al-maqāl* and *al-Kashf ʿan manāhij al-adilla*. Ibn Rushd's traditionalism is found in his return to the "original, authentic, not distorted and not interpreted" texts of Aristotle and the Koran.[89] Furthermore, both Ibn Rushd

---

85 Ibid., pp. 176–177. See Ibn Rushd, *al-Kashf*, pp. 166–169, 193–194; Ibn Taymiyya, *al-Radd*, p. 315/270.

86 Al-Ṣaghīr, Mawāqif, pp. 177–178.

87 Ibid., p. 179. On Ibn Sīnā's position and Ibn Rushd's critique of it see Davidson, Herbert A.: *Proofs for Eternity, Creation and the Existence of God in Medieval Islamic and Jewish Philosophy*, New York and Oxford 1987, pp. 281–335.

88 Al-Ṣaghīr, Mawāqif, p. 180.

89 Ibid., p. 181.

and Ibn Taymiyya view the history of ideas as a history of decline. Al-Ṣaghīr suggests that the latter remains within the framework of the former's critique of Muslim theologians and philosophers, insofar as he aimed to restore them to their respective origins: the Koran and Aristotle. Ibn Taymiyya, who knew that Ibn Rushd was the closest Muslim philosopher to Aristotle, considered him also to be "the closest philosopher to Islam" – "a testimony which Ibn Rushd would have most liked!"[90] In his final remarks, al-Ṣaghīr assumes that the striking similarities of both positions are traceable to common sources of thought or to Ibn Rushd's influence on Ibn Taymiyya, which, of course, the latter did not display openly. Ibn Taymiyya would be, thus, like Thomas Aquinas – "one of the firstlings of Averroism in a different environment than its first Moroccan milieu."[91]

In conclusion, al-Ṣaghīr presents Ibn Taymiyya's position as "an echo, application and extension of Ibn Rushd's philosophical critique" to previous Muslim philosophers and *kalām*-theologians. He does this in order to make a case for Ibn Rushd's uninterrupted influence in the Islamic East (*al-mashriq*).[92] In his view, Ibn Taymiyya's propagated agreement of "clear reason and sound traditional knowledge" is identical with Ibn Rushd's principle of the oneness of truth. Al-Ṣaghīr, however, by means of the interrogative form of the title as well as several cautious statements within the study itself, demonstrates his awareness of the highly hypothetical nature of his arguments and conclusions.

Nevertheless, al-Ṣaghīr is silent about Ibn Taymiyya's explicit accusation that Ibn Rushd, in his writings, concealed his true belief in the so-called "double truth": that the truth of theological teachings is reserved exclusively for philosophers, while common people are fed pious fictions. Al-Ṣaghīr likewise completely ignores the numerous polemical attacks against the Córdoban philosopher in Ibn Taymiyya's works.[93] Obviously, Ibn Taymiyya does not take Ibn Rushd's profes-

---

90 Ibid., p. 182. In her abovementioned study, Anke von Kügelgen, Dialogpartner, pp. 472–475, states that Ibn Taymiyya does not treat Ibn Rushd in a better way than al-Ghazālī deals with his predecessors. She, furthermore, briefly indicates major points of agreement and disagreement between both thinkers, referring to relevant passages in Ibn Taymiyya's works.

91 Al-Ṣaghīr, Mawāqif, p. 182.

92 Ibid., p. 165.

93 For instance: Ibn Taymiyya, *Dar*ʾ, edited by Muḥammad Rashād Sālim, vol. 1, p. 11 et passim, vol. 11, s. v. Ibn Rushd.

sion of the oneness of truth seriously.[94] As the study makes clear, some of his positions can be considered "Averroistic"; these positions, nonetheless, serve Ibn Taymiyya's fundamental conviction of the absolute primacy of Koran and *sunna* over philosophical reasoning – and this is doubtlessly *contra* Averroes.

3. Ibn Taymiyya's Resumption of the Philosophical Discourse in Islam

In a monograph on the resumption of philosophy in Islam, the Moroccan scholar ʿAbd al-Ḥakīm Ajhar extensively examines a number of Ibn Taymiyya's teachings.[95] His analysis includes Ibn Taymiyya's concept of God's oneness (*tawḥīd*), the relationship between God's essence and attributes,[96] and Ibn Taymiyya's teaching in regards to God's eternal creation of the world and to locating the accidents (*ḥawādith*) in the divine essence.[97] Through this selection of purely metaphysical topics, the author intends to demonstrate that Ibn Taymiyya revived Islamic philosophy after it was stalemated by the death of Ibn Rushd. After presenting Ajhar's conception of Ibn Taymiyya as a philosopher and the justification he offers for this view, I will present a summary of his analysis of Ibn Taymiyya's main philosophical assertions.

Ibn Taymiyya, so Ajhar, possesses "an intellectual project" and "a philosophical position which resembles any other philosophical position in the history of philosophy in Islam". His worldview is coherent and "based on clear and solid philosophical and logical foundations". Ajhar describes this aspect of Ibn Taymiyya's thought as "the other hidden side" which is difficult to discover because of Ibn Taymiyya's use of "a twofold language",[98] with which he articulated one truth in a philosophical and a religious way. Unlike Ibn Rushd, however, he did not attempt to establish a philosophical system paralleling religion; rather, moving uniquely and rationally, he treated highly speculative

94 A similar conclusion is in von Kügelgen, Dialogpartner, p. 476.

95 Ajhar, ʿAbd al-Ḥakīm: *Ibn Taymiyya wa-stiʾnāf al-qawl al-falsafī fī al-Islām*, Casablanca and Beirut 2004.

96 Ibid., pp. 43–93.

97 Ibid., pp. 145–226. The middle chapter (pp. 97–141) deals with several theological and philosophical teachings on the originating of the world (*ḥudūth*) and causality, which build Ibn Taymiyya's background in dealing with the topic.

98 Ibid., p. 13.

topics within a religious system utilizing, therewith, the same arguments and Koranic statements used by Ibn Rushd.[99]

Although Ibn Taymiyya explicitly rejected *taʾwīl* (the interpretation of the Koran), he actually developed his position through practicing *taʾwīl*, as he steadily claimed to be "correcting the philosophers' and theologians' misunderstanding" of the sacred and philosophical texts to which they referred. In doing so, he considered reason to be the "activity of interpreting the text [of the Koran]" (*al-nashāṭ al-taʾwīlī lil-naṣṣ*).[100] This unique understanding of rationality, intrinsically connected to the Scripture, enabled him, furthermore, to "justify his philosophy as the harmony (*insijām*) and congruence (*muṭābaqa*) between clear reason and true text." Ibn Taymiyya's "clear reason" (*ṣarīḥ al-maʿqūl*) is nothing else but philosophy, as he knew it through Ibn Rushd and Abū al-Barakāt al-Baghdādī (d. after 560/1164); he, however, avoids using this term because of its negative connotations in Islam.[101] Ibn Taymiyya's philosophy can, thus, be considered as a project of "rational interpretation (*taʾwīl ʿaqlī*) which goes beyond the outward of the text (*ẓāhir al-naṣṣ*) to its rational interior (*bāṭinihi al-ʿaqlī*)." Ibn Taymiyya's project closely resembles that of Ibn Rushd, who, however, did not conceal it as he himself did.[102] Ibn Taymiyya's philosophy is a reformatory enterprise; its purpose is to return reason and religious tradition to the original concord that existed before they were misconceived in philosophy and theology as "two antipodes."[103] Ibn Taymiyya formulates

> a position which is totally in agreement with the rational norms of his time regarding the questions of God's unity and His creation [of the world], [His] being somewhere (*al-jiha*), the teaching of causality and the concept of eternity. In order to justify his 'implied' philosophical system (*manẓūmatahu al-falsafiyya 'al-ḍimniyya'*) [...] he resorted to the text [of the Koran].[104]

The "philosopher" Ibn Taymiyya develops a two-track strategy. On one hand, regarding almost all matters of society, history, politics and eschatology, he rejects any philosophical interpretation of the Koran

99 Ibid., p. 16.
100 Ibid., pp. 16–17, n. 1.
101 Ibid., p. 218, n. 174.
102 Ibid., p. 17 and footnote.
103 Ibid., p. 16.
104 Ibid., pp. 16–17.

and accepts literally-stated religious views exclusively; on the other hand, "in rare rational boldness [...] he establishes a creative ontology which combines oneness and multiplicity in a way which goes beyond former philosophical schools."[105] When dealing with philosophical-theological matters such as God's unity and the creation of the world, however, he utilizes an exoteric-esoteric style that enables him to express ideas in a way that corresponds with a traditional religious understanding.

Ibn Taymiyya employs his exoteric-esoteric approach, according to Ajhar, especially in regards to the rejection of the metaphorical interpretation of God's anthropomorphic attributes; it also is demonstrated by his particularly vehement critique of foregoing Muslim rational philosophers and *kalām*-theologians. In both cases, Ibn Taymiyya followed the traditionalist strand in Islam *expressis verbis*.[106] A more careful reading of his work, however, reveals him to be a "philosopher" who attempted to "revive and activate rational thinking in Islam", utilizing, like the philosophers, the method of rational argumentation and critique.[107] In many other cases, "he justifies his real intentions, as he declares that he does not reject *kalām* and philosophy as a whole, but rather particular formulas and concepts" in these disciplines. This means that he is not hostile to rational discourses as such, but rather objects "to the way *kalām*-theologians and philosophers [discussed] essential ontological issues." In this sense, he rebukes them for their failure "to defend Islam by means of reason."[108]

In Ajhar's view, Ibn Taymiyya consciously and deliberately employed such a style; its vagueness allowed him to establish rational and philosophical foundations for Sunni Islam without being counted among the philosophers or *kalām*-theologians. Besides this, the obscurity of his discourse can be attributed to the historical fact that his ideas are spread out within polemical debates requiring deep knowledge of their historical and intellectual backgrounds; it is this polemical context that primarily determines the tone of his arguments.[109] Furthermore, Ibn Taymiyya negotiates complicated philosophical topics in an unusual and untraditional way – this approach was an additional reason for the obscurity of his style. By negotiating these topics, his

105 Ibid., p. 17.
106 Ibid., p. 22.
107 Ibid., p. 23.
108 Ibid., pp. 83–84 and n. 100.
109 Ibid., pp. 24–25, 218.

"philosophical reason" was open to the philosophers – even to those whom he considered enemies.[110]

Of basic relevance for Ibn Taymiya's project is his conception of knowledge as a special relation between man and the world with no other medium but universal notions, which are based on "real objects". Human knowledge is, thus, "a totally objective process which is determined by the essential epistemological factors which human reason creates through its relation with the world", such as logic.[111] Knowledge

> is a process which is limited to the realm of this world; it is rational in the Aristotelian sense, stripped of metaphysics. This is the reason why Ibn Taymiyya always asserts that knowledge has to be formulated through meaningful expressions of real significance.[112]

Such a concept of knowledge does not play any role in man's relation to God, which is distinctively a religious relation based upon worship "and the fulfillment of the religious laws conveyed by the Prophet Muhammad, which have been formulated and fixed by the jurists and the Hadith-scholars in reliance upon revelation." Ibn Taymiyya, so Ajhar, separates clearly between rational knowledge and religion; "each one of the two has its own field and practices."[113]

In a critical hint, Ajhar states that Ibn Taymiyya's emphasis on reason and its agreement with the text of the Koran did not lead to the revival of rational thought in Islam; on the contrary, it became common among Muslims to reject all forms of rational thinking in the name of good religious tradition. Ibn Taymiyya contributed to this negative development in Islamic intellectual history through his use of "a double-leveled language" which attacked the philosophers and theologians on one hand and adopted "the most daring philosophical opinions in the history of Islamic thought" on the other. As such, his discourse was "ambiguous" and difficult to understand.[114]

Ajhar extensively presents Ibn Taymiyya's philosophical views on the topics which are addressed in the following chapters.

---

110 Ibid., pp. 21–22.
111 Ibid., p. 230.
112 Ibid., p. 231.
113 Ibid.
114 Ibid., p. 23.

3.1. God's Oneness, His Attributes and the Multiplicity of Created Beings

It was hard for *kalām*-theologians to explain how God's absolute oneness could be reconciled with His creation of multiple existents. Muslim philosophers, such as al-Fārābī, adopted the Neoplatonic theory of emanation, which allowed the multiplicity of existents to originate in the first intellect, not in God, preserving thus His absolute oneness.[115] According to Ibn Taymiyya, multiplicity originates in God's attributes, which are one with God's essence. Being the highest universals, they are, at the same time, not separate from their particulars. This double-sided function enables God's attributes to establish, in a rationally explicable way, the relationship between God's absolute oneness and the multiplicity of world affairs; the oneness, transcendence and eternity of God's divine essence remain, thus, unaffected. What comes into being within the divine essence is the "divine action" (*al-fiʿl al-ilāhī*) itself, which means the transformation of the universals to a less universal status through particularization. It is a "conceptual creation" (*ḥudūth mafhūmī*) which preserves the ontological difference between the transcendental divine essence and the world of being and corruption.[116]

Following the Aristotelian strand pursued by Ibn Rushd, Ibn Taymiyya does not consider God's essence as an *abstractum*, void of attributes, but as an objective reality which includes the attributes (*al-ṣifāt*) as a real part.[117] Therefore, he rejects the Muʿtazilī attempt to divest God of His attributes, dismissing this as a way of annihilating the idea of God; yet, he also rejects God's anthropomorphism.[118] For him, God, who is free of corporeal attributes, is not located at a certain space; the world is of a planetary shape, and God encompasses it from all sides infinitely. Though encompassing the world, God is always above it; this is actually an attribute of His transcendence. Even if God is apart from the world, He is at the same time not careless about it. His relation to the world is carried out by His attributes.[119]

115 See Fakhry, Majid: *A History of Islamic Philosophy*, New York 2004, pp. 121–128; Davidson, Herbert: *Alfarabi, Avicenna, and Averroes on Intellect*, New York and Oxford 1992, pp. 44–126.

116 Ajhar, *Ibn Taymiyya*, pp. 19–20.

117 Ibid., pp. 50–51.

118 See van Ess, Josef: Tashbīh wa-tanzīh, in: *EI*^{2}, vol. 10 (2000), pp. 341–342.

119 Ajhar, *Ibn Taymiyya*, pp. 60–61. See Ibn Taymiyya, *Darʾ taʿāruḍ al-ʿaql wal-naql aw muwāfaqat ṣaḥīḥ al-manqūl li-ṣarīḥ al-maʿqūl*, edited by ʿAbd al-Laṭīf

According to Ajhar, Ibn Taymiyya dealt with the complicated relationship between God's attributes and His essence in a "unique and courageous way" which deserves to be considered not only as a contribution "to the formulation of the original philosophical problem; it also breaks with intellectual premises which remained untouched throughout a long period of Islamic thought." In regards to the topics he treated, Ibn Taymiyya was clearly concerned with developing a logical justification of his opinions. Dealing critically with former philosophers and *kalām*-theologians on this topic, he rejected some of their views while adopting many others. This philosophical act of selection makes it difficult for the reader to discover which philosophical views he "put in a different philosophical framework" and adopted, especially since his views are scattered throughout several books. As "his new concepts and ideas" demonstrate, however, Ibn Taymiyya remains both "a *mutakallim* and a philosopher" deeply immersed in both *kalām* and *falsafa*.[120]

Ibn Taymiyya considers God's essence and attributes to be one, forming together "God's oneness and objective existence". In order to define the nature of the divine attributes and their relation to the divine essence, he utilized a philosophical rather than a philological approach, declaring God an inseparable unity consisting of both the essence and the attributes. In this sense, God's attributes, such as His omniscience, omnipotence, life, hearing, seeing etc., are actually not additions (*zāʾida*) to His essence nor different from it (*ghayr*). They possess a "conceptual being" (*al-kaynūna al-mafhūmiyya*)[121] and, as such, they are universals, both genera and species. Together with God's essence, these constitute a unified one being. In this regard, Ibn Taymiyya's teaching that "God and the attributes are one" appears to be very close to the teaching developed by the Muʿtazilī theologian Abū al-Hudhayl al-ʿAllāf (d. 841), stating that the attributes are God Himself (*hiya huwa*).[122] For the Ḥanbalī scholar, however, God's oneness is not merely imagined

ʿAbd al-Raḥmān, Beirut 1417/1997, vol. 3, pp. 277–293. See in general the illuminating study by Jan Hoover, *Ibn Taymiyya's Theodicy of Perpetual Optimism*, Leiden 2007.

120 Ajhar, *Ibn Taymiyya*, p. 83. See on this Özervarli, M. Sait: The Qurʾānic Rational Theology of Ibn Taymiyya and His Criticism of the *Mutakallimūn*, in: Yossef Rapoport and Shahab Ahmad (eds.): *Ibn Taymiyya and His Times*, Oxford 2010, pp. 78–100.

121 Ajhar, *Ibn Taymiyya*, p. 85.

122 Ibid., pp. 86–88. See Ibn Taymiyya, *Darʾ*, edited by ʿAbd al-Laṭīf ʿAbd al-Raḥmān, vol. 5, pp. 328–329; Nyberg, Henrik Samuel: Abu'l-Hudhayl al-ʿAllāf, in: *EI*², vol. 1 (1960), pp. 127–129; see Ibn Rushd's critique of the

but is also objective; although not composite, it is the source of an eternal agency that does not begin or end in time.[123]

This ingenious philosophical concept, combining God's oneness with the plurality of His attributes intends, according to Ajhar, to offer a rational explanation for the creation of the manifold world by the one God. Ibn Taymiyya rejects, therefore, the classical theological classification of God's attributes into essential (*dhātiyya*) and abstract (*maʿnawiyya*) qualities, claiming an equality for all divine attributes as eternal universals in perpetual action united with the divine essence. Each one of these attributes produces its particulars according to specific functions.[124]

Separating himself from traditional *kalām's* view on God's oneness, Ibn Taymiyya obviously aimed to "establish a new philosophical position" different from mainstream *kalām* and *falsafa*. His "philosophical principles" are the unity of God's essence and attributes; the eternity of the divine attributes which are both genera and species; and the eternity of the divine agency.[125] Ajhar states that such a view is "unique in the history of Islamic thought and particularly in the history of Islamic theology".[126] Distinguishing between Ibn Taymiyya's divine attributes and Plato's ideas, he states that the divine attributes do not, like Plato's forms, exist autonomously beyond time and space, with real existents seeming to be no more than their pale imitations. On the contrary, the divine attributes exist in the very essence of God united with His essence, and this unification produces God's oneness. All existents in the material world have their origin in the divine attributes through an eternal process of creation.

Another focus of Ibn Taymiyya's philosophical endeavor is the nature of God's knowledge, which he considers to be, like the divine attributes, one genus with multiple manifestations that cause the objects of knowledge (*al-maʿlūmāt*).[127] It is, once again, God's will which plays a mediating role in relating God's knowledge to the perceptible world. As Ajhar relates, Ibn Taymiyya uniquely offers "a systematic

---

Muʿtazila on this point, which has been criticized by Ibn Taymiyya, *al-Kashf*, pp. 134–136.

123 Ajhar, *Ibn Taymiyya*, p. 89. See Ibn Taymiyya, *Darʾ*, edited by ʿAbd al-Laṭīf ʿAbd al-Raḥmān, vol. 1, p. 215.

124 Ajhar, *Ibn Taymiyya*, p. 90. See Ibn Taymiyya, *Darʾ*, edited by ʿAbd al-Laṭīf ʿAbd al-Raḥmān, vol. 2, pp. 108–109.

125 Ajhar, *Ibn Taymiyya*, p. 91.

126 Ibid., p. 92.

127 Ibid., pp. 181–182; Ibn Taymiyya, *Darʾ*, edited by ʿAbd al-Laṭīf ʿAbd al-Raḥmān, vol. 5, pp. 262–263.

philosophical critique" of the theologians who, in their conceptions of divine knowledge, neglected the role of the divine will. Based on premises borrowed from philosophy, Ibn Taymiyya states that God's will, just as it acts in harmony with the other attributes, also acts in concord with His knowledge. This cooperation makes it possible that God both creates and knows the particulars.[128] God's knowledge, however, acts in eternal succession, which Ibn Taymiyya often describes as "self-renewal" (*tajaddud*).[129] Ajhar points out that Ibn Taymiyya was primarily concerned with offering the most rational explanation of the process of creation, even if doing so "would lead [him] to destroy all foundations of Islamic *kalām*." Ibn Taymiyya's "intellectual and philosophical adventure could have been easier and 'safer', in a religious dogmatic sense, if he would have determined his premises arbitrarily, without philosophical justification, as his predecessors used to do." In regards to the teaching of creation, however, Ibn Taymiyya "was, on a philosophical level, committed to the rational and logical demands which he held to be in agreement with the Koran and the Sunna in a state of real purity."[130]

3.2. Creation of the World

Ibn Taymiyya's views regarding the creation of the world are to be situated, according to Ajhar, in the context of the intensive debate on this topic between Muslim philosophers and theologians. By emphasizing God's will and power as the means by which God created the world, the *kalām*-theologians were unable to develop a worldview which could include causal relations between the existents. According to the theologians, existents – being totally dependent on divine will – are void of any latent ability to come into being or influence other existents. This is in sharp contrast with the philosophers' view, which saw the world as subordinated to a determined order due to a natural causality actually reflective of God's eternal plan for the world.[131]

128 Ajhar, *Ibn Taymiyya*, 188; Ibn Taymiyya, *Darʾ*, edited by ʿAbd al-Laṭīf ʿAbd al-Raḥmān, vol. 5, pp. 295–296.

129 Ajhar, *Ibn Taymiyya*, p. 189. Ibn Taymiyya, *Jāmiʿ al-Rasāʾil*, edited by Muḥammad Rashād Sālim, Cairo 1969, p. 180.

130 Ibid., pp. 189–190.

131 See, for instance, Davidson, *Proofs for Eternity*, pp. 147–172; Fakhry, Majid: *Islamic Occasionalism and Its Critique by Averroës and Aquinas*, London and

Ibn Taymiyya, of course, did not wish to diminish God's absolute power and freedom. He sought, therefore, a rationally accepted explanation of how existence occurred, and developed a unique model wherein the act of creation functions as a mediator between the creator and the created. In order to illustrate how the act of creation fulfills this function, Ajhar expounds Ibn Taymiyya's theory on divine actions and their operation in the world.

For Ibn Taymiyya, divine actions (*afʿāl Allāh*) have a mediatory status between God and the world. These are actually the divine attributes, as they have moved from their universal status as genera to their particular status as species. Divine actions emerge, thus, from God's eternal attributes; they are connected to them and follow them in time. This interval is the time needed for a universal divine attribute to become a particular divine action, occurring outside the divine essence. As Ajhar states, divine actions play "a double philosophical role": they connect the agent, i. e. the divine essence together with the attributes, to the perceptible world, on one hand, and separate both sides from each other, on the other, thus preventing God and the world from being inevitably conceptualized as one being. Due to the divine act of creation, which originally occurred in God's essence, the origin of the created world can be found nowhere else save within the divine essence itself. This is the only way, as Ajhar represents Ibn Taymiyya's view, to reconcile causality with the divine will: God must possess temporal priority against the world.[132] Nevertheless, by these Peripatetic gymnastics, Ibn Taymiyya exceeds all Muslim theologians – including al-Ghazālī – in the "philosophical effort" he expends.[133]

The divine will plays a central role in Ibn Taymiyya's conception of eternal creation, as "it brings forth out of each one of God's attribute

New York 2008; idem: The Classical Islamic Arguments for the Existence of God, in: *The Muslim World* 47 (1957), pp. 133–145; Frank, Richard M.: *The Metaphysics of Created Being According to Abū L-Hudhayl al-ʿAllāf. A Philosophical Study of the Earliest Kalām*, Istanbul 1966; idem: *Beings and Their Attributes. The Teaching of the Basrian School of the Muʿtazila in the Classical Period*, Albany 1978.

132 Ajhar, *Ibn Taymiyya*, pp. 145–146.

133 Ibid., p. 150. Al-Ghazālī's concept of causality has been extensively studied in a large number of articles and monographs. See e. g. Griffel, Frank: *Al-Ghazālī's Philosophical Theology*, Oxford 2009, pp. 147–149, 175–177, 215–217, and the bibliography; Daiber, Hans: God versus Causality. Ghazālī's Solution and Its Historical Background, in: Georges Tamer (ed.): *Islam and Rationality. The Impact of al-Ghazālī*, vol. 1 Leiden (forthcoming).

its own single elements." Thus, the divine will functions as a mediator between the attributes and the particulars resulting from them. Fulfilling this function means that the divine will acts according to a certain logic. At this very point, Ibn Taymiyya is radically different from the *kalām*-theologians, especially the Ashʿarīs and Māturīdīs, who ascribe unrestricted freedom of action to God's will. He, in contrast, believed that genera and species produce only that which logically belong to them. Thus, "the sperm of man produces nothing else but man, the egg nothing else but a bird, the seed nothing else but a tree, and the tree nothing else but fruits."[134] The divine will also

> does not function but according to a definite logic (*manṭiq muḥaddad*) which consists in bringing that which exists in the attributes potentially (*mawjūd bil-quwwa*) to actual existence (*al-wujūd bil-fiʿl*). Consequently, there is no cosmic arbitrariness in creation. The idea of the absolute freedom of the divine will does not bear with chaos, and the idea of miracle cannot be generally applied to the entire divine creation. […] God's voluntative actions subsist in His essence through His will and His power.[135]

Distinguishing the divine action (*al-fiʿl*) from both the subject (*al-fāʿil*) and the object (*al-mafʿūl*) and depicting it as a mediator between them, Ibn Taymiyya rejects the temporal correlation between God and the world, linking them, however, "according to the logic of necessity (*wifqa manṭiq al-ḍarūra*)".[136] Thus, that God's actions begin in His essence does not impair His transcendence. In this sense, Ibn Taymiyya, like Ibn Rushd, suggests that God's creation of the world is eternal, inasmuch this act did not begin and will not end at a certain moment of time. God's eternal creation of the world is intrinsically related to His eternal activity, which itself is without beginning or end.[137] Ajhar makes clear that the connecting role between the one God and the world of multiplicity, which Ibn Taymiyya ascribes to the

---

134 Ajhar, *Ibn Taymiyya*, pp. 160–161; Ibn Taymiyya, *Darʾ*, edited by ʿAbd al-Laṭīf ʿAbd al-Raḥmān, vol. 3, p. 399.

135 Ajhar, *Ibn Taymiyya*, p. 161. See also Hoover, Jon: God Acts by His Will and Power. Ibn Taymiyya's Theology of a Personal God in His Treatise on the Voluntary Attributes, in: Yossef Rapoport and Shahab Ahmad (eds.): *Ibn Taymiyya and His Times*, pp. 55–77.

136 Ajhar, *Ibn Taymiyya*, p. 165; Ibn Taymiyya: *Majmūʿat al-rasāʾil wal-masāʾil*, edited by Rashīd Riḍā, Beirut 1983, vol. 5, p. 371. In this context, Ajhar points out especially Ibn Rushd's influence on Ibn Taymiyya.

137 Ajhar, *Ibn Taymiyya*, p. 166.

divine actions, is the same role Muslim philosophers ascribed to the heavenly spheres.[138]

Ibn Taymiyya's philosophical explanation of creation – that is, as an eternal action involving the particularization of universal divine attributes which are located and united with God's essence – goes, as Ajhar states, beyond all former theological attempts to explain the relationship between God and the world. Clearly, though, this explanation had no adverse effects on the divine transcendence. Ibn Taymiyya accomplishes this through distinguishing between two kinds of coming into being (*ḥudūth*): one is related to the genera (*al-ajnās, jins al-ḥawādith*), i.e. the divine attributes, and one is related to the particular accidents (*al-aʿrāḍ al-khāṣṣa al-muḥaddada*) which come into being and perish in time.[139] His philosophical conception integrates various elements taken from the works of former philosophers and *kalām*-theologians, such as Abū al-Ḥusayn al-Baṣrī (d. 436/1044) and Abū al-Barakāt al-Baghdādī; it is, however, especially indebted to Ibn Rushd. As such, it earned vehement critique from his contemporary theologians.[140]

According to Ajhar's interpretation, Ibn Taymiyya's world is in perpetual renewal due to a continuous state of agency (*fāʿiliyya*). This agency "is the divine creation and the motion through which the existents move from one state into another. Each state is a necessary condition for the following state which results from it."[141] This perspective is a result of Ibn Taymiyya's "philosophical courage", which also manifests in his bold connection of his own philosophical views to major authorities of Hadith, such as al-Bukhārī, and traditional *kalām*, such as Aḥmad b. Ḥanbal. In referring to them, he aims not only to support his position, but also to impute his own philosophical views on creation and divine actions to the traditionalists.[142] Ibn Taymiyya's philosophical ideas seem to be "a creative synthesis of the views of former philosophers", through which he succeeded in negotiating topics crucial to the Muslims of his time. In particular,

---

138 Ibid., p. 167.

139 Ibid., pp. 171–173.

140 Ibid., pp. 174–175. For an overview of the conflicts around Ibn Taymiyya, see Bori, Caterina: Ibn Taymiyya *wa-Jamāʿatuhu*. Authority, Conflict and Consensus in Ibn Taymiyya's Circle, in: Yossef Rapoport and Shahab Ahmad (eds.): *Ibn Taymiyya and His Times*, pp. 23–52.

141 Ajhar, *Ibn Taymiyya*, p. 190.

142 Ibid., p. 191.

Abū al-Barakāt al-Baghdādī provided Ibn Taymiyya with significant rational support.[143]

As Ibn Taymiyya emphasizes God's eternal agency, he also negates the theological teaching of *creatio ex nihilo*. For him, the state of non-existence is nothing but

> a state of being in potentia (*bil-quwwa*) [...]. Ibn Taymiyya does not acknowledge at all a state of nonexistence preceding existence as a whole. Even a particular existent is not preceded by nonexistence, but it was latent (*kāmin*) [...] in a preceding thing which constitutes its condition from which it results. The state of nonexistence which precedes the existent is for Ibn Taymiyya nothing but a state of latency.[144]

Ajhar points out, furthermore, that Ibn Taymiyya utilizes the same Koranic verses used by Ibn Rushd in his treatise *Faṣl al-maqāl* to assert that the world was not created out of nothing.[145]

In contrast to the philosophers, Ibn Taymiyya understands causality in a way that maintains a temporal difference between God and the world, therefore upholding God's temporal priority. Against the *kalām*-theologians, he acknowledges the eternity of God's agency and acknowledges its connection to His eternal will and power.[146] Accordingly, Ibn Taymiyya argues both rationally and philosophically for the infinite regress of the causes as an inevitable premise for God's eternal agency. As infinite as the chain of causes could be, each one of the causes is naturally in a state of potential existence and necessarily requires another cause to move it into the state of actual existence. God remains, thus, the absolute cause of the world; He brings all existents into being through their immediate natural causes.[147] In his view, the cause (*ʿilla*) does not create an existent, but it functions as a "necessary condition" (*sharṭ ḍarūrī*) for it to come into being.[148] God's will and

143 Ibid., pp. 197–198. For his views see al-Baghdādī, Abū al-Barakāt Hibat Allāh b. ʿAlī b. Malkā: *Kitāb al-Muʿtabar fī al-ḥikma al-ilāhiyya*, Haydarabad 1357–1358/1938–1939.

144 Ajhar, *Ibn Taymiyya*, p. 213; Ibn Taymiyya, *Darʾ*, edited by ʿAbd al-Laṭīf ʿAbd al-Raḥmān, vol. 5, p. 217.

145 Ajhar, *Ibn Taymiyya*, p. 217. See Koran (11:7; 14:48; 41:11); Ibn Rushd, *Faṣl*, pp. 21–22; Ibn Taymiyya, *Majmūʿat al-rasāʾil*, vol. 5, p. 352.

146 Ajhar, *Ibn Taymiyya*, p. 21.

147 Ibid., pp. 199–201; Ibn Taymiyya, *Darʾ*, edited by ʿAbd al-Laṭīf ʿAbd al-Raḥmān, vol. 2, pp. 198–199.

148 Ajhar, *Ibn Taymiyya*, pp. 204–206. The *kalām*-theologians denied the immediate effect of natural causes, seeing God to be the immediate cause of everything in the world. They often illustrated their position by saying that man

His agency are for him "a continuous force pushing the beings so that they do not stop and maintain their efficiency."[149]

Maintaining a position close to Ibn Rushd's conception of double causality, Ibn Taymiyya believes that every existent "is a condition or an instrument for the divine activity (*sharṭ aw āla lil-fāʿiliyya al-ilāhiyya*)". Each caused existent results from two things: "the existent which precedes it and is a condition for its existence, and the divine action which occurred in God's essence for the sake of bringing that existent into being."[150] Through His actions, God operates as the causal core of "an infinite chain of causes [...] due to the fact that each existent has necessarily to be conditioned through another existent which has, again, to be conditioned through another existent *ad infinitum*." Ibn Taymiyya attempts, thus, to reconcile God's role as creator of the world with natural causality. This attempt, properly considered, is also an effort to reconcile theology with philosophy.[151]

Ibn Taymiyya's theory of God's eternal and continuous creation of the world offers, so Ajhar, a major contribution to the explanation of important dogmatic and philosophical questions in Islam. In most cases, Ibn Taymiyya avoids employing terminology used by the philosophers in order to distinguish himself from them; in other cases, he attacks the philosophers vigorously. Sometimes he agrees with them; suddenly he changes his attitude and opposes them. He obviously was convinced that "clear reason" corresponded with the majority of the philosophers' ideas. He, however, was also aware of the bad reputation philosophers had among Muslims; this led him to articulate, within his own works, the accumulated historical animosity against philosophy found in Islamic thought. Yet, this side of his writings, adopted and further developed by his students, is merely the external one. Exam-

---

becomes sated *upon* (*ʿinda*) eating bread and quenches his thirst *upon* (*ʿinda*) drinking water. It is God, however, who causes the state of being sated and quenched. Ibn Taymiyya, in contrast, rejects this idea, substituting the preposition *ʿinda* by the preposition *bi-* which expresses a causal relationship. Thus, man becomes sated *through* eating bread and quenched *through* drinking water: ibid., p. 222; Ibn Taymiyya, *Majmūʿat al-rasāʾil*, vol. 1, p. 100; vol. 5, p. 330. See el Omari, Racha: Ibn Taymiyya's "Theology of the Sunna" and His Polemics with the Ashʿarites, in: Yossef Rapoport and Shahab Ahmad (eds.): *Ibn Taymiyya and His Times*, pp. 101–119.

149 Ajhar, *Ibn Taymiyya*, p. 223.

150 Ibid., p. 209. For Ibn Rushd's "double causality" see Arnaldez, Roger: Ibn Rushd, in: *EI²*, vol. 3 (1971), pp. 909–920.

151 Ajhar, *Ibn Taymiyya*, pp. 210, 219.

ined in depth, Ibn Taymiyya's writings betray the strong influence of the philosophers. The hidden side of his work "was probably not known to any of his followers, or it might have been known to some of them, who, nevertheless, kept silent about it for the same reasons which forced their master to hide it."[152]

4. Ibn Taymiyya's Nominalism and the Renaissance of Arabic Philosophy

The previously discussed scholars are primarily interested in presenting the historical value of Ibn Taymiyya's philosophical thought in the context of theological-philosophical discourses of Islamic thinking in the past. In contrast, the Tunisian professor of philosophy Abū Yaʿrub (Muḥammad al-Ḥabīb) al-Marzūqī (b. 1947) ascribes to Ibn Taymiyya and Ibn Khaldūn the development of a new stream of modern, nominalistic Arabic-Islamic philosophy that supersedes Plato's and Aristotle's realism and the modern philosophy influenced by them in the West.[153]

According to al-Marzūqī, the philosophy of Ibn Taymiyya and Ibn Khaldūn represents the "ultimate stage" (*al-manzila al-ghāya*) of Arabic philosophy in regards to defining the nature of the theoretical and the practical Universal (*al-kullī*). Both thinkers belong to the realm of philosophy in its theoretical and practical dimensions as known in Greek civilization, inasmuch as they belong to the realm of

152 Ibid., p. 226.

153 Al-Marzūqī presents his interpretation extensively in his monograph *Iṣlāḥ al-ʿaql fī al-falsafa al-ʿarabiyya. Min wāqiʿiyyat Arisṭū wa-Aflāṭūn ilā ismiyyat Ibn Taymiyya wa-Ibn Khaldūn* (Reformation of Reason in Arabic Philosophy. From the Realism of Aristotle and Plato to the Nominalism of Ibn Taymiyya and Ibn Khaldūn), Beirut 1996^2. This book builds upon the earlier voluminous work *Manzilat al-kullī fī al-falsafa al-ʿarabiyya fī al-Aflāṭūniyya wal-ḥanīfiyya al-muḥdathatayn al-ʿarabiyyatayn* (The Position of the Universal in Arabic Philosophy in Arabic Neoplatonism and Neohanifism), Tunis 1994. Both books are part 1 and 2 of al-Marzūqī's lengthy Ph.D. thesis with over 1000 pages. A concise article, Fikr Ibn Taymiyya al-iṣlāḥī. Abʿāduhu al-falsafiyya (Ibn Taymiyya's Reformatory Thought. Its Philosophical Dimensions), published in the Moroccan periodical *al-Munʿaṭaf* 18–19 (2001), and made available online: http://www.alfalsafa.com/fikr ibn taymia.html (accessed on August 16, 2011), contains a useful summary of al-Marzūqī's understanding of Ibn Taymiyya. It is widely published on several Arabic websites.

theology (*kalām*) in its theoretical and practical dimensions as known in Arabic civilization. Thus, Ibn Taymiyya and Ibn Khaldūn represent the utmost convergence of philosophy and theology, theory and practice, "Arabic Neoplatonism" (*al-aflāṭūniyya al-muḥdatha al-ʿarabiyya*) and "Arabic Neohanifism" (*al-ḥanīfiyya al-muḥdatha al-ʿarabiyya*).[154]

Al-Marzūqī defines Arabic Neoplatonism as the entirety of premodern Arabic philosophy, which he divides into a connective (*al-waṣliyya*) and a separative (*al-faṣliyya*) part. The connective part includes, with Ikhwān al-Ṣafāʾ (Brethren of Purity) a Platonic branch, and with the Peripatetics, such as al-Fārābī, an Aristotelian branch. The separative part, again, includes a Platonic branch with al-Suhrawardī's (d. 587/1191) Illuminationist philosophy, and an Aristotelian branch with Ibn Rushd's philosophy.[155] Arabic Neohanifism signifies

> all theological (*kalāmiyya*) and mystical (*ṣūfiyya*) intellectual attempts whose authoritative text are the Koran and Hadith, as Islam is the neo-ḥanīf religion which goes back to the 'true' (*ḥanīf*) religion following Judaism[156] and Christianity[157] and the alteration (*taḥrīf*) they caused, as stated in the Koran.[158]

Al-Marzūqī likewise divides Arabic Neohanifism into a connective part, which encompasses the two branches of pre-Ghazalian theology (*kalām*) and mysticism (*taṣawwuf*), and a separative part, which includes the two branches of theology and mysticism, which flourished in the time between al-Ghazālī and Ibn Taymiyya.

Through this structural and historical mapping of Arabic philosophy, al-Marzūqī aims to define the "reformatory attempts" of Ibn Taymiyya and Ibn Khaldūn at the end of the medieval period and the beginning of the Arab Renaissance.[159] He calls their philosophical position "nominalism" (*ismiyya*), which he describes as the negation of the jump from general concepts to universal concepts on an epistemological and an

---

154 Al-Marzūqī, *Iṣlāḥ*, p. 13.

155 Al-Marzūqī also subsumes practices like magic and astrology under the category of Arabic Neoplatonism: ibid., p. 15, n. 6.

156 According to al-Marzūqī: "*al-tawrātiyya*," "Torahism". Ibid., p. 15, n. 7.

157 According to al-Marzūqī: "*al-injīliyya*," "Evangelism". Ibid., p. 15, n. 7.

158 Al-Marzūqī, *Iṣlāḥ*, p. 15, n. 7.

159 Ibid., p. 15. The Arab Renaissance begins, according to al-Marzūqī, in the 19th century following four centuries of decline (*ʿaṣr al-inḥiṭāṭ*), which he subsequently reduces to two centuries, the 16th and 17th: ibid., p. 15, n. 8.

existential level.[160] In the way they deal with philosophical problems, both thinkers appear to be "philosophically closer to Plato and Aristotle, and religiously closer to Moses and Jesus" than earlier philosophers and theologians of both Arabic Neoplatonism and Neohanifism.[161]

As this overview makes clear, al-Marzūqī's presentation of Ibn Taymiyya's philosophy is heavily loaded with conceptual and philosophical-historical arguments. A full analysis of his model would go beyond the scope of the present study.[162] Therefore, I will discuss, in the following passages, only the main aspects of al-Marzūqī's interpretation of Ibn Taymiyya's "nominalistic philosophy", leaving aside his discussion of Ibn Khaldūn.

In al-Marzūqī's view, Ibn Taymiyya might be the most important philosopher in the history of Islam; he

> abolished the realism of the natural Universal through presenting its positivistic character and let theoretical science become historical [...] the act of philosophy (*al-tafalsuf*) became a historical science [...]. Ibn Taymiyya's work theorized, first, theory and, consequently, it also theorized practice.[163]

Ibn Taymiyya's nominalistic understanding of the definition leads, furthermore, to the abolishment of the traditional difference between the outward (*al-ẓāhir*) and inward (*al-bāṭin*) levels in both natural and religious knowledge as well.[164] In opposition to that what was predominant in philosophy before his time, Ibn Taymiyya's approach led to

---

160 Ibid., p. 20 and n. 17. Al-Marzūqī discusses the concept of the Universal in Arabic philosophy extensively in his abovementioned book *Manzilat al-kullī fī al-falsafa al-ʿarabiyya.*

161 Ibid., p. 22.

162 According to al-Marzūqī, "Plotinus turned philosophy into religion, and Muhammad turned religion into philosophy. The first made religion the ultimate purpose of philosophy through sealing science and putting an end to it (*bi-khatm al-ʿilm wa-qatlih*). The second made religion into philosophy by sealing revelation and putting an end to it (*bi-khatm al-waḥy wa-qatlih*)." While Plotinus, by sealing science, cast man out of history in regards to science and practice, Muḥammad brought man back into history in regards to science and practice, as it was necessary for revelation to be sealed: ibid., 37, n. 34. Ibn Taymiyya put an end to Neoplatonism, and, presumably without being aware it, also put an end to Neohanifism: ibid., p. 38. Such over-generalizations characterize al-Marzūqī's method in dealing with the history of philosophy and religion.

163 Al-Marzūqī, *Iṣlāḥ*, p. 71.

164 Ibid., p. 78, with reference to Ibn Taymiyya, *al-Radd*, pp. 81–82/39–40.

a new situation in which language, pronounced and written, became decisive for determining cognitive concepts.[165] Theoretical and practical meanings, accordingly, were demoted to mere symbols[166]; absolute congruence exists between the written form of a word, its pronunciation and its meaning.[167] With definitions and theoretical concepts proclaimed by Ibn Taymiyya as "human inventions" (*mukhtaraʿāt insāniyya*), the traditional dichotomy of theory and practice loses its foundation; both become interdependent – a development which is truly "an epistemological coup".[168]

Furthermore, al-Marzūqī describes Ibn Taymiyya's work as "a practical spiritual revolution" (*thawra ʿamaliyya rūḥiyya*) which is based on redefining the status of the "theoretical Universal" (*al-kullī al-naẓarī*). Ibn Taymiyya challenged the "spiritual priestly rule" (*sulṭān al-kahanūt al-rūḥī*) which collaborated with the "temporal military rule" (*sulṭān al-ʿaskarūt al-zamānī*) and obtained, consequently, unrestricted power on the life of the people through "negating the command of the religious law" (*nafī al-amr al-sharʿī*) and being restricted to universal "pure determinism" (*al-jabriyya al-khāliṣa*).[169]

Al-Marzūqī states that Ibn Taymiyya resolved the main dilemma of Arabic-Islamic thought, which he describes as an intellectual "dissociation" resulting in an ongoing "cold war" between reason and the worldly sciences, on one side, and religious tradition and the sciences of the Hereafter on the other. Ibn Taymiyya achieved, thus, the goal which al-Ghazālī and other Muslim thinkers had failed to accomplish.[170] Ibn Taymiyya, however, did not leave systematic philosophical writings, but "philosophical seeds"; these are spread throughout

165 Ibid., p. 80, referring to Ibn Taymiyya, *Darʾ*, edited by Muḥammad Rashād Sālim, vol. 3, p. 216.

166 Ibid., p. 81.

167 Ibid., pp. 105–106, 176–177; Ibn Taymiyya, *Darʾ*, edited by Muḥammad Rashād Sālim, vol. 3, p. 216.

168 Ibid., pp. 118–119. In his enthusiastic account of Ibn Taymiyya's "philosophy", al-Marzūqī neglects to mention that much of Ibn Taymiyya's arguments against Aristotle's logic can be found in works of *kalām*-theologians, especially the Ashʿarīs, although he refers to a passage in Ibn Khaldūn's *Muqaddima*, in which this pre-Taymiyyan critique is precisely summarized: ibid, p. 190. See Ibn Khaldūn: *The Muqaddimah. An Introduction to History*, translated from the Arabic by Franz Rosenthal, New York 1958, vol. 3, chapter 6, section 22, pp. 143–147.

169 Al-Marzūqī, *Iṣlāḥ*, p. 394.

170 The following presentation of al-Marzūqī's interpretation of Ibn Taymiyya's thought is based on the abovementioned article: Fikr Ibn Taymiyya al-iṣlāḥī.

his books – some of which bear a philosophical touch – as well as in fatwas and in isolated statements. Despite this enticing trail of clues, however, there are "substantial" (*dhātiyya*) obstacles that make a philosophical reading of his work difficult. These impediments are the fragmented nature of Ibn Taymiyya's philosophical writing and his "practical" interest in calumniating the arguments of his opponents without systematically discussing their positions. These hurdles cause, furthermore, two "accidental" (*ʿāriḍa*) deterrents: 1) that the Islamic institutions of some countries have employed Ibn Taymiyya's thought to abolish true theoretical religious and philosophical thinking; and 2) that Islamic opposition movements fighting against secular ideas use only negative aspects of his thought. Therefore, a penetrating reading of Ibn Taymiyya's works must first eliminate all of these hindrances in order to extract the philosophical essence that reveals Ibn Taymiyya's identity as "a great philosopher".

Indeed, Ibn Taymiyya's writings contain "the project of a philosophical revolution which, had it been realized, would have saved Arabic-Islamic thought from the theoretical and practical dilemmas which deactivated its scientific creativity." Indeed, this very lack of creativity affected Muslims' reactions to natural and historical phenomena. The modern interpreter has to define the "necessary and sufficient conditions" (*al-shurūṭ al-ḍarūriyya wal-kāfiya*) of the normative critique Ibn Taymiyya applied against the philosophical and religious thought predominant in his age, as presented in the works of Ibn Rushd, al-Suhrawardī, Ibn ʿArabī (d. 638/1240), and al-Rāzī, on the other.

Al-Marzūqī connects these Muslim thinkers to dilemmas caused in Islamic philosophical and religious thought on a theoretical and practical level. These dilemmas led to Ibn Taymiyya's critique of their ideas, through which he attempted to revive the "Muhammedan Reformation" (*al-iṣlāḥ al-muḥammadī*) in its rejection of the religious distortion that had happened in the Torah and the Gospels. Analogously, Ibn Taymiyya campaigned, as abovementioned, against the philosophical distortion of the philosophy of Plato by Ikhwān al-Ṣafāʾ, and against the deformation of the philosophy of Aristotle by Peripatetics such as Ibn Rushd. In opposition, Ibn Taymiyya endeavored to develop an alternative metaphysics and an alternative meta-history, deriving their sources from the reinterpretation of the Koran and the prophetic tradi-

---

Abʿāduhu al-falsafiyya, available online: http://www.alfalsafa.com/fikr ibn taymia.html, accessed on August 16, 2011.

tion (*sunna*) in a way that illuminated the scientific-theoretical and the practical-ethical dimensions of the "Islamic revolution".

Al-Marzūqī asserts that this twofold endeavor, if fulfilled, could save humanity from the "evils of globalism" (*shurūr al-ʿawlama*). Manifesting through philosophical teachings which declared existence to be a natural unity – as in the works of the Peripatetics and the Brethern of Purity – or a historical unity – as in the works of Ibn ʿArabī and al-Rāzī – the evil of globalism had already become visible in Ibn Taymiyya's age.

According to al-Marzūqī, Ibn Taymiyya's critical treatment of logic and metaphysics located the origin of philosophical thought within an endogenous Arabic-Islamic epistemological practice. Exceeding the superficial opposition of philosophy and religion, this practice claimed to establish the theoretical correspondence of "true religious tradition and clear reason." This was a reaction to the hermeneutical norm predominant in *kalām* and philosophy, which divided human knowledge into esoteric and exoteric strata. On the contrary, "the Muhammedan revolution" (*al-thawra al-muḥammadiyya*), by declaring Islam the religion of human disposition (*al-fiṭra*) and elevating religious thought to a universal state, abolished the contradiction between the natural and the revealed religion: this stratification of knowledge was thus rendered obsolete.[171] Through a "methodological revolution", Ibn Taymiyya was able to remove all accretions in order to reveal the real harmony of clear reason and true religious tradition. His method led to removing falsification (*taḥrīf*) from philosophy, as it eliminated the "metaphysical absolutization" which made religious law appear to contradict cosmological necessity. Ibn Taymiyya's diagnosis of metaphysics distinguishes between cosmological necessity and "religious command" (*al-amr al-sharʿī*), ascribing to this the prerequisite of human freedom, as the fulfillment of religious commands is based on free choice.[172]

Al-Marzūqī states, furthermore, that Ibn Taymiyya articulates his critique of both philosophy and religious thought on A) an epistemological and B) an existential level. On the epistemological level, he deals with the traditionally pretended opposition of analysis (*taḥlīl*) and interpretation (*taʾwīl*) of objects of knowledge; on the existential level, he deals with the traditionally pretended opposition of truth

171 Al-Marzūqī refers to Koran (7:172–173).

172 Al-Marzūqī, Fikr Ibn Taymiyya al-iṣlāḥī, http://www.alfalsafa.com/fikr ibn taymia.html, accessed on August 16, 2011.

(*ḥaqīqa*) and metaphor (*majāz*) in regards to the Koran. The goal of Ibn Taymiyya's critique is to abolish the "dualism of knowledge" so that "monotheism (*al-tawḥīd*) becomes philosophical monotheism which fulfills what Islam proclaims, which is to be the theory of the universal religion". This universal religion includes, as its primary attribute, the congruence of "the sealing revealed religion" and "the rational natural religion, meaning the religion of natural disposition (*fiṭra*)".[173]

A. Ibn Taymiyya's epistemological critique, again, is divided into two parts:

1. The first part deals with "clear reason" and includes the clearness of pure and applied rational knowledge. Ibn Taymiyya aims here at "reforming the theory of rational knowledge, logic, metaphysics and natural philosophy."[174]

2. The second part deals with "sound religious tradition" and includes the soundness of pure and applied traditional knowledge. Ibn Taymiyya aims here at "reforming the theory of traditional religious knowledge, history, meta-history and the philosophy of history and civilization based on that."[175]

Through his comprehensive treatment of the relationship between analysis and interpretation, Ibn Taymiyya was able to free Arabic thought from the false assumption that analysis and truth represent rational sciences, while interpretation and metaphor represent religious sciences. Demonstrating that this dichotomy is superficial, Ibn Taymiyya's treatment of this issue occurred on two levels:

1. Through his critique of Aristotle's logic and the metaphysics based on it, Ibn Taymiyya declares that the essential attributes and definitions, i. e. the primary truths which are the principles of logic and metaphysics, are no more than "cognitive values" (*muqaddarāt dhihniyya*) set in relation to the existents so that these can be known. As a result, definitions (*ḥudūd*) do not establish the essence and the truth of existents; they are mere "scientific names" (*asmāʾ ʿilmiyya*) which occur in the human mind. Demonstrative knowledge, exalted in Peripatetic philosophy as

---

173 Al-Marzūqī, Fikr Ibn Taymiyya al-iṣlāḥī, http://www.alfalsafa.com/fikr ibn taymia.html, accessed on August 16, 2011, *al-Maqāla al-thāniya. Kayfa ṣāra fiʾl al-tafalsuf mumkinan.*

174 Al-Marzūqī, Fikr Ibn Taymiyya al-iṣlāḥī, http://www.alfalsafa.com/fikr ibn taymia.html, accessed on August 16, 2011.

175 Al-Marzūqī, Fikr Ibn Taymiyya al-iṣlāḥī, http://www.alfalsafa.com/fikr ibn taymia.html, accessed on August 16, 2011.

the most accurate form of human knowledge, consists, thus, of nothing else but "cognitive values"; this renders knowledge (*al-ʿilm*), as such, to be "hypothetic and deduced" (*faraḍī istintājī*). Related to the form of an existent, it is equally as approximate in regards to its matter. Aristotelian demonstration is, thus, changed into the relative epistemological outcome of a nominalistic process. An analytical result is reduced to a formal one; its truth is merely a subject of cognitive evaluation. Consequently, science cannot be absolute, as the pure rational axiomatic principles are not part of the external existents, but belong to the realm of subjective "cognitive values". Analytical systems, then, are developed out of optional starting points, each according to a specific practice, in order to explain certain phenomena. Analysis (*taḥlīl*) results necessarily from interpretation (*taʾwīl*) and is not opposite to it.

2. On the second level, Ibn Taymiyya attempted to achieve a "revolution" seeking to overthrow the "theory of science inherited from the Greeks and the theory of existence supporting it, as well". The outcome of his endeavor is the knowledge that both religious and rational sciences can share the same object, as religious sciences (*al-ʿulūm al-naqliyya*) can deal with natural phenomena and rational sciences (*al-ʿulūm al-ʿaqliyya*) can deal with religious issues as well. All objects of knowledge are nothing but rational, as reason is the only organ of knowledge – which is also valid in regards to religious knowledge as well. In this sense, religious sciences, such as the interpretation of the Koran, do not differ from rational sciences except in regards to the subject matter handled.

B. The second problem Ibn Taymiyya addresses on an existential level is the traditionally imagined opposition of truth (*ḥaqīqa*) and metaphor (*majāz*) in regards to the Koran. This topic is actually "the center of his works and the theoretical pillar of his responses to *kalām*, mysticism and especially philosophy". This occurs, again, on two levels:

1. On the first level, Ibn Taymiyya rejects the opposition of truth and metaphor as a later invention, baseless and unknown as it was to the early great authorities of philology, *tafsīr* and *uṣūl al-fiqh*.

2. On the second level, Ibn Taymiyya rejects the concept of interpretation which "determines the truth of that what an issue, in itself or in its reference, results in"[176], without taking into account the capability

176 Al-Marzūqī, Fikr Ibn Taymiyya al-iṣlāḥī, http://www.alfalsafa.com/fikr ibn taymia.html, accessed on August 16, 2011.

of human languages when describing objects the Koran considers as unseen. Only God knows objects such as sanctions in the Hereafter, God's essence, and God's attributes. Ibn Taymiyya also rejects the act of interpretation as the search for a truth beyond the metaphor, which ascribes to the text an outward level in opposition to an inward one. Dismissing this opposition as invalid, Ibn Taymiyya raises awareness of the fact that the metaphorical and real meanings of expressions are bound to "verbal conditions" (*quyūd lafẓiyya*); he utilizes Arabic philological and linguistic materials in his argumentation in a way that, according to al-Marzūqī, should help resolve the contemporary dilemma of Koranic exegesis. Ibn Taymiyya develops, furthermore, a philosophical theory of language according to which single expressions do not have significance except when constrained by linguistic evidence and the state of discourse of which they are part. This achievement is important for the understanding of science, as such: based on this premise, a science is "an artificial language whose function is to analyze a phenomenon in a way presupposing that its logical and analytical system consists of pure cognitive values"[177].

5. Conclusions

Contemporary Muslim authors overwhelmingly intrigued by philosophical elements in Ibn Taymiyya's works do not limit his impact to his critique of past philosophers and *kalām*-theologians; on the contrary, they ascribe specific philosophical qualities to him, qualifying him as a philosopher in his own right. What's more, some of these authors widely extend his philosophical impact to include theoretical alternatives he suggested, which, they allege, possess worth beyond their historical value in regards to the establishment of modern Islamic philosophy. Naturally, imputing the status of a philosopher to Ibn Taymiyya means connecting him to former and later philosophers; his refutation of Aristotelian logic is seen, therefore, both as a continuation of Stoic and Skeptic positions and as a predecessor of early modern empiricism. Furthermore, his nominalistic interpretation of basic elements of logic and his realistic conception of existence are presented as an ambitious philosophical project, based on the founda-

177 Al-Marzūqī, Fikr Ibn Taymiyya al-iṣlāḥī, http://www.alfalsafa.com/fikr ibn taymia.html, accessed on August 16, 2011.

tion of Koran and Sunna, whose aim was to correct the Platonic and Aristotelian schools. According to another strand of interpretation, the most manifest point is Ibn Taymiyya's philosophical connection to Ibn Rushd's philosophy, whose powerful spell Ibn Taymiyya was not able to completely break and which thus, confers on Ibn Taymiyya the identity of an Averroist – even if he would not admit it.

Ibn Taymiyya is one of the giants of Islamic intellectual history. His writings clearly display his exemplary mastery of Islamic religious sciences, philosophy and *kalām*-theology. Furthermore, he was a prolific *mujtahid* who did not slavishly follow the Ḥanbalī school of *fiqh*, but developed his own views on important religious, social and political topics.[178] His striving to present the unity of rationality and religion and to defend faith against the attacks of critical philosophers is conducted through intensive usage of philosophical terminology and argumentation.

Nevertheless, how much of a philosopher is Ibn Taymiyya, actually? Ibn Taymiyya was an extremely committed Muslim who endeavored with the utmost effort to defend Sunni Islam with both sword and pen: having courageously fought with the Mamluk army against the Crusaders, the Tatars, the Shiites and the Armenians, he enthusiastically wrote against every idea and practice in which he saw a threat against orthodox Islam. For him, writing was just as much a form of holy jihad as military service. This might be an explanation for his dedicating a major part of his legal statements (*fatwās*) to important doctrinal topics. Hereby, Ibn Taymiyya departed from the traditional style of theologians and philosophers alike, who were primarily interested in addressing their peers while preventing the uneducated majority (*al-ʿawāmm*) from taking part in specialized debates.[179] On the contrary, Ibn Taymiyya made doctrinal discussions not only a privilege for scholars, but also a matter for the public sphere. Combining great zeal for his religion with a vast and deep knowledge of philological and religious tradition, theology and philosophy, he unfolded many of his teachings in sharp polemical writings which unmistakably reflect, besides his erudition, his deep faith and piety.

Ibn Taymiyya's methodological principle that clear reason and sound tradition necessarily agree is fundamentally based on his belief

178 Al-Matroudi, *The Ḥanbalī School*, pp. 186–191.

179 A prime example of this attitude is al-Ghazālī's treatise *Iljām al-ʿawāmm ʿan ʿilm al-kalām* (Restraining the Ordinary People from the Science of *Kalām*), edited by Muḥammad al-Muʿtaṣim bi-llāh al-Baghdādi, Beirut 1406/1985.

that whatever contradicts the literal text of Koran and Hadith cannot be rational at all. In this, he diametrically opposes Ibn Rushd who, in the case of disagreement between the Koran and the requirements of rationality, argues for interpreting the Koranic text in a way that favors rationality. For Ibn Taymiyya, it is the revealed text and the statements of the prophet which ultimately determine what is rational and what is not. Pure rationality is embodied in the Koran and Hadith; what is not in agreement with them is both unoriginal and rationally corrupt. Accordingly, true knowledge is that which is taken directly from Koran and Hadith, and there is no certain evidence other than what is included in the revealed corpus as transmitted by the infallible prophet Muḥammad. Whatever does not agree with this corpus is disqualified from the realm of reason. As philosophy is essentially a rational activity of investigation and critique independent of the authority of revelation, Ibn Taymiyya's conception of rationality as part of the outcome of revelation provides just the opposite of that what philosophy is.[180]

Indeed, Ibn Taymiyya's works include philosophical components appropriately assimilated into a comprehensive theological image, different aspects of which are spread throughout his numerous writings. These philosophical components are utilized to support his theological arguments and to attack the philosophers with their own weapons. It has also been stated that, beyond his deep knowledge of philosophy, he "shares with the philosophers the philosophical spirit" which strives to penetrate thoroughly into the essence of subjects, and like them he is mindful of "determining the meaning of words accurately".[181] Despite this shared spirit, however, Ibn Taymiyya's

---

180 Abrahamov, Binyamin: Ibn Taymiyya on the Agreement of Reason with Tradition, in: *The Muslim World* 82 (1992), pp. 256–272, presents Ibn Taymiyya's arguments rejecting the preference of reason to tradition, as they are included in *Darʾ taʿāruḍ al-ʿaql wal-naql*, and locating the truth exclusively in revelation. On this intensively debated question in Islamic philosophy and theology, see, for instance: Arberry, Arthur J.: *Revelation and Reason in Islam*, London 1957; Frank, Richard M.: Reason and Revealed Law. A Sample of Parallels and Divergences in Kalām and Falsafa, in: Roger Arnaldez and Simone van Riet (eds.): *Recherches d'Islamologie. Recueil d'articles offert à Georges C. Anawati et Louis Gardet par leur collègues et amis*, Louvain 1978.

181 Fu'ād, ʿAbd al-Fattāḥ Aḥmad: *Ibn Taymiyya wa-mawqifuhu min al-fikr al-falsafī*, Alexandria 1980, p. 273. In a more recent publication, Fu'ād declares Ibn Taymiyya as the representative of *ahl al-sunna* in their critique of "the philosophers of Islam and the Sufis": Fu'ād, ʿAbd al-Fattāḥ Aḥmad: *Falāsifat*

religious understanding of rationality makes it difficult to label him as a philosopher. While the philosophers held that the highest happiness could be achieved by the intellectual contemplation of non- or extra-doctrinal metaphysical truths, Ibn Taymiyya, in contrast, held that true happiness comes from knowledge of God and the perfection and salvation of the soul in the afterlife. The Koran – not human reason – was the appropriate guide on this path; as such, scripture was the ultimate basis for all truth and took direct precedence if in conflict with reason. In this context, Ibn Taymiyya would consider it a curse to be called a philosopher.

Despite obvious historical and cultural differences as well as the different theological conception of scriptures in Christianity and Islam, Ibn Taymiyya's usage of philosophy reminds me of the way the Church Fathers of the East used Platonic, Aristotelian, Stoic and Neoplatonic concepts to articulate Christian doctrines. The work of these Fathers cannot be considered philosophy; Ibn Taymiyya, compared to them, is just as unqualified to be called a philosopher as they are. Furthermore, Thomas Aquinas called philosophy the maid of theology, thus giving philosophy a separate though subordinate state in relation to theology. Ibn Taymiyya, in fundamentally subsuming rationality to the words of Koran and Hadith, goes farther to deny rationality a similar state.

In this context, the role Ibn Taymiyya ascribes to the prophet Muhammad is pivotal. As Muhammad is the deliverer of revelation, he is the absolute authority in regards to the truth: what he said is true and serves as criterion to determine the truth of theological and philosophical statements. Muḥammad's authority passes to the body of religious scholars (*ʿulamāʾ*), who are "the heirs of the prophets" (*al-ʿulamāʾ warathat al-anbiyāʾ*) according to a famous tradition in Islam.[182] Yet, the articulated truth of these scholars depends on their participation in the community consensus (*ijmāʿ*) founded exclusively on the ultimate source of this spiritual lineage: namely, the Koran and Hadith. Ibn Taymiyya's reasoning, therefore, reveals its conclusively circular form.

---

al-islām wal-ṣūfiyya wa-mawqif ahl al-sunna minhum, Alexandria 2006, pp. 10–11, 98–100, 120–122, 129–130, 133–136 et passim.

182 Rosenthal, Franz: *Knowledge Triumphant. The Concept of Knowledge in Medieval Islam; with an introduction by Dimitri Gutas*, Leiden and Boston 2007, p. 38.

In making Ibn Taymiyya a philosopher, which consequences arise for the conception of philosophy? Ibn Taymiyya unwaveringly asserts in his writings that the text of the Koran and the Sunna are the sole, solid, and unquestionable fundament of truth. Intrinsically, then, it seems that depicting him as a philosopher necessarily leads to a unique concept of "islamicized philosophy" totally dependent on Islamic sacred writings. Such a philosophy is stripped of its most significant qualities, viz., the search for truth through critical investigation of traditions and the quest to intellectually penetrate the essence of things. This quintessentially philosophical quest must continue even if this means challenging established religious doctrine. When philosophy looses this piercing motion, it looses its meaning and essence; it is transformed into a specialized way of thinking whose main goal is to satisfy religious restrictions epitomized in the concept of the fear of God known analogously to Judaism, Christianity and Islam. Such a philosophy looses, furthermore, its status as a critical power in society. It becomes a sterile enterprise, loaded with predetermined conclusions, with no promise of growth and no energy to change.

Celebrating Ibn Taymiyya as a philosopher bears, furthermore, an important symptomatic value for the assessment of contemporary Islamic thought. In general, the authors who contributed to creating his philosophical identity represent an influential trend in conservative groups. These groups consider the only worthwhile rationality to be the religious rationality originating solely from Koran and Sunna. However, while authors like ʿAbd al-Ḥakīm Ajhar label Ibn Taymiyya a philosopher in his own intellectual context, authors like Abū Yaʿrub al-Marzūqī tend to attribute a creative role to Ibn Taymiyya in the development of modern Islamic philosophy. Keeping in mind that Ibn Taymiyya's conception of rationality is strictly bound to revelation, whatever this group of contemporary Muslim authors labels as Ibn Taymiyya's philosophy can only be a "scriptural philosophy" deriving its theoretical principles and basic arguments exclusively from scripture and tradition.

How, and, indeed, to what extent is this "philosophy" different from theology? Wouldn't it be more appropriate to call Ibn Taymiyya a theologian, instead? This would, in a much more satisfying way, suit Ibn Taymiyya's self-understanding and, at the same time, preserve the nature of philosophy from violation. Ultimately, considering Ibn Taymiyya a philosopher is part of a political ideology that describes traditional Islam as perfectly matched with modernity; oddly and astoundingly, this mindset represents a pre-modern state of Islamic thought that somehow, anachronistically, manages to hold power over the minds of contemporary Muslims. In the end, we must conclude that calling Ibn Taymiyya a "philosopher" is a case of imputed – not actual – identity.[183]

183 Against the background of claiming for Ibn Taymiyya being a philosopher, a valiant attempt to present the historical context of his critical attitude towards philosophy and the negative influence of his views on the status of the study of philosophy at Saudi universities is provided by the Saudi author Saʿūd al-Sarḥān in his monograph *al-Ḥikma al-maṣlūba. Madkhal ilā mawqif Ibn Taymiyya min al-falsafa* (Crucified Wisdom. An Introduction to Ibn Taymiyya's Attitude from Philosophy), Beirut 2008. He asserts that, based on Ibn Taymiyya's views, philosophy is viewed in Saudi Arabia as "disbelief and error" (*kufr wa-ḍalāl*). As a consequence, philosophy is still not taught there; ibid., p. 12. According to the author, Ibn Taymiyya did not study philosophy systematically and for its own purpose, but eclectically in order to obtain arguments against *kalām*-theologians, Sufis and Shii scholars. He, thus, instrumentalized philosophy for his polemical purposes (pp. 20, 35–36). Although Ibn Taymiyya predominantly accused philosophers of disbelief (pp. 37–39), he, in contrast to former critics of philosophy, utilized philosophical terminology in order to address philosophers critically "in their language" (p. 76). See Ibn Taymiyya, *Darʾ*, edited by Muḥammad Rashād Sālim, vol. 1, p. 43.

Section 4: Inclusion and Exclusion in Islamic Theology and Law

Against Islamic Universalism

ʿAlī al-Ḥarbī's 1990 Attempt to Prove That Ibn Taymiyya and Ibn Qayyim al-Jawziyya Affirm the Eternity of Hell-Fire

Jon Hoover

Introduction

This is companion piece to my earlier study "Islamic Universalism. Ibn Qayyim al-Jawziyya's Salafī Deliberations on the Duration of Hell-Fire."[1] There, I analyze three major considerations of the duration of the Fire in the works of Ibn Qayyim al-Jawziyya and examine their debt to Ibn Taymiyya's *Fanāʾ al-nār* (The Passing Away of the Fire).[2] *Fanāʾ al-nār* is the last treatise that Ibn Taymiyya wrote before his death in 728/1328, and it makes a strong case for eventual salvation of even unbelievers from the Fire in the hereafter. Ibn Taymiyya sets aside the classical Sunni consensus that unbelievers and associators (*mushrikūn*) will suffer eternal chastisement in the Fire by citing lack of agreement on this matter among the early Muslims, the *salaf*. Moreover, he argues, God will eventually bring chastisement and the Fire to an end in accord with His mercy and wise purpose. Some years later, Ibn al-Qayyim devoted a chapter to this question in *Ḥādī al-arwāḥ* (Spurring the Souls), a major work on eschatology.[3] This discussion follows the structure of Ibn Taymiyya's *Fanāʾ al-nār*, quotes it extensively, and greatly elaborates its arguments for the limited duration of Hell-Fire.

1 Hoover, Jon: Islamic Universalism. Ibn Qayyim al-Jawziyya's Salafī Deliberations on the Duration of Hell-Fire, in: *The Muslim World* 99 (2009), pp. 181–201.

2 *Fanāʾ al-nār* is short for Ibn Taymiyya: *al-Radd ʿalā man qāla bi-fanāʾ al-janna wal-nār* (Refutation of Whoever Says that the Garden and the Fire Will Pass Away), ed. by Muḥammad b. ʿAbd Allāh al-Samharī, Riyadh 1415/1995.

3 Ibn Qayyim al-Jawziyya, Shams al-Dīn Muḥammad: *Ḥādī al-arwāḥ ilā bilād al-afrāḥ*, ed. by Ṭāhā ʿAbd al-Raʾūf Saʿd, Cairo n.d., pp. 307–341 (in chapter 67).

Ibn al-Qayyim provides a similar treatment in *Shifāʾ al-ʿalīl* (Healing of the Sick) that is less beholden to the structure and wording of *Fanāʾ al-nār*, suggesting that it is later than *Ḥādī al-arwāḥ*.[4] Rather unexpectedly, the discussions in both *Ḥādī al-arwāḥ* and *Shifāʾ* end with Ibn al-Qayyim backing away from the force of his arguments and leaving the duration of the Fire to God's will. Ibn al-Qayyim also gives much attention to this topic in *al-Ṣawāʿiq al-mursala* (The Thunderbolts Sent Out).[5] The second half of this work has not been found, but we know that the second half includes a long deliberation on the duration of the Fire from the abridgement of the whole *Mukhtaṣar al-Ṣawāʿiq*.[6] Here, Ibn al-Qayyim no longer withholds judgment on the duration of the Fire but argues that chastisement in the Fire will indeed pass away even for unbelievers and associators. There is little question that all three of these works come from Ibn Qayyim al-Jawziyya's mature years before his death in 751/1350. *Ḥādī al-arwāḥ*, which appears to be the earliest of the three, may date to 745/1344–1345.[7]

My earlier study examines only those explicit deliberations on the duration of the Fire located in Ibn Taymiyya's and Ibn al-Qayyim's writings by previous scholars. It does not canvas the full range of their vast oeuvres in order to attempt a definitive assessment of their positions. Nonetheless, the evidence might be thought sufficient to report that Ibn Taymiyya and Ibn al-Qayyim believe that the Fire will pass away. This is indeed the conclusion that many scholars have drawn, sometimes on the basis of Ibn al-Qayyim's *Ḥādī al-arwāḥ* alone.[8]

4 Idem: *Shifāʾ al-ʿalīl fī masāʾil al-qaḍāʾ wal-qadar wal-ḥikma wal-taʿlīl*, ed. by al-Sayyid Muḥammad al-Sayyid and Saʿīd Maḥmūd, Cairo 1414/1994, pp. 540–565 (in chapter 22, part way into aspect (*wajh*) 36).

5 Idem: *Kitāb al-Ṣawāʿiq al-mursala ʿalā al-jahmiyya wal-muʿaṭṭila*, ed. by ʿAlī b. Muḥammad al-Dakhīl Allāh, Riyadh 1408/1987–1988.

6 Idem: *Mukhtaṣar al-Ṣawāʿiq al-mursala ʿalā al-jahmiyya wal-muʿaṭṭila*, abridgement (*ikhtiṣār*) by Muḥammad b. al-Mawṣilī, ed. by al-Ḥasan b. ʿAbd al-Raḥmān al-ʿAlawī, Riyadh 1425/2004, pp. 642–685, pdf online: http://www.archive.org/details/muktsr_swaik_mursla, accessed December 18, 2012.

7 A marking on a manuscript of *Ḥādī al-arwāḥ* (ms. 6/2) found in the collection of the Mosul Library of Public Endowments indicates that Ibn al-Qayyim finished his book in 745 A.H. See Aḥmad, Sālim ʿAbd al-Razzāq: *Fihris makhṭūṭāt maktabat al-awqāf al-ʿāmma fī al-Mawṣil*, Baghdad 1982–1983, vol. 2, p. 31.

8 Relying solely on *Ḥādī al-arwāḥ*, the following attribute the passing away of the Fire to Ibn al-Qayyim: el-Ṣāleḥ, Ṣoubḥī: *La vie future selon le Coran*, Paris 1971, pp. 56–60; Idleman Smith, Jane and Yazbeck Haddad, Yvonne: *The Islamic Understanding of Death and Resurrection*, Albany 1981, p. 94; and Abrahamov, Binyamin: The Creation and Duration of Paradise and Hell in Islamic Theol-

There is, however, a minority of specifically Muslim scholars who set forth several brief passages of apparently contrary evidence in an effort to align Ibn Taymiyya and Ibn Qayyim al-Jawziyya with the classical Sunni doctrine. The fullest attempt to make this case that I have found is a short book by ʿAlī al-Ḥarbī called *Kashf al-astār li-ibṭāl iddiʿāʾ fanāʾ al-nār. Al-mansūb li-shaykh al-islām Ibn Taymiyya wa-tilmīdhihi Ibn Qayyim al-Jawziyya* (Lifting the Veils to Invalidate the Contention that the Fire will Pass Away, which is Attributed to *shaykh al-islām* Ibn Taymiyya and his Disciple Ibn Qayyim al-Jawziyya) published in Saudi Arabia in 1990.[9] The present study examines al-Ḥarbī's arguments to see what we might learn from his efforts. It will become clear that al-Ḥarbī's account of Ibn Taymiyya is untenable. However, al-Ḥarbī's findings do prevent us from concluding that Ibn Qayyim al-Jawziyya ultimately denies the eternity of the Fire, and they push us to reconsider the trajectory of his later thought on this issue.

---

ogy, in: *Der Islam* 79 (2002), pp. 87–102. Muslim scholars often add a doctrinal judgment to their reports. Relying on a wider range of evidence than the preceding scholars, al-Ḥumayd, ʿAbd al-Karīm b. Ṣāliḥ: *al-Inkār ʿalā man lam yaʿtaqid khuld wa taʾbīd al-kuffār fī al-nār*, Burayda 1422/2001, observes that both Ibn Taymiyya and Ibn al-Qayyim say that the Fire will pass away, and he affirms it as correct Islamic doctrine. The following denounce the passing of the Fire as erroneous Islamic doctrine, and, in some cases, attribute it to Ibn Taymiyya and/or Ibn al-Qayyim: al-Subkī, Abū Ḥasan ʿAlī Taqī al-Dīn (d. 756/1355): *al-Iʿtibār bi-baqāʾ al-janna wal-nār*, ed. by Ṭāhā al-Dasūqī Ḥubayshī, Cairo 1987; al-Dimashqī al-Ḥiṣnī, Taqī al-Dīn Abū Bakr (d. 829/1425–6): *Dafʿ shubah man shabbaha wa-tamarrada wa-nasaba dhālik ilā al-Sayyid al-Jalīl al-Imām Aḥmad*, Cairo 1350/1931–32; al-Ṣanʿānī, Muḥammad b. Ismāʿīl (d. 1182/1768): *Rafʿ al-astār li-ibṭāl adillat al-qāʾilīn bi-fanāʾ al-nār*, ed. by Muḥammad Nāṣir al-Dīn al-Albānī, Beirut 1405/1984; al-Ashqar, ʿUmar Sulaymān ʿAbd Allāh: *al-Janna wal-nār*, Cairo 1426/2005 [date of al-Ashqar's introduction and, presumably, the date of original publication: 1406/1986], pp. 39–46, in English as al-Ashqar, ʿUmar S.: *Paradise and Hell in the Light of the Qur'an and Sunnah*, transl. by Nasiruddin al-Khattab, Riyadh 2002, pp. 57–65; al-Hararī al-Ḥabashī, ʿAbd Allāh: *al-Maqālāt al-sunniyya fī kashf ḍalālāt Aḥmad b. Taymiyya*, Beirut 1425/2004, pp. 170–73.

9 Al-Ḥarbī, ʿAlī b. ʿAlī Jābir: *Kashf al-astār li-ibṭāl iddiʿāʾ fanāʾ al-nār. Al-mansūb li-shaykh al-islām Ibn Taymiyya wa-tilmīdhihi Ibn Qayyim al-Jawziyya*, Mecca 1410/1990. See also the internet fatwa arguing that Ibn Taymiyya and Ibn al-Qayyim uphold the eternity of the Fire; Markaz al-fatwā: *Fanāʾ al-nār ʿind Ibn Taymiyya wa-Ibn al-Qayyim. Fatwa No. 64739*, 16 July 2005, online: http://www.islamweb.net/fatwa/index.php?page=showfatwa&lang=A&Id=64739&Option=FatwaId, accessed December 18, 2012.

1. ʿAlī al-Ḥarbī's Predicament

ʿAlī al-Ḥarbī is generous in detailing the circumstances that led him to try to demonstrate Ibn Taymiyya's and Ibn Qayyim al-Jawziyya's adherence to classical Sunni doctrine, and the narrative of his travail is a major rhetorical feature of *Kashf al-astār*. To fully appreciate al-Ḥarbī's story, however, it must be kept in mind that Ibn Taymiyya's *Fanāʾ al-nār* was not clearly identified or published in its entirety until 1995, well after al-Ḥarbī completed his *Kashf al-astār* in 1990. Moreover, while Ibn Taymiyya does appear in Ibn Qayyim al-Jawziyya's *Ḥādī al-arwāḥ* by name, *Ḥādī al-arwāḥ*'s debt to *Fanāʾ al-nār* is not apparent without direct comparison to the latter text. Nor can Ibn Taymiyya's views be ascertained with any degree of confidence solely from *Ḥādī al-arwāḥ*.

Al-Ḥarbī reports that he initially encountered the problem of the duration of the Fire while preparing his doctoral thesis at the Umm al-Qurā University in Mecca on the theological doctrines of Ibn al-Wazīr (d. 840/1436). Ibn al-Wazīr was first in the line of traditionalist scholars that emerged out of the Zaydī scholarly tradition in Yemen and later produced Muḥammad al-Shawkānī (d. 1250/1834).[10] According to al-Ḥarbī, Ibn al-Wazīr first leaned toward belief in the Fire's eventual passing but then decided to withhold judgment on the matter. Ibn al-Wazīr also said that Ibn Taymiyya and his followers argued that God's mercy and wise purpose precluded everlasting chastisement and eternal Fire.[11]

Ibn al-Wazīr's claim about Ibn Taymiyya alarms al-Ḥarbī because it renders two of his basic convictions contradictory. First, he believes that Islamic doctrine teaches the eternity of the Fire, and, second, he considers Ibn Taymiyya a great rejuvenator of Islam. Thus, for al-Ḥarbī, it is simply unthinkable that such an eminent reformer of the faith as Ibn Taymiyya could deny so basic an Islamic doctrine as the eternity of Hell-Fire. The fact that Ibn al-Wazīr states otherwise precipitates a cognitive crisis and spurs al-Ḥarbī to seek some kind of resolution.[12]

---

10 Al-Ḥarbī's thesis is entitled *Ibn al-Wazīr wa-ārāʾuhu al-iʿtiqādiyya*. For basic information on Muḥammad b. Ibrāhīm al-Wazīr, see Haykel, Bernard: *Revival and Reform in Islam. The Legacy of Muhammad al-Shawkānī*, Cambridge 2003, pp. 10, 41, 108.

11 Al-Ḥarbī, *Kashf al-astār*, pp. 6, 17–18, 25–28.

12 Ibid., pp. 4–5.

Al-Ḥarbī first elaborates the magnitude of the problem. He found the assertion that Ibn Taymiyya supported the passing away of the Fire in a number of works from the fourteenth century down to the present.[13] Moreover, he encountered it so often among his contemporaries that it seemed that only those who had heard him refute it at his doctoral defence thought otherwise.[14] Al-Ḥarbī relates a few anecdotes to underline the severity of the situation. In 1406/1985–1986, a certain Muḥammad Abū Raḥīm attributed the passing away of the Fire to Ibn Taymiyya when defending his doctorate. A member of the examining committee asked Abū Raḥīm where he had obtained his information. He replied that he had found it in Ibn Qayyim al-Jawziyya's *Ḥādī al-arwāḥ*. The examiner responded that this matter had been much discussed and that al-Ḥarbī, who was present at the defence, had already dealt with it earlier.[15] In a second anecdote, al-Ḥarbī quizzed several scholars during a hajj season in Mecca. Most of them attributed the Fire's passing away or at least the sense of it to Ibn Taymiyya, but they could not provide relevant evidence. Others preferred not to comment or encouraged al-Ḥarbī to look in the vast collection of Ibn Taymiyya's writings *Majmūʿ al-Fatāwā*.[16] In a third incident, a teacher at the Umm al-Qurā University told al-Ḥarbī that a relative of his had found Ibn Taymiyya supporting the limited duration of the Fire. Al-Ḥarbī expressed great interest in seeing the references, but none were forthcoming.[17]

As these anecdotes illustrate, one of al-Ḥarbī's fundamental complaints is that scholars fail to cite any texts from Ibn Taymiyya supporting an end to the Fire. However, he does point to Ibn Taymiyya's disciple Ibn Qayyim al-Jawziyya and especially his book *Ḥādī*

13 Ibid., pp. 15–22.

14 Ibid., pp. 4, 9.

15 Ibid., pp. 22–23. It is perhaps this same incident that al-Ḥarbī refers to at another place in his book. An unnamed researcher defending his doctorate at the Umm al-Qurā University attributed the passing away of the Fire to Ibn Taymiyya. At this, one of al-Ḥarbī's professors, Rāshid al-Rājiḥ, encouraged him to write a separate treatise on the subject to settle the matter (ibid., p. 9). On yet another occasion, al-Ḥarbī relates how a certain Fayṣal ʿAbd Allāh argued in a master's thesis defense at the Umm al-Qurā University that the Fire would likely pass away. ʿAbd Allāh explained that this best accords with God's mercy, pardon and wise purpose. However, he did not make reference to Ibn Taymiyya or Ibn Qayyim al-Jawziyya (ibid., p. 22).

16 Ibid., p. 7.

17 Ibid., p. 23.

al-arwāḥ as the main sources of the difficulties.[18] Al-Ḥarbī suspects that Ibn al-Wazīr and others who attribute the passing away of the Fire to Ibn Taymiyya rely on Ibn al-Qayyim for their judgments but have no evidence from Ibn Taymiyya himself. He cites as an obvious example the 18th century Yemenite scholar Muḥammad b. Ismāʿīl al-Ṣanʿānī (d. 1182/1768) who quotes Ibn al-Qayyim's *Ḥādī al-arwāḥ* extensively in his *Rafʿ al-astār* but attributes the ideas that he found there directly to Ibn Taymiyya. This problem had been observed earlier in 1984 by Muḥammad Nāṣir al-Dīn al-Albānī, the editor of al-Ṣanʿānī's work.[19] As I indicated above, Ibn al-Qayyim does not make entirely clear in *Ḥādī al-arwāḥ* what position Ibn Taymiyya holds.

The task that al-Ḥarbī sets for himself in writing *Kashf al-astār* is replacing widespread belief that Ibn Taymiyya and Ibn al-Qayyim say that the Fire will pass away with solid evidence that these two Ḥanbalīs affirm the Fire's eternity.[20] Al-Ḥarbī bemoans how difficult it was to extricate the pertinent material from his thesis on Ibn al-Wazīr. He tells how he immersed himself in the sea of Ibn Taymiyya's knowledge – he who was not accustomed to waves and diving – and how God rescued him when he called out just as God saved the Prophet Jonah.[21] This bit of melodrama provides the clue to al-Ḥarbī's strategy. He searches for texts from Ibn Taymiyya and his disciple affirming the eternity of the Fire and tries to show that these represent their most mature views. Before proceeding to those passages, we will first examine what al-Ḥarbī does with those texts that clearly do not support his argument, namely, Ibn al-Qayyim's *Ḥādī al-arwāḥ*, *Shifāʾ al-ʿalīl* and *Mukhtaṣar al-Ṣawāʿiq*.

2. Ibn Qayyim al-Jawziyya's Passages that Do Not Affirm the Eternity of the Fire

Al-Ḥarbī begins with an overview of Ibn al-Qayyim's discussion of the duration of the Fire in *Ḥādī al-arwāḥ*. His aim is not so much to

18 Ibid., pp. 9, 15, 24–25, 34, 78.

19 Ibid., pp. 29–30; al-Ṣanʿānī, *Rafʿ al-astār*, p. 63, n. 7. For an introduction to the life and thought of the controversial Hadith scholar al-Albānī (d. 1999), see Brown, Jonathan: *The Canonization of al-Bukhārī and Muslim. The Formation and Function of the Sunnī Ḥadīth Canon*, Leiden 2007, pp. 321–334.

20 Al-Ḥarbī, *Kashf al-astār*, pp. 10–11.

21 Ibid., p. 8.

refute Ibn al-Qayyim point by point as to illustrate how his writing can lead to confusion and to clarify his final position in this text. First, as al-Ḥarbī observes, Ibn al-Qayyim in *Ḥādī al-arwāḥ* reports from Ibn Taymiyya that two different views on the duration of Fire have been known since the very early generations of Islam, that is, from the time of the *salaf*. Ibn al-Qayyim himself identifies seven different views in the wider tradition, the seventh being that the Fire will pass away. Ibn al-Qayyim adds that, according to Ibn Taymiyya, this latter view was transmitted from several early Muslims, including the Companions of the Prophet ʿUmar, Ibn Masʿūd, Abū Hurayra and Abū Saʿīd al-Khuḍrī.[22]

Ibn al-Qayyim then cites texts supporting the passing of the Fire. Al-Ḥarbī highlights two of these. The first is a tradition from ʿUmar that reads, "Even if the People of the Fire stayed in the Fire like the amount of sand of *ʿĀlij*,[23] they would have, despite that, a day in which they would come out." This tradition would seem to be saying that every last person in the Fire will eventually come out of it, even if after a very long time. However, al-Ḥarbī protests that this tradition speaks of people coming out of the Fire, not of the Fire's passing away, and more to the point it applies only to disobedient monotheists who deserve eventual reward for their belief. It certainly does not apply to unbelievers. Moreover, he says, this tradition has a weak chain of transmitters and is in fact forged.[24] The second text that Ibn al-Qayyim cites in favor of the passing of the Fire is a Koranic verse that makes duration of punishment in the Fire contingent on God's will: "As for those who are wretched, they will be in the Fire, moaning and sighing, abiding in it, as long as the Heavens and the Earth endure, except as your Lord wills. Surely, your Lord does whatever He wills."[25] Al-Ḥarbī does not here counter Ibn al-Qayyim's interpretation of this text, but he later asserts that the texts of the Koran and the Sunna supporting the opposite position of the eternity of the Fire are peremptory (*qaṭʿī*).[26]

22 Ibid., pp. 35–36; Ibn Qayyim al-Jawziyya, *Ḥādī al-arwāḥ*, pp. 311–313.

23 *ʿĀlij* is the name of a large expanse of sand on the route to Mecca. See al-Ḥamawī, Yāqūt b. ʿAbd Allāh: *Kitāb Muʿjam al-buldān*, Cairo 1324/1906, part 6, p. 99.

24 Al-Ḥarbī, *Kashf al-astār*, pp. 36, 53, see 84. Al-Ḥarbī earlier quotes and then reinterprets or rejects other traditions supporting the passing away of the Fire; ibid., pp. 20, 31–32.

25 Koran (11:106–107); al-Ḥarbī, *Kashf al-astār*, pp. 36–37; Ibn Qayyim al-Jawziyya, *Ḥādī al-arwāḥ*, pp. 313–318.

26 Al-Ḥarbī, *Kashf al-astār*, p. 43.

Ibn al-Qayyim goes on in the following section of his *Ḥādī al-arwāḥ* to list and refute arguments for the eternity of the Fire. Al-Ḥarbī quotes from this extensively and observes that Ibn al-Qayyim dismisses any claim to consensus among the Companions and the Successors on the eternity of the Fire. In fact, Ibn al-Qayyim argues, not one of the Companions said that the Fire will last forever. Moreover, the texts of the Koran stipulate that the People of the Fire abide in it only as long as it lasts, not forever.[27]

The last section of *Ḥādī al-arwāḥ* on the duration of the Fire is long and provides 25 arguments for the Fire's passing away. Al-Ḥarbī shows little interest in this section, and he records only the concluding argument, namely, that God could have no wise purpose in chastisement that never ends. Al-Ḥarbī is much more anxious to underline the fact that Ibn al-Qayyim backs away from these arguments in the end, withholds judgment, and leaves the duration of the Fire to God's will.[28]

Al-Ḥarbī claims that Ibn al-Qayyim also withholds judgment in another long discussion of the Fire's duration found in *Mukhtaṣar al-Ṣawāʿiq*.[29] Al-Ḥarbī quotes the following from *Mukhtaṣar al-Ṣawāʿiq* to substantiate this point:

> If the dawn of what is correct shines on you, [that is good]. If not, then ascribe the judgment to what God ascribes it in His statement, 'surely your Lord does whatever He wills' (11:107), and hold firm to the statement of ʿAlī b. Abī Ṭālib – May God be pleased with him. He mentioned that the People of the Garden enter the Garden and the People of the Fire enter the Fire. He described their state. Then he said, 'After that, God does what He wills'.[30]

At first glance, this citation might appear to support leaving the ultimate destiny of those in the Fire to God's will. However, al-Ḥarbī fails to note that Ibn al-Qayyim in the immediately preceding lines urges his readers to consider the arguments for an end to chastisement in the Fire very seriously. The beginning of the above quoted text, "If the dawn of what is correct shines on you, [that is good]", refers back to those arguments. With this Ibn al-Qayyim is claiming that the correct

27 Ibid., pp. 37–39; Ibn Qayyim al-Jawziyya, *Ḥādī al-arwāḥ*, pp. 318–322.
28 Al-Ḥarbī, *Kashf al-astār*, pp. 39–40; Ibn Qayyim al-Jawziyya, *Ḥādī al-arwāḥ*, pp. 322–341.
29 Al-Ḥarbī, *Kashf al-astār*, pp. 9, 34–35, 40.
30 Ibid., p. 40; Ibn Qayyim al-Jawziyya, *Mukhtaṣar al-Ṣawāʿiq*, pp. 663, as transl. in Hoover, Islamic Universalism, p. 196.

view is that chastisement in the Fire will come to an end for everyone. However, in the passage quoted above he allows those unable to see this truth simply to leave the matter to God's will. With this, it cannot be said that Ibn al-Qayyim himself withholds judgment in *Mukhtaṣar al-Ṣawāʾiq*. He only counsels that position for those who are unable to grasp arguments for the passing away of the Fire.[31]

After reviewing *Ḥādī al-arwāḥ* and *Mukhtaṣar al-Ṣawāʾiq*, al-Ḥarbī examines the treatment of the Fire found in Ibn al-Qayyim's *Shifāʾ al-ʿalīl*. Only the end of this discussion concerns him. Here, Ibn al-Qayyim relates how he twice asked Ibn Taymiyya about the duration of the Fire. The first time, Ibn Taymiyya gave no answer except to say that it was a big question. The second time, during his "last session" (*fī majlisihi al-akhīr*), Ibn Taymiyya wrote a treatise on the subject that Ibn al-Qayyim calls "famous" (*mashhūr*).[32] Al-Ḥarbī states that this work has not been found, but he supposes that it probably supports the eternity of the Fire and that it might be a work mentioned by Ibn Taymiyya's biographer Ibn ʿAbd al-Hādī called *Qāʾida fī al-radd ʿalā man qāla bi-fanāʾ al-janna wal-nār* (A Rule in Refutation of Whoever Says that the Garden and the Fire will Pass Away).[33] As I show in my earlier study, we now know that Ibn Taymiyya's "famous" work is in fact *Fanāʾ al-nār* and that it does *not* affirm the eternity of the Fire.

In the *Shifāʾ al-ʿalīl* passage quoted by al-Ḥarbī, Ibn al-Qayyim goes on to explain that he withholds judgment on the question of the Fire's duration, leaving the matter to God's will. He also states that there is no support for everlasting Fire in authoritative texts. Al-Ḥarbī observes that Ibn al-Qayyim here again withholds judgment, even after confusing his readers by arguing that the Fire will pass away and betraying a preference for that view.[34]

Having come to the conclusion that Ibn al-Qayyim withholds judgment on the duration of the Fire in *Ḥādī al-arwāḥ*, *Mukhtaṣar al-Ṣawāʾiq* and *Shifāʾ al-ʿalīl*, al-Ḥarbī sees in this a sign that Ibn al-Qayyim, as well as Ibn Taymiyya, might ultimately uphold the eter-

31 For fuller discussion, see ibid., pp. 194–196.

32 Al-Ḥarbī, *Kashf al-astār*, pp. 42–43; Ibn Qayyim al-Jawziyya, *Shifāʾ al-ʿalīl*, pp. 564–565.

33 Al-Ḥarbī, *Kashf al-astār*, pp. 43–44, 48, 83; Ibn ʿAbd al-Hādī, Muḥammad b. Aḥmad: *al-ʿUqad al-durriyya min manāqib shaykh al-islām Aḥmad b. Taymiyya*, Beirut n. d., p. 67.

34 Al-Ḥarbī, *Kashf al-astār*, pp. 42–43; Ibn Qayyim al-Jawziyya, *Shifāʾ al-ʿalīl*, p. 565.

nity of the Fire. This, he explains, spurred him to search widely for texts in support of that view:

> Emanating from Ibn al-Qayyim's withholding judgment on this great issue is the scent of a new position for him concerning it. On the basis of my knowledge acquired from the writings of *shaykh al-islām* Ibn Taymiyya and his disciple *imām* Ibn Qayyim al-Jawziyya that they rank among the rejuvenators of Salafi doctrine and those who raise its banner, this is what prompted me to search anew in the books of Ibn al-Qayyim and his Shaykh. By the success of God – Exalted and majestic is He – I arrived at the desired objective, which is the agreement of the two Shaykhs and [their] unity in maintaining the everlastingness of the Fire.[35]

Al-Ḥarbī overstates the extent of his new search in Ibn Taymiyya's and Ibn al-Qayyim's works. Most of the texts and arguments that he employs are already considered in al-Albānī's introduction to al-Ṣanʿānī's *Rafʿ al-astār*,[36] and, as we will see, al-Ḥarbī is well aware of this discussion even if he does not acknowledge his full debt to it. However, al-Albānī and al-Ḥarbī offer opposing assessments of the evidence. While al-Albānī cites texts in which Ibn Taymiyya and Ibn al-Qayyim affirm the eternity of the Fire, he is not certain that these indicate their final views, and he criticizes them for otherwise slipping into serious error. Al-Albānī concludes that however great Ibn Taymiyya and Ibn al-Qayyim might have been, their opinions must be treated with caution. Al-Ḥarbī on the other hand insists that such great reformers must certainly have believed in the eternity of the Fire. We will first examine how al-Ḥarbī tries to prove this for Ibn Taymiyya and then for Ibn al-Qayyim.

3. Trying to Demonstrate that Ibn Taymiyya Upholds the Eternity of the Fire

Al-Ḥarbī states frequently that there is no evidence in Ibn Taymiyya's corpus showing that he believes in the passing away of the Fire. However, in a nod to the witness of Ibn al-Qayyim's *Ḥādī al-arwāḥ* that Ibn Taymiyya reported two views from the Salaf on this issue, al-Ḥarbī imagines that he might first have leaned toward the passing away of the Fire and then shifted to the "correct" view. To make this plausible,

35 Al-Ḥarbī, *Kashf al-astār*, p. 49.
36 Al-Albānī's introduction is found in al-Ṣanʿānī, *Rafʿ al-astār*, pp. 5–51.

al-Ḥarbī notes other cases in which Ibn Taymiyya changed his position. Al-Ḥarbī explains, for example, that Ibn Taymiyya first believed that the mythical Khiḍr was still alive but then later came to the view that he had died. Similarly, Ibn Taymiyya said early in his career that oil became unclean if something unclean fell into it, but then he changed his mind later on. Whatever its merits, al-Ḥarbī does not think that the theory that Ibn Taymiyya also changed his mind on the duration of the Fire is very likely because none of his texts speak of it. Al-Ḥarbī allows that he may have missed something in the course of his research, but he doubts it. Moreover, if Ibn Taymiyya does say somewhere that the Fire will pass away, this would contradict the Shaykh's clear affirmation of its eternity that al-Ḥarbī claims to have found elsewhere.[37]

Al-Ḥarbī's evidence for Ibn Taymiyya's belief in the eternity of the Fire consists of 15 short passages gathered from his corpus. Although not always obvious from al-Ḥarbī's discussion, what is at issue in all but two of these passages is the possibility of an infinite series of events. The early *kalām* theologian Jahm b. Ṣafwān (d. 128/745) denies that an infinite series of events is possible and concludes from this that the Garden and the Fire cannot possibly last forever. They must come to an end and pass away. Abū al-Hudhayl b. ʿAllāf (d. 227/841?) also denies the possibility of an infinite series. However, this leads him to a less radical conclusion than it does Jahm. For Abū al-Hudhayl motion in the Garden and the Fire must eventually cease, but the Garden and the Fire themselves will remain in existence. Ibn Taymiyya rejects the fundamental premise of these arguments. He affirms the possibility of an infinite series, and he condemns Jahm and Abū al-Hudhayl for their views. Al-Ḥarbī interprets Ibn Taymiyya's censure to be clear affirmation that both the Fire and the Garden will last forever.[38] This, however, is an overinterpretation. In context, these passages are better understood as no more than condemnations of those who deny the

37 Al-Ḥarbī, *Kashf al-astār*, pp. 44–48, 58–59.

38 Ibid., pp. 59–70. Al-Ḥarbī's twelfth text comes from Ibn Taymiyya: *Darʾ taʿāruḍ al-ʿaql wal-naql*, ed. by Muḥammad Rashād Sālim, n.p. n.d., vol. 2, p. 358, and provides what appears to be a firm affirmation that the Fire will remain forever. However, al-Ḥarbī fails to note that Ibn Taymiyya is simply quoting from al-Ashʿarī's *Maqālāt al-islāmiyyīn* in the context of a discussion on the possibility of an infinite series. Al-Ḥarbī observes that his 13 text from Ibn Taymiyya's *Muwāfaqat ṣaḥīḥ al-manqūl* is identical to his 14 text from *Darʾ al-taʿāruḍ*, but he fails to realize that these two titles are simply different names for the same work. These two passages also come from the same context in *Darʾ al-taʿāruḍ* as al-Ḥarbī's twelfth text.

possibility of an infinite series. The limited duration of the Fire may be argued by other means, as will become clearer below.

The remaining two texts do affirm the eternity of the Fire plainly but very briefly. In the first, Ibn Taymiyya is asked to comment on the tradition, "Seven things will neither die, nor pass away, nor taste passing away: the Fire, its residents, the Tablet, the Pen, the Footstool, and the Throne." He responds in a short fatwa that this tradition does not come from the Prophet but from some scholars. Nonetheless, he affirms its content: "The Salaf of the nation, its Imams, and the rest of the People of the Sunna and the Community hold that some created things will not go out of existence and will not pass away entirely, like the Garden, the Fire, the Throne and so forth." Ibn Taymiyya then condemns Jahm and like-minded Muʿtazilīs who say that all created things will pass away.[39]

The second passage comes from Ibn Taymiyya's *Bayān talbīs al-jahmiyya*, a work that dates to his stay in Egypt from 705/1306 to 712/1313. While discussing God's creation of the world, Ibn Taymiyya states, "[God] has informed that the Garden and the Fire will remain absolutely (*baqāʾan muṭlaqan*)." This affirmation of the Fire's perpetuity could not be stronger, but Ibn Taymiyya does not elaborate further.[40]

From these sundry texts, al-Ḥarbī concludes that Ibn Taymiyya definitely adheres to the eternity of the Fire and thereby agrees with the consensus of the *salaf* and the entire Muslim community. It is thus entirely inappropriate, according to al-Ḥarbī, to speak of this great rejuvenator of the Islamic faith believing that the Fire will pass away.[41]

Al-Ḥarbī's evidence for Ibn Taymiyya's belief in the eternity of the Fire is meagre, but it might carry the day were it not for impor-

39 Al-Ḥarbī, *Kashf al-astār*, p. 66; Ibn Taymiyya: *Majmūʿ Fatāwā shaykh al-islām Aḥmad b. Taymiyya*, ed. by ʿAbd al-Raḥmān b. Muḥammad b. Qāsim and Muḥammad b. ʿAbd al-Raḥmān b. Muḥammad, Cairo n. d., vol. 18, p. 307. Neither al-Ḥarbī nor Ibn Taymiyya comment on the fact that only six items are listed in the tradition prompting the fatwa.

40 Al-Ḥarbī, *Kashf al-astār*, p. 66; Ibn Taymiyya: *Bayān talbīs al-jahmiyya fī taʾsīs bidaʿihim al-kalāmiyya aw Naqḍ Taʾsīs al-jahmiyya*, ed. by Muḥammad b. ʿAbd al-Raḥmān b. Qāsim, n. p. n. d., vol. 1, p. 157. The editor adds a footnote to the effect that this counters those who charge Ibn Taymiyya with saying that the Fire will pass away. Ibn Rajab, ʿAbd al-Raḥmān b. Aḥmad: *Kitāb al-Dhayl ʿalā ṭabaqāt al-ḥanābila*, ed. by Muḥammad Ḥāmid al-Fiqī, Cairo 1372/1953, part 2, p. 403, lists this among the works that Ibn Taymiyya wrote during his seven years in Egypt.

41 Al-Ḥarbī, *Kashf al-astār*, pp. 59, 69–71.

tant counter-evidence that he struggles to marginalize. As mentioned above, al-Albānī edited a text by al-Ṣanʿānī in 1984 refuting the passing away of the Fire. In the introduction to this edition, al-Albānī suggests that Ibn al-Qayyim got his basic ideas on the duration of the Fire from Ibn Taymiyya. To back up his claim, he prints three pages from a previously unknown manuscript containing a text by Ibn Taymiyya called *Fī al-radd ʿalā man qāla bi-fanāʾ al-janna wal-nār* (Concerning the Refutation of Whoever Maintains the Passing Away of the Garden and the Fire). Al-Albānī surmises that the Arabic handwriting comes from the 11th/17th century, and he adds that the name of the scribe is unknown.[42]

Al-Ḥarbī reports briefly that these pages speak of two views on the duration of the Fire among the *salaf* and later generations, but he devotes little effort to describing their contents. Instead, he seeks to discredit their authenticity: these unknown fragments oppose what Ibn Taymiyya says elsewhere in his corpus; al-Albānī's edition of them fails to meet scholarly standards; and it is not known who copied them. Moreover, they do not state unequivocally that the Fire will end, and their title speaks of refuting those who say that the Fire will pass away, not of affirming them. Al-Ḥarbī also accuses al-Albānī of trying to discredit Ibn Taymiyya by publishing these pages.[43] He adds that if the pages quoted by al-Albānī truly came from Ibn Taymiyya, his enemies would have long quoted them and distributed them widely to discredit him.[44] At the very end of his treatise, al-Ḥarbī is more open to the possibility that these pages might come from Ibn Taymiyya, but he is no more eager to read them. Rather, he suggests that they might come from the same treatise mentioned in Ibn ʿAbd al-Hādī's list of Ibn Taymiyya's works noted previously and called *Qāʿida fī al-radd ʿalā man qāla bi-fanāʾ al-janna wal-nār* (A Rule in Refutation of Whoever Says that the Garden and the Fire will Pass Away). Based on this title, al-Ḥarbī again says that it is very likely that the treatise denies that the Fire will pass away.[45]

As I have already indicated above, Ibn Taymiyya did in fact write a treatise called *al-Radd ʿalā man qāla bi-fanāʾ al-janna wal-nār*, which I have been calling *Fanāʾ al-nār* for short. The entire work was published in Saudi Arabia in 1995, and, as the editor argues, its authenticity is

42 Al-Albānī in his introduction to al-Ṣanʿānī, *Rafʿ al-astār*, pp. 8–14.
43 Al-Ḥarbī, *Kashf al-astār*, pp. 32–33.
44 Ibid., pp. 58, 82.
45 Ibid., pp. 83–84.

beyond serious doubt.[46] Writing in 1990, al-Ḥarbī did not have access to this, but it is the same work from which al-Albānī quotes.

Ibn Taymiyya's *Fanāʾ al-nār* does three things. First, it refutes the view of Jahm b. Ṣafwān that both the Garden and the Fire will pass away and the view of Abū al-Hudhayl b. ʿAllāf that motion in the Garden and the Fire will come to a halt even though both remain forever. As indicated above, Jahm and Abū al-Hudhayl adopt these positions because they deny the possibility of an infinite series of events.[47] It is important to note that Ibn Taymiyya here denies that *both* the Garden and the Fire will pass away. However, this does not preclude the Fire *alone* passing away, which is what Ibn Taymiyya goes on to argue. Al-Ḥarbī fails to make this distinction, and he erroneously takes Ibn Taymiyya's many condemnations of Jahm to prove that Ibn Taymiyya affirms the eternity of the Fire. Second, *Fanāʾ al-nār* outlines and then dismisses mainstream Sunni arguments for the eternity of the Fire. These include arguments from the Koran and the consensus (*ijmāʿ*) of the community.[48] Third, *Fanāʾ al-nār* argues that the Koran and its interpretation by the *salaf*, that is, the early Muslims, do not support the eternity of the Fire. On the contrary, God's mercy and wise purpose in creation preclude punishing anyone forever. Although Ibn Taymiyya does not say clearly in *Fanāʾ al-nār* that the Fire will pass away, he leaves little doubt that he favours this view.[49]

The pages of *Fanāʾ al-nār* that al-Albānī quotes include Ibn Taymiyya's key arguments for an end to chastisement in the Fire.[50] Perhaps al-Ḥarbī can be excused for dismissing these pages because they were incomplete. Now, however, with the full *Fanāʾ al-nār* available and our knowledge that it was the last treatise Ibn Taymiyya wrote, it is apparent that al-Ḥarbī's attempt to demonstrate his belief in the eternity of the Fire fails. Even though Ibn Taymiyya very briefly affirmed the eternity of the Fire in a few earlier writings, it appears that he worked through the implications of his theology of God's mercy

46 Al-Samharī, the editor of Ibn Taymiyya's *Fanāʾ al-nār*, discusses its authenticity on pp. 12–16.

47 Ibn Taymiyya, *Fanāʾ al-nār*, pp. 42–52.

48 Ibid., pp. 71–79.

49 Ibid., pp. 52–70, 80–83.

50 Al-Albānī quotes these pages in his introduction to Ṣanʿānī, *Rafʿ al-astār*, pp. 9–14, and includes photographs of the source manuscript on pp. 53–55. Al-Albānī's printed text corresponds to al-Samharī's edition of *Fanāʾ al-nār*, pp. 52–57 and 80–83.

and wise purpose to a doctrine of universal salvation at the end of his life. His final testimony in *Fanāʾ al-nār* is that God's mercy and wise purpose will bring an end to chastisement in the Fire for all.

4. Trying to Demonstrate that Ibn al-Qayyim Upholds the Eternity of the Fire

Al-Ḥarbī's work on Ibn al-Qayyim is more fruitful. His argumentation is not persuasive in itself, but, combined with additional evidence and analysis, it does require us to be more cautious about Ibn al-Qayyim's mature views on the matter. Al-Ḥarbī presents four passages as proof that Ibn al-Qayyim eventually came to uphold everlasting chastisement of unbelievers and associators in the Fire. These are found in Ibn al-Qayyim's *Zād al-maʿād* (Provision for the Hereafter), *Ijtimāʿ al-juyūsh* (Gathering of the Armies), *Ṭarīq al-hijratayn* (The Road of the Two Migrations) and *al-Wābil al-ṣayyib* (The Heavy Shower). I will examine each of these works in turn.

Al-Ḥarbī quotes the following passage from *Zād al-maʿād* and takes it to be an indicator, but not a clear declaration, of Ibn al-Qayyim's belief in the eternity of the Fire:

> When an associator (*mushrik*) is foul in constitution and foul in essence, the Fire does not cleanse his foulness. On the contrary, if he were to come out of it, he would return as foul as he was [before], like a dog when it enters the sea and then comes out of it. Therefore, God – Most High is He – forbade the Garden to the associator.[51]

When set in its context in *Zād al-maʿād*, this passage provides stronger evidence for al-Ḥarbī's case than he realizes. *Zād al-maʿād* is an extensive compilation of Hadith on the Prophet's practice and instruction on everything from the ritual prayer to medicine.[52] Al-Ḥarbī's evidence comes from the introductory section of the book where Ibn al-Qayyim ties happiness in this world and the hereafter to following the Prophet. In the course of his discussion, Ibn al-Qayyim observes that

51 Al-Ḥarbī, *Kashf al-astār*, pp. 49–50, 79; Ibn Qayyim al-Jawziyya: *Zād al-maʿād fī hady khayr al-ʿibād*, ed. by Shuʿayb al-Arnaʾūṭ and ʿAbd al-Qādir al-Arnaʾūṭ, Beirut 1414/1994, vol. 1, p. 68.

52 See Krawietz, Birgit: Ibn Qayyim al-Jawzīyah. His Life and Works, in: *Mamlūk Studies Review* 10 (2006), pp. 19–64, for fuller overviews of *Zād al-maʿād* (pp. 57–59) and Ibn al-Qayyim's other books discussed in this study.

God in the perfection of His wisdom and power chooses some things – such as angels, prophets, communities, places, nights and days – over others. Likewise, God in his wisdom creates the fair, for whom is fitting only what is fair (*ṭayyib*), and the foul, for whom is fitting only what is foul (*khabīth*). While the fair and the foul are mixed together in this present world, God will distinguish the fair from the foul in the hereafter, placing the fair in the Garden and the foul in the Fire. It is in this context that Ibn al-Qayyim pens the passage quoted above, which offers no hope that the foul might one day become fair. The possibility of universal salvation is not broached.[53]

Al-Ḥarbī's second quotation comes from *Ijtimāʿ al-juyūsh*. The bulk of this book consists of quotations from the Koran, the Hadith and other texts brought together to prove that God is on His Throne. The passage in question comes from a creedal statement attributed to the two Hadith scholars Abū Zurʿa al-Rāzī (d. 264/878) and Abū Ḥātim al-Rāzī (d. 277/890), not to be confused with the Ismāʿīlī scholar of the same name (d. 322/933). In addition to affirming that God is on His throne, this statement mentions numerous other doctrines not relevant to the topic of the book, among them that the Garden and the Fire "both will never pass away".[54] Al-Ḥarbī reckons that Ibn al-Qayyim's citation of this statement without comment indicates his approval.[55] This is perhaps more than one can safely conclude because Ibn al-Qayyim appeals to this text for other purposes and also does not comment on a great deal else that he quotes in this book.

The third piece of evidence that al-Ḥarbī cites comes from Ibn al-Qayyim's *Ṭarīq al-hijratayn*, a large work outlining human need for and fulfilment in God. About one-third of the way through the book is a several-page section explaining that God in His wise purpose created the two abodes of the Garden and Hell. The first abode is for those seeking God's good pleasure, and it is the place of everything good and fair. The second is for those who rouse God's anger and wrath, and it is the place for everything evil and foul. Then comes the key line that al-Ḥarbī quotes, "These two abodes are the two abodes of permanence (*dārā al-qarār*)".[56] The text continues on to distinguish the two abodes

53 Ibn Qayyim al-Jawziyya, *Zād al-maʿād*, pp. 42–68.
54 Idem: *Ijtimāʿ al-juyūsh al-islāmiyya ʿalā ghazw al-muʿaṭṭila wal-jahmiyya*, Beirut 1404/1984, p. 145.
55 Al-Ḥarbī, *Kashf al-astār*, p. 50.
56 See Koran (40:39).

in several ways, affirming all the while that everything occurs in accord with God's wise purpose and His sundry other attributes.[57]

There is a significant point about *Ṭarīq al-hijratayn* that al-Ḥarbī does not make. Whereas *Ḥādī al-arwāḥ*, *Shifāʾ al-ʿalīl*, and *Mukhtaṣar al-Ṣawāʾiq* elaborate substantial arguments from God's attributes – especially God's wise purpose – for the passing away of the Fire, there is no hint of these in *Ṭarīq al-hijratayn*. The duration of the Fire is never put in question, and the reader is left to understand that God's wise purpose entails that those who incur God's vengeance will do so forever. Al-Ḥarbī also does not notice that the last major section of *Ṭarīq al-hijratayn* is of considerable interest. Here, Ibn al-Qayyim outlines 18 levels of humans and jinn in the hereafter, ranging from God's messengers at the top in the Garden on down to hypocrites and other unbelievers at the bottom in the Fire. In this section, the length of punishment in the Fire for unbelievers is never discussed. It is simply assumed that their eternity destiny is the Fire.[58] It is apparent that the subject matter of *Ṭarīq al-hijratayn* provides Ibn al-Qayyim ample opportunity to bring up the controversy over the Fire's duration. However, he does not do so, and he gives the reader no reason to doubt that the chastisement of unbelievers in the Fire will continue forever.

Al-Ḥarbī's fourth quotation comes from Ibn al-Qayyim's *al-Wābil al-ṣayyib*, and it is his clearest piece of evidence.[59] *Al-Wābil al-ṣayyib* is devoted to the remembrance (*dhikr*) of God, and the passage in question occurs in a brief commentary on the difference between a monotheist (*muwaḥḥid*) and an associator. According to Ibn al-Qayyim, an associator cannot enter the Garden because monotheism (*tawḥīd*) is the only key (*miftāḥ*) to the Garden. If the sins of some monotheists have not been completely removed by the time of their deaths, they must first spend some time in the Fire to be cleansed before entering the Garden.[60] Ibn al-Qayyim then elaborates on the Fire:

> As for the Fire, it is the abode of what is foul in words, deeds, foods and drinks and the abode of those who are foul. [God – Most High is

57 Al-Ḥarbī, *Kashf al-astār*, pp. 50–51; Ibn Qayyim al-Jawziyya: *Ṭarīq al-hijratayn wa-bāb al-saʿādatayn*, ed. by Abū Ḥafṣ Sayyid Ibrāhīm b. Ṣādiq b. ʿImrān, Cairo 1991, pp. 135–140 (quote on p. 135).

58 Ibid., pp. 331–405.

59 Al-Ḥarbī, *Kashf al-astār*, pp. 51–52.

60 Ibn Qayyim al-Jawziyya: *al-Wābil al-ṣayyib min al-kalim al-ṭayyib*, ed. by Sayyid Ibrāhīm, Cairo 1991, pp. 19–20.

> He – said, "That God may distinguish the foul (*khabīth*) from the fair (*ṭayyib*) and stack the foul one upon another, pile them up all together and put them in Hell. Those are the losers" (Koran 8:37).] God – Most High is He – gathers the foul one to another and piles them up as something composed is piled one part upon another. Then, He puts them in Hell with their people. There is no one in it but the foul. As people are of three levels – [1] fair, unmarred by something foul, [2] foul, in whom there is nothing fair, and [3] others in whom is both something foul and something fair – their abodes are three: [1] the abode of pure fairness, [2] the abode of pure foulness – these two abodes will not pass away (*hātān al-dārān lā tafnayān*) – and [3] an abode for those accompanied by something foul and something fair, which is the abode that passes away. This is the abode of the disobedient. None of the disobedient among those who confess [God's] unity will remain in Hell. When they have been chastised according to the measure of their recompense, they will be brought out of the Fire and brought into the Garden. Only the abode of pure fairness and the abode of pure foulness will remain.[61]

In this text, Ibn al-Qayyim sets out classical Sunni eschatology in terms of the fair and the foul, and he asserts plainly in his own voice that the Fire, "the abode of pure foulness", will not pass away. This is exactly what al-Ḥarbī is looking for, and he writes triumphantly: "This is what befits *imām* Ibn al-Qayyim and his like because it agrees with the two revelations [of the Koran and the Sunna], the doctrine of the *salaf* and their followers."[62]

Al-Ḥarbī then raises the obvious question. Does Ibn al-Qayyim first trot out arguments for limited duration of the Fire in *Ḥādī al-arwāḥ*, *Shifāʾ al-ʿalīl* and *Mukhtaṣar al-Ṣawāʿiq al-mursala* and then later affirm the Fire's eternity in *al-Wābil al-ṣayyib* and *Ṭarīq al-hijratayn*? Or is it the other way around with Ibn al-Qayyim first affirming the Fire's eternity and then producing arguments to the contrary later on? Al-Ḥarbī first observes that Ibn al-Qayyim's books contain no dates. The only thing scholars have been able to determine about the order of these texts is that *Ḥādī al-arwāḥ* precedes *al-Ṣawāʿiq al-mursala*. Al-Ḥarbī adds that *Shifāʾ al-ʿalīl* is probably later than these two texts because it enumerates fewer arguments for the passing away of the Fire and thus reveals Ibn al-Qayyim's weakening inclination toward this

61 Al-Ḥarbī, *Kashf al-astār*, pp. 51–52 (al-Ḥarbī's quotation of this text includes the Koranic verse given here in brackets); Ibn Qayyim al-Jawziyya, *al-Wābil al-ṣayyib*, p. 20.

62 Al-Ḥarbī, *Kashf al-astār*, p. 53.

view.[63] Unfortunately for al-Ḥarbī, this argument is specious because Ibn al-Qayyim argues the same basic points in all three texts no matter how he enumerates the arguments.

Be that as it may, al-Ḥarbī continues on that he thinks it likely that *al-Wābil al-ṣayyib*, *Ṭarīq al-hijratayn* and even *Ijtimāʿ al-juyūsh* come after the other three books and present Ibn al-Qayyim's final view that the Fire is eternal. Al-Ḥarbī gives seven arguments for this. First, the sharpness and length of the arguments found in *Ḥādī al-arwāḥ* come only from the vigour of youth. Second, as just noted, al-Ḥarbī thinks that the arguments in *Shifāʾ al-ʿalīl* are weaker than those in *Ḥādī al-arwāḥ* because they are fewer in number. Third, Ibn al-Qayyim's focus on pietistic practice and the hereafter in *al-Wābil al-ṣayyib* and *Ṭarīq al-hijratayn* are characteristic of someone nearing life's end. Fourth, and in line with the preceding argument, *al-Wābil al-ṣayyib* and *Ṭarīq al-hijratayn* are much less dialectical in style than *Ḥādī al-arwāḥ* and the other texts. Fifth, if *al-Wābil al-ṣayyib* and *Ṭarīq al-hijratayn* were early works, Ibn al-Qayyim would have noted in the other three books that he had previously held to the eternity of the Fire and then changed his position. Sixth, Ibn al-Qayyim in his book *Ijtimāʿ al-juyūsh* cites a report that the Garden and the Fire will both pass away. Ibn al-Qayyim uncharacteristically accepts this text without debate and does not deal with it in earlier works. According to al-Ḥarbī, this indicates that he has come to accept the eternity of the Fire. The seventh argument is simply a challenge to produce decisive evidence to disprove the above arguments if they are found unconvincing.[64] Al-Ḥarbī sums up:

> Ibn al-Qayyim does not affirm that the Fire will pass away categorically, neither in *al-Ḥādī* nor in *al-Ṣawāʿiq* nor in *al-Shifāʾ*. Rather, everything is support for and inclination toward saying the Fire will pass away, then withholding judgment, and then expressing his final view – God knows best – which agrees with the view of his Shaykh, which agrees with the texts of the Book and the authentic Sunna, the sayings of the righteous *salaf*, and, even more, the consensus of the Muslims.[65]

Al-Ḥarbī's argumentation portrays Ibn al-Qayyim as a young and prolific firebrand with strong ideas who gradually settles down to a pious life of less dialectical writing and adherence to "correct" doctrine

63 Ibid., pp. 53–54.
64 Ibid., pp. 54–56.
65 Ibid., pp. 59, see 78–82.

in his later years. This narrative of Ibn al-Qayyim's development permits al-Ḥarbī to supplant three long and sophisticated discussions of the duration of the Fire with a few short indications of the Fire's eternity elsewhere that have not been independently dated. It also enables him to reconcile Ibn al-Qayyim's prestige as a rejuvenator of Sunni doctrine with the fact that a number of the Ḥanbalī scholar's books contain material that does not agree with what al-Ḥarbī believes that doctrine teaches.

5. Further Consideration of the Possibility that Ibn al-Qayyim Upholds the Eternity of the Fire

Al-Ḥarbī's overall argumentation is weak insofar as he first projects how the great Muslim scholar Ibn Qayyim al-Jawziyya must turn out and then dates the texts on that basis. If, by some other means, *Zād al-maʿād*, *Ijtimāʿ al-juyūsh*, *Ṭarīq al-hijratayn* and *al-Wābil al-ṣayyib* could be dated prior to *Ḥādī al-arwāḥ*, *Shifāʾ al-ʿalīl* and *al-Ṣawāʿiq al-mursala*, al-Ḥarbī's thesis would fall flat and we could posit development in Ibn al-Qayyim's thought from belief in the Fire's eternity to belief that God's mercy and wise purpose will bring the Fire to an end. However, that scenario would be just as arbitrary as al-Ḥarbī's in the absence of an adequate chronology of Ibn al-Qayyim's works. Such a chronology remains a desideratum in the field, but enough work has been done by Joseph Bell and later Livnat Holtzman to give al-Ḥarbī's hypothesis another chance.[66]

Ijtimāʿ al-juyūsh may be safely excluded from the present discussion because it does not provide serious evidence for Ibn al-Qayyim's belief in the eternity of the Fire. According to both Bell and Holtzman, *Ijtimāʿ al-juyūsh* is also a fairly early work. Holtzman includes *al-Wābil al-ṣayyib* and *Ḥādī al-arwāḥ* among Ibn al-Qayyim's middle works. In my view *al-Wābil al-ṣayyib* is difficult to place, and it could be a bit later. As noted above, *Ḥādī al-arwāḥ* may date to 745/1344–45. Holtzman assigns *Shifāʾ al-ʿalīl* and *al-Ṣawāʿiq al-mursala* to the later

66 Bell, Joseph Norment: *Love Theory in Later Ḥanbalite Islam*, Albany 1979, pp. 95–103; and Holtzman, Livnat: Ibn Qayyim al-Jawziyyah, in: Devin Stewart and Joseph Lowry (eds.): *Essays in Arabic Literary Biography 1350–1850*, Wiesbaden 2009, pp. 202–223.

period of Ibn al-Qayyim's life along with *Ṭarīq al-hijratayn*, and *Zād al-maʿād*, which she says is most likely his last work.[67]

As I noted above, both *Zād al-maʿād* and *Ṭarīq al-hijratayn* display much stronger support for the eternity of the Fire than al-Ḥarbī recognizes. Now, if indeed *Zād al-maʿād* is Ibn al-Qayyim's last work and if perhaps *Ṭarīq al-hijratayn* and *al-Wābil al-ṣayyib* are later than *Shifāʾ al-ʿalīl* and *al-Ṣawāʿiq al-mursala*, it appears that Ibn al-Qayyim thought better of his earlier deliberations on the Fire and retreated to simple affirmation of the Fire's eternity. Contextual factors lend further plausibility to this scenario. In 1345 Taqī al-Dīn al-Subkī (d. 756/1355), the Shāfiʿī chief judge in Damascus, attacked Ibn al-Qayyim over the latter's views on the legalities of horse races, and Ibn al-Qayyim had to acquiesce to al-Subkī's views. The two had another disagreement later on, apparently over divorce procedures, and had to be publicly reconciled in 1349.[68] Additionally, in 1348, Taqī al-Dīn al-Subkī wrote a refutation of *Fanāʾ al-nār*, which forcefully sets aside Ibn Taymiyya's arguments for the passing away of the Fire as unbelief (*kufr*).[69] It is certainly conceivable that al-Subkī composed his treatise in response to Ibn al-Qayyim's use of *Fanāʾ al-nār* and its arguments in *Ḥādī al-arwāḥ*, *Shifāʾ al-ʿalīl*, and *al-Ṣawāʿiq al-mursala*. It is also plausible that Ibn al-Qayyim stopped arguing – in writing at least – against the eternity of the Fire to ward off al-Subkī's charge of unbelief.

We are now in position to sum up what seems to have happened. Inspired by Ibn Taymiyya's *Fanāʾ al-nār*, Ibn Qayyim al-Jawziyya greatly elaborated arguments for the limited duration of Hell-Fire in *Ḥādī al-arwāḥ* apparently around 1345, and then a bit later in *Shifāʾ*

---

67 According to Bell, *Love Theory*, p. 103, Ibn al-Qayyim's major work on morality and spirituality *Madārij al-sālikīn* is also very late and includes references to *al-Ṣawāʿiq al-mursala* and *Ṭarīq al-hijratayn*. Additionally, *Madārij al-sālikīn*, ed. by ʿImād ʿĀṣ, Cairo 1416/1996, vol. 2, p. 404 (in the section on *dhikr*), mentions *al-Wābil al-ṣayyib*. I am grateful to Gino Schallenbergh for this reference. Holtzman, Ibn Qayyim al-Jawziyyah, p. 217, explains that *Zād al-maʿād* is likely Ibn al-Qayyim's last work because it is the only work to mention the very late *Madārij al-sālikīn*. I also explain in my earlier work, Islamic Universalism, why *Shifāʾ al-ʿalīl* and *al-Ṣawāʿiq al-mursala* come after *Ḥādī al-arwāḥ*.

68 These events are given in more detail in Laoust, Henri: Ibn Ḳayyim al-Djawziyya, in: *EI²*, vol. 3 (1986), pp. 821–822, and Holtzman, Ibn Qayyim al-Jawziyyah, pp. 220–221.

69 Al-Subkī, *al-Iʿtibār bi-baqāʾ al-janna wal-nār*. Al-Subkī provides the date of writing in his text as Dhū al-Ḥijja 748/1348 (p. 90). For further discussion of this work, see Hoover, Islamic Universalism.

al-ʿalīl. In both books, however, Ibn al-Qayyim backed away from the force of his arguments in the end and took an agnostic position on the question. At about the same time, the powerful Damascene chief judge Taqī al-Dīn al-Subkī began to harass Ibn al-Qayyim. In 1345 al-Subkī took Ibn al-Qayyim to task over legal matters pertaining to horse racing, and Ibn al-Qayyim had to back down. In the meantime Ibn al-Qayyim continued his theological reflection on the Fire in *al-Ṣawāʿiq al-mursala*. There he abandoned his earlier agnostic view on the duration of the Fire and affirmed that indeed chastisement in the Fire will end. This is likely what prompted al-Subkī to write a refutation of Ibn Taymiyya's *Fanāʾ al-nār* in 1348. That is, al-Subkī refuted Ibn Taymiyya's tract in order to make clear to Ibn al-Qayyim that he must stop his speculation and believe in the eternity of the Fire. This appears to have worked, with Ibn al-Qayyim again backing down. Ibn al-Qayyim stopped speculating on the duration of the Fire in his latest works, and he wrote as if the Fire were eternal in his last work *Zād al-maʿād*, as well as in two other works that may also be late: *Ṭarīq al-hijratayn* and *al-Wābil al-ṣayyib*. Further disagreement between al-Subkī and Ibn al-Qayyim in 1349 over divorce procedures confirms that tension between al-Subkī and Ibn al-Qayyim was ongoing through the late 1340s.

Conclusion

In conclusion we return to ʿAlī al-Ḥarbī's mission. His aim is to show that Ibn Taymiyya and Ibn Qayyim al-Jawziyya uphold the eternity of the Fire so that they conform to classical Sunni doctrine and thereby to his, that is, al-Ḥarbī's, preconceived notion of what such great Muslim scholars and rejuvenators of the faith should believe. In the case of Ibn Taymiyya, al-Ḥarbī's efforts fall short in the view of the fact that the Shaykh's last work *Fanāʾ al-nār* argues for the passing away of the Fire. With respect to Ibn al-Qayyim, al-Ḥarbī draws our attention to the distinct possibility of a late-life turn in the Ḥanbalī scholar's writing toward affirming the eternity of the Fire. Al-Ḥarbī's case remains very weak on its own because he fails to provide concrete evidence that Ibn al-Qayyim's works upholding the Fire's eternity are later than those that do not. However, two things add considerably to the credibility of al-Ḥarbī's hypothesis: first the fact that some of these texts do indeed appear to be later – especially *Zād al-maʿād* – and second the late-life difficulties that Ibn al-Qayyim suffered at the hands of

Taqī al-Dīn al-Subkī. These factors lead us to conclude that after Ibn al-Qayyim withheld judgment on the duration of the Fire in *Ḥādī al-arwāḥ* and *Shifāʾ al-ʿalīl* and then argued for the passing away of the Fire in *Mukhtaṣar al-Ṣawāʿiq* he stopped discussing this issue and unassumingly affirmed the eternity of the Fire in his latest works in order to evade al-Subkī's wrath.

One wonders what similar contextual factors might lie behind al-Ḥarbī's own passion to get his theological exemplars to uphold certain doctrines? Is this simply a religious and intellectual crisis faced by a particular individual, or is it part of the wider contemporary politicization of Ibn Taymiyya and Ibn al-Qayyim? I am not in position to answer these questions, but perhaps research into the 1980s social and intellectual environment of the Umm al-Qurā University in Mecca would yield further insight. At the least, al-Ḥarbī's travail supplies not only an intriguing episode in contemporary Islamic theological discourse that draws inspiration from Ibn Qayyim al-Jawziyya and his teacher Ibn Taymiyya. Al-Ḥarbī's pains also stir us to better understand these two figures themselves.

Addendum

Clear evidence of specifically theological conflict between Ibn Qayyim al-Jawziyya and Taqī al-Dīn al-Subkī in the late 1340s came to my attention too late to include in the body of this article. In 1348 or 1349, soon after al-Subkī wrote his refutation of Ibn Taymiyya's *Fanāʾ al-nār*, he wrote another refutation against Ibn al-Qayyim's anti-Ashʿarī theological poem *al-Kāfiya al-shāfiya* (also known as *al-Qaṣīda al-nūniyya*). This strongly suggests that Ibn al-Qayyim's poem and his theological ideas more generally had become sufficiently popular that al-Subki saw need to halt their spread, and it further supports the thesis that al-Subkī's real target in his refutation of Ibn Taymiyya's *Fanāʾ al-nār* was Ibn al-Qayyim.[70]

70 For further details, see the editors' introduction in Bori, Caterina and Holtzman, Livnat (eds.): *A Scholar in the Shadow: Essays in the Legal and Theological Thought in Ibn Qayyim al-Ǧawziyyah*, *Oriente Moderno* 90:1 (2010), pp. 22–26.

Law and Order According to Ibn Taymiyya and Ibn Qayyim al-Jawziyya

A Re-Examination of *siyāsa sharʿiyya*

Abdessamad Belhaj

Introduction

In this paper, my purpose is to investigate the relationship between Sharia and public order as understood by Ibn Taymiyya (d. 728/1328) and Ibn Qayyim al-Jawziyya (d. 751/1350). For the sake of focus, I limit the scope of my study to Ibn Taymiyya's *al-Siyāsa al-sharʿiyya fī iṣlāḥ al-rāʿī wal-raʿiyya* (Islamic Public Policy for the Righteousness of the Ruler and the Ruled)[1] and Ibn al-Qayyim's *al-Ṭuruq al-ḥukmiyya fī al-siyāsa al-sharʿiyya* (The Judicial Methods in Islamic Public Policy).[2] In more than one way, these two books have considerably influenced other works on *siyāsa sharʿiyya*, Islamic public policy,[3] up to modern times. I do not intend to explore in detail the contents of the two works. Rather, I will focus, first, on their scholarly reception and the prob-

1 It has been translated into French by Henri Laoust as *Le traité de droit public*, Beirut 1948. My translation here of *fī* as *for* is based on the fact that the title of the book appears in some biographies of Ibn Taymiyya as *li-iṣlāḥ*. See Ibn Taymiyya, Taqī al-Dīn: *al-Siyāsa al-sharʿiyya fī iṣlāḥ al-rāʿī wal-raʿiyya*, ed. by ʿAlī b. Muḥammad al-ʿUmrān, Mecca 1429/2008, p. 19 of the editor's introduction. The book is also available in English under the title *Ibn Taymiyya on Public and Private Law in Islam or Public Policy in Islamic Jurisprudence*, transl. by ʿUmar Farrūkh, Beirut 1966.

2 Ala'eddin Kharofa translated this into English as *The Legal Methods in Islamic Administration*, Kuala Lumpur 2000.

3 The subject-matter of *siyāsa sharʿiyya* is the description and the justification of a set of public coercive regulations that derive their authority from *sharīʿa*. Most of these regulations are discussed in the discipline of Islamic jurisprudence, *fiqh* as judiciary or criminal law issues. Chiefly, *siyāsa sharʿiyya* deals with issues of administration, market, judiciary system, crimes and rebellion.

lems they raised. Afterwards, I deal with the two authors' approach to morals. Chiefly, they identify *fasād*, corruption, as the cause of the decline of Muslim public order, in its social and political expressions alike. I therefore highlight the conservative and moral criticism that Ibn Taymiyya and Ibn al-Qayyim addressed to the society they lived in. They came to see the reason for its "moral corruption" in the lack of order, which was endangering the very existence of the Islamic system. Hence the solution proposed by both authors is to extend the authority of judges and rulers so that it can regulate order and ensure the higher objectives of Islamic law. Subsequently, I reconsider classifying the ethico-political views of the two authors, who are usually depicted as anti-system and radical thinkers. Above all, I attempt to reframe their ideas in in two directions. On the one hand, I show their reconciliatory character with regard to relations with the state. On the other, I highlight their moral tendency to preserve the *status quo*.

The present study argues that the *siyāsa sharʿiyya* of Ibn Taymiyya and Ibn al-Qayyim are primarily concerned with an efficient public order that reflects the norms of Sharia. What interests the two jurists in the first place is how to prevent excluding Sharia from the public space. This could happen either if the corruption of the society infiltrates all aspects of public life irreversibly or if the rulers, in their public policy, take recourse to measures that do not stem from Sharia. Correspondingly, Ibn Taymiyya and Ibn al-Qayyim, each in his own style, produced an advisory piece of literature that gives judges and rules more authority over public order. By doing so, they extend the authority of Sharia and its control over a corrupt society. In fact, from the perspective of the two authors, the authority of Islamic law is to be considered not only in its texts but also in its application and its spirit. Besides putting emphasis on the moralistic-conservative motivations of Ibn Taymiyya and Ibn al-Qayyim, I am making the point that they sought the re-establishment of an Islamic public order. As a result, they moved to a more coercive approach that seemed to them the best way for Sharia to regain control over the public order. For the simple reason that the function of regulating the public life belongs to the rulers, and because Islamic law defines the scope and the authority of rulers, Ibn Taymiyya and Ibn al-Qayyim were compelled to renegotiate the relationship between Sharia and public order in favour of a legitimized and extended authority of the state.

To begin with, the term *siyāsa* refers to any form of management, be it private or public. As such, it defines the application of practical reason to a body for the sake of its promotion (the managed body could be an animal, a human, individuals or groups).[4] Therefore, *siyāsa* is, on the one hand, the formulation of an active behaviour in a way that considers appropriately its consequences. On the other hand, it implies a certain pragmatic rationalism in overseeing affairs that is, above all, present in *siyāsa* as political management. In regard to this latter meaning, *siyāsa* was used interchangeably in early Islam to denote statecraft, government, the manner of governing or the ability to govern. Often, the practice of *siyāsa* was understood as a mixture of both wisdom and craft – hence Bernard Lewis' conclusion that *siyāsa* denotes "a skill or a craft rather than a doctrine or a philosophy".[5] At this point, one could ask whether Muslim jurists and theologians did not attempt to formulate a political doctrine before the Muslim assimilation of the Greek philosophy in the tenth century. One probable answer is that the jurists did not feel the need to "invent" their own field of political theory. Through Islamic jurisprudence (*fiqh*) and Islamic theology (*kalām*), they were able to express the general principles of Sharia on the subject of politics. The opposition between Muslim political factions was theorized in *kalām*, whereas important institutions of the state such as finance and courts were discussed in detail in *fiqh* books. Nevertheless, things changed with the assimilation of Greek political philosophy, which became a competing model that rallies adepts and may even threaten the order of the Caliphate.[6] Most likely, this cleavage of opposing political visions pushed the jurists to take political theory seriously and compose works dedicated specially to political subjects from a juristic standpoint.

As for the term *siyāsa sharʿiyya* itself, to the best of my knowledge it was used for the first time by Ibn ʿArabī (d. 638/ 1240). Nonetheless, later sources on *siyāsa sharʿiyya* rely heavily on Ibn Taymiyya.[7] At first,

4 Tamer, Georges: *Islamische Philosophie und die Krise der Moderne. Das Verhältnis von Leo Strauss zu Alfarabi, Avicenna, und Averroes*, Leiden and Boston 2001, pp. 239–240. See also Najjar, Fauzi M.: *Siyāsa* in Islamic Political Philosophy, in: Michael E. Marmura (ed.): *Islamic Theology and Philosophy. Studies in Honor of George F. Hourani*, Albany 1984, pp. 92–93.

5 Lewis, Bernard: *Political Words and Ideas in Islam*, Princeton 2007, pp. 32–33. See also Lewis' brief notes on *siyāsa* in idem: *The Political Language of Islam*, Chicago 1988, pp. 11, 19.

6 On *siyasā* in the Muslim philosophical perspective, see Tamer, *Islamische Philosophie*, pp. 202–204.

7 Ibn al-Qayyim quotes the Ḥanbalī jurist Abū al-Wafāʾ ʿAlī b. ʿAqīl (d. 513/1119), who seems to have used *siyāsa sharʿiyya* with the same meaning as that of Ibn

this could seem paradoxical, since Ibn Taymiyya was a fierce opponent of Ibn ʿArabī's legacy. Still, let us not forget that, in his formative years, Ibn Taymiyya was a great admirer of Ibn ʿArabī. That being the case, he might have read *al-Futūḥāt al-makkiyya*, Ibn ʿArabī's masterpiece.[8] In the 66th chapter of his book, the great mystic discusses prophecy as being justified by the legal management and the divine laws, *al-siyāsa al-sharʿiyya wal-nawāmīs al-ilāhiyya*.[9] Here, Ibn ʿArabī used *siyāsa sharʿiyya* in a double sense: on the one hand, in a practical/political sense referring to the way the Prophet rules over his community; on the other hand, he also intended a metaphysical sense in which God manages his universe, choosing a messenger by way of emanation (*fayḍ ilāhī*). In addition, Ibn ʿArabī distinguished between prophetic policies (*siyāsāt nabawiyya*, revealed by God) and wisdom policies (*siyāsāt ḥikmiyya*), inspired by reason. Compared to the latter, the main characteristic of the former is that it encompasses both worldly human affairs and those of the hereafter.[10] As such, it is the expression of the divine management of the world.[11] In a similar fashion, Ibn Taymiyya describes his book as being a short treatise containing epitomes of divine management and prophetic rule (*risāla mukhtaṣara fīhā jawāmiʿ min al-siyāsa al-ilāhiyya wal-ināba al-nabawiyya*).[12] Conversely, Ibn Taymiyya followed a different line of reasoning. As I will show later, Ibn Taymiyya focused mainly on the conduct of human affairs as essential for the divine order. As a result, his work has much in common with juridical works concerned with administrative, financial and criminal laws. In particular, *siyāsa sharʿiyya* draws on the political literature of *al-Aḥkām al-sulṭāniyya* by such jurists as ʿAlī b. Muḥammad al-Māwardī (d. 450/1058) and al-Qāḍī Abū Yaʿlā b. al-Farrāʾ (d. 458/ 1066).[13]

Taymiyya and Ibn al-Qayyim. In the absence of the original source, we cannot be sure whether Ibn ʿAqīl was the first to use the term. See Ibn Qayyim al-Jawziyya, Shams al-Dīn: *al-Ṭuruq al-ḥukmiyya fī al-siyāsa al-sharʿiyya*, ed. by Nāyif b. Aḥmad al-Ḥamad, Mecca 1428/2008, p. 29.

8 On the place of Sufism in the life and ideas of Ibn Taymiyya, see Makdisi, George: Ibn Taymīya. A Ṣūfi of the Qādiriya Order, in: *American Journal of Arabic Studies* 1 (1973), pp. 118–129.

9 Ibn ʿArabī, Muḥyī al-Dīn: *al-Futūḥāt al-makkiyya*, Cairo 1405/1985, vol. 1, p. 100.

10 Ibid., pp. 102–103.

11 Ibid., pp. 100–101.

12 Ibn Taymiyya, *al-Siyāsa al-sharʿiyya*, p. 4.

13 Nimrod Hurvitz recently wrote a comparative study of these two works (the content of al-Māwardī's book being the most original); see Hurvitz, Nimrod:

1. Review of Contemporary Literature

The modern Arabic literature on *siyāsa sharʿiyya* is quite abundant and needs a separate critical evaluation. It suffices here to review two recent contributions on the subject. First, the work of Ibrāhīm ʿAbd al-Raḥīm[14] seems to represent the normative line of Islamic reasoning on *siyāsa sharʿiyya*, with its long chapters that gather every material possible on the subject without being able to link them either to the context or to medieval sources. He reads these materials ahistorically in a way that allows him to "theorize" and to establish a normative model of how policies should be executed if they are to be considered Islamic. In fact, the chief focus of the author is to make Sharia relevant as a source of politics. Thus, he considers *siyāsa sharʿiyya* to be politics based on the rules of Islamic law, its judgments and its orientation in opposition to positive policies (*siyāsa waḍʿiyya*).[15] For him, *siyāsa sharʿiyya* is a subcategory of Islamic law that concerns itself with political issues. All things considered, the literature of Ibn Taymiyya and Ibn al-Qayyim on the subject does not support the sharp distinction that ʿAbd al-Raḥīm establishes between positive politics and legal politics. On the contrary, if his concern was to undermine (human) positive politics and therefore to show that it is less valuable and advisable than legal politics (supposed to be divine),[16] Ibn Taymiyya and Ibn al-Qayyim insisted that positive politics, as long as they serve the authority of Islamic law, should be considered equally as important as legal politics. Above all, he does not seem to be aware of the common ground between positive and legal politics, while, before modern times, Sunni jurists never questioned that there was common ground.

Abū ʿUmar al-Tamīmī's contribution, though a radical standpoint, is not very different in its results. A Saudi radical operative and jurist in the North Caucasus, he was killed in 2005. Among the radical Chechen fighters, he enjoyed a high religious authority as the Mufti of Chechnya. He embodies how radical activists and intellectuals equate

Competing Texts. The Relationship between al-Mawardi's and Abu Yaʿla's al-Ahkam al-sultaniyya, Cambridge 2007.

14 An Egyptian professor and vice-director of the Center of Islamic Studies and Research at Cairo University. He teaches *siyāsa sharʿiyya* at the famous Dār al-ʿUlūm.

15 ʿAbd al-Raḥīm, Ibrāhīm: *al-Siyāsa al-sharʿiyya. Mafhūmuhā, maṣādiruhā, majālātuhā*, Cairo 2006, pp. 19–20.

16 Ibid., p. 49.

siyāsa sharʿiyya with the perfect Salafi state. An example of his understanding of *siyāsa sharʿiyya* emerges from the chapter he devotes to Muslim external relations, in which he states that "the fruit of jihad is the application of Islamic law".[17] In the Koran and Sunna, al-Tamīmī sees references to the principles of foreign policy of an Islamic state. Unsurprisingly, he cites the theological credo of association (*walāʾ*) with believers and dissociation (*barāʾ*) from non-believers as an essential feature if not the most important of Muslim policy.[18] Islamic government, he asserts, "cannot claim to be Muslim without following this creed, and by virtue of it, it constitutes alliances and friendships with Muslims, assists them and at the same time refrains from polytheism and polytheists and shows them enmity".[19] All the same, the Muslim state should seek reconciliation with unbeliever states if legal interests require it.[20] Furthermore, al-Tamīmī allows the Muslim state even to conclude trade agreements with these countries and be beneficial to unbelievers who do not fight the Muslims. Similarly, the Muslim state should discuss with unbelievers and interact with them respectfully, calling them to Islam.[21] Obviously, *siyāsa sharʿiyya* becomes the focus of all political desires. Nevertheless, in this radical literature of *siyāsa sharʿiyya*, the reader could identify a certain tension between imagination and Islamic law. To put it differently, the legacy of *siyāsa sharʿiyya*, being developed mainly among jurists, acquired a legal authority that limits the political imagination of modern Islamic interpretations. Due to this tension between *siyāsa sharʿiyya* as a text and as an imaginary, al-Tamīmī is bewildered in the circles of faith, law and interest; on the one hand, faith requires him to call to Islamize the whole world and, on the other, law allows the fighting only of aggressors and this with restrictions, and finally, the interest of political and economic stability further restricts the authority of faith.

Western scholarship has primarily interpreted *siyāsa sharʿiyya* of Ibn Taymiyya and Ibn al-Qayyim as a normative Muslim political governance. As such, this concept represents somewhat a competing juristic model of the philosophical perfect state, *al-madīna al-fāḍila*. In this regard, Frank Vogel argues that *siyāsa sharʿiyya* is "a harmonization between procedures of Islamic jurisprudence (*fiqh*) and the practi-

17 Al-Tamīmī, Abū ʿUmar: *al-Siyāsa al-sharʿiyya*, Beirut 2007, p. 4.
18 Ibid., p. 426.
19 Ibid.
20 Ibid., pp. 428–429.
21 Ibid.

cal demands of governance (*siyāsa*)".[22] He sees a conflict between the jurists and the rulers that *siyāsa sharʿiyya* takes on to solve. In brief, the reconciliation surmised between Sharia and *siyāsa* would take the shape of "a constitutional theory by which the excesses of rulers may be curtailed and *sharīʿa* legitimacy extended to actual states".[23] To put it differently, the jurists offer rulers legitimacy "in return for a greater share of power".[24] More recently, Benjamin Jokisch argued that *siyāsa sharʿiyya* "indicates a state model in which political or executive authority is clearly separated from legal authority".[25] He added that *siyāsa sharʿiyya* refers to a stage in the development of Islamic law in which "it is no longer the ruler who creates, changes or abrogates law, but it is the law defined and controlled by the jurists that sets limits to the political activities of the ruler".[26] His understanding reiterates the supposed everlasting conflict between jurists and rulers already emphasized by Frank Vogel. Many authors, be they Muslim jurists or Islamic intellectuals, adopt this interpretation of *siyāsa sharʿiyya* as an Islamic governance without any critical reading.[27] Not to mention the multitude of "think tankers" who explain current ideas and activities of radical Islamism by its ideological roots in *siyāsa sharʿiyya*. For example, Mohammad Hashim Kamali perceives *siyāsa sharʿiyya* as "a *sharīʿa*-oriented policy or government in accordance with *sharīʿa*".[28] For the most part, similar uncritical interpretations assume the existence of Muslim political governance that is defended by Ibn Taymiyya and Ibn al-Qayyim against "non-Islamic" political systems.

The second reading of the legacy of the writings of Ibn Taymiyya and Ibn al-Qayyim on *siyāsa sharʿiyya* highlights the coercive nature

---

22 Vogel, Frank E.: *Siyasa shar'iyya* [Governance in Accordance with Divine Law], in: *EI*[2], vol. 9 (1960), p. 694.

23 Ibid., p. 695.

24 Ibid.

25 Jokisch, Benjamin: *Islamic Imperial Law. Harun-al-Rashid's Codification Project*, Berlin and New York 2007, p. 396.

26 Ibid. In essence, his thesis is an attempt to establish a parallel between, if not a direct influence of the Byzantine "society of law" on *siyāsa sharʿiyya*. Though such influence is not excluded, *siyāsa sharʿiyya* trusts society less, instead making the state the major agent of Sharia.

27 For an example of a Muslim jurist interpreting *siyāsa sharʿiyya*, see Khallāf, ʿAbd al-Wahhāb: *al-Siyāsa al-sharʿiyya aw niʿam al-dawla al-islāmiyya*, Cairo 1977. For an example of a Muslim intellectual reflecting on the same subject, see al-Nafīsī, ʿAbd Allāh: *Fī al-Siyāsa al-sharʿiyya*, Kuwayt 1984.

28 Kamali, Mohammad Hashim: *Shari'ah Law. An Introduction*, Oxford 2008, pp. 225–226.

of their approach. From this judicial perspective, they emphasize the extended authority given to judges and rulers in the interpretation of penal punishments. In this reading, *siyāsa sharʿiyya* is a "coercive policy" concerned primarily with criminal procedures.[29] Especially in Ibn al-Qayyim's work, *siyāsa sharʿiyya* appears to be a set of principles for forensic evidence examination.[30] By the same token, the current of the penal approach is counter-balanced by a "public interest" conception of *siyāsa sharʿiyya.* For instance, Muhammad Khalid Masud acknowledges that, for Ibn Taymiyya, "*siyāsa* is related to the need for discipline and order and that discipline can be achieved best by assimilating the practice of *siyāsa* into *sharīʿa*".[31] However, Ibn Taymiyya conceives order as a means of realizing the public interest (*maṣlaḥa*).[32] Emile Tyan raised this point and clearly stated that *siyāsa sharʿiyya*, after all, is not a new method or source of Islamic law. Rather, in its legal reasoning and application, it functions the same way as public interest (*istiṣlāḥ*) or juristic preference (*istiḥsān*). According to Tyan, *siyāsa sharʿiyya* consists in applying rules and legal solutions that consider practical utility, independently from strict legality.[33] Still, Tyan asserts that the laws of *siyāsa sharʿiyya* are consistent with the fundamental principles of the law, since they are intended to achieve its essential goals.[34]

Baber Johansen stands out conspicuously among the Western scholars who showed a particular interest in the legacy of Ibn Taymiyya and

29 Ibrahim, Saeed Hasan: Basic Principles of Criminal Procedure under Islamic Shari'a, in: Muhammad A. Abdel Haleem, Adel Omar Sharif and Kate Daniels (eds.): *Criminal Justice in Islam. Judicial Procedure in the Sharīʿah*, London 2003, pp. 17–34, here pp. 24–25.

30 Al-Sulamī, ʿAbd al-Raḥmān Nāfiʿ: al-Siyāsa al-sharʿiyya ʿinda al-imām Ibn Qayyim al-Jawziyya, in: *Majallat Jāmiʿat al-Malik ʿAbd al-ʿAzīz. Al-Ādāb wal-ʿUlūm al-Insāniyya* 16 (2008), pp. 317–356, here p. 325. Ann Lambton expressed this view as follows: "through *al-Siyāsa al-sharʿiyya* there runs like a thread the theme of the need for coercive power to maintain discipline and enforce order", Lambton, Ann K. S.: *State and Government in Medieval Islam. An Introduction to the Study of Islamic Political Theory; the Jurists*, Oxford and New York 1981, p. 145.

31 Masud, Muhammad Khalid: The Doctrine of *Siyāsa* in Islamic Law, in: *Recht van de Islam* 18 (2001), pp. 1–29, here pp. 11–12.

32 Ibid., p. 12. See also: Layish, Aharon: Saudi Arabian Legal Reform as a Mechanism to Moderate Wahhabi Doctrine, in: *Journal of the American Oriental Society* 107 (1987), pp. 279–292, here p. 284.

33 Tyan, Emile: Méthodologie et sources du droit en Islam (*Istiḥsān*, *Istiṣlāḥ*, *Siyāsa sharʿiyya*), in: *Studia Islamica* 10 (1959), pp. 79–109, here p. 101.

34 Ibid., p. 104.

Ibn al-Qayyim on *siyāsa sharʿiyya*. On balance, he approached the subject from a different angle each time he dealt with it, leaving the reader with many unanswered questions. However, one notes an evolution (or rather an overlapping) in his treatment of *siyāsa sharʿiyya*. In the first place, he adopted a kind of "juridical" perspective that emphasizes the coercive meaning of the term coupled with an attention to "legal argumentation"[35] (legal evidence/proof). While one must agree with Johansen that for certain Muslim jurists *siyāsa* meant exclusively an equality of undefined criminal punishment (*taʿzīr*) it seems hard to accept his statement that this meaning is a forerunner of a special form of *siyāsa sharʿiyya* that includes *siyāsa* in the Sharia.[36] All the same, the coercive aspect of *siyāsa* is only one dimension among others found in the literature of *siyāsa sharʿiyya*. That being the case, the majority of Muslim jurists did not consider the punitive competence of the state as being the same as government's management of the public order. Manuals of *fiqh* mention other state functions, depending on the juridical question at stake, such as the financial function (in the chapter on almsgiving, *zakāt*) or the defensive function (in the chapter on jihad). Similarly, when dealing with issues of criminal punishment (in the chapter of *ḥudūd*), the state appears, first and foremost, as a necessary coercive agent. Therefore, *siyāsa* cannot be understood as an exclusively criminal punishment, aside from the juridical chapter of criminal punishment. Still, in his recent writings, Johansen focused rather on certain "politico-moralistic" aspects of *siyāsa sharʿiyya*.[37] With this intention, he was more attentive to Ibn Taymiyya's politico-social system, framing his ideas within the Mamluk context. With this in mind, I shall now turn to the main legal and moral problems of *siyāsa sharʿiyya* as discussed by Ibn Taymiyya and Ibn al-Qayyim.

35 Johansen, Baber: Signs as Evidence. The Doctrine of Ibn Taymiyya (1263–1328) and Ibn Qayyim al-Jawziyya (d. 1351) on Proof, in: *Islamic Law and Society* 9 (2002), pp. 168–193. Ovamir Anjum has criticized Johansen's approach to the legacy of Ibn Taymiyya as being too legalistic: Anjum, Ovamir: *Reason and Politics in Medieval Islamic Thought. The Taymiyyan Moment*, Madison 2008, pp. 62–66.

36 Johansen, Baber: *Contingency in a Sacred Law. Legal and Ethical Norms in the Muslim Fiqh*, Boston and Leiden 1999, p. 217.

37 Idem: A Perfect Law in an Imperfect Society. Ibn Taymiyya's Concept of "Governance in the Name of the Sacred Law", in: Peri Bearman, Wolfhart Heinrichs and Bernard G. Weiss (eds.): *The Law Applied. Contextualizing the Islamic Shari'a; a Volume in Honor of Frank E. Vogel*, London and New York 2008, pp. 259–294.

2. A Corrupted Society (*fasād*)

Fasād is a highly negative concept in the Koran. Often, it indicates the spiritual decay of a community that chose to move from a state of belief to disbelief. The Koran also links religious *fasād* with earthly destruction, disorder and chaos, which lead to the absence of security for people and property, in a direct cause/effect relationship.[38] In its manifestation, *fasād* refers to corruption, ruination, the taking of someone's property or violent action.[39] All these calamities come as a consequence of man's disobedience to his creator. Since man destroys the divine order by seeking wealth and power, these two desires are associated with *fasād*.[40] According to Muslim legal terminology, *fasād* means nullity. That is, all religous, commercial or social legal acts that are not fully legal are null and void, or corrupt. The usage of *fasād* in Islamic law goes beyond this specific meaning. Thus, the jurists use the expression of *fasād al-zamān* to deplore the deterioration of the times[41] or any corruption of the body politic such as dissidence or rebellion.[42] Any divergence from the social, religious or political behaviour prescribed by Islamic law is an act of *fasād*. Though the concept has been extended to encompass political and economic corruption, it has kept its religious and moral connotations.[43] In the religious rhetoric of *ahl al-ḥadīth*,[44] the partisans of traditions and the main reference point of Ibn Taymiyya and Ibn al-Qayyim, *fasād* is associated with all aspects of innovation (*bidʿa*). At a certain point, *ahl al-ḥadīth* tend to consider any reform as a kind of corruption and disorder. Thus, they incarnate the most conservative current of ideas within Muslim movements and sects.

Likewise, Ibn Taymiyya perceives *fasād* as a consequence of disabling Sharia. For him, there is no doubt that Sharia preserves the

38 Fāliḥ, Āmir ʿAbd-Allāh: *Muʿjam alfāẓ al-ʿaqīda*, Riyadh 1997, p. 853, e. g.: Koran (6:33).

39 Penrice, John: *A Dictionary and a Glossary of the Qur'an*, Delhi 2002, p. 110.

40 Rahman, Fazlur: *Major Themes of the Qur'an*, Chicago 2009, p. 56.

41 Gerber, Haim: *Islamic Law and Culture. 1600–1840*, Leiden 1999, p. 124.

42 Bennison, Amira K.: *Jihad and its Interpretations in Pre-Colonial Morocco. State-Society Relations During the French Conquest of Algeria*, London 2002, p. 167.

43 On this aspect, see al-Ghazālī, Muḥammad: *al-Fasād al-siyāsī fī al-mujtamaʿāt al-ʿarabiyya wal-islāmiyya*, Cairo 2005, p. 7.

44 On this traditionalist school of thought in Islam, see Schacht, Joseph: Ahl al-Ḥadīth, in: *EI*², vol. 1 (1960), pp. 258–259.

inner state of belief among the community members and looks after their well-being as well. Ibn Taymiyya says, "much of the corruption in people's affairs goes back to the disabling (*taʿṭīl*) of criminal punishments".[45] He is even more critical of people taking recourse to money or nobility to escape such punishment. For him, this is one of the main reasons for corruption.[46] With regard to *fasād*, Ibn Taymiyya distinguishes between four categories of people:

> Those who seek ascendancy over people and corruption on earth. Indeed, these people commit a sin and are the corrupted kings and chiefs, like pharaoh and his party;
> who crave for corruption without ascendancy such as thieves, criminals among abject people and the like;
> who aspire to ascendancy without corruption like those who have religious authority or scholarship. This category is common among the scholars and the pious;
> The people of Paradise who want neither ascendancy nor corruption on earth, though they may deserve a higher rank than the others.[47]

From this categorization, Ibn Taymiyya draws the conclusion,

> [i]f the intent of political and financial power is to be closer to God and keep on the divine path, this would lead to righteousness of life in this world and in the hereafter. Conversely, if political power breaks away from religion or vice versa, public affairs will be corrupted.[48]

What relationship does Ibn Taymiyya establish between *fasād* as public corruption and as religious corruption? It seems that he considers the corruption of the rulers as a cause of the corruption of the ruled. Here again, the rulers are seen as the "guardians" of the Islamic public order and not simply sultans or commanders of worldly affairs. Nevertheless, the condition of the people could remain partially uncorrupted. Things could be worse in the absence of rulers, who incarnate order.[49] Identically, Ibn al-Qayyim condemns immoral conduct within the community. Above all, he reprobates the mixture of men and women which, for him, is the origin of all sins. Judging from *al-Ṭuruq*

---

45 Ibn Taymiyya, *al-Siyāsa al-sharʿiyya*, p. 91.
46 Ibid.
47 Ibid., p. 238.
48 Ibid., p. 240.
49 Bori, Caterina: Théologie politique et Islam à propos d'Ibn Taymiyya (m. 728/1328) et du sultanat mamelouk, in: *Revue de l'histoire des religions* 224 (2007), pp. 5–46, here p. 24.

al-ḥukmiyya, Ibn al-Qayyim seems to pay more attention to the social aspects of corruption than Ibn Taymiyya did. As an illustration, in the following passage, he states:

> There is no doubt that enabling women to mix with men is the root of all calamities and evils. It is also one of the greatest causes of disaster affecting everybody. In addition, it is one of the causes of corruption in public and private affairs, and the mixing of men and women causes the spread of immorality, adultery, pandemics and plagues.[50]

Additionally, Ibn al-Qayyim appears to be more concerned with legal evidence in dealing with anti-system political violence. As a result, he considers that the testimony of convinced heterodox theological followers including Shiites and Muʿtazilīs could be accepted in the court. He justifies such an exceptional judicial solution with the necessity to uphold a judicial system. If the country is predominantly populated or governed by heterodox sects or if the judges and the muftis belong to such sects, he asserts, then one cannot reject their witnesses. Doing so would disable the whole judicial procedure and eventually lead to great corruption.[51] Thus, the prior function of any public policy is to keep the community away from corruption. Barber Johansen points out that what is at stake in *siyāsa sharʿiyya* is "not a system of rules and norms but the religious purpose underlying these norms in its practical political form".[52] To put it another way, what is important to Ibn al-Qayyim is how to prevent *fasād* as a chaotic situation in which religion loses control over people.

In a similar vein, but in the opposite way, Ibn Taymiyya adopts a preventive approach to *fasād* by assimilating a political assassin to a bandit, since the former creates a state of a public corruption (*al-fasād al-ʿāmm*).[53] On this point, Ibn Taymiyya seems to come under al-Ghazālī's influence. Ann Lambton noted that the latter, "impelled by the fear of civil war (*fitna*) and corruption (*fasād*) leading to disorder and anarchy […] attempted to incorporate the sultanate into the Caliphate and thereby to maintain the religious unity of

50 Ibn Qayyim al-Jawziyya, *al-Ṭuruq al-ḥukmiyya*, p. 724.
51 Ibid., p. 465.
52 Johansen, Signs as Evidence, p. 181.
53 Abou El Fadl, Khaled: *Rebellion and Violence in Islamic Law*, Cambridge and New York 2001, p. 277. In addition, see Bin Mohd Sharif, Mohd Farid: *Baghy* in Islamic Law and the Thinking of Ibn Taymiyya, in: *Arab Law Quarterly* 20 (2006), pp. 289–305.

the Caliphate".[54] What probably lies behind this Sunni concept of *fasād* is the belief that public corruption changes the *fiṭra*, which is creation's original state of being disposed to monotheism.[55] In short, there is a sort of contraction and expansion of Sharia with attention to corruption; eventually, Sharia concedes certain of its rules to prevent the spread of corruption in the public order. By the same token, it is extended to "non-Sharia" areas for the same reason.

3. The Coercive Order Extended

Even more, Ibn Taymiyya and Ibn al-Qayyim were worried that the Muslim rulers continuously took recourse to non-Sharia procedures and principles of coercion in the public order. Moreover, the rulers cited the limits of public policy coercion procedures offered by Sharia as justification for the importation of these legal methods. If rulers decide to exclude Sharia from public order because of its lack of pragmatism or to employ a substitute for it as a source of authority, Sharia runs the risk of vanishing. Ibn al-Qayyim's pragmatic approach is found in a central passage of his text where he relates a debate between Ibn ʿAqīl (d. 513/1119) and an anonymous Shāfiʿī lawyer. In the course of the debate, the Shāfiʿī defines *siyāsa sharʿiyya* as "everything that agrees with sharia".[56] His Ḥanbalī opponent, by contrast, suggested looking at Islamic public policy as "an act that leads people closer to righteousness and further away from corruption, even if it has not been decreed by the Prophet and does not originate from the Koran".[57] Ibn ʿAqīl objects to the definition given by the Shāfiʿī asserting

> [i]f by "whatever agrees with sharia" you mean that it is not in opposition to the express instructions of the divine law, then you are right; but if you meant that there is no other (acceptable) public policy except that which is revealed in the sharia, that is an error and presupposes that the early Muslims were mistaken, since it is well known to all those familiar with

54 Lambton, Ann K.S.: Changing Concepts of Authority in the Late Ninth/Fifteenth and Early Tenth/Sixteenth Centuries, in: Alexander S. Cudsi and ʿAlī al-Dīn Hilāl (eds.): *Islam and Power*, Baltimore 1981, p. 49.

55 Griffel, Frank: The Harmony of Natural Law and Shari'a in Islamist Theology, in: Abbas Amanat and Frank Griffel (eds.): *Shari'a. Islamic Law in the Contemporary Context*, Stanford 2007, p. 46.

56 Ibn Qayyim al-Jawziyya, *al-Ṭuruq al-ḥukmiyya*, p. 29.

57 Ibid.

> the traditions that the first caliphs killed some people to set an example. If nothing else had happened but that the caliph ʿUthmān (d. 35/656) burned the Koranic manuscripts (which were widespread but different in some features from the authorised one), that in itself is (a good example of) the realisation of views based on the interests of the community.[58]

This debate illustrates the two opposing viewpoints of the experts on religious law on the relationship between politics and Sharia: the first accepts the compromises made with the rulers' politics, as long as they serve a common good that is recognisable from the point of view of the Sharia; according to the other viewpoint, the politics of ruling is in opposition to the politics of religious law. Therefore, Sharia is perfect and does not need any external legitimacy or effectiveness. One can consider the first current of ideas as pragmatic in the sense that the jurists recognize the important role rulership plays in shaping the public order.

Other juridical schools, seemingly facing the same challenge, developed the traditional principle of necessity (*ḍarūra*) whereas others theorized public interest (*maṣlaḥa*).[59] Nevertheless, these secondary and contested sources of legal judgements and procedures did not seem sufficient to maintain Sharia as the main source of authority for the policies adopted by Mamluk rulers. Therefore, the scope of *siyāsa sharʿiyya* had to be much broader than that of *maṣlaḥa* or *ḍarūra*. On the one hand, it seeks to justify the coercive public policy adopted by Muslim rulers. On the other, it makes any similar procedure or principle, by way of extension, a part of Sharia.

Pursuing this further, Ibn Taymiyya attempts to justify coercive public policy by stating that political authority is a duty.[60] He uses mostly a textual reasoning from which he concludes that the author-

58 Ibid.

59 Similarly, Antony Black noticed the response of the Twerlver Shiism to the same challenge when "the Old Twelver view allowed only the imam himself to use coercive force, al-Karakī extended this to the Mujtahid, *qua* Deputy, when he was delivering judgment and imposing Legal Penalties"; Black, Antony: *The History of Islamic Political Thought. From the Prophet to the Present*, New York 2001, p. 229. On *ḍarūra* see Krawietz, Birgit: *Ḍarūra* in Modern Islamic Law. The Case of Organ Transplantation, in: Robert Gleave and Eugenia Kermeli (eds.): *Islamic Law. Theory and Practice*, London and New York 1997, pp. 185–193. On *maṣlaḥa* see Opwis, Felicitas Meta Maria: *Maṣlaḥa and the Purpose of the Law. Islamic Discourse on Legal Change from the 4th/10th to 8th/14th Century*, Leiden and Boston 2010.

60 Ibn Taymiyya, *al-Siyāsa al-sharʿiyya*, p. 232.

ity of the state over the community should be extended because the purposes and interests of Islamic law include political authority.[61] For him, the ultimate objective in legal coercion is commanding right and forbidding wrong.[62] Consequently, the ruler should make prayers compulsory and punish delayers as much as he should use power to enforce order and law.[63] Ibn Taymiyya does not call to an ideal Islamic policy that would replace the policies adopted by the Mamluks. Rather, he appears to be in favour of a strict public ethics supervised by existing states. However, Ibn Taymiyya underlines the limits of this extended authority he offers rulers. Unsurprisingly, he goes back again to Muslim ethics criticising the political and moral corruption of some princes and commanders.[64] He does not condemn the Mamluks as such or any other Muslim sultanate. Rather, he emphasizes two features that should qualify a good ruler: power (*quwwa*) and honesty (*amāna*).[65] In other words, he perceived legal coercive public policy as a combination of force and responsibility. For the most part, Ibn Taymiyya tries to deal with a *de facto* situation. He did not perceive the state as suspect or view it as a necessary evil, as is argued by Sachedina.[66] What remains essential for him is Sharia as an ultimate source of authority.

In the same way, Ibn al-Qayyim argued in favour of extending the authority of the judges for the sake of the effectiveness of the judicial system. Nevertheless, he also underlines the necessity for a judge to understand the context in which he applies *fiqh*. That is to say, the judge should consider the public order before implementing Sharia rules. Hence the importance of contextual evidence (*qarāʾin*) and signs (*amārāt*) in the judicial process. Admittedly, Ibn al-Qayyim strongly defends the normative dimension of Sharia; but since the subject of judicial procedures is, by nature, a technical subject, *al-Ṭuruq al-ḥukmiyya* has much in common with the manuals on judicature

61 Ibid., p. 30.

62 Ibid., p. 96. See Ibn Taymiyya on forbidding wrong, in: Cook, Michael A.: *Commanding Right and Forbidding Wrong in Islamic Thought*, Cambridge 2000, pp. 151–158. See also: Laoust, Henri: *Essai sur les doctrines sociales et politiques de Taki-al-Din Ahmad b. Taimiya, canoniste Ḥanbalite. Né à Ḥarrān en 661/1262, mort à Damas en 728/1328; thèse pour le doctorat*, Cairo 1939.

63 Ibn Taymiyya, *al-Siyāsa al-sharʿiyya*, p. 96.

64 Ibid., pp. 240–243.

65 Ibid., p. 17.

66 Sachedina, Abdulaziz: Guidance or Governance? A Muslim Conception of "Two Cities", in: *George Washington Law Review* 68 (2000), pp. 1079–1097, here p. 1087.

(*adab al-qāḍī*). Thus, Ibn al-Qayyim's book covers mainly the traditional judicial themes discussed by Ḥanafī jurists. Nevertheless, he differs in that he defends a more pro-active role for the judge. Notably, he authorises judges to use torture "in order to obtain confession that indicates the location of the stolen things whose existence can convict the suspected person".[67] If the stolen goods, he goes on to say, "are not in the place indicated by the suspect, the victim has the right to ask the judge to beat the thief until he leads to the rest of the stolen things".[68] If the suspect has the money but hides it somewhere, the general rule is to beat him. If he denies the accusation, then he should be beaten undoubtedly to force him to recognize his responsibility. Ibn al-Qayyim justifies beating a thief by asserting that the suspect has the duty to give back the money.[69] Similarly, someone who refuses to carry out his financial responsibilities could be beaten. Ibn al-Qayyim relies on the consensus of the jurists to justify physical punishment until the accused can pay.[70] Indeed, Ibn al-Qayyim is concerned with the outcomes of an inefficient public order. To make sure that the justice of Sharia is applied, the judges have full authority to solve cases. Incidentally, Ibn al-Qayyim touches on the subject of politics. He points out that the reason some rulers dare to show disrespect for Islamic law is the ignorance of certain jurists. The latter think that the scope of Sharia does not go beyond what is revealed in the Koran and Sunna. By doing so, the jurists encourage the political authorities to take recourse to non-Islamic measures in order to be effective in their political rule. At this point, Ibn al-Qayyim reminds the jurists that a just public policy (*siyāsa ʿādila*) is a part of the spirit of Islamic law, in its indications and its moral objectives. In like manner, Ibn al-Qayyim argues for the coherence of law (*sharīʿa*) and public policy (*siyāsa*). Thus, he who has a deep understanding of Sharia and knowledge of its completeness (and of the fact that Sharia ensures the interests of people in this world and in the hereafter) knows that just public policy is Sharia and does not need any other public policy than what Sharia promotes. Remaining strictly within the judicial realm of his analysis, he defines just public

67 Johansen, Baber: La découverte des choses qui parlent. La légalisation de la torture judiciaire en droit musulman (XIIIe–XIVe siècles), in: *Enquête, anthropologie, histoire, sociologie* 7 (1998), pp. 175–202, here p. 197. See also his discussion of torture and "Trials of suspicion", in: idem, Signs as Evidence, pp. 189–192.

68 Ibn Qayyim al-Jawziyya, *al-Ṭuruq al-Ḥukmiyya*, p. 287.

69 Ibid.

70 Ibid., p. 278.

policy as the policy that allows rights to be restored from the unjust sinner. As such, justice has two roles for him; on the one hand, it should restore the rights of the victim and correct the injurer. On the other hand, it should be punitive to the vicious.[71] Despite its importance, the distinction made by Ibn al-Qayyim between a just public policy and an unjust one (*siyāsa ẓālima*), was not a starting point of reflection on the mechanisms of unjust policies applied in his time.

Furthermore, Ibn al-Qayyim draws attention to the understanding faculties of the judge (*fiqh al-ḥākim*) stating that the judge should be perspicacious in understanding the signs and the verbal and the contextual proofs as much as the general rules of law. Otherwise, he would be guided by prejudices and would violate common sense. He certainly would do so if he considered only the apparent elements of a case rather than paying attention to the conditions of legal evidence as well.[72] Equally, Ibn al-Qayyim distinguishes between two legal understandings: first, the one that is related to the general elements of a legal case; and the other, an understanding of the reality of the case and of human psychology. In the second understanding, the judge should be aware of the difference between the truth and lies, right and wrong; he should compare this and give legal judgement in accordance with reality; the judge does not regard duty and the reality as two different things.[73]

Ḥisba (an agency that controls commercial practices as well as moral conduct in public space), one of Islamic public policy's main institutions supporting the principle of commanding right and forbidding wrong, did not appear in Ibn Taymiyya's *al-Siyāsa al-sharʿiyya*. Bearing in mind that he already dealt with this subject in a separate treatise, *Risālat al-Ḥisba*, he probably did not want to repeat himself. At any rate, more than a few studies have analyzed the conception of *ḥisba* in Ibn Taymiyya's understanding. Notably, Ahmed Abdelsalam draws the conclusion that Ibn Taymiyya forbids the use of violence against rulers, as long as they practice praying. Likewise, he warns "against the offensive practice of *iḥtisāb* without specific knowledge, mildness and patience".[74] Ibn al-Qayyim devoted a long chapter to the subject of *ḥisba*.[75] Ibn al-Qayyim briefly reminds us of the *muḥtasib*'s authority

71 Ibid., pp. 7–8.
72 Ibid., pp. 6–7.
73 Ibid., p. 7.
74 Abdelsalam, Ahmed: The Practice of Violence in the *ḥisba*-Theories, in: *Iranian Studies* 38 (2005), pp. 547–554, here p. 552.
75 Ibn Qayyim al-Jawziyya, *al-Ṭuruq al-ḥukmiyya*, pp. 620–683.

to inflict punishment. In particular, he states that a *muḥtasib* is allowed to beat or imprison those who do not pray at the proper time or who fail to respect other religious duties, such as the Friday prayer, group prayer.[76] Nevertheless, he informs us in detail about different kinds of fraud in Muslim society that necessitate the *muḥtasib*'s hard intervention. Having dedicated his book to cases of litigation before a judge, he found it out of place to give more attention to the subject of *ḥisba*, a local executive institution that resolves conflicts between people without trial.[77]

The main issue raised by Ibn Taymiyya and Ibn al-Qayyim, as formulated by An-Na'im, is the extent to which "any *sharīʿa* principle that is enforced through the coercive authority of the state ceases to be part of the normative system of Islam".[78] In other words, could *siyāsa sharʿiyya* be the bridge, so to speak, between the normative system of Islam and the state? If that is possible, *siyāsa sharʿiyya* could be a sort of positive law. Let us not forget that these coercive policies are, in the first place, caliphal practices that were adopted as personal opinions or *ad hoc* decisions. Though they have the legal legitimacy as norms in the Sunni juridical schools, they originated in the practices, if not in the customs of early Muslim communities. An-Na'im opposes this possibility, asserting:

> A principle or rule of *sharīʿa*, as the religious law of Islam, cannot become positive law unless the legislative authority of the state. When so enforced by the coercive authority of the state, however, that principle or rule ceases to be religious, as its binding force becomes dependent on the political authority of the state and not the moral authority of religion.[79]

The essence of An-Na'im's point is based on the belief that coercion and religion are by nature opposed to each other. Ibn Taymiyya and Ibn al-Qayyim, however, were realists and defended the inseparability of religion and coercion. Neither author perceives the state as an inherently corrupted political form. Instead, Ibn Taymiyya defends the state as one of the greatest religious duties: "Religion cannot be maintained

76 Ibid., pp. 627–628.

77 Ibid., p. 620.

78 An-Na'im, Abdullahi Ahmed: *Sharīʿa* in the Secular State. A Paradox of Separation and Conflation, in: Bearman et al., *The Law Applied*, pp. 321–341, here p. 322.

79 Idem: Religion, the State and Constitutionalism in Islamic and Comparative Perspectives, in: *Drake Law Review* 57 (2009), pp. 829–850, here p. 831.

without the state (*lā qiyām illā bihā*) because humans cannot achieve their interests unless they gather as they need each other. Once assembled, they need a leader."[80]

Indeed, Ibn Taymiyya and later Ibn al-Qayyim emphasize that the state is necessary for religion and order, which makes them traditional Sunni political jurists.[81] While Muʿtazilī political ideas highlight the capacity of humans to manage themselves by way of reason and the universal principle of justice, Sunnis are less optimistic and rely on law to command right and forbid wrong in the society. Consequently, they need a political body able to apply law. That being the case, there is no similarity between the juristic need for a state and the idea of a contract between the society, Sharia and the state. Rather, one should think of a compromise between Sharia and the state. However, Ibn Taymiyya and Ibn al-Qayyim were not considering an Islamic state that would enforce Sharia. For them, the state is a tool that allows Sharia to control the public order. In a similar way, Ibn al-Qayyim puts the accent on the necessity for a judge to be close to reality. Thus, he praised the quality of being able to understand the reality of cases (*fahm fī nafs al-wāqiʿ*), while criticizing many judges who lacked this quality.[82] Moreover, he made the point that those who do consider *siyāsa* to be part of Sharia "lack not only a real knowledge of Islamic law and the reality, but also the capacity to apply each to the other, as well".[83]

4. A Comparison Between Ibn Taymiyya and Ibn al-Qayyim on *siyāsa sharʿiyya*

As a final point, I would like to briefly compare the two works of Ibn Taymiyya and Ibn al-Qayyim on *siyāsa sharʿiyya*. At this stage,

80 Ibn Taymiyya, *al-Siyāsa al-sharʿiyya*, p. 217.

81 On the judicial necessity of the state according to Ibn Taymiyya see Khan, Qamaruddin: *The Political Thought of Ibn Taymiyah*, Lahore 1983, p. 125.

82 Ibn Qayyim al-Jawziyya, *al-Ṭuruq al-ḥukmiyya*, p. 7.

83 Ibid., p. 31. Frank Vogel summarizes the sense of reality in Ibn al-Qayyim's judicial philosophy as follows: "He advanced the idea, learned from Ibn Taymiyya, that the justice sought by the *sharīʿa* cannot be found just in doctrine with no concern for reality and practical implementation. *Sharīʿa* demands justice realized in the world, as far as human capacities allow," see Vogel, Frank: *Islamic Law and Legal System. Studies of Saudi Arabia*, Leiden and Boston 2000, p. 145.

it is necessary to consider the difference between the motivations of the two authors in taking up the task of writing on the subject. Ibn Taymiyya seems to have composed his treatise as advice (*nuṣḥ*) to the Mamluk prince Jamāl al-Dīn Āqqush al-Manṣūrī (d. 720/1320–21), the governor of Damascus, who requested the author to write a treatise on *siyāsa*.[84] As such, it can be considered a piece of juristic political advice. For his part, Ibn al-Qayyim was also asked by an anonymous person from Tripoli about the validity of a judgment by a judge or a governor who judges according to the physiognomy (*firāsa*) and contextual evidence (*qarāʾin*) and who might use violence to investigate the case.[85] The difference between these purposes probably explains the difference in the structure of the books: Ibn Taymiyya touches upon several points such as rulership, criminal punishments, jihad, whereas Ibn al-Qayyim focuses mainly on the judicial methods that enable an effective legal investigation. In this sense, Ibn Taymiyya tackled the theoretical background of the discussion of socio-political questions, remaining careful because his primary audience was the political authority. In contrast, Ibn al-Qayyim had to explicate a rather limited and technical question that could be useful only if applied in a judicial system.

Accordingly, when Ibn al-Qayyim, on the margin of his main purpose, discusses general questions of *siyāsa*, he quotes or paraphrases the style of his teacher.[86] Conversely, when he remains focused on judicial questions, he reveals much broader knowledge of *fiqh* and hadith than his master. With this in mind, Ibn al-Qayyim did not challenge the methodology of Ibn Taymiyya. For the most part, it is a scriptural reasoning methodology that relies mostly on the Koran, the traditions and the Companions' judicial and political practices. The two authors intervene rarely to only "glorify" or to draw conclusions from these precedents. Besides, they emphasize the qualities of legal knowledge and moral authority of the *salaf*, early pious Muslims, as models of just rulers and judges. If we assume with Wael Hallaq that, in early Islam, legal authority was "personal and private and that it was in the persons of the individual jurists (be they laymen or on occasion caliphs)",[87] then we can note at this level that the contribution of Ibn Taymiyya and Ibn al-Qayyim is to have shifted the embodiment of the authority

84 Ibn Taymiyya, *al-Siyāsa al-sharʿiyya*, p. 4.
85 Ibn Qayyim al-Jawziyya, *al-Ṭuruq al-ḥukmiyya*, pp. 3–4.
86 Ibid., p. 245.
87 Hallaq, Wael: *An Introduction to Islamic Law,* Cambridge and New York 2009, p. 35.

of Sharia from an individual moralistic/juristic sphere to an approach that is concerned rather with public order. Nevertheless, their approach strengthened the tyranny of the state in the Muslim world.[88] In the 16th-19th centuries, *siyāsa sharʿiyya* continued to figure in political as well as in juridical books.[89] Chiefly Ḥanafī jurists showed a particular interest in its concepts and doctrines, since they were in charge of official judicial institutions and kept in close contact with political authorities.[90]

Conclusion

A closer look at the "political ideas" of Ibn Taymiyya and Ibn al-Qayyim reveals that what seems to be the main reference point of an "Islamic state" or "Islamic government", a cornerstone of much of the Islamist political discourse today, is a myth. Not only is the assumption of the radicalism of the two authors unfounded; as was previously stated, they also reproduced a conservative schema similar to other conservative Sunni jurists. For them, two salient facts prevail: the first is that there is a corrupted public order that challenges the legitimacy and the survival of Sharia and the second is that only by conceding more authorised coercion to the state could Sharia's control of the society be re-established. Ultimately, *siyāsa sharʿiyya* is an ethical criticism of the community and of the state with a strong emphasis on coercive justice. Both authors were concerned about the state of morals in the community, which, in the orthodox Ḥanbalī view, had reached an intolerable level of corruption (*fasād*). So they highlighted a normative solution to bring the governors and the community back to the right way (*iṣlāḥ al-rāʿī wal-raʿiyya*) as the title of Ibn Taymiyya's *siyāsa sharʿiyya* work

88 Ibn Taymiyya himself, being a victim of the coercive order ruled by the Mamluk state, ended by calling for the limiting of state jurisdiction. See Jackson, Sherman A.: *Islamic Law and the State. The Constitutional Jurisprudence of Shihāb al-Dīn al-Qarāfī*, Leiden and New York 1996, pp. 205–206.

89 For an overview of *siyāsa sharʿiyya* see Masud, The Doctrine of *Siyāsa*, pp. 1–29.

90 Examples of later *siyāsa sharʿiyya* books include: Dadah Khalīfa Afandī, Ibrāhīm (d. 973/1565, Ḥanafīte school): *al-Siyāsa al-sharʿiyya*, ed. by Fu'ād ʿAbd al-Munʿim Aḥmad, Alexandria 1411/1991. Ṭūghān Shaykh Muḥammadī (d. 878/1473, Ḥanafīte school): *al-Muqaddima al-sulṭāniyya fī al-siyāsa al-sharʿiyya*, ed. by ʿAbd Allāh Muḥammad ʿAbd Allāh, Cairo 1997. Bayram, Muḥammad ibn al-Ḥusayn (d. 1214/1800, Ḥanafī school): *Risāla fī al-Siyāsa al-sharʿiyya*, ed. by Muḥammad Ṣāliḥ al-ʿAsalī, Dubai 2002.

further runs.[91] One main difference stands between Ibn Taymiyya and Ibn al-Qayyim. If Ibn Taymiyya focuses more on what is to be done to correct errors, Ibn al-Qayyim was preoccupied rather with the ways to do it (*ṭuruq*, sg. *ṭarīq*). Thus, in *al-Ṭuruq al-ḥukmiyya* he mainly discussed the methods that allow judges to impose a moral order within the community.[92] In addition, Ibn Taymiyya did not deal with *ḥisba*, probably because his main addressee was a high governor who might not have been interested in questions of market control. Conversely, Ibn al-Qayyim, writing on the judicial field, felt the necessity to treat, even if at a limited scale, an institution that resolves conflicts.

In the final analysis, Ibn Taymiyya and Ibn al-Qayyim do not offer an Islamic model of governing. Assuredly, at points they deal with some political concerns for modern Islamic political thought, but the framework is entirely different. They did not attempt to prove the existence of an Islamic political theory in opposition to the political practice of the Mamluks. At best, in calling for a *siyāsa sharʿiyya* as a coercive policy or a set of coercive judicial measures, they advanced a harsh moral criticism of the public order. It is a sort of extension of a judge's or a governor's power on the one hand and a legitimation of this power on the other hand. Consequently, the widely accepted interpretation of *siyāsa sharʿiyya* as "governance in accordance with the *sharīʿa*" does not seem to adequately render the social and political ideas of Ibn Taymiyya and Ibn al-Qayyim. In addition, I showed that the ultimate objective of *siyāsa sharʿiyya* is to make the community respect the rules of Sharia. My conclusion is that despite the negative ideological inflation that surrounds their writings, the works of Ibn al-Qayyim and Ibn Taymiyya are scientifically important for our understanding of the Sunni authority concept and deserve much of the interest in them increasing today. At any rate, we should review their legacy in a way that includes the conservative and moralistic character of their approach.

91 Compare n. 1.
92 Compare n. 2.

Ibn Qayyim al-Jawziyya's Attitude Toward Christianity in *Hidāyat al-ḥayārā fī ajwibat al-yahūd wal-naṣārā**

Dominik Schlosser

Introduction

When different religions encounter each other, they can deal with this situation in various ways. If they take the position that the respective other religions also offer legitimate paths to salvation, they generally regard the coexistence of different religious systems as an acceptable state. But if they lay an absolute claim to their own definite superiority to all other religions, then they regard themselves as being in competition on principle. Well into the 20th century, Christianity and its historically younger competitor Islam were especially characterized by this latter stance. It is well known and has often been taken as a theme that, in the Middle Ages,[1] the conflict between Islam and Christianity as systems of meaning was conducted not only militarily and politically, but also in theological controversies with the respective other religious community, and that debates and polemical writings both functioned as vehicles for this.[2] The function and aim of such works has also often been a focus of interest – though usually only in relation to the respec-

---

* This paper is based on a MA thesis presented at the Institute for Religious Studies at the University of Leipzig in 2004. I would like to express my gratitude to Birgit Krawietz and Georges Tamer for their readiness to incorporate it in the present volume. Special thanks are also due to the Zentrum Moderner Orient (ZMO), Berlin, for financing the English translation.

1 In the following, I use the term "Middle Ages" to designate the period from the middle of the 1st/7th century until the end of the 9th/15th century, although I am aware that it is doubtless problematic to apply the term – a creation of the European Enlightenment and Romantic Period – to Islamic (intellectual) history.

2 On this, see, for instance, Busse, Heribert: *Die theologischen Beziehungen des Islam zu Judentum und Christentum*, 2nd ed., Darmstadt 1991, pp. 1–2.

tive political-social and religious situation in which they were composed.[3] If one tries to determine their function as generally as possible, i. e., without reference to their concrete historical circumstances, then, taking recourse to Niklas Luhmann's systems theory, we can name two tendencies that can be made out in almost every medieval Muslim polemical script directed against Christianity:[4] first, we can note that the Muslim anti-Christian polemicists of the Middle Ages integrate the other religion in the specific worldview of their own religion, for the purpose of cognitive coping: they do not generally grasp and depict Christianity as an independent religion. Asserting a claim for the exclusive truth of Islam as the last of the revelatory religions, they instead classify it within Islamic salvatory history by declaring that, in its current form, the Christian religion is a corrupted version of the religion revealed by God, a version that, in a way, has been abrogated by the Koranic revelation. This procedure can be described, with Luhmann, as a self-referential operation of a system, i. e., as a systemic activity in which the system refers to itself, thereby seeking to preserve itself as such.[5] According to Luhmann, a self-generating and self-maintaining system must therefore find identities in its environment that serve

3 This is the case, for example, in the two essays by Charfi, Abdelmajid: La fonction historique de la polémique islamochrétienne à l'époque abbaside, in: Samir Khalil Samir and Jørgen S. Nielsen (eds.): *Christian Arabic Apologetics During the Abbasid Period*, Leiden 1994, pp. 44–56, and Charfi, Abdelmajid: Polémiques islamo-chrétiennes à l'époque médiévale, in: Jacques Waardenburg (ed.): *Scholarly Approaches to Religion, Interreligious Perspectives and Islam*, Bern, Berlin and Frankfurt a. M. 1995, pp. 261–274.

4 The following train of thought is owed to the article by Schmid, Hansjörg: Gegner werden gemacht. Neutestamentliche, religionsgeschichtliche und aktuelle Perspektiven, in: *Zeitschrift für Katholische Theologie* 124 (2002), pp. 385–396, here in particular pp. 386–390.

5 The fundamental distinction between system and environment is constitutive of Niklas Luhmann's functional-structural systems theory. The system – which Luhmann understands as a regulated relation among elements (see Luhmann, Niklas: *Soziale Systeme. Grundriß einer allgemeinen Theorie*, 5th ed., Frankfurt a. M. 1994, p. 44) – is characterized by being separate from its environment; see ibid., p. 35. According to Luhmann – greatly simplified – the system acts in its elementary operations in such a way that it system-immanently registers and processes the system/environment difference it produces, thereby referring to itself; the environment is thus integrated in the system's world of language; see ibid., p. 64. Luhmann uses the term "self-reference" for the system's constant referring to itself; ibid., p. 58.

> as points of repulsion and as control factors for its own operations. But they have this function not as something solid by nature or as a resisting core of reality; they fulfill this function only because they are constituted in the system for this function.[6]

To mention the second tendency, this is true also of the medieval Islamic anti-Christian polemics, because when the authors of the writings in this genre refute the Christian religion, they are interested in far more than merely proving its implausibility and insubstantiation. The reference to and debate with Christianity serves not least to display the plausibility and especially the superiority of their own religious convictions and thus fulfills the purpose of clarifying and solidifying a Muslim identity, of whatever kind, which can be directly deduced from the fact that hardly any of the Muslim anti-Christian polemicists of the Middle Ages neglects to provide a favorable depiction of his own religious convictions.

These tendencies appear not latently, but very explicitly, in the example of a treatise apparently composed in the 730s/1330s,[7] the *Hidāyat al-ḥayārā fī ajwibat al-yahūd wal-naṣārā* (The Guidance for the Confused in Answering the Jews and Christians)[8] by Ibn Taymiyya's leading student Ibn Qayyim al-Jawziyya (d. 751/1350). Despite indi-

6 Luhmann, Niklas: Identitätsgebrauch in selbstsubstitutiven Ordnungen, besonders Gesellschaften, in: Odo Marquard and Karlheinz Stierle (eds.): *Identität*, 2nd ed., Munich 1979, pp. 315–345, here pp. 337–338.

7 See Hoover, Jon: The Apologetic and Pastoral Intentions of Ibn Qayyim al-Jawziyya's Polemic against Jews and Christians, in: *Muslim World* 100 (2010), pp. 476–489, here p. 477. It cannot be said with certainty when the *Hidāyat al-ḥayārā* was composed, because Ibn al-Qayyim undertook no clear dating and contemporaneous events are not mentioned in his treatise. An aid to dating is offered, however, by the knowledge that Ibn al-Qayyim is supposed to have compiled all of his works after his teacher's death in 728/1328 (see Bell, Joseph Norment: *Love Theory in Later Ḥanbalite Islam*, Albany 1979, p. 95; Holtzman, Livnat: Ibn Qayyim al-Jawziyyah, in: Joseph E. Lowry and Devin J. Stewart (eds.): *Essays in Arabic Literary Biography 1350–1850*, Wiesbaden 2009, pp. 202–223, here p. 206). This year can therefore be considered a terminus *post quem*. The *Hidāyat al-ḥayārā* is named in another work of Ibn al-Qayyim, the *Aḥkām ahl al-dhimma* (Regulations for the People of the Convenant) (see Ibn al-Qayyim: *Aḥkām ahl al-dhimma*, edited by Ṭāha ʿAbd al-Raʾūf Saʿd, Beirut 1415/1995, part 1, p. 204), but since its date of composition is equally indeterminable, this mention provides no indication of the terminus *ante quem*.

8 In the following, this will be abbreviated as *Hidāyat al-ḥayārā* in the text. The 1417/1996 edition of Muḥammad Aḥmad al-Ḥājj is used for the present paper. On the manuscripts al-Ḥājj used for his edition of the *Hidāyat al-ḥayārā*, see his *Dirāsa ḥawla al-kitāb*, in: Abū ʿAbd Allāh Muḥammad b. Abī Bakr b. Qayyim

vidual passages that remain sober and neutral, this work is in no way a religious-historical book in the sense of a primarily descriptive and indifferent depiction of the Jewish and Christian religion. Rather, the *Hidāyat al-ḥayārā* is a scathing polemic directed equally against Judaism and Christianity that takes, as Martin Accad points out, a "hostile and insulting tone [...] against Christians and Jews in general".[9]

A large part of the overview depictions of Muslim perception of Christianity or of medieval Muslim polemics against Judaism and Christianity refer to the *Hidāyat al-ḥayārā*,[10] but the number of works that go beyond merely mentioning it is relatively low, and studies in which Ibn al-Qayyim's polemic is comprehensively evalu-

al-Jawziyya: *Hidāyat al-ḥayārā fī ajwibat al-yahūd wal-naṣārā*, edited by Muḥammad Aḥmad al-Ḥājj, Damascus 1416/1996, pp. 15–214, here pp. 14–15.

9 Accad, Martin: The Ultimate Proof-Text. The Interpretation of John 20.17 in Muslim-Christian Dialogue (Second/Eighth-Eighth/Fourteenth Centuries), in: David Thomas (ed.): *Christians at the Heart of Islamic Rule*, Leiden and Boston 2003, pp. 199–214, here pp. 211–212.

10 See amongst others: Goldziher, Ignaz: Ueber muhammedanische Polemik gegen Ahl al-kitâb, in: *Zeitschrift der Deutschen Morgenländischen Gesellschaft* 32 (1878), pp. 341–387, here pp. 343, 373, 375; Steinschneider, Moritz: *Polemische und apologetische Literatur in arabischer Sprache, zwischen Muslimen, Christen und Juden*, Leipzig 1877, p. 108; Fritsch, Erdmann: *Islam und Christentum im Mittelalter. Beiträge zur Geschichte der muslimischen Polemik gegen das Christentum in arabischer Sprache*, Breslau 1930, p. 33; Anawati, Georges. C.: Polémique, apologie et dialogue islamo-chrétiens. Positions classiques médiévales et positions contemporaines, in: *Euntes Docete* 22 (1969), pp. 375–452, here pp. 411–412; Charfi, Abdelmajid: Bibliographie du dialogue islamo-chrétien, in: *Islamochristiana* 4 (1978), pp. 247–267, here p. 259; Waardenburg, Jacques: World Religions in the Light of Islam, in: Alford T. Welch and Pierre Cachia (eds.): *Islam*, Edinburgh 1979, pp. 245–275, here p. 261; Perlmann, Moshe: Muslim-Jewish Polemics, in: *Encyclopedia of Religion and Ethics*, New York 1987, vol. 11, pp. 396–401, here p. 399; Lazarus-Yafeh, Hava: Some Neglected Aspects of Medieval Muslim Politics Against Christianity, in: *Harvard Theological Review* 89 (1996), pp. 61–84, here pp. 63, 65, n. 12, p. 68, n. 27, 81–82; Waardenburg, Jacques: Muslim Studies of Other Religions. The Medieval Period; 650–1500, in: idem (ed.): *Muslim Perceptions of Other Religions*, New York and Oxford 1999, pp. 18–69, here p. 45; Adang, Camilla and Schmidtke, Sabine, Polemics (Muslim-Jewish), in: Norman A. Stillman (ed.): *Encyclopedia of Jews in the Islamic World*, Leiden and Boston 2010, vol. 4, pp. 82–89, here 84. Indirect reference to the *Hidāya al-ḥayārā* is found in Zebiri, Kate: *Muslims and Christians Face to Face*, Oxford 1997, p. 138, Perlmann, Moshe: Islam. Polemics Against Judaism, in: *Encyclopedia Judaica*, Jerusalem 1996, vol. 9, pp. 101–102, here p. 102; and Gaudeul, Jean-Marie: *Encounters and Clashes. Islam and Christianity in History*, Rome 2000, vol. 1, p. 190.

ated are almost lacking. In this respect, Martin Accad's 2005 essay on "Muḥammad's Advent as the Final Criterion for the Authenticity of the Judeo-Christian Tradition" has to be named as a positive exception.[11] The same is true for Jon Hoover's article "The Apologetic and Pastoral Intentions of Ibn Qayyim al-Jawziyya's Polemic against Jews and Christians" (2010)[12] and the entry "Ibn Qayyim al-Jawziyya" in *Christian-Muslim Relations. A Bibliographical History* written by the same author.[13]

That Western research has thus far paid less attention to the *Hidāyat al-ḥayārā* is not because access to it is difficult; Ibn al-Qayyim's treatise appeared in various editions, and an English translation is available as well.[14] One reason for this remarkable reticence may be that the *Hidāyat al-ḥayārā* is not a high-level philosophical-theological polemic: in it, Ibn al-Qayyim mostly eschews any argumentation based on logical proof, being content to polemicize against Christianity and Judaism on a popular level; for example, he does not shy from castigating. In addition, Ibn al-Qayyim's polemic sometimes takes on the character of a sermon, as the Damascene scholar repeatedly turns directly to the reader and calls on him, for example, to compare the teachings of Christianity with Muḥammad's message.[15] Adding to the *Hidāyat al-ḥayārā*'s character as a sermon are the questions, liberally strewn in the text[16] and the frequent direct addresses to the Christians.[17] That the *Hidāyat al-ḥayārā* has so far received little attention has probably to do with the fact that it depends on Ibn Taymiyya's (d. 728/1328) much more extensive work *al-Jawāb al-ṣaḥīḥ li-man baddala dīn al-masīḥ* (The Correct Answer to the One Who Has

11 Accad, Martin: Muḥammad's Advent as the Final Criterion for the Authenticity of the Judeo-Christian Tradition. Ibn Qayyim al-Jawziyya's *Hidāyat al-ḥayārā fī ajwibat al-Yahūd wa-'l-Naṣārā*, in: Barbara Roggema, Marcel Poorthuis, Pim Valkenberg (eds.): *The Three Rings. Textual Studies in the Historical Trialogue of Judaism, Christianity and Islam*, Leuven 2005, pp. 217–236.

12 Hoover, The Apologetic and the Pastoral, pp. 476–489.

13 Hoover, Jon: Ibn Qayyim al-Jawziyya, in: David Thomas and Alex Mallett (eds.): *Christian-Muslim Relations. A Bibliographical History, Vol. 4 (1200–1350)*, Leiden and Boston 2012, pp. 989–1002, here 996–1002.

14 Ibn Qayyim al-Jawziah, Imam Allamah Shamsuddeen ibn abi Bakr: *Guidance to the Uncertain in Reply to the Jews and the Nazarenes*, translated by Abdedelhay El-Masri, n.p. 1428/2007.

15 Ibn Qayyim al-Jawziyya, *Hidāyat al-ḥayārā*, pp. 228, 338, 341, 347, 575.

16 Ibid., pp. 225, 243, 245–246, 252, 338, 415, 445.

17 See, for example, ibid., pp. 497, 529.

Altered Christ's Religion),[18] which has sometimes even led to the remark that large parts of its content can be regarded as a plagiarism of Ibn Taymiyya's polemical treatise, at best.[19] It can be considered certain that Ibn al-Qayyim used his master's anti-Christian polemic for his refutation of Christianity in the *Hidāyat al-ḥayārā*, but the judgment that the *Hidāyat al-ḥayārā* is a mere plagiarism of *al-Jawāb al-ṣaḥīḥ* is already problematic because large parts of the *Hidāyat al-ḥayārā* are devoted to a polemic against Judaism, thus going beyond the content of Ibn al-Qayyim's principal teacher's exhaustive writing.

The idea that the *Hidāyat al-ḥayārā* is a plagiarism implies not only that its substantive and argumentative breadth and depth does not essentially go beyond *al-Jawāb al-ṣaḥīḥ* of Ibn al-Qayyim's master Ibn Taymiyya and thus, in a certain way, can be regarded as a contribution to the history of the latter's reception. At the same time, it underscores that in this work Ibn al-Qayyim does not show himself to be an original thinker, but rather (and not least because some passages of *al-Jawāb al-ṣaḥīḥ* are adopted verbatim – usually without being labeled as such) moves within the framework of the field of Muslim anti-Christian polemics already surveyed by his predecessors, which in turn entails two consequences. First, *a priori* prejudgments are adopted by Ibn al-Qayyim; and second, a good part of the themes, arguments,

18 For details about this work, see especially Michel, Thomas F.: *A Muslim Theologian's Response to Christianity. Ibn Taymiyya's al-Jawab al-Sahih*, Delmar 1984, pp. 99–135; Roberts, Nancy N.: Reopening the Muslim-Christian Dialogue of the 13–14th Centuries. Critical Reflections on Ibn Taymiyyah's Response to Christianity in *al-Jawāb al-ṣaḥīḥ li man baddala dīn al-Masīḥ*, in: *Muslim World* 84 (1996), pp. 342–366; Thomas, David: Apologetic and Polemic in the Letter from Cyprus and Ibn Taymiyya's *al-Jawāb al-ṣaḥīḥ li man baddala dīn al-Masīḥ*, in: Yossef Rapoport and Shahab Ahmed (eds.): *Ibn Taymiyya and His Times*, Karachi 2010, pp. 247–265, here pp. 255–262; Hoover, Jon: Ibn Taymiyya, in: David Thomas and Alex Mallett (eds.): *Christian-Muslim Relations. A Bibliographical History; Vol. 4 (1200–1350)*, Leiden and Boston 2012, pp. 824–878, here 834–844.

19 Proponents of this view include besides Ignazio di Matteo, Erdmann Fritsch, Carl Brockelmann, and Abdelmajid Charfi, whereby none of these went to the trouble to adduce evidence to support this judgment. See di Matteo, Ignazio: *Tahrif* or the Alteration of the Bible According to the Moslems, in: *Muslim World* 14 (1924), pp. 61–84, here p. 80; Fritsch, *Islam und Christentum*, p. 33; Brockelmann, Carl: *Geschichte der arabischen Litteratur*, 2nd ed., Leiden 1996, suppl. vol. 2, p. 126; Charfi, Bibliographie du dialogue islamo-chrétien, p. 259. In this regard, see also Ljamai, Abdelilah: *Ibn Ḥazm et la polémique islamo-chrétienne dans l'histoire de l'islam*, Leiden and Boston 2003, pp. 183–184.

and accusations reproduced in the *Hidāyat al-ḥayārā* are only too well known,[20] since they belonged for several centuries to the basic stock of seldom questioned Muslim polemics against Christianity[21] and, considering their veritably habitual employment, they possess a character as topos. Viewed in this light, the real achievement of Ibn al-Qayyim and his originality in selecting such platitudes as the accusation of falsifying scripture (*taḥrīf*) or the thesis that the appearance of the Prophet Muḥammad is already prophesied in the revelatory scriptures of the People of the Book (*ahl al-kitāb*) is that he provided bolstering content and combined them in a more or less coherent whole.

However, the present paper will not attempt to make the doubtless instructive comparison between Ibn al-Qayyim's polemical writing and the works of his predecessors in the area of Muslim polemics against Christianity and the delineation of continuities, parallels, and characteristic divergences. The primary interest here is rather a text-immanent analysis of the *Hidāyat al-ḥayārā* in regard to central aspects of the depiction and refutation of Christianity as well as the tendencies underlying it. Additionally, the question of the sources Ibn al-Qayyim consulted when composing the *Hidāyat al-ḥayārā* and the occasion for writing this treatise and its "place in life" will be briefly touched upon.

1. Sources of the *Hidāyat al-ḥayārā*

The first source for the *Hidāyat al-ḥayārā* that should be mentioned is Ibn Taymiyya's voluminous *al-Jawāb al-ṣaḥīḥ*: Ibn al-Qayyim not only takes up the themes and arguments of the anti-Christian polemical writing of his teacher. As a close comparison of the texts of the two works shows, he also adopts passages almost verbatim, only in the rarest cases marking them as such with formulations like *qāla shaykh al-islām*.[22] Dependent on Ibn Taymiyya's work are, for instance, the passage treating

20 See Cohen, Mark R.: *Under Crescent and Cross. The Jews in the Middle Ages*, Princeton 1994, p. 151.

21 Instructive lists of the objections to Christianity that were part of the standard repertoire of Muslim anti-Christian polemics in the Middle Ages, taking up Erdmann Fritsch, are offered in Wilms, Franz-Elmar: *Al-Ghazālīs Schrift wider die Gottheit Jesu*, Leiden 1966, pp. 223–243; and Waardenburg, Muslim Studies of Other Religions, pp. 49–51.

22 Ibn Qayyim al-Jawziyya, Shams al-Dīn Muḥammad: *Hidāyat al-ḥayārā fī ajwibat al-yahūd wal-naṣārā*, edited by Muḥammad Aḥmad al-Ḥājj, Damascus and Beirut 1416/1996, pp. 323–341.

the Paraclete's sayings in the Johannine Gospel,[23] individual passages of elucidations of Deuteronomy 33:2,[24] Psalm 45:2–5,[25] and sections of the summary of the first main section of the *Hidāyat al-ḥayārā*.[26] Except for the information on the councils following the Ephesinum of 431 A.D., the historical overview of the genesis of Christianity until 691–692 A.D. that is contained in the *Hidāyat al-ḥayārā* does not seem to take recourse to the universal chronicle *Naẓm al-jawhar*[27] (The String of Pearls) of the Melkite patriarch of Alexandria Saʿīd b. al-Baṭrīq (d. 328/940),[28] bet-

---

23 Ibid., pp. 323–341. The section received by Ibn al-Qayyim is found in Ibn Taymiyya, Aḥmad ʿAbd al-Ḥalīm: *al-Jawāb al-ṣaḥīḥ li-man baddala dīn al-masīḥ*, edited by ʿAlī al-Sayyid Ṣubḥ al-Madanī, Cairo 1383/1964, vol. 4, pp. 6–19.

24 Ibn Qayyim al-Jawziyya, *Hidāyat al-ḥayārā*, pp. 345–347. See the passages in Ibn Taymiyya, *al-Jawāb al-ṣaḥīḥ*, vol. 3, pp. 300–302.

25 Ibn Qayyim al-Jawziyya, *Hidāyat al-ḥayārā*, p. 353. See Ibn Taymiyya, *al-Jawāb al-ṣaḥīḥ*, vol. 3, pp. 318–319.

26 Ibn Qayyim al-Jawziyya, *Hidāyat al-ḥayārā*, p. 574. See Ibn Taymiyya, *al-Jawāb al-ṣaḥīḥ*, vol. 2, p. 360. On Ibn al-Qayyim's borrowings from *al-Jawāb al-ṣaḥīḥ*, see Hoover, The Apologetic and Pastoral, pp. 486–487, 485, n. 24.

27 The Arabic text of Eutychios' *Annales* is included in Saʿīd b. al-Baṭrīq: *Eutychii Patriarchae Alexandrini Annales*, edited by Louis Cheikho, Bernard Carra de Vaux, Habib Zayyat, Louvain 1954.

28 On Ibn al-Baṭrīq, see Brockelmann, *Geschichte der Arabischen Litteratur*, vol. 1, pp. 154–155; idem, *Geschichte der Arabischen Litreratur*, suppl., vol. 1, p. 228; Graf, Georg: *Geschichte der christlichen arabischen Literatur*, vol. 2: Die Schriftsteller bis zur Mitte des 15. Jahrhunderts, Vatican City 1947, pp. 32–39; Breydy, Michael: *Études sur Saʿīd ibn Baṭrīq et ses sources*, Louvain 1983, pp. 1–11; idem: *Das Annalenwerk des Eutychios von Alexandrien. Ausgewählte Geschichten und Legenden kompiliert von Saʿīd ibn Baṭrīq um 935 A.D.*, Louvain 1983, pp. vi–ix (with corrigenda to Graf); idem: Eutychios von Alexandrien, in: *Lexikon für Theologie und Kirche*, Freiburg, Basel and Rome 1995, vol. 3, p. 1023; Griffith, Sidney H.: Eutychios of Alexandria, in: Alexander P. Kazhdan (ed.): *The Oxford Dictionary of Byzantinum*, New York and Oxford 1991, vol. 2, p. 760; Micheau, Françoise: Said b. al-Bitrik, in: *EI*², vol. 8 (1995), pp. 853–856; Simonsohn, Uriel: Saʿīd b. al-Baṭrīq, Eutychius of Alexandria, in: David Thomas and Alex Mallett (eds.): *Christian-Muslim Relations. A Bibliographical History, Vol. 2 (900–1050)*, Leiden and Boston 2011, pp. 224–233, here 224–226. On the textual history of the *Kitāb al-Taʾrīkh al-majmūʿ ʿalā al-taḥqīq wal-taṣdīq*, see Breydy, *Saʿīd ibn Baṭrīq*, pp. 29–87; for its structure and content, see Radtke, Bernd: *Weltgeschichte und Weltbeschreibung im mittelalterlichen Islam*, Stuttgart 1992, pp. 133–134. See also Griffith, Sidney H.: Apologetics and Historiography in the Annals of Eutychius of Alexandria. Christian Self-Definition in the World of Islam, in: Rifaat Ebied and Herman Teule (eds.): *Studies on the Christian Arabic Heritage. In Honour of Father Prof. Dr. Samir Khalil Samir S.I. at the Occasion of His Sixty-Fifth Birthday*, Louvain 2004, pp. 65–90.

ter known as Eutychios of Alexandria, although Ibn al-Qayyim prefaces many passages with the formulation *qāla Ibn al-Baṭrīq*, thereby suggesting a direct quotation. The high degree of congruence in wording and in the selection of events treated suggests that this outline is a distillation of the corresponding sections of *al-Jawāb al-ṣaḥīḥ* that are based on the *Annales* of Eutychios.[29] But speaking against this finding is the fact that Ibn al-Qayyim's elucidations on the councils of the years 449–691/692 A.D. have no correspondence in *al-Jawāb al-ṣaḥīḥ* and yet exhibit parallels to Eutychios' *Annales*. The aforementioned conclusion could, however, be maintained if one postulated, for example, that Ibn al-Qayyim had consulted an intermediary source here, as well.

That Ibn al-Qayyim also employed the *Kitāb al-Fiṣal fī al-milal wal-ahwāʾ wal-niḥal* (The Book of Opinions on Religions, Heresies, and Sects) of the Andalusian Ẓāhirī scholar Ibn Ḥazm (d. 457/1064)[30] as a source for his polemical treatise[31] can be deduced from the fact that the his formal presentation of the Gospels[32] is congruent in all points with those in Ibn Ḥazm's heresiographical writing.[33] In addition, it can be assumed that the anti-Jewish polemic *Ifḥām al-yahūd* (Silencing the Jews), composed by the Jewish convert to Islam, Samaw'al al-Maghribī (d. ca. 570/1175), around 559/1163, served as a source for Ibn al-Qayyim,[34] because the section found in the *Hidāyat al-ḥayārā*

29 This is conceded even by Muḥammad Aḥmad al-Ḥājj, who otherwise strives to underscore Ibn al-Qayyim's independence and who judges his originality as greater than Western research generally does. See al-Ḥājj, *Dirāsa ḥawla al-kitāb*, pp. 138, 164. In this regard, see also Accad, Muḥammad's Advent, p. 220; and Hoover, The Apologetic and Pastoral Intentions, p. 488.

30 For the content and meaning of this work, see in particular Gaudeul, *Encounters and Clashes*, pp. 116–119 and the literature cited there. On Ibn Ḥazm's criticism of Christianity in general, see Arnaldez, Roger: *Grammaire et théologie chez Ibn Ḥazm de Cordoue. Essai sur la structure et les conditions de la penseé musulmane*, Paris 1956, pp. 305–313; and Ljamai, *Ibn Ḥazm et la polémique islamo-chrétienne*, pp. 83–139.

31 See ibid., pp. 183–187, 190.

32 Ibn Qayyim al-Jawziyya, *Hidāyat al-ḥayārā*, pp. 310–311.

33 See the passages in Ibn Ḥazm al-Ẓāhirī, Abū Muḥammad ʿAlī b. Aḥmad: *al-Fiṣal fī al-milal wal-ahwāʾ wal-niḥal*, edited by Muḥammad Ibrāhīm Naṣr and ʿAbd al-Raḥmān ʿUmayra, Beirut n.d., vol. 2, pp. 13–14.

34 See Perlmann, Moshe: *Ifḥām al-yahūd. Silencing the Jews*, New York 1964, pp. 24, 95, B33. On this, see also by the same author: Ibn Qayyim and Samʿaul al-Maghribi, in: *Journal of Jewish Bibliography* 3 (1942), pp. 71–74. On Ibn al-Qayyim's dependence on Ibn al-Maghribī's work, see also Lazarus-Yafeh, Hava: *Intertwined Worlds. Medieval Islam and Bible Criticism*, Princeton 1992, pp. 53, n. 8, 133, n. 8, 138–139; and Cohen, *Crescent and Cross*, 1994, p. 152.

on the loss of the original text of the Torah in Babylonian exile and on its reconstitution by the biblical Ezra[35] differs only slightly from the parallel passage in Ibn al-Maghribī's anti-Jewish treatise.[36] Another source for the *Hidāyat al-ḥayārā* that Ibn al-Qayyim cites in the text as little as he does Ibn Ḥazm's *Kitāb al-Fiṣal* and *Ifḥām al-yahūd*, is *Tathbīt dalāʾil al-nubuwwa* (The Establishment of the Proofs of the Prophethood) by the Muʿtazilī theologian ʿAbd al-Jabbār b. Aḥmad al-Hamadhānī (d. 415/1025),[37] from which he has evidently worked into his own text among other things both the section on the so-called Council of Jerusalem (in about 50 A. D.) and the supposed discrepancy between Jesus' religious practices and those of Christians.[38]

It is not clear whether Ibn al-Qayyim had access to an Arabic translation of the Old and New Testament scriptures[39] or if the Bible quotations in the *Hidāyat al-ḥayārā*[40] are taken from the writings of his predecessors in the field of Muslim anti-Christian polemics such as Naṣr b. Yaḥyā b. ʿĪsā b. Saʿīd al-Mutaṭabbib's (588/589/1193) *al-Naṣīḥa al-īmāniyya fī faḍīḥat al-milla al-naṣrāniyya* (Faithful Advice about Corruption of the Christian Religion).[41] The conclusion that Ibn al-Qayyim's at least passing knowledge of the biblical writings is based on his reception of such works of his predecessors, as Alphonse Min-

35 Ibn Qayyim al-Jawziyya, *Hidāyat al-ḥayārā*, pp. 420–422.

36 The passages reproduced by Ibn al-Qayyim are found in Perlmann, *Ifḥām al-yahūd*, pp. 48–52 (Arabic text).

37 About this work see especially Reynolds, Gabriel Said: *A Muslim Theologian in the Sectarian Milieu. ʿAbd al-Jabbār and the Critique of Christian Origins*, Leiden 2004; al-Hamadhānī, ʿAbd al-Jabbār b. Aḥmad: *Critique of Christian Origins. A Parallel English-Arabic Text*; edited, translated, and annotated by Gabriel Said Reynolds and Samir Khalil Samir, Provo 2010, pp. xxi–lxxv.

38 Ibn Qayyim al-Jawziyya, *Hidāyat al-ḥayārā*, pp. 483–487. See the note in Stern, Samuel M.: ʿAbd al-Jabbār's Account of How Christ's Religion was Falsified by the Adoption of Roman Customs, in: *Journal of Theological Studies* 19 (1968), pp. 128–185, here p. 131, n. 1. This essay also contains a translation of the corresponding passages; see ibid., pp. 131–133. On other passages Ibn al-Qayyim lifted from the *Tathbīt dalāʾil al-nubuwwa*, see idem: Quotations from Apocryphal Gospels in ʿAbd al-Jabbār, in: *Journal of Theological Studies* 18 (1967), pp. 34–57, here pp. 35, 38. See also Reynolds, *A Muslim Theologian*, pp. 77–79.

39 On this, see, for example, Lazarus-Yafeh, *Intertwined Worlds*, p. 126.

40 The term "quotation" here does not mean to imply that Ibn al-Qayyim reproduces biblical pericopes absolutely faithfully; rather, I use the expression to designate passages whose wording and/or structure deviates from the biblical original, but nonetheless presents the content of the passage in question.

41 See Accad, Muḥammad's Advent, pp. 229–230.

gana already conjectured,[42] suggests itself when one considers that the evidence that Ibn al-Qayyim presents for the biblical pericopes in the *Hidāyat al-ḥayārā* repeatedly proves to be inaccurate, for example when he classifies a passage from the First Epistle of John as part of the Acts of the Apostles.[43] Supporting this assumption, for instance, is the fact that, in the *Hidāyat al-ḥayārā*, Ibn al-Qayyim keeps Shihāb al-Dīn al-Qarāfī's[44] (d. 683–684/1285) and his teacher's erroneous identification of the "Ruler of the World" with the promised Paraclete.[45] It must also be noted that, to support his own positions, Ibn al-Qayyim presents in the *Hidāyat al-ḥayārā* pseudo-biblical material, i. e., text passages that are of neither Old nor New Testament origin, nor taken from apocryphal writings, but that he nonetheless identifies as Bible quotations.[46] Finally, it should be mentioned that in the *Hidāyat al-ḥayārā* Ibn al-Qayyim also implies that he has gained knowledge first-hand, for example when he reproduces a disputation (*munāẓara*) that he claims to have conducted with unnamed scholarly Jews during one of his visits to Egypt[47] and cites Muslim converts as guarantors of information noted in the *Hidāyat al-ḥayārā*.[48]

2. Reasons for Composing the *Hidāyat al-ḥayārā*

What was Ibn al-Qayyim's main intention in composing the *Hidāyat al-ḥayārā* and what group of readers was his intended audience? A text-immanent answer to the question of its place in life is offered, first, by the programmatic title, which suggests that Ibn al-Qayyim's aim with the *Hidāyat al-ḥayārā* was to strengthen the faith of the ordinary Mus-

42 Alphonse Mingana postulates that Ibn al-Qayyim used the *Kitāb al-Dīn wal-dawla* (The Book of Religion and Empire) by the erstwhile Nestorian ʿAlī b. Rabban al-Ṭabarī (d. 250/864) for his Bible quotations; see Mingana, Alphonse: Remarks on Ṭabari's Semi-official Defence of Islam, in: *Bulletin of the John Rylands Library* 9 (1925), pp. 236–240, here p. 237. On this, see generally Lazarus-Yafeh, *Intertwined Worlds*, p. 118; Accad, Muḥammad's Advent, pp. 229–230.

43 Ibn Qayyim al-Jawziyya, *Hidāyat al-ḥayārā*, p. 342.

44 See al-Qarāfī, Shihāb al-Dīn Aḥmad b. Idrīs: *Kitāb al-Ajwiba al-fākhira ʿan al-asʾila al-fājira*, printed on the margins of Bājajizāda, ʿAbd al-Raḥmān: *al-Fāriq bayna al-khāliq wal-makhlūq*, Cairo 1322/1904, pp. 2–265, here p. 245.

45 Ibn Qayyim al-Jawziyya, *Hidāyat al-ḥayārā*, pp. 223, 340–341.

46 See, for example, ibid., p. 494.

47 Ibid., pp. 384–385.

48 See, for example, ibid., pp. 370, 420.

lims of his time and at the same time to provide them with an argumentative toolbox for discursive debate with Christians and Jews, and second, by a separate section of the extensive prolegomenon of the *Hidāyat al-ḥayārā* in which the Damascene scholar goes into his motives for writing. This section makes it clear that Ibn al-Qayyim regards it as God's unchanging right, and thus his own duty as a Muslim before God, to refute those who denigrate the Koran, the Prophet Muḥammad, and Islam and to combat them with words as well as with force of arms.[49]

Along with the motive of providing his co-religionists with material for possible disputations with Christians and Jews, here I would like to focus attention also on at least one other impulse that could have moved Ibn al-Qayyim to compose the *Hidāyat al-ḥayārā*. First, it should be considered that, from the Muslim viewpoint, the debate with Christians and Jews in the theological-dogmatic area in the time when the *Hidāyat al-ḥayārā* was written was not a virulent and immediate challenge, as it was for example in the early Abbasid period, but rather a theoretical issue. Another aspect joins this: despite the backdrop of certain historical events like the Crusades, the brief Mongol occupation of Damascus in 699/1300, in which both Armenian and Georgian auxiliary troops took part,[50] the Cypriot military expeditions against the Syro-Palestinian littoral,[51] and the fact that, in his *Aḥkām ahl al-dhimma*, Ibn al-Qayyim accuses Oriental Christians of collaborating with the Frankish Crusaders,[52] it is incorrect to assume that the *Hidāyat al-ḥayārā* also

---

49 Ibid., p. 232.

50 See, for instance, Raff, Thomas: *Das Sendschreiben nach Zypern. Ar-Risāla al-Qubruṣīya von Taqī al-Dīn Aḥmad Ibn Taymiyya (661–728 A.H. = 1263–1328 A.D.)*; Edition, Übersetzung und Kommentar, Ph.D. thesis (Bonn) 1971, pp. 42–49 and the literature named in its footnotes; Spuler, Bertold: *Die Mongolen im Iran*, 4th ed., Leiden 1985, pp. 84–85; Holt, Peter M.: *The Age of the Crusades*, London and New York 1986, pp. 110–111; Pouzet, Louis: *Damas au VIIe/XIIIe siècle. Vie et structure religieuse d'une métropole islamique*, 2nd ed., Beirut 1991, pp. 290–303; and Degeorge, Gérard: *Damas. Des origines aux Mamluks*, Paris 1997, pp. 258–260. For this occupation see also Amitai, Reuven: The Mongol Occupation of Damascus in 1300. A Study of Mamluk Loyalities, in: Michael Winter and Amalia Levanoni (eds.): *The Mamluks in Egyptian and Syrian Politics and Society*, Leiden 2004, pp. 21–41.

51 On this, see Fuess, Albrecht: *Verbranntes Ufer. Auswirkungen mamlukischer Seepolitik auf Beirut und die syro-palästinensische Küste (1250–1517)*, Leiden 2001, pp. 160–166.

52 See Ibn Qayyim al-Jawziyya, *Aḥkām ahl al-dhimma*, part 1, pp. 187–188, in which the Damascene theologian argues that Christian writers stood in correspondence with the Crusaders in hopes that the latter would annihilate Islam

refers to current or recent events or a concrete situation. Ibn al-Qayyim's treatment of Christianity is not without historical references – he offers an outline of the historical development of Christianity extending as far as the year 691–982 A.D. and refers to the early period of Islam – but beyond that, the *Hidāyat al-ḥayārā* presents no recognizable references to historical events, so that the criticism it expresses of Christianity is in a certain way timeless. If one views the *Hidāyat al-ḥayārā*'s depiction of Christianity in this light, one must suspect that Ibn al-Qayyim's writing on the "Guidance of the Confused in Answering the Jews and Christians" does not reflect a current discussion, but belongs in the category of literary debates with Christianity. Not least for this reason, the question arises whether the condemnation of the Christian religion is only the primary goal of the *Hidāyat al-ḥayārā* and whether it also and equally functions as a self-referential operation of a system in Luhmann's sense. In other words: Ibn al-Qayyim's criticism of Christians not only had the function of disqualifying them, but also aimed to use the negative example of the *ahl al-kitāb* to point out to Muslims teachings and religious practices that had found favor within the Muslim community, but that he regarded as incompatible with correct Islamic belief; to warn fellow Muslims against assimilating to Christian practice, and implicitly to demonstrate to them the supremacy of their own religious confession, provided it was the "true" form of Islam as Ibn al-Qayyim saw it. The multiple references to the religious disparity among Christians,[53] which Ibn al-Qayyim stylizes as the epitome of Christianity,[54] the tradition he cites with the accusation that both Jews and Christians had used the graves of their prophets as prayer sites,[55] his criticism of the Jahmiyya's, i.e., especially the Ashʿarīs' conception of God, which he rejects as being in the same line as Christian ideas of God,[56] his catalog of the essential divine attributes (*ṣifāt Allāh*),[57] his remark that God knew how to prevent any falsifica-

and its adherents; he provides the example of an incident that allegedly happened during the rule of Sultan al-Malik al-Ṣāliḥ Ayyūb (ruling 638–647/1240–1249). This may be the passage that Jean-Maurice Fiey had in mind when, without citing evidence, he attributes to Ibn al-Qayyim "the accusation(s) […] of active collusion of the Christians with the Crusader enemy"; see Fiey, Jean-Maurice: Naṣārā, in: *EI²*, vol. 7 (1993), pp. 970–973, here p. 972.

53 Ibn Qayyim al-Jawziyya, *Hidāyat al-ḥayārā*, pp. 533, 574–575.

54 Ibid., p. 533.

55 Ibid., p. 574. See *Ṣaḥīḥ Muslim*, *Kitāb al-Masājid wa-mawāḍiʿ al-ṣalāt*, no. 530.

56 Ibn Qayyim al-Jawziyya, *Hidāyat al-ḥayārā*, pp. 220, 343.

57 Ibid., pp. 522–525.

tion of the Koran,[58] and a large number of other passages in the *Hidāyat al-ḥayārā* make this assumption seem very plausible.[59]

3. Ibn al-Qayyim's Depiction and Refutation of Christianity in the *Hidāyat al-ḥayārā*

Since every terminology already implies valuations, as is well known, it is appropriate to cast a glance at the various designations applied to Christians in the *Hidāyat al-ḥayārā*. Three tendencies can be made out: first, to a limited extent, Ibn al-Qayyim uses primarily neutral expressions to refer to Christians, like the Koranic term for Christians, *naṣārā*,[60] and the umbrella term *ahl al-kitāb*,[61] which, it is noteworthy, includes in his case along with Christians only Jews (in accordance with his diction, which has a very broad interpretation of the term *zanādiqa* – understood as the religious communities that possess no revealed scripture.[62] In one passage of the *Hidāyat al-ḥayārā*, Ibn al-Qayyim even concedes that the *ahl al-kitāb* are to be preferred to the *zanādiqa*,[63] among whom he groups not only idolators (*ʿubbād al-awthān*) and devil worshippers, but also Zoroastrians, Sabians, and finally the "unbelieving philosophers" (*malāḥidat al-falāsifa*).[64] However, he immediately relativises the dichotomy in the non-Muslim religious communities between the *ahl al-kitāb* and *zanādiqa* and notes that, just like the latter, Jews and Christians were definitely to be regarded as adherents of false religions.[65] In view of the doctrines and practices that the *Hidāyat al-ḥayārā* presents as constitutive of Christianity, Ibn al-Qayyim also – and much more frequently – refers to Christians with simple, denigrating epithets like "tritheists" or "trinitarians" (*muthallitha*),[66] "Cross worshippers" (*ʿubbād aṣ-ṣalīb*)[67] or

58 Ibid., p. 315.
59 For a discussion of the actual reasons for the composition of the *Hidāyat al-ḥayārā*, see also Hoover, The Apologetic and Pastoral Intentions, pp. 479–482.
60 See, for instance, ibid., p. 236.
61 See, for instance, ibid., p. 227.
62 Ibid.
63 Ibid.
64 Ibid., p. 228.
65 Ibid., p. 229.
66 See, for example, ibid., p. 491.
67 See, for example, ibid., p. 537.

"brothers of the swine" (*ikhwān al-khanāzīr*).[68] The Damascene theologian unmistakably expresses his judgment of the Christian faith as a wrong path that leads directly to the fires of hell,[69] not least by repeatedly using the pejorative term borrowed from the *Fātiḥa* "those who have strayed [from the right path]" (*al-ḍāllūn*)[70] and "the community of error" (*ummat al-ḍalāl*).[71]

Preferring such generalizing terms, Ibn al-Qayyim puts those so designated into three or four specific categories only when he examines the differences in the Christological and Mariological doctrines among the Christian denominations. Here he takes recourse to the terms customary in the Christian historiography of dogma and the Church: "Jacobites", "Melkites", "Nestorians", and "Arians".

3.1. The Historical Genesis of Christianity Until 691/692 A.D.

The argumentative power that Ibn al-Qayyim attributes to a discussion of the constitution and development of Christianity in the context of a critical debate with it can be judged by the fact that he presents a self-contained outline of the early history of Christianity in the *Hidāyat al-ḥayārā*. For this historical overview, he adapts parts of the *Annales* of Eutychios, whom – as mentioned above – he apparently did not receive directly, but via Ibn Taymiyya's *al-Jawāb al-ṣaḥīḥ*, whereby he deals with his model independently in that he occasionally abridges it or slightly changes its wording. Beginning with what he calls the supposed crucifixion of Jesus, he not only focuses on it as the beginning of Christianity, but also traces Christianity's genesis against the background of the councils up to the year 691/692 A.D. in particular. For the most part, Ibn al-Qayyim eschews adding commentary to the material that Ibn Taymiyya presents from Eutychios' *Annales*, making a judgment all the clearer in his concluding remarks. It is less the form of depiction than the emphases he places and the aforementioned announcement that make it clear that his viewpoint (of the early history) of Christianity is based on a particular idea that he sees confirmed in Eutychios' description of Church history. Presenting it is the only reason why he includes such a historical overview in the *Hidāyat al-ḥayārā*: this is the presentation of, in Ibn al-Qayyim's

68 See ibid., p. 432.
69 Ibid., p. 225.
70 See, for example, ibid., p. 425.
71 See, for instance, ibid., p. 480.

diction, the *tark dīn al-masīḥ wal-insilāḥ minhu jumlatan*,[72] the idea of a not unintentional, but variously motivated distortion of the "true religion of Jesus",[73] i.e., of the religion that is to be equated with the religion revealed in the Koran.[74] Ibn al-Qayyim's claim is that the divinely commanded doctrines, which Jesus and his predecessors in the office of prophet tirelessly propounded, and the forms of practicing faith directed by God, strict adherence to which Jesus repeatedly inculcated in his apostles, were replaced by doctrines and practices deviating from them.[75] Ibn al-Qayyim does not place the responsibility for this solely on the participants at the councils.[76] He also blames, first, the Christian clergy,[77] whom he accuses of and arbitrarily – as if claiming divine authority – replacing God's commandments to human beings with their own commandments and prohibitions, which the faithful in turn regard as binding, and, second, the Christians *per se*, who, he contends, reject *in toto* the divine commandments contained in the revelatory scriptures and instead orient their actions toward the directives of the clergy.[78]

The verdict that the Christians had willfully corrupted Jesus' promulgations and had thus deviated from the "true religion of Jesus" and that Christianity in its current form is therefore nothing but a degeneration – a verdict that many of Ibn al-Qayyim's predecessors in the intellectual debates with Christianity had asserted in various degrees of intensity[79] – shapes not only Ibn al-Qayyim's condensed depiction of the first centuries of Christianity; it also functions as the basis of his critique of the substance and practices of Christian belief. As the basic theme underlying the *Hidāyat al-ḥayārā* would have it and as shown not least by many passages in which Ibn al-Qayyim calls the Christians *ummat al-ḍalāl*, the history of the first centuries of Christianity appears almost exclusively as the history of the "Christians' deviation from the right path": according to Ibn Qayyim's depiction, the distortion of Jesus' promulgations began already in "pre-Constantine" times, for example with the 3rd-century theologian and patriarch of Antioch,

72 Ibid., p. 486.
73 Ibid., p. 487.
74 Ibid., p. 338; see also pp. 425, 577.
75 Ibid., pp. 486–488.
76 Ibid., p. 539; see also p. 584.
77 Ibid., p. 574.
78 Ibid., p. 228.
79 In this context, Erdmann Fritsch speaks of the "common denominator of all individual polemics"; see Fritsch, *Islam und Christentum*, p. 46.

Paul of Samosata, who, as the Damascene scholar argues, started the doctrine of Jesus' divine and human nature, and proceeded rapidly as a result of Constantine's turn to the Christian faith, motivated by a vision of the cross, and the corresponding public recognition of Christianity. As a consequence of the controversies publicly conducted at the councils about Christological issues and of the doctrinal decisions promulgated at them, as well as of the resulting schisms into various churches and groups, this development – according to Ibn al-Qayyim's presentation – finally led to a situation in which "each of them [...] [took] his God freely as he wished and damned those who followed another [God] and permitted him to dissociate from him".[80]

Regarding Ibn al-Qayyim's explications (based on Ibn Taymiyya's depiction) of the young Christian communities up to Constantine's acceptance of Christianity,[81] two thematic complexes show that he considered the genesis of early Christianity a conclusive means of argumentation against Christian doctrines and Christians and that he applies it as such in the *Hidāyat al-ḥayārā*: on the one hand, Ibn al-Qayyim speaks about two of the events that Eutychios mentions in his *Annales*,[82] in which he more or less explicitly ascertains the gradually beginning falsification of the "true religion of Jesus": first, the shifting of Easter from the 14th of Nisan to the following Sunday in the communities outside of Asia Minor, which, according to Eutychios, transpired in the period of Marcus Aurelius' rule;[83] and second, the teaching of Paul of Samosata. In Ibn al-Qayyim's depiction the rescheduling of Easter appears as the work of several bishops and patriarchs that grew out of the Christians' striving to separate themselves from the Jewish practice of Pesach.[84] Figuring in the *Hidāyat al-ḥayārā* as a protagonist of the falsification of "true" Christianity is, remarkably, Paul of Samosata, whose doctrine is described in other medieval Muslim anti-Christian polemics – for example, Ibn Ḥazm's *Kitāb al-Fiṣal* and *al-Jawāb al-ṣaḥīḥ* of Ibn Taymiyya – as an avowal of the unity of God and the mere creatureliness of Jesus and which is thus moved into proximity with Islamic teachings.[85] Ibn al-Qayyim, by contrast, goes

80 Ibn Qayyim al-Jawziyya, *Hidāyat al-ḥayārā*, p. 573.

81 See the corresponding sections in Ibn Taymiyya, *al-Jawāb al-ṣaḥīḥ*, vol. 3, pp. 5–19. On this, see Ibn al-Baṭrīq, *Annales*, vol. 1, pp. 93–121.

82 See ibid., pp. 104–105, 114.

83 See ibid., p. 104.

84 Ibn Qayyim al-Jawziyya, *Hidāyat al-ḥayārā*, p. 545.

85 See Ibn Ḥazm, *al-Fiṣal fī al-milal*, vol. 1, pp. 109–110. In the *Jawāb al-ṣaḥīḥ* Ibn Ḥazm's remarks on Paul of Samosata are quoted verbatim, see Ibn Taymiyya, *al-Jawāb al-ṣaḥīḥ*, vol. 2, p. 312.

beyond Ibn Taymiyya's presentation,[86] remarking that the Antiochian patriarch was the first to corrupt the Christians and their religion. Before Paul of Samosata (Būlus as-Shimshāṭī) spread his teachings, Ibn al-Qayyim states, the Christian communities had, unanimously and without making exceptions, adhered to the precept that Jesus was merely a servant and messenger of God, whereas Paul of Samosata had forwarded the teaching of Jesus' divine and human nature.[87] The reason for this conspicuous difference might be that Ibn al-Qayyim erroneously confounded Paul of Samosata with his namesake, the apostle Paul,[88] which latter in turn is occasionally blamed in numerous medieval Muslim anti-Christian polemics for the falsification of the "original" Christianity, for instance in Ibn Ḥazm's *Kitāb al-Fiṣal*[89] and in the work of the Mālikī jurist al-Qarāfī, *al-Ajwiba al-fākhira ʿan al-asʾila al-fājira* (The Excellent Replies to the Execrable Enquiries).[90]

At the center of Ibn al-Qayyim's description of the period between Jesus' assumption into heaven and Constantine's conversion to Christianity, however, are fewer events that he designates as the Christians' corruption of the divine revelation brought by Jesus or as deviations from his religious conduct. Instead, adopting Ibn Taymiyya's representations[91] that in large part follow Eutychios' *Annales*,[92] Ibn al-Qayyim extensively treats the persecution of the Christians at the hands of the Roman state, whereby he paints a picture of Christian communities' constant tribulations as a result of their persecution and does not neglect to mention that the Gospels were composed in this conflict situation.[93] But the idea implicit in this depiction – that under these circumstances the Christians could hardly have preserved the Gospel sent down to Jesus – remains unspoken. To take away the impression that Ibn al-Qayyim's historical outline extended attention to the

86 See the section in ibid., vol. 3, pp. 14–15.
87 Ibn Qayyim al-Jawziyya, *Hidāyat al-ḥayārā*, p. 548.
88 On this, see especially van Koningsveld, Pieter Sjörd: The Islamic Image of Paul and the Origin of the Gospel of Barnabas, in: *Jerusalem Studies in Arabic and Islam* 20 (1996), pp. 200–228, here pp. 206–207.
89 See Ibn Ḥazm, *al-Fiṣal fī al-milal*, vol. 2, p. 204. On this, see also van Koningsveld, The Islamic Image of Paul, pp. 210–212.
90 See al-Qarāfī, *Kitāb al-Ajwiba*, pp. 171–175.
91 See the corresponding passages in Ibn Taymiyya, *al-Jawāb al-ṣaḥīḥ*, vol. 3, pp. 7–14.
92 See Ibn al-Baṭrīq, *Annales*, vol. 1, pp. 96–123.
93 Ibn Qayyim al-Jawziyya, *Hidāyat al-ḥayārā*, pp. 541–543.

Roman emperors' persecution of Christians[94] means that he intended with these descriptions to evoke sympathy with the Christians in his Muslim readership – an impression that might arise if one read these passages out of context – would be to mistake his intention completely. Rather, they show that Ibn al-Qayyim, without explicitly saying so in this context, adduces the early recognition by individual rulers as an argument for the superiority of Islam over Christianity: it was not until three centuries after its birth (the argument can be traced) that a ruler in the person of Constantine, adopted the Christian religion. By contrast, Islam and Muḥammad's status as prophet were already acknowledged during the latter's lifetime by individual regents, like the Amharic Negus and the Byzantine emperor Heraklios, as is found in reports on the early period of Islam that Ibn al-Qayyim mentions in other passages of the *Hidāyat al-ḥayārā*.[95]

In Ibn al-Qayyim's description, which is dependent on Ibn Taymiyya's work,[96] the reign of Constantine appears as a watershed in the history of early Christianity in two ways. First, he points out that the state persecution of Christians ended with Constantine's official adoption of Christianity, which, in his presentation, was owed solely to a vision of the cross in the sky. In this connection, the Damascene theologian argues that due to Constantine's conscious fostering of the Christian confession, Christianity was even able to establish itself.[97] Ibn al-Qayyim also regards Constantine's reign as the period in which the already previously emerging *tabdīl*, the deformation of the "original" religion of Jesus finally solidified under changed conditions – the Christians now had their own state[98] – finally prevailed. Ibn al-Qayyim then contends that 15 years after the beginning of Constantine's rule, the dispute over Christological questions openly broke out, and the emperor convened the First Council of Nicaea (325 A.D.).[99]

After noting this, Ibn al-Qayyim shifts to treat the further development of Christianity, which he traces until the year 691/692 A.D., primarily against the background of the councils and the doctrines debated in them. At least in regard to the Council of Ephesus, he there-

94 Ibid., pp. 543–548.

95 Ibid., pp. 257–263, 275–286.

96 See Ibn Taymiyya, *al-Jawāb al-ṣaḥīḥ*, vol. 3, pp. 20–25. On this, see the passages in Ibn al-Baṭrīq, *Annales*, vol. 1, pp. 123–129.

97 Ibn Qayyim al-Jawziyya, *Hidāyat al-ḥayārā*, p. 552.

98 Ibid., p. 573.

99 Ibid., p. 552.

by also works on the basis of Ibn Taymiyya's *al-Jawāb al-ṣaḥīḥ*, from which he adopts portions of the corresponding sections, themselves dependent on the *Annales* of Eutychios – whereby he offers no own interpretations of the passages he copies; so that while events that are not directly connected to the councils may not be omitted entirely, they play a markedly subordinate role in this section.

Two tendencies are crucial to Ibn al-Qayyim's depiction of the councils,[100] in which he treats the Councils of Nicaea, Constantinople (381 A.D.) and Ephesus, the Second Council of Ephesus, which is also called the Robber Synod (449 A.D.), the Council of Chalcedon (451 A.D.), the fifth general Council of Constantinople (553 A.D.), and the two Councils in Trullo (680 A.D. and 691/692 A.D.). First, his depiction underscores how the clerics who appeared at the councils as authorized representatives of Christianity dissented over a central component of the Christian faith, namely Christology. Second, he sketches therein the disputes that resulted from doctrinal differences and that were publicly conducted in advance of and at the councils over the proper understanding of the person of Jesus, which in his depiction culminated in individual groups' doctrinal opinions advancing to dogmas not least because the state takes their side, while others are condemned and rejected as error. On the whole, in this section Ibn al-Qayyim conveys the impression that the history of Christianity since Constantine's assumption of power was a series of vehement disputes among theologians anathematizing each other – disputes that sometimes led to violent conflicts or even deaths.

Ibn al-Qayyim's overview of the first centuries of Christianity concludes with a summary in which he takes up essential elements of his basic view of Christianity and makes an overall evaluation of the Christian religion and its adherents. It begins with the observation that the religion of the Christians is based on nothing else than the reciprocal damnation of the council participants. Afterwards, Ibn al-Qayyim states that despite their temporal proximity to Jesus' life and working, the existence of a Christian state, a flourishing scholarship, and their intense concern for the preservation of their religion, the councils participants did not reach any unified statement about the object of their worship.[101] In this context, Ibn al-Qayyim once again notes

100 On Ibn al-Qayyim's perception of the councils, see also his *Ighāthat al-lahfān min maṣā'id al-shayṭān*, edited by Muḥammad Ḥāmid al-Fiqī, Beirut n.d., vol. 2, pp. 270–281.

101 Ibn Qayyim al-Jawziyya, *Hidāyat al-ḥayārā*, p. 573.

that Christianity is characterized neither by a certain degree of inner cohesion, nor by theological unity. Rather, as he sees it, the disunity of its adherents in central religious convictions is constitutive of the Christian religion[102] – a dissent, he suggests to the reader between the lines, that should be seen as a symptom of the baselessness of Christian doctrine and that he pins on the Christological positions of the various Christian denomination.[103] The Christians cling to Jesus, his Gospel, and his apostles, but they disagree in their valuation of his person: among the Christians, the view that Jesus should be considered solely God's servant can be found, as well as the idea that he is a God; some affirm that he is the Son of God or believe in him as one of three godheads. Others, in turn, see in Jesus two natures and two hypostases (*uqnūmān*), whereas others deny this idea and see in Jesus one nature and one hypostasis. Aside from that, he avers, the Christians propound a number of other views on the person of Jesus, views adopted from their forefathers (*aslāfihim*).[104] Ibn al-Qayyim's emphasis on the Christians' disagreement about the figure of Jesus finally culminates in the assertion that this disunity would have the effect that a people that had no knowledge of God and that came into contact with Christianity would under no circumstances take on the Christian religion.[105]

3.2. The Christian View of the Person of Jesus

Strewn throughout the entire work, the critical viewing of Christian Christology as well as the refutation of the faith in the divinity of Jesus and his being the Son of God, a refutation unsurprisingly based especially on the postulate of God's unity, takes a large role in the *Hidāyat al-ḥayārā*. With this interest and approach, Ibn al-Qayyim follows predetermined paths; more remarkable is the fact that he hereby tacks between sometimes aggressive polemic and elucidations full of bitter ridicule, on the one hand, and more sober-neutral depictions with implicit or postponed valuations and answers, on the other.

In consideration of the countless repetitions that Ibn al-Qayyim uses in his depiction of the Christian view of the figure of Jesus in the *Hidāyat al-ḥayārā*, the following will examine only a short section of

102 Ibid., p. 533.
103 Ibid., p. 574.
104 Ibid.
105 Ibid., p. 575.

text in which – without referring to Christian theologians, their writings, or any other source – he concisely speaks about what he sees as the common foundations of the Christian denominations concerning the person and nature of Jesus and presents the doctrinal differences about this that, as can be read between the lines, are a visible expression of the implausibility of Christian belief. In Ibn al-Qayyim's presentation, what Christians have in common is that they do not see in Jesus a messenger of God. Rather, as he states, they unanimously declare that Jesus is verily God, primally eternal (*qadīm*), and timeless (*azalī*), and that they attribute to him the creation of heaven and earth, the angels and the prophets, and the sending of the envoys whom he has empowered to perform miraculous acts as proof of their prophetic mission. The Christians, Ibn al-Qayyim maintains, also agree that Mary was pregnant with Jesus and gave birth to him as her corporeal son, so that he sojourned among the humans and they thereby were able to see him.[106] Despite these doctrinal views, which are affirmed by all Christian groups along with the doctrine of the Trinity, notes Ibn al-Qayyim, the Christians do not take a unified standpoint in essential questions of belief. He strongly affirms that no community can be found in which there is a greater conflict of views in regard to its object of veneration and worship, to its prophets and their religion than among the Christians.[107]

Ibn al-Qayyim explicitly identifies this alleged intramural dispute with the ideas that the Jacobites, Melkites, Nestorians, and Arians have about Jesus' nature, whereby he sketches the Arian confession – which he summarizes as maintaining that Jesus is just a servant of God and a created being – as a positive deviation for which the other Christian denominations had threatened the Arians with death.[108] By contrast and without exception, he devalues as "drivel" (*hadhayānāt*) the Christological teachings of the Jacobites, Melkites, and Nestorians,[109] which he argues were formulated by the scholarly elite (*khawāṣṣ*) of the respective denominations but are incomprehensible to the broad masses of the faithful. The latter, Ibn al-Qayyim contends, hold that God lay with Mary and that she bore him a son; he also accuses them of agreeing to the doctrines of the *khawāṣṣ* without intellectually penetrating them.[110]

106 Ibid., p. 533.
107 Ibid.
108 Ibid., p. 536.
109 Ibid., p. 537.
110 Ibid.

Considering both his resolute adherence to the notion of the absolute unity of God and his view of the creatureliness of Jesus, with which he is also in agreement with Muslim *plebeia opinio*, Ibn al-Qayyim's judgment of the belief in Jesus' divinity and of his status as Son of God is predetermined. Such viewpoints that he castigates as already untenable since they are in his understanding unacceptable to human rationality and unprejudiced intuition[111] are to his mind not only an affront to Jesus,[112] but primarily a negation of the *tawḥīd*,[113] and are for him thus tainted with the verdict of *shirk*, having other divinities beside God.[114] So it is not surprising that Ibn al-Qayyim campaigns against them in the *Hidāyat al-ḥayārā* with words whose clarity leaves nothing to be desired: he speaks of the "most ignominious blasphemy against the Lord of the worlds" (*masabbati rabb al-ʿālamīn aqbaḥ masabbatin*)[115] and rebukes the Christians for attributing to God qualities whose shamefulness, in his perspective, cannot be surpassed.[116]

Ibn al-Qayyim's dispute with Christological views is not, of course, limited to damning the Christians lock, stock, and barrel with such epithets; it is also carried out on three other levels. First, he lists a wealth of relevant passages from the canonical Gospels as evidence that Jesus did not claim any divine status, but rather understood himself as an envoy of God and bore witness to God's absolute oneness and uniqueness. Second, Ibn al-Qayyim undertakes to refute, step by step, a series of potential arguments for Jesus' divinity, including the miracles the Gospels say Jesus performed and Old Testament passages that are interpreted as predictions fulfilled by Jesus. On the third level, finally, Ibn al-Qayyim counters the doctrine of Jesus being divine or the Son of God with his own absolutist idea of God. On all three levels, unlike his teacher Ibn Taymiyya[117] and the unknown author of the *Radd al-jamīl li-ilāhiyyat ʿĪsā bi-ṣarīḥ al-Injīl* (A Fitting Refutation of the Divinity of Jesus from

111 Ibid., p. 538.
112 Ibid., p. 501.
113 Ibid., p. 228.
114 Ibid., p. 343. On *shirk* in general, see Hawting, Gerald R.: Širk and 'Idolatry' in Monotheist Polemic, in: Uri Rubin and David J. Wasserstein (eds.): *Dhimmis and Others. Jews and Christians and the World of Classical Islam*, Winona Lake 1997, pp. 107–126.
115 Ibn Qayyim al-Jawziyya, *Hidāyat al-ḥayārā*, p. 251.
116 Ibid., p. 585.
117 See Ibn Taymiyya, *al-Jawāb al-ṣaḥīḥ*, vol. 3, pp. 39–122. On this, see also Troupeau, Gérard: Ibn Taymiyya et sa réfutation d'Eutychès, in: *Bulletin d'études orientales* 30 (1978), pp. 209–220.

the Evidence of the Gospel), which is attributed, very probably falsely, to Abū Ḥāmid al-Ghazālī (d. 505/1111),[118] Ibn al-Qayyim does not deign to dispute in detail the Christologies of the three great Eastern denominations, contenting himself instead with disproving the notion of Jesus' divinity in general expressions. Without seeking to underscore that Ibn al-Qayyim's polemic is qualitatively inferior to Ibn Taymiyya's *al-Jawāb al-ṣaḥīḥ* and especially to *al-Radd al-jamīl* in terms of debating with the various Christologies, it is surely not misplaced to note that the refutation of Christianity in the *Hidāyat al-ḥayārā* oscillates between two poles. On the one hand, Ibn al-Qayyim does not entirely eschew a philosophical-rational proof, since he insists in several passages that the Christian religious ideas are incompatible with human reason or with unprejudiced intuition;[119] on the other hand, however, his argumentation is based strongly on quotations from the Gospels and from Koranic verses and on the Muslim *opinio communis*. He thus refrains from grappling with a rationally-argued refutation of the Trinitarian dogma, which he identifies as the basic Christian religious conviction. Following Suras (5:17 and 116), he grasps the Christian concept of a triune God as a profession of belief in a trio of God, Mary as his companion, and Jesus as God's own son[120] and he is content to apodictically counter it with Koranic verses and even to place it in the neighborhood of *shirk*.[121] By contrast, Ibn al-Qayyim gives more attention to disputing that

> the Lord of Heaven and Earth [...] entered into the pudenda of a woman, [...] incarnated himself in her womb (*fa-iltaḥama bi-baṭnihā*), and spent nine months there, whereby he laid himself between excrement, urine, blood, and menstrual blood (*ṭamth*)[122]

118 See al-Ghazālī, Abū Ḥāmid Muḥammad b. Muḥammad: *Réfutation excellente de la divinité de Jésus-Christ d'après les évangiles. Texte établi, traduit et commenté par Robert Chidiac*, Paris 1939, pp. 26–37 (Arabic text). On the author of *al-Radd al-jamīl*, see Lazarus-Yafeh, Hava: Étude sur la polémique islamo-chrétienne. Qui était l'auteur de *al-Radd al-jamīl li-ilāhiyyat ʿĪsā bi-ṣarīḥ al-Injīl* attribué à al-Gazzali?, in: *Revue des Sciences Religieuses* 37 (1969), pp. 219–238, here pp. 236–237; Reynolds, Gabriel Said: The Ends of *al-Radd al-Jamīl* and Its Portrayal of Christian Sects, in: *Islamochristiana* 25 (1999), pp. 45–65; El Kaisy-Friemuth, Maha: *Al-Radd al-Jamīl*: al-Ghazālī's or Pseudo-Ghazālī's?, in: David Thomas (ed.): *The Bible in Arab Christianity*, Leiden and Boston 2005, pp. 275–295.

119 Ibn Qayyim al-Jawziyya, *Hidāyat al-ḥayārā*, p. 522; see also p. 538.

120 Ibid., p. 228.

121 Ibid.

122 Ibid., p. 480.

– thus his polemically pointed reference to the doctrine of Incarnation, toward which he takes a rejecting stance *eo ipso*. Considering his postulation of the absolute sublimity and utter perfection of God, Ibn al-Qayyim argues that the idea that a woman's pudenda could contain God is as ridiculous and unacceptable as the thought that God would have himself born from a woman in order to come to earth as a bawling newborn that had to be suckled. Ibn al-Qayyim does not explicitly make the self-suggesting accusation that the Christian notion that God had been conceived and born implies a definite doubt as to God's omnipotence, which eliminates the distance between the Creator and his creatures and thereby degrades him to their level, but this indictment can be found between the lines and a Muslim readership probably automatically associated (and associates) it.

Ibn al-Qayyim counters the qualification of the person of Jesus as a godhead, which he reproves as unjustifiably attributing human traits and passions to the one God,[123] by referring to the perfection of God, who is, in his view, free of needs like nutrition and sleep[124] that burden the beings he created in their imperfection. Quite in contrast to God, who, if he were to descend to earth, would neither sleep nor eat, much less defecate, Jesus – as Ibn al-Qayyim presents it, citing the unanimous conviction of the Christians – did all of this.[125] His argumentation here aims at the conclusion that Jesus is therefore to be considered a mere creature of God and in no way to be worshipped as a God become a human being.

As can be expected, for Ibn al-Qayyim, the reprehensibility of Christian doctrine is expressed not least in the belief in Jesus' death by crucifixion. The Damascene scholar decries the adherence to a God humiliated and tormented by human beings, his creatures, a God hanging helplessly on the cross and suffering death on it, as inescapably questioning God's sovereignty (*rubūbiyya*) as creator of the world.[126] Tellingly, however, Ibn al-Qayyim does not anticipate a possible rejoinder that would point out that the divine nature of Jesus, who, unlike the human, created nature, neither suffers nor dies, even though he is familiar with the doctrine of Jesus' twofold nature, as other passages in the *Hidāyat al-ḥayārā* make clear.[127]

123 Ibid., p. 254.
124 Ibid., p. 523.
125 Ibid., p. 497.
126 Ibid., p. 427; see also pp. 497–480.
127 Ibid., pp. 535–536; see also p. 574.

3.3. Mariology

Ibn al-Qayyim not only treats Christian doctrine and Christology primarily in terms of the violation of the profession of God's absolute unity through the practice of *shirk*, he also discusses Christian Mariological views primarily from this viewpoint. But the *Hidāyat al-ḥayārā's* treatment of Christian Mariology is much less extensive and much shallower than its critical examination of the doctrine of Jesus' divinity.

Ibn al-Qayyim's depiction creates the impression that the Christians were fairly united in their doctrinal views of Mary. He maintains that they profess that Mary, chosen by God from among all other women, became pregnant with a son, Jesus, and gave birth to him.[128] Along with these teachings, Ibn al-Qayyim accuses the Christians of raising Mary above the angels and envoys and, above all, of worshipping her. He implicitly condemns the latter practice as an attack on God's omnipotence by pointing out that the Christians' prayers to Mary for livelihood (*rizq*), well-being (*ʿāfiya*), and the forgiveness of sin should be addressed exclusively to God.[129] As a proponent of the idea of God's absolute transcendence, Ibn al-Qayyim decidedly negates what he presents as the Christian consensus of Mariological convictions, including the accompanying veneration of Mary. It and the Christian view of God are reason enough for him to accuse them not only of reviling God and having another deity beside him, but also, in the same breath, of unbelief (*kufr*).[130]

3.4. Christian Religious Practices

Ibn al-Qayyim's standpoint toward Christian religious practices is that a judicious person (*al-ʿāqil*) who compares the doctrines, ritual duties (*furūʿ*) and legal ordinances (*sharāʾiʿ*) of the Christians with those of Islam could ultimately come only to the conclusion that the Christian clergy, and even more so the great mass of common believers, had preferred deviation from the proper path to right divine guidance and had adopted the falsest and most disgraceful of doctrines (*ʿaqāʾid*) and

128 Ibid., p. 481.
129 Ibid.
130 Ibid., p. 482.

actions (*aʿmāl*).[131] Considering this judgment, it is no wonder that, in the *Hidāyat al-ḥayārā*, the Damascene theologian does not stop at his critique of Christian doctrines, but also takes umbrage at certain Christian rituals and practices. In his striving to denigrate them, Ibn al-Qayyim makes no effort to reflect on their meaning, nor does his depiction aim to provide more evidence of the intra-Christian divergence he notes[132] in the area of everyday religious practices. Rather, Ibn al-Qayyim aims to construe a discrepancy between a number of Christian religious practices and the forms of practicing faith that Jesus cultivated and thereby to make the Christians appear as a community that is guilty of corrupting the "true religion of Jesus" and of an obvious violation of his directives. In order to argue in accordance with this intention that the religious conduct of Jesus was norm-setting for Christians in directly analogy to the Sunna and that it was a behavior that corresponded in every way to the example of the earlier prophets and the precepts of the Torah, Ibn al-Qayyim cites the view, which he presents as the Christian consensus, that Jesus had called for the retention of the precepts of the Torah and of his predecessors in the role of prophet. Without providing a legitimation for this statement, he also underscores that Jesus explicitly told the apostles not only to emulate his own behavior, but also to make the precepts he imposed upon them into obligations for all human beings. Along with the relinquishing of circumcision, a practice that Jesus, in agreement with Moses, Aaron, and the other prophets before him, had explicitly prescribed,[133] and the celebration of Sundays instead of the Sabbath, which he had kept as long as he lived,[134] Ibn al-Qayyim here names three other points that display the divergence between the precepts of the preceding prophets, which Jesus adhered to, and the usage of the Christians. As an especially obvious deviance, he pillories the Christian approach to bodily-cultic purity. In his view, Jesus propounded ritual purity (*ṭahāra*), always carried out a complete washing (*ghusl*) under conditions of major ritual impurity (*janāba*), and prescribed purification after menstruation, whereas the Christians do not regard these ordinances as obligatory. Indeed, they even believe, as he claims, that a prayer spoken after relieving oneself without washing and while excrements still adhere to certain parts of the body does not lose its validity and – so Ibn al-Qayyim's visibly

131 Ibid., pp. 255–256.
132 Ibid., p. 533.
133 Ibid., p. 484.
134 Ibid., p. 485.

exaggerated presentation – even regard it as more meritorious (*afḍal*) than a prayer spoken in a state of ritual purity because it is not compatible with Jewish and Muslim customs.[135] Beyond this, Ibn al-Qayyim notes that the Christians' behavior while praying deviates from what Jesus felt bound by. He maintains that, following the example of the chain of prophets before him, Jesus recited the Torah and Psalter when praying; whereas Christians, when they pray, repeat words recited by their clergy (lit.: *alladhīna yataqaddamūna*), thereby resembling loud sobbing and songs, and cross themselves at the beginning of the prayer, which is in his view less a veneration than a mockery of God.[136] Ibn al-Qayyim also clearly contrasts Jesus' alleged attitude toward the consumption of pork meat, which he argues the Christians not only declare permissible, but had even raised to the sign of their religion.[137] Here he claims that although Jesus had not only forbidden, but even cursed the consumption of pork, the Christians forthrightly claim that the pig is to be considered one of the purest, most beautiful, and best animals.[138] But to discredit the eating of pork, Ibn al-Qayyim is not satisfied to adduce an unambiguous prohibition by Jesus and also notes Jesus' proscription of the pig as an impure animal by weaving Mark 16:9 respectively Luke 8:2 into Matthew 8:28–34 or Mark 5:1–15 respectively Luke 8:27–35 to create a narrative according to which Jesus drove seven devils out of Mary Magdalene and ordered them to enter a pig.[139]

Among the forms of Christian religiosity that Ibn al-Qayyim does not brand aberrations from Jesus' own example but nevertheless condemns is, to provide only one example, confession and the associated acts of expiation. He expresses his rejection implicitly when he notes that infractions like drunkenness (*sukr*) and adultery or fornication (*zinā*) are not punished among the Christians, who do not even believe that these infractions lead to punishment in the afterlife. Rather, he argues, the Christian clergy forgive believers such offenses, which the latter in turn repay with gifts, money, or the like.[140] For a Muslim reading public that, in accordance with the Sharia, regards these offenses as a violation of a right of God (*ḥaqq Allāh*), and thus to be corporeally

135 Ibid., pp. 483–484.
136 Ibid., p. 484.
137 Ibid., p. 486.
138 Ibid., pp. 484–485.
139 Ibid., p. 485.
140 Ibid.

punished, the only possible conclusion is that the Christian practice of confession violates God's will and his commandments.

In the *Hidāyat al-ḥayārā*, Ibn al-Qayyim is not content to accuse the Christians of turning away from the forms of religious practice that Jesus adhered to and prescribed. At the same time, he tries to show that the Christians do not do this through ignorance, but knowingly, and he names two reasons for this, both of which, significantly, he regards as valid.[141] First, referring to the report in the Acts of the Apostles about the so-called Apostles' Council and its resolutions, Ibn al-Qayyim suggests a causal connection between the alleged deviation and the still-young Christian community's strivings to expand its circle of adherents.[142] As the etiology for this, Ibn al-Qayyim sees, among other things, the Christian strivings to dissociate themselves from Judaism. About three hundred years after Jesus' lifetime, the Christians began consciously dissociating themselves from the Jews in cult practices and in legal regulations.[143] As an expression and mere result of such strivings for separation, Ibn al-Qayyim mentions not only the eschewal of Sabbath observation, the omission of circumcision, and the lack of dietary prohibitions.[144] Similarly, he incriminates the Christians for permitting their patriarchs and bishops to pronounce commandments and prohibitions at their own discretion.[145] Ibn al-Qayyim presents it as certain that the doctrine of Jesus' divine sonship was rooted in a retort to the Jewish taunt that Jesus was a "skilled sorcerer and bastard". In this connection, he also maintains that the Christians' raising the cross to the status of a cult object was based solely on the Jews' abhorrence of it, which in turn is based on the Torah's cursing of death on the cross.[146] Following this, Ibn al-Qayyim declares that instead of regarding the cross with extreme contempt and burning all the crosses they could get their hands on,[147] the Christians responded to the Jewish stance by venerating and worshipping the cross on which the one they prayed to and worshipped had died such a shameful death.[148]

141 Ibid., pp. 486–487.
142 Ibid., p. 487.
143 Ibid., p. 486.
144 Ibid.
145 Ibid.
146 In this passage, Ibn al-Qayyim refers to the phrase in Deuteronomy 21:23, which he reproduces as "Cursed is he who hangs on the cross".
147 Ibid., p. 252.
148 Ibid., p. 486.

As shown above, in his critique of both Christian rituals and practices Ibn al-Qayyim makes use primarily of two argumentative procedures. First, he condemns them against the background of his own vision of Jesus' behavior, which he applies as a yardstick for Christian religious conduct.[149] Second, he criticizes certain forms of Christian religious practice with the remark that they are not based on right divine guidance, but have arisen from human initiative with the primary goal of conforming with the customs and traditions of the environment[150] or of dissociation from the Jews.[151] To be able to condemn them, Ibn al-Qayyim also takes supplementary recourse to another pattern of argumentation. This consists in taking the maxims of the *tawḥīd*, which for him comprises professing belief in God and serving God alone, as the sole criterion for judging Christian cult and belief. Accordingly, religious doctrines and practices that he regards as failing to fulfill this criterion are condemned as a violation of the worship of the one God, that is to say, as *shirk*. Ibn al-Qayyim makes use of this argumentation, for example, when he rebukes the Christians for idolatry. Thus, he unambiguously says that "pictures painted by hand on walls",[152] which dogs could urinate on when they approach them, function as objects of veneration among the Christians. He claims that they turn to the pictures with their pleas for forgiveness of sins, for mercy, for livelihood, and for succor and that they approach them with the utmost subservience, humility, and abasement.[153] With such a depiction, the Damascene scholar attempts to create the impression that the Christians do attribute a higher rank to images – his elucidations do not make it clear whether he is here alluding to cult images in the narrow sense – than to God, in that they show a veneration to them that he regards as due God alone, and that they also turn to the images with wishes and interests whose fulfillment lies solely in God's power.

---

149 Ibid., p. 485; see also p. 487.
150 Ibid.
151 Ibid., pp. 486–487.
152 Ibid., p. 343.
153 Ibid., p. 254.

3.5. Authenticity of the Gospels

The charge that the Christians were guilty of the alteration (*tabdīl*) and modification (*taghyīr*) of the "true religion of Jesus" by deviating from the forms of religious practice that Jesus observed and from the doctrines he proclaimed is coupled in the *Hidāyat al-ḥayārā* with the accusation that the Christians had falsified the divine revelation given to Jesus, i.e., the Gospel (*Injīl*). This verdict entered the canon of the themes treated in Muslim anti-Christian polemics with Ibn Ḥazm's *Kitāb al-Fiṣal* at the latest,[154] but is already implicit in the Koran. Accordingly, Ibn al-Qayyim's elucidations on the question of the *taḥrīf* of the Torah and the Gospels also point out that God had reproved the *ahl al-kitāb* for falsifying their respective divine scriptures and concealing the real truth of God's revelation; he supports this assertion with Suras (2:159 and 3:171).[155]

It is noteworthy that Ibn al-Qayyim tries to grasp the theme of scripture falsification fundamentally by distinguishing among various kinds of the People of the Book's unsuitable dealings with the wording of the genuine divine revelation: concealing the truth of the revelation (*ikhfāʾ al-ḥaqq*) and keeping it secret (*kitmān*), darkening it with lies and deception (*labs al-ḥaqq bil-bāṭil*), falsifying the wording (*taḥrīf lafẓ al-kalim*), falsely interpreting the text (*taḥrīf maʿnā al-kalim*), and, finally, twisting the words (lit.: *layy al-lisān*).[156] But he does not take up this differentiation in the further progress of his depiction and, in addition, refrains from providing some examples of these kinds of falsifications of the Judeo-Christian scriptures, so that the terminology for scripture falsification retains a certain fuzziness in the *Hidāyat al-ḥayārā*, which is reinforced by the fact that Ibn al-Qayyim also makes use of the terms *tabdīl*, elimination (*izāla*), and *taghyīr* without defining them. Remarkably enough, contrary to what might be expected, there is no trace in the *Hidāyat al-ḥayārā* of Ibn Taymiyya's view, which undertakes a differentiation between the historical (*khabariyyāt*) and the preceptive statements (*amriyyāt*) in the

154 See along with Lazarus-Yafeh, *Intertwined Worlds*, p. 13; idem: Taḥrīf, in: *EI*², vol. 10 (1998), pp. 111–112; also Waardenburg, Muslim Studies of Other Religions, p. 24; and Accad, Martin: Corruption and/or Misinterpretation of the Bible. The Story of the Islāmic Usage of *Taḥrīf*, in: *The Near East School of Theology Theological Review* 24 (2003), pp. 67–97.

155 Ibn Qayyim al-Jawziyya, *Hidāyat al-ḥayārā*, pp. 311–312.

156 Ibid., p. 312.

Bible and postulates that the falsification of the text (*taḥrīf al-alfāẓ*) is limited to the first kind, whereas the *amriyyāt* are affected solely by falsified interpretations (*taḥrīf al-maʿānī*).[157]

According to Ibn al-Qayyim, the views of the Muslims diverge on the question of the authenticity and integrity of the revelatory scriptures of the *ahl al-kitāb*. On the one hand, he reports, there are voices that claim that no changes were made to the wording of the Torah and Gospel and that they are therefore present in an unfalsified state – a standpoint that the Damascene scholar does not consider valid, since he regards it as tantamount to accusing Muḥammad of having lied when he blamed the Christians and Jews for falsifying their revelatory scriptures. Ibn al-Qayyim goes on in the *Hidāyat al-ḥayārā*, to emphasize that on the other hand, some Muslims postulate that the *ahl al-kitāb* had falsified their divine scriptures in various ways and made numerous changes in the text.[158] Ibn al-Qayyim's personal stance toward the issue of *taḥrīf* tends toward the latter view. For him, the fact that the present Gospels speak of Jesus' death on the cross and about his burial and resurrection is sufficient evidence that the currently existing Gospels cannot be equated with the one he thinks Jesus promulgated[159] in the Hebrew language.[160] Rather, he expounds that the Gospels as possessed by the Christians in his day are scriptures that have taken up parts of the Gospel sent down to Jesus and of his apostles' dictums.[161]

In his evaluation of the four canonical Gospels, Ibn al-Qayyim sees himself completely confirmed by the Christian understanding of them, which he summarizes to the effect that all Christian groups agree that the Gospels are neither a scripture revealed to Jesus by God, nor God's speech (*kalām Allāh*), but four Gospels written down by four different persons at different times and at a marked temporal remove from the life and workings of Jesus.[162]

That, in the Christians' own view, the Gospels that all Christians regard as authoritative are not the result of divine inspiration, but rather of human endeavor (this is the conclusion to be drawn from Ibn al-Qayyim's remarks on the Christian understanding of the Gos-

157 See Ibn Taymiyya, *al-Jawāb al-ṣaḥīḥ*, vol. 2, p. 118. In this regard, see also Michel, *A Muslim Theologian's Response*, pp. 112–120.
158 Ibn Qayyim al-Jawziyya, *Hidāyat al-ḥayārā*, p. 415.
159 Ibid., p. 309.
160 Ibid., p. 326.
161 Ibid., pp. 309–310.
162 Ibid., p. 310.

pels) is not the only thing that drastically compromises them in his eyes. He also adduces the situation of the apostles as an argument for a critical view of the canonical Gospels and points out that only two of the writers of the Gospels, namely the evangelists Matthew and John, were Jesus' apostles and could therefore be regarded as eyewitnesses to the events they describe, whereas this is not true of Mark and Luke.[163] This shows that, in analogy to the procedures of Muslim Hadith criticism, Ibn al-Qayyim makes the degree of reliability of the writers of the Gospels into the touchstone of the textual authenticity of the Gospels.[164]

But Ibn al-Qayyim's negative judgment of the canonical Gospels is primarily based on his conviction that each of the four evangelists has added to and abridged the text and also included passages that contradict the other Gospels.[165] With his elaborations on the development of the Gospels and their authors, Ibn al-Qayyim evokes a comparison between them and the Koran – a comparison of the normative scriptures of the two religious communities that, from the perspective of Muslim readers whom the *Hidāyat al-ḥayārā* directly addresses, can favor only the Koran, which, as he underscores elsewhere, is a scripture revealed by God and that is also inimitable and whose equal no human being can place beside it.[166] Of course, in the *Hidāyat al-ḥayārā*, Ibn al-Qayyim is not content with the mere accusation that, ultimately, the four evangelists had corrupted the divinely revealed Gospel when they recorded it, rather than preserving it unfalsified. With the implication that Christian doctrines like the belief in Jesus' death on the cross are based on scriptures whose credibility is discredited by the contradictions they contain as well as by additions and abridgements, and which are therefore necessarily baseless, he lists, in a section of the *Hidāyat al-ḥayārā* devoted precisely to this, the contradictory statements within one and the same Gospel as well as the statements and reports of individual evangelists that contradict those of other evangelists. But for reasons of space, there will be no treatment here of this catalog, whose breadth and depth cannot compete with the lists of an Ibn Ḥazm, for instance, whose *Kitāb al-Fiṣal* comprises a critique of the Gospel text that examines a total of 78 passages as well as

163 Ibid., p. 426.
164 On this procedure in general, see Fritsch, *Islam und Christentum*, p. 64.
165 Ibn Qayyim al-Jawziyya, *Hidāyat al-ḥayārā*, pp. 426–427.
166 Ibid., pp. 441–442.

the contradictions between the Torah and the Gospels.[167] Since for Ibn al-Qayyim it is thoroughly unimaginable that the agglomeration of contradictions and incongruities found in the four canonical Gospels could come from God, he sees it as conclusive evidence that numerous changes have been made to the original text of the Gospel and that the Christians therefore invoke a scripture corrupted by text falsifications and replacements.[168] But this finding does not prevent him from quoting, as needed, verses from the Gospels as Jesus' authentic utterances, using them as correctives to Christian standpoints, and thereby underpinning his own *a priori* positions by recourse to the canonical writings of the rival party. Like his predecessors in the field of Muslim polemics against Christianity, Ibn al-Qayyim thus does not eschew citing certain logoi, like the promise of the "Paraclete" in the Gospel of John, as testimonies to the prophetic mission of Muḥammad,[169] and he cites Jesuanic statements to prove that Jesus' understanding of himself reduces to absurdity the strivings of individual Christian denominations to attribute to him a sonship of God or a divine nature.[170] But Ibn al-Qayyim does not fail to notice the inconsistency of this approach: this is shown by the fact that, in regard to the passages in the Gospels that he claims foretell the coming of Muḥammad, he takes recourse to the apodictic statement that the four evangelists had managed to keep these annunciations of Muḥammad secret, but that God had prevented the exchange and elimination of individual text passages[171] or that the wealth of such passages had made it impossible to replace them entirely with others.[172]

167 On Ibn Ḥazm's attack on the integrity of the Gospels, see especially Behloul, Samuel-Martin: *Ibn Ḥazms Evangelienkritik. Eine methodische Untersuchung*, Leiden, Boston and Cologne 2002, pp. 135–221. See also Pulcini, Theodore and Laderman, Gary: *Exegesis as Polemical Discourse. Ibn Hazm on Jewish and Christian Scriptures*, Atlanta 1998, pp. 97–128; Kassis, Hanna E.: Critique of Scriptures. Polemics of al-Jâhiz and Ibn Hazm Against Christianity and Judaism, in: Yossef Schwartz and Volkhard Krech (eds.): *Religious Apologetics. Philosophical Argumentation*, Tübingen 2004, pp. 237–250, here pp. 245–249; and Aasi, Haider Ghulām: *Muslim Understanding of Other Religions. A Study of Ibn Hazm's Kitāb al-Faṣl fī al-Milal wa al-Ahwāʾ wa al-Niḥal*, New Delhi 2007, pp. 115–187.

168 Ibn Qayyim al-Jawziyya, *Hidāyat al-ḥayārā*, p. 429.

169 Ibid., pp. 323–341.

170 Ibid., pp. 492–493.

171 Ibid., p. 416.

172 Ibid., p. 415.

Concluding Remarks

At the beginning of the present study, medieval Muslim anti-Christian polemic writings were examined from the standpoint of system-environment difference, resulting in the insight that two fundamental tendencies are inherent in this genre: on the one hand, the interpretation and evaluation of Christianity within the Islamic intellectual framework – a framework composed of, among other things, Koranic premises and the valuations arrived at by the respective predecessors in the field of Muslim anti-Christian polemics; and on the other hand, the use of the other religious system as a foil against whose background the superiority of one's own religious faith was more or less explicitly highlighted. Further, it was postulated at the beginning that Ibn al-Qayyim's *Hidāyat al-ḥayārā* is no exception to this and that these two tendencies find flagrant expression in it. Now, in all brevity, this claim will be proven. The first of the two tendencies is effective in Ibn al-Qayyim's interpretation of Christianity, an interpretation that is based in turn on the idea the *Hidāyat al-ḥayārā* develops of the history of the revelation of God. According to the *Hidāyat al-ḥayārā*, in order to lead humanity, which has remained in the darkness of ignorance since its creation, into the "light of knowledge, of wisdom, of belief, and of right divine guidance" (*nūr al-ʿilm wal-maʿrifa wal-īmān wal-hudā*) and thereby to help it attain blessedness (*saʿāda*),[173] in the past God has repeatedly sent prophets to the earth, who proclaimed to the individual peoples[174] one and the same religion, that is: Islam.[175] Not surprisingly, Ibn al-Qayyim's viewpoint also comprises the notion that Muḥammad is one of a chain of prophets that includes Jesus and that, on the one hand, Muḥammad confirms the annunciations of his predecessors in the office of prophet[176] as "seal of the prophets and envoys" (*khātim al-anbiyāʾ wal-rusul*) and, on the other hand, he has received the concluding divine revelation and promulgated the Islamic religion in its final form.[177] Ibn al-Qayyim further propounds the view that Muḥammad's status as prophet is distinguished from that of the other messengers of God in that the divine revelation to Muḥammad is universal in character. In contrast to the preceding prophets (for example,

173 Ibid., pp. 591–592.
174 Ibid., p. 381.
175 Ibid., p. 425.
176 Ibid., p. 577.
177 Ibid., p. 330; see also p. 424.

as Ibn al-Qayyim explains by invoking both Sura 3:49 and Matthew 10:5–6, Jesus' proclamation addressed solely the Jewish people[178]) Muḥammad proclaims the divine revelation to the entirety of humankind, i.e., also to the Jews and Christians, as well as to the *jinn*[179] – a statement that is to be understood as an implicit presentation of Islam's claim to universal validity. According to this view of the history of revelation, Islam (as the one divinely revealed religion, annunciated by all prophets and envoys, and solely valid) stands in contrast to the non-Islamic religions – in principle and without any limitation. Accordingly, for Ibn al-Qayyim, the question of the meaning and value of the Christian religion is superfluous. As he sees it, Christianity as it actually exists is nothing but a distorted form of Jesus' original religion,[180] and the revelation of God given to Muḥammad and fixed in writing in the Koran has proven its obvious baselessness.[181]

That Islam forms the matrix upon which Ibn al-Qayyim reads Christian faith is also manifested in the fact that, in the framework of his doubting of the genuineness of the Gospels, which ultimately insinuates that they are partially falsified, he notes that neither Luke nor Mark were among Jesus' apostles and thus cannot have been eyewitnesses to the events they narrate in their Gospels; this is a critique based upon the idea familiar to Hadith science that an interrupted chain of tradition (*isnād munqaṭiʿ*) is not sufficient to ensure an accurate transmission. Ibn al-Qayyim's Islamic interpretation of Christianity is expressed even more conspicuously in the fact that his argumentation involves Jesus' alleged practice in the sense of a counterpart to the Sunna, in that he applies it as a criterion for judging Christian religious practice. To be considered in this context is also the parallel he draws between the "original" Gospel and the Koran, which enables him to deny *a priori* the integrity of the canonical Gospels, since they are writings that originated from a human hand.

The *Hidāyat al-ḥayārā* resembles other medieval Muslim polemics against Christianity not least in that – to come to the second tendency – Ibn al-Qayyim ties his refutation of Christian belief and rites to a positive presentation of his own religious convictions and in that Christianity thereby functions as a negative contrast to Islam, i.e., as the system's repulsion point in Luhmann's sense. Thus, embedded in

178 Ibid., p. 381.
179 Ibid., p. 222; see also pp. 381, 385.
180 Ibid., p. 487.
181 Ibid., p. 388.

the text of the *Hidāyat al-ḥayārā* as separate sections are elucidations of the repentance (*tawba*), by means of which the believer can redeem his failings and sins or by means of which God will forgive him, of the attributes of God, and of the Muslim understanding of Jesus, which implicitly refer to contrary Christian or Jewish viewpoints and which are thus part of a riposte to them. As a result, numerous sections of Ibn al-Qayyim's polemical treatise read like a positive presentation of Islamic religious doctrines and practices that, at least in the author's evident intention, shine in the brightest light when placed against the background of incriminated Christian teachings and religious practices. The most eloquent example of this is the passage in which Ibn al-Qayyim presents the Christians' prayer behavior antithetically to and immediately after the Muslim practice.[182]

In conclusion, let it be emphasized that, although Ibn al-Qayyim's œuvre is extensive,[183] consideration of the *Hidāyat al-ḥayārā* alone already permits general statements about his understanding of Christianity. But for a more detailed analysis of his view of the Christian religion, it would be necessary to go beyond the *Hidāyat al-ḥayārā* and to include in the examination – more than has been done here – at least the equally relevant writings *Aḥkām ahl al-dhimma* and *Ighāthat al-lahfān min maṣāʾid al-shayṭān* (Rescuing the Distressed from Satan's Snares).

182 Ibid., pp. 254–255.

183 For an overview of Ibn al-Qayyim's literary production, see Bell, *Love Theory*, pp. 95–103; Krawietz, Birgit: Ibn Qayyim al-Jawzīyah. His Life and Works, in: *Mamlūk Studies Review* 10 (2006), pp. 19–64, here pp. 28–60; Holtzman, Ibn Qayyim al-Jawziyyah, pp. 212–221.

Section 5: Creative Reception Outside the Arab World

Ibn Taymiyya and Ibn Qayyim al-Jawziyya as Changing Salafi Icons[1]

Annabelle Böttcher

Introduction

The Sunni scholar and Ḥanbalī legal expert Taqī al-Dīn Ibn Taymiyya (d. 1328) has become known in the non-Muslim world as a reference for radical Sunni Muslims, who frequently take recourse to him when searching for religious and historical justifications for their violent acts.[2] This has led terrorist hunters and experts to identify him as *the* negative icon of the Salafi jihadi movement. His works have been described as one of the "obscure sources" used to justify rebellion in a tradition of submission to the ruler in Sunni political theory.[3] However, reducing his influence to one of the catalyzing factors for radical Islam and so-called Islamic terrorism[4] does not at all grasp the

---

1 This article is the fruit of many years of intensive discussions and research with and about armed and unarmed Salafis in Germany, Jordan, and Iraq. Even though I was often struck by the violence of their discourses, I was always welcomed to share in the thoughts and pains of those who suffered and made others suffer even more.

2 See for example Worth, Robert: The Deep Intellectual Roots of Islamic Terror, in: *The New York Times* (Oct. 13, 2001), online: http://www.nytimes.com/2001/10/13/arts/13ROOT.html, accessed Dec. 2, 2010. Jansen, Johannes J. G.: *The Dual Nature of Islamic Fundamentalism*, Ithaca 1997, pp. 32–33; Krawietz, Birgit: Ibn Taymiyya, Vater des islamischen Fundamentalismus? Zur westlichen Rezeption eines mittelalterlichen Schariatsgelehrten, in: Manuel Atienza, Enrico Pattaro, Martin Schulte, Boris Topornin and Dieter Wyduckel (eds.): *Theorie des Rechts in der Gesellschaft*, Berlin 2003, pp. 39–62, here pp. 50–52.

3 Sivan, Emmanuel: Sunni Radicalism in the Middle East and the Iranian Revolution, in: *International Journal of Middle East Studies* 21 (1989), pp. 1–30, here p. 9.

4 Bascio, Patrick: *Defeating Islamic Terrorism. The Wahhabi Factor*, Wellesley 2007; Brewer, Paul and Downing, David: *September 11 and Radical Islamic Terrorism*, Strongsville 2005; Taheri, Amir: *Holy Terror. Inside the World of Islamic Terrorism*, Bethesda 1987.

broad scale of Ibn Taymiyya's attraction among Salafis. Ibn Taymiyya is a household name in the Islamic world with a popularity reaching far beyond the circles of radical Islam on the one hand and advanced scholarship on the other. While the historian and famous traveler Ibn Baṭṭūṭa (d. 1217), who met Ibn Taymiyya during a stay in Damascus, said his behavior made it seem as if he had "a screw loose"[5], others have bestowed the honorary title of *shaykh al-islām* on him,[6] thus acknowledging his contributions to the Sunni scholarly tradition. Apart from being recognized as an erudite scholar, theologian, and jurist among Sunni Muslims in general, he and his students turned into positive icons for a growing puritanical reform movement with deep roots in the Islamic Salafi tradition. Citing their names has become a trademark in the Salafi global "reference space of the soul", in which humans, goods, ways of thinking, ritual practices, political and cultural values, and ideas circulate irrespective of national, ethnic, and linguistic barriers.[7] In this reference space, Salafis are engaged in the production and maintenance of meaning, which social movement scholars call a "framing process".[8] In this process, Salafis diagnose political, economic, and social problems and reach some sort of consensus about their causes and the need to alter them. These changes target their own private lives as well as those of others. Some might even feel obliged to urge others to act according to their recommendations. The means of implementing change vary from peaceful to violent, representing a wide spectrum of Salafis from the pacifist citizen to the armed combatant engaged in violent opposition to the state structure. In this process, the works of Ibn Taymiyya and his students play an important role even though they are not easy to understand for the average reader. Salafi framing efforts are embedded in a particular environment with varying sets of political, social, and economic factors and actors.[9] In the Islamic world, the latter represent the political power-holders, the army, and non-state

5 Little, Donald P.: Did Ibn Taymiyya Have a Screw Loose?, in: *Studia Islamica* 41 (1975), pp. 93–111, here p. 95.
6 Ibid., p. 99.
7 Allievi, Stefano: Islam in the Public Space. Social Networks, Media and Neo-Communities, in: Stefano Allievi and Jorgen S. Nielsen (eds.): *Muslim Networks and Transnational Communities in and across Europe*, Leiden and Boston 2003, pp. 1–27, here p. 10.
8 Benford, Robert D. and Snow, David A.: Framing Processes and Social Movements. An Overview and Assessment, in: *Annual Review of Sociology* 26 (2000), pp. 611–639, here pp. 614–615.
9 Ibid., p. 628.

actors such as tribes and religious networks, all of whom are entangled in a complex struggle for religious, economic, and political legitimacy. Salafis are part of this struggle. In many countries they are becoming a growing political force mostly organized in informal networks, which are viewed as a challenge to the religious and consequently the political legitimacy of the mostly authoritarian regimes. In response, these regimes have taken advantage of the political, ideological, and military consequences of the 9/11 events and the subsequent "Global War on Terrorism" by portraying Salafis as a threat to national and global stability. Thus, they are often used as a pretext to silence political opposition and a scapegoat for the shortcomings of these regimes. The result is that Salafis have come under immense pressure globally, which strongly affects their framing processes and their choice of religious authorities as well as the modalities of accessing religious expertise.

The purpose of this article is to analyze the ways Ibn Taymiyya and his students, notably Ibn Qayyim al-Jawziyya (d. 1350), are integrated into the self-representations and daily lives of Salafis. Under what circumstances are they referred to? What parts of their oeuvre do Salafis pick up? What aspects of their biographies do Salafis highlight, and how are such choices presented?

The bulk of the Western secondary literature on Ibn Taymiyya and Ibn Qayyim al-Jawziyya deals with their world of ideas expressed within the different genres of "late medieval" scholarly writing and the contribution these two authors have made to the history of Islamic thought in general. However, incomparably less attention has been paid to the different types of surroundings that enhance and prestructure the receptiveness for certain of Ibn Taymiyya's and Ibn Qayyim al-Jawziyya's ideas or for ideas attributed to them. The present article is therefore not concerned with what these two authors "really" meant, on which previous experts they relied, or which subsequent scholars they impacted with their writings. Instead, it is argued that certain social circumstances call for specific justifications or theoretical reflections. Not only for Ḥanbalī adepts but also for Salafis in general, Ibn Taymiyya and Ibn al-Qayyim represent a huge reservoir and resource that is actively used on demand. In this regard, there seem to be fewer boundaries than one would assume.

The article argues that, under certain circumstances, one of Ibn Taymiyya's students, Ibn al-Qayyim, is almost as popular as his master himself – if not, at times, even more. The two are often cited together; however, as will likewise be shown, they satisfy quite different needs of the same broad target group. In the following, less attention is paid to the contents of their writings and more to factors such as the political environment and participation, respect for human rights, religious legitimacy of the ruling elite, the overall economic situation, and its effects on the everyday life of the people. In order to find out how these external factors influence a Salafi's interest in turning to Ibn Taymiyya and/or Ibn Qayyim al-Jawziyya, I have focused on two fundamentally different settings: one of political stability and security, the other one of conflict or even violence. In the first setting, Salafis live as recognized citizens in a democratic European country, where they are able to pursue their activities and studies without being under close scrutiny, let alone pressure from any state institution or religious competitor. A Salafi community in the eastern German city of Leipzig has been chosen. Salafis, like many other Muslims, have come to occupy niches within the German Islamic topography, where they seem to feel relatively comfortable and are able to design their own world. The depicted Salafi community in Leipzig is led by a German Salafi couple of Syrian descent (like Ibn Taymiyya and Ibn al-Qayyim themselves). Interestingly, political pressure on this particular group has been mounting since the research period from 2003 to 2008. The research also considers the approach to religious authority within a strictly gender segregated network. The second setting, in contrast, shows Salafis in situations of intense pressure from outside, either under persecution or in detention. This might be inflicted by a ruling political power and its coercive apparatus or by raging battles in a war zone like Iraq, Afghanistan, or Somalia. Under such circumstances, Salafis can be arrested, detained, tortured, and kept without a trial for longer durations. Such forms of intense pressure strongly affect their mode of recourse to their Salafi teachings, notably the works of Ibn Taymiyya and Ibn Qayyim al-Jawziyya.

These two fundamentally different settings represent two important poles around which Salafi references to Ibn Taymiyya and co. often develop and evolve nowadays. Taking the social conditions of Salafi adepts into closer consideration means transcending the realm of mere ideas and challenging the often essentializing statements about what the authors in question represent. A serious intellectual history of the modern impact of Ibn Taymiyya or Ibn al-Qayyim should include such dimensions.

1. Salafis in Germany and the Remoteness of Ibn Taymiyya

The majority of Muslims has moved to Germany since 1961 through work force migration from Turkey.[10] As a result, about 2.5 to 2.7 million of a total of approximately 3.8 to 4.3 million Muslims in Germany are from Turkey.[11] About 2.64 million are Sunnis mostly from the Ḥanafī school of law (*madhhab*) and about 300,000 are Sunni Shāfiʿīs, mostly of Kurdish origin.[12] Many of the Sunni Muslims originally came from Anatolia and are predominantly oriented toward Sufism.[13] It is impossible to pinpoint the percentage in exact figures, but the biggest organizations of Muslims in Germany are Sufi-inspired if not dominated by Sufism, such as Milli Görüş (Avrupa Milli Görüş Teşkilatları e. V.),[14] the Suleiman community (*Verein Islamischer Kulturzentren*, VIKZ),[15] and the Nūr community. Their institutional form of organization avoids showing structural features of a classic Sufi order, because they have had to adapt to the political and legal demands of secular Turkey.[16] Still, these organizations are deeply

10 Smaller numbers of Muslims came as labourers from Morocco, Tunisia, and former Yugoslavia. See Heimbach, Marfa: *Die Entwicklung der islamischen Gemeinschaft in Deutschland seit 1961*, Berlin 2001, p. 61.

11 Federal Office for Migration and Refugees: *Muslim Life in Germany*, Nürnberg 2009, p. 11.

12 Religionswissenschaftlicher Medien- und Informationsdienst e. V.; online: http://www.remid.de/remid_info_zahlen.htm, accessed Dec. 2, 2010.

13 Böttcher, Annabelle: Vielfältige islamische Traditionen in Deutschland, in: *Neue Züricher Zeitung* 298 (Dec. 21, 2004), p. 5.

14 Jonker, Gerdien: The Evolution of the Naqshbandi-Mujaddidi. Sulaymançis in Germany, in: Jamal Malik and John Hinnells (eds.): *Sufism in the West*, London 2006, pp. 71–85, here p. 73.

15 See Jonker, Gerdien: *Eine Wellenlänge zu Gott. Der Verband der Islamischen Kulturzentren in Europa*, Berlin 2002; Gökalp, Altan: Les fruits de l'arbre plutôt que ses racines. Le Suleymanisme, in: Marc Gaborieau, Alexandre Popovic and Thierry Zarcone (eds.): *Naqshbandis. Cheminements et situation actuelle d'un ordre mystique musulman*, Istanbul and Paris 1990, pp. 421–435; Lemmen, Thomas: *Islamische Organisationen in Deutschland*, ed. by Friedrich-Ebert-Stiftung (Abt. Arbeit und Sozialpolitik), Bonn 2000, pp. 48–52, online: http://www.fes.de/fulltext/asfo/00803toc.htm, accessed Dec. 03, 2010.

16 Jonker, Gerdien: Die Verortung der islamischen Gemeinden im deutschen Umfeld, in: idem (ed.): *Kern und Rand. Religiöse Minderheiten aus der Türkei in Deutschland*, Berlin 1999, pp. 131–146, here pp. 134–135.

rooted in the Sufi tradition of the Naqshbandiyya-Mujaddidiyya.[17] In addition to the influx from Turkey, political and economic refugees and students from Lebanon, Palestine, Iran, Afghanistan, Syria, Pakistan, Iraq, Bosnia-Herzegovina, and the Kosovo started trickling into Germany in the 1970s.[18] Among the Lebanese, Iranian, and Iraqi refugees were a large number of Shiites. The Muslims from the other countries were mainly Sunni. There are no figures available for Salafis, even though it is quite probable that some Sunnis from Middle Eastern countries such as Iraq, Syria, Lebanon, etc. were Salafis. Very few Salafis are from Turkey.[19] Official figures about Salafi presence do not even exist for members of radical Salafi groups in Germany, according to the "Annual Report of the Office for the Protection of the Constitution" of the Ministry of the Interior in Germany. This source mentions activities of radical Salafi groups, for example those belonging to various branches of al-Qaida, to the Algerian Groupe Salafiste pour la Prédication et le Combat (GSPC), and the Salafi Kurdish/Iraqi groups Anṣār al-Islām, Islamic Jihad Union, Anṣār al-Sunna, and Jamāʿat Anṣār al-Sunna.[20]

In 2009, an increase of anti-German media statements by al-Qaida and homegrown militant Islamists groups started to worry German authorities. This was connected to the German elections to the Bundestag and to Germany's mounting military presence in Afghanistan. In April 2009, legal proceedings were started against the Islamic Jihad Union also called "Sauerland-group", whose members travelled to the border region between Pakistan and Afghanistan to received military training.[21]

Apart from this violence-espousing minority among Salafis, there are groups that are not necessarily less radical in their discourse, but

17 Böttcher, Vielfältige islamische Traditionen, p. 5. The Naqshbandiyya-Mujaddidiyya is as Sufi tradition named after Aḥmad al-Farūqī al-Sirhindī, known as the *mujaddid.*

18 Heimbach, *Entwicklung der islamischen Gemeinschaft*, pp. 63–64; Lemmen, *Islamische Organisationen*, p. 18.

19 Some Salafi websites are also presented in Turkish. The Salafi community in Leipzig addressed some of its mails to Turkish-speaking members. See Mail "Salaf.de News" dated Nov. 16, 2003, accessed Dec. 03, 2010. In another mail they asked for financial support for a number of sick Turkish students and their family members in Saudi Arabia. See Mail "Salaf.de News" dated June 7, 2003, accessed Dec. 03, 2010.

20 Bundesministerium des Innern: *Verfassungsschutzbericht 2009*, Berlin 2009, pp. 216–247.

21 Ibid., pp. 212–220.

that reject violent means. They are dispersed all over Germany in cities, such as Münster, Karlsruhe, Berlin, and Leipzig. Each group finds its geographical niche from where it pursues its activities relatively freely, because competition from other Salafi groups is quite small and not comparable to the situation in many other parts of the Islamic world. However, the political and social environment imposes two constraints on their activities: one is the fact that many of these Salafi groups are under surveillance by the respective province's Office for the Protection of the Constitution (*Landesverfassungsschutz*) and other foreign secret services. Another constraint for Salafis in Germany is inherent to the topography of the Islamic landscape. The strong presence of Sufi Islam in Germany hamper Salafi expansionist strategies, because they usually entertain a strained relationship with Sufis. The Sufi influence poses a major obstacle to the expansion of Salafism in Germany, unlike in neighboring France, which is dominated by an Arab Sunni Islam from Maghreb countries that is receptive to Salafi Islam. As a result, the number of Salafi groups and circles in Germany is small.[22] There is also a probability that the strong Naqshbandī influence on German Sufi Islam might influence this relationship favorably, because Salafis tend to coexist more easily with Naqshbandīs than with representatives of other Sufi traditions, because of the Naqshbandīs' sober approach to certain Sufi practices. This and the low number of Salafis in Germany mean there seems to be no room for an extensive reappraisal of Ibn Taymiyya's famous harsh criticism of Sufism. Also in regard to other aspects, Ibn Taymiyya's impact is relatively modest among Salafi authorities in Germany.

1.1. The Salafis in Leipzig

The Salafi community of Leipzig is presented here as a case study. Leipzig has more than half a million inhabitants and is the largest city in the federal state of Saxony in eastern Germany. One can speculate

22 The "Hamburg cell" of the 9/11 bombers was an exception that gained wide publicity. For more details, see National Commission on Terrorist Attacks Upon the United States: *The 9/11 Commission Report. Final Report of the National Commission on Terrorist Attacks upon the United States*, Washington D.C. 2004, pp. 160–169. However, in this report no explicit reference is made to Salafism. See also Sageman, Marc: *Understanding Terror Networks*, Philadelphia 2004, pp. 103–107.

why the Salafis have chosen this location in eastern Germany. It probably facilitates the community's expansion because there are few others in this part of Germany, which means that Salafis do not have to compete in an environment with previously established Sufi-oriented Turkish or Kurdish Islamic communities. In Germany, the right of religious freedom is stipulated in the constitution. This also applies to Muslims residing in Germany, but until now the German government and associated institutions, such as the political parties and their foundations, have persistently resisted recognizing institutional Islam as a "*Körperschaft des öffentlichen Rechts*" (body under public law), and as a consequence the Islamic community is not recognized as having equal standing with the Catholic and the Protestant Church or the Jewish communities.[23] Institutionalized Islam in Germany usually appears as a "registered association" (*eingetragener Verein*). Mosques and Islamic centres function on the basis of this legal concept.

This is also the case for the Salafi community in Leipzig. The centre of their institutionalized network is the al-Raḥmān mosque not far from Leipzig's main train station.[24] It was founded by Ḥasan Dabbāgh, a German national of Syrian origin, and his wife, Umm ʿAbd Allāh in 1995.[25] They form a sort of Salafi dual-career couple. Ḥasan Dabbāgh came to Germany to study medicine but never finished. Looking for an alternative professional pathway in the stagnating German economy, he found a niche on the Islamic religious market and managed to successfully establish himself as a religious entrepreneur. In 1995 he assumed the position of a prayer leader and manager of al-Raḥmān Mosque in Leipzig and in 1998 he opened a mosque, where he has since been lecturing and preaching in Arabic and staccato German.[26]

Ḥasan Dabbāgh never studied Islamic law or theology in an accredited Islamic institution such as the Faculty of Islamic Law in Damas-

23 For this problem, consult Rohe, Mathias: *Zur öffentlich-rechtlichen Situation von Muslimen in ausgewählten europäischen Ländern*, Vienna 2006, pp. 11–15.

24 Spiewak, Martin: Vorbeter aus der Fremde, in: *DIE ZEIT* 39 (Sept. 21, 2006); online: http://www.zeit.de/2006/39/Imame_2?page=all, accessed Dec. 03, 2010.

25 For more details about mosque associations in Germany, see Marfa, *Entwicklung der islamischen Gemeinschaft*, pp. 70–74.

26 See for example his Friday prayers under: http://www.gamesfather.com/video/Search-Chutba-updated-1.htm, accessed Dec. 03, 2010. His Friday sermons can also be downloaded as video clips from the website of "as-Sunna-Verlag.de". For example Dabbāgh, Ḥasan: *Das Loben, eine Waffe mit zwei Seite. Friday prayer dated Jan. 25, 2008*; online: http://www.as-sunna-verlag.de/index.php?cat_c55_Scheich-Dr-Hassan-Dabbagh.html, accessed May 30, 2008.

cus or al-Azhar in Cairo, nor did he participate in informal study circles with renowned Muslim scholars over a period of several years. His credentials are based on an approximately two-month Islamic dogma (*ʿaqīda*) crash course in Saudi Arabia with a Muslim religious scholar and professor at a Saudi University named Muḥammad Saʿīd al-Qaḥṭānī (b. 1956).[27] The latter was a student of the late Saudi Grand Mufti ʿAbd al-ʿAzīz Ibn Bāz (1909–1999).[28] Shaykh Ḥasan openly admitted not being an Islamic scholar and frequently challenged his followers to verify his statements. For example, when he was invited to present Salafi Islam at a seminar at the Free University of Berlin in the summer of 2003, he arrived with an entourage of young male Arab and European Salafis, who sat in the back of the room with the Koran and Hadith books on their laps – always at the ready to look up the answers to questions. In the course of that lecture, Dabbāgh frequently asked them to verify his statements, which gave his teachings an egalitarian touch.[29] Despite his lack of academic credentials, his noisy appearances have a certain impact. Since March 2006, Dabbāgh made it into several discussion rounds on German TV channels.[30] Hence, despite their small number, Salafis do have some possibilities to insert their statements into the public discourse. About 300 followers regularly attend the mosque,[31] which is under surveillance of the "Office for the Protection of the Constitution of Sachsen" (*Landesamt für Verfassungsschutz in Sachsen*).[32] In April 2008 Dabbāgh's mosque and his private residence – together with other Salafi centres in four of 16

27 Muḥammad Saʿīd al-Qaḥṭānī is a Saudi scholar specialized in Islamic dogma who graduated with an MA from the Umm al-Qurā University in Mecca in 1401/1980. He currently teaches as an Assistant Professor at the Umm al-Qurā University. See http://www.islamtoday.net/questions/muftee.cfm?Sch_ID=121, accessed July 30, 2008.

28 Informal conversation with Umm ʿAbd Allāh on May 29, 2004 in al-Nūr Mosque in Berlin. ʿAbd al-ʿAzīz Ibn Bāz was Grand Mufti of Saudi Arabia from 1993 to 1999.

29 Lecture of Shaykh Ḥasan Dabbāgh at the Free University of Berlin on June 12, 2003.

30 Musharbash, Yassin: Maischberger, Christiansen und der doppelte Imam, in: *Spiegel-Online* (Sept. 14, 2006); online: http://www.spiegel.de/kultur/gesellschaft/0,1518,437136,00.html, accessed Dec. 11, 2010.

31 Figure given by the Religionswissenschaftliche Forum e.V. from the University of Leipzig. See http://www.reform-leipzig.de/web/index.php/Religionen_in_Leipzig.html, accessed Dec. 11, 2010.

32 See its report on the internet: Landesamt für Verfassungsschutz: *Islamische Gemeinde in Sachsen. Al-Rahman Moschee e.V.*; online: http://www.verfas-

German locations – were searched by the German police to look for evidence of their adherence to radical Salafi networks.[33] In May 2009, he was accused of encouraging German converts to become radical Muslims[34], of having spread hatred against non-Muslims through his publishing houses As-Sunna and Al-Tamhid and of having glorified jihad and terror.[35] The charges were later suspended.[36] In an interview given to the *Leipziger Volkszeitung* in May 2009, Dabbāgh expressed his frustration about the surveillance and "misunderstandings".[37]

1.2. Gendered Access to Salafi Islam

An autodidactic approach to Islamic learning is a feature of Salafi Islam and also practised by Shaykh Ḥasan's wife, Umm ʿAbd Allāh, who is a key player in this centre. Meanwhile a German national, she is a native of Qamishly, a Syrian town in a predominantly Kurdish area of Syria. Originally, she came to Germany to study business computing, hence her excellent German.[38] She described herself as a convert to Salafi Islam but unlike other "female Salafi converts", she did not adopt the Salafi dress code. Instead, she continues to wear the Syrian fashion: a black long coat, a black veil, and a typically Syrian face veil (*mandīl*) in black, covering the lower part of her face. This dress code does not signal the

sungsschutz.sachsen.de/download/al-Rahman-Moschee_e._V._HB_2009.pdf, accessed Dec. 11, 2010.

33 Musharbash, Yassin: Staatsanwalt sucht Beweise gegen Radikalisierer-Netzwerk, in: *Der Spiegel* (April 23, 2008); online: http://www.spiegel.de/politik/deutschland/0,1518,549200,00.html, accessed Dec. 11, 2010.

34 Leipziger Imam unter Verdacht, in: *Focus Online* (May 5, 2009); online: http://www.focus.de/politik/deutschland/volksverhetzung-leipziger-imam-unter-verdacht_aid_402279.html, accessed Dec. 10, 2010; Landesamt für Verfassungsschutz Sachsen: *Kurzinformationen*, Dresden Sept. 22, 2009; online: http://www.verfassungsschutz.sachsen.de/download/MoBe_08_2009.pdf, accessed Dec. 11, 2010.

35 Anklage gegen Missionare des Terrors, in: *Focus Online* (Aug. 29, 2009); online: http://www.focus.de/politik/deutschland/islamisten-anklage-gegen-missionare-des-terrors_aid_430708.html, accessed Dec. 11, 2010.

36 Statement on the Salafi internetforum Dawa-news.net; online: http://dawa-news.net/tag/hassan-dabbagh/, accessed Dec. 11, 2010.

37 Krutsch, Peter: Ich fuehle mich als Suendenbock missbraucht, in: *Leipziger Volkszeitung* (May 26, 2009).

38 Informal conversation with Umm ʿAbd Allāh on May 29, 2004 in al-Nūr Mosque in Berlin.

adherence to a particular confessional group within Islam. Umm ʿAbd Allāh met her husband in Germany. Their marriage was not arranged by either of their families. What brought them together is their common origin and their quest for true Islam. Umm ʿAbd Allāh described her marriage as an ongoing and heated discussion about Islam because in the beginning the two of them could never agree on anything. In the end, her husband often succeeds in coming up with the necessary evidence from the holy sources of Koran and Hadith to convince her of his arguments.[39] Both Shaykh Ḥasan and Umm ʿAbd Allāh are the main actors for shaping Salafi religious knowledge emanating from this centre. They also strongly influence the choice of religious authorities and the modalities of access to them.

Since the process of acquiring Salafi religious knowledge is, as a rule, gender-segregated and because relevant female activities have been neglected in the academic literature, I will focus in this section on Umm ʿAbd Allāh. What seems to fascinate her most about Salafi Islam is the direct access to the sources of Islam, the Koran and the Sunna of the Prophet Muḥammad. The Koran is God's revelation to mankind in the Arabic language; the theological, legal and other rules are derived from it. As an additional source, the Sunna of the Prophet, which includes narratives of statements and actions of the Prophet Muḥammad, is consulted. Because the Prophet Muḥammad is the seal of a long chain of prophets, his behaviour serves as model for all Muslims; this model is called the Sunna. He was followed by his companions and other meritorious members of the two following generations, called "the pious ancestors" (*al-salaf al-ṣāliḥ*). Umm ʿAbd Allāh tries to discover these sources on her own as a way of self-empowerment. Instead of relying entirely on (male) Muslim legal scholars and theologians for references and thus submitting to their monopoly of interpretation, she is making an effort to assume this time-consuming challenge of verifying the sources. As will be outlined further on, she does accept a certain tradition of legal scholars and theologians. Her aim is to reconstruct every detail of the Prophet Muḥammad's life from the Koran and the Prophetic traditions (*aḥādīth*) in order to derive a proper code of conduct for her personal orientation. Since many of these traditions are forgeries, Umm ʿAbd Allāh is particularly sceptical about the trustworthiness and reliability of Hadith-collections;

39 Informal conversation with Umm ʿAbd Allāh on May 29, 2004 in al-Nūr Mosque in Berlin.

therefore Hadith-research is in the centre of her interest. It is also the pillar of the Salafi methodology[40] and gives her the possibility to discard certain doctrines she regards as weak or forged, since the literalist reading of the sources requires that only authentic and thus trustworthy texts serve as a normative basis for religious practice or social behaviour. Any interpretation of these sources is subject to error and represents an innovation (*bidʿa*).[41] Umm ʿAbd Allāh's methodology is illustrated by her e-learning course material, which she developed for her lessons with female students on "Paltalk". Generally, Umm ʿAbd Allāh's materials deal with the basics, such as warning against polytheism (*shirk*). She explained, for instance, that it is polytheism to believe in the healing effects of medicine, because only God can heal, while medical treatment is just a tool. Another topic elaborated further is the duty to invite people to (Salafi) Islam (*daʿwa*), an offer people are free to accept.[42] In one script entitled "Going to the Toilet", she elaborates 15 points on proper conduct in the restroom. Each gesture and saying upon entering, using, and leaving the toilet is explained and cemented by traditions transmitted from the Prophet. Among these traditions are two that were narrated by the Prophet's favourite wife, ʿĀʾisha.[43] Ritual purity (*ṭahāra*) in Islam is explained and references from the Koran and the Prophetic traditions are cited that are narrated by females, such as one of the Prophet's companions, Umm ʿAtiyya al-Anṣāriyya.[44] She told that the Prophet Muḥammad entered the women's space when his daughter Zaynab died and recommended clean but used water.[45] In another tradition, one of the Prophet's wives was mentioned as having done the ablution together with him using water that showed traces of dough. That is to say that, in this German Muslim community centre, Umm ʿAbd Allāh strategically transcends her position as a mere spouse within the framework of shared teaching tasks to postulate her version of liberation-theological access to the holy sources. The choice of

40 Informal conversation with Umm ʿAbd Allāh on May 29, 2004 in al-Nūr Mosque in Berlin.

41 For a definition of "Salafī literalism" as opposed to "Salafī Reformism", see Ramadan, Tariq: *Western Muslims and the Future of Islam*, Oxford 2004, pp. 25–27.

42 Course material distributed by email on June 19, 2004 by Umm ʿAbd Allāh.

43 Course material distributed by email on June 19, 2004 by Umm ʿAbd Allāh.

44 Umm ʿAṭiyya al-Anṣāriyya is a companion of the Prophet Muḥammad and a narrator of a Hadith. She was also cited by Saudi scholars. See ʿAbd al-ʿAzīz Ibn ʿAbd Allāh Ibn Bāz, Muḥammad b. ʿAbd al-ʿAzīz: *Islamic Fatawa Regarding Women*, London 1996, p. 125.

45 Course material distributed by email on June 19, 2004 by Umm ʿAbd Allāh.

topics, such as ritual purity, allows her to convey the implicit and, in fact, central message of the existence of indispensable first-hand *female* knowledge. Also her habitus of empowerment, self-fashioning techniques, and the challenging attitude of always demanding convincing indicators from the holy sources for each and every situation in human life would very much astonish a resurrected – and throughout his lifetime reportedly misogynous – Ibn Taymiyya.

1.3. Female Approach to Salafi Religious Authorities

Umm ʿAbd Allāh imagines herself as belonging to an existing female scholarly tradition within Salafi Islam, of which she heard some rumours. According to this discourse, the former Saudi Arabian state mufti Ibn Bāz graduated a female scholar with a license to teach students of her own (*ijāza*). She is said to have established her own teaching institution for female Salafis in Saudi Arabia.[46] For Umm ʿAbd Allāh, this is just one example of a nascent female Salafi teaching tradition in the heartland of Islam, Saudi Arabia, of which nothing is known outside. She interprets this as a natural historic continuation of the strong role women fulfilled in transmitting reliable information about the Prophet, foremost his own wife ʿĀʾisha. Umm ʿAbd Allāh says this tradition has to be rediscovered and revived. Searching for it and collecting books written by female Salafi scholars has therefore become one of her passions.[47] However, this conviction of hers seems to be more an individual attitude than to be accompanied by a serious in-depth search, comparable to her quest for specific Hadith information, since she does not mention (and might not even be aware of) the strong female Salafi tradition in northern Yemen. Nevertheless, references to the Prophet's wife ʿĀʾisha, and her jurisprudential input are quite frequent among Salafi males and females in Germany. Such allusions greatly help to attract the attention of female adepts. Umm ʿAbd Allāh, for her part, even has a distinctly female approach when it comes to challenging the male leadership in her community. During her husband's frequent absences, she replaces him, even though it has been very difficult for her husband's male followers to accept

46 Informal conversation with Umm ʿAbd Allāh on May 29, 2004 in al-Nūr Mosque in Berlin.
47 Informal conversation with Umm ʿAbd Allāh on May 29, 2004 in al-Nūr Mosque in Berlin.

her. Since she shares responsibilities with her husband, she is the only one who has an overview of his time schedule, the contacts, finances, etc. This tight grip on information and decision-making helps her defend her position in this male-dominated environment. Nevertheless, there are limitations to such an endeavour. For instance, Umm ʿAbd Allāh expressed her disappointment that she could not assume her husband's position as a preacher in the mosque.[48] While her husband calls himself a Shaykh even though he lacks the academic credentials, Umm ʿAbd Allāh behaves very modestly. She does not claim any other title than that of the mother of her son ʿAbd Allāh. This is a frequent characteristic of female Muslim students and scholars all over the Islamic world.[49]

Umm ʿAbd Allāh is still at the beginning of her scholarly career. Since there are not enough female Salafis to get together for a teaching lesson, Umm ʿAbd Allāh has resorted to virtual teaching in the Internet.[50] She regularly "meets" with about 20 German-speaking Salafi-oriented ladies in "Paltalk" for e-learning lessons. Access is restricted to females, who have to authenticate themselves with voicesamples in order to get access to this study group. This oral approach corresponds to what Gary R. Bunt called "voiced Islam".[51] Umm ʿAbd Allāh also regularly sends out homework to her students. Her course materials are available on a webpage that she has meticulously developed over time.[52] Interestingly, this virtual space reflects the same features as the real space, where strict gender segregation is imposed. In spite of her efforts, Umm ʿAbd Allāh is still in the early stages of this discovery process and far from being able to challenge on her own the soundness of these Prophetic traditions or other sources. She claims that her

---

48 Informal conversation with Umm ʿAbd Allāh on May 29, 2004 in al-Nūr Mosque in Berlin.

49 For modesty in female religious authority in Sufism, see Böttcher, Annabelle: Portraits of Kurdish Women in Contemporary Sufism, in: Shahrzad Mojab (ed.): *Women of a Non-State Nation. The Kurds*, Costa Mesa 2001, pp. 195–208, here pp. 197–203; Böttcher, Annabelle: Religious Authority in Transnational Sufi Networks, in: Gudrun Krämer and Sabine Schmidtke (eds.): *Speaking for Islam. Religious Authorities in Muslim Societies*, Leiden and Boston 2006, pp. 241–268, here pp. 261–263.

50 Böttcher, Vielfältige islamische Traditionen, p. 5.

51 Bunt, Gary R.: *Virtually Islamic. Computer-mediated Communication and Cyber Islamic Environments*, Cardiff 2000, p. 9.

52 Informal conversation with Umm ʿAbd Allāh on May 29, 2004 in al-Nūr Mosque in Berlin.

main references are the Koran and the Prophetic traditions. References to Ḥanbalī/Salafi sources are missing. This remoteness from the main Ḥanbalī/Salafi figureheads in her discourse, might be part of a much broader phenomenon in Salafi circles in Germany or even the West at large. To shed more light on this, I will analyze the process of how Salafis actually refer to concrete religious authorities by looking at their (re)production of religious knowledge on the Internet.

1.4. The Salafis from Leipzig and the Internet

As Gary Bunt pointed out, Salafis generally have a strong presence in the Internet.[53] Shaykh Ḥasan, his wife, and their followers are extremely active in the Internet and maintain several websites. First of all, they had a homepage in German language for their mosque,[54] with a header reading "Qur'ān, authentic Sunna and the way of the companions".[55] The front page had links to four other websites, which all belonged to the same group, as will be shown below. At this first website, the mosque welcomed the visitor and presented itself as an "interest group of Muslims, which tries to transfer Islam on the basis of authentic sources".[56] Another website of theirs, www.salaf.de, presents itself on the front page as "authentic and informative".[57] It is more of a virtual bookshelf, where texts – mainly smaller, easily digestible units – from the Salafi tradition are deposited and made available in the German language. In the introductory text, the homepage – after a praise to God – announces its intention of "passing authentic knowledge about Islam through its modest contributions".[58] Under the categories dogma, Koran, Sunna, religious duty and Islamic jurisprudence, education and purification, sermon, method (*manhaj*), biography of the Prophet and Islamic history, society and life, language, and a section "for non-Muslims", a wide variety of texts is made accessible to the reader. However, the core titles of Salafi teachings are written in Arabic language, which creates an obstacle for those who do not

53 Bunt, *Virtually Islamic*, pp. 37–38.
54 http://www.alrahman-moschee.de/home.html, accessed May 30, 2008.
55 Ibid.
56 Ibid.
57 See front-page http://www.salaf.de, accessed Dec. 03, 2010.
58 See front-page http://www.salaf. de/startseite/html, accessed Dec. 03, 2010.

read Arabic. Therefore, those communities or institutions that wish to engage in the transfer of religious knowledge either teach Arabic or go through great pains translating Salafi works into other languages. This immense investment in translations has also been displayed by the Leipzig Salafis. Many of their texts are painstakingly translated (from English, Turkish or even from Bosnian) into German to make their selection of texts accessible to non-Arabic-speaking communities and thus expand the transnational Salafi networks. Strikingly, they do not take their texts directly from the Arabic originals as one would expect from a group that claims to always go back to the sources. This raises questions about the group's definition of "sources". This feature rather reinforces the impression that its insistence on authentic sources has much more to do with a self-emancipating habitus than with realities on the ground. The authors displayed on their websites are, on the one hand, well-known scholars from the Salafi tradition and, on the other, quite unknown names, most probably members or sympathizers of the Leipzig mosque. The selection presents a global Salafi community from many different countries such as India, South Africa, the United States, Europe and the Balkans. It reveals a clear preference for authors from the Ḥanbalī school of law. Nevertheless, in the section on the life of the Prophet and Islamic history there are also a number of biographies of representatives from other schools of law, among them the founder of the Ḥanafī school, Abū Ḥanīfa,[59] the founder of the Shāfiʿī school, al-Shāfiʿī,[60] and Ibn Kathīr (d. 1373), also a Shāfiʿī scholar with Ḥanbalī leanings.[61]

During a surveil in August 2008, a total of 65 authors appeared in August 2008. While some texts do not mention any author at all, Muḥammad Ṣāliḥ al-Munajjid, a well-known contemporary Saudi Muslim scholar, is the person with the largest number of texts on the website. He studied with the Wahhabi state establishment, including

59 Salaf.de: *Kurzbiographie von Imam Abu Hanifa (80–150 n. H.). Excerpt taken from* Siyar A'lamun-Nubala; translated from English into German by Abū Imrān, 2004; online: http://www.salaf.de/swf/sir0009.swf, accessed Dec. 04, 2010, five pages.

60 Salaf.de: *Kurzbiographie von Imam asch-Schafi'i (132–204 n. H.). Excerpt taken from* Siyar A'lamun-Nubala Siyar A'lamun-Nubala; translated from English into German by Abū Imrān, 2004; online: http://www.salaf.de/swf/sir0015.swf, accessed Dec. 04, 2010.

61 Salaf.de: *Kurzbiographie von Imam Ibn Kathir*, translated from English into German by Azad Ibn Muhammad, 2004; online: http://www.salaf.de/swf/sir0017.swf, accessed Dec. 04, 2010, three pages.

such teachers as ʿAbd al-ʿAzīz b. ʿAbd Allāh Ibn Bāz, Muḥammad Ṣāliḥ al-ʿUthaymīn, and ʿAbd Allāh Ibn Jibrīn. Later he was a preacher in a mosque in Khobar. On the German Salafi website in early 2009, Shaykh Munajjid was well-represented with a total of twelve texts. He appeared, for instance, in the dogma section with two texts, one entitled "What is Aqida?"[62] and the other one on the eschatological topic of the *dajjāl*.[63] He reappeared in the section "Ritual Duty and Islamic Jurisprudence" with a text on "How to behave in the following situations"[64] and one on "Muharram and Ashura".[65] Interestingly, the latter describes the virtues of fasting during the mourning month of Muḥarram in a very sober way. In a chapter about "Wide-spread innovations (*bidʿa*) on Aschura", excerpts from Ibn Taymiyya's fatwas are cited, which also make reference to his rejection of Twelver Shiite rituals such as flagellations.[66] With the presence of a tiny Shiite community in Leipzig, the anti-Shiite polemics do not reflect any local tensions, but insert themselves into a broader strong anti-Shiite sentiment among Salafis.

Another scholar, who is almost equally well-represented with eleven texts on the website, is the late Muḥammad Nāṣir al-Dīn al-Albānī (1909–1999).[67] He was the son of a clockmaker from Albania[68] and had a reputation of being the Hadith scholar of his time (*muḥaddith al-ʿaṣr*).[69] He is followed by the Saudi scholar, Muḥammad Ibn Ṣāliḥ

62 Al-Munadschid, Scheich Muhammad Salih: *Was ist Aqida?*, translated from English by Abu Imran, 2006; online: http://www.salaf.de/swf/aqd0001.swf, accessed Dec. 03, 2010, three pages.

63 A central evil figure in Islamic eschatology, see Al-Munadschid, Scheich Muhammad Salih: *Der Dadschal*, 2006; online: http://www.salaf.de/swf/aqd0011.swf, accessed Dec. 05, 2010, eleven pages.

64 Al-Munadschid, Scheich Muhammad Salih: *Wie man sich in folgenden Situationen verhält*, translated from English to German by Azad ibn Muhammad, 2002; online: http://www.salaf.de/swf/ibd0012.swf, accessed Dec. 04, 2010, 31 pages.

65 Al-Munadschid, Scheich Muhammad Salih: *Muharram und Aschura*, translated from the English by Somaya K. Lemcke, 2006; online: http://www.salaf.de/swf/ibd0009.swf, accessed Dec. 04, 2010, 13 pages.

66 Ibid.

67 Al Albānī , Muḥammad Nāṣiruddīn: *The Face Veil* (*Der Gesichtsschleier*), translated from Arabic by Dr. Bilāl Philip and translated from English into German by Umm Laysa', 2008; online: http://www.salaf.de/swf/ges0015.swf, accessed Dec. 04, 2010, twelve pages.

68 *An Introduction to the Salafī Daʿwa*; online: http://www.qss.org/articles/salafi/text.html, accessed Dec. 03, 2010.

69 On his political stance, see Lacroix, Stéphane: Al-Albani's Revolutionary Approach to Hadith, in: *ISIM Review* 21 (2008), pp. 6–7.

al-ʿUthaymīn (1926–2001) with ten texts. Notably, only then comes Ibn Qayyim al-Jawziyya with more than eight texts followed by Bilāl Philips (b. 1947), an American convert, with six texts.[70] Muḥammad b. ʿAbd al-Wahhāb (1703–1792)[71] and ʿAbd al-ʿAzīz Ibn Bāz[72] are each represented with four texts on the website. The Shāfiʿī scholar Ibn Kathīr appears three times[73] as does the Saudi Arabian scholar ʿAbd Allāh al-Fawzān (b. 1933).[74] Other authors appear only once.[75]

Conspicuous in all of this is the overall dominance of state-approved scholars from the time when Ḥasan Dabbāgh carried out his crash-course in Saudi Arabia. In sharp contrast to the official iconic status of Ibn Taymiyya, his student Ibn Qayyim al-Jawziyya is represented more often than his famous teacher from whom this website offers only two texts. The majority of Ibn al-Qayyim's texts are located in the section on education and self-purification (*tazkiya*) that deals with monitoring one's hidden desires and inclinations in order to direct them in a pious

70 Philipps, Abu Ameenah Bilal: *Die Bereiche des Tauhid*; online: http://www.salaf.de/swf/aqd0014.swf; idem: *Zakah al-fiṭr*; online: http://www.salaf.de/swf/ibd0016.swf; idem: *Die Verhaertung des Herzens*; online: http://www.salaf.de/swf/tarb0025.swf; idem: *Lehrbuch des Islam*, Bd. 1; online: http://www.salaf.de/swf/ver0002.swf; idem: *Die wahre Religion Gottes*; online: http://www.salaf.de/swf/fue0002.swf, all accessed Dec. 04, 2010.

71 Shaykh al-Islām Ibn ʿAbd al-Wahhāb, Muḥammad: *Religiöse Erscheinungen der Dschahiliya*, translated from English to German by Azad Ibn Muhammad, 2004; online: http://www.salaf.de/swf/ver0001.swf, accessed August 1, 2008, 31 pages; idem: *Die Bedingungen, Säulen und Pflichten des Gebetes*, translated from English into Germany by Abu Imran, 2005; online: http://www.salaf.de/swf/ibd0002.swf, accessed Dec. 04, 2010, 13 pages.

72 bin Baz, Abdul Aziz: *Wichtige Lektionen für die Muslimische Gemeinschaft*, translated by Umm Amani al-Akad, 2003; online: http://www.salaf.de/swf/tarb0023.swf, accessed Dec. 04, 2010, twelve pages; Ibn Baz, Abdu-l-Aziz Ibn Abdullah: *Die Art des Propheten, das Gebet zu verrichten*, translated from English into German by K. al-Akad, 2004; online: http://www.salaf.de/swf/ibd0001.swf, accessed Dec. 04, 2010, ten pages.

73 Ibn Kathir, Imam: *Erläuterung von missverstandenen Versen*, 2001; online: http://www.salaf.de/swf/qur0008.swf, accessed Dec. 04, 2010, five pages.

74 Ibn Salih al-Fawzan, 'Abdullah: *Die Nacht von al-Qadr. From Ahadith as-Siyam; Ahkam wa Adab* (pp. 141–143, translated from English to German by Amr Abdullah, 2002; online: http://www.salaf.de/swf/ibd0011.swf, accessed Dec. 04, 2010, five pages. Here the author is most probably the Saudi scholar Shaykh Ṣāliḥ Ibn Fawzān Ibn ʿAbd Allāh.

75 Among them are Aḥmad b. Ḥanbal (780–855) himself, the Saudi scholar Muḥammad Saʿīd al-Qaḥṭānī, the deceased Yemenite scholar Muqbil al-Wādiʿī, the South African Salafi Ahmad Didat (b. 1926) and the Indian Salafi Zakir Naik (b. 1965) from Mumbai.

direction. It comprises smaller pieces taken from the author's works, such as "The Love for Allah",[76] a section from his patchwork monograph *al-Fawāʾid*,[77] "*al-ʿUbūdiyya*",[78] "Diseases of the Heart and their Cure",[79] "The Patience of Noble and not Noble Human Beings",[80] "Emigration to God",[81] and "The Eminent Position of the Scholars".[82] The section "Biography and History" has a refutation entitled "Al-Khidr"[83] which denounces the belief in *al-Khiḍr*, a positive legendary figure.

Ibn Taymiyya is mentioned in the section "For Non-Muslims/General" in relation to his text entitled "This is the Straight Religion".[84] This text is an online version of a book printed in 1984. It is the German translation of a letter written by Ibn Taymiyya to the King

---

76 Ibnul Qayyim, Imam: *Die Liebe zu Allah*, excerpt of the third volume of *Madārij al-Sālikīn*; translated from English to German by Azad Ibn Muhammad, 2005; online: http://www.salaf.de/swf/tarb0013.swf, accessed Dec. 04, 2010, three pages.

77 Ibnul Qayyim al-Dschawziyya, Imam: *al-Fawa'id – Anmerkungen des Nutzens*, in: Al-Ibānah, Issue No. 2, Dhul-Qa'dah 1416H/April 1996, translated by K. Akad, 2004; online: http://www.salaf.de/swf/tarb0001.swf, accessed Dec. 01, 2010.

78 Idem: *Al 'Ubudiyyah. Aus der Fussnote von "Die Schande von Al-Hawa (Leidenschaft) [Madaridsch as-Salikin 1/100–101, 105], geringfügig angepasst von Dr. Saleh As-Saleh*, translated from English into German by Azad Ibn Muhammad, 2004; online: http://www.salaf.de/swf/tarb0003.swf, accessed Dec. 04, 2010.

79 Idem: *Krankheiten des Herzens und ihre Heilung. Auszug aus Kapitel 1 von "Heilung mit der Medizin des Propheten – Allahs Heil und Segen auf ihm"*, translated from English to German by Azad Ibn Muhammad, 2004; online: http://www.salaf.de/swf/tarb0018.swf, accessed Dec. 04, 2010, four pages.

80 Idem: *Die Geduld edler und unedler Menschen*, excerpt from Uddat as-Sabririn wa Dharikat (*Patience and Gratitude*), translated from English into German by Nizar Abu Suhail, 2006; online: http://www.salaf.de/swf/tarb0027.swf, accessed Dec. 04, 2010, seven pages.

81 Idem: *Die Auswanderung zu Allah,* excerpt from Risala at-Tabukiyya, translated from English to German by Azad Ibn Muhammad, 2007; online: http://www.salaf.de/swf/tarb0029.swf, accessed Dec. 04, 2010.

82 Idem: *Die herausragende Stellung der Gelehrten*, excerpt from Miftah Dar as-Sa'ada, from English to German by Umm Amani al-Akad, 2003; online: http://www.salaf.de/swf/tarb0012.swf, accessed Dec. 04, 2010.

83 Idem: *Al-Chidr. Second Chapter of* Al-Manaru l-Munif fi s-Sahih wa-d-Da'if, translated from Turkish into German by Eser Ebu Zeyneb, 2005; online: http://www.salaf.de/swf/sir0023.swf, accessed Dec. 04, 2010, nine pages.

84 Ibn Taymiya: *Das ist die aufrechte Religion. Brief des Ibn Taymiya an den König von Zypern*; online: http://www.salaf.de/swf/fue0020.swf, accessed Dec. 04, 2010.

of Cyprus under the aforementioned title.[85] The translation was carried out by a convert named Sahib Mustaqim Bleher and published in 1984 by a person named Darunnur in the city of Würselen near Aachen in North Rhine-Westphalia. In the short introduction on the back of the book cover, Ibn Taymiyya is presented as "one of the most important scholars and renewers of Islam". In addition, some information is given about the translator, the printer, and the publisher. According to the publisher, this work by Ibn Taymiyya was chosen for translation because it describes the relationship between Islam and Christianity in a way "which has lost nothing of its attraction and relevance to the current situation".[86] Since the booklet was already available in the German language, the Salafis from Leipzig merely made it accessible on the Internet. In the section "Biography and History/General", one finds a document about Ibn Taymiyya entitled "The Virtues of Ahmad Ahmad Taqiyuddin ibn Taymiyya".[87] It is a collection of statements made by famous scholars and assembled by a certain Abu Imran, most probably a member of the group.[88] Ibn Kathīr, also a student of Ibn Taymiyya, appears once with a text entitled "Explanation of Misunderstood Verses" in the "Qur'an" section of this website.[89]

All in all, the Salaf.de website under discussion is simply a virtual library offering a selection of translated texts of an admonishing nature from a wide historical and geographic spectrum of the *modern* Salafi tradition. For a group that is deeply suspicious of "innovations" and distortions, the website reflects surprisingly little effort to go directly to the sources. The Hadith-section is poorly developed apart from a number of charts about how to check their soundness. For this reason, the outlined selection of texts is a contradiction in

85 Raff, Thomas: *Das Sendschreiben nach Zypern. Ar-Risaala al-Qubrusiyya von Taqī ad-Dīn Ibn Taymiyya (661–728 A. H.=1263–1328 A. D.); Edition, Übersetzung und Kommentar*, Ph. D. thesis, Bonn 1971.

86 Ibn Taymiyya, Taqī al-Dīn: *Das ist die aufrechte Religion. Brief des Ibn Taymiya an den König von Zypern*; aus dem Arabischen von Sahib Mustaqim Bleher, Würselen 1984.

87 Abu Imran: *Die Vorzüge von Schaich al-Islam Ahmad Taqiyuddin Ibn Taymiyya (1263–1328) anhand Aussagen berühmter Gelehrter*, compiled by Abu Imran, 2002; online: http://www.salaf.de/swf/sir0021.swf, accessed Dec. 04, 2010.

88 http://www.salaf.de/hp/Muslima/muslima.html, accessed Dec. 04, 2010.

89 Ibn Kathir: *Erläuterung von missverstandenen Versen*, 2001; online: http://www.salaf.de/swf/qur0008.swf, accessed Dec. 04, 2010, five pages.

itself. In addition, the scarcity of Ibn Taymiyya's texts is stunning. A possible explanation is that the website reflects to some extent the level of scholarship within the group. It is unlikely that other texts circulate in hardcopy because those who engage in the effort of translating certainly would want their texts to be made available to a wider German-speaking audience. The website is a tool in their own learning and framing process. It provides them with information about their "space of reference". According to their website, they are still in the early phase of Salafi scholarship. At this stage, Ibn al-Qayyim's pious pedagogical texts are more attractive to them than the much harsher Ibn Taymiyya, who quite obviously does not have much to offer to them so far. This impression is also confirmed by an analysis of the other websites the group entertains: sections with audio-units, legal judgments (*fatāwā*), and products for sale are dispersed on the group's other websites. Instead of including all in one website, the group opened a website for each category. This is most likely not a coincidence, but might be the result of a conscious division of labour among the members of the group. A website offering legal judgments (*fatāwā*) was opened in February 2004 under www.fataawa.de.[90] It contains a small collection of juridical opinions in accordance with the principles of Islamic jurisprudence. On the front page, an anonymous author advertises the website as the "first fataawawebsite in the German language".[91] In it is explained that since "we" cannot make legal judgments on our own, "we" have to revert to the "scholars of Islam". And, the editor goes on to explain: they are the scholars of "Ahlal Sunna wal Dschama'a",[92] the synonym of "Ahlal Hadith",[93] not to be confounded with those of the "Ahlal Bida'a".[94] These legal judgments are taken from Saudi websites, such as the one from Muḥammad Ṣāliḥ al-Munajjid (b. 1961/1381)[95] and are translated into German, sometimes very amateurishly. By providing access to a small selection of judgments issued by former students of famous representatives of Saudi state Islam, like Ibn Bāz, Ibn ʿUthaymīn, and others,

90 Announcement to subscribers of the electronic newsletter *Salaf.de News* dated February 9, 2004.
91 http://www.fataawa.de/index02.html, accessed Dec. 04, 2010.
92 People of the Sunna and the Community.
93 People of the Prophetic traditions.
94 People of deviation. See http://www.fataawa.de/index02.html, accessed Dec. 04, 2010.
95 For his homepage see http://www.islam-qa.com/ar, accessed Dec. 04, 2010.

the operator of this website clearly inserts himself into the Saudi-style Salafi tradition. The topics cover a range from the permissibility of certain fashion items to prayer and fasting. In the translations, the name of a certain Abū Bakr al-Almānī frequently appears; this is the pseudonym of a German convert and one of Shaykh Ḥasan's followers. Most likely the "we" is actually Abū Bakr al-Almānī, who maintains the website by himself.

The group's former online shop www.al-tamhid-verlag.eu offered books, DVDs, and CDs in German, Turkish, French, and Arabic. Another online shop under www.as-sunna-verlag.de/as-sunna-verlag/index.php has become the main platform for books, DVDs, and CDs from two Salafi publishing houses: As-Sunna-Verlag and Al-Tamhid-Verlag. According to information available on the website of As-Sunna Publishers, 295,916 hits were registered from February 2007 to May 2008.[96] Products range from Koranic recitations on CDs to introductions to prayer such as the night prayer during the month of Ramadan[97] and a book on fasting by Ḥasan Dabbāgh. In mid-2008, a selection of his lectures on topics such as fasting in Ramadan, Hadith, arrogance, pilgrimage, and Islamic jurisprudence was available on CD.[98] His lectures are also accessible in abundance as audio units on Youtube since early 2008. Providers of these video-clips appear under names such as "FlaggeDerSunna" (FlagOfTheSunna), "AufWegDerGefaerten2" [sic!] (OnPathOfCompanions2) and "VideoIslaam". The provider "FlaggeDerSunna" (FlagOfTheSunna) offered 119 videos with lectures by Shaykh Ḥasan in Arabic and German since February 2008.[99]

The websites and the publishing house officially propagate an entirely male Salafi production, that even makes authoritative statements about exclusively female topics such as the veil[100] including the

96 See http://www.as-sunna-verlag.de/index.php, accessed Dec. 10, 2010.

97 See ibid.

98 See http://www.as-sunna-verlag.de/index.php?cat=c39_Scheich-Dr--Hassan-Dabbagh.html, accessed Dec. 10, 2010.

99 See http://www.youtube.com/user/FlaggeDerSunna, accessed Dec. 10, 2010.

100 *Der Hidschab ist schön!*, translated from English into German by Umm Amani al-Akad, 2004; online: http://www.salaf.de/swf/ges0003.swf, accessed Dec. 11, 2010, six pages; *Die Tugenden des Hidschab*, translated from English into German by Umm Amani al-Akad, 2004; online: http://www.salaf.de/swf/ges0004.swf, accessed Dec. 11, 2010, five pages; *Warum soll ich den Hidschab tragen?*, translated from English into German by Umm Amani al-Akad, 2004; online: http://www.salaf.de/swf/ges0005.swf, accessed Dec. 11, 2010, five pages; *Die Wirklichkeit des Hidschab. Die Kleidung einer muslimischen Frau*,

face veil,[101] menstruation, and birth.[102] Only one text entitled "The one who fasts – surrounded by many merits" (Der Fastende – umgeben von vielen Vorzügen) was written by two ladies, Umm Bilāl and Umm ʿUmayr.[103] However, the occasional appearance of female translators indicates that women actively participate in the design and maintenance of these websites and engage in transmitting religious Salafi knowledge.

Within the dichotomy of the male and female social sphere in orthodox Islam, this webspace belongs to the public, male-dominated sphere. The female Salafis seem to be subordinate to males, but this hypothesis might be too hasty and needs to be verified by detailed ethnographic research. A patronizing tone can be detected, such as in texts by a certain "Abu Jamal", whose works frequently appear on the websites of this Salafi group. In two lectures entitled "Admonishing examples for the women" in which he tries to encourage his female audience to follow the female role models provided during the lifetime of the Prophet Muḥammad,[104] he candidly admits having noticed "that there are wonderful stories about women, of which some excel the men". During the recitations of these stories he is sometimes surprisingly explicit and descriptive about female sexual desires and relationships.[105] Obviously,

---

translated from English into German by Umm Amani al-Akad, 2004; online: http://www.salaf.de/swf/ges0006.swf, accessed Dec. 11, 2010, five pages; *Die verbindlichen Bedingungen für einen islamischen Hidschab*, translated from English into German by Umm Amani al-Akad, 2004; online: http://www.salaf.de/swf/ges0007.swf, accessed Dec. 11, 2010, five pages; *Worte an meine muslimische Schwester*, translated from English into German by Umm Amani al-Akad, first published in: *Muslim Creed* 3 (1995); online: http://www.salaf.de/swf/ges0008.swf, accessed Dec. 11, 2010.

101 Al Albani, Muḥammad Nāṣiruddīn: *The Face Veil* (*Der Gesichtsschleier*), translated from Arabic by Dr. Bilāl Philip and translated from English into German by Umm Laysa', 2008; online: http://www.salaf.de/swf/ges0015.swf, accessed Dec. 11, 2010, twelve pages.

102 Ibn Salih al-'Uthaimin, Schaich Muhammad: *60 Fragen zu Menstruation und Wochenbett*, translated from Arabic into German by Abu Julaybib, 2004; online: http://www.salaf.de/swf/ges0011.swf, accessed Dec. 11, 2010, 31 pages.

103 http://www.salaf.de/ibada&fiqh/ibada&fiqh_fasten.thml, accessed Dec. 11, 2010.

104 Abu Jamal: *Ermahnende Beispiele für die Frauen*, part 1; online: http://www.al-tamhid.net and idem: *Ermahnende Beispiele für die Frauen*, part 2; online: http://www.al-tamhid.net, both accessed Dec. 11, 2010.

105 Abu Jamal: *Ermahnende Beispiele für die Frauen*, part 1; online: http://www.al-tamhid.net and idem: *Ermahnende Beispiele für die Frauen*, part 2; online: http://www.al-tamhid.net, both accessed Dec. 11, 2010.

also German Salafis have to cater to the demands of a growing female audience that asks for religious explanations, justifications, and role models.

1.5. Saudi Religious Authorities

In their effort to establish religious legitimacy in Leipzig and its surroundings or in – via Internet – the German-speaking Muslim world in general, the group inserted itself within the official Wahhabi scholarly tradition. Interestingly, the couple did not turn to a religious authority in their country of origin, Syria, as is frequently the case with immigrant Muslims.[106] Instead, they reverted to the representatives of the Saudi clerical establishment. At the same time, they do not accept the term "Wahhabi" for themselves, as a text on their website by a certain Abu Hamad al-Kashmiri,[107] with comments added by Abu Imran, indicates. In a footnote (by Abu Imran?) the term is rejected because "those who follow the Qur'an and the Sunna according to the understanding of the first three generations, who have been praised by the Prophet – PBH – never call and never called themselves 'Wahhabi'". And it is added: "With Wahhabi all these groups, governments and Sufi sects actually mean the way of the good Salaf (the pious forefathers; companions, prophets, students of the companions etc.), to which people like us invite."[108] The commentator continues that they as a group accept the denomination "Salafi" out of the necessity to distinguish themselves from other groups, which call themselves "Ahlu Sunna" or simply Muslim.[109] Since the group could not provide their own experts in Islamic religious knowledge, they took the initiative of staking out a place in the Salafi tradition. This lack of religious Islamic authorities is a major challenge for the Islamic community in Germany. Many preachers and teachers in mosque associations lack qualification for these positions. They have taught themselves the basics of Islam and assume these positions in their free time alongside their professional careers. This lack also provided a favourable environment for autodi-

106 Allievi, Islam in the Public Space, p. 8.
107 Al-Kashmiri, Abu Hamad: *Wahhabismus enthüllt*, translated from English into Arabic by Azad Ibn Muhammad, comments by Abu Imran, 2002; online: http://www.salaf.de/swf/man0016.swf, accessed Dec. 03, 2010.
108 Al-Kashmiri, Wahhabismus enthüllt, p. 3.
109 Ibid.

dactic strategies in acquiring religious learning as part of extended individual solution-finding. Another result is that Muslims in Germany show a strong transnational orientation toward renowned religious authorities residing outside Europe. While in general Muslims take recourse to the religious authority in their country of origin, this is not the case for Shaykh Ḥasan and his al-Raḥmān Mosque. It is hardly imaginable that he would have been able to achieve a similar type of "career" either in his home state Syria or in Saudi Arabia itself. Rather, it is the convenient German setting with its various options and amenities that allows adepts of Salafi doctrines to fashion themselves and carve out a niche.

2. Salafi Religious Authorities in Combat Zones

In the second scenario, the focus is on a political setting where Salafis come under intense outside pressure, whether because they are engaged in armed struggle in combat zones such as Iraq or because they are persecuted for adhering to some Salafi interpretation of Islam. What religious authorities do such Salafis tend to rely on in a setting of this type? Do Ibn Taymiyya and his students come to constitute a source of inspiration? A study entitled "Militant Ideology Atlas" by a group of researchers of the "Combating Terrorism Center" at the U.S. military academy West Point very meticulously documents the sources used by scholars and activists generally believed to be members of al-Qāʿida. Unlike the Salafis in Leipzig, many of those scholars and activists have a solid Islamic education. It is a compilation of the "most popular texts" by Salafi intellectuals read by radical Salafis.[110] Ibn Taymiyya is among the most frequently cited references in al-Qāʿida's most widely read texts.[111] The texts of radical authors, such as ʿAbd Allāh ʿAzzām, Abū Baṣīr al-Ṭarṭūsī, Abū Qaṭādā al-Filisṭīnī, Abū Muḥammad al-Maqdisī, and Usāma b. Lādin were screened according to their reference to other authors. The study revealed that out of a total of 95 texts, Ibn Taymiyya was cited in 47 and Ibn Qayyim al-Jawziyya in 25 of them. When it comes to the frequency of authors cited, Ibn Taymiyya was referred to in 25 writings. His student Ibn al-Qayyim was cited in

110 McCants, William: *Militant Ideology Atlas. Research Compendium*, New York 2006, p. 7.
111 Ibid, pp. 8–23.

eight writings. This shows that a hierarchy exists with Ibn Taymiyya and his student Ibn al-Qayyim. The aforementioned Palestinian ʿAbd Allāh ʿAzzām is among those authors who like to refer to Ibn Taymiyya, but less so to Ibn Qayyim al-Jawziyya.[112] The Jordanian radical Abū Muḥammad al-Maqdisī also cites Ibn Taymiyya amply. Among 20 of his works analyzed in the study, 15 cited Ibn Taymiyya and 14 Ibn Qayyim al-Jawziyya. Ibn Taymiyya is among those mentioned most frequently.[113] A clearcut rule concerning the presence of texts, direct quotations from, or references to Ibn Taymiyya on militant websites cannot be formulated, since the interest of their average readers to study the classic sources of Ḥanbalī-Salafi Islam is not quite clear. Al-Maqdisī posted a number of Ibn Taymiyya's texts and fatwas in the Arabic language on his homepage and the hits and downloads of these sources, which went into the thousands, seem to indicate a strong interest by the viewers.[114] The website is currently no longer available, but his publications are accessible on other websites.[115]

It is not surprising that radical Salafis feel attracted to Ibn Taymiyya's personality, his scholarship, and his political attitudes. He was frequently in conflict with the Mamluk rulers and their allies and did not hesitate to articulate his criticism in public. As a result, he was imprisoned for his convictions six times during his lifetime.[116] He was first arrested in 1294 for a short time, then in 1305 for about a year and a half. Less than a year after his release, he was again imprisoned for another two years. In 1318, in 1320–21, and in 1326 he was again jailed.[117] But interestingly enough according to Johansen, it was Ibn Taymiyya and Ibn al-Qayyim who were instrumental in legitimizing judicial torture as a means of providing proof in a legal procedure.[118]

112 Ibid, pp. 37–48.

113 Ibid, pp. 161–221.

114 For a list of Ibn Taymiyya's publications and fatwas see http://almaqdese.net/c?i=30, accessed January 9, 2009.

115 Such as the website "Pulpit of Monotheism and Jihad"; online: http://www.tawhed.ws/a?a=2qrikosd, accessed Dec. 10, 2010.

116 Little, Donald P.: *History and Historiography of the Mamlūks*, London 1986, p. 181.

117 Idem: The Historical and Historiographical Significance of the Detention of Ibn Taymiyya, in: *International Journal of Middle East Studies* 4 (1973), pp. 311–327, here p. 312.

118 Johansen, Baber: Signs as Evidence. The Doctrine of Ibn Taymiyya (1263–1328) and Ibn Qayyim al-Jawziyya (d. 1351) on Proof, in: *Islamic Law and Society* 9 (2002), pp. 168–193, here pp. 191–193.

The fact that in at least one trial in Cairo in 1302, he was accused of collaborating with the Mongols is never examined carefully.[119] Contemporary Salafis like to refer to Ibn Taymiyya's detention experiences. The fact that he lived in a time of political turmoil and that he did not shun from political and military involvement makes him even more attractive as a role model. However, as mentioned earlier, here again the Salafis' perception of Ibn Taymiyya is very selective. Ibn Taymiyya often supported the political regime in place. In 1300, he was said to have even participated in an expedition organized by the Mamluks into the neighboring Kaswrawān mountains to punish the Shiite population for having cooperated with the Mongols and Franks.[120] Later that year he called for jihad against the Mongol invaders and for support of the Mamluk governor.[121] This reflects his uncontrolled rage, anger, and hostility against his adversaries.[122] Ibn Taymiyya's dedication to a cause also appeals to radical Salafis. He was described as taking pleasure in nothing but propagating and recording religious learning and acting in accordance with it. He never married and whenever he had any money he gave it away.[123]

As a contested scholar and personality, Ibn Taymiyya seems to be much more attractive as a role model to Salafis under intense pressure than Salafis who enjoy the setting of a pluralistic society with judicial guarantees of their freedom. Citizens who live under an authoritarian regime experience its unrestricted powers in the form of arbitrary arrests, torture, and appalling conditions in places of detention without trial. The use of systematic physical and psychological torture is widespread among police and security services and often replaces investigations. This widespread disrespect for human rights is even reflected in the literary production of the Islamic world. Detention and torture have been described by the Egyptian Muslim Sister Zaynab al-Ghazālī[124] for the Egyptian security apparatus and by Hiba Dabbāgh, a Sunni girl, for the Syrian detention system.[125] While Hiba Dabbāgh's account first had to be published anonymously, decades lat-

119 Jackson, Sherman A.: Ibn Taymiyyah on Trial in Damascus, in: *Journal of Semitic Studies* 39 (1994), pp. 41–85, here p. 50.
120 Laoust, Henri: *La profession de foi d'Ibn Taymiyya*, Paris 1986, pp. 15–16.
121 Ibid, p. 15.
122 Little, Did Ibn Taymiyya Have a Screw Loose, p. 109.
123 Ibid, p. 105.
124 Al-Ghazālī, Zaynab: *Ayyām min ḥayātī*, Cairo 1988.
125 Dabbāgh, Hiba: *Khams daqā'iq wa-ḥasab*, n.p. n.d.

er the Egyptian bestselling novel "The Yacoubian Building" *(ʿImārat Yaʿqūbiyān)* by ʿAlāʾ al-Aswānī is much more outspoken. The novel's character Ṭāhā al-Shādhilī saw his aspirations for entry into the police academy frustrated and he became a Muslim orthodox. In the end, after sexual abuse and severe beatings at the hands of the Egyptian security forces, he resorted to violence.[126] The Qatari TV channel al-Jazeera has also addressed the topic of detention and torture on several occasions. In 2006, it aired a series entitled "Literature of the Prisons" (*Adab al-sujūn*) dealing with the prison and torture experience of Arab intellectuals.[127] With the "War on Terrorism", the situation worsened and Salafis have become its main target. Their lives are strongly influenced by this experience of persecution, combat, arbitrary detention, interrogation, and torture. Ayman al-Ẓawāhirī (b. 1951), one of the religious authorities of al-Qāʿida, seems to have been radicalized during his imprisonment in the 1980s in Egypt. During these torture sessions, he divulged information leading to the arrest, torture, and trial of his closest friend.[128] Al-Ẓawāhirī's public statements often include remarks about torture.[129] A document allegedly used as a training manual for members of al-Qāʿida entitled "Military Studies in Jihad against the Tyrants", also referred to as the "Manchester Document" because it was found by the British Manchester Metropolitan Police during a search, includes references to torture: some are directed specifically at the Egyptian regime, which is addressed as "apostate rulers" who "threw thousands of the Haraka Al-Islamiyia (Islamic Movement) youth in gloomy jails and detention centers that were equipped with the most modern torture devices and [manned with] experts of oppression and torture".[130] According to the author, it was unbelief, that

---

126 Al-Aswānī, ʿAlāʾ: *The Yacoubian Building*, Cairo and New York 2004.

127 Mishbāl, Muḥammad: *Tajribat al-iʿtiqāl wal-taʿdhīb*; online: www.aljazeera.net, accessed May 17, 2006; al-Mukhtār, Ḥamīd: *Riwāyāt min qalb al-muʿtaqal*; online: www.aljazeera.net, accessed May 8, 2005.

128 Al-Zayyaat, Montasser: *The Road to Al-Qaeda. The Story of bin Laaden's Right-Hand Man*, London 2002, pp. 30–31, 106–107; Wright, Lawrence: *The Looming Tower. Al-Qaeda and the Road to 9/11*, New York 2007, pp. 51–58.

129 Zambelis, Chris: Is there a Nexus between Torture and Radicalization?, in: *Jamestown Terrorism Monitor* 6 (June 13, 2008); online: http://www.jamestown.org/terrorism/news/article.php?articleid=2374266, accessed July 15, 2008.

130 *Declaration of Jihad against the Country's Tyrants Military Series*. UK/BM-7 Translation; online: http://www.fas.org/irp/world/para/manualpart1_1.pdf, accessed August 2010.

"drove Sadat, Hosni Mubarak, Gadhafi, Hafez Assad, Saleh, Fahed – Allah's curse be upon the non-believing leaders – and all the apostate Arab rulers to torture, kill, imprison, and torment Moslems".[131] Ibn Taymiyya is quoted by Ibrahim al-Masri as saying that Muslims have to assemble, cooperate, and assist each other under a chosen leader in order to govern their affairs. Hereby God's commands have to be implemented, be it by force, jihad, justice, pilgrimage, or otherwise.[132]

One of the leading Salafi religious authorities, the Jordanian Abū Muḥammad al-Maqdisī, described how often his house in Jordan was searched and his personal belongings confiscated.[133] After his arrests, he and his followers lived in solitary confinement "isolated from the outside world for periods unmatched by prisoners before them in this country except for a few" and "experiencing a range of mental and physical torture crafted by the authorities, who were forced to hide many brothers from the occasional visits of international organisations".[134] Under such circumstances, detainees often (re-)discover Ibn Taymiyya and his students. They might be able to access religious books during or after their initial period of interrogation. Depending on whether or not they are held in solitary confinement or in collective cells, they can have books through family visits or they exchange them with other detainees.[135]

One rare piece of evidence of reading experiences in detention is given by a young Salafi of Yemeni descent named Anwar al-Awlaki. He was born in 1971 in Las Cruces, New Mexico, and later studied civil engineering and education in the United States. He also worked as the Imam of an Islamic centre in Virginia.[136] In 2006 he returned to Yemen and was subsequently arrested and imprisoned for more than 18 months without

131 Ibid, p. 9.

132 Ibid., p. 12.

133 Al-Maqdisī, Shaykh Abū Muḥammad ʿĀsim (May Allāh hasten his escape): *This is Our ʿAqīdah*, n. p. n. d., p. 6.

134 Ibid, p. 4.

135 In Guantanamo, one of the requests by the detainees after the hunger strike in the first half of the year 2006 was for the circulation of religious books. See Golden, Tim: The Battle for Guantanamo, in: *The New York Times* (Sept. 17, 2006); online: http://www.nytimes.com/2006/09/17/magazine/17guantanamo.html?pagewanted=print, accessed Dec. 10, 2010.

136 Al-Awlaki, Anwar: Understandig Ramadan. The Muslim Month of Fasting, in: *Washington Post* (Nov. 19, 2001); online: http://www.washingtonpost.com/wp-srv/liveonline/01/nation/ramadan_awlaki1119.htm, accessed July 8, 2008.

charges. After his release, he remained in Yemen. In November 2009, he has been the focus of intense scrutiny since he was linked to an army psychiatrist accused of killing 13 people at Fort Hood, Tex., and then to Umar Faruk Abdulmutallab, the Nigerian, charged with trying to blow up a Detroit-bound airliner in December 2009. American counterterrorism officials accuse al-Awlaki of being an operative of al-Qāʿida on the Arab Peninsula.[137] The Obama administration even authorized the targeted killing of Anwar al-Awlaki in Yemen.[138] During his detention, he was first in solitary confinement in an underground basement in a prison in Sanaa with little light and no books. Later he could get some books through his family. Among them were the Koran, Ibn Kathīr's historic work in ten volumes entitled *al-Bidāya wal-nihāya*, and Ibn Qayyim al-Jawziyya's book *Madārij al-sālikīn* in three volumes.[139] From Shaykh al-Awlaki's description it is clear that he greatly appreciated the *spiritual* dimension of Ibn al-Qayyim's work. It is quite possible that after interrogations with torture experience and a period of solitary confinement with no access to daylight and sunshine, a detainee either may find Ibn Taymiyya too legalistic or no longer appreciates his harsh calls. Instead, he seeks comfort to strengthen his faith. For some, the mystically tinged writings of an Ibn al-Qayyim offer much more relief in such situations than the unforgiving rhetoric of an Ibn Taymiyya. However, both general options are possible as a reaction to the haunting experiences in prison. When Ibn Taymiyya was imprisoned in Cairo, he was said to have converted the prison into an institute of religious study and devotion, turning the inmates away from futile games to prayer.[140] A similar agenda along the lines of Ibn Taymiyya's prison activities seems to be implemented nowadays by observant Muslims in detention. If detainees are not held in solitary confinement but in collective cells, they might participate in informal teaching lessons given by an Islamic scholar or someone more advanced in Islamic religious

137 Anwar al-Awlaki, in: *The New York Times* (Dec. 07, 2010); online: http://topics.nytimes.com/topics/reference/timestopics/people/a/anwar_al_awlaki/index.html, accessed Dec. 11, 2010.

138 Savage, Charlie: Suit Over Targeted Killings Is Thrown Out, in: *The New York Times* (Dec. 07, 2010); online: http://www.nytimes.com/2010/12/08/world/middleeast/08killing.html?_r=1&ref=anwar_al_awlaki, accessed Dec. 12, 2010.

139 Begg, Moazzam: Moazzam Begg Interviews Imam Anwar Al Awlaki, in: *Cageprisoners*, (Dec. 31, 2007); online: http://www.cageprisoners.com/articles.php?id=22926, accessed July 5, 2008.

140 Little, Did Ibn Taymiyya Have a Screw Loose, p. 107.

science either in their cells or in the recreation areas. In Guantanamo, a half-dozen more learned detainees have served the others as a source of religious rulings.[141]

U.S. detention authorities have recently become aware of the influence of Islamic books and teaching circles in U.S. prisons. In a hearing, Senator Schumer from the State of New York noted that what he called "Wahhabi literature" was readily available in federal prisons.[142] In 2007, the Bureau of Prisons started carrying out an inventory of books in chapel libraries and main prison libraries.[143] A "Wahhabi/Salafi" version of the Koran in English was cited as being widely available in U.S. prisons. It had an appendix entitled "The Call to Jihad". Among detainees in prison, age-old conflicts between Sunnis and Shiites may flare up and (re-)kindle interest especially in Ibn Taymiyya's harsh rhetoric against Shiite Islam and its deviances. Another popular Salafi publication distributed among detainees was written by Saeed Ismaeel and entitled "The Differences between the Sheeah and Muslims Who Follow the Sunnah" was provided in English.[144]

Conclusion

This excursion into two different settings of the Salafi "reference space of the soul"[145] shed some light on the role major scholars such as Ibn Taymiyya and Ibn Qayyim al-Jawziyya play in the Salafi framing process.

In both settings, the complexity and depth of their works remain beyond reach for the Salafi laymen and -women because they require

141 Tim Golden, "The Battle for Guantanamo," The New York Times, 17 September 2006, online: http://www.nytimes.com/2006/09/17/magazine/17guantanamo.html?pagewanted=all&_r=0, accessed August 3, 2008.

142 *Terrorism. Radical Islamic Influence of Chaplaincy of the U.S. Military and Prisons.* Hearing before the Subcommittee on Terrorism, Technology and Homeland Security of the Committee on the Judiciary United States Senate, October 14, 2003, Serial No. J-108–44, Washington D.C. 2004, pp. 5–6; online: http://bulk.resource.org/gpo.gov/hearing/108s/93254.pdf, accessed August 3, 2008.

143 *Prison Radicalization. Are Terrorist Cells Forming in U.S. Cell Blocks?;* Hearing before the Committee on Homeland Security and Governmental Affairs United States Senate; September 19, 2006, Washington D.C. 2007, p. 32; online: http://www.access.gpo.gov/congress/senate, accessed July 20, 2008.

144 Ibid, p. 44.

145 Allievi, Islam in the Public Space, p. 10.

many years of systematic and intensive studies. Just as certain exclusive brands in the world of consumerism remain beyond reach of those, who do not have the financial capacity. Instead of freezing in respectful admiration of the exclusivity of these eminent scholars, Salafis show a refreshing creativity by creating their proper versions of the inaccessible originals and integrating them into the self-representation of their daily routines. Each one, Ibn Taymiyya and Ibn al-Qayyim, represents a reference of its own depending on the needs of Salafis. In the first setting of the German city of Leipzig, Salafis live in a politically stable and relatively secure environment. They have the time and the means to develop their autodidactic approach to Islamic learning. In this sense, Leipzig is a veritable laboratory of Salafi grassroot scholarship in its infancy. In their endeavour to insert themselves into the broader Salafi networks, these German Salafis have invested much to develop their internet presence, where they proudly display the first results of their modest contributions to the broader Salafi reference space. Translations of well-known (Ḥanbalī and Saudi) scholars are mixed with the writings of local laymen (and more seldomnly women). Ibn Taymiyya and Ibn al-Qayyim are mentioned, but remain part of a broader collection of references.

In the second setting, Salafis are persecuted, arrested, detained, tortured and kept without proper legal proceedings. Global Salafi networks are exposed to these two poles of external influences and integrate this experience into their daily lives. It is the feeling of intense political pressure and being exposed to the centre of political turmoil in this waging "War against Terrorism" that explains the preference of Ibn Taymiyya and Ibn Qayyim al-Jawziyya. Ibn Taymiyya is clearly one of the heroes of those engaged in armed struggle because of certain elements of his biography. His student Ibn Qayyim al-Jawziyya offers a more spiritual dimension in times of inner recollection and faith renewal.

Ibn Taymiyya's Worldview and the Challenge of Modernity

A Conflict Among the Ahl-i Ḥadīth in British India

Martin Riexinger

Considered an – albeit brilliant – eccentric, Ibn Taymiyya was a figure at the margin of Islamic intellectual life for centuries until his ideas became a major source of inspiration for a number of political *cum* religious movements from the 18th century onwards. In the 20th century he finally emerged as one of the most important intellectual authorities in the Islamic world.[1] The fact that the rediscovery of Ibn Taymiyya coincided with the increasing dominance of European powers over the Muslim World and the ensuing radical social change lent support to the idea that his religious ideas were positively affiliated to "modernity". This concept was reinforced by the fact that his puritan thought seemed to appear as Islamic parallel to Protestantism which allegedly set in motion the development toward a rational modernity in the West. Do his polemics against saint worship and popular cults not resemble the attacks against the Catholic Church in the age of Reformation? Does his insistence on the importance of proof texts from the primary sources Koran and Hadith not correspond to the Protestant principle of *sola scriptura*? This idea was not promoted by Western scholars in the first instance. Already the educationist and

1 Already early contemporary Western observers have perceived this development: Goldziher, Ignaz: *Die Richtungen der islamischen Koranauslegung*, Leiden 1920, pp. 339–340; and Laoust, Henri: *Essai sur les doctrines sociales et politiques de Takī-d-dīn Aḥmad Ibn Taimīya, canoniste Ḥanbalite. Né à Ḥarrān en 661/1262, mort à Damas en 728/1328; thèse pour le doctorat*, Cairo 1939, pp. 557–575. For a recent assessment see Krawietz, Birgit: Ibn Taymiyya. Vater des islamischen Fundamentalismus? Zur westlichen Rezeption eines mittelalterlichen Schariatsgelehrten, in: Enrico Pattaro, Martin Schulte, Boris Topornin and Dieter Wyduckel (eds.): *Theorie des Rechts und der Gesellschaft. Festschrift für Werner Krawietz zum 70. Geburtstag*, Berlin 2003, pp. 39–62, here pp. 41–42.

modernist reformer Sayyid Aḥmad Khān (1817–1898) had stated with broader reference to the puritan tradition: "In my opinion what the Protestant is to the Roman Catholic so (*sic*) is the Wahabi to the other Mahomedan creeds."[2] In recent decades the Pakistani reformer Fazlur Rahman (1919–1988) insisted "we shall argue that for a genuine reconstruction of Islam to occur, the threads have to be traced back to Ibn Taymiyya with certain considerations."[3] Egyptian professor of philosophy Ḥasan Ḥanafī (b. 1935) lists Ibn Taymiyya and Muḥammad b. ʿAbd al-Wahhāb as ancestors of his project "The Islamic Left" which is supposed to bring about a revival of the Islamic world vis à vis a decaying West.[4] Although rarely with special reference to Ibn Taymiyya, a number of recent scholars have argued that remarkable parallels between Protestantism and puritan or fundamentalist Islamic movements exist.[5] Fieldwork among puritan movements reveals that

2 Sayyid Aḥmad Khān (Syed Ahmed Bahadoor): *Dr. Hunter's "Our Indian Mussulmans. Are they Bound in Conscience to Rebel Against the Queen?"; Compiled by a Mahomedan*, London 1872, pp. 7, 11–14; Sayyid Aḥmad Khān hailed from a family affiliated to the Ṭarīqa-yi Muḥammadiyya (see below); Pearson, Harlan Otto: *Islamic Reform and Revival in Nineteenth Century India*, New Delhi 2008, pp. 204–209 (originally PhD thesis, Duke University 1979). He had even written *Rāh-i sunnat awr radd-i bidʿat* in 1950 where he does, however, not quote Ibn Taymiyya: Sayyid Aḥmad Khān: *Maqālāt-i Sar Sayyid*, ed. by Muḥammad Ismāʿīl Pānīpatī, Lahore 1990, vol. 5 *akhlāqī awr iṣlāḥī maḍāmīn*, pp. 354–429. Although his theological outlook changed dramatically after 1857, he followed the Ahl-i Ḥadīth in rituals matters all his life (Riexinger, Martin: *Ṣanāʾullāh Amritsarī (1868–1948) im Punjab unter britischer Herrschaft*, Würzburg 2004, pp. 167, 171). Furthermore he defended the Ahl-i Ḥadīth against the accusation that they were seditious: Sayyid Aḥmad Khān: Wahhābī. Ahl-i Ḥadīth yā muttabiʿ-i ḥadīth, in: idem: *Maqālāt-i Sar Sayyid*, Lahore 1992, vol. 9 *mulkī u siyāsī maḍāmīn*, pp. 210–212; even before, British travellers and Protestant missionaries had equated puritan Muslims to Protestants: Pearson, *Islamic Reform*, pp. 147, 191, 194, 229.

3 Rahman, Fazlur: *Revival and Reform in Islam*, ed. by Ebrahim Moosa, Oxford 1999, p. 132.

4 Riexinger, Martin: Nasserism Revitalized. A Critical Reading of Ḥasan Ḥanafī's Projects "The Islamic Left" and "Occidentalism" (and their Uncritical Reading), in: *Die Welt des Islams* 47 (2007), pp. 63–117, here pp. 74–74, 93.

5 Gellner, Ernest: *Muslim Society*, Cambridge 1981, pp. 131–148; Utvik, Bjørn Olav: A Pervasive Seriousness Invaded the Country. Islamism, Cromwell's Ghost in the Middle East, in: Prijo Markkola & Stein Tønnesson (eds.): *Between National Histories and Global History*, Helsinki 1997, pp. 129–142; more cautious: Loimeier, Roman: Is There Something Like "Protestant Islam"?, in: *Die Welt des Islams* 45 (2005), pp. 216–254; Schöller, Marco: Ibn Taymīyah und nochmals die Frage nach einer Reformation im Islam, in: Otto Jastrow, Shabo Talay and Herta Hafenrichter

this equation is common among both their members and local outside observers.[6]

Apart from the fact that the connection between Protestantism and modernization in Europe is less certain than the plethora of unreflected reiterations of Weber's thesis on the connection between Protestantism and capitalism suggest,[7] the alleged affinity of Ibn Taymiyya to modernity is rather problematic. One reason for this is an hitherto neglected aspect: his theology and his interpretation of the Koran. The conflict among the Ahl-i Ḥadīth on the interpretation of certain verses of Koran (*āyāt*) in early 20th century British India may serve as instructive example. The emergence and expansion of this school of thought coincided with the colonial penetration of the subcontinent by the British, but it was promoted by traditional scholars who paid little attention to intellectual developments outside the Islamic realm. However the conflict discussed caused repercussions among circles who consciously adopted Ibn Taymiyya's thought in their attempt to come to grips with the challenge of Western civilization.

1. The Ahl-i Ḥadīth: Origins and Doctrines

The Ahl-i Ḥadīth emerged between the 1830s and the 1860s out of a larger puritan trend in South Asian Islam that had begun with Walī

(eds.): *Studien zur Semitistik und Arabistik. Festschrift für Hartmut Bobzin zum 60. Geburtstag*, Wiesbaden 2008, pp. 363–384, here pp. 373–384; Peters (Peters, Rudolph: Islamischer Fundamentalismus. Glaube, Handeln, Führung, in: Wolfgang Schluchter (ed.): *Max Webers Sicht des Islams. Interpretation und Kritik*, Frankfurt/Main 1987, pp. 217–241, here p. 229) takes the opposite approach and presents the parallels between puritan Islamic movements and Protestantism as counter-evidence for the latter's pivotal role in the making of capitalism.

6 For Subsaharan Africa see Loimeier, Protestant Islam, pp. 217–219; I myself heard this remark in conversation with the foremost collector of Ahl-i Ḥadīth materials, Ziaullah Khokhar in Gujranwala as well as from Muhammad Khalid Masud.

7 The counter-evidence for Weber's thesis is summed up by Hamilton, Richard F.: *The Social Misconstruction of Reality. Validity and Verification in the Scholarly Community*, New Haven and London 1996, pp. 32–107; recent scholarship on the Reformation tends to stress that it was rather the "taming" of puritan tendencies that turned the Netherlands into the laboratory of modernity: MacCulloch, Diarmaid: *The Reformation. A History*, London 2003, pp. 371–373, 590; Reinhardt, Volker: *Die Tyrannei der Tugend. Calvin und die Reformation in Genf*, Munich 2009, pp. 249; Skovgaard-Petersen, Jakob: Islam og vulgær-weberianisme, in: *Kritik* 10 (2010), pp. 20–28.

Allāh Dihlawī (1703–1763) who, after returning from his studies in the Hijaz, rejected the Islamic law schools (*madhāhib*) and the veneration of saints and their tombs.[8] Although the latter already betrays the influence of Ibn Taymiyya whose ideas he might have encountered as student of the Kurānī family and the South Asian émigré Muḥammad Ḥayyāt al-Sindī (d. 1750), his religious thought differs in many aspects from Ibn Taymiyya's teachings.[9] In particular he remained deeply

8 Shāh Walī Allāh Dihlawī: *ʿIqd al-jīd fī aḥkām al-ijtihād wal-taqlīd*, Cairo 1385 a.h.; idem: *al-Inṣāf fī bayān asbāb al-ikhtilāf*, Cairo 1950; Baljon, Johannes Marinus Simon: *Religion and Thought of Shāh Walī Allāh Dihlawī (1703–1762)*, Leiden 1986; idem: Shāh Waliullah and the Dargah, in: Christian W. Troll (ed.): *Muslim Shrines in India. Their Character, History and Significance*, Delhi 1989, pp. 189–197; Hermansen, Marcia: Translator's Introduction, in: Walī Allāh: *The Conclusive Argument from God. Wali Allah of Dehli's Hujjat Allah al-Baligha*, translated by Marcia K. Hermansen, Leiden 1996, pp. xv–xl.

9 Voll, John O.: Muḥammad Ḥayyāt al-Sindī and Muḥammad b. ʿAbd al-Wahhāb. Analysis of an Intellectual Group in Eighteenth Century Medina, in: *Bulletin of the School of Oriental and African Studies* 38 (1975), pp. 32–39; Voll, John O.: Linking Groups in the Networks of Eighteenth-Century Revivalist Scholars, in: John O. Voll and Nehemia Levtzion (eds.): *Eighteenth-Century Renewal and Reform in Islam*, Syracuse 1987, pp. 69–92; Voll's theory of a reformist network based on common teachers in the Hijaz has been criticized by Ahmad Dallal (The Origins and Objectives of Islamic Revivalist Thought, in: *Journal of the American Oriental Society* 113 (1993), pp. 341–359) due to the neglect of decisive differences between figures like Shāh Walī Allāh (1703–1762) and Muḥammad b. ʿAbd al-Wahhāb (1703–1792) and Muḥammad b. ʿAlī al-Sanūsī (1787–1860). Although this position has its merits, especially with regard to completely contrary attitudes to Sufism, Dallal goes to the other extreme by belittling actual correspondences. Furthermore the incorporation of al-Shawkānī and Ṣāliḥ al-Fullānī in the comparison would have resulted in a wider spectrum of common points, Riexinger, *Sanāʾullāh Amritsarī*, pp. 66–68, 71; that certain issues relevant for these puritan reformers were discussed in the Ḥijāz is undeniable. For example the rejection of *taqlīd* with reference to Ibn Taymiyya and Ibn al-Qayyim can be traced back to Muḥammad Ḥayyāt al-Sindī: Ibn Taymiyya, Taqī al-Dīn: *Tuḥfat al-anām fī ʿamal bil-ḥadīth al-nabī ʿalayhi al-salām*, adjunct to Ṣadr al-Dīn b. ʿAbd al-ʿAzīz: *al-Ittibāʿ*, Lahore 1401/1980, pp. 72–103, 98–99; Ibn Taymiyya, Taqī al-Dīn: *al-Īqāf ʿalā sabab al-ikhtilāf*, adjunct to Ṣadr al-Dīn b. ʿAbd al-ʿAzīz: *al-Ittibāʿ*, Lahore 1401 a.h., pp. 104–115, here p. 115; Nafiʿ, Basheer M.: A Teacher of Ibn ʿAbd al-Wahhāb. Muḥammad Ḥayāt al-Sindī and the Revival of *aṣḥāb al-ḥadīth*'s Methodology, in: *Islamic Law and Society* 13 (2006), pp. 208–233, here pp. 223–230). Moreover Dallal's objection that the respective reformists did not hold one consistent set of beliefs can not disprove that they drew inspiration from certain scholars, as Ibrāhīm al-Kūrānī himself did at the same time hold positions derived from Ibn Taymiyya and Ibn ʿArabī. And both Ibn ʿArabī's strong admirer of al-Barzanjī and his fierce detractor

committed to Sufi concepts. Due to this intellectual influence he did not subscribe to anthropomorphist concepts of God. Instead he distinguished strictly between the physical world (*ʿālam al-ajsād*) and the spiritual world (*ʿālam al-arwāḥ*) which can not be aptly described with categories usually applied to the former.[10] After his death his successors seem not to have been particularly interested in the teachings of Ibn Taymiyya. His son ʿAbd al-ʿAzīz even denounced him as an extremist.[11]

Walī Allāh's grandson Shāh Ismāʿīl founded the Ṭarīqa-yi Muḥammadiyya, which called for the purge of "non-Islamic" accretions. He allied himself with Sayyid Aḥmad Barelwī (1786–1831), a former mercenary in the army of the princely state of Tonk (Rajasthan), which was disbanded by the British. They and their followers embarked for the Hajj in 1821.[12] On this occasion they passed through Yemen where at that time Muḥammad Ibn ʿAlī al-Shawkānī (1760–1834) was the leading scholar and a figure of considerable political influence.[13] Shāh Ismāʿīl and Sayyid Aḥmad returned to India and migrated from the territory ruled by the East India Company to the no man's land

al-Maqbalī saw no problem in studying with Ibrāhīm al-Kūrānī; Nafiʿ, Basheer M.: Taṣawwuf and Reform in Pre-Modern Islamic Culture. In Search of Ibrāhīm al-Kūrāni, in: *Die Welt des Islams* 42 (2002), pp. 307–355, here pp. 334–342.

10 Baljon, *Religion and Thought*, pp. 21–23.

11 Dihlawī, ʿAbd al-ʿAzīz: *Fatāwā-i ʿazīzī*, Delhi 1311/1893, vol. 2, pp. 71–72.

12 Bari, M. A.: A Nineteenth Century Muslim Reform Movement in India, in: George Makdisi (ed.): *Arabic and Islamic Studies in Honor of Hamilton A. R. Gibb*, Leiden 1965, pp. 85–102; Pearson, *Islamic Reform*; Gaborieau, Marc: A Nineteenth Century Indian "Wahhabi" Tract Against the Cult of Muslim Saints, in: Troll, *Muslim Shrines in India*, pp. 198–256; Gaborieau, Marc: Late Persian, Early Urdu. The Case of "Wahhabi" Literature (1818–1857), in: Françoise Delvoye (ed.): *Confluence of Culture. French Contributions to Indo-Persian Studies*, Delhi 1994, pp. 170–196; Gaborieau, Marc: Criticizing the Sufis. The Debate in Early Nineteenth Century India, in: Frederick de Jong and Bernd Radtke (eds.): *Islamic Mysticism Contested. Thirteen Centuries of Controversies and Polemics*, Leiden 1999, pp. 452–467; Riexinger, *Sanāʾullāh Amritsarī*, pp. 103–108; see Preckel in this volume. Various South Asian publications suffer from major politically motivated distortions. Whereas most pre-World War I texts aim at dispelling the suspicion that the Ṭarīqa-yi Muḥammadiyya was "seditious" most post-World War I publications portray them a forerunners of either Indian nationalism or Muslim separatism. This trend was initiated in 1940 by one of the foremost Muslim activists in the Indian National Congress: Sindhī, ʿUbayd Allāh: *Shāh Walī Allāh awr un kī siyāsī taḥrīk*, Lahore 1965.

13 Haykel, Bernard: *Revival and Reform in Islam. The Legacy of Muhammad al-Shawkānī*, Cambridge 2003.

between the Sikh empire in the Punjab and Afghanistan.[14] They finally fell in their ill-fated jihad against the Sikhs in the battle at Balakot in 1832. Some of their followers, however, had stayed behind in Sanaa to study under al-Shawkānī. After returning to India they propagated his legal theories and his anti-Sufi stance which both betray the influence of Ibn Taymiyya. But in the fields of theology and exegesis of the Koran al-Shawkānī was not a follower of the Damascene rigorist as his non-literal interpretation of verse 7:54 testifies (see below).

After their return from Yemen the Indian scholars installed themselves in their hometowns in the Eastern Gangetic plain where they began to propagate their new religious ideas.[15] Soon they also gained a following in Delhi among those who were influenced by the school of Shāh Walī Allāh.[16] In the next decades the newly emerged school of the Ahl-i Ḥadīth spread to various parts of India, especially the princely state of Bhopal,[17] and to the Punjab, where Amritsar became its second most important centre after Delhi.[18] Already the Ṭarīqa-yi Muḥammadiyya was denounced by its Sufi and Shia opponents as "Wahhābī", a designation which the British rulers adopted.[19] Nev-

14 See the article by Claudia Preckel in this volume.

15 ʿAẓīmābādī, ʿAbd al-Raḥīm: *al-Durr al-manthūr fī tarājim ahl al-Ṣādiqfūr*, Delhi 1927.

16 Bihārī, Faḍl-i Ḥusayn: *al-Ḥayāt baʿd al-mamāt*, Delhi 1908 (reprint Sangla Hil 1982).

17 Saeedullah: *The Life and Works of Siddiq Hasan Khan, Nawwab of Bhopal (1248–1307/1832–1890)*, Lahore 1973; see also Preckel, Claudia: *Islamische Bildungsnetzwerke und Gelehrtenkultur im Indien des 19. Jahrhunderts. Muḥammad Ṣiddīq Ḥasan Ḫān (st. 1890) und die Entstehung der Ahl-e Ḥadīṯ-Bewegung in Bhopal*, Dissertation (Ruhr-Universität Bochum) 2005, online: http://www-brs.ub.ruhr-unibochum.de/netahtml/HSS/Diss/PreckelClaudia/diss.pdf, accessed April 2008; and her article in this volume.

18 Preckel, *Islamische Bildungsnetzwerke*, pp. 179–221; this is primarily due to the activities of ʿAbd Allāh Ghaznawī (1811–1881). He had to flee Afghanistan because he objected to the *taqlīd* of the Ḥanafī *madhhab* and settled in Amritsar where he founded a *madrasa* that was continued by his family until the expulsion of the Muslims from the city in 1947. He corresponded with Ṣiddīq Ḥasan Khān and tried to propagate the ideas of the Ahl-i Ḥadīth in Afghanistan and Central Asia: Riexinger, *S̱anāʾullāh Amritsarī*, pp. 181–183; Preckel, *Islamische Bildungsnetzwerke*, pp. 307–308.

19 Hunter, William: *Our Indian Musalmans. Are they Bound in Conscience to Rebel against the Queen?*, London 1876; protests of the Ahl-i Ḥadīth led by Muḥammad Ḥusayn Batʾālwī resulted in the ban of the term from official correspondence in 1890. Nevertheless it was used in secret correspondence like police files until the 1920s, Riexinger, *S̱anāʾullāh Amritsarī*, pp. 218–219.

ertheless they were definitely not influenced by the Najdīs. Their undeniable common traits were due to the inspiration from the same sources. Whereas leading figures of the Ahl-i Ḥadīth like Ṣiddīq Ḥasan Khān (1832–1890), Muḥammad Ḥusayn Bat'ālwī (1840–1920) and Thanā' Allāh Amritsarī (1867–1948) denied any relationship between their movement and the followers of Muḥammad b. ʿAbd al-Wahhāb until the 1920s,[20] members of the movement who were less eager to please the British showed no reluctance to stress the affinity: ʿAbd al-Wāḥid and ʿAbd al-Raḥīm Ghaznawī from an outstanding family of Ahl-i Ḥadīth scholars of Afghan origin in Amritsar and Delhi were the first to print works of Muḥammad b. ʿAbd al-Wahhāb[21] whereas Bashīr Aḥmad Sahaswānī (d. 1908), a scholar from the Eastern Gangetic plain published an apology of the Wahhabis in 1908.[22] In addition a number of young Wahhabis studied at *madrasas* of the Ahl-i Ḥadīth.[23]

Quite early the Ahl-i Ḥadīth made use of the printing press and it seems that their share in the Muslim printing activities continued to exceed their percentage of the population by far.[24] This was at least in part due to the fact that many of the early Ahl-i Ḥadīth came from the urban upper classes of North Indian Muslim society, and therefore the rate of literacy among them was above average. In areas where their followers hailed from a more modest, sometimes rural, background their emphasis on religious learning had a positive influence on the

20 Ibid., pp. 523–524.

21 Ghaznawī, ʿAbd al-Wāḥid and ʿAbd al-Raḥīm: *Majmūʿat al-tawḥīd*, Delhi n.d., title page (reproduced in Riexinger, *Sanāʾullāh Amritsarī*, p. 644); Bʰaṭī, Muḥammad Isḥāq: *Nuqūsh-i ʿaẓmat-i rafta*, Lahore 1996, p. 67.

22 Al-Sahaswānī, Muḥammad Bashīr: *Ṣiyānat al-insān ʿan waswasat al-shaykh Daḥlān*, Riyadh 1975. In Arabic sources the *nisba* is usually vocalized as al-Sahsuwānī, but the Uttar Pradesh town (*qaṣba*) it refers to is called Sahaswān. For an explanation of the importance of these Mulism towns, see Preckel in this volume.

23 Bihārī, *al-Ḥayāt baʿd al-mamāt*, p. 265; Salafī, Munīr Aḥmad: *Ḥāfiẓ ʿAbd al-Mannān Wāzīrābādī*, Lahore 1994, p. 27; Schulze, Reinhard: *Islamischer Internationalismus im 20. Jahrhundert. Untersuchungen zur Geschichte der Islamischen Weltliga*, Leiden 1990, p. 133, n. 416; Wasella, Jürgen: *Vom Fundamentalisten zum Atheisten. Die Dissidentenkarriere des ʿAbdallāh al-Qaṣīmī (1907–1996)*, Gotha 1997, pp. 34–35.

24 Churchill, Edward: Printed Literature of the Punjabi Muslims. 1860–1900, in: W. Eric Gustafson and Kenneth W. Jones (eds.): *Sources on Punjab History*, Delhi 1975, pp. 276–282; in this respect they continued what the Ṭarīqa-yi Muḥammadiyya had begun: Pearson, *Islamic Reform*, pp. 101–112, 117–126; Gaborieau, Late Persian, Early Urdu.

rate of literacy among the respective groups, as the various "Ahl-i Ḥadīth-villages" in the Punjab testify.[25] The importance of print for the Ahl-i Ḥadīth motivated some of their scholars to choose a different career path than that of a teacher in a *madrasa*: they became religious publishers instead. In 1874 Muḥammad Ḥusayn Bat'ālwī started the monthly *Ishā'at ul-sunnat* (Propagation of the Sunna) one of the very first Islamic magazines worldwide.[26] It was followed in 1904 by the weekly *Ahl-i Ḥadīth* published by his former student Thanā' Allāh Amritsarī.[27]

Right from the beginning the Ahl-i Ḥadīth accepted Ibn Taymiyya's objections against Sufi rituals, many of his legal rulings like the rejection of the *ṭalāq al-bid'a* (i. e. the validity of the repudiation if expressed on one occasion)[28] and his insistence on the demand that any legal ruling has to be based on one of the primary sources Koran and Hadith and not on *ijmā'* or *taqlīd*. In one further respect he served as an important role model for them. The vision of Islamic history the Ahl-i Ḥadīth propagated consisted of the constant struggle of the *ahl al-ḥadīth* renouncing *taqlīd* and the *madhāhib* against the *ahl al-bid'a* who place humans like jurists (*fuqahā'*) and Sufi leaders (*pīr*s) in a position of authority that ought to be exclusively occupied by God and his messenger. Constantly the *ahl al-ḥadīth* suffered persecution at the hands of the innovators (*bid'atīs*). Hence Ibn Taymiyya was exiled and incar-

25 Riexinger, *Ṣanā'ullāh Amritsarī*, pp. 189–195.

26 Ibid., pp. 13, 213. The magazine was published until 1920, however, quite irregularly. The content was primarily polemic, first directed against Mirzā Ghulām Aḥmad, after 1904 primarily against Thanā' Allāh Amritsarī.

27 Unlike Muḥammad Ḥusayn Bat'ālwī, Thanā' Allāh Amritsarī was able to secure the continuous regular publication of this weekly until his expulsion from Amritsar in August 1947. In addition to religious subjects he and his contributors frequently commented on politics especially after World War I when Thanā' Allāh supported for some time the Indian National Congress and the Khilafat Movement.

28 Ibn Taymiyya, Taqī al-Dīn: *Majmū' al-Fatāwā lil-shaykh Taqī al-Dīn Ibn Taymiyya*, Beirut 1978, vol. 32, pp. 131–135, vol. 33, pp. 12–13, 30–33; on his views also Laoust, *Essai sur les doctrines sociales et politiques*, pp. 429, 614; both Shāh Walī Allāh Dihlawī, *Ḥujjat Allāh al-bāligha*, Cairo 1977, vol. 2, p. 139, and Muḥammad b. 'Alī al-Shawkānī, *Nayl al-awṭār*, Cairo 1993, vol. 6, pp. 274–276, agree with Ibn Taymiyya in this respect; Ṣiddīq Ḥasan Khān, Muḥammad: *Ḥusn al-uswa bi-mā thabata min Allāh wa-rasūlihi fī al-niswa*, Constantinople 1301/1883/84, pp. 16–17. Amritsarī, Thanā' Allāh: *Fatāwā-i thanā'iyya*, Sargodha 1972, vol. 2, pp. 214–225, with quotations of earlier Ahl-i Ḥadīth scholars, idem: *Ahl-i Ḥadīth kā madhhab*, Sargodha 1986, pp. 115–117.

cerated for their uncompromising stance (like other *ahl al-ḥadīth* as for example Ibn Ḥanbal and Ibn Ḥazm).[29] The Ahl-i Ḥadīth in British India saw themselves confronting a similar hostility when they were thrown out of mosques because they used to pray with their hands at their ears during most positions (*rafʿ al-yadayn*) and dared to speak the *amen* aloud (*āmīn bil-jahr*) or denounced the veneration of saints.[30]

However, the theological concepts of the Ahl-i Ḥadīth were "taymiyyanized" much more slowly. Early representatives like Nadhīr Ḥusayn Dihlawī (d. 1805–1902) – known as *shaykh al-kull* because almost all leading Ahl-i Ḥadīth scholars of the 19th and early 20th century had been his students – did not advocate the literal interpretation of the Koranic statements on God's attributes.[31] Furthermore he was favourably inclined towards Sufism. He demanded that his disciples offer him oath of allegiance (*bayʿa*) and he praised Ibn ʿArabī, claiming that unity of being (*waḥdat al-wujūd*) understood as unity of divine manifestations (*waḥdat al-shuhūd*) was totally in accordance with the doctrines of the *ahl al-sunna*.[32] In the last decades of the 19th century, however, most scholars of the Ahl-i Ḥadīth seem to have agreed that God had corporeal features and hence a spatial relation (*jiha*) to all other things. He is localized above the heavens and the earth (*ʿuluww*), comes down in the night (*nuzūl*) and he sits on the throne (*istawā ʿalā al-ʿarsh*). Those who did not subscribe to these positions were denounced as Muʿtazilīs or even Jahmīs "whose rank and file believes in everything and whose elite believes in nothing".[33] The exact course of this development remains to be analyzed on the basis of respective literature, but it may be suspected that Ṣiddīq Ḥasan Khān, well known for his mate-

29 On the invented tradition of the Ahl-i al-Ḥadīth in general: Riexinger, *S̱anāʾullāh Amritsarī*, pp. 142–154; a fine example for the self-identification of the Ahl-i Ḥadīth with the persecuted Ibn Taymiyya: Ṣiddīq Ḥasan Khān, Muḥammad: *Itḥāf al-nubalāʾ al-muttaqīn bi-iḥyāʾ al-fuqahāʾ al-muḥaddithīn*, Kanpur 1282/1865/66, pp. 207–209; idem: *Abjad al-ʿulūm*, Lahore 1983, vol. 3, pp. 133–134.

30 Metcalf, Barbara: *Islamic Revival in British India. Deoband 1860–1900*, Princeton 1982, pp. 285–289; Riexinger, *S̱anāʾullāh Amritsarī*, pp. 165–167.

31 Dihlawī, Nadhīr Ḥusayn: *Fatāwā-yi nadhīriyya*, Gujranwālā n. d., vol. 1, pp. 3–4.

32 Bihārī, *al-Ḥayāt baʿd al-mamāt*, pp. 123–125.

33 Ṣiddīq Ḥasan Khān, Muḥammad: *Bughyat al-rāʾid fī sharḥ al-ʿaqāʾid*, Lucknow n. d., pp. 11, 17, 26 (quotation). On the *jahmiyya* see van Ess, Josef: Ḍirār b. ʿAmr und die "Cahmīya". Die Biographie einer vergessenen Schule, in: *Der Islam* 43 (1967), pp. 241–279; 44 (1968), pp. 1–70.

rial support for the publication of Ibn Taymiyya's works in the Middle East and the acquisition of manuscripts of his writings played a considerable role in this process.[34] Moreover it is noteworthy that the first published translation into Urdu of a work by Ibn Taymiyya was the treatise *al-ʿAqīda al-ḥamawiyya al-kubrā*.[35]

2. The Controversies about Thanāʾ Allāh Amritsarī's *tafsīr*

Soon after the theological ideas of Ibn Taymiyya had been widely accepted by the Ahl-i Ḥadīth scholars one of them dared to disagree again. From 1898 onwards Thanāʾ Allāh Amritsarī, a young religious scholar (*mawlwī*) from a modest Kashmiri background published an eight-volume Urdu *tafsīr* (completed in 1938) and an Arabic commentary on the Koran in 1902. Especially the latter stirred a major controversy because Thanāʾ Allāh had dared to paraphrase the sentence *thumma istawā ʿalā al-ʿarsh* in (7:54) as "he executed his decisions (*naffaẓa aḥkāmahu*) with regard to what he had created and administered his orders (*dabbara amrahu*)". In a footnote he justified his interpretation:

> The first of these verses [i. e. Koran 7:54, 10:3 and 32:4] hints at the impossibility of *istiwāʾ* [in the literal sense] with regard to God because he is the creator of everything but himself. And that what is below him is something that has emerged in time on which he can not come to a rest (*lā yumkinu an yastaqirra ʿalayhi*). In the case of the second and the first verse there are indications in the context which corroborate our interpretation, because God mentions *istiwāʾ* in connection with the terms administration (*tadbīr*) and government (*ḥukūma*) and the non-

34 See Preckel in this volume; Commins, David Dean: *Islamic Reform. Politics and Social Change in the Late Ottoman Syria*, Oxford 1990, pp. 24–28, 40, 60; the autograph of *al-Radd ʿalā al-manṭiqiyyīn* is in the library at Bhopal: Hallaq, Wael B.: Introduction, in: idem (ed.): *Ibn Taymiyya Against the Greek Logicians, Translated with Introduction and Notes*, Oxford 1993, pp. xi–lviii, here pp. lv–lvi. However, the cosmological concepts Ṣiddīq Ḥasan Khān (or rather his ghost-writers) expresses in his writings are rather inconsistent. Especially in *Abjad al-ʿulūm* (vol. 1, pp. 437–440) he offers rationalizing explanations for astronomical and meteorological phenomena.

35 According to an advertisement (in: Ṣiddīq Ḥasan Khān , Muḥammad: *al-Iḥtiwāʾ ʿalā masʾalat al-istiwāʾ*, Lahore 1291/1874–75, p. 36) it was published in Amritsar by Ghulām al-ʿAlī in 1872. It is noteworthy that at that point of time Ibn Taymiyya had to be introduced to the Indian Muslim audience as the teacher of the teacher (i. e. Ibn Kathīr) of the lexicographer al-Fīrūzābādī.

> existence of an intercessor. This hints at that with [the word] *istiwāʾ* a notion is intended which comes close to "steering" as ʿIzz al-Dīn al-Miṣrī [i.e. ʿIzz al-Dīn b. ʿAbd al-Salām][36] writes in his book *Ishārat al-īʿjāz ilā baʿḍ al-anwāʿ al-majāz*: "The 16th metaphor is *istiwāʾ*. It is a metaphor for his accession to power (*istīlāʾ ʿalā ḥukmihi*) and its exercise, to speak with the poet: *istawāʾ Bishrun ʿalā al-ʿIrāqī bi-ghayri sayfin wa-damin muhraq* [Bishr gained power of the Iraq without sword or bloodshed]. It is an equation (*tamthīl*) because the kings govern their realm sitting on the throne.[37]

Several members of the Ghaznawī family mobilized scholars from the Punjab in order to force Thanāʾ Allāh to recant. In addition to his stance with regard to the issue of *istīwāʾ* they reproached him with diverging from the exegetical path of the *salaf* in 40 cases where he interpreted a verse without referring to a respective Hadith or a saying of a companion.[38] In some of the cases Thanāʾ Allāh did not affirm a miracle which the wording of the Koran suggests. Instead he proposed a "natural" interpretation as in the case of (2:260) where Ibrāhīm according to Thanāʾ Allāh called four living birds placed on four hills to come to him and not the 16 pieces of four dead birds in order to prove that the resurrection is possible.[39] In other cases he did not affirm miracles which were not explicitly mentioned in the verse itself but in certain exegetical traditions, as in the case of Maryam in her seclusion (3:37) who answered to the question from where she had received food *min ʿinda Allāh* which is often understood as "the fruits of summer in winter and the fruits of winter in summer". For Thanāʾ Allāh this simply represents a statement of Maryam's gratefulness to God for receiv-

36 Hirschler, Konrad: Pre-Eighteenth Century Traditions of Revivalism. Damascus in the Thirteenth Century, in: *Bulletin of the School for Oriental and African Studies* 68 (2005), pp. 195–214.

37 Amritsarī, Thanāʾ Allāh: *Tafsīr al-Qurʾān bi-kalām al-Raḥmān*, Amritsar 1902 (1st ed.), p. 149, l. 10–13 and n. 1.

38 Ghaznawī, ʿAbd al-Ḥaqq: *Kitāb al-Arbaʿīn fī anna Thanāʾ Allāh laysa ʿalā madhhab al-muḥaddithīn fī al-dīn bal ʿalā madhhab al-jahmiyya wal-muʿtazila wal-qadariyya al-muḥarrifīn*, Amritsar n.d.

39 Amritsarī, Thanāʾ Allāh: *Tafsīr al-Qurʾān bi-kalām al-Raḥmān*, Amritsar 1348/1929 (2nd ed.), p. 44, ll. 21–23; idem: *Tafsīr-i Thanāʾī*, Amritsar 1348/1929, vol. 1, p. 172, n. 1. He argues that the uncommon verb *ṣāra/yaṣūru* (*fa-ṣurhunna*) has to be understood as "to team" (Ur. *jʰāknā*) not as "to slaughter", and *juzʾan minhum* as "each one of them". In this case he is notably at odds even with al-Rāzī, Fakhr al-Dīn: *al-Tafsīr al-kabīr*, Cairo n.d., vol. 7, p. 41, ll. -5-p. 42.

ing food in a normal way (*bil-ʿāda*).[40] Similarly Thanāʾ Allāh shuns to project Hadith based eschatological or cosmological content into certain verses as in the case of (6:158) where he considered *yawma yaʾtī baʿḍu āyāti rabbika* as a reference to every human's individual death and not a hint at the sunrise from the West on the Day of Judgment,[41] or in the case of the *bayt maʿmūr* (Koran 52:4) which Thanāʾ Allāh understands as the totality of the mosques on Earth not as a building in one of the seven heavens from which according to reports from the ascent to heavens (*miʿrāj*) every day angels do descend who will not return until the day of Judgment.[42] When the Ghaznawīs presented their complaints in writing, *istiwāʾ*, the initial and foremost bone of contention, was excluded, since they sought the support of Deobandīs, a group of Ḥanafīs critical of Sufi practices, which was named after the town (*qaṣba*) Deoband north of Delhi where they had founded their *Dār al-ʿUlūm* in 1867. They shared the ideas of the majority of Ahl-i Ḥadīth scholars with regard to miracles and eschatology, but who as Ḥanafīs and Māturīdīs rejected their corporeal concept of God.[43]

For Thanāʾ Allāh the fact that he deviated from the exegesis of the *salaf* posed no major problem. He insisted that it was permissible to pass over what the first generations had to say. According to him the excellence of the *salaf* was exclusively due to their loyalty to the prophet not to their superior knowledge, hence everybody with a sound knowledge of Arabic is entitled to interpret the Koran.[44] This idea is also the reason for the title of his Arabic commentary *Tafsīr al-qurʾān bi-kalām al-raḥmān* (Interpretation of the Koran With the Words of the Compassionate (God)), suggesting that his interpretation is based on the general linguistic conventions of the Holy Book. Furthermore he defended his understanding of *istiwāʾ* with extensive references to leading figures from various branches of Islamic thought. Did the imams of the four schools of law as well as al-Juwaynī (1028–1085), al-Ghazālī (1058–1111) and Ibn Taymiy-

40 Amritsarī, *Tafsīr al-Qurʾān bi-kalām al-Raḥmān* (1st ed.), Amritsar 1902, p. 56, ll. 14–15. In this case he is again at odds even with al-Rāzī, *al-Tafsīr al-kabīr*, vol. 8, p. 30, l. 5 - p. 32, l. 10.

41 Amritsarī, *Tafsīr al-Qurʾān bi-kalām al-Raḥmān* (2nd ed.), p. 120, ll. 17–19; Amritsarī, *Tafsīr-i Thanāʾī*, vol. 3, pp. 104–106.

42 Amritsarī, *Tafsīr al-Qurʾān bi-kalām al-Raḥmān* (1st ed.), p. 436, l. 13.

43 Ghaznawī, *Kitāb al-Arbaʿīn*, pp. 29, 31 and especially 54–55: signatures of Rashīd Aḥmad Gangohī and Maḥmūd al-Ḥasan.

44 Amritsarī, Thanāʾ Allāh: *Āyāt-i mutashābihāt?*, Amritsar 1904, pp. 30–31.

ya not agree upon the fact that the Koranic expressions for God's attributes may not be specified (*bi-lā kayf*)? He passed over the fact that these different scholars used the same phrase to legitimize totally different concepts. Unlike Thanā᾽ Allāh suggested, Ibn Taymiyya explicitly rejected the interpretation of *istiwā᾽* as *istīlā᾽* (also "to rule", but usually "to take over rule") with reference to the very *bayt* the Indian "*muṣannif*–publisher" quoted to justify his interpretation. According to the latter the verb has to be understood ingressively in the given context: Bishr takes power, which he did not possess before. Of course such a statement is clearly unacceptable with regard to God.[45] For al-Ghazālī *bi-lā kayf* implied the rejection of corporealism instead.[46] By quoting Abū Muslim al-Iṣfahānī (d. 934) as authority for his interpretations Thanā᾽ Allāh provoked the most hostile reactions, because this scholar, whose ideas are only known from citations by Shii authors in particular, was a Muʿtazilī (in)famous for his strong tendency to allegorize. But Thanā᾽ Allāh declared that the general affiliation of a particular author with a heretical movement does not as such undermine the value of his single statements. If they accord to the Koran and the general conventions of the Arabic language their interpretations ought to be accepted.[47]

In general al-Ghazālī and al-Rāzī (d. 1210) were the authorities whom Thanā᾽ Allāh most often referred to. In spite of all their differences they had consciously engaged in the intellectual struggle with philosophy. In this context they both stressed that a strong line should be drawn between the exegesis of the Koran and issues raised by science. For al-Ghazālī whoever insists that scriptural evidence overrules findings gained by geometrical evidence does a disservice to religion for he ridicules it in the eyes of the educated, whereas al-Rāzī insisted that the main intention of the Koran is to teach religious duties (*takālīf*) not astronomy. For Thanā᾽ Allāh's opponents these role models were one more reason to denounce him. His staunchest enemy, ʿAbd al-Aḥad Khānpūrī (1852–1928), who was, due to his fierce polemics and harsh

45 Ibn Taymiyya, *Majmūʿ al-Fatāwā*, vol. 5, pp. 144, 226, 232; *al-ʿAqīda al-ḥamawiyya*, p. 53; al-Shawkānī justified his non-literal interpretation of *istiwā᾽* with this verse; al-Shawkānī, Muḥammad b. ʿAlī: *Fatḥ al-qadīr*, vol. 2, p. 219, vol. 3, p. 66.

46 Al-Ghazālī, Muḥammad b. ʿAlī, Abū Ḥāmid: *Iljām al-ʿawāmm min ʿilm al-kalām*, Miṣr 1350/1931–32, pp. 2, 5, 30.

47 Amritsarī, Thanā᾽ Allāh: *al-Kalām al-mubīn bi-jawāb al-arbaʿīn*, Amritsar 1904, p. 15.

behavior, nicknamed as "Ibn Taymiyya of Rawalpindi"[48] with reference to his place of residence wrote a 450 page attack on Thanā' Allāh, motivated by his opinion that in the India of his day the efforts of Ibn Ḥanbal had to be repeated. Hence he wanted to subject Thanā' Allāh to "the judgment of Ibn Taymiyya",[49] who extensively criticized al-Ghazālī and al-Rāzī for partially accepting philosophical arguments. He mainly attacked Thanā' Allāh's stance on *ʿuluww* and *fawqiyya*. By ridding God of his attributes, he declared, Thanā' Allāh deprives him of his divinity.[50] But apart from that the vitriolic diatribe consisted mainly of unfounded allegations such as the denial of the Judgment and the Resurrection[51] or God's will because the "philosopher" Thanā' Allāh allegedly considers him someone who makes the existence of something necessary due to his own essence (*mūjib bil-dhāt*).[52]

The harsh opposition of many scholars did not at all isolate Thanā' Allāh among the Ahl-i Ḥadīth. To outsiders he even became their main representative, thanks to his magazine *Haftroza Ahl-i Ḥadīth* (published without major interruption from 1904–1947, possibly a unique case among South Asian Islamic periodicals) and his leading role in Ahl-i Ḥadīth organizations. He founded the All India Ahl-i Ḥadīth Conference in 1912. The first initiatives in this direction date back to 1906, hence to those years in which the conflict on Koran exegesis (*tafsīr*) began.[53] Furthermore he was a religious scholar whom the Muslim educational organizations throughout India liked to invite to lecture at their annual sessions. Notably both his activities as a magazine editor and his efforts to create an effective organizational structure for the Ahl-i Ḥadīth were directed at non-scholars whose participation in the affairs of the community Thanā' Allāh encouraged. In addition to his activities among the Ahl-i Ḥadīth Thanā' Allāh was an ardent supporter of the many local associations (most of them called *anjuman-i islāmiyya*) which consisted mainly of businessmen, professionals and members of the civil service who intended to overcome the

48 For a biography see Khānpūrī, Muḥammad ʿAbd Allāh: *Tadhkira-i ʿulamā'-i Khānpūr*, Lahore 1985, pp. 35–142, on his battlesome behaviour, here pp. 132–134.

49 Khānpūrī, ʿAbd al-Aḥad: *Kitāb al-Tawḥīd wal-sunna fī radd al-ilḥād wal-bidʿa*, Rāwalpindī n. d., p. 3.

50 Ibid., pp. 11–13, 36–37, 42.

51 Ibid., pp. 140, 252–254.

52 Ibid., p. 139.

53 Riexinger, *S̱anā'ullāh Amritsarī*, pp. 513–521.

educational gap separating the Muslims from the Sikhs and the Hindus in particular as well as the resulting under-representation of Muslims in the civil service, the professions and the business community. For this reason they propagated secular education among the Muslims and they collected funds for the establishment of educational institutions which would end the dependence on schools and colleges operated by Christian missionaries or Āryā Samāj, a Hindu reform movement (see below). Against this the party of his opponents consisted mainly of scholars who were reinforced by a few lay figures with a high social standing. For them secular learning was not a major concern.[54]

The fact that Thanāʾ Allāh and his opponents addressed two different audiences is the main clue to understanding the ambivalent relationship between the modernization of Islamic societies and the rising influence of Ibn Taymiyya in the intellectual field. In his introduction to Ibn Taymiyya's refutation of the Greek logicians Hallaq argues that Ibn Taymiyya's argument that logical conclusions can never generate content resembles the intellectual foundation of Western empiricism. Although Hallaq misses the decisive point completely, his argument contains a kernel of truth. For Hume and his ilk the alternative to deductive reasoning is empirical, for Ibn Taymiyya it is scriptural evidence. But insofar Ibn Taymiyya and al-Shawkānī insist that any legal ruling has to be justified before the laymen with a proof text, their position strengthens the laymen with regard to the scholar who can no longer claim authority based on conclusions comprehensible exclusively to a learned elite. In this respect one might indeed see parallels with the development of a meritocratic understanding of religious office during the Reformation.[55]

Whereas in the field of law the insistence on proof texts appealed to those claiming intellectual maturity due to their secular education, in the field of theology and *tafsīr* the application of the same scripturalist principle would imply the rejection of fundamental scientific findings, not only such that have been made in the West since 1500, because the corporeal concept of God implies elements of the Sunna-cosmology, especially the notion of seven worlds layered one above the other, and

54 On the social background of the dispute see Riexinger, Martin: How Favourable is Puritan Islam to Modernity. A Case Study on the Ahl-i Hadis in British India, in: Gwilym Beckerlegge (ed.): *Colonialism, Modernity and Religious Identities. Religious Reform Movements in South Asia*, New Delhi and New York 2008, pp. 147–165.

55 See Reinhardt, *Tyrannei der Tugend*, pp. 255–256.

of seven heavens at the top of which Paradise, the Footstool and the Throne are located "above everything created", just above an ocean (*baḥr*). Earth itself is a sphere, but surrounded for the largest part by water, which implies that God can be considered to reside literally "high above" all mankind (*ʿuluww, fawqiyya*). This holds true even if Ibn Taymiyya did not subscribe to concepts like the origin of rain in an ocean in the heavens, or that the Earth rests on the mountain Qāf and even though his explanation for the angel Raʿd's voice is ambiguous: thunder may be his voice but the idea that it is generated in the clouds themselves is no contradiction, because every movement in the upper and the lower world is brought about by angels.[56] However, such ideas were propagated by Thanāʾ Allāh's opponents as Ibn Taymiyya's position and propagated under the label *tafsīr al-salaf*[57] whereas he wanted to avoid an embarrassment for Islam in the age of expanding secular education. Unlike the aggressive reactions of his opponents make believe Thanāʾ Allāh was far from radical in this respect. He did not accept that Earth orbits around the sun before the 1940s although he always disputed that this issue was a matter of belief and unbelief.[58] Furthermore he devoted extensive space to polemics against the much more radical interpretations of certain *āyas* by the *necharī* Sayyid Aḥmad Khān.[59]

56 Ibn Taymiyya, *Majmūʿ al-Fatāwā*, vol. 6, pp. 550–559, 586, 596–597 (cosmology in general); vol. 24, pp. 262–262 (*raʿd*, rain). Fakhr al-Dīn al-Rāzī presents the spherical nature of Earth as the 13th (and shortest) reason to reject the literal interpretation of *istiwāʾ* (*Tafsīr al-kabīr*, vol. 14, p. 109, ll. 13–14). On Sunna-cosmology in general see Heinen, Anton: *Islamic Cosmology. A Study of as-Suyūṭī's* al-Hay'a as-Saniyya fī l-hay'a as-sunniyya, Stuttgart 1982; Radtke, Bernd: *Weltgeschichte und Weltbeschreibung im mittelalterlichen Islam*, Stuttgart 1992.

57 An illustrative example of extremely conservative attitudes is a controversy in the magazine *Haft Roza Ahl-i Ḥadīth* lasting from February 1938 until July 1939. For his opponents see Riexinger, *Ṣanāʾullāh Amritsarī*, pp. 381–384.

58 Ibid., pp. 375–378.

59 Christian W. Troll who is unaware of the controversy stirred by Thanāʾ Allāh's *Tafsīr al-qurʾān* stresses exclusively this aspect, see Christian W. Troll: A Note on the *Tafsīr-i Thanāʾī* of Thanā Allāh Amritsārī and His Criticism of Sayyid Aḥmad Khān's Tafsīr-i Aḥmadī, in: *Islamic Culture* 59 (1984), pp. 29–44; *necharī* is the common term for Sayyid Aḥmad Khān because he taught that there is no difference between the "Work of God" and the "Word of God" and that the Koran should hence be interpreted in accordance with the laws of *nature*. His terminology (he uses the English words in Urdu texts) betrays the influence of English deism: Riexinger, Martin: South Asian Muslim Responses to the Theory of Evolution, in: *Die Welt des Islams* 49 (2009), pp. 212–247, here p. 217.

But it was not the intellectual comfort of the *taʿlīm yāfte* (those with a secular education) alone that motivated Thanāʾ Allāh to deviate from the teachings of Ibn Taymiyya. His prominence among the Ahl-i Ḥadīth and the high esteem of a larger part of the Muslim public was also due to his role as a controversialist who successfully confronted "heretics" like the Aḥmadīs and the Ahl-i Qurʾān (deniers of Hadith) on the one hand and proselytizing non-Muslims like the Christian missionaries and the Hindu reformists of the Āryā Samāj on the other in public debates (*munāẓaras*).[60] The latter deviated from the traditional non-proselytism of Hinduism and tried to "reconvert" Indian Muslims and Christians in a purification ceremony called *shuddʰī*.[61] In order to achieve this aim they denounced both monotheist religions as assemblages of irrational nonsense. In the case of Islam they ridiculed *āyas* implying cosmological statements, by suggesting that they were commonly understood literally. In his famous *munāẓaras* the records of which were published as booklets, he demonstrated that the respective terms were literary conventions of the Arab language. His most famous anti-Āryā pamphlet *Turk-i Islām ba-jawāb-i Tark-i Islām* is a refutation of many literal interpretations on which his opponents insisted.[62]

But Thanāʾ Allāh's approach to the Āryās was not purely defensive with regard to cosmology, instead he attacked their core beliefs not because they are at odds with the Koran but because they allegedly contradict "science" (*sāʾins*) and "reason". In order to unmask the idea of the pre-eternity of matter and the soul he took recourse to the argumentation of classical *kalām*, according to which everything that carries a form, has changing qualities or is composed, is contingent and can

60 Riexinger, *Sanāʾullāh Amritsarī*, pp. 229–336; actually Thanāʾ Allāh's frequent success as controversialist (*munāẓir*) contributed significantly to the acceptance of the once despised Ahl-i Ḥadīth by the Muslim community in general.

61 On the Āryā Samāj in general Jones, Kenneth W.: *Arya Dharm. Hindu Consciousness in the 19th Century Punjab*, Cambridge 1976; Llewellyn, John E.: *The Arya Samaj as a Fundamentalist Movement. A Study in Comparative Fundamentalism*, Delhi 1993. On the impact of the *shuddʰī* campaigns on Muslim public see Sikand, Yoginder: *The Origins of Development of the Tablighi Jama'at. A Cross-country Comparative Study*, Hyderabad 2002, pp. 26–32, 50–54, 62–63; Riexinger, *Sanāʾullāh Amritsarī*, pp. 281–295.

62 The book is directed against the pamphlet *Tark-i Islām* by the ex-Muslim Dʰarampal, whom Thanāʾ Allāh and his associates could regain for Islam later. "Turk" stands for the Central Asian soldier spreading Islam in India. At the same time it alludes to the use of the word as common term of abuse for Muslims among Hindus.

hence not be pre-eternal.[63] This idea which was commonly considered as Ashʿarī by Indian Muslims at that time, was originally brought forth by Abū al-Hudhayl (d. 841).[64] Mostly used to prove the necessity of a non-contingent God for the creation of contingent beings, it was used by al-Ghazālī, Thanāʾ Allāh's big role model, to refute the philosphers' concept of the eternity of matter.[65] Ibn Taymiyya[66] and Ibn al-Qayyim[67] on the contrary completely rejected this argument, insisting that if it was impossible for something pre-eternal to acquire temporal attributes then God could not have a confined body and he could not adopt a specific spatial relation (*jiha*) to anything created like the throne.

This strong literalist tendency among the Ahl-i Ḥadīth which can be traced back to their reception of Ibn Taymiyya, highlights one aspect that is usually passed over, whenever puritan Islamic movements and Protestantism, Calvinism in particular, are equated: the totally different approach to secular learning with its consequences for the interpretation of the sacred scripture. Calvin did not consider the Bible a handbook of astronomy. Therefore he argued in favour of allegorical interpretation when particular verses were at odds with astronomical findings. Hence, he might rather be regarded as a counterpart of al-Ghazālī than of Ibn Taymiyya in this respect. According to Hooykaas this approach of Calvin facilitated, the reformer's objection to Copernicus notwithstanding, the reception and acceptance of heliocentrism and enabled the countries where his theology flourished to take the lead in the development of science in the West.[68]

63 Amritsārī, Thanāʾ Allāh: *Uṣūl-i Āryā*, Amritsar 1929, pp. 8–15; Amritsārī, Thanāʾ Allāh: *Ḥaqq-i Prakāsh ba-jawāb-i satyārt*[h] *prakāsh*, Amritsar 1928, pp. 41–42.

64 Ess, Josef van: *Theologie und Gesellschaft im 2. und 3. Jahrhundert Hidschra. Eine Geschichte des religiösen Denkens im frühen Islam*, Berlin and New York 1991, vol. 3, p. 231.

65 Al-Ghazālī, Abū Ḥāmid: *Tahāfut al-falāsifa*, ed. by Sulaymān Dunyā, Cairo 1980, pp. 143–144.

66 Shāh Walī Allāh Dihlawī: *al-Inṣāf fī bayān asbāb al-ikhtilāf*, Cairo 1950, vol. 1, p. 68, vol. 4, pp. 268–269.

67 Ibn Qayyim al-Jawziyya, Shams al-Dīn: *Ijtimāʿ al-juyūsh al-islāmiyya ʿalā ghazw al-muʿaṭṭila wal-jahmiyya*, Mecca and Riyadh 1996, pp. 68–69. This book which is for the most part a listing of sayings of the *ṣaḥāba*, *tābiʿūn* and *atbāʿ al-tābiʿīn*, takes a surprising turn in the last chapter where Ibn al-Qayyim shows that Ibn Rushd al-Ḥafīd (*al-Kashf ʿan manāhij al-adilla*, in: Ibn Rushd, Abū l-Walīd Muḥammad: *Falsafat Ibn Rushd*, Beirut 1982, pp. 83–84) has demonstrated the impossibility of the existence of something without confinement.

68 Calvinus, Iohannes: *Mosis libri V cum Iohannis Calvini Commentariis*, Geneva 1558, p. 6; Hooykaas, Reijer: *Religion and the Rise of Modern Science*, Edin-

3. The Development of the Controversy and Its Settlement at the Islamic World Conference in 1926

His strong position among the laymen and the Islamic public in general notwithstanding, Thanāʾ Allāh had to suffer setbacks whenever he confronted an audience consisting of Ahl-i Ḥadīth scholars. The controversy should have been settled in 1904 at a major convention in the Ahl-i Ḥadīth stronghold Arrah (province of Bihar). However Thanāʾ Allāh simply ignored the mediation and continued in the same vein. Therefore a second attempt at mediation was prepared at the meeting of the All India Ahl-i Ḥadīth Conference at Madras 14 years later. Whereas Thanāʾ Allāh pledged to follow the method of the *muḥaddithūn*, his opponents promised to abstain from denouncing him as beyond the pale of the Ahl-i Ḥadīth. This mediation was again to no avail because Thanāʾ Allāh regarded it as licence to continue as he pleased. This behaviour motivated ʿAbd al-Aḥād Khānpūrī as one of those who had signed the agreement as a representative of Thanāʾ Allāh's opponents, to write his 450 page attack against the alleged heretic. Finally the controversy calmed down due to the mediation of an outsider and probably because certain arguments of Thanāʾ Allāh's opponents had become less and less convincing.[69]

To understand this we must take a short glimpse at Thanāʾ Allāh's political attitudes. Before World War I he was a pro-British loyalist. Therefore he shunned any association with the Saudi Wahhabis, because sympathy for them was considered seditious by the colonial authorities.[70] However, at the end of World War I he changed into an ardent nationalist because of his abhorrence at the anti-Ottoman policies of the British. He became a leading figure of the Khilafat committee in Punjab. This political organisation was made up primarily of Deobandī and Ahl-i Ḥadīth scholars strove for the preservation

burgh 1972, pp. 117–134; Crottet, Bernard: *Calvin. Biographie*, Paris 1995, p. 290–291. Rienk Vermij (*The Calvinist Copernicans. The Reception of the New Astronomy in the Dutch Republic; 1575–1750*, Amsterdam 2002, pp. 239–333), stresses, however, that the resistance to post Copernican astronomy in the Dutch Reformed Church was much stronger than Hooykaas' presentation suggests. Nevertheless, he too confirms that the advocates of the new astronomy took recourse to Calvin's arguments to justify their approach; MacCulloch, *Reformation*, pp. 685–688.

69 Riexinger, *S̱anāʾullāh Amritsarī*, pp. 356–364.

70 Ibid., p. 523.

of the Ottoman Caliphate, and for this purpose cooperated with the Hindu dominated Indian National Congress whereas it shunned the traditionally pro-British Muslim elite.[71] The emergence of the ʿAbd al-ʿAzīz b. Saʿūd as major antagonists of the Hashimites, whom many Indian Muslims regarded as puppets of the British, led Thanāʾ Allāh to renounce his earlier anti-Wahhabi stance in 1924. In his publications he defended their policy which had caused hostile reactions among Indian Shiis and Sufi-oriented Muslims because of the destruction of the graves of many highly esteemed if not venerated figures from the history of Islam. When Ibn ʿAbd al-ʿAzīz summoned the Islamic World Conference in Mecca in 1926 Thanāʾ Allāh headed a delegation of the Ahl-i Ḥadīth (one of three delegations from India, the other two were sent by the Jamʿiyyat ul-ʿulamāʾ-i Hind and the Khilafat Committee, the latter being very critical of Saudi policies). His opponents among the Ahl-i Ḥadīth at home were shocked because they regarded themselves as the true allies of the new guardians of the Holy Places. Therefore they immediately organised a delegation of their own in order to counter Thanāʾ Allāh's attempt to pose as the foremost representative of their school of thought. They attempted to discredit him by alerting the Wahhabi scholars to his contentious *tafsīr*.

Finally the parties agreed to settle their dispute via mediation by the king. In the meanwhile both had gained eminent supporters. As had to be expected the Wahhabi *ʿulamāʾ* as well as Ḥasan b. Yūsuf, the Ḥanbalī mufti of Damascus, sided with the Ghaznawīs whereas Thanāʾ Allāh's position was defended by the most important journalistic ally of the *amīr*, Muḥammad Rashīd Riḍā (1865–1935), the Lebanese born editor of the Cairo-based reformist magazine *al-Manār* (1898–1935). ʿAbd al-ʿAzīz b. Saʿūd avoided to side with one party and issued a declaration in which he ordered them to renew the earlier pact.[72]

---

71 Ibid., pp. 449–458; on this movement in general Minault, Gail: *The Khilafat Movement. Religious Symbolism and Political Mobilization in India*, New York 1999.

72 Amritsarī, *Tafsīr al-Qurʾān bi-kalām al-Raḥmān* (2nd ed.), backcover, reproduced in Riexinger, *Sanāʾullāh Amritsarī*, p. 643; it is worthy to note that in the context of a refutation of "Shiism and Zaydism" ʿAbd Allāh b. Muḥammad b. ʿAbd al-Wahhāb (*Jawāb ʿalā al-shīʿa wal-zaydiyya*, in: Rashīd Riḍā, Muḥammad (ed.): *Majmūʿat al-Tawḥīd*, Cairo 1346/1927, pp. 128–159) dedicates a considerable amount of attention – an attack on "jahmism" as arch-heresy included – to the refutation of the allegorical interpretation of the *istiwāʾ* and other attributes of God; on Rashīd Riḍā and his relations with the Saudis: Boberg, Dirk: *Ägypten, Naǧd und der Ḥiǧāz. Eine Untersuchung zum religiös-politischen Verhält-*

The affair did not calm down in the immediate aftermath. Thanā' Allāh demonstrated that he had found an eminent supporter abroad. Thanā' Allāh's son ʿAṭā' Allāh sent Rashīd Riḍā an extensive request for a legal opinion (*istiftā'*) written by Thanā' Allāh's best friend and most important collaborator Ibrāhīm Mīr Siyālkothī (d. 1874–1956), in which he asked whether the metaphorical interpretation of *istiwā'* as proposed by the speculative theologians (*mutakallimūn*) was acceptable. Rashīd Riḍā endorsed their point of view and justified his position also with references to figures revered by the Ahl-i Ḥadīth such as al-Shawkānī and Walī Allāh.[73] In 1930 he advertised in *al-Manār* that the new edition of the *Tafsīr al-qur'ān bi-kalām ar-raḥmān* was available from his office.[74]

Thanā' Allāh's opponents bothered to demonstrate that he misinterpreted the spirit of the mediation document. ʿAbd al-Aḥad wrote a pamphlet titled *al-Fayṣla al-ḥijāziyya al-sulṭāniyya bayn ahl al-sunna wal-jahmiyya al-thanā'iyya* (The Hijazi Decision by the Sultan between the Followers of the Prophetic Tradition and the Thanā'ian Jahmism) in which he drew again the conclusion that Thanā' Allāh was a "heretic to be decapitated" (*zindīq maʿnūq*). Finally, in 1929 Thanā' Allāh and his main opponents the Ghaznawīs signed a pledge to abstain from further defamations which they finally both kept.[75]

4. Beyond the Punjab: The Global Significance of a Local Conflict

The line of conflict in this controversy can be summed up as follows: a scholar coming from a tradition imbued with the ideas of Ibn Taymiyya

nis zwischen Ägypten und den Wahhābiten, 1923–1936, anhand von in Kairo veröffentlichten pro- und antiwahhābitischen Streitschriften und Presseberichten, Frankfurt/Main 1991; see also Ende, Werner: Rashīd Riḍā, Muḥammad, in: *EI*², vol. 8 (1994), pp. 446–448 and Jomier, Jacques: al-Manār, in: *EI*², vol. 6, pp. 360–361; Yasushi, Kosugi: *al-Manār* Revisited. The „Lighthouse" of the Islamic Revival, in: Stéphane A. Dudoignon and Komatsu Hisao (eds.): *Intellectuals in the Modern Islamic World. Transmission, Transformation, Communication*, Abingdon 2006, pp. 3–39.

73 Istiftā' fī fatwā wa-ṭalab iqrāriha wa-taṣḥīḥiha, in: *al-Manār* 28 (1927/1928), pp. 261–271.

74 Taqrīẓ al-maṭbūʿāt al-jadīda, in: *al-Manār* 31 (1930/1931), pp. 396–397.

75 Riexinger, *Sanā'ullāh Amritsarī*, p. 362. ʿAbd al-Aḥad did not realize that *fayṣla* (decision/judgment) does not exist in Arabic.

had to distance himself from the latter's theology when he addressed an audience from the newly emerging middle class with secular education. In the 1920s a conflict with similar characteristics arose in the realm of the future Saudi kings. The fact that the ʿAbd al-ʿAzīz did not fully endorse the position of the Wahhabi *ʿulamāʾ* with regard to Thanāʾ Allāh's *tafsīr* reflects that the new Saudi administration had to come to terms with a similar problem when it started a secular system of education in the mid 1920s. The Egyptian Salafi Ḥāfiẓ Wahba, one of the ruler's key advisors, recounts that he was taken aback by the ultra-conservative mindset of the *ʿulamāʾ* on the Arabian Peninsula which reminded him of the European Middle Ages. According to him, many scholars protested vehemently against geography text-books which did not accord to the concepts of Sunna-cosmology.[76] In the Saudi case the creation of an administrative élite fitting the most important needs of a modern state, demanded that certain elements had to be introduced into the system of education which did not conform to Ibn Taymiyya's worldview. Therefore it may be suspected that Ibn ʿAbd al-ʿAzīz regarded attempts to accommodate Salafi creeds to the exigencies of a modern state and secular education with some sympathy.[77] As a result of Ibn ʿAbd al-ʿAzīz's reforms *jahmī* thought seems to have made considerably inroads into the staunchest Wahhabi circles. Today even in this milieu the interpretation of *istiwāʾ* as physical sitting is no longer defended. ʿAbd al-ʿAzīz Ibn Bāz (d. 1999), chief mufti of Saudi Arabia and (in)famous for his 1964 fatwa in which he declares everybody claiming that Earth orbits around the sun an unbeliever (*kāfir*) merely interprets the term as attribute of God's governance, because even he had given up the idea of compact heavens.[78]

Like those who came from a tradition imbued by the ideas of Ibn Taymiyya, and wanted to accommodate it to modern challenges, the

76 Wahba, Hafiz: *Arabian Days*, London 1964, pp. 48–52.

77 Salmān Sulaymān Manṣūrpūrī (1867–1930), a lawyer, civil servant and one of Thanāʾ Allāh's most prominent lay supporters was according to his son invited to serve in the administration of the kingdom, however, he died during the passage (Manṣūrpūrī, Salmān Sulaymān and Manṣūrpūrī, ʿAbd al-Bāqī: *Safarnāma-i ḥijāz maʿahu sīrat-i Salmān*, Lahore n. d., p. 278).

78 Ibn Bāz, ʿAbd al-ʿAzīz: *al-Adilla al-naqliyya wal-ḥissiyya ʿalā imkān al-ṣuʿūd ilā al-kawākib wa-ʿalā jarayān al-shams wal-qamar wa-sukūn al-arḍ*, Riyadh 1982, pp. 7–17; on the controversy stirred by this fatwa: Ende, Werner: Religion, Politik und Literatur in Saudi-Arabien. Der geistesgeschichtliche Hintergrund der heutigen religiösen und kulturpolitischen Situation, in: *Orient* 22 (1981), pp. 377–390; 23 (1982), pp. 21–35, 378–393, here pp. 381–385.

modernists who praised him as their role model in fact chose a rather selective approach. Rashīd Riḍā admired the legal theory of Ibn Taymiyya,[79] appreciated his opposition against most aspects of Sufism and even praised him and Ibn Ḥanbal for defending the integrity of Islamic beliefs against the influx of non-Islamic ideas.[80] However the stance he took on the interpretation of the Koran exposes this adulation as lip service, because he cautiously avoided any reference to their exegetical concepts when he had to cope with concrete issues like the *istiwāʾ*.[81] When readers asked for his counsel with regard to the interpretation of cosmological verses, he denied the validity of the respective Hadiths and claimed – alluding to al-Ghazālī like Thanāʾ Allāh

79 Rashīd Riḍā, Muḥammad: Tafsīr al-Qurʾān, *al-Manār* 9 (1906/07), p. 44; 18 (1915), pp. 321–352, here pp. 342–344, 327–329, 334–336. The outstanding example for the influence of Ibn Qayyim al-Jawziyya is the fictional *Muḥāwarat al-muṣliḥ wal-muqallid* (Dialogue between a Reformer and an Imitator) resp. *Munāẓara bayn al-muqallid wa-ṣāḥib ḥujja* (Debate between an Imitator and the Possessor of a Proof), which *al-Manār* began to publish when Muḥammad ʿAbduh was still alive: Riexinger, *Sanāʾullāh Amritsarī*, p. 53. Similar texts were also produced by the Ahl-i Ḥadīth: Anonymous: Taqlīd awr ʿamal bil-ḥadīth, in: *Haft Roza Ahl-i Ḥadīth*, Nov. 15/22 (1912), pp. 6–8; ul-Mulk, Muḥsin: *Taqlīd awr ʿamal bil-ḥadīth*, Amritsar 1909, pp. 57–59. This author (1837–1907) was the successor of Sayyid Aḥmad Khān as director of the Anglo-Muhammadan College at Aligarh; Riexinger, *Sanāʾullāh Amritsarī*, pp. 171–173. These texts follow the model of Ibn Qayyim al-Jawziyya, Shams al-Dīn: *Iʿlām al-muwaqqiʿīn*, Cairo 1374/1955, vol. 2, pp. 182–196. However, Rashīd Riḍā's *muḥāwara* differs in so far he proceeds from reforms in legal theory to social reform and political awareness, on this also: Skovgaard-Petersen, Jakob: Portrait of the Intellectual as a Young Man. Rashīd Riḍā's *Muḥāwarat al-muṣliḥ wal-muqallid* (1906), in: *Islam and Christian-Muslim Relations* 12 (2001) pp. 93–104; via *al-Manār* these fictional discussions became also popular among Ottoman Turkish Islamic intellectuals: Anonymous: Muhavara, bir muhakkık ile mukallid arasında, in: *Sebilürreşad* 222 (Nov. 11, 1328), pp. 250–252, 223; (Dec. 6, 1328), pp. 265–268; see also Uçar, Bülent: *Recht als Mittel zur Reform von Religion und Gesellschaft. Die türkische Debatte um die Scharia und die Rechtsschulen im 20. Jahrhundert*, Würzburg 2005, p. 139; another approach in legal theory which Rashīd Riḍā appreciated like the Ahl-i Ḥadīth were the Ẓāhirī ideas of Ibn Ḥazm and al-Shawkānī: Rashīd Riḍā, Muḥammad: al-Asʾila al-jāwiyya fī samāḥat al-lahw, in: *al-Manār* 9 (1906/1907), pp. 35–51, here pp. 37, 43–44; Rashīd Riḍā, Muḥammad: Ḥukm man radda kalām al-ulamāʾ alladhī lā dalāl ʿalayhi, in: *al-Manār* 9 (1906/1907), pp. 139–147, here pp. 144–147; Rashīd Riḍā, Muḥammad, Tafsīr al-Qurʾān, in: *al-Manār* 9 (1906/1907), pp. 327–328, 334–342; Rashīd Riḍā, Muḥammad: Uṣūl al-fiqh ʿinda al-Ẓāhiriyya, in: *al-Manār* 18 (1915), pp. 379–386, 423–431.

80 Preface to al-Sahaswānī, *Ṣiyānat al-insān*, pp. 7–9.

81 Rashīd Riḍā, Muḥammad: *Tafsīr al-Qurʾān al-ḥakīm al-shahīr bi-tafsīr al-Manār*, n.p. 1973, vol. 8, pp. 451–453.

did – that anybody arguing against scientific findings with reference to the literal meaning of verses from the Koran would embarrass Islam instead of defending it.[82]

In the South Asian context Abū al-Kalām Āzād praised Ibn Taymiyya as outstanding intellectual hero who dismantled the arguments of the Muʿtazilīs and philosophers as no one else had done before and he equated his intellectual struggle to Ibn Ḥanbal's resistance to the "pagan" ideas supported by the caliph al-Ma'mūn.[83] His image of these two figures and other puritan authors betray unmistakably that he was acquainted with the "invented tradition" of the Ahl-i Ḥadīth, in particular with the respective writings of Ṣiddīq Ḥasan Khān. However, like Rashīd Riḍā he too avoided any reference to the theologians he praised when he interpreted the Koran. In fact, his ideas were even more radical than those of the editor of *al-Manār*. Teaching that the Koran did not deal at all with scientific issues he rejected literalist interpretations and he even accepted the theory of evolution which Rashīd Riḍā rejected.[84] Decades later the Pakistani modernist Fazlur Rahman displayed an equally inconsistent attitude. On the one hand he applauded Ibn Taymiyya as opponent of Sufism, which he saw as the root cause for the prevailing passivity in the Muslim world (see above). On the other hand to free Islamic thought from the limitations enforced by the Hadith was the major objective of Fazlur Rahman.[85]

---

82 Rashīd Riḍā, Muḥammad: Ithbāt istidārat al-arḍ wa-dawrāniha min al-qur'ān, in: *al-Manār* 7 (1904/05), pp. 260–262; Rashīd Riḍā, Muḥammad: As'ila min Jāwah/Ajwibat al-Manār, in: *al-Manār* 12 (1909/10), pp. 260–270, here pp. 260, 269–270; Rashīd Riḍā, Muḥammad: ʿIlm al-hay'a wal-sunna al-nabawiyya, in: *al-Manār* 13 (1910/11), pp. 117–119; Rashīd Riḍā, Muḥammad: Ḥarakat al-arḍ wa-dawarāniha, in: *al-Manār* 13 (1910/11), p. 119. These fatwas show, that also in the Middle East and South East Asia, where some of the petitioners (*mustaftīs*) resided, the interpretation of cosmological verses of the Koran was a contentious issue before World War I.

83 Khānpūrī, Muḥammad ʿAbd Allāh, *Tadhkira-i ʿulamā'*, pp. 175–177, 222–224, 245–246.

84 Āzād, Abū l-Kalām: Madhhab-i nushū' u irtiqā kā ek ṣafḥa, in: *al-Hilāl* (Dec. 10, 1913), pp. 14–16; (Dec. 17, 1913), pp. 8–9. Rashīd Riḍā did not accept the theory of evolution, however, he refused to denounce someone who did so as an unbeliever: Rashīd Riḍā, Muḥammad: Naẓariyyat Dārwīn wal-islām, in: *al-Manār* 30 (1930/31), pp. 593–600; Rashīd Riḍā, Muḥammad: Iḥtiḍār madhhab ʿilmī, in: *al-Manār* 31 (1931/32), pp. 131–134; Rashīd Riḍā, Muḥammad: al-Maqāl al-thālith ʿashar, in: *al-Manār* 33 (1933/34), pp. 58–64.

85 Rahman, Fazlur: *Islamic Methodology in History*, Islamabad 1995, pp. 27–84, esp. pp. 75, 80.

Whether Ibn Taymiyya would have tolerated such a selective approach is highly doubtful. He considered Islam as one coherent system combining a worldview and a legal system based on the revelation, that means the Sunna in particular,[86] and he tended to attack his opponents harshly and not to show reluctance to denounce opponents as unbelievers (*takfīr*). Whenever modernists want to liberate Islamic law from the boundaries imposed by the Hadith in order to make Islamic law more flexible or to overcome a literalist interpretation of the Koran and praise Ibn Taymiyya as well, their adulation should rather be regarded as a sign of naiveté than as proof for their intellectual affinity.

---

86 Nagel, Tilman: *Staat und Glaubensgemeinschaft im Islam*, Zürich 1981, vol. 2, pp. 109–140.

Bibliography

1. Primary Sources

[Pseudo-] Ibn Qayyim al-Ǧauziyya, Muḥammad b. Abī Bakr: *Über die Frauen. Liebeshistorien und Liebeserfahrung aus dem arabischen Mittelalter*, transl. by Johannes Bellmann, Leipzig and München 1986.

Ibn Qayyim al-Jawziah, Imam Allamah Shamsuddeen ibn abi Bakr: *Guideance to the Uncertain in Reply to the Jews and the Nazarenes*, translated by Abdelhay El-Masri, n. p. 1428/2007.

Ibn Qayyim al-Jawziyya: *al-Muhadhdhab min Madārij al-sālikīn*, Beirut 2005.

Ibn Qayyim al-Jawziyya: *Le paradis. Hadi el arwah ila bilad el afrah; résumé par Fdal Haja and trad. Hébri Bousserouel*, Paris 1995.

Ibn Qayyim al-Jawziyya: *Patience and Gratitude. An Abridged Translation of ʿUddat as-sabirin wa dhakhirat as-shakirin*, edited by ʿAbdassamad Clarke and Nasiruddin al-Khattab, London 1997, reprint 1998.

Ibn Qayyim al-Jawziyya: *The Soul's Journey After Death. An Abridgement of Ibn al-Qayyim's Kitab ar-Ruh with a Commentary of Layla Mabrouk*, London 1987.

Ibn Qayyim al-Jawziyya, Shams al-Dīn Muḥammad b. Abī Bakr: *Aḥkām ahl al-dhimma*, ed. by Ṣubḥī al-Ṣāliḥ, 2 vols., n. p. 1381/1961 (reprint Beirut 1401/1981).

Ibn Qayyim al-Jawziyya, Shams al-Dīn: *Aḥkām ahl al-dhimma*, 2 parts, ed. by Ṭāhā ʿAbd al-Raʾūf Saʿd, Beirut 1415/1995.

Ibn Qayyim al-Jawziyya, Shams al-Dīn: *Āthār al-imām Ibn Qayyim al-Jawziyya wa-mā laḥiqahā min aʿmāl. Ighāthat al-lahfān fī ḥukm ṭalāq al-ghaḍbān*, ed. by ʿAbd al-Raḥmān b. Ḥasan b. Qāʾid, Jeddah n. d.

Ibn Qayyim al-Jawziyya, Shams al-Dīn: *Badāʾiʿ al-fawāʾid*, ed. by ʿAlī b. Muḥammad al-ʿImrān, Jedda 1424/2003.

Ibn Qayyim al-Jawziyya, Shams al-Dīn: *al-Dāʾ wal-dawāʾ aw al-jawāb al-kāfī li-man saʾala ʿan al-dawāʾ al-shāfī*, ed. by ʿAbd al-Ghaffār Sulaymān al-Bundārī, Cairo 1411/1999.

Ibn Qayyim al-Jawziyya, Shams al-Dīn: *al-Fawāʾid*, ed. by Muṣṭafā b. al-ʿAdawī, Mansoura 1422/2001.

Ibn Qayyim al-Jawziyya, Shams al-Dīn: *al-Furūq al-nafsiyya bayn ṣifāt al-nafs al-ṭayyiba wal-khabītha*, ed. by Abū Ḥudhayfa Ibrāhīm b. Muḥammad, Ṭanṭā n. d.

Ibn Qayyim al-Jawziyya, Shams al-Dīn: *Ḥādī al-arwāḥ ilā bilād al-afrāḥ*, ed. by Ṭāhā ʿAbd al-Raʾūf Saʿd, Cairo n. d.

Ibn Qayyim al-Jawziyya, Shams al-Dīn: *Hidāyat al-ḥayārā fī ajwibat al-yahūd wal-naṣārā*, ed. by Abū ʿAbd al-Raḥmān ʿĀdil b. Saʿd, Cairo n. d.

Ibn Qayyim al-Jawziyya, Shams al-Dīn: *Hidāyat al-ḥayārā fī ajwibat al-yahūd wal-naṣārā*, ed. by Muḥammad Aḥmad al-Ḥājj, Damascus 1416/1996.

Ibn Qayyim al-Jawziyya, Shams al-Dīn: *Ibn Qayyim al-Jawziyya on the Invocation of God. Al-Wābil al-Ṣayyib min al-Kalim al-Ṭayyib*, transl. by Michael Abdurrahman Fitzgerald and Moulay Youssef Sitine, Cambridge 2000.

Ibn Qayyim al-Jawziyya, Shams al-Dīn: *Ighāthat al-lahfān min maṣāʾid al-shayṭān*, 2 vols., ed. by Muḥammad Ḥāmid al-Fiqī, Beirut n. d.

Ibn Qayyim al-Jawziyya, Shams al-Dīn: *Ighāthat al-lahfān min maṣāyid al-shayṭān*, ed. by Muḥammad Bayūmī, Cairo 1996.

Ibn Qayyim al-Jawziyya, Shams al-Dīn: *Ijtimāʿ al-juyūsh al-islāmiyya ʿalā ghazw al-muʿaṭṭila wal-jahmiyya*, Beirut 1404/1984.

Ibn Qayyim al-Jawziyya, Shams al-Dīn: *Ijtimāʿ al-juyūsh al-islāmiyya ʿalā ghazw al-muʿaṭṭila wal-jahmiyya*, Mecca and Riyadh 1996.

Ibn Qayyim al-Jawziyya, Shams al-Dīn: *Iʿlām al-muwaqqiʿīn*, 4 vols., Cairo 1374/1955.

Ibn Qayyim al-Jawziyya, Shams al-Dīn: *Iʿlām al-muwaqqiʿīn ʿan rabb al-ʿālamīn*, 4 vols., ed. by Muḥammad ʿAbd al-Salām Ibrāhīm, Beirut 1414/1993.

Ibn Qayyim al-Jawziyya, Shams al-Dīn: *al-Kāfiya al-shāfiya fī intiṣār al-firqa al-nājiya. Al-Qaṣīda al-nūniyya*, ed. by ʿAbd Allāh b. Muḥammad al-ʿUmayr, Riyadh 1416/1996.

Ibn Qayyim al-Jawziyya, Shams al-Dīn: *Madārij al-sālikīn*, 3 vols., ed. by ʿImād ʿĀṣ, Cairo 1416/1996.

Ibn Qayyim al-Jawziyya, Shams al-Dīn: *Madārij al-sālikīn fī manāzil iyyāka naʿbudu wa-iyyāka nastaʿīn*, 3 vols., Beirut n. d.

Ibn Qayyim al-Jawziyya, Shams al-Dīn: *Madārij al-sālikīn fī manāzil iyyāka naʿbudu wa-iyyāka nastaʿīn*, ed. by Muḥammad al-Fiqī, Beirut 1412/1992.

Ibn Qayyim al-Jawziyya, Shams al-Dīn: *Maḥabbat Allāh ʿazza wa-jalla*, Damascus and Beirut 2002.

Ibn Qayyim al-Jawziyya, Shams al-Dīn: *Miftāḥ dār al-saʿāda wa-manshūr wilāyat al-ʿilm wal-irāda*, ed. by Maḥmūd Ḥasan Rabīʿ, Cairo 1358/1939.

Ibn Qayyim al-Jawziyya, Shams al-Dīn: *Miftāḥ dār al-saʿāda wa-manshūr wilāyat al-ʿilm wal-irāda*, 2 vols., ed. by Sayyid Ibrāhīm and ʿAlī Muḥammad, Cairo 1418/1997.

Ibn Qayyim al-Jawziyya, Shams al-Dīn: *Rawḍat al-muḥibbīn wa-nuzhat al-mushtāqīn*, ed. by Sayyid Jamīlī, Beirut 1987.

Ibn Qayyim al-Jawziyya, Shams al-Dīn: *Kitāb al-Rūḥ*, Hyderabad 1324/1906–1907 and 1357/1938–1939 (reprint of 1318/1900–1901).

Ibn Qayyim al-Jawziyya, Shams al-Dīn: *Kitāb al-Rūḥ*, Cairo 1979.

Ibn Qayyim al-Jawziyya, Shams al-Dīn: *Kitāb al-Rūḥ*, ed. by Abū ʿAbd al-Raḥmān al-Makkī, Mecca 1425/2004.
Ibn Qayyim al-Jawziyya, Shams al-Dīn: *Kitāb al-Ṣawāʾiq al-mursala ʿalā al-jahmiyya wal-muʿaṭṭila,* 4 vols., ed. by ʿAlī b. Muḥammad al-Dakhīl Allāh, Riyadh 1408/1987–1988.
Ibn Qayyim al-Jawziyya, Shams al-Dīn: *Mukhtaṣar al-Ṣawāʾiq al-mursala ʿalā al-jahmiyya wal-muʿaṭṭila*, abridgement (*ikhtiṣār*) by Muḥammad b. al-Mawṣilī, ed. by al-Ḥasan b. ʿAbd al-Raḥmān al-ʿAlawī, Riyadh 1425/2004, pp. 642–685.
Ibn Qayyim al-Jawziyya, Shams al-Dīn: *Shifāʾ al-ʿalīl fī masāʾil al-qaḍāʾ wal-qadar wal-ḥikma wal-taʿlīl*, ed. by Muḥammad Badr al-Dīn Abū Firās al-Naʿsānī, Cairo 1323/1903.
Ibn Qayyim al-Jawziyya, Shams al-Dīn: *Shifāʾ al-ʿalīl fī masāʾil al-qaḍāʾ wal-qadar wal-ḥikma wal-taʿlīl*, ed. by al-Sayyid Muḥammad al-Sayyid and Saʿīd Maḥmūd, Cairo 1414/1994.
Ibn Qayyim al-Jawziyya, Shams al-Dīn: *Ṭarīq al-hijratayn wa-bāb al-saʿādatayn*, Cairo n. d.
Ibn Qayyim al-Jawziyya, Shams al-Dīn: *Ṭarīq al-hijratayn wa-bāb al-saʿādatayn*, ed. by Abū Ḥafṣ Sayyid Ibrāhīm b. Ṣādiq b. ʿImrān, Cairo 1991.
Ibn Qayyim al-Jawziyya, Shams al-Dīn: *Ṭarīq al-hijratayn wa-bāb al-saʿādatayn,* ed. by ʿAmr b. Muḥammad, Riyadh 1414/1994.
Ibn Qayyim al-Jawziyya, Shams al-Dīn: *Tuḥfat al-mawdūd bi-aḥkām al-mawlūd*, ed. by Muḥammad ʿAlī Abū al-ʿAbbās, Cairo 1987.
Ibn Qayyim al-Jawziyya, Shams al-Dīn: *al-Ṭuruq al-ḥukmiyya fī al-siyāsa al-sharʿiyya*, ed. by Nāyif b. Aḥmad al-Ḥamad, Mecca 1428/2008.
Ibn Qayyim al-Jawziyya, Shams al-Dīn: *ʿUddat al-ṣābirīn wa-dhakhīrat al-shākirīn,* Cairo 1993.
Ibn Qayyim al-Jawziyya, Shams al-Dīn: *al-Wābil al-ṣayyib min al-kalim al-ṭayyib*, ed. by Sayyid Ibrāhīm, Cairo 1991.
Ibn Qayyim al-Jawziyya, Shams al-Dīn: *Zād al-maʿād fī hady khayr al-ʿibād*, 6 vols., ed. by Shuʿayb al-Arnaʾūṭ and ʿAbd al-Qādir al-Arnaʾūṭ, Beirut 1414/1994.
Ibn Qayyim al-Jawziyya, Shams al-Dīn: *Zād al-maʿād fī hady khayr al-ʿibād*, 4 vols., Cairo 1425/2004.
Ibnu Qayyim Al Jauziyah: *Mendulang Faidah dari Lautan Ilmu,* translated by Kathur Suhardi, Jakarta 1998.
Ibnu Qayyim Al Jauziyah: *Rahasia Dibalik Shalat,* translated by Amir Hamzah Fachruddin and Kamaluddin Sadiatulharamain, Jakarta 2000.
Ibnu Qayyim Al Jauziyah: *Sabar Perisai Seorang Mukmin,* Pustaka 2000.
Ibnul Qayyim al Dschauziyah, Imam: *Al-ʿUbudiyyah. Aus der Fußnote von: Die Schande von Al-Hawa (Leidenschaft) [Madaridsch as-Salikin 1/100–101, 105]*, adopted by Dr. Saleh As-Saleh, translated from English into German by Azad Ibn Muhammad, 2004.

Ibnul Qayyim al-Dschawziyya, Imam: *Al-Chidr. Second Chapter of* Al-Manaru l-Munif fi s-Sahih wa-d-Daʿif, translated from Turkish into German by Eser Ebu Zeyneb, 2005.

Ibnul Qayyim al-Dschawziyya, Imam: *Die Auswanderung zu Allah,* excerpt from Risala at-Tabukiyya, translated from English to German by Azad Ibn Muhammad, 2007.

Ibnul Qayyim al-Dschawziyya, Imam: *Die Geduld edler und unedler Menschen*, excerpt from Uddat as-Sabririn wa Dhakirat (*Patience and Gratitude*), translated from English into German by Nizar Abu Suhail, 2006.

Ibnul Qayyim al-Dschawziyya, Imam: *Die herausragende Stellung der Gelehrten*, excerpt from Miftah Dar as-Saʿada, from English to German by Umm Amani al-Akad, 2003.

Ibnul Qayyim al-Dschawziyya, Imam: *al-Fawaʾid. Anmerkungen des Nutzens*; erschienen in: Al-Ibānah, Issue No. 2, Dhul-Qaʿdah 1416H/April 1996, translated by K. Akad, 2004.

Ibnul Qayyim al-Dschawziyya, Imam: *Krankheiten des Herzens und ihre Heilung. Auszug aus Kapitel 1 von* "Heilung mit der Medizin des Propheten – Allahs Heil und Segen auf ihm", translated from English to German by Azad Ibn Muhammad, 2004.

Ibnul Qayyim, Imam: *Die Liebe zu Allah*, excerpt of the third volume of Madārij al-Sālikīn, translated from English to German by Azad Ibn Muhammad, 2005.

Ibn Taymiyya, Taqī al-Dīn: *A Muslim Theologian's Response to Christianity. Ibn Taymiyya's* al-Jawāb al-ṣaḥīḥ, edited and translated by Thomas F. Michel, Delmar 1984.

Ibn Taymiyya, Taqī al-Dīn: *Bayān muwāfaqat ṣarīḥ al-maʿqūl li-ṣaḥīḥ al-manqūl*, Cairo 1321–1322/1903–1905.

Ibn Taymiyya, Taqī al-Dīn: *Bayān talbīs al-jahmiyya fī taʾsīs bidaʿihim al-kalāmiyya aw Naqḍ Taʾsīs al-jahmiyya*, 2 vols., ed. by Muḥammad b. ʿAbd al-Raḥmān b. Qāsim, n. p. n. d.

Ibn Taymiyya, Taqī al-Dīn: *Darʾ taʿāruḍ al-ʿaql wal-naql*, ed. by Muḥammad Rashād Sālim, n. p. n. d.

Ibn Taymiyya, Taqī al-Dīn: *Darʾ taʿāruḍ al-ʿaql wal-naql*, 11 vols., ed. by Muḥammad Rashād Sālim, Riyadh 1399–1400/1979–1980.

Ibn Taymiyya, Taqī al-Dīn: *Darʾ taʿāruḍ al-ʿaql wal-naql*, 11 vols., ed. by Muḥammad Rashād Sālim, Riyadh 1399–1403/1979–1983.

Ibn Taymiyya, Taqī al-Dīn: *Darʾ taʿāruḍ al-ʿaql wal-naql aw muwāfaqat ṣaḥīḥ al-manqūl li-ṣarīḥ al-maʿqūl*, 5 vols., ed. by ʿAbd al-Laṭīf ʿAbd al-Raḥmān, Beirut 1417/1997.

Ibn Taymiyya, Taqī al-Dīn: *Das ist die aufrechte Religion. Brief des Ibn Taymiya an den König von Zypern;* from the Arabic by Sahib Mustaqim Bleher, Würselen 1984.

Ibn Taymiyya, Taqī al-Dīn: *Kitāb al-Īmān*, ed. by Muḥammad Zabīdī, Beirut 1414/1993.

Ibn Taymiyya, Taqī al-Dīn: *Ibn Taymiyya on Public and Private Law in Islam or Public Policy in Islamic Jurisprudence*, translated by ʿUmar Farrūkh, Beirut 1966.

Ibn Taymiyya, Taqī al-Dīn: al-Īqāf ʿalā sabab al-ikhtilāf, adjunct to Ibn ʿAbd al-ʿAzīz, Ṣadr al-Dīn: *al-Ittibāʿ*, Lahore, 1401/1980, pp. 104–115.

Ibn Taymiyya, Taqī al-Dīn: *Jāmiʿ al-Rasāʾil*, ed. by Muḥammad Rashād Sālim, Cairo 1969.

Ibn Taymiyya, Taqī al-Dīn: *al-Jawāb al-ṣaḥīḥ li-man baddala dīn al-masīḥ*, 4 vols., ed. by ʿAlī al-Sayyid Ṣubḥ al-Madanī, Cairo 1383/1964.

Ibn Taymiyya, Taqī al-Dīn: *Le Traité de droit public d'Ibn Taimīya*, translated by Henri Laoust, Beirut 1948.

Ibn Taymiyya, Taqī al-Dīn: *Le Traité de droit public d'Ibn Taimīya*, translated by Henri Laoust, Damascus 1952.

Ibn Taymiyya, Taqī al-Dīn: *Majmūʿ al-Fatāwā lil-shaykh Taqī al-Dīn Ibn Taymiyya*, 37 vols., Beirut 1978.

Ibn Taymiyya, Taqī al-Dīn: *Majmūʿ Fatāwā*, 37 vols., ed. by ʿAbd al-Raḥmān b. Muḥammad b. Qāsim al-ʿĀṣimī al-Najdī, Riyadh 1991.

Ibn Taymiyya, Taqī al-Dīn: *Majmūʿ Fatāwā Ibn Taymiyya*, 37 vols., Riyadh 1416/1995.

Ibn Taymiyya, Taqī al-Dīn: *Majmūʿ Fatāwā shaykh al-islām Aḥmad Ibn Taymiyya*, 37 vols., ed. by ʿAbd al-Raḥmān b. Muḥammad b. Qāsim and Muḥammad b. ʿAbd al-Raḥmān b. Muḥammad, Cairo n. d.

Ibn Taymiyya, Taqī al-Dīn: *Majmūʿ Fatāwā shaykh al-islām Aḥmad Ibn Taymiyya*, 37 vols., ed. by ʿAbd Allāh b. Qāsim, Rabat 1961.

Ibn Taymiyya, Taqī al-Dīn: *Majmūʿat al-Fatāwā li-shaykh al-islām Ibn Taymiyya*, 37 vols., vol. 4, ed. by ʿAbd al-Raḥmān b. Muḥammad b. Qāsim and Muḥammad b. ʿAbd al-Raḥmān, Cairo n. d. (reprint of the Riyadh edition 1381–1386/1961–1967).

Ibn Taymiyya, Taqī al-Dīn: *Majmūʿat al-Fatāwā li-shaykh al-islām Taqī al-Dīn Aḥmad b. Taymiyya al-Ḥarrānī*, 37 vols., ed. by ʿĀmir al-Jazzār and Anwar al-Bāz, Riyadh and Mansoura 1419/1998.

Ibn Taymiyya, Taqī al-Dīn: *Majmūʿat al-Fatāwā li-shaykh al-islām Taqī al-Dīn Aḥmad b. Taymiyya al-Ḥarrānī*, 37 parts in 20 vols., vol. 9, ed. by ʿĀmir al-Jazzār and Anwar al-Bāz, Mansoura and Cairo 1421/2001.

Ibn Taymiyya, Taqī al-Dīn: *Majmūʿat al-Rasāʾil al-kubrā*, Cairo 1323/1905–1906.

Ibn Taymiyya, Taqī al-Dīn: *Majmūʿat al-Rasāʾil al-kubrā*, Beirut 1972.

Ibn Taymiyya, Taqī al-Dīn: *Majmūʿat al-Rasāʾil wal-masāʾil*, 5 vols., ed. by Muḥammad Rashīd Riḍā, Beirut 1983.

Ibn Taymiyya, Taqī al-Dīn: *Majmūʿat al-Rasāʾil wal-masāʾil*, 5 vols., ed. by Muḥammad Rashīd Riḍā, 2nd ed. Beirut 2001.

Ibn Taymiyya, Taqī al-Dīn: *Majmūʿat Tafsīr*, ed. by ʿAbd al-Ṣamad Sharaf al-Dīn, Mumbai 1993.
Ibn Taymiyya, Taqī al-Dīn: *al-Masāʾil al-māradīniyya*, ed. by Muḥammad Ḥāmid al-Fiqī, Cairo 1980.
Ibn Taymiyya, Taqī al-Dīn: *Minhāj al-sunna al-nabawiyya fī naqḍ kalām al-shīʿa wal-qadariyya*, 10 vols., ed. by Muḥammad Rashād Sālim, Riyadh n.d.
Ibn Taymiyya, Taqī al-Dīn: *Minhāj al-sunna al-nabawiyya fī naqḍ kalām al-shīʿa wal-qadariyya*, Cairo 1370/1950–51 (reprint: Beirut 1985).
Ibn Taymiyya, Taqī al-Dīn: *Minhāj al-sunna al-nabawiyya fī naqḍ kalām al-shīʿa wal-qadariyya*, 9 vols., ed. by Muḥammad Rashād Sālim, Cairo 1989.
Ibn Taymiyya, Taqī al-Dīn: *Minhāj al-sunna* and *Majmūʿat al-Rasāʾil al-kubrā*, 2 vols. in one, Cairo 1323/1905.
Ibn Taymiyya, Taqī al-Dīn: *Naqḍ al-manṭiq*, ed. by Muḥammad b. ʿAbd al-Razzāq Ḥamza, Sulaymān b. ʿAbd al-Raḥmān al-Ṣanīʿ and Muḥammad Ḥāmid al-Fīqī, Cairo 1370/1951.
Ibn Taymiyya, Taqī al-Dīn: *Naṣīḥat ahl al-imān fī al-radd ʿalā manṭiq al-yūnān / al-Radd ʿalā al-manṭiqiyyīn*, ed. by ʿAbd al-Ṣamad Sharaf al-Dīn al-Kutubī, reviewed by Muḥammad Ṭalḥa Bilāl Minyār, with an introduction by al-Sayyid Sulaymān al-Nadwī, Beirut 1426/2005 (reprint of Bombay 1368/1949).
Ibn Taymiyya, Taqī al-Dīn: *Kitāb al-Nubuwwāt*, Cairo 1346/1927–1928.
Ibn Taymiyya, Taqī al-Dīn: *Kitāb al-Nubuwwāt,* Beirut 1985.
Ibn Taymiyya, Taqī al-Dīn: *al-Qawāʿid al-nūrāniyya al-fiqhiyya*, ed. by Muḥammad Ḥāmid al-Fiqī, Cairo 1370/1951.
Ibn Taymiyya, Taqī al-Dīn: Public *Duties in Islam. The Institution of the Ḥisba*, translated by Muhtar Holland, Leicester 1982.
Ibn Taymiyya, Taqī al-Dīn: *al-Radd ʿalā al-manṭiqiyyīn*, edited by ʿAbd al-Ḥamad Sharaf al-Dīn al-Kutubī, reviewed by Muḥammad Ṭalḥa Bilāl Minyār, with an introduction by al-Sayyid Sulaymān al-Nadwī, Beirut 1426/2005.
Ibn Taymiyya, Taqī al-Dīn: *al-Radd ʿalā al-manṭiqiyyīn*, ed. by ʿAbd al-Ṣamad Sharaf al-Dīn al-Kutubī, Bombay 1368/1949.
Ibn Taymiyya, Taqī al-Dīn: *al-Radd ʿalā man qāla bi-fanāʾ al-janna wal-nār*, ed. by Muḥammad b. ʿAbd Allāh al-Samharī, Riyadh 1415/1995.
Ibn Taymiyya, Taqī al-Dīn: Risāla fī al-Kalām ʿalā al-fiṭra, in: Ibn Taymiyya, Taqī al-Dīn: *Majmūʿat al-Rasāʾil al-kubrā*, part 2, Beirut 1972, pp. 333–349.
Ibn Taymiyya, Taqī al-Dīn: Risālat al-Qiyās, in: Ibn Taymiyya, Taqī al-Dīn: *Risālatān fī Maʿnā al-qiyās li-shaykhay al-islām Ibn Taymiyya wa-Ibn al-Qayyim*, ed. by ʿAbd al-Fattāḥ Maḥmūd ʿUmar, Amman 1407/1987, pp. 11–89.
Ibn Taymiyya, Taqī al-Dīn: *al-Siyāsa al-sharʿiyya fī iṣlāḥ al-rāʿī wal-raʿiyya*, ed. by ʿAlī b. Muḥammad al-ʿUmrān, Mekka 1429/2008.

Ibn Taymiyya, Taqī al-Dīn: *The Legal Methods in Islamic Administration*, translated by Ala'eddin Kharofa, Kuala Lumpur 2000.
Ibn Taymiyya, Taqī al-Dīn: *Kitāb Tafsīr sūrat al-ikhlāṣ*, ed. by al-Sayyid Muḥammad Badr al-Dīn al-Naʿsānī al-Ḥalabī, Cairo 1323/1905.
Ibn Taymiyya, Taqī al-Dīn: *Tuḥfat al-anām fī al-ʿamal bi-ḥadīth al-nabī ʿalayhi al-salām*, adjunct to Ṣadr al-Dīn b. ʿAbd al-ʿAzīz: *al-Ittibāʿ*, Lahore, 1401/1980, pp. 72–103.
Ibn Taymiyya, Taqī al-Dīn Aḥmad: *al-Fatwā al-ḥamawiyya al-kubrā*, Beirut [around 1984].
Ibn Taymiyya, Taqī al-Dīn Aḥmad b. ʿAbd al Ḥalīm: *al-Fatwā al-ḥamawiyya al-kubrā*, Beirut n. d. [around 1984].

2. Secondary Sources

Aasi, Haider Ghulām: *Muslim Understanding of Other Religions. A Study of Ibn Hazm's Kitāb al-Faṣl fī al-Milal wa al-Ahwāʾ wa al-Niḥal*, New Delhi (Adam) 2007.
Abaza, Mona: *Indonesian Students in Cairo. Islamic Education, Perceptions and Exchanges*, Paris 1994.
ʿAbd al-Ḥāfiẓ, Chawharī: *Taʿārif-i Jamāʿat-i mujtahidīn*, Lahore n. d.
al-ʿAbd, ʿAbd al-Laṭīf Muḥammad: *al-Tafkīr al-manṭiqī bayna al-manhaj al-qadīm wal-manhaj al-jadīd*, Cairo 1977.
ʿAbd al-Ḥaqq, Ghaznawī: *Kitāb al-Arbaʿīn fī anna Thanāʾ Allāh laysa ʿalā madhhab al-muḥaddithīn fī al-dīn bal ʿalā madhhab al-jahmiyya wal-muʿtazila wal-qadariyya al-muḥarrifīn*, Amritsar n. d.
ʿAbd al-Raḥīm, Ibrāhīm: *al-Siyāsa al-sharʿiyya. Mafhūmuhā, maṣādiruhā, majālātuhā*, Cairo 2006.
ʿAbd al-Raʾūf al-Munāwī, Zayn al-Dīn: *al-Kawākib al-durriyya fī tarājim al-sāda al-ṣūfiyya*, 5 vols., ed. by Muḥammad Adīb al-Jādir, Beirut 1999.
ʿAbd al-Rāziq, Muṣṭafā: *Khamsa min aʿlām al-fikr al-Islāmī*, Cairo n. d.
Abdelsalam, Ahmed: The Practice of Violence in the *ḥisba*-Theories, in: *Iranian Studies* 38 (2005), pp. 547–554.
ʿAbd al-Salām, ʿAbd al-ʿAẓīm: *Ibn Qayyim al-Jawziyya*, Kuwait 1984.
Abdillah, Mujiyono: *Dialektika Hukum Islam dan Perubahan Sosial. Sebuah Refleksi sosiologis atas pemikiran Ibn Qayyim al-Jauziyyah*, Surakarta 2003.
Abdul-Mawjûd, Salâhud-Dîn ʿAlî: *The Biography of Imâm Ibn al-Qayyim*, transl. by Abdul-Râfi Adewale Imâm, Riyadh: Darrussalam, 2006.
Abou El Fadl, Khaled: *Rebellion and Violence in Islamic Law*, Cambridge and New York 2001.
Abrahamov, Binyamin: *Al-Ḳāsim b. Ibrāhīm on the Proof of God's Existence*, Leiden 1990.

Abrahamov, Binyamin: A Re-examination of al-Ashʿarī's Theory of *Kasb* according to *Kitāb al-Lumaʿ*, in: *Journal of the Royal Asiatic Society* 1–2 (1989), pp. 210–221.

Abrahamov, Binyamin: Ibn Taymiyya on the Agreement of Reason with Tradition, in: *The Muslim World* 82 (1992), pp. 256–272.

Abrahamov, Binyamin: *Islamic Theology. Traditionalism and Rationalism*, Edinburgh 1998.

Abrahamov, Binyamin: The Creation and Duration of Paradise and Hell in Islamic Theology, in: *Der Islam* 79 (2002), pp. 87–102.

Abū al-Barakāt Aḥmadī: *Fatāwā-yi Ahl-i ḥadīth al-maʿrūf bihi Fatāwā Barakatiyya*, Delhi 1992.

Abū Zahra, Muḥammad: *Ibn Taymiyya. Ḥayātuhu wa-ʿaṣruhu wa-ārāʾuhu wa-fiqhuhu*, Cairo 1952.

Abū Zayd, Bakr b. ʿAbd Allāh: *Ibn Qayyim al-Jawziyya. Ḥayātuhu, āthāruhu, mawāriduhu*, Riyadh 1400/1980.

Abū Zayd, Bakr b. ʿAbd Allāh: *Ibn Qayyim al-Jawziyya. Ḥayātuhu, āthāruhu, mawāriduhu*, Riyadh 1412/1991–92.

Abū Zayd, Bakr b. ʿAbd Allāh: *Ibn Qayyim al-Jawziyya. Ḥayātuhu, āthāruhu, mawāriduhu*, Riyadh 1423/2002.

Accad, Martin: Corruption and/or Misinterpretation of the Bible. The Story of the Islāmic Usage of *Taḥrīf*, in: *The Near East School of Theology Theological Review* 24 (2003), pp. 67–97.

Accad, Martin: Muḥammad's Advent as the Final Criterion for the Authenticity of the Judeo-Christian Tradition. Ibn Qayyim al-Jawziyya's *Hidāyat al-ḥayārā fī ajwibat al-Yahūd wa-ʾl-Naṣārā*, in: Barbara Roggema, Marcel Poorthuis and Pim Valkenberg (eds.): *The Three Rings. Textual Studies in the Historical Trialogue of Judaism, Christianity and Islam*, Leuven 2005, pp. 217–236.

Accad, Martin: The Ultimate Proof-Text. The Interpretation of John 20.17 in Muslim-Christian Dialogue (Second/Eighth-Eighth/Fourteenth Centuries), in: David Thomas (ed.): *Christians at the Heart of Islamic Rule*, Leiden and Boston 2003, pp. 199–214.

Adamek, Gerhard: *Das Kleinkind in Glaube und Sitte der Araber im Mittelalter*, Ph. D. thesis, Bonn 1968.

Ahmad, Furqan and Ali, Firasat: *Divorce in Mohammedan Law. The Law of "Triple Divorce"*, New Delhi 1988.

Ahmad, Imtiaz (ed.): *Divorce and Remarriage Among Muslims in India*, New Delhi 2003.

Ahmad, Qeyamuddin: *The Wahhabi Movement in India*, Calcutta 1966.

Aḥmad, Sālim ʿAbd al-Razzāq: *Fihris makhṭūṭāt maktabat al-awqāf al-ʿāmma fī al-Mawṣil*, 8 vols., Baghdad 1982–83.

Ahmed, Shahab: Ibn Taymiyyah and the Satanic Verses, in: *Studia Islamica* 87 (1988), pp. 67–124.

Ahsan, Sayyid: *Life and Thoughts of Muhammad Ibn Abd al-Wahhab*, Aligarh 1988.
Aigner, Anita: Einleitung. Von 'architektonischer Moderne' zu 'Architektur in der Moderne'. Kulturelle Grenzüberschreitungen, in: ibid. (ed.): *Vernakulare Moderne. Grenzüberschreitungen in der Architektur um 1900*; das Bauernhaus und seine Aneignung, Bielefeld 2010, pp. 7–35.
Ajhar, ʿAbd al-Ḥakīm: *Ibn Taymiyya wa-stiʾnāf al-qawl al-falsafī fī al-islām*, Casablanca and Beirut 2004.
al-Ājurrī, Abū Bakr: *Kitāb al-Sharīʿa*, Beirut 1421/2000.
Āl al-Shaykh, ʿAbd al-Raḥmān b. ʿAbd al-Laṭīf: *Mashāhīr ʿulamāʾ Najd wa-ghayrihim*, Riyadh 1394/1974.
Al Albanī, Muḥammad Nāṣiruddīn: *The Face Veil* (*Der Gesichtsschleier*), translated from Arabic by Dr. Bilāl Philip and translated from English into German by Umm Laysa', 2008.
al-Albanī, Nāṣir al-Dīn: *The Prayer as Offered by Allah's Messenger* (*Kitāb Ṣifāt ṣalāṭ al-nabī*), translated from Arabic into English by A.Q. Naqvi, Delhi 2002.
Alam, Muzaffar: *The Crisis of Empire in Mughal North India*, Delhi 1986.
Alavi, Seema: *Islam and Healing. Loss and Recovery of an Indo-Muslim Medical Tradition; 1600–1900*, New York 2008.
ʿAlī Ḥasan Khān: *Maʾāthir-i Ṣiddīqī. Sīrat-i Walājāhī*, 4 parts, Lucknow 1924.
Al-Alousī, Husām Muhī Eldīn: *The Problem of Creation in Islamic Thought, Qurʾān, Hadith, Commentaries, and Kalam*, Baghdad 1968.
Allāhābādī, Raḥmat Allāh Rabbānī: *Masʾalat rafʿ al-yadayn maʿa āmīn bil-jahr*, Delhi 1983.
Allievi, Stefano: Islam in the Public Space. Social Networks, Media and Neo-Communities, in: Stefano Allievi and Jorgen S. Nielsen (eds.): *Muslim Networks and Transnational Communities in and across Europe*, Leiden and Boston 2003, pp. 1–27.
Alvi, Sajida: Qāẕī Sanāʾ Allāh Pānīpatī. An Eighteenth-Century *ṣūfī ʿālim*; a Study of His Writings in Their Sociopolitical Context, in: Wael B. Hallaq and Donald Little (eds.): *Islamic Studies Presented to Charles J. Adams*, Leiden 1991, pp. 11–26.
Amitai, Reuven: The Mongol Occupation of Damascus in 1300. A Study of Mamluk Loyalities, in: Michael Winter and Amalia Levanoni (eds.): *The Mamluks in Egyptian and Syrian Politics and Society*, Leiden 2004, pp. 21–41.
al-Amri, Husayn Ibn-Abdullah: *The Yemen in the 18th and 19th Centuries. A Political and Intellectual History*, London 1985.
Amritsarī, Thanāʾ Allāh: *Ahl-i Ḥadīth kā madhhab*, Sargodha 1986.
Amritsarī, Thanāʾ Allāh: *Āyāt-i mutashābihāt*, Amritsar 1904.
Amritsarī, Thanāʾ Allāh: *Fatāwā-yi thanāʾiyya*, 2 vols., Sargodha 1972.
Amritsarī, Thanāʾ Allāh: *Ḥaqq-i Prakāsh ba-jawāb-i satyārth prakāsh*, Amritsar 1928.

Amritsarī, Thanā' Allāh: *al-Kalām al-mubīn bi-jawāb al-arbaʿīn*, Amritsar 1904.

Amritsarī, Thanā' Allāh: *Tafsīr al-Qur'ān bi-kalām al-Raḥmān*, Amritsar 1902.

Amritsarī, Thanā' Allāh: *Tafsīr al-Qur'ān bi-kalām al-Raḥmān*, 2nd ed. Amritsar 1929.

Amritsarī, Thanā' Allāh: *Tafsīr-i Thanā'ī*, 8 vols., Amritsar 1929.

Amritsarī, Thanā' Allāh: *Uṣūl-i Āryā*, Amritsar 1929.

An-Na'im, Abdullahi Ahmed: Religion, the State and Constitutionalism in Islamic and Comparative Perspectives, in: *Drake Law Review* 57 (2009), pp. 829–850.

An-Na'im, Abdullahi Ahmed: Shariʿa in the Secular State. A Paradox of Separation and Conflation, in: Peri Bearman, Wolfhart Heinrichs and Bernard G. Weiss (eds.): *The Law Applied*, pp. 321–341.

Anawati, George C.: Polémique, apologie et dialogue islamo-chrétiens. Positions classiques médiévales et positions contemporaines, in: *Euntes Docete* 22 (1969), pp. 375–452.

Anjum, Ovamir: *Reason and Politics in Medieval Islamic Thought. The Taymiyyan Moment*, Ph.D. thesis, Madison 2008.

Anjum, Ovamir: Sufism without Mysticism. Ibn Qayyim al-Ǧawziyya's Objectives in Madāriǧ al-sālikīn, in: Bori and Holtzman, A Scholar in the Shadow, pp. 161–188.

al-Anṣārī al-Harawī, ʿAbd Allāh: *Trois traités spirituels*, Paris 1985.

al-Anṣārī, Abū Ismaʿīl: *Manāzil al-sā'irīn ilā al-ḥaqq al-mubīn*, ed. by ʿAbd al- Ḥāfī Manṣūr, Tunis 1989.

al-Anṣārī, Ḥusayn b. Muḥsin: *Asānīd al-shaykh Ḥusayn Ibn Muḥsin*, manuscript, Lucknow n. d.

al-Anṣārī, Ḥusayn b. Muḥsin: *al-Fatḥ al-rabbānī al-radd ʿalā al-Qādiyānī*, Delhi 1309/1892.

al-Anṣārī, Ḥusayn b. Muḥsin: *Nūr al-ʿayn min fatāwā shaykh Ḥusayn*, Lucknow 1339/1921.

Anshari, Endang Saifuddin: *The Jakarta Charter of June 1945. A History of the Gentlemen's Agreement Between the Islamic and the Secular Nationalists in Modern Indonesia*; M.A. thesis, Montreal 1976.

Apaydın, H. Yunus: İbn Kayyim el-Çevziyye, in: *Islām Ansiklopedisi*, Istanbul (Türkiye Diyanet Vakfı) 1999, vol. 20, pp. 109–123.

Arberry, Arthur John: *Revelation and Reason in Islam*, London 1957.

Arberry, Arthur J.: *The Koran Interpreted*, Oxford 1962.

Aristotle: *Topica et Sophistici Elenchi*, ed. by Sir William David Ross, Oxford 1979.

Arnaldez, Roger: Apories sur la prédestination et le libre arbitre dans le commentaire de Razi, in: *Mélanges de l'institut dominicain d'études orientales* 6 (1959/61), pp. 123–126.

Arnaldez, Roger: *Grammaire et théologie chez Ibn Ḥazm de Cordoue. Essai sur la structure et les conditions de la penseé musulmane*, Paris 1956.

Arnaldez, Roger: L'oeuvre de Fakhr al-Dīn al-Rāzī. Commentateur du Coran et philosophe, in: *Cahiers de Civilisation Médiévale Xe-XIIe siècles* 3 (1960), pp. 307–323.
Arnold, Thomas W.: *The Preaching of Islam*, London 1935 (repr. Lahore 1979).
Asad, Muhammad (transl.): *The Message of the Qur'ān*, Bristol 2003.
al-Ashʿarī, Abū al-Ḥasan: *Kitāb al-Lumaʿ fī al-radd ʿalā ahl al-zaygh wal-bidaʿ*, ed. by ʿAbd al-Azīz ʿIzz al-Dīn al-Sayrawān, Beirut 1987.
al-Ashqar, ʿUmar S.: *Paradise and Hell in the Light of the Qur'an and Sunnah*, transl. by Nasiruddin al-Khattab, Riyadh 2002.
al-Ashqar, ʿUmar Sulaymān ʿAbd Allāh: *al-Janna wal-nār*, Cairo 1426/2005.
As'ila min Jāwah/Ajwibat al-Manār, in: *al-Manār* 12 (1909/10), pp. 260–270.
al-Aswānī, ʿAlā': *The Yacoubian Building*, Cairo and New York 2004.
Atademir, Hamdi R.: Porphyrios ve Ebherî'nin İsagoci'leri, in: *Ankara Üniversitesi Dil ve Tarih-Coğrafya Fakültesi Dergisi* 6 (1948), p. 468.
al-Atharī, Muḥammad Bahjat: *Aʿlām al-ʿIrāq*, Cairo 1345/1926.
al-Attas, Syed Muhammad al Naquib: *A Commentary on the Ḥujjat al-Ṣiddīq of Nūr al-Dīn al-Rānīrī*, Kuala Lumpur 1986.
al-Attas, Syed Muhammad al Naquib: *Preliminary Statement on a General Theory of the Islamization of the Malay-Indonesian Archipelago*, Kuala Lumpur 1969.
al-Attas, Syed Muhammad al Naquib: *Rānīrī and the Wujūdiyyah of 17th-Century Acheh*, Singapore 1966.
al-Attas, Syed Muhammad al Naquib: *The Mysticism of Ḥamzah Fanṣūrī*, Kuala Lumpur 1970.
Attewell, Guy: *Refiguring Unani tibb. Plural Healing in Late Colonial India*, New Delhi 2007.
Audi, Robert: *The Cambridge Dictionary of Philosophy*, Cambridge 1996.
Averroès: *Tafsīr mā baʿd al-ṭabīʿa*, ed. by Maurice Bouyges, 4 vols., 2nd ed., Beirut 1967–1973.
Avicenna: *Remarks and Admonitions*, part 1: *Logic*, transl. by Shams Constantine Inati, Toronto 1984.
Awang, Omar: The Major Arabic Sources which Determined the Structure of Islamic Thought in the Malay Archipelago Before the Nineteenth Century A.D. in the Field of Law, Theology and Sufism, in: Lutpi Ibrahim (ed.): *Islamika. Esei-esei Sempena Abad ke-15 Hijrah*, Kuala Lumpur 1981, pp. 80–85.
ʿAẓīmābādī, ʿAbd al-Raḥīm: *al-Durr al-manthūr fī tarājim ahl al-Ṣādiqfūr*, Delhi 1927.
al-ʿAẓma, ʿAzīz: *Ibn Taymiyya*, Beirut 2000.
Azra, Azyumardi: *Jaringan Ulama Nusantara*, Bandung 1995.
Azra, Azyumardi: Opposition to Sufism in the East Indies in the Seventeenth and Eighteenth Centuries, in: Frederick de Jong and Bernd Radtke (eds.):

Islamic Mysticism Contested. Thirteen Centuries of Controversies and Polemics, Leiden 1999, pp. 665–686.

Azra, Azyumardi: *The Origins of Islamic Reformism in Southeast Asia*, Leiden 2004.

Bacon, Francis: *Novum Organon/The New Organon*, ed. by Lisa Jardine and Michael Silverthorne, Cambridge and New York 2000.

al-Baghdādī, Abū al-Barakāt Hibat Allāh b. ʿAlī b. Malkā: *Kitāb al-Muʿtabar fī al-ḥikma al-ilāhiyya*, 3 vols., Haydarabad 1357–1358/1938–1939.

al-Baghdādī, Abū Manṣūr ʿAbd al-Qāhir al-Tamīmī: *Kitāb Uṣūl al-dīn*, Beirut 1401/1981 (reprint of Istanbul (Maṭbaʿat al-Dawla) 1346/1928).

Ibn Bakar, Osman: Sufism in the Malay-Indonesian World, in: Seyyed Hossein Nasr (ed.): *Islamic Spirituality. Manifestations*, London 1991, pp. 259–263.

Baljon, Johannes Marinus Simon: *Religion and Thought of Shāh Walī Allāh Dihlawī* (1703–1762), Leiden 1986.

Baljon, Johannes Marinus Simon: Shāh Waliullah and the Dargah, in: Christian W. Troll (ed.): *Muslim Shrines in India. Their Character, History and Significance*, Delhi 1989, pp. 189–197.

al-Baqarī, Aḥmad Maḥmūd Māhir: *Ibn Qayyim al-Jawziyya. Min āthārihi al-ʿilmiyya*, Beirut 1404/1984 and Alexandria 1407/1987.

al-Bāqillānī, Abū Bakr: *Tamhīd al-awāʾil wa-talkhīṣ al-dalāʾil*, ed. by ʿImād al-Dīn Aḥmad Ḥaydar, Beirut 1987.

al-Baqrī, Aḥmad Maḥmūd: *Ibn al-Qayyim min āthārihi al-ʿilmiyya*, Beirut 1404/1984.

Bari, M. A.: A Nineteenth Century Muslim Reform Movement in India, in: George Makdisi (ed.): *Arabic and Islamic Studies in Honor of Hamilton A. R. Gibb*, Leiden 1965, pp. 85–102.

Barton, Greg: *Jemaah Islamiyah. Radical Islamism in Indonesia*, Sydney 2004.

Bascio, Patrick: *Defeating Islamic Terrorism. The Wahhabi Factor*, Wellesley 2007.

Basham, Arthur Llewellyn: *The Wonder that was India*, New Delhi 1981, vol. 1.

Bauer, Carmen: Zurück zum Quellcode. Salafistische Wissenspraktiken im Internet, in: *Inamo* [Informationsprojekt Naher und Mittlerer Osten e. V.] 57 (2009), pp. 37–42.

Bauer, Thomas: Mamluk Literature. Misunderstandings and New Approaches, in: *Mamlūk Studies Review* 9 (2005), pp. 105–132.

Bayazeed Khan Panni, Mohammad: *Dajjal. The Judeo-Christan 'Civilization'*, translated from Bangla by Ummut Tijah Makhduma Panni, Dhaka 2008.

Bayram, Muḥammad ibn al-Ḥusayn: *Risāla fī al-Siyāsa al-sharʿiyya*, ed. by Muḥammad Ṣāliḥ al-ʿAsalī, Dubai 2002.

Bearman, Peri, Bianquis, Thierry, Bosworth, Charles, van Dozel, E. and Heinrichs, Wolfhart (eds): *Encyclopaedia of Islam*, 2nd ed. [= EI^2], 12 vols., Leiden 1954–2004.

Bearman, Peri J., Heinrichs, Wolfhart and Weiss, Bernard G. (eds.): *The Law Applied. Contextualizing the Islamic Sharīʿa; a Volume in Honor of Frank E. Vogel*, London and New York 2008.

de Beaurecueil, Serge: Esquisse d'une biographie de Anṣārī, in: *Mélanges de l'institut dominicain d'études orientales* 4 (1957), pp. 95–140; 5 (1958), pp. 47–113; 6 (1959), pp. 387–402.

de Beaurecueil, Serge: La structure du *Livre des Etapes* de Khwaja Abdallah Ansari, in: *Mélanges de l'institut dominicain d'études orientales* 11 (1972), pp. 77–125.

de Beaurecueil, Serge: Le langage imagé du livre des étapes de Khwāja Abdullah Anṣārī, mystique hanbalite du V-e/XI-e s., in: *Bulletin d'études orientales* 30 (1978), pp. 32–44.

de Beaurecueil, Serge: Les déficiences des demeures, in: ʿAbd Allāh al-Anṣārī al-Harawī: *Trois traités spirituels*, Paris 1985, pp. 233–237.

de Beaurecueil, Serge: Un petit traité de ʿAbdallāh al-Anṣārī sur les deficiences a certaines demeures spirituelles, in: Dominique Sourdel (ed.): *Mélanges Louis Massignon*, Damascus 1957, pp. 154–169.

Begg, Moazzam: Moazzam Begg Interviews Imam Anwar Al Awlaki, in: *Cageprisoners* (December 31, 2007).

Bēgum, Sikander: *A Pilgrimage to Mecca*, Calcutta 1906, new edition by Siobhan Lambert-Hurley, Bloomington 2008.

Behloul, Samuel-Martin: *Ibn Ḥazms Evangelienkritik. Eine methodische Untersuchung*, Leiden, Boston and Cologne 2002.

Bell, Joseph Norment: *Love Theory in Later Ḥanbalite Islam*, Albany 1979.

Benford, Robert D. and Snow, David A.: Framing Processes and Social Movements. An Overview and Assessment, in: *Annual Review of Sociology* 26 (2000), pp. 611–639.

Benjamin, Daniel and Simon, Steven: *Age of Sacred Terror*, New York 2002.

Benjamin, Daniel, Kirby, Aidan and Smith, Julianne: *Currents and Crosscurrents of Radical Islamism. A Report of the CSIS (Center for Strategic and International Studies) Transatlantic Dialogue on Terrorism; April 2006*, Washington 2006.

Bennison, Amira K.: *Jihad and Its Interpretations in Pre-Colonial Morocco. State-Society Relations During the French Conquest of Algeria*, London 2002.

van den Bergh, Simon: *Averroes' Tahafut Al-Tahafut (The Incoherence of the Incoherence)*, Cambridge 1987.

Bhaṭṭī, Muḥammad Isḥāq: *Nuqūsh-i ʿaẓmat-i rafta*, Lahore 1996.

Bihārī, Fal-i Ḥusayn: *al-Ḥayāt baʿd al-mamāt*, Delhi 1908 (reprint Sangla Hil 1982).

Bin Mohd Sharif, Mohd Farid: *Baghy* in Islamic Law and the Thinking of Ibn Taymiyya, in: *Arab Law Quarterly* 20 (2006), pp. 289–305.

Bin Ngah, Mohd Nor: *Kitab Jawi. Islamic Thought of the Malay Muslim Scholars*, Singapore 1983.

Bisri, Affandi: *Shaikh Aḥmad al-Shurkātī. His Role in the al-Irshād Movement*, unpublished M. A. thesis, Montreal 1976.

Black, Antony: *The History of Islamic Political Thought. From the Prophet to the Present*, New York 2001.

Blake, Stephen: *Shahjahanabad. The Sovereign City of Mughal India 1639–1739*, Cambridge 1991.

Bluhm-Warn, Jutta: Al-Manar and Ahmad Soorkattie, in: Peter G. Riddell and Tony Street (eds.): *Islam. Essays on Scripture, Thought and Society*, Leiden 1997, pp. 295–308.

Boberg, Dirk: *Ägypten, Naǧd und der Ḥiǧāz. Eine Untersuchung zum religiös-politischen Verhältnis zwischen Ägypten und den Wahhābiten, 1923–1936, anhand von in Kairo veröffentlichten pro- und antiwahhābitischen Streitschriften und Presseberichten*, Frankfurt/Main 1991.

Boddy, Janice Patricia: *Civilizing Women. British Crusades in Colonial Sudan*, Princeton 2007.

Boland, Bernard Johan: *The Struggle of Islam in Modern Indonesia*, The Hague 1971.

Bori, Caterina: A New Source for the Biography of Ibn Taymiyya, in: *Bulletin of the School of Oriental and African Studies* 67 (2004), pp. 321–348.

Bori, Caterina: Ibn Taymiyya. Una vita esemplare; analisi delle fonti classiche della sua biografia, in: *Rivista degli Studi Orientali* 76 (2003).

Bori, Caterina: Ibn Taymiyya *wa-Jamāʿatuhu*. Authority, Conflict and Consensus in Ibn Taymiyya's Milieu, in: Rapoport and Ahmad, *Ibn Taymiyya and His Times*, pp. 32–52.

Bori, Caterina: The Collection and Edition of Ibn Taymiyya's Works. Concerns of a Disciple, in: *Mamlūk Studies Review* 13 (2009), pp. 47–67.

Bori, Caterina: Théologie politique et Islam à propos d'Ibn Taymiyya (m. 728/1328) et du sultanat mamelouk, in: *Revue de l'histoire des religions* 224 (2007), pp. 5–46.

Bori, Caterina and Holtzman, Livnat (eds.): *A Scholar in the Shadow. Essays in the Legal and Theological Thought of Ibn Qayyim al-Ǧawziyyah*, [*Oriente Moderno* 90:1 (2010)], Rome 2010.

Bori, Caterina and Holtzman, Livnat: [Introduction] A Scholar in the Shadow, in: idem: *A Scholar in the Shadow*, pp. 13–44.

Böttcher, Annabelle: Portraits of Kurdish Women in Contemporary Sufism, in: Shahrzad Mojab (ed.): *Women of a Non-state Nation. The Kurds*. Costa Mesa 2001, pp. 195–208.

Böttcher, Annabelle: Religious Authority in Transnational Sufi Networks, in: Gudrun Krämer and Sabine Schmidtke (eds.): *Speaking for Islam. Religious Authorities in Muslim Societies*, Leiden and Boston 2006, pp. 241–268.

Böttcher, Annabelle: Vielfältige islamische Traditionen in Deutschland, in: *Neue Züricher Zeitung* 298 (Dec. 21, 2004), p. 5.

Bradely, Raymond D.: Infinite Regress Argument, in: Robert Audi: *The Cambridge Dictionary of Philosophy*, Cambridge 1996, pp. 429–430.
Breydy, Michael: *Das Annalenwerk des Eutychios von Alexandrien. Ausgewählte Geschichten und Legenden kompiliert von Saʿīd ibn Baṭrīq um 935 A. D.*, Louvain 1983.
Breydy, Michael: *Études sur Saʿīd ibn Baṭrīq et ses sources*, Louvain 1983.
Breydy, Michael: Eutychios von Alexandrien, in: *Lexikon für Theologie und Kirche*, paperback ed. of the 2nd ed. by Josef Höfer and Karl Rahner, Freiburg im Breisgau, Basel and Rome, vol. 3 (1995), p. 1023.
Brockelmann, Carl: *Geschichte der arabischen Litteratur, Supplementbände I-III*. Leiden 1937–1942.
Brockelmann, Carl: *Geschichte der arabischen Litteratur*, 2. den Supplementbänden angepasste Auflage, Leiden 1943.
Brown, Jonathan: *The Canonization of al-Bukhārī and Muslim. The Formation and Function of the Sunnī Ḥadīth Canon*, Leiden 2007.
Brewer, Paul and Downing, David: *September 11 and Radical Islamic Terrorism*, Strongsville 2005.
vom Bruck, Gabriele: Regimes of Piety Revisited. Zaydī Political Moralities in Republican Yemen, in: *Die Welt des Islams* 50 (2010), pp. 185–223.
van Bruinessen, Martin: Genealogies of Islamic Radicalism in Post-Suharto Indonesia, in: *South East Asia Research* 10 (2002), pp. 117–154.
van Bruinessen, Martin: Kitab Kuning. Books in Arabic Script Used in the Pesantren-Milieu, in: *Bijdragen van het Koninklijk Instituut voor de Taal-, Land- en Volkenkunde* 146 (1990), pp. 249–250.
Brunner, Anette: Der zum Himmel erhobene Blick als Ausdruck enthusiastischen Schöpfertums. Die Darstellung der Invention im Künstlerbildnis der Goethezeit, in: *Paragrana. Internationale Zeitschrift für Historische Anthropologie*, suppl. 2 (2006), pp. 57–72.
Brunschvig, Robert: Los teólogos-juristas del islam en pro o en contra de la lógica griega, Ibn Ḥazm, al-Ġazālī, Ibn Taymiyya, in: *al-Andalus* 35 (1970), pp. 143–177.
Brunschvig, Robert: Pour ou contre la logique grecque chez les théologiens juristes de l'Islām. Ibn Ḥazm, al-G͟hazālī, Ibn Taymiyya, in: Robert Brunschvig (ed.): *Études d'Islamologie*, Paris 1979, pp. 303–327.
Buelow, George J.: Originality, Genius, Plagiarism in English Criticism of the Eighteenth Century, in: *International Review of the Aesthetics and Sociology of Music* 21 (1990), pp. 117–128.
Bulkeley, Kelly: *Dreaming in the World Religions*, New York 2008.
Bundesministerium des Innern: *Verfassungsschutzbericht 2009*, Berlin 2009.
Bunt, Gary R.: *Virtually Islamic. Computer-mediated Communication and Cyber Islamic Environments*, Cardiff 2000.
Busse, Heribert: *Die theologischen Beziehungen des Islam zu Judentum und Christentum*, 2nd ed. Darmstadt 1991.

Calder, Norman: Al-Nawawi's Typology of *muftīs* and its Significance for a General Theory of Islamic Law, in: *Islamic Law and Society* 3 (1996), pp. 137–164.
Calder, Norman: Tafsīr from Ṭabarī to Ibn Kathīr. Problems in the Description of a Genre; Illustrated with Reference to the Story of Abraham, in: Gerald R. Hawting and Abdul-Kader A. Shareef (eds.): *Approaches to the Qurʾān*, London 1993, pp. 101–140.
Calder, Norman: The Law (in History of Islamic Philosophy), in: Seyyed Hossein Nasr and Oliver Leaman (eds.): *History of Islamic Philosophy*, London 1996, pp. 979–998.
Calvin, Johannes: *Institutes of the Christian Religion*, 2 vols., Philadelphia 1975.
Calvinus, Iohannes: *Mosis libri V cum Iohannis Calvini Commentariis*, Geneva 1558.
Center for Strategic and International Studies: *Currents and Crosscurrents of Radical Islamism. A Report of the CSIS Transatlantic Dialogue on Terrorism*, April 2006, Washington 2006.
de Certeau, Michel: *Kunst des Handelns*, Berlin 1988.
Charfi, Abdelmajid: Bibliographie du dialogue islamo-chrétien, in: *Islamochristiana* 4 (1978), pp. 247–267.
Charfi, Abdelmajid: La fonction historique de la polémique islamochrétienne à l'époque abbaside, in: Samir Khalil Samir and Jørgen S. Nielsen (eds.): *Christian Arabic Apologetics During the Abbasid Period*, Leiden 1994, pp. 44–56.
Charfi, Abdelmajid: Polémiques islamo-chrétiennes à l'époque médiévale, in: Jacques Waardenburg (ed.): *Scholarly Approaches to Religion, Interreligious Perspectives and Islam*, Bern, Berlin, Frankfurt am Main, New York, Paris and Wien 1995, pp. 261–274.
Chejne, Anwar G.: Ibn Ḥazm of Cordova on Logic, in: *The Journal of the American Oriental Society* 104 (1984), pp. 52–72.
Chishtī, Wahhāj al-Dīn: *Bēgamāt-i Bhōpāl* (The Begamat of Bhopal), Karachi 1981.
Chittick, William C.: *The Sufi Path of Love. The Spiritual Teachings of Rumi*, New York 1983.
Chodkiewicz, Michel: *Le sceau des saints. Prophétie et sainteté dans la doctrine d'Ibn Arabî*, Paris 1986.
Chumaidy, A. Farichin: *The Jamʿiyyah Nahdlatul ʿUlama. Its Rise and Early Development* (1926–1945); unpublished M. A. thesis, Montreal 1976.
Churchill, Edward: Printed Literature of the Punjabi Muslims. 1860–1900, in: W. Eric Gustafson and Kenneth W. Jones (eds.): *Sources on Punjab History*, Delhi 1975, pp. 276–282.
Cohen, Mark R.: *Under Crescent and Cross. The Jews in the Middle Ages*, Princeton 1994.
Colvin, John Russell: Notice of the Peculiar Tenets Held by the Followers of Syed Ahmed. Taken Chiefly from the "Sirát-úl-Mústaqím", a Principal

Treatise of That Sect, Written by Moulaví Mahommed Ismaíl, in: *Journal of the Asiatic Society of Bengal* 1 (1832) pp. 479–498.
Commins, David Dean: *Islamic Reform. Politics and Social Change in the Late Ottoman Syria*, Oxford 1990.
Commins, David: *The Wahhabi Mission and Saudi Arabia*, London 2006.
Conermann, Stephan and El Hawary, Amr: Ausklang. Das Problem der Gattungsbestimmung in transkultureller Perspektive, in: idem (eds.): *Was sind Genres? Nicht-abendländische Kategorisierungen von Gattungen*, Schenefeld 2009, pp. 316–324.
Cook, David: *Studies in Muslim Apocalyptic*, Princeton 2002.
Cook, Michael A.: *Commanding Right and Forbidding Wrong in Islamic Thought*, Cambridge 2000.
Cooke, Francis T.: Ibn al-Qaiyim's Kitāb al-Rūḥ, in: *The Muslim World* 25 (1935), pp. 129–144.
Cooperson, Michael: *Classical Arabic Biography. The Heirs of the Prophets in the Age of al-Ma'mūn*, Cambridge 2000.
Copleston, Frederick S.J.: *A History of Philosophy*, vol. 5: *Hobbes to Hume*, London 1959.
Craig, William Lane: *The Kalām Cosmological Argument*, New York 1979.
Crottet, Bernard: *Calvin. Biographie*, Paris 1995.
Çağrıcı, Mustafa: İbn Teymiyye'nin bakışıyla Gazzâlî-Ibn Rüşd tartışması, in: *İslam Tetkikleri Dergisi* (*Review of Islamic Studies*) 9 (1995), pp. 77–126
Çelebī, Kātib: *Keşf al-zunun*, ed. by Şerefettin Yaltkaya and Rifat Bilge, 2 vols., Istanbul (Maarif Matbaası) 1941/1943.
Dabbāgh, Ḥasan: *Das Loben, eine Waffe mit zwei Seite* [sic!]. *Friday prayer dated Jan. 25, 2008.*
Dabbāgh, Hiba: *Khams daqā'iq wa-ḥasab*, n.p. n.d.
Dadah Khalīfa Afandī, Ibrāhīm: *al-Siyāsa al-sharʿiyya*, ed. by Fu'ād ʿAbd al-Munʿim Aḥmad, Alexandria 1411/1991.
Daiber, Hans: *Bibliography of Islamic Philosophy*, 2 vols., Leiden 1999.
Daiber, Hans: God versus Causality. Ghazālī's Solution and Its Historical Background, in: Georges Tamer (ed.): *Islam and Rationality. The Impact of al- Ghazālī*, vol. 1 , Leiden (forthcoming).
Dallal, Ahmad: Appropriating the Past. Twentieth Century Reconstruction of Premodern Islamic Thought, in: *Islamic Law and Society* 7 (2000), pp. 325–358.
Dallal, Ahmad: The Origins and Objectives of Islamic Revivalist Thought, in: *Journal of the American Oriental Society* 113 (1993), pp. 341–359.
Davidson, Herbert A.: Alfarabi and Avicenna on the Active Intellect, in: *Viator* 3 (1972), pp. 109–178.
Davidson, Herbert A.: *Alfarabi, Avicenna and Averroes on Intellect. Their Cosmologies, Theories of the Active Intellect and Theories of Human Intellect*, New York and Oxford 1992.

Davidson, Herbert A.: *Proofs for Eternity, Creation and the Existence of God in Medieval Islamic and Jewish Philosophy*, New York and Oxford 1987.

Degeorge, Gérard: *Damas. Des origines aux Mamluks*, Paris 1997.

Derenbourg, Hartwig: *Les manuscrits arabes de l'Escurial*, Paris 1884.

Desker, Barry and Ramakrishna, Kumar: Forging an Indirect Strategy in Southeast Asia, in: *The Washington Quarterly* 25 (2002), pp. 161–176.

al-Dhahabī, Shams al-Dīn: *al-Naṣīḥa al-dhahabiyya li-Ibn Taymiyya*, ed. by Muḥammad Zāhid al-Kawtharī, Damascus 1347/1928–29.

Dihlawī, ʿAbd al-ʿAzīz: *Fatāwā-i ʿazīzī*, 2 vols., Delhi 1311/1893.

Dihlawī, Shāh Ismāʿīl Shahīd: *Taqwiyat al-Īmān*, English translation, Delhi 1998, and Arabic/English, Riyadh 1995.

Dihlawī, Shāh Walī Allāh: *al-Inṣāf fī bayān asbāb al-ikhtilāf*, Cairo 1950.

Dihlawī, Shāh Walī Allāh: *Ḥujjat Allāh al-bāligha*, 2 vols., Cairo 1977.

Dihlawī, Shāh Walī Allāh: *ʿIqd al-jīd fī aḥkām al-ijtihād wal-taqlīd*, Cairo 1385 a. h./1965–1966.

al-Dimashqī al-Ḥiṣnī, Taqī al-Dīn Abū Bakr: *Dafʿ shubah man shabbaha wa-tamarrada wa-nasaba dhālik ilā al-Sayyid al-Jalīl al-Imām Aḥmad*, Cairo 1350/1931–32.

Djajadiningrat, P. A. Hoesein: Islam in Indonesia, in: Kenneth W. Morgan (ed.): *Islam. The Straight Path; Islam Interpreted by Muslims*, New York 1958, pp. 375–402.

Dobbin, Christine: *Islamic Revivalism in a Changing Peasant Economy. Central Sumatra; 1784–1847*, London 1983.

Dutton, Yasin: *ʿAmal* v. *ḥadīth* in Islamic Law. The Case of *sadl al-yadayn* (Holding One's Hands by One's Sides) When Doing the Prayer, in: *Islamic Law and Society* 3 (1996), pp. 13–40.

EI² = Peri Bearman, Thierry Bianquis, Charles Bosworth, E. van Dozel and Wolfhart Heinrichs (eds.): *Encyclopaedia of Islam*, 2nd ed., 12 vols., Leiden 1954–2004.

Eich, Thomas: Die Diskussion islamischer Rechtsgelehrter um pre-marital screening und die Abtreibung behinderter Embryonen, in: Thomas Eich and Thomas Sören Hoffmann (eds.:) *Kulturübergreifende Bioethik. Zwischen globaler Herausforderung und regionaler Perspektive*, Freiburg and Munich 2006, pp. 152–178.

El Azhary Sonbol, Amira: *Women, the Family, and Divorce Laws in Islam*, Syracuse 1996.

El Kaisy-Friemuth, Maha: *Al-Radd al-Jamīl*: al-Ghazālī's or Pseudo-Ghazālī's?, in: David Thomas (ed.): *The Bible in Arab Christianity*, Leiden and Boston 2005, pp. 275–295.

El Omari, Racha: Ibn Taymiyya's 'Theology of the Sunna' and His Polemics with the Ashʿarites, in: Rapoport and Ahmad, *Ibn Taymiyya and His Times*, pp. 101–119.

Ende, Werner: Religion, Politik und Literatur in Saudi-Arabien. Der geistesgeschichtliche Hintergrund der heutigen religiösen und kulturpolitischen Situation, in: *Orient* 22 (1981), pp. 377–390; 23 (1982) pp. 21–35, 378–393.

Endress, Gerhard: Die wissenschaftliche Literatur, in: Wolfdietrich Fischer (ed.): *Grundriss der Arabischen Philologie*, Wiesbaden 1992, suppl., vol. 3, pp. 25–57.

Endress, Gerhard: Grammatik und Logik. Arabische Philologie und griechische Philosophie im Widerstreit, in: Burkhard Mojsisch (ed.): *Sprachphilosophie in Antike und Mittelalter*, Amsterdam 1986, pp. 163–299.

Endress, Gerhard: The Defense of Reason. The Plea for Philosophy in the Religious Community, in: *Zeitschrift für Geschichte der arabisch-islamischen Wissenschaften* 6 (1990), pp. 1–49.

van Ess, Josef: *Die Erkenntnislehre des ʿAḍudaddīn al-Īcī, Übersetzung und Kommentar des ersten Buches seiner Mawāqif*, Wiesbaden 1966.

Van Ess, Josef: Ḍirār b. ʿAmr und die "Cahmīya". Die Biographie einer vergessenen Schule, in: *Der Islam* 43 (1967), pp. 241–279; 44 (1968), pp. 1–70.

van Ess, Josef: Skepticism in Islamic Religious Thought, in: Charles Malik (ed.): *God and Man in Contemporary Islamic Thought*, Beirut 1972, pp. 83–98.

van Ess, Josef: The Logical Structure of Islamic Theology, in: Gustave Edmund von Grunebaum (ed.): *Logic in Classical Islamic Culture. First Giorgio Levi della Vida Biennial Conference*; May 12, 1967, Wiesbaden 1970, pp. 21–50.

van Ess, Josef: *Theologie und Gesellschaft im 2. und 3. Jahrhundert Hidschra. Eine Geschichte des religiösen Denkens im frühen Islam*, 6 vols., Berlin and New York 1991–1997.

van Ess, Josef: *Zwischen Ḥadīṯ und Theologie. Studien zum Entstehen prädestinatianischer Überlieferung*, Berlin and New York 1975.

Fakhry, Majid: *A History of Islamic Philosophy*, 2nd ed. London 2004.

Fakhry, Majid: *Islamic Occasionalism and its Critique by Averroës and Aquinas*, London and New York 2008.

Fakhry, Majid: The Classical Islamic Arguments for the Existence of God, in: *The Muslim World* 47 (1957), pp. 133–145.

Fāliḥ, Āmir ʿAbd-Allāh: *Muʿjam alfāẓ al-ʿaqīda*, Riyadh 1997.

al-Fārābī, Abū Naṣr: *Iḥṣāʾ al-ʿulūm*, ed. by Angel González Palencia, Madrid 1932.

al-Fārābī, Abū Naṣr: Kitāb al-Qiyās and Kitāb al-Qiyās al-ṣaghīr, in: idem: *al-Manṭiq ʿind al-Fārābī*, vol. 2, pp. 11–93.

al-Fārābī, Abū Naṣr: *al-Madīna al-fāḍila. Al-Farabi on the Perfect State*; Abū Naṣr al-Fārābī's Mabādiʾ ārāʾ ahl al-madīna al-fāḍila, ed. by Richard Walzer, Oxford 1985.

al-Fārābī, Abū Naṣr: *al-Manṭiq ʿind al-Fārābī*, 3 vols., ed. by Rafīq al-ʿAjam, Beirut 1985–1986.

al-Fārābī, Abū Naṣr: *Risāla fī al-ʿAql*, ed. by Maurice Bouyges, Beirut 1938.

al-Fawzan, ʿAbdullah Ibn Salih: *Die Nacht von al-Qadr. From Ahadith as-Siyam*; Ahkam wa Adab (p. 141–143), translated from English to German by Amr Abdullah, 2002.

Fealy, Greg: *Ulama and Politics in Indonesia. A History of Nahdlatul Ulama (1952–1967)*; Ph.D thesis, Victoria 1988.

Federal Office for Migration and Refugees: *Muslim Life in Germany*, Nürnberg 2009.

Fierro, Maribel: La polémique à propos de rafʿ al-yadain fī l-ṣalāt dans al-Andalus, in: *Studia Islamica* 65 (1987), pp. 69–90.

Fierro, Maribel: The Treatises against Innovations (*Kutub al-bidʿa*), in: *Der Islam* 69 (1992), pp. 204–246.

Flasch, Kurt: Attributionsatheismus in Boccaccios Decameron VI 9. Guido Cavalcanti, in: Friedrich Niewöhner and Olaf Pluta (eds.): *Atheismus im Mittelalter und in der Renaissance*, Wiesbaden 1999, pp. 115–127.

Frank, Richard: *Al-Ghazālī and the Ashʿarite School*, Durham 1994.

Frank, Richard M.: Reason and Revealed Law. A Sample of Parallels and Divergences in Kalām and Falsafa, in: Roger Arnaldez and Simone van Riet (eds.): *Recherches d'Islamologie. Recueil d'articles offert à Georges C. Anawati et Louis Gardet par leur collègues et amis*, Louvain 1978.

Franke, Patrick: *Mullā ʿAlī al-Qārī. Textproduktion und Gedankenwelt eines mekkanischen Religionsgelehrten der islamischen Jahrtausendwende* (forthcoming).

Freitag, Ulrike: Der Orientalist und der Mufti. Kulturkontakt im Mekka des 19. Jahrhunderts, in: *Die Welt des Islams* 43 (2003), pp. 37–60.

Frenkel, Yehoshua: Islamic Utopia under the Mamluks. The Social and Legal Ideals of Ibn Qayyim al-Ǧawziyyah, in: Bori and Holtzman, *Scholar in the Shadow*, pp. 67–87.

Fritsch, Erdmann: *Islam und Christentum im Mittelalter. Beiträge zur Geschichte der muslimischen Polemik gegen das Christentum in arabischer Sprache*, Breslau 1930.

Fu'ād, ʿAbd al-Fattāḥ Aḥmad: *Falāsifat al-Islām wal-ṣūfiyya wa-mawqif ahl al-sunna minhum*, Alexandria 2006.

Fu'ād, ʿAbd al-Fattāḥ: *Ibn Taymiyya wa-mawqifuhu min al-fikr al-falsafī*, Alexandria 1980.

Fuess, Albrecht: *Verbranntes Ufer. Auswirkungen mamlukischer Seepolitik auf Beirut und die syro-palästinensische Küste (1250–1517)*, Leiden 2001.

Füssel, Marian: Die Rückkehr des Subjekts in der Kulturgeschichte. Beobachtungen aus praxeologischer Perspektive, in: Stefan Deines, Stephan Jaeger and Ansgar Nünning (eds.): *Historisierte Subjekte. Subjektivierte Historie*; Zur Verfügbarkeit und Unverfügbarkeit von Geschichte, Berlin 2003, pp. 141–159.

Gaborieau, Marc: A Nineteenth Century Indian "Wahhabi" Tract Against the Cult of Muslim Saints, in: Christian W. Troll (ed.): *Muslim Shrines in India. Their Character, History and Significance*, Delhi 1989, pp. 198–256.

Gaborieau, Marc: Criticizing the Sufis. The Debate in Early Nineteenth Century India, in: Frederick de Jong and Bernd Radtke (eds.): *Islamic Mysticism Contested. Thirteen Centuries of Controversies and Polemics*, Leiden 1999, pp. 452–467.
Gaborieau, Marc: Late Persian, Early Urdu. The Case of "Wahhabi" Literature (1818–1857), in: Françoise Delvoye (ed.): *Confluence of Culture. French Contributions to Indo-Persian Studies*, Delhi 1994, pp. 170–196.
Galen: *al-Ṣināʿa al-ṣaghīra*, ed. by M. S. Sālim, Cairo 1988.
Galigo, Andi Syamsul Bahri: *Pemikiran Tasauf Syeikh Abu Mahasin Yusuf al-Taj*, Kuala Lumpur 2004.
Galston, Miriam: al-Fārābī on Aristotle's Theory of Demonstration, in: Parviz Morewedge (ed.): *Islamic Philosophy and Mysticism*, Delmar and New York 1981, pp. 23–24.
Gardet, Louis, and Anawati, Georges C.: *Introduction à la théologie musulmane. Essai de théologie comparée*, Paris 1948.
Gardet, Louis, and Anawati, Georges C.: *Les grands problèmes de la théologie musulmane. Dieu et la destine de l'homme*, Paris 1967.
Gaudeul, Jean-Marie: *Encounters and Clashes. Islam and Christianity in History*, 2 vols., Rome 2000.
Gellner, Ernest: *Muslim Society*, Cambridge 1981.
Gerber, Haim: *Islamic Law and Culture. 1600–1840*, Leiden 1999.
al-Ghannūshī, Rāshid: *al-Qadar ʿind Ibn Taymiyya*, London 1999.
al-Ghazālī, Abū Ḥāmid: *Iḥyāʾ ʿulūm al-dīn*, 5 vols., Cairo 1933.
al-Ghazālī, Abū Ḥāmid: *Iljām al-ʿawāmm min ʿilm al-kalām*, Egypt 1931–32.
al-Ghazālī, Abū Ḥāmid: *Miḥakk al-naẓar*, ed. by Rafīq al-ʿAjam, Beirut 1994.
al-Ghazālī, Abū Ḥāmid: *Miʿyār al-ʿilm fī fann al-manṭiq*, Beirut 1983.
al-Ghazālī, Abū Ḥāmid: *Kitāb al-Mustaṣfā min ʿilm al-uṣūl*, bi-sharḥ Muḥibb Allāh b. ʿAbd al-Shakūr (al-Bihārī), Cairo 1322–1324/1904–1906.
al-Ghazālī, Abū Ḥāmid: *Tahāfut al-falāsifa*, ed. by Sulaymān Dunyā, Cairo 1980.
al-Ghazālī, Abū Ḥāmid: *Deliverance from Error. An Annotated Translation of "al-Munqidh min al-ḍalāl" and other Relevant Works of al-Ghazālī*, transl. by Richard Joseph McCarthy, Louisville 1980.
al-Ghazālī, Abū Ḥāmid: *Réfutation excellente de la divinité de Jésus-Christ d'après les évangiles. Texte établi, traduit et commenté par Robert Chidiac*, Paris 1939.
al-Ghazālī, Muḥammad: *al-Fasād al-siyāsī fī al-mujtamaʿāt al-ʿarabiyya wal-islāmiyya*, Cairo 2005.
al-Ghazālī, Zaynab: *Ayyām min ḥayātī*, Cairo 1988.
Ghaznawī, ʿAbd al-Ḥaqq: *Kitāb al-Arbaʿīn fī anna Thanāʾ Allāh laysa ʿalā madhhab al-muḥaddithīn fī al-dīn bal ʿalā madhhab al-jahmiyya wal-muʿtazila wal-qadariyya al-muḥarrifīn*, Amritsar n. d.
Giladi, Avner: *Children of Islam. Concepts of Childhood in Medieval Muslim Society*, New York 1968.

Giladi, Avner: Gender Differences on Child Rearing and Education. Some Preliminary Observations with Reference to Medieval Muslim Thought, in: *al-Qantara* 16 (1995), pp. 291–301.

Giladi, Avner: Some Notes on Taḥnīk in Medieval Islam, in: *Journal of Near Eastern Studies* 47 (1988), pp. 175–179.

Gimaret, Daniel: *Les noms divins en Islam. Exégèse lexicographiqe et théologique*, Paris 1988.

Gimaret, Daniel: Théories de l'acte humain dans l'école hanbalite, in: *Bulletin d'études orientales* 28 (1977), pp. 165–78.

Gimaret, Daniel: *Théories de l'acte humain en théologie musulmane*, Paris 1980.

Girdner, Scott Michael: *Reasoning with Revelation. The Significance of the Koranic Contextualization of Philosophy in al-Ghazālī's* Mishkāt al-Anwār (the Niche of Lights), unpublished dissertation, Boston University 2010.

Glasmeier, Michael: *Loop. Zur Geschichte und Theorie der Endlosschleife am Beispiel Rodney Grahams*, key note speech, May 5, 2011 in the course of the conference "Wiederaufgelegt. Zur Appropriation von Texten und Büchern in Büchern" (May 5–7, 2011) organized by Annette Gilbert, Peter Szondi-Institute, Free University, Berlin.

Gobillot, Geneviève: *La fiṭra. La conception originelle*; ses interprétations et functions chez les penseurs musulmans, Cairo 2000.

Gobillot, Geneviève: L'Épitre du discours sur la fiṭra (*Risāla fī-l-kalām ʿalā-l-fiṭra*) de Taqī-l-Dīn Aḥmad Ibn Taymīyya (661/1262–728/1328). Présentation et traduction annotée, in: *Annales Islamologiques* 20 (1984), pp. 29–53.

Gökalp, Altan: Les fruits de l'arbre plutôt que ses racines. Le Suleymanisme, in: Marc Gaborieau, Alexandre Popovic and Thierry Zarcone (eds.): *Naqshbandis. Cheminements et situation actuelle d'un ordre mystique musulman*, Istanbul and Paris 1990, pp. 421–435.

Goldziher, Ignaz: *Die Richtungen der islamischen Koranauslegung*, Leiden 1920.

Goldziher, Ignaz: Neuplatonische und gnostische Elemente im Ḥadīṯ, in: Joseph Desomogyi (ed.): *Ignaz Goldziher. Gesammelte Schriften*, Hildesheim 1970 (reprint), vol. 5, pp. 108–114.

Goldziher, Ignaz: Stellung der alten islamischen Orthodoxie zu den antiken Wissenschaften, in: Joseph Desomogyi (ed.): *Ignaz Goldziher. Gesammelte Schriften*, Hildesheim 1970, vol. 5, pp. 357–400.

Goldziher, Ignaz: The Attitude of Orthodox Islam Toward the "Ancient Sciences", in: Merlin L. Swartz (ed.): *Studies on Islam*, New York and Oxford 1981, pp. 185–215.

Goldziher, Ignaz: *The Ẓāhirīs. Their Doctrine and Their History; a Contribution to the History of Islamic Theology*, Leiden 2007.

Goldziher, Ignaz: Ueber muhammedanische Polemik gegen Ahl al-kitâb, in: *Zeitschrift der Deutschen Morgenländischen Gesellschaft* 32 (1878), pp. 341–387.

Graf, Georg: *Geschichte der christlichen arabischen Literatur*, vol. 2: Die Schriftsteller bis zur Mitte des 15. Jahrhunderts, Vatican City 1947.

Griffel, Frank: Al-Ghazālī's Appropriation of Ibn Sīnā's Views on Causality and the Development of the Science in Islam, in: *Uluslararası İbn Sīnā sempozyumu bildiriler* (May 22–24, 2008), vol. 2, pp. 105–115.

Griffel, Frank: *Al-Ghazālī's Philosophical Theology*, Oxford 2009.

Griffel, Frank: *Apostasie und Toleranz im Islam. Die Entwicklung zu al-Ghazālīs Urteil gegen die Philosophie und die Reaktionen der Philosophen*, Leiden, Bosten and Cologne 2000.

Griffel, Frank: The Harmony of Natural Law and Shari'a in Islamist Theology, in: Abbas Amanat and Frank Griffel (eds.): *Shari'a. Islamic Law in the Contemporary Context*, Stanford 2007, pp. 38–61.

Griffith, Sidney H.: Apologetics and Historiography in the Annals of Eutychius of Alexandria. Christian Self-Definition in the World of Islam, in: Rifaat Ebied and Herman Teule (eds.): *Studies on the Christian Arabic Heritage. In Honour of Father Prof. Dr. Samir Khalil Samir S. I. at the Occasion of his Sixty-Fifth Birthday*, Louvain 2004, pp. 65–90.

Griffith, Sidney H.: Eutychios of Alexandria, in: Alexander P. Kazhdan (ed.): *The Oxford Dictionary of Byzantinum*, New York and Oxford 1991, vol. 2, p. 760.

Gupta, Narayani: *Delhi Between Two Empires. 1803–1931. Society, Government and Urban Growth*, Delhi 1981.

Gutas, Dimitri: Aspects of Literary Form and Genre in Arabic Logical Works, in: Charles Burnett (ed.): *Glosses and Commentaries on Aristotelian Logical Texts. The Syriac, Arabic and Medieval Latin Traditions*, London 1993, pp. 29–76.

Gutas, Dimitri: *Avicenna and the Aristotelian Tradition. Introduction to Reading Avicenna's Philosophical Works*, Leiden 1988.

Gutas, Dimitri: Fārābī, Abū Naṣr i. Biography, in: Ehsan Yarshater (ed.): *Encyclopedia Iranica*, vols. 1–14, London 1985–2008, vol. 9, New York 1999, pp. 208–213.

Gutas, Dimitri: *Greek Thought, Arabic Culture. The Graeco-Arabic Translation Movement in Baghdad and Early ʿAbbāsid Society (2nd–4th/8th–10th Centuries)*, London and New York 1998.

Gutas, Dimitri: Pre-Plotinian Philosophy in Arabic (other than Platonism and Aristotelianism). A Review of the Sources, in: Wolfgang Haase (ed.): *Aufstieg und Niedergang der Römischen Welt*, Berlin and New York 1994, vol. II. 361, pp. 4939–4973.

Gutas, Dimitri: The Heritage of Avicenna. The Golden Age of Arabic Philosophy, 1000 – ca. 1350, in: Jules Janssens and Daniel De Smet (eds.): *Avicenna and His Heritage. Acts of the International Colloquium, Leuven – Louvain-la-Neuve September 8–11, 1999*, Leuven 2002, pp. 81–97.

Gutas, Dimitri: The Logic of Theology (*kalām*) in Avicenna, in: Dominik Perler and Ulrich Rudolph (eds.): *Logik und Theologie. Das* Organon *im arabischen und im lateinischen Mittelalter*, Leiden and Boston 2005, pp. 59–72.

Gutas, Dimitri: The Study of Arabic Philosophy in the Twentieth Century. An Essay on the Historiography of Arabic Philosophy, in: *British Journal of Middle Eastern Studies* 29 (2002), pp. 5–25.

al-Ḥājj, Muḥammad Aḥmad: Dirāsa ḥawla al-kitāb, in: Ibn Qayyim al-Jawziyya, Shams al-Dīn Muḥammad: *Hidāyat al-ḥayārā fī ajwibat al-yahūd wal-naṣārā*, ed. by Muḥammad Aḥmad al-Ḥājj, Damascus 1416/1996, pp. 15–214.

Ḥājjī Khalīfa (Kātib Çelebi): *Kashf al-ẓunūn ʿan asāmī al-kutub wal-funūn*, 6 vols., ed. by Şerefeddin Yaltakaya and Rifat Bilge, Istanbul 1941–1955.

Hakkı, İzmirli İsmail: *Yeni İlm-i Kelam*, 2 vols., Istanbul 1920.

Hallaq, Wael B.: *A History of Islamic Legal Theories. An Introduction to Sunnī* uṣūl al-fiqh, Cambridge 1997.

Hallaq, Wael B.: *An Introduction to Islamic Law,* Cambridge and New York 2009.

Hallaq, Wael B.: *Authority, Continuity and Change in Islamic Law*, Cambridge 2001.

Hallaq, Wael B.: *Ibn Taymiyya Against the Greek Logicians. Translated with an Introduction and Notes*, Oxford 1993.

Hallaq, Wael B.: Ibn Taymiyya on the Existence of God, in: *Acta Orientalia* 52 (1991), pp. 49–69.

Hallaq, Wael B.: Logic. Formal Arguments and Formalization of Arguments in Sunnī Jurisprudence, in: *Arabica* 37 (1990), pp. 315–358.

al-Hamadhānī, ʿAbd al-Jabbār b. Aḥmad: *Critique of Christian Origins. A Parallel English-Arabic Text*; ed., transl. and annotated by Gabriel Said Reynolds and Samir Khalil Samir, Provo 2010.

al-Ḥamawī, Yāqūt b. ʿAbd Allāh: *Kitāb Muʿjam al-buldān*, 10 parts, Cairo 1324/1906.

Ḥāmid, Raḍiyya: *Nawwāb Sayyid Ṣiddīq Ḥasan Khān*, Delhi 1983.

Hamilton, Richard F.: *The Social Misconstruction of Reality. Validity and Verification in the Scholarly Community*, New Haven and London 1996.

Haqq, Sirajul: Ibn-Taimiyya's Conception of Analogy and Consensus, in: *Islamic Culture* 17 (1943), pp. 77–87.

Haqque, Serajul: Ibn Taimīyyah, in: Mian Mohammad Sharif (ed.): *A History of Muslim Philosophy. With Short Accounts of Other Disciplines and the Modern Renaissance in Muslim Lands*, 2 vols., Wiesbaden 1963–1966, vol. 2, pp. 796–819.

al-Hararī al-Ḥabashī, ʿAbd Allāh: *al-Maqālāt al-sunniyya fī kashf ḍalālāt Aḥmad ibn Taymiyya*, Beirut 1425/2004.

Harās, Muḥammad Khalīl: *Bāʿith al-nahḍa al-islāmiyya. Ibn Taymiyya al-salafī; naqduhu li-masālik al-mutakallimīn wal-falāsifa fī al-ilāhiyyāt*, Beirut 1984.

al-Ḥarbī, ʿAlī b. ʿAlī Jābir: *Kashf al-astār li-ibṭāl iddiʿāʾ fanāʾ al-nār. Al-mansūb li-shaykh al-islām Ibn Taymiyya wa-tilmīdhihi Ibn Qayyim al-Jawziyya*, Mecca 1410/1990.

Haroon, Sana: *Frontier of Faith. Islam in the Indo-Afghan Borderland*, New York 2007.

Hartmann, Angelika: *an-Nāṣir li-Dīn Allāh (1180–1225). Politik, Religion, Kultur in der späten ʿAbbāsidenzeit*, Berlin and New York 1975.

Hartmann, Angelika: Bemerkungen zu Handschriften ʿUmar as-Suhrawardīs, echten und vermeintlichen Autographen, in: *Der Islam* 60 (1983), pp. 112–142.

Hartmann, Angelika: Eine orthodoxe Polemik gegen Philosophen und Freidenker – Eine zeitgenössische Schrift gegen Ḥāfiẓ? – Muʿīn ud-Dīn Yazdī und sein "Tarǧama-yi rašf an-naṣā'iḥ", in: *Der Islam* 56 (1979), pp. 274–293.

Hartmann, Angelika: Ismāʿīlitische Theologie bei sunnitischen ʿulamā' des Mittelalters?, in: Ludwig Hagemann and Ernst Pulsfort (eds.): *"Ihr alle aber seid Brüder". Festschrift für A. Th. Khoury zum 60. Geburtstag*, Würzburg and Altenberge 1990, pp. 190–206.

Hartmann, Angelika: Kosmogonie und Seelenlehre bei ʿUmar as-Suhrawardī (st. 632/1234), in: Dieter Bellmann (ed.): *Gedenkschrift Wolfgang Reuschel, Akten des III. Arabistischen Kolloquiums, Leipzig, 21.-22. November 1991*, Stuttgart 1994, pp. 135–156.

Hartmann, Angelika: La prédication islamique au moyen age. Ibn al-Ǧauzī et ses sermons (fin du 6/12e siècle), in: *Quaderni di Studi Arabi* 5–6 (1987–88), pp. 337–345.

Hartung, Jan-Peter: *Viele Wege und ein Ziel. Leben und Wirken von Sayyid Abū al-Ḥasan ʿAlī al-Ḥasan Nadwī (1914–1999)*, Würzburg 2004.

Harun, Nasrun: *Ijtihad Ibn Qayyim al-Jauziyyah dalam Konteks Perubahan Sosial*, Ph.D. thesis, Jakarta 1997.

Hasan, Mushirul: *From Pluralism to Seperatism. Qasbas in Colonial Awadh*, New Delhi 2004.

Ḥasanī, ʿAbd al-Ḥayy: *Nuzhat al-khawāṭir wa-bahjat al-masāmiʿ wal-nawāẓir*, 8 vols., Hyderabad 1402/1981.

Hawting, Gerald R.: Širk and 'Idolatry' in Monotheist Polemic, in: Uri Rubin and David J. Wasserstein (eds.): *Dhimmis and Others. Jews and Christians and the World of Classical Islam*, Winona Lake 1997, pp. 107–126.

Haykel, Bernard: *Revival and Reform in Islam. The Legacy of Muhammad al-Shawkānī*, Cambridge 2003.

Heer, Nicholas: Ibn Taymiyah's Empiricism, in: Farhad Kazemi and Robert Duncan McChesney (eds.): *A Way Prepared. Essays on Islamic Culture in Honor of Richard Bayly Winder*, New York and London 1988, pp. 109–115.

Heer, Nicholas: The Priority of Reason in the Interpretation of Scripture. Ibn Taymiyyah and the Mutakallimun, in: Mustansir Mir (ed.): *Literary Heritage of Classical Islam. Arabic and Islamic Studies in Honor of James A. Bellamy*, Princeton 1993, pp. 181–195.

Heimbach, Marfa: *Die Entwicklung der islamischen Gemeinschaft in Deutschland seit 1961*, Berlin 2001.

Heinen, Anton: *Islamic Cosmology. A Study of as-Suyūṭī's* al-Hay'a as-Saniyya fī l-hay'a as-sunniyya, Stuttgart 1982.

Hermansen, Marcia K.: Dreams and Dreaming in Islam, in: Kelly Bulkeley (ed.): *Dreams. A Reader in the Religious, Cultural and Psychological Dimensions of Dreaming*, New York 2001.

Hermansen, Marcia K.: Translator's Introduction, in: Walī Allāh: *The Conclusive Argument from God. Shāh Walī Allāh of Delhi's* Ḥujjat Allāh al-Bāligha, transl. by Marcia K. Hermansen, Leiden 1995, pp. xv–xl.

Hick, John: *Arguments for the Existence of God*, London 1970.

Ḥijāzī, ʿIwaḍ Allāh Jād: *Ibn al-Qayyim wa-mawqifuhu min al-tafkīr al-islāmī*, Cairo 1960.

Hirschler, Konrad: Pre-Eighteenth Century Traditions of Revivalism. Damascus in the Thirteenth Century, in: *Bulletin of the School for Oriental and African Studies* 68 (2005), pp. 195–214.

Holland, Muhtar (transl.): *Public Duties in Islam. The Institution of the Ḥisba*, Leicester 1982.

Holmes Katz, Marion: *The Birth of the Prophet Muhammad*, Leiden 2007.

Holt, Peter M.: *The Age of the Crusades*, London and New York 1986.

Holthuis, Susanne: *Intertextualität. Aspekte einer rezeptionsorientierten Konzeption*, Tübingen 1993.

Holtzman, Livnat: Human Choice, Divine Guidance and the *Fiṭra* Tradition. The Use of Ḥadīth in Theological Treatises by Ibn Taymiyya and Ibn Qayyim al-Jawziyya, in: Rapoport and Ahmed, *Ibn Taymiyya and His Times*, pp. 163–188.

Holtzman, Livnat: Ibn Qayyim al-Jawziyyah, in: Joseph Lowry and Devin Stewart (eds.): *Essays in Arabic Literary Biography 1350–1850*, Wiesbaden 2009, pp. 201–223.

Hoover, Jon: God Acts by His Will and Power. Ibn Taymiyya's Theology of a Personal God in His Treatise on the Voluntary Attributes, in: Rapoport and Ahmad, *Ibn Taymiyya and His Times*, pp. 55–77.

Hoover, Jon: *Ibn Taymiyya's Theodicy of Perpetual Optimism*, Leiden and Boston 2007.

Hoover, Jon: Islamic Universalism. Ibn Qayyim al-Jawziyya's Salafī Deliberations on the Duration of Hell-Fire, in: *The Muslim World* 99 (2009), pp. 181–201.

Hoover, Jon: Perpetual Creativity in the Perfection of God. Ibn Taymiyya's Hadith Commentary on God's Creation of this World, in: *Journal of Islamic Studies* 15 (2004), pp. 287–329.

Hoover, Jon: The Apologetic and Pastoral Intentions of Ibn Qayyim al-Jawziyya's Polemic against Jews and Christians, in: *The Muslim World* 100 (2010), pp. 476–489.

Hooykaas, Reijer: *Religion and the Rise of Modern Science*, Edinburgh 1972.

Hourani, George F.: *Arab Seafaring in the Indian Ocean in Ancient and Early Medieval Times*, Princeton 1995.

Howell, Julia Day: Sufism and the Indonesian Islamic Revival, in: *The Journal of Asian Studies* 60 (2001), pp. 701–729.

al-Ḥumayd, ʿAbd al-Karīm b. Ṣāliḥ: *al-Inkār ʿalā man lam yaʿtaqid khuld wa taʾbīd al-kuffār fī al-nār*, Burayda 1422/2001.

Hunter, William W.: *Our Indian Muslims, are They Bound in Conscience to Rebel Against the Queen?*, Delhi 1969. [1st ed. 1876]

Hurgronje, C. Snouck: *Mekka in the Latter Part of the 19th Century. Daily Life, Customs and Learning of the Moslims of the East-India-Archipelago*, Leiden 1970.

Hurvitz, Nimrod: *Competing Texts. The Relationship between al-Mawardi's and Abu Ya'la's* al-Ahkam al-sultaniyya, Cambridge 2007.

Hurvitz, Nimrod: The *Mukhtaṣar* of al-Khiraqī, in: Ron Shaham (ed.): *Law, Custom and Statute in the Muslim World*, Leiden 2007, pp. 1–16.

Ḥusayn Dihlawī, Nadhīr: *Fatāwā-yi nadhīriyya*, 3 vols., Gujranwālā n. d.

Husson, Lawrence: Indonesians in Saudi Arabia. Worship and Work, in: *Studia Islamika* 4 (1997), pp. 109–135.

Ibn ʿAbbās al-Wājih, ʿAbd al-Salām: *Aʿlām al-muʾallifīn al-Zaydiyya*, Sanaa 1420/1999.

Ibn ʿAbd al-Hādī, Muḥammad b. Aḥmad: *al-ʿUqūd al-durriyya min manāqib shaykh al-islām Aḥmad ibn Taymiyya*, Beirut n. d.

Ibn ʿAbd al-Wahhāb, ʿAbd Allāh b. Muḥammad: Jawāb ʿalā al-shīʿa wal-zaydiyya, in: Ibn ʿAbd al-Wahhāb, ʿAbd Allāh b. Muḥammad: *Majmūʿat al-Tawḥīd*, Cairo 1346/1927, pp. 128–159.

Ibn Abdil-Wahab, Imam Muhammad: *Die Bedingungen, Säulen und Pflichten des Gebetes*, translated from English into Germany by Abu Imran, 2005.

Ibn Abdil-Wahab, Imam Muhammad: *Religiöse Erscheinungen der Dschahiliya*, translated from English to German by Azad Ibn Muhammad, 2004.

Ibn ʿAqīl, Abū al-Wafāʾ: *al-Taʿlīqāt al-musammāt "Kitāb al-Funūn"*, 2 vols., ed. by George Makdisi, Beirut 1970–1971.

Ibn ʿArabī, Muḥyī al-Dīn: *al-Futūḥāt al-Makkiyya*, 4 vols., Cairo 1405/1985.

Ibn al-ʿArīf, Abū al-ʿAbbās: *Maḥāsin al-majālis*, Paris 1939.

Ibn al-ʿArīf, Abū al-ʿAbbās: *The Attractions of Mystical Sessions*, London 1980.

Ibn ʿAtīq, Ismāʿīl b. Saʿd b. Ḥamad: *Introduction to al-Majmūʿ al-Mufīd min rasāʾil wa-fatāwā al-Shaykh Saʿd b. Ḥamad b. ʿAtīq*, Riyadh 1415/1995.

Ibn Badrān, ʿAbd al-Qādir: *al-Madkhal ilā madhhab al-imām Aḥmad ibn Ḥanbal*, Cairo n. d.

Ibn Baṭṭūṭa, Abū ʿAbd Allāh Muḥammad: *Riḥlat Ibn Baṭṭūṭa*, Beirut 1960.

Ibn al-Baṭrīq, Saʿīd: *Eutychii Patriarchae Alexandrini Annales*, 2 vols., ed. by Louis Cheikho, Carra de Vaux and Habib Zayyat, Louvain 1954.

Ibn Bāz, ʿAbd al-ʿAzīz: *al-Adilla al-naqliyya wal-ḥissiyya ʿalā imkān al-ṣuʿūd ilā al-kawākib wa-ʿalā jarayān al-shams wal-qamar wa-sukūn al-arḍ*, Riyadh 1982.

Ibn Bāz, ʿAbd al-Azīz: *Bayān* of the *Madhhab ahl al-sunna fī al-istiwāʾ* (Explanation of the People of the Sunna's Teachings of the *istiwāʾ*), in: *Majallat al-Buḥūth al-Islāmiyya* 8 (1403/1983), pp. 169–172.

Ibn Bāz, ʿAbd al-ʿAzīz b. ʿAbd Allāh: *Islamic Fatawa Regarding Women*, London 1996.

Ibn Baz, Abdu-l-Aziz Ibn Abdullah: *Die Art des Propheten, das Gebet zu verrichten*, translated from English into German by K. al-Akad, 2004.

(I)bin Baz, Abdul Aziz: *Wichtige Lektionen für die Muslimische Gemeinschaft*, translated by Umm Amani al-Akad, 2003.

Ibn al-Farrāʾ, Abū Yaʿlā: *al-Masāʾil al-ʿaqdiyya min Kitāb al-Riwāyatayn wal-wajhayn*, ed. by Saʿūd ibn ʿAbd al-ʿAzīz al-Khalaf, Riyadh 1419/1999.

Ibn Ḥajar al-ʿAsqalānī: *al-Durar al-kāmina fī aʿyān al-miʾa al-thāmina*, 7 vols., ed. by M. S. Jād al-Ḥaqq, Cairo 1966.

Ibn Ḥanbal, Aḥmad: *Musnād*, 6 vols., Istanbul 1992.

Ibn Ḥanbal, Aḥmad: *al-Radd ʿalā al-zanādiqa wal-jahmiyya*, ed. by ʿAlī Sāmī al-Nashshār, Alexandria 1971.

Ibn Ḥazm al-Ẓāhirī, Abū Muḥammad ʿAlī b. Aḥmad: *al-Fiṣal fī al-milal wal-ahwāʾ wal-niḥal*, 5 vols., ed. by Muḥammad Ibrāhīm Naṣr and ʿAbd al-Raḥmān ʿUmayra, Beirut n. d.

Ibn al-Jawzī, Abū al-Faraj ʿAbd al-Raḥmān: *Talbīs Iblīs*, ed. by Khayr al-Dīn ʿAlī, Beirut n. d.

Ibn al-Jawzī: *The Devil's Delusion*, transl. by David Samuel Margoliouth, in: *Islamic Culture* 9 (1935), pp. 1–21, 10 (1935) pp. 20–39.

Ibn Kathīr, Aḥmad al-Dīn Ismāʿīl: *al-Bidāya wal-nihāya*, 7 vols., Cairo 1939.

Ibn Kathir: *Erläuterung von missverstandenen Versen*, translated from Bosnian into German by S. D., 2001.

Ibn Khaldūn: *The Muqaddimah. An Introduction to History*, 3 vols., transl. by Franz Rosenthal, New York 1974.

Ibn Khaldūn: *Muqaddimat Ibn Khaldūn. Prolégomènes d'Ebn-Khaldoun; texte arabe publié d'après les manuscrits de la Bibliothèque Impériale par M. Quatremère*, 3 vols., Beirut 1970 (reprint of Paris 1858).

Ibn Khallikān: *Kitāb Wafayāt al-aʿyān. Biographical Dictionary*; transl. from the Arabic by Mac Guckin de Slane, 4 vols., Beirut 1970.

Ibn Khallikān: *Wafayāt al-aʿyān*, ed. by Iḥsān ʿAbbās, 8 vols., Beirut 1977.

Ibn al-Mawṣilī, Muḥammad: *Mukhtaṣar al-Ṣawāʾiq al-mursala ʿalā al-jahmiyya wal-muʿaṭṭila li-Ibn Qayyim al-Jawziyya*, ed. by al-Ḥasan b. ʿAbd al-Raḥmān al-ʿAlawī, 4 vols., Riyadh 1425/2004.

Ibn Murrī, Shihāb al-Dīn: Athāra min al-taʾrīkh, in: *al-Manār* 10 (1325/1907), pp. 616–621.

Ibn Nizar, Tamar Jaya: *Pemikiran Kalām Ibn Qayyim al-Jauziyyah*, Ph. D. thesis Jakarta 1999.

Ibn Qudāma, Muwaffaq al-Dīn ʿAbd Allāh b. Aḥmad: *al-Mughnī*, 15 vols., ed. by ʿAbd Allāh ʿAbd al-Muḥsin al-Turkī and ʿAbd al-Fattāḥ Muḥammad al-Ḥulw, Cairo 1406–1411/1986–1990.

Ibn Rajab, Zayn al-Dīn ʿAbd al-Raḥmān b. Aḥmad: *Kitāb al-Dhayl ʿalā ṭabaqāt al-ḥanābila*, ed. by Muḥammad Ḥāmid al-Fiqī, 2 vols., Cairo 1372/1952–53 (reprint Beirut n. d.).

Ibn Rushd al-Ḥafīd: *Falsafat Ibn Rushd*, Beirut 1982.

Ibn Rushd (Averroes): *al-Kashf ʿan manāhij al-adilla fī ʿaqāʾid al-milla*, ed. by Muṣṭafā Ḥanafī and Muḥammad ʿĀbid al-Jābirī, Beirut 1998.

Ibn Rushd (Averroes): *Kitāb Faṣl al-maqāl with its Appendix (ḍamīma) and an Extract from kitāb al-Kashf ʿan manāhiğ al-adilla*, Arabic text edited by George F. Hourani, Leiden 1959.

Ibn al-Ṣalāḥ: *Fatāwā Ibn al-Ṣalāḥ fī al-tafsīr wal-ḥadīth wal-uṣūl wal-fiqh*, ed. by ʿAbd al-Muʿṭī Amīn Qalʿajī, Cairo 1403/1983.

Ibn Sīnā, Abū ʿAlī: *Avicenna's De Anima (Arabic Text) Being the Psychological Part of* Kitāb al-Shifāʾ, ed. by Fazlur Rahman, London, New York and Toronto 1959.

Ibn Sīnā, Abū ʿAlī: *al-Ishārāt wal-tanbīhāt, maʿa sharḥ Naṣīr al-Dīn al-Ṭūsī*, ed. by Sulaymān Dunyā, Cairo 1971.

Ibn Sīnā, Abū ʿAlī: *Ithbāt al-nubuwwāt (Proof of Prophecies)*, ed. by Michael E. Marmura, Beirut 1968.

Ibn Sīnā, Abū ʿAlī: *Livre des directives et remarques* (*Kitāb al-Ishārāt wa l-tanbīhāt*), traduction avec introduction et notes par A. M. Goichon, Beyrut and Paris 1951.

Ibn Sīnā, Abū ʿAlī: *al-Shifāʾ, al-Ilāhiyyāt*, 2 vols., ed. by Ibrāhīm Madkūr, al-Ab Qanawātī, Saʿīd Zāyid, Cairo 1380/1960.

Ibrahim, Mohd. and Takiyuddin, H.: *Konsep Tauhid dan Sifat-sifat Allah Menurut Ibn Qayyim al-Jawziyya*, M. A. thesis, Kuala Lumpur 1999.

Ibrahim, Saeed Hasan: Basic Principles of Criminal Procedure under Islamic *Sharīʿa*, in: Muhammad A. Abdel Haleem, Adel Omar Sharif and Kate Daniels (eds.): *Criminal Justice in Islam. Judicial Procedure in the Sharīʿah*, London 2003, pp. 17–34.

Idleman Smith, Jane and Yazbeck Haddad, Yvonne: *The Islamic Understanding of Death and Resurrection*, Albany 1981.

al-Iṣfahānī, Rāghib: *al-Iʿtiqādāt*, ed. by Shamrān al-ʿAjli, Beirut 1988.

Islahi, Abdul Azim: *Economic Thought of Ibn al Qayyim (1292–1350 A. D.)*, Jeddah 1984.

Ismail, Masthurah: *Analisis Terhadap Pandangan Ibn Qayyim al-Jawziyya mengenai Hak Beragama Orang bukan Islam di dalam Negara Islam. Kajian dalam Aḥkām ahl al-Dhimmah*, M. A. thesis, Kuala Lumpur 2007.

Izutsu, Toshihiko: *The Structure of Ethical Terms in the Koran. A Study in Semantics*, Tokyo 1959.

İzgi, Cevat: *Osmanlı Medreselerinde İlim*, Istanbul 1997.

al-Jābirī, Muḥammad ʿĀbid: *Naḥnu wal-turāth*, 6th ed. Beirut 1993.

Jackson, Sherman A.: Ibn Taymiyyah on Trial in Damascus, in: *Journal of Semitic Studies* 39 (1994), pp. 41–85.

Jackson, Sherman A.: *Islamic Law and the State. The Constitutional Jurisprudence of Shihāb al-Dīn al-Qarāfī*, Leiden and New York 1996.

Jackson, Sherman A.: The Alchemy of Domination? Some Asharite Responses to Mutazilite Ethics, in: *International Journal of Middle Eastern Studies* 31 (1999), pp. 185–201.

Jadaane, Fehmi: *L'influence du stoícisme sur la pensé musulmane*, Beirut 1968.

Jaffe, Kineret S.: The Concept of Genius. Its Changing Role in Eighteenth-Century French Aesthetics, in: *Journal of the History of Ideas* 41 (1980), pp. 579–599.

al-Jāḥiz, Abū ʿUthmān ʿAmr b. Baḥr: *al-Dalāʾil wal-iʿtibār ʿalā al-khalq wal-tadbīr*, Beirut 1988.

Jalbani, Ghulam Husain: *Teachings of Shāh Walīyullāh of Delhi*, Lahore 1967.

Jansen, Johannes J. G.: Ibn Taymiyyah and the Thirteenth Century. A Formative Period of Modern Muslim Radicalism, in: *Quaderni di Studi Arabi* 5–6 (1987–88), pp. 391–396.

Jansen, Johannes J. G.: The Creed of Sadat's Assassins. The Contents of "The Forgotten Duty" Analyzed, in: *Die Welt des Islams* 25 (1985), pp. 1–30.

Jansen, Johannes J. G.: *The Dual Nature of Islamic Fundamentalism*, Ithaca 1997.

Jansen, Johannes J. G.: *The Neglected Duty. The Creed of Sadat's Assassins and Islamic Resurgence in the Middle East*, New York 1986.

Jawādī Amlī, Āyat Allāh: *al-ʿAqīda min khilāl al-fiṭra fī al-Qurʾān*, Beirut 1994.

Jedrej, Marian Charles and Shaw, Rosalind (eds.): *Dreaming, Religion, and Society in Africa*, Leiden 1993.

Johansen, Baber: A Perfect Law in an Imperfect Society. Ibn Taymiyya's Concept of "Governance in the Name of the Sacred Law", in: Peri Bearman, Wolfhart Heinrichs and Bernard G. Weiss (eds.), *The Law Applied*, pp. 259–294.

Johansen, Baber: *Contingency in a Sacred Law. Legal and Ethical Norms in the Muslim Fiqh*, Boston and Leiden 1999.

Johansen, Baber: La découverte des choses qui parlent. La légalisation de la torture judiciaire en droit musulman (XIIIe–XIVe siècles), in: *Enquéte, anthropologie, histoire, sociologie* 7 (1998), pp. 175–202.

Johansen, Baber: Signs as Evidence. The Doctrine of Ibn Taymiyya (1263–1328) and Ibn Qayyim al-Jawziyya (d. 1351) on Proof, in: *Islamic Law and Society* 9 (2002), pp. 168–193.

Johns, Anthony H.: Friends in Grace. Ibrāhīm al-Kūrānī and ʿAbd al-Raʾūf al-Singkelī, in: Saifuddin Udin (ed.): *Spectrum. Essays Presented to Sutan Takdir Alisjahbana*, Jakarta 1978, pp. 469–485.

Johns, Anthony H.: From Coastal Settlement to Islamic School and City. Islamization in Sumatra, the Malay Peninsula and Java, in: *Hamdard Islamicus* 4 (1981), pp. 3–28.

Johns, Anthony H.: Islam in Southeast Asia. in: Mircea Eliade (ed.): *The Encyclopedia of Religion*, 16 vols., New York 1987, vol. 7, pp. 410–411.

Johns, Anthony H.: *Nur al-Daqa'iq* by Shams al-Din of Pasai, in: *Journal of Royal Asiatic Society* 73 (1953), pp. 137–151.
Johns, Anthony H.: Sufism as a Category in Indonesian Literature and History, in: *Journal of Southeast Asian History* 2 (1961), pp. 10–23.
Johns, Anthony H.: *The Gift Addressed to the Spirit of the Prophet*, Canberra 1965.
Jokisch, Benjamin: *Ijtihād* in Ibn Taymiyya's *Fatāwā*, in: Robert Gleave and Eugenia Kermeli (eds.): *Islamic Law. Theory and Practice*, London and New York 1997, pp. 119–137.
Jokisch, Benjamin: *Islamic Imperial Law. Harun-al-Rashid's Codification Project*, Berlin and New York 2007.
Jokisch, Benjamin: *Islamisches Recht in Theorie und Praxis. Analyse einiger kaufrechtlicher Fatwas von Taqī'd-Dīn Aḥmad b. Taymiyya*, Berlin 1996.
Jones, Kenneth W.: *Arya Dharm. Hindu Consciousness in the 19th Century Punjab*, Cambridge 1976.
Jonker, Gerdien: Die Verortung der islamischen Gemeinden im deutschen Umfeld, in: idem (ed.): *Kern und Rand. Religiöse Minderheiten aus der Türkei in Deutschland*, Berlin 1999, pp. 131–146.
Jonker, Gerdien: *Eine Wellenlänge zu Gott. Der Verband der Islamischen Kulturzentren in Europa*, Berlin 2002.
Jonker, Gerdien: The Evolution of the Naqshbandi-Mujaddidi. Sulaymançis in Germany, in: Jamal Malik and John Hinnells (eds.): *Sufism in the West*, London 2006, pp. 71–85.
al-Jurjānī, Muḥammad al-Sharīf: *Kitāb al-Taʿrīfāt*, Beirut 1969.
al-Juwaynī, ʿAbd al-Malik b. Yūsuf: *al-ʿAqīda al-niẓāmiyya*, ed. by Aḥmad Ḥijāzī al-Saqqā, Cairo 1979.

Kamali, Mohammad Hashim: *Shari'ah Law. An Introduction*, Oxford 2008, pp. 225–226.
Kaptein, Nico: Meccan Fatwas from the End of the Nineteenth Century on Indonesian Affairs, in: *Studia Islamika* 2 (1995), pp. 141–160.
Kaptein, Nico J. G.: *Muhammad's Birthday Festival. Early History in the Central Muslim Lands and the Development in the Muslim West until the 10th/16th Century*, Leiden 1993.
Karamustafa, Ahmet: *Sufism. The Formative Period*, Edinburgh 2007.
al-Karmī, Marʿī b. Yūsuf: *al-Kawākib al-durriyya fī manāqib al-mujtahid Ibn Taymiyya*, ed. by Najm ʿAbd al-Raḥmān Khalaf, Beirut 1406/1986.
al-Kashmiri, Abu Hamad: *Wahhabismus enthüllt*, translated from English into Arabic by Azad Ibn Muhammad, comments by Abu Imran, 2002.
Kassis, Hanna E.: Critique of Scriptures. Polemics of al-Jâhiz and Ibn Hazm Against Christianity and Judaism, in: Yossef Schwartz and Volkhard Krech (eds.): *Religious Apologetics. Philosophical Argumentation*, Tübingen 2004, pp. 237–250.

Katz, Marion Holmes: *The Birth of the Prophet Muhammad*, Leiden 2007.

Kennedy-Day, Kiki: *Books of Definition in Islamic Philosophy. The Limits of Words*, London and New York 2003.

Kerr, Malcolm H.: *Islamic Reform. The Political and Legal Theories of Muhammad ʿAbduh and Rashid Rida*. Berkeley and Los Angeles 1966.

Khalid, Anas: *The Mukhtasar of Al-Khiraqi*, Ph.D thesis, New York University 1992.

Khallāf, ʿAbd al-Wahhāb: *al-Siyāsa al-sharʿiyya aw niẓam al-dawla al-islāmiyya*, Cairo 1977.

al-Khallāl, Abū Bakr: *al-Sunna*, 3 vols., ed. by ʿAṭiya al-Zahrānī, Riyadh 1410/1989.

Khan, Qamaruddin: *The Political Thought of Ibn Taymiyah*, Lahore 1983.

Khan, Shaharyar Muhammad: *Begums of Bhopal*, London 2000.

Khānpūrī, ʿAbd al-Aḥad: *Tadhkira-i ʿulamāʾ-i Khānpūr*, Lahore 1985.

Khānpūrī, ʿAbd Allāh: *Kitāb al-Tawḥīd wal-sunna fī radd al-ilḥād wal-bidʿa*, Rāwalpindī n. d.

al-Khiraqī, Abū al-Qāsim: *al-Matn*, ed. by Abū Ḥudhayfa Ibrāhīm b. Muḥammad, Tanta 1413/1993.

al- Khiraqī, Abū al-Qāsim: *Mukhtaṣar*, ed. by Muḥammad Zuhayr al-Shāwīsh, Damascus 1378/1958.

Kitchlu, T. N.: *Widows in India*, New Delhi 1993.

Knysh, Alexander D.: *Ibn ʿArabī in the Later Islamic Tradition. The Making of a Polemical Image in Medieval Islam*, Albany 1999.

Knysh, Alexander D.: *Islamic Mysticism. A Short History*, Leiden 2000.

van Koningsveld, Pieter Sjörd: The Islamic Image of Paul and the Origin of the Gospel of Barnabas, in: *Jerusalem Studies in Arabic and Islam* 20 (1996), pp. 200–228.

Kratz, E. Ulrich: Malay as Lingua Franca. A Historical Survey, in: *Malay Literature* 12 (1999), pp. 46–57.

Kraus, Paul: Les "Controverses" de Fakhr al-Dīn Rāzī, in: *Bulletin de l'Institut d'Égypte* 19 (1937), pp. 187–214.

Krawietz, Birgit: *Ḍarūra* in Modern Islamic Law. The Case of Organ Transplantation, in: Robert Gleave and Eugenia Kermeli (eds.): *Islamic Law. Theory and Practice*, London and New York 1997, pp. 185–193.

Krawietz, Birgit: Ibn Qayyim al-Jawzīyah. His Life and Works, in: *Mamlūk Studies Review* 10 (2006), pp. 19–64.

Krawietz, Birgit: Ibn Taymiyya, Vater des islamischen Fundamentalismus? Zur westlichen Rezeption eines mittelalterlichen Schariatsgelehrten, in: Manuel Atienza, Enrico Pattaro, Martin Schulte, Boris Topornin and Dieter Wyduckel (eds.): *Theorie des Rechts in der Gesellschaft. Festschrift für Werner Krawietz zum 70. Geburtstag*, Berlin 2003, pp. 39–62.

Krawietz, Birgit: Transgressive Creativity in the Making. Ibn Qayyim al-Ǧawziyyah's Reframing within Ḥanbalī Legal Methodology, in: Bori and Holtzman, *A Scholar in the Shadow*, pp. 43–62.

von Kügelgen, Anke: *Averroes und die arabische Moderne. Ansätze zu einer Neubegründung des Rationalismus im Islam*, Leiden 1994.

von Kügelgen, Anke: Dialogpartner im Widerspruch. Ibn Rushd und Ibn Taymīya über die „Einheit der Wahrheit", in: Rüdiger Arnzen and Jörn Thielmann (eds.): *Words, Texts and Concepts Cruising the Mediterranean Sea. Studies on the Sources, Contents and Influences of Islamic Civilization and Arabic Philosophy and Science Dedicated to Gerhard Endress on His Sixty-fifth Birthday*, Leuven 2004, pp. 455–481.

von Kügelgen, Anke: Ibn Taymīyas Kritik an der aristotelischen Logik und sein Gegenentwurf, in: Dominik Perler and Ulrich Rudolph (eds.): *Logik und Theologie. Das* Organon *im arabischen und lateinischen Mittelalter*, Leiden and Boston 2005, pp. 167–225.

Kühn, Wilfried: Die Rehabilitierung der Sprache durch den arabischen Philologen as-Sīrāfī, in: Burkhard Mojsisch (ed.): *Sprachphilosophie in Antike und Mittelalter*, Amsterdam 1986, pp. 301–402.

Lacroix, Stéphane: Al-Albani's Revolutionary Approach to Hadith, in: *ISIM Review* 21 (2008), pp. 6–7.

Laffan, Michael F.: *Islamic Nationhood and Colonial Indonesia. The Umma Below the Winds*, London and New York 2003.

Lambert-Hurley, Siobhan: *Muslim Women, Reform and Princely Patronage. Nawab Sultan Jahan Begam of Bhopal*, London 2007.

Lambton, Ann K. S.: Changing Concepts of Authority in the Late Ninth/Fifteenth and Early Tenth/Sixteenth Centuries, in: Alexander S. Cudsi and ʿAlī al-Dīn Hillal (eds.): *Islam and Power*, Baltimore 1981, pp. 49–71.

Lambton, Ann K. S.: *State and Government in Medieval Islam. An Introduction to the Study of Islamic Political Theory*, Oxford and New York 1981.

Landau-Tesseron, Ella: The Cyclical Reform. A Study of the Mujaddid Tradition, in: *Studia Islamica* 79 (1989), pp. 79–119.

Langermann, Tzvi: Abū al-Faraj Ibn al-Ṭayyib on Spirit and Soul, in: *Le Muséon* 122 (2009), pp. 149–159.

Langermann, Tzvi: David Ibn Shoshan on Spirit and Soul, in: *European Journal of Jewish Studies* 1 (2007), pp. 63–86.

Langermann, Tzvi: Ibn Kammūna and the "New Wisdom" of the Thirteenth Century, in: *Arabic Sciences and Philosophy* 15 (2005), pp. 277–327.

Langermann, Tzvi: The Naturalization of Science in Ibn Qayyim al-Ǧawziyyah's *Kitāb al-Rūḥ*, in: Bori and Holtzman, *A Scholar in the Shadow*, pp. 211–228.

Laoust, Henri: *Essai sur les doctrines sociales et politiques de Taḳī-d-Dīn Aḥmad Ibn Taimīya, canoniste Ḥanbalite. Né à Ḥarrān en 661/1262, mort à Damas en 728/1328; thèse pour le doctorat*, Cairo 1939.

Laoust, Henri: La biographie d'Ibn Taymīya d'après Ibn Kathīr, in: *Bulletin d'études orientales* 9 (1942), pp. 115–162.

Laoust, Henri: *La profession de foi d'Ibn Baṭṭa. Traditionniste et jurisconsulte musulman d'école hanbalite mort en Irak à ʿUkbarâ en 387/997*, Damascus 1958.

Laoust, Henri: *La profession de foi d'Ibn Taymiyya. Texte, traduction et commentaire de la Wāsiṭiyya*, Paris 1986.

Laoust, Henri: Le Hanbalisme sous le califat de Bagdad (241/855–656/1258), in: *Revue des études islamiques* 1 (1959), pp. 67–128.

Laoust, Henri: Le Hanbalisme sous les mamlouks bahrides (658–784/1260–1382), in: *Revue des études islamiques* 28 (1960), pp. 1–71.

Laoust, Henri (transl.): *Le traité de droit public d'Ibn Taimīya*, Damascus (Institut Français) 1952.

Laoust, Henri: *Les schismes dans l'Islam. Introduction à une étude de la religion musulmane*, Paris 1965.

Laoust, Henri: L'influence d'Ibn-Taymiyya, in: Alford T. Welch and Pierre Cachia (eds.): *Islam. Past Influence and Present Challenge*, New York 1979, pp. 15–33.

Laoust, Henri (trans.): Traité sur la Ḥisba/*al-ḥisba fī al-islām aw waẓīfat al-ḥukūma al-islāmiyya*, in: *Revue des études islamique* 52 (1984), pp. 17–208.

Lapidus, Ira M.: *A History of Islamic Societies*, Cambridge 1988.

Layish, Aharon: Saudi Arabian Legal Reform as a Mechanism to Moderate Wahhabi Doctrine, in: *Journal of the American Oriental Society* 107 (1987), pp. 279–292.

Lazarus-Yafeh, Hava: Étude sur la polémique islamo-chrétienne. Qui était l'auteur de *al-Radd al-ǧamīl li-ilāhiyyat ʿĪsā bi-ṣarīḥ al-Injīl* attribué à al-Ġazzalī?, in: *Revue des Sciences Religieuses* 37 (1969), pp. 219–238.

Lazarus-Yafeh, Hava: *Intertwined Worlds. Medieval Islam and Bible Criticism*, Princeton 1992.

Lazarus-Yafeh, Hava: Some Neglected Aspects of Medieval Muslim Politics Against Christianity, in: *Harvard Theological Review* 89 (1996), pp. 61–84.

Leder, Stefan: Postklassisch und vormodern. Beobachtungen zum Kulturwandel in der Mamlūkenzeit, in: Stephan Conermann and Anja Pistor-Hatam (eds.): *Die Mamlūken. Studien zu ihrer Geschichte und Kultur zum Gedenken an Ulrich Haarmann (1942–1999)*, Hamburg 2003, pp. 289–312.

Lemmen, Thomas: *Islamische Organisationen in Deutschland*, Bonn 2000.

Lewis, Bernard: *Political Words and Ideas in Islam*, Princeton 2007.

Lewis, Bernard: *The Political Language of Islam*, Chicago 1988.

Lewy, Hans: *Chaldean Oracles and Theurgy*, Paris 1978.

de Libera, Alain: *La querelle des universaux de Platon a la fin du Moyen Age*, Paris 1996.

Little, Donald P.: Did Ibn Taymiyya Have a Screw Loose?, in: *Studia Islamica* 41 (1975), pp. 93–111.

Little, Donald P.: *History and Historiography of the Mamlūks*, London 1986.

Little, Donald P.: The Historical and Historiographical Significance of the Detention of Ibn Taymiyya, in: *International Journal of Middle East Studies* 4 (1973), pp. 311–327.

Livingston, John W.: Ibn Qayyim al-Jawziyyah. A Fourteenth Century Defense Against Astrological Divination and Alchemical Transmutation, in: *Journal of the American Oriental Society* 91 (1971), pp. 96–103.

Livingston, John W.: Science and the Occult in the Thinking of Ibn Qayyim al-Jawziyya, in: *Journal of the American Oriental Society* 112 (1992), pp. 598–610.

Ljamai, Abdelilah: *Ibn Ḥazm et la polémique islamo-chrétienne dans l'histoire de l'islam*, Leiden and Boston 2003.

Llewellyn, John E.: *The Arya Samaj as a Fundamentalist Movement. A Study in Comparative Fundamentalism*, Delhi 1993.

Locke, John: *An Essay Concerning Human Understanding*. Collated *and* Annotated *with* Biographical, Critical *and* Historical Prolegomena *by Alexander Campbell Fraser*, 2 vols., New York 1959.

Lohlker, Rüdiger: „Unstatthafte Neuerungen“ oder das Feld der religiösen Diskussion im Islam, in: *Zeitschrift der Deutschen Morgenländischen Gesellschaft* 149 (1999), pp. 221–244.

Loimeier, Roman: Is there something like "Protestant Islam"?, in: *Die Welt des Islams* 45 (2005), pp. 216–254.

Loth, Otto: *A Catalogue of the Arabic Manuscripts in the Library of the India Office*, London 1877.

Luhmann, Niklas: Identitätsgebrauch in selbstsubstitutiven Ordnungen, besonders Gesellschaften, in: Odo Marquard and Karlheinz Stierle (eds.): *Identität*, Munich 1979, 2nd ed., pp. 315–345.

Luhmann, Niklas: *Soziale Systeme. Grundriß einer allgemeinen Theorie*, 5th ed. Frankfurt am Main 1994.

Luqmān, Akhtar J.: *al-Sayyid Ṣiddīq Ḥasan al-Qannawjī*, Riyadh 1996.

Luqmān al-Salafī, Muḥammad: *Fatāwā barāy-i khawātīn-i Islām*, Delhi n. d.

Luther, Martin: *Martin Luther's Basic Theological Writings*, ed. by Timothy F. Lull, Minneapolis 1989.

al-Manār

MacCulloch, Diarmaid: *The Reformation. A History*, London 2003.

Macdonald, Duncan B.: The Development of the Idea of Spirit in Islam, in: *Acta Orientalia* 9 (1931), pp. 307–351.

Mach, Rudolph: *Catalogue of Arabic Manuscripts (Yahuda Section) of the Garrett Collection*, Princeton 1977.

Madelung, Wilferd: The Late Muʿtazila and Determinism. The Philosophers' Trap, in: Biancamaria Scarcia Amoretti and Lucia Rostagno (eds.): *Yād-Nāma in memoria di Alessandro Bausani*, Rome 1991, vol. 1, pp. 245–257.

Madjid, Nurcholis: *Ibn Taymiyya on Kalām and Falsafa. A Problem of Reason and Revelation in Islam*, unpublished Ph. D. thesis, University of Chicago 1984.

Madkour, Ibrahim: *L'Organon d'Aristote dans le monde arabe, ses traductions, son étude et ses applications*, Paris 1969.

Mahdi, Muhsin: *Alfarabi's Philosophy of Plato and Aristotle*, New York 1962.

Mahdi, Muhsin: *Ibn Khaldūn's Philosophy of History. A Study in the Philosophic Foundation of the Science of Culture*, London 1957.

Maḥmūd, ʿAbd al-Qādir: *al-Fikr al-islāmī wal-falsafāt al-muʿāriḍa fī al-qadīm wal-ḥadīth*, Cairo 1986.

Maimonides, Moses: *Dalālat al-ḥāʾirīn*, ed. by Ḥussayn Atay, Cairo n. d.

Maimonides, Moses: *The Guide of the Perplexed*, translated by Shlomo Pines, Chicago 1963.

Makari, Victor E.: *Ibn Taymiyyah's Ethics. The Social Factor*, Chico 1983.

Makdisi, George: Hanbalite Islam, in: *Studies on Islam*, transl. and ed. by Merlin L. Swartz, New York and Oxford 1981, pp. 216–274.

Makdisi, George: *Ibn ʿAqīl et la résurgence de l'Islam traditionaliste au XIe siécle (Ve siécle de l'Hégire)*, Damascus 1963.

Makdisi, George: *Ibn ʿAqīl. Religion and Culture in Classical Islam*, Edinburgh 1997.

Makdisi, George: Ibn Taymīya. A Ṣūfī of the Qādiriya Order, in: *The American Journal of Arabic Studies* 1 (1973), pp. 118–129.

Makdisi, George: The Hanbali School and Sufism, in: *Boletin de la Asociacion Española de Orientalistas* 15 (1979), pp. 115–126.

Makdisi, George: *The Rise of Colleges. Institutions of Learning in Islam and the West*, Edinburgh 1981.

al-Makkī, Abū Ṭālib: *Qūṭ al-qulūb*, 3 vols., ed. by ʿAbd al-Munʿim al-Ḥinfī, Cairo 1991.

Malik, Jamal: *Islam in South Asia. A Short History*, Leiden 2008.

Malik, Jamal: *Islamische Gelehrtenkultur in Nordindien. Entwicklungsgeschichte und Tendenzen am Beispiel von Lucknow*, Leiden 1997.

Manji, Irshad: *The Trouble with Islam Today. A Muslim's Call for Reform*, Toronto 2005.

Mansurnoor, Iik Arifin: Muslims in Modern Southeast Asia. Radicalism in Historical Perspectives, in: *Taiwan Journal of Southeast Asian Studies* 2 (2005), pp. 3–54.

Manṣūrpūrī, ʿAbd al-Bāqī: *Safarnāma-i ḥijāz maʿahu sīrat-i Salmān*, Lahore n. d.

Ibn al-Manẓūr, Jamāl al-Dīn: *Lisān al-ʿarab*, Beirut 2000.

al-Maqdisī, Muṭahhar b. Ṭāhir: *Kitāb al-Badʾ wal-taʾrīkh*, 3 vols., ed. by Clément Huart, Baghdad n. d.

al-Maqdisī, Shaykh Abū Muḥammad ʿĀṣim: *This is our ʿAqīdah*, n. p. n. d.

Marcotte, Roxanne D.: Ibn Taymiyya et sa critique des produits de la faculté d'estimation (Wahmiyyāt) dans le *Darʾ taʿāruḍ al-ʿaql wa al-naql*, in: *Luqmān* 18 (2002), pp. 43–58.

al-Mardāwī, ʿAlāʾ al-Dīn ʿAlī b. Sulaymān: *al-Inṣāf fī maʿrifat al-rājiḥ min al-khilāf ʿalā madhhab al-imām Aḥmad b. Ḥanbal*, ed. by Muḥammad Ḥāmid al-Fiqī, 12 vols., Cairo 1955–1958 (reprint Beirut 1419/1998).

al-Mardāwī, ʿAlāʾ al-Dīn ʿAlī b. Sulaymān: Qāʿida nāfiʿa jāmiʿa li-ṣifat al-riwāyāt al-manqūla ʿan al-imām Aḥmad, appended to al-Mardāwī, ʿAlāʾ al-Dīn: *al-Inṣāf fī maʿrifat al-rājiḥ*, vol. 12, pp. 177–218.

Margoliouth, David Samuel: The Discussion Between Abū Bishr Mattā and Abū Saʿīd al-Sīrāfī on the Merits of Logic and Grammar, in: *Journal of the Royal Asiatic Society NS*, 37 (1905), pp. 79–129.

Marmura, Michael E.: Ghazali's Attitude to the Secular Sciences and Logic, in: Hourani, George F. (ed.): *Essays on Islamic Philosophy and Science*, Albany 1975, pp. 100–111.

Marmura, Michael E.: The Metaphysics of Efficient Causality in Avicenna (Ibn Sina), in: idem (ed.): *Islamic Theology and Philosophy. Studies in Honor of George F. Hourani*, Albany 1984, pp. 172–187.

Marty, Martin E. and Appleby, R. Scott: *Fundamentalisms Observed. Fundamentalism Project 1,* Chicago 1991.

al-Marzūqī, Abū Yaʿrub: Fikr Ibn Taymiyya al-iṣlāḥī. Abʿāduhu al-falsafiyya, in: *al-Munʿaṭaf* 18–19 (2001).

al-Marzūqī, Abū Yaʿrub: *Iṣlāḥ al-ʿaql fī al-falsafa al-ʿarabiyya. Min wāqiʿiyyat Arisṭū wa-Aflāṭūn ilā ismiyyat Ibn Taymiyya wa-Ibn Khaldūn*, Beirut 1996.

al-Marzūqī, Abū Yaʿrub: *Manzilat al-kullī fī al-falsafa al-ʿarabiyya fī al-Aflāṭūniyya wal-ḥanīfiyya al-muḥdathatayn al-ʿarabiyyatayn*, Tunis 1994.

Masud, Muhammad Khalid: The Definition of *bidʿa* in the South Asian *fatāwā* Literature, in: *Annales Islamologiques* 27 (1993), pp. 55–75.

Masud, Muhammad Khalid: The Doctrine of *Siyāsa* in Islamic Law, in: *Recht van de Islam* 18 (2001), pp. 1–29.

Masʿūd Ālam Nadwī, Ibn ʿAbd: *Ibn ʿAbd al-Wahhāb, Muḥammad. Ek maẓlūm awr badnām muṣliḥ*, Lahore n. d.

Matheson, Virginia and Hooker, Michael B.: Jawi Literature in Patani. The Maintenance of an Islamic Tradition, in: *Journal of the Malaysian Branch of the Royal Asiatic Society* 60/61 (1988), pp. 1–86.

Al-Matroudi, Abdul Hakim I.: *The Ḥanbalī School of Law and Ibn Taymiyyah. Conflict or Conciliation*, London and New York 2006.

Ibn Mattawayh, Abū Muḥammad Ḥasan b. Aḥmad: *al-Majmūʿ fī al-Muḥīṭ bil-taklīf*, 2 vols., ed. by Jean Joseph Houben and Daniel Gimaret, Beirut 1986.

di Matteo, Ignazio: *Tahrif* or the Alteration of the Bible According to the Moslems, in: *The Muslim World* 14 (1924), pp. 61–84.

al-Māturīdī, Abū Manṣūr: *Kitāb al-Tawḥīd*, ed. by Bekir Topaloğlu and Muhammed Aruçi, Ankara 2003.

McCants, William: *Militant Ideology Atlas. Research Compendium,* November 2006, New York 2006.

McCarthy, Richard Joseph: *The Theology of al-Ashʿarī. The Arabic Texts of al-Ashʿarī's Kitāb al-Lumaʿ and Risālat Istiḥsān al-khawḍ fī ʿilm al-kalām; With Briefly Annotated Translations, and Appendices Containing Material Pertinent to the Study of al-Ashʿarī*, Beirut 1953.

Mehr, Ghulām Rasūl: *Sayyid Aḥmad Shahīd*, Lahore n. d.
Meier, Fritz: Eine auferstehung Muḥammads bei Suyūṭī, in: *Der Islam* 62 (1985), pp. 20–58.
Meier, Fritz: *Zwei Abhandlungen über die Naqschbandiyya*, Stuttgart 1994.
Melchert, Christopher: *Ahmad ibn Hanbal*, Oxford 2006.
Melchert, Christopher: The Formation of the Sunnī Schools of Law, in: Wael B. Hallaq (ed.): *The Formation of Islamic Law*, Aldershot 2004, pp. 351–66.
Melchert, Christopher: The Meaning of *qāla al-Shāfiʿī* in Ninth-century Sources, in: James E. Montgomery (ed.): *Abbasid Studies*, Leuven 2004, pp. 277–301.
Memon, Muhammad Umar: *Ibn Taimiyya's Struggle Against Popular Religion. With an Annotated Translation of the* Kitāb iqtidāʾ al-ṣirāṭ al-mustaqīm fī mukhālafat aṣḥāb al-jaḥīm, The Hague 1976.
Messer, Richard: *Does God's Existence Need Proof?*, Oxford 1993.
Metcalf, Barbara Daly: *Islamic Revival in British India. Deoband*; 1860–1900, Princeton 1982.
Michel, Thomas (ed. and transl.): *A Muslim Theologian's Response to Christianity. Ibn Taymiyya's* al-Jawāb al-ṣaḥīḥ, Delmar 1984.
Michel, Thomas: Ibn Taymiyya's Critique of Falsafa, in: *Hamdard Islamicus* 6 (1983), pp. 3–14.
Michel, Thomas: Ibn Taymiyya's *Sharḥ* on the *Futūḥ al-Ghayb* of ʿAbd al-Qādir al-Jīlānī, in: *Hamdard Islamicus* 4 (1981), pp. 3–12.
Michot, Jean R.: *Ibn Taymiyya. Lettre à Abû l-Fidâʾ; traduction de l'arabe, présentation, notes et lexique*, Louvain-la-Neuve 1994.
Michot, Yahya J.: A Mamlūk Theologian's Commentary on Avicenna's *Risāla aḍḥawiyya* Being a Translation of a Part of the *Darʾ taʿāruḍ al-ʿaql wal-naql* of Ibn Taymiyya, With Introduction, Annotation and Appendices, in: *Journal of Islamic Studies* 14 (2003), pp. 149–203.
Michot, Yahya: Between Entertainment and Religion. Ibn Taymiyya's Views on Superstition, in: *The Muslim World* 99 (2009), pp. 1–20.
Michot, Yahya J.: *Ibn Taymiyya (d. 728/1328). Against Extremisms; Texts Transl., Annotated and Introduced by Yahya M. Michot, With a Foreword by Bruce B. Lawrence*, Beirut 2012.
Michot, Yahya J.: Ibn Taymiyya. Les intermédiaires entre dieu et l'homme (*Risâlat al-wâsiṭa bayna al-khalq wal-ḥaqq*). Traduction française suivie de le shaykh de l'Islam Ibn Taymiyya; chronique d'une vie de théologien militant, in: *Le Musulman* Numéro hors-série (1417/1996), pp. 1–27.
Michot, Yahya J.: Ibn Taymiyya on Astrology. Annotated Translation of Three Fatwas, in: *Journal of Islamic Studies* 11 (2000), pp. 147–208.
Michot, Yahya: Ibn Taymiyya's "New Mardin Fatwa." Is Genetically Modified Islam Carcinogenic?, in: *The Muslim World* 101 (2011), pp. 130–181.
Michot, Yahya J.: Textes spirituels d'Ibn Taymiyya. XIV. Raison, confession, loi; une typologie musulmane du religieux, in: *Le Musulman* 27 (1996), pp. 24–29.

Michot, Yahya J.: Vanités intellectuelles... L'impasse des rationalismes selon le *Rejet de la contradiction* d'Ibn Taymiyyah, in: *Oriente Moderno* 19 (2001), pp. 597–617.

Mill, John Stuart: *A System of Logic*, New York 1919.

Miller, Judith: The Challenge of Radical Islam, in: *Foreign Affairs* 72 (1993), pp. 47–56.

Minault, Gail: *Secluded Scholars. Women's Education and Muslim Social Reform in Colonial India*, Delhi 1999.

Minault, Gail: *The Khilafat Movement. Religious Symbolism and Political Mobilization in India*, New York 1999.

Mingana, Alphonse: Remarks on Ṭabari's Semi-official Defence of Islam, in: *Bulletin of the John Rylands Library* 9 (1925), pp. 236–240.

Mohd Yusof, Mohd Izwan: *Metodologi Ibn Qayyim al-Jawziyya dalam* Kitāb al-Amthāl fī al-qur'ān, M. A. thesis, Kuala Lumpur 2007.

Mujahid, Abdul-Malik: Publishers Note, in: Shah Ismail Shaheed: *Taqwiyat al-īmān*, Riyadh 1995.

ul-Mulk, Muḥsin: *Taqlīd aw ʿamal bil-ḥadīth*, Amritsar 1909.

al-Munadschid, Scheich Muhammad Salih: *Der Dadschal*, translated from English by S. D., 2006.

al-Munadschid, Scheich Muhammad Salih: *Muharram und Aschura*, translated from the English by Somaya K. Lemcke, 2006.

al-Munadschid, Scheich Muhammad Salih: *Was ist Aqida?*, translated from English from Abu Imran, 2006.

al-Munadschid, Scheich Muhammad Salih: *Wie man sich in folgenden Situationen verhält*, translated from English to German by Azad ibn Muhammad, 2002.

Ibn al-Murtaḍā, Aḥmad b. Yahya: *al-Munya wal-amal fī sharḥ al-milal wal-niḥal*, ed. by Muḥammad Jawād Mashkūr, Beirut 1410/1990.

Muslim b. al-Ḥajjāj al-Qushayrī, Abū al-Ḥusayn: *Ṣaḥīḥ Muslim*, 2 vols., Liechtenstein 2000.

n. a.: *Der Hidschab ist schön!*, translated from English into German by Umm Amani al-Akad, 2004.

n. a.: *Die Tugenden des Hidschab*, translated from English into German by Umm Amani al-Akad, 2004.

n. a.: *Die verbindlichen Bedingungen für einen islamischen Hidschab*, translated from English into German by Umm Amani al-Akad, 2004.

n. a.: *Die Wirklichkeit des Hidschab. Die Kleidung einer muslimischen Frau*, translated from English into German by Umm Amani al-Akad, 2004.

n. a.: ʿIlm al-hayʾa wal-sunna al-nabawiyya, in: *al-Manār* 13 (1910–11), pp. 117–119.

n. a.: Istiftāʾ fī fatwā wa-ṭalab iqrārihā wa-taṣḥīḥihā, in: *al-Manār* 28 (1927–28), pp. 261–271.

n. a.: Ithbāt istidārat al-ar wa-dawrānihā min al-qur'ān, in: *al-Manār* 7 (1904–05), pp. 260–162.

n. a.: *Masāʾil al-imām Aḥmad b. Ḥanbal wa-Isḥāq b. Rāhawayh*, recension of al-Kawsaj, ed. by Abū al-Ḥusayn Khālid b. Maḥmūd al-Rabāt, Wiʿām al-Hāwishī and Jumʿa Fatḥī, 2 vols., Riyadh 1425/2004.

n. a.: *Masāʾil al-imām Aḥmad b. Muḥammad b. Ḥanbal wa-Isḥāq b. Rāhawayh*, recension of Ḥarb b. Ismāʿīl al-Kirmānī, ed. by Nāṣir b. Saʿūd b. ʿAbd Allāh al-Salāma, Riyadh 1425.

n. a.: *Worte an meine muslimische Schwester*, translated from English into German by Umm Amani al-Akad, first published in: *Muslim Creed* 3 (1995).

Nadhīr Ḥusayn Dihlawī, Muḥammad: *Fatāwā-yi nadhīriyya*, Gujranwālā n. d.

Nadvi, Syed Sulaiman: Muslims and Greek Schools of Philosophy, in: *Islamic Culture* 1 (1927), pp. 85–91.

Nadwī, Abū al-Ḥasan ʿAlī: *Sīrat Sayyid Aḥmad Shahīd*, Lucknow 1986.

Nadwi, Abul Hasan Ali: *Saviours of Islamic Spirit*, 4 vols., Lucknow 1993 (1st Engl. ed.).

Nadwī, Masʿūd ʿĀlam: *Ibn ʿAbd al-Wahhāb, Muḥammad. Ek maẓlūm awr bad-nām muṣliḥ*, Lahore n. d.

Nadwī, Masʿūd ʿĀlam: *Mohammad Bin Abdul Wahhab. A Slandered Reformer*, transl. by Muhammad Rafiq Khan, Benaris 1982.

Nadwī, Muḥammad: *al-Amīr Sayyid Ṣiddīq Ḥasan Khān*, Beirut 1999.

Nadwī, Sayyid Abū al-Ḥasan ʿAlī: *Naqd al-falsafa wal-manṭiq wa-ʿilm al-kalām wa-tarjīḥ uslūb al-kitāb wal-sunna*, transl. into Arabic by Saʿīd al-Aʿẓamī al-Nadwī, in: *Majallat al-Baʿth al-Islāmī* 18 (1973), pp. 49–63.

Nadwī, Sayyid Abū al-Ḥasan ʿAlī: *Taʾrīkh daʿwa wa-ʿazīma*, Lucknow 1419/1998.

Nafi, Basheer M.: Salafism Revived. Nuʿmān al-Ālūsī and the Trial of Two Ahmads, in: *Die Welt des Islams* 49 (2009), pp. 49–97.

Nafiʿ, Basheer M.: A Teacher of Ibn ʿAbd al-Wahhāb. Muḥammad Ḥayāt al-Sindī and the Revival of *aṣḥāb al-ḥadīth*'s Methodology, in: *Islamic Law and Society* 13 (2006), pp. 208–241.

Nafiʿ, Basheer M.: Taṣawwuf and Reform in Pre-Modern Islamic Culture. In Search of Ibrāhīm al-Kūrāni, in: *Die Welt des Islams* 42 (2002) pp. 307–355.

Nagel, Tilman: *Allahs Liebling*, München 2008.

Nagel, Tilman: *Staat und Glaubensgemeinschaft im Islam*, 2 vols., Zürich 1981.

Najjar, Fauzi M: *Siyāsa* in Islamic Political Philosophy, in: Michael E. Marmura (ed.): *Islamic Theology and Philosophy. Studies in Honor of George F. Hourani*, Albany 1984, p. 92–110.

Nash, Manning: Islamic Resurgence in Malaysia and Indonesia, in: Martin E. Marty and Scott E. Appleby (eds.): *Fundamentalism Observed*, Chicago and London 1991, pp. 691–739.

al-Nashshār, ʿAlī Sāmī: *Manāhij al-baḥth ʿind mufakkirī al-islām wa-naqd al-muslimīn lil-manṭiq al-arisṭuṭālīsī*, 4th ed. Cairo 1978.

National Commission on Terrorist Attacks Upon the United States: *The 9/11 Commission Report. Final Report of the National Commission on Terrorist Attacks Upon the United States*, Washington D. C. 2004.

Nawshahrawī, Abū Yaḥyā Imām Khān: *Hindustān mēn Ahl-i ḥadīth kī ʿilmī khidmāt*, Lāʾilpūr 1352/1934.
Nawshahrawī, Abū Yaḥyā Imām Khān: *Tarājim-i ʿulamāʾ-i ḥadīth-i Hind*, Lahore 1992.
van Niewenhuijze, Christoffel A. O.: *Samsu'l-Din van Pasai*, Leiden 1945.
al-Niffarī, Muḥammad ʿAbd Allāh: *Kitāb al-Mawāqif*, ed. by Arthur J. Arberry, London 1935.
al-Niffarī, Muḥammad ʿAbd al-Jabbār: *Kitāb al-Nuṭq wal-ṣamṭ. Nuṣūṣ ṣūfiyya*, ed. by Muḥammad ʿAbbās Qāsim, Amman 2001.
Nizami, Khaliq Ahmad: The Impact of Ibn Taimiyya on South Asia, in: *Journal of Islamic Studies* 1 (1990), pp. 120–149.
Noer, Deliar: *The Modernist Muslim Movement in Indonesia, 1900–1942*, Singapore 1973.
Ibn Nubāta, Jamāl al-Dīn: *Sarḥ al-ʿuyūn fī sharḥ risālat Ibn Zaydūn*, Beirut 1986.
Nuʿmānī, ʿAllāma Shiblī: *al-Kalām*, Karachi 1979.
Nwyia, Paul: Une cible d'Ibn Taymiya, le moniste al-Tilimsani, in: *Bulletin d'études orientales* 30 (1978), pp. 127–145.

Ohlander, Erik S.: Fear of God (*taqwā*) in the Qurʾān. Some Notes on Semantic Shift and Thematic Context, in: *Journal of Semitic Studies* 50 (2005), p. 137–152.
Olesen, Niels Henrik: Etude comparée des idées d'Ibn Taymiyya (1263–1328) et de Martin Luther (1483–1546) sur le culte des saints, in: *Revue des études islamiques* 50 (1982), pp. 175–206.
Opwis, Felicitas Meta Maria: *Maṣlaḥa and the Purpose of the Law. Islamic Discourse on Legal Change from the 4th/10th to 8th/14th Century*, Leiden and Boston 2010.
Ormsby, Eric: *Ghazali. The Revival of Islam*, Oxford 2008.
Özervarlı, M. Sait: İbn Teymiyye. İtikadī Görüşleri, in: *Türkiye Diyanet Vakfı İslâm Ansiklopedisi*, vol. 20, Istanbul 1999, pp. 409–411.
Özervarlı, M. Sait: *İbn Teymiyye'nin Düşünce Metodolojisi ve Kelamcılara Eleştirisi*, Istanbul 2008.
Özervarli, M. Sait: The Qurʾānic Rational Theology of Ibn Taymiyya and His Criticism of the *Mutakallimūn*, in: Rapoport and Ahmad, *Ibn Taymiyya and His Times*, pp. 78–100.

Peacock, James L.: *Purifying the Faith. The Muḥammadiyyah Movement in Indonesian Islam*, Menlo Park 1978.
Pearson, Harlan Otto: *Islamic Reform and Revival in Nineteenth-century India*, New Delhi 2008 (Ph.D thesis, Durham 1979).
Penrice, John: *A Dictionary and a Glossary of the Qur'an*, Delhi 2002.
Perho, Irmeli: Climbing the Ladder. Social Mobility in the Mamluk Period, in: *Mamlūk Studies Review* 15 (2011), pp. 19–35.

Perho, Irmeli: Man Chooses His Destiny. Ibn Qayyim al-Jawziyya's Views on Predestination, in: *Islam and Christian-Muslim Relations* (12) 2001, pp. 61–70.
Perho, Irmeli: *The Prophet's Medicine. A Creation of the Muslim Traditionalist Scholars*, Helsinki 1995.
Perlmann, Moshe: Ibn al-Qayyim and Samau'al al-Maghribi", in: *Journal of Jewish Bibliography* 3 (1942), pp. 71–74.
Perlman, Moshe: Ibn Qayyim and the Devil, in: *Studi orientalistici in onore di Giorgio Levi Della Vida*, 2 vols. Rome, 1956, pp. 330–337.
Perlman[n], Moshe: Ifḥām al-yahūd. *Silencing the Jews*, New York 1964.
Perlman, Moshe: Islam. Polemics Against Judaism, in: *Encyclopedia Judaica*, Jerusalem 1996, vol. 9, pp. 101–102.
Perlman, Moshe: Muslim-Jewish Polemics, in: *Encyclopedia of Religion and Ethics*, New York and London 1987, vol. 11, pp. 396–401.
Perlman, Moshe: Samau'al al-Maghribī. Ifḥām al-Yahūd; Silencing the Jews, in: *American Academy of Jewish Research Proceedings* 32 (1964), pp. 1–104.
Pernau, Margrit: *Bürger mit Turban. Muslime in Delhi im 19. Jahrhundert*, Göttingen 2008.
Peshāwārī, ʿAbd al-Ṣamad: *Ṭalab al-arab min Adab al-ṭalab*, Bhopal 1878.
Peskes, Esther: *Muḥammad b. ʿAbdalwahhāb im Widerstreit*, Stuttgart 1993.
Peters, Rudolph: Islamischer Fundamentalismus. Glaube, Handeln, Führung, in: Wolfgang Schluchter (ed.): *Max Webers Sicht des Islams. Interpretation und Kritik*, Frankfurt/Main 1987, pp. 217–241.
Pines, Shlomo: *Studies in Islamic Atomism*, Jerusalem 1997.
Pīrzāda, Shams: *Ikaṯṯhī tīn ṭalāqīn*, Bombay 1997.
Plantinga, Alvin: Reason and Belief in God, in: Alvin Plantinga and Nicholas Wolterstorff (eds.): *Faith and Rationality*, Notre Dame and London 1991, pp. 16–93.
Pollock, Sheldon I.: *Literary Cultures in History. Reconstructions from South Asia*, Berkeley 2003.
Polo, Marco: *The Travel of Marco Polo*, translated by Aldo Ricci, London 1950.
Pouzet, Louis: *Damas au VIIIᵉ/XIIIᵉ siècle. Vie et structure religieuse d'une métropole islamique*, 2nd ed. Beirut 1991.
Preckel, Claudia: *Begums of Bhopal*, New Delhi 2000.
Preckel, Claudia: Interpretations of Widow Remarriage and Divorce. Shah Jahan Begum's (d. 1901) *Tahdhib an-Niswan* and the *Ahl-e hadith* Movement in 19th-century Bhopal, in: *Pakistan Journal of Women's Studies* 11 (2004), pp. 41–51.
Preckel, Claudia: *Islamische Bildungsnetzwerke und Gelehrtenkultur im Indien des 19. Jahrhunderts. Muḥammad Ṣiddīq Ḥasan Ḫān (st. 1890) und die Entstehung der Ahl-e ḥadīṯ-Bewegung in Bhopal*, Ph.D. thesis, Bochum 2005.
Prison Radicalization. Are Terrorist Cells Forming in U.S. Cell Blocks?, Hearing Before the Committee on Homeland Security and Governmental Affairs United States Senate; September 19, 2006. Washington D.C. 2007, p. 32.

Pulcini, Theodore and Laderman, Gary: *Exegesis as Polemical Discourse. Ibn Hazm on Jewish and Christian Scriptures*, Atlanta 1998.

Qadir, Chaudry Abdul: An Early Islamic Critique of Aristotelian Logic. Ibn Taymiyyah, in: *International Philosophical Quarterly* 8 (1968), pp. 498–512.

al-Qarāfī, Shihāb al-Dīn Aḥmad b. Idrīs: *Kitāb al-Ajwiba al-fākhira ʿan al-asʾila al-fājira*, printed on the margins of ʿAbd al-Raḥmān Bājajizāda: *al-Fāriq bayna al-khāliq wal-makhlūq*, Cairo 1322/1904.

al-Qāshānī, ʿAbd al-Razzāq: *Iṣṭilāḥāt al-ṣūfiyya*, ed. by Muḥammad Adīb Jadir, Cairo 1981.

al-Qāshānī, ʿAbd al-Razzāq: *Laṭāʾif al-iʿlām*, 2 vols., Cairo 1995.

al-Qāsimī, Jamāl al-Dīn: *Dalāʾil al-tawḥīd*, Cairo 1986.

al-Qazwīnī, Zakariyyā: *Mufīd al-ʿulūm wa-mubīd al-humūm*, ed. by Muḥammad ʿAbd al-Qādir ʿAṭāʾ, Beirut n. d.

al-Qushayrī, Abū al-Qāsim: *Risāla fī ʿIlm al-taṣawwuf*, Cairo n. d.

Radtke, Bernd: *The Exoteric Aḥmad Ibn Idrīs. A Sufi's Critique of the Madhāhib and the Wahhābīs*, Leiden 2000.

Radtke, Bernd: *Weltgeschichte und Weltbeschreibung im mittelalterlichen Islam*, Stuttgart 1992.

Raff, Thomas: *Das Sendschreiben nach Zypern. Ar-Risāla al-Qubruṣīya von Taqī al-Dīn Aḥmad Ibn Taymiyya (661–728 A. H. = 1263–1328 A. D.); Edition, Übersetzung und Kommentar*, Ph. D. thesis, Bonn 1971.

Rahbar, Daud: *God of Justice. A Study in the Ethical Doctrine of the Qurʾān*, Leiden 1960.

Rahbar, Mohammad Daud: Shah Waliullah and Ijtihad, in: *The Muslim World* 45 (1955), pp. 346–358.

Rahman, Fazlur: *Islam*, Chicago 1979.

Rahman, Fazlur: *Islamic Methodology in History*, Islamabad 1995.

Rahman, Fazlur: *Major Themes of the Qur'an*, Chicago 2009.

Rahman, Fazlur: *Revival and Reform in Islam*, ed. by Ebrahim Moosa, Oxford 1999.

Ramadan, Tariq: *Western Muslims and the Future of Islam*, Oxford 2004.

Rapoport, Yossef: Ibn Taymiyya on Divorce Oaths, in: Michael Winter and Amalia Levanoni (eds.): *The Mamluks in Egyptian and Syrian Politics and Society*, Leiden and Boston 2004, pp. 191–217.

Rapoport, Yossef: Ibn Taymiyya's Radical Legal Thought. Rationalism, Pluralism and the Primacy of Intention, in: Rapoport and Ahmad, *Ibn Taymiyya and His Times*, pp. 191–228.

Rapoport, Yossef: *Marriage, Money and Divorce in Medieval Islamic Society*, Cambridge 2005.

Rapoport, Yossef and Ahmed, Shahab (eds.): *Ibn Taymiyya and His Times*, Karachi 2010.

Rapoport, Yossef and Ahmed, Shahab: Introduction, in: idem: *Ibn Taymiyya and His Times*, pp. 3–20.

al-Rāzī, Fakhr al-Dīn: *Iʿtiqādāt firaq al-muslimīn wal-mushrikīn wa-maʿahu baḥth fī al-ṣūfiyya wal-firaq al-islāmiyya li-Muṣṭafā Bek ʿAbd al-Rāzī*, ed. by ʿAlī Sāmī al-Nashshār, Cairo 1356/1938.

al-Rāzī, Fakhr al-Dīn: *Kitāb al-Arbaʿīn fī uṣūl al-dīn*, 2 vols., ed. by Aḥmad Ḥijāzī al-Saqqā, Cairo (Maktabat al-Kulliyya al-Azhariyya) 1986. Rep. Beirut 1424/2004.

al-Rāzī, Fakhr al-Dīn: *Kitāb al-Mabāḥith al-mashriqiyya fī ʿilm al-ilāhiyyāt wal-ṭabīʿiyyāt*, ed. by Muḥammad al-Muʿtaṣim bi-llāh al-Baghdādī, Beirut 1990.

al-Rāzī, Fakhr al-Dīn: *Kitāb Maʿālim uṣūl al-dīn*, ed. by Samīḥ Dughaym, Beirut 1992.

al-Rāzī, Fakhr al-Dīn: *al-Maḥṣūl fī ʿilm uṣūl al-fiqh*, 6 vols., ed. by Jābir Fayyāḍ al-ʿAlwānī, Beirut 1412/1992.

al-Rāzī, Fakhr al-Dīn: *al-Maṭālib al-ʿāliya min al-ʿilm al-ilāhī*, 5 vols., ed. by Aḥmad Ḥijāzī al-Saqqā, Beirut 1407/1987.

al-Rāzī, Fakhr al-Dīn: *Muḥaṣṣal afkār al-mutaqaddimīn wal-mutaʾakhkhirīn min al-ʿulamāʾ wal-ḥukamāʾ wal-mutakallimīn*, ed. by Samīḥ Dughaym, Beirut 1992.

al-Rāzī, Fakhr al-Dīn: *Muḥaṣṣal afkār al-mutaqaddimīn wal-mutaʾakhkhirīn min al-ʿulamāʾ wal-ḥukamāʾ wal-mutakallimīn*, ed. by Ṭāhā ʿAbd al-Raʾūf Saʿd, Cairo n. d.

al-Rāzī, Fakhr al-Dīn: *Tafsīr al-Fakhr al-Rāzī al-mushtahar bil-tafsīr al-kabīr wa-mafātīḥ al-ghayb*, 17 vols., Beirut 1414/1993.

al-Rāzī, Fakhr al-Dīn: *al-Tafsīr al-kabīr*, 32 vols., Cairo n. d.

Reichmuth, Stefan: Bildungskanon und Bildungsreform aus der Sicht eines islamischen Gelehrten der anatolischen Provinz. Muḥammad al-Sājaqlī (Saçaqlızāde, gest. um 1145/1733) und sein *Tartīb al-ʿulūm*, in: Rüdiger Arnzen and Jörn Thielmann (eds.): *Words, Texts and Concepts Cruising the Mediterranean Sea. Studies on the Sources, Contents and Influences of Islamic Civilization and Arabic Philosophy and Science Dedicated to Gerhard Endress on His Sixty-fifth Birthday*, Leuven 2004, pp. 493–520.

Reichmuth, Stefan: *The World of Murtaḍā al-Zabīdī (1732–1791). Studies on the Life, Networks and Writings of an Islamic Humanist Scholar of the 18th Century*, Cambridge 2009.

Reinhardt, Volker: *Die Tyrannei der Tugend. Calvin und die Reformation in Genf*, München 2009.

Reynolds, Gabriel Said: *A Muslim Theologian in the Sectarian Milieu. ʿAbd al-Jabbār and the Critique of Christian Origins*, Leiden 2004.

Ricci, Ronit: *Islam Translated. Literature, Conversion and the Arabic Cosmopolis of South and Southeast Asia*, Chicago 2011.

Ricklefs, Merle Calvin: *A History of Modern Indonesia since c. 1200*, Palo Alto 2001.

Riḍā, Muḥammad Rashīd: al As'ila al-jāwiyya fī samāḥat al-lahw, in: *al-Manār* 9 (1906–1907), pp. 35–51.
Riḍā, Muḥammad Rashīd: Ḥukm man radda kalām al-ulamā' alladhī lā dalāl ʿalayhi, in: *al-Manār* 9 (1906–1907), pp. 139–147.
Riḍā, Muḥammad Rashīd: Tafsīr al-Qur'ān, in: *al-Manār* 9 (1906–1907), pp. 44, 18; (1915), pp. 321–352.
Riḍā, Muḥammad Rashīd: *Tafsīr al-Qur'ān al-ḥakīm al-shahīr bi-tafsīr al-Manār*, n. p. 1973.
Riddell, Peter G.: The Sources of ʿAbd al-Ra'ūf's *Tarjumān al-Mustafīd*, in: *Journal of the Malaysian Branch of the Royal Asiatic Society* 57 (1984), pp. 113–118.
Riexinger, Martin: How Favourable is Puritan Islam to Modernity. A Case Study on the Ahl-i Hadis in British India, in: Gwilym Beckerlegge (ed.): *Colonialism, Modernity and Religious Identities. Religious Reform Movements in South Asia*, New Delhi and New York 2008, pp. 147–165.
Riexinger, Martin: Legalist Sufis and Sufi Legalists in British India, in: Alfonso Carmona (ed.): *El Sufismo y las Normas del Islam. Trabajados del IV Congreso Internacional des Estudios Jurídicos Islámicos; Derecho y Sufismo*, Murcia 2006, pp. 409–420.
Riexinger, Martin: Nasserism Revitalized. A Critical Reading of Ḥasan Ḥanafī's Projects "The Islamic Left" and "Occidentalism" (and Their Uncritical Reading), in: *Die Welt des Islams* 47 (2007), pp. 63–117.
Riexinger, Martin: *Sanā'ullāh Amritsarī (1868–1948) und die Ahl-i Ḥadis im Punjab unter britischer Herrschaft*, Würzburg 2004.
Riexinger, Martin: South Asian Muslim Responses to the Theory of Evolution, in: *Die Welt des Islams* 49 (2009) pp. 212–247.
Roberts, Nancy N.: Reopening the Muslim-Christian Dialogue of the 13–14th Centuries. Critical Reflections on Ibn Taymiyyah's Response to Christianity in *al-Jawāb al-ṣaḥīḥ li man baddala dīn al-Masīḥ*, in: *The Muslim World* 84 (1996), pp. 342–366.
Robinson, Francis: *Islam and Muslim History in South Asia*, Delhi 2000.
Robinson, Francis: *'Ulama of Farangi Mahall*, Delhi 2001.
Robinson, Richard: *Definition*, Oxford 2003 (reprint).
Rohe, Mathias: *Zur öffentlich-rechtlichen Situation von Muslimen in ausgewählten europäischen Ländern*, Vienna 2006.
Rosenthal, Franz: *Knowledge Triumphant. The Concept of Knowledge in Medieval Islam; With an Introduction by Dimitri Gutas*, Leiden and Boston 2007.
El-Rouayheb, Khaled: From Ibn Ḥajar al-Haytamī (d. 1566) to Khayr al-Dīn al-Ālūsī (d. 1899). Changing Views of Ibn Taymiyya among Non-Ḥanbalī Sunni Scholars, in: Rapoport and Ahmed, *Ibn Taymiyya and His Times*, pp. 296–318.
El-Rouayheb, Khaled: Opening the Gate of Verification. The Forgotten Arab-Islamic Florescence of the 17th Century, in: *International Journal of Middle Eastern Studies* 38 (2006), pp. 263–281.

El-Rouayheb, Khaled: Was there a Revival of Logical Studies in Eighteenth-century Egypt?, in: *Die Welt des Islams* 45 (2005), pp. 1–19.
Rudolph, Ulrich and Perler, Dominik: *Occasionalismus. Theorien der Kausalität im arabisch-islamischen und im europäischen Denken*, Göttingen 2000.
Rudolph, Ulrich: Die Neubewertung der Logik durch al-Ġazālī, in: Dominik Perler and Ulrich Rudolph (eds.): *Logik und Theologie. Das* Organon *im arabischen und lateinischen Mittelalter*, Leiden and Boston 2005, pp. 73–97.

Sachedina, Abdulaziz: Guidance or Governance? A Muslim Conception of "Two Cities", in: *George Washington Law Review* 68 (2000), pp. 1079–1097.
Saʿd, al-Ṭablāwī Maḥmūd: *Mawqif Ibn Taymiyya min falsafat Ibn Rushd fī al-ʿaqīda wa-ʿilm al-kalām wal-falsafa*, Cairo 1409/1989.
Saeed, Abdullah and Saeed, Hassan: *Freedom of Religion, Apostasy and Islam*, Aldershot and Burlington 2004.
Saeedullah: The Life and Works of Muhammad Siddiq Hasan Khan, Nawab of Bhopal (1248–1307/1832–1890), Lahore 1973.
al-Ṣafadī, Ṣalāḥ al-Dīn Khalīl b. Aybak: *al-Wāfī bil-wafayāt*, Istanbul n. d.
Sageman, Marc: *Understanding Terror Networks*, Philadelphia 2004.
al-Ṣaghīr/al-Ṣughayyir, ʿAbd al-Majīd: Mawāqif "rushdiyya" li-Taqī al-Dīn Ibn Taymiyya?, in: *Dirāsāt Maghribiyya muhdāt ilā al-mufakkir al-Maghribī Muḥammad ʿAzīz al-Ḥabbābī*, Casablanca 1987, pp. 164–182.
al-Sahsawānī [or al-Sahaswānī], Muḥammad Bashīr: *Ṣiyānat al-insān ʿan waswasat al-Shaykh Daḥlān*, foreword by Muḥammad Rashīd Riḍā, 5th ed. n. p. 1395/1975.
al-Sahsawānī, Muḥammad Nadhīr: *Munāẓara Aḥmadiyya*, Kanpur 1289/1871–1872.
Saiful Anam, Ahmad: *Kriteria Kesahihan Hadis menurut Ibn Qayyim al-Jawziyya*, Ph. D. thesis, Jakarta 1997.
al-Salafī, Abū al-Mukarram ʿAbd al-Jalīl: *Daʿwat al-imām Muḥammad b. ʿAbd al-Wahhāb fī shibh al-qārra al-hindiyya*, Riyadh 1413/1993.
Salafī, Munīr Aḥmad: *Ḥāfiẓ ʿAbd al-Mannān Wāzīrābādī*, Lahore 1994.
el-Ṣāleḥ, Ṣoubḥī: *La vie future selon le Coran*, Paris 1971.
al-Ṣanʿānī, Muḥammad b. Ismāʿīl: *Rafʿ al-astār li-ibṭāl adillat al-qāʾilīn bi-fanāʾ al-nār*, ed. by Muḥammad Nāṣir al-Dīn al-Albānī, Beirut 1405/1984.
Sanyal, Usha: *Devotional Islam and Politics in British India. Ahmad Riza Khan Barelwi and His Movement, 1870–1920*, Delhi 1999.
al-Sarḥān, Saʿūd: *al-Ḥikma al-maṣlūba. Madkhal ilā mawqif Ibn Taymiyya min al-falsafa*, Beirut 2008.
al-Sarrāj, ʿAbd Allāh Abū Naṣr: *Kitāb al-Lumaʿ*, ed. by Reynold Nicholson, Leiden 1914.
Sartain, Elizabeth M. (ed.): *Jalāl al-Dīn al-Suyūṭī*, 2 vols., Cambridge 1975.
Sayf, Muḥammad Aslam: *Taḥrīk-i Ahl-i ḥadīth*, Delhi 1999.

Sayyid Aḥmad Khān (Syed Ahmed Bahadoor): *Dr. Hunter's "Our Indian Mussulmans. Are they Bound in Conscience to Rebel Against the Queen?"; Compiled by a Mahomedan*, London 1872.
Sayyid Aḥmad Khān: *Maqālāt-i Sar Sayyid*, 16 vols., ed. by Muḥammad Ismāʿīl Pānīpatī, Lahore 1990.
Schallenbergh, Gino: Ibn Qayyim al-Jawziyya on Sufi Terminology. The Concept of the Spiritual Path (*ṭarīq*), in: Kristof D'Hulster and Jo Van Steenbergen (eds.): *Continuity and Change in the Realms of Islam. Studies in Honour of Professor Urbain Vermeulen*, Leuven 2008, pp. 555–565.
Schallenbergh, Gino: Ibn Taymīya on the 'Ahl al-Bayt', in: Urbain Vermeulen and Jo van Steenbergen (eds.): *Egypt and Syria in the Fatimid, Ayyubid and Mamluk Eras*, vol. 3 (Proceedings of the 6th, 7th and 8th International Colloquium organized at the Katholieke Universiteit Leuven in May 1997, 1998 and 1999), Leuven 2001, pp. 407–420.
Schallenbergh, Gino: Intoxication and Ecstasy. Sufi Terminology in the Work of Ibn Qayyim al-Djawzīya, in: Urbain Vermeulen and Jo van Steenbergen (eds.): *Proceedings of the 6th, 7th and 8th Colloquium on the History of Egypt and Syria in the Fatimid, Ayyubid and Mamluk Eras*, Leuven 2005, p. 459–474.
Schmid, Hansjörg: Gegner werden gemacht. Neutestamentliche, religionsgeschichtliche und aktuelle Perspektiven, in: *Zeitschrift für Katholische Theologie* 124 (2002), pp. 385–396.
Schöck, Cornelia: *Koranexegese, Grammatik und Logik. Zum Verhältnis von arabischer und aristotelischer Urteils-, Konsequenz- und Schlusslehre*, Leiden and Boston 2006.
Schöller, Marco: Ibn Taymīyah und nochmals die Frage nach einer Reformation im Islam, in: Otto Jastrow, Shabo Talay and Herta Hafenrichter (eds.): *Studien zur Semitistik und Arabistik. Festschrift für Hartmut Bobzin zum 60. Geburtstag*, Wiesbaden 2008, pp. 363–384.
Schulze, Reinhard: *Islamischer Internationalismus im 20. Jahrhundert*, Leiden 1990.
Schwer, Thilo: Persönliche Aneignung versus kommerzielle Verwertung im Möbeldesign, in: Birgit Richard and Alexander Ruhl (eds.): *Konsumguerilla. Widerstand gegen Massenkultur?*, Frankfurt am Main and New York 2008, pp. 55–68.
Seljuq, Affan: Relations Between the Ottoman Empire and the Muslim Kingdoms in the Malay-Indonesian Archipelago, in: *Der Islam* 57 (1980), pp. 301–310.
al-Shahrastānī, Muḥammad: *Struggling with the Philosopher. A Refutation of Avicenna's Metaphysics*; a new Arabic edition and English translation of Muḥammad b. ʿAbd al-Karīm b. Aḥmad al-Shahrastānī's *Kitāb al-Muṣāraʿa* by Wilferd Madelung and Toby Mayer, London and New York 2001.
al-Shahrastānī, Muḥammad b. ʿAbd al-Karīm: *Kitāb Muṣāraʿat al-falāsifa*, edited by Suhayr Muḥammad Mukhtār, Cairo 1976/1396.

al-Shaʿrānī, ʿAbd al-Wahhāb: *al-Ṭabaqāt al-kubrā*, 2 vols., ed. by ʿAbd al-Raḥmān Maḥmūd, Cairo 1993.
al-Shawkānī, Muḥammad b. ʿAlī: *Adab al-ṭalab wa-muntahā al-arab*, Sanaa 1419/1998.
al-Shawkānī, Muḥammad b. ʿAlī: *al-Badr al-ṭāliʿ*, Cairo 1929.
al-Shawkānī, Muḥammad b. ʿAlī: *Fatḥ al-qadīr*, 6 vols., al-Mansoura 1994.
al-Shawkānī, Muḥammad b. ʿAlī: *Nayl al-awṭār*, 8 vols., Cairo 1993.
Shayzari, Abd al-Rahman b. Nasr: *The Book of the Islamic Market Inspector. Nihayat al-rutba fi talab al-hisba*, transl. by Ronald Paul Buckley, Oxford 1999.
Shepard, William: 'Fundamentalism' Christian and Islamic, in: *Religion* 17 (1987), pp. 355–378.
Shihadeh, Ayman: *The Teleological Ethics of Fakhr al-Dīn al-Rāzī*, Leiden and Boston 2006.
Ṣiddīq Ḥasan Khān, Muḥammad: *Abjad al-ʿulūm*, 3 vols., Lahore 1403/1983.
Ṣiddīq Ḥasan Khān, Muḥammad: *Bughyat al-rāʾid fī sharḥ al-ʿaqāʾid*, Lucknow n. d.
Ṣiddīq Ḥasan Khān, Muḥammad: *al-Dīn al-khāliṣ*, Cairo 1959.
Ṣiddīq Ḥasan Khān, Muḥammad: *Fatḥ al-bayān fī maqāṣid al-qurʾān*, Cairo ca. 1965 (reprint of the 1884 Bulāq edition).
Ṣiddīq Ḥasan Khān, Muḥammad: *Ḥujaj al-kirāma fī āthār al-qiyāma*, Bhopal 1874.
Ṣiddīq Ḥasan Khān, Muḥammad: *Ḥusn al-uswa bi-mā thabata min Allāh wa-rasūlihi fī al-niswa*, Constantinople 1883/1884.
Ṣiddīq Ḥasan Khān, Muḥammad: *al-Idhāʿa li-mā kāna wa-mā yakūnu bayna yaday al-sāʿa*, n. p. n. d. [ca. 1980].
Ṣiddīq Ḥasan Khān, Muḥammad: *al-Iḥtiwāʾ ʿalā masʾalat al-istiwāʾ*, Lahore 1291/1874–1875.
Ṣiddīq Ḥasan Khān, Muḥammad: *Iqtirāb al-sāʿa* , n. p. n. d.
Ṣiddīq Ḥasan Khān, Muḥammad: *Iqtirāb al-sāʿa*, Kanpur 1301/1883.
Ṣiddīq Ḥasan Khān, Muḥammad: *Itḥāf al-nubalāʾ al-muttaqīn bi-iḥyāʾ al-fuqahāʾ al-muḥaddithīn*, Kanpur 1282/1865–1866.
Ṣiddīq Ḥasan Khān, Muḥammad: *Qurrat al-aʿyān wa-masarrāt al-ādhān fī maʾāthir al-malik al-jalīl al-Nawwāb Muḥammad Ṣiddīq Ḥasan Khān*, Constantinople 1298/1881.
Ṣiddīq Ḥasan Khān, Muḥammad: *Riḥlat al-Ṣiddīq ilā bayt Allāh al-ʿatīq*, Lucknow 1289/1872.
Ṣiddīq Ḥasan Khān, Muḥammad: *Silsilat al-ʿasjad fī dhikr mashāʾikh al-sanad*, Bhopal 1293/1876.
Ṣiddīq Ḥasan Khān, Muḥammad: *al-Tāj al-mukallal min jawāhir maʾāthir al-ṭirāz al-ākhir wal-awwal*, 2nd ed. Bombay 1383/1963.
Ṣiddīq Ḥasan Khān, Muḥammad: *Tarjumān al-Wahhābiyya*, Benares 1898.
al-Sijistānī, Abū Dāʾūd: *Sunan Abī Dāʾūd*, ed. by Aḥmad Saʿd ʿAlī, Cairo 1952.

Sikand, Yoginder: *The Origins of Development of the Tablighi Jama'at. A Cross-country Comparative Study*, Hyderabad 2002.

Sila, Muhammad Adlin: *Tasawuf Perkotaan. Kasus Pusat Kajian Tasawuf (PKT) Tazkiyah Sejati Jakarta*, Jakarta 2000.

Sindhī, ʿUbayd Allāh: *Shāh Walī Allāh awr un kī siyāsī taḥrīk*, Lahore 1965.

Sivan, Emmanuel: Ibn Taymiyya. Father of the Islamic Revolution; Medieval Theology and Modern Politics, in: *Encounter* 60 (1983), pp. 41–50.

Sivan, Emmanuel: *Radical Islam. Medieval Theology and Modern Politics*, New Haven 1990.

Sivan, Emmanuel: Sunni Radicalism in the Middle East and the Iranian Revolution, in: *International Journal of Middle East Studies* 21 (1989), pp. 1–30.

Siyālkotī, Muḥammad Ibrāhīm Mīr: *Ta'rīkh-i Ahl-i ḥadīth*, New Delhi 1995.

Skovgaard-Petersen, Jakob: Islam og vulgær weberianisme, in: *Kritik* 10 (2010), pp. 20–28.

Skovgaard-Petersen, Jakob: Portrait of the Intellectual as a Young Man. Rashīd Riḍā's *Muḥāwarat al-muṣliḥ wal-muqallid* (1906), in: *Islam and Christian-Muslim Relations* 12 (2001) pp. 93–104.

Sourdel, Dominique and Sourdel-Thomine, Janine: Henri Laoust 1905–1983, in: *Revue des études islamiques* 52 (1984), pp. 3–16.

Spuler, Bertold: *Die Mongolen im Iran*, 4th ed., Leiden 1985.

Ssekamanya, Siraje Abdullah: Ibn Taymiyya's Theological Approach Illustrated. On the Essence (*Dhat*) and the Attributes (*Sifat*) of Allah, in: *al-Shajarah* 9 (2004), pp. 43–61.

Steigerwald, Diane: *La pensée philosophique et théologique de Shahrastānī (m. 548/1153)*, Laval 1997.

Steinberg, Guido: *Religion und Staat in Saudi-Arabien*, Würzburg 2002.

Steinschneider, Moritz: *Polemische und apologetische Literatur in arabischer Sprache, zwischen Muslimen, Christen und Juden*, Leipzig 1877.

Stern, Samuel M.: ʿAbd al-Jabbār's Account of How Christ's Religion was Falsified by the Adoption of Roman Customs, in: *Journal of Theological Studies* 19 (1968), pp. 128–185.

Stern, Samuel M.: Quotations from Apocryphal Gospels in ʿAbd al-Ǧabbār, in: *Journal of Theological Studies* 18 (1967), pp. 34–57.

Street, Tony: Arabic Logic, in: Peter Adamson and Richard C. Taylor (eds.): *The Cambridge Companion to Arabic Philosophy*, Cambridge 2005, pp. 572–579.

al-Subkī, Abū Ḥasan ʿAlī Taqī al-Dīn: *al-Iʿtibār bi-baqāʾ al-janna wal-nār*, ed. by Ṭāhā al-Dasūqī Ḥubayshī, Cairo 1987.

al-Subkī, Tāj al-Dīn Abū Naṣr ʿAbd al-Wahhāb: *Kitāb Muʿīd al-niʿam wa-mubīd al-niqam. The Restorer of Favours and the Restrainer of Chastisements*, ed. by David W. Myhrman, London 1968.

al-Subkī, Tāj al-Dīn Abū Naṣr ʿAbd al-Wahhāb: *Ṭābaqāt al-shāfiʿiyya al-kubrā*, 10 vols., ed. by ʿAbd al-Fattāh al-Ḥilw and Maḥmūd al-Ṭanāḥī, Cairo 1992.

al-Subkī, Tāj al-Dīn Abū Naṣr ʿAbd al-Wahhāb: Tâj Eddîn Es-Subkî's Muʿîd en-niʿam wa mubîd en-niqam. Über die moralischen Pflichten der verschiedenen islamischen Bevölkerungsklassen; mit Kürzungen aus dem Arabischen übersetzt von Oskar Rescher, in: Oskar Rescher (ed.) *al-Subkī. Gesammelte Werke*, sect. II, vol. 2, Osnabrück 1980 (reprint of Constantinople 1925), pp. 71–74.

al-Ṣughayyir, ʿAbd al-Majīd: Mawāqif „rushdiyya" li-Taqī al-Dīn Ibn Taymiyya? Mulāḥaẓāt awwaliyya, in: al-Ṭāhir Waʿzīz (ed.): *Dirāsāt maghribiyya. Muhdāt ilā al-mufakkir al-maghribī Muḥammad ʿAzīz al-Ḥabbābī (Lahbabi)*, Casablanca 1987, pp. 176–177.

al-Suhrawardī, Abū Ḥafṣ ʿUmar: *ʿAwārif al-maʿārif*, 2 vols., Cairo n. d.

al-Sulamī, ʿAbd al-Raḥmān Nāfiʿ: al-Siyāsa al-sharʿiyya ʿinda al-Imām Ibn Qayyim al-Jawziyya, in: *Majallat Jāmiʿat al-Malik ʿAbd al-ʿAzīz. Al-Ādāb wal-ʿUlūm al-Insāniyya* 16 (2008), pp. 317–356.

al-Suyūṭī, Jalāl al-Dīn: *al-Ḥāwī lil-fatāwā fī al-fiqh wa-ʿulūm al-tafsīr wal-ḥadīth wal-uṣūl wal-naḥw wal-iʿrāb wa-sāʾir al-funūn*, 2 vols., Beirut 1395/1975.

al-Suyūṭī, Jalāl al-Dīn: *Jahd al-qarīḥa fī tajrīd al-naṣīḥa*, ed. by ʿAlī Sāmī al-Nashshār, Cairo 1947.

al-Suyūṭī, Jalāl al-Dīn: *Jahd al-qarīḥa fī tajrīd al-naṣīḥa*, ed. by Suʿād ʿAbd al-Rāziq and ʿAlī Sāmī al-Nashshār, Cairo 1970.

al-Suyūṭī, Jalāl al-Dīn: al-Qawl al-mushriq fī taḥrīm al-ishtighāl bil-manṭiq, in: al-Suyūṭī, Jalāl al-Dīn: *al-Ḥāwī lil-fatāwā*, Beirut 1395/1975, pp. 255–257.

al-Suyūṭī, Jalāl al-Dīn: *Ṣawn al-manṭiq wal-kalām ʿan fann al-manṭiq wal-kalām wa-yalīhī Mukhtaṣar al-Suyūṭī li-kitāb naṣīḥat ahl al-īmān fī al-radd ʿalā manṭiq al-yūnān li-Taqī al-Dīn Ibn Taymiyya. Jahd al-qarīḥa fī tajrīd al-naṣīḥa*, ed. by ʿAlī Sāmī al- Nashshār, Cairo 1366/1947.

Swartz, Merlin: Acquisition (kasb) in Early Kalām, in: Samuel Miklos Stern, Albert Hourani and Vivian Brown (eds.): *Islamic Philosophy and the Classical Tradition. Essays Presented by His Friends and Pupils to Richard Walzer on His Seventieth Birthday*, Columbia 1972, pp. 355–387.

Swartz, Merlin: *Ibn al-Jawzī's* Kitāb al-Quṣṣāṣ wal-mudhakkirīn, Beirut 1971.

Swartz, Merlin: A Seventh-century (A. H.) Sunni Creed. The *ʿAqīda wāsiṭiyya* of Ibn Taymīya, in: *Humaniora Islamica* 1 (1973), pp. 91–131.

Ṭabāṭabāʾī, Muṣṭafā: *al-Mufakkirūn al-muslimūn fī muwājahat al-manṭiq al-yūnānī*; translated into Arabic by ʿAbd al-Raḥīm M. al-Balūshī, Beirut 1990.

al-Ṭablāwī, Maḥmud Saʿd: *Mawqif Ibn Taymiyya min falsafat Ibn Rushd fī al-ʿaqīda wa-fī ʿilm al-kalām wal-falsafa*, Cairo 1409/1989.

al-Taftazānī, Saʿd al-Dīn: *Sharḥ al-Maqāṣid*, 5 vols., ed. by ʿAbd al-Raḥmān ʿUmayra, Beirut 1989.

Taheri, Amir: *Holy Terror. Inside the World of Islamic Terrorism*, Bethesda 1987.

Talmon-Heller, Daniella: Fidelity, Cohesion and Conformity within Madhhabs in Zangid and Ayyubid Syria, in: Peri Bearman, Wolfhart Heinrichs and Bernard G. Weiss (eds.): *The Islamic School of Law*, Cambridge 2005, pp. 94–116.

Tamer, Georges: *Islamische Philosophie und die Krise der Moderne. Das Verhältnis von Leo Strauss zu Alfarabi, Avicenna und Averroes*, Leiden and Boston 2001.

al-Tamīmī, Abū ʿUmar: *al-Siyāsa al-sharʿiyya*, Beirut 2007.

Ṭāshköprü-Zāda: *al-Shaqāʾiq al-nuʿmāniyya fī ʿulamāʾ al-dawla al-ʿuthmāniyya*, ed. by Aḥmad Ṣubḥī Furāt, Istanbul 1985.

al-Tawḥīdī, Abū Ḥayyān: *Kitāb al-Imtāʿ wal-muʾānasa*, ed. by Aḥmad Amīn and Aḥmad al-Zayn, Beirut n. d.

Taylor, Christopher S.: *In the Vicinity of the Righteous.* Ziyāra *and the Veneration of Muslim Saints in Late Medieval Egypt*, Leiden 1999.

Terrorism. Radical Islamic Influence of Chaplaincy of the U.S. Military and Prisons; Hearing Before the Subcommittee on Terrorism, Technology and Homeland Security of the Committee on the Judiciary United States Senate, October 14, 2003, Serial No. J-108–44. Washington D.C. 2004.

Theurgus, Iulianus: *The Chaldean Oracles. Text, translation and commentary by Ruth Majercik*, Leiden 1989.

Thomas, David: Apologetic and Polemic in the Letter from Cyprus and Ibn Taymiyya's *al-Jawāb al-ṣaḥīḥ li man baddala dīn al-Masīḥ*, in: Rapoport and Ahmed, *Ibn Taymiyya and His Times*, pp. 247–265.

al-Tilimsānī, ʿAfīf al-Dīn Sulaymān: *Sharḥ manāzil al-sāʾirīn*, Cairo n. d.

al-Tilimsānī, ʿAfīf al-Dīn Sulaymān: *Sharḥ mawāqif al-Niffarī*, ed. by Jamāl al-Marzūqī, Cairo 1997.

Titus, Murray T.: *Indian Islam*, Delhi 1979.

Troll, Christian W.: A Note on the *Tafsīr-i Thanāʾ* of Thanā Allāh Amritsārī and His Criticism of Sayyid Aḥmad Khān's *Tafsīr-i Aḥmadī*, in: *Islamic Culture* 59 (1984), pp. 29–44.

Troupeau, Gérard: Ibn Taymiyya et sa réfutation d'Eutychès, in: *Bulletin d'études orientales*, 30 (1978), pp. 209–220.

Ṭūghān Shaykh Muḥammadī: *al-Muqaddima al-sulṭāniyya fī al-siyāsa al-sharʿiyya*, ed. by ʿAbd Allāh Muḥammad ʿAbd Allāh, Cairo 1997.

Türker, Mubahat: *Üç Tehâfüt Bakımından Felsefe ve Din Münasebeti*, Ankara 1956.

Tyan, Emile: Méthodologie et sources du droit en Islam (*Istiḥsān*, *Istiṣlāḥ*, *Siyāsa sharʿiyya*), in: *Studia Islamica* 10 (1959), pp. 79–109.

ʿUbayd Allāh Khān, Sulṭān Jahān Bēgum: *Ḥayāt-i Sikanderī*, Bhopal 1921.

Uçar, Bülent: *Recht als Mittel zur Reform von Religion und Gesellschaft. Die türkische Debatte um die Scharia und die Rechtsschulen im 20. Jahrhundert*, Würzburg 2005.

al-ʿUlaymī, ʿAbd al-Raḥmān: *al-Manhaj al-Aḥmad fī tarājim aṣḥāb al-imām Aḥmad*, 6 vols., ed. by ʿAbd al-Qādir al-Arnāʾūt, Beirut 1997.

al-Urmawī, Sirāj al-Dīn: *al-Taḥṣīl fī al-maḥṣūl*, ed. by ʿAbd al-Ḥamīd ʿAlī Abū Zayd, Beirut 1408/1988.

Utvik, Bjørn Olav: A Pervasive Seriousness Invaded the Country. Islamism, Cromwell's Ghost in the Middle East, in: Juhani Koponen (ed.): *Between National Histories and Global History*, Helsinki 1997, pp. 129–142.

Vajda, George: La connaissance naturelle de Dieu selon al-Ǧāḥiẓ critiqueé par les muʿtazilites, in: *Studia Islamica* 24 (1966), pp. 19–33.

Valiuddin, Mir: *Love of God. The Sufi Approach*, Lahore 1979.

Vermij, Rienk: *The Calvinist Copernicans. The Reception of the New Astronomy in the Dutch Republic; 1575–1750*, Amsterdam 2002.

Vikør, Knut S.: *Between God and the Sultan. A History of Islamic Law*, London 2005.

Vogel, Frank E.: *Islamic Law and Legal System. Studies of Saudi Arabia*, Leiden and Boston 2000.

Voll, John O.: *Islam. Continuity and Change in the Modern World*, Syracuse 1982.

Voll, John O.: Linking Groups in the Networks of Eighteenth-century Revivalist Scholars. The Mizjaji Family in Yemen, in: Nehemia Levtzion and John O. Voll (eds.): *Eighteenth-century Renewal and Reform in Islam*, Syracuse 1992, pp. 69–92.

Voll, John O.: Muḥammad Ḥayyā al-Sindī and Muḥammad b. ʿAbd al-Wahhāb. An Analysis of an Intellectual Group in Eighteenth Century Medina, in: *Bulletin of the School of Oriental and African Studies* 38 (1975), pp. 32–39.

Voorhoeve, Petrus: *Handlist of Arabic Manuscripts in the Library of the University of Leiden*, Leiden 1957.

Vredenbregt, Jacob: The Haddj. Some of Its Features and Functions in Indonesia, in: *Bijdraagen tot de Taal-, Land- en Volkenkunde de Koninlijke Institut* 118 (1962), pp. 91–154.

Waardenburg, Jacques: Muslim Studies of Other Religions. The Medieval Period; 650–1500, in: idem. (ed.): *Muslim Perceptions of Other Religions*, New York and Oxford 1999, pp. 18–69.

Waardenburg, Jacques: World Religions in the Light of Islam, in: Alford T. Welch and Pierre Cachia (eds.): *Islam*, Edinburgh 1979, pp. 245–275.

al-Wābil, Yūsuf b. ʿAbd Allāh b. Yūsuf: *Qiyāmat kī nishāniyān*, translated by Muḥammad Muqīm b. Ḥāmid ʿAlī Fayḍī, Delhi 2003.

Wahba, Hafiz: *Arabian Days*, London 1964.

al-Wardī, ʿAlī: *Muqaddima li-Dirāsat al-manṭiq al-ijtimāʿī. Manṭiq Ibn Khaldūn fī ḍawʾ ḥaḍāratihi wa-shakhṣiyyatihi; muḥāḍarāt*, Cairo 1962.

Wasella, Jürgen: *Vom Fundamentalisten zum Atheisten. Die Dissidentenkarriere des ʿAbdallāh al-Qaṣīmī (1907–1996)*, Gotha 1997.

Watson, C. William: Islamic Books and Their Publishers. Notes on the Contemporary Indonesian Scene, in: *Journal of Islamic Studies* 16 (2005), pp. 177–210.

Watt, W. Montgomery: *Free Will and Predestination in Early Islam*, London 1948.

Watt, W. Montgomery: *Islamic Creeds*, Edinburgh 1994.

Watt, W. Montgomery: Khārijite Thought in the Umayyad Period, in: *Der Islam* 36 (1961), pp. 215–231.

Watt, W. Montgomery: *The Formative Period of Islamic Thought*, Edinburgh 1973.

Weismann, Itzhak: *Taste of Modernity. Sufism, Salafiyya, and Arabism in Late Ottoman Damascus*, Leiden and Boston 2001.

Weiss, Bernard G.: Ibn Taymiyya on Leadership in the Ritual Prayer, in: Muhammad Khalid Masud, Brinkley Messick and Davis Stephan Powers (eds.): *Islamic Legal Interpretation. Muftis and Their Fatwas*, Cambridge MA and London 1996, pp. 63–71.

Weiss, Bernard G.: *The Spirit of Islamic Law. The Spirit of the Laws*, Athens 1998.

Weisser, Ursula: Ibn Qaiyim al-Ǧauzīya über die Methoden der Embryologie, in: *Medizinhistorisches Journal* 16 (1981), pp. 227–239.

Wensinck, Arent Jan: *Concordance et indices de la tradition musulmane*, 8 vols., Leiden 1936–1988.

Wensinck, Arent Jan: *The Muslim Creed. Its Genesis and Historical Development*, London 1965.

Wilms, Franz-Elmar: *Al-Ghazālīs Schrift wider die Gottheit Jesu*, Leiden 1966.

Winstedt, Richard O.: *A History of Classical Malay Literature*, Kuala Lumpur 1969.

Winstedt, Richard O.: The Advent of Muhammadanism in the Malay Peninsula and Archipelago, in: *Journal of the Straits Branch of the Royal Asiatic Society* 77 (1917), pp. 171–175.

Wolfson, Harry Austryn: *The Philosophy of the Kalam*, Cambridge and London 1976.

Wood, Robert: *An Essay on the Original Genius and Writings of Homer. With a Comparative View of the Ancient and Present State of the Troade*, London 1769.

Wright, Lawrence: *The Looming Tower. Al-Qaeda and the Road to 9/11*, New York 2007.

al-Yāfiʿī, ʿAbd Allāh b. Asʿad: *Nashr al-maḥāsin al-ghāliya fī faḍl mashāyikh al-maqāmāt al-ʿāliya*, ed. by Aḥmad Saʿdī, Cairo 2004.

Yāfūt, Sālim: *Ibn Ḥazm wal-fikr al-falsafī bil-maghrib wal-andalus*, Casablanca 1986.

al-Yasīn, Muḥammad Ḥasan: *Allāh bayna al-fiṭra wal-dalīl*, Beirut 1972.

Yasushi, Kosugi: *al-Manār* Revisited. The „Lighthouse“ of the Islamic Revival, in: Stéphane A. Dudoignon and Komatsu Hisao (eds.): *Intellectuals in the Modern Islamic World. Transmission, Transformation, Communication*, Abingdon 2006, pp. 3–39.

Yatīm, Muḥammad: Ibn Taymiyya wa-mas'alat al-ʿaql wal-naql, in: *al-Furqān* 3 (1407/1987), pp. 16–24.

Yule, Sir Henry: *Hobson-Jobson. A Glossary of Colloquial Anglo-Indian Words and Phrases and of Kindred Terms*, ed. by William Crooke, London 1903.

Yusof, Ahmad Ikbal: *Ibn Qayyim's Critique of Philosophical Sufism. The Refutation of al- Tilimsānī's Version of Waḥdat al-Wujūd*, Surakarta 2003.

Yusof, Ahmad Ikbal b. Mohd: *Ibn Qayyim's Critique of Philosophical Sufism. The Refutation of al-Tilimsānī's Version of Waḥdat al-Wujūd*, M. A. Thesis, Kuala Lumpur 2004.

al-Zabīdī, Murtaḍā: *Kitāb Itḥāf al-sāda al-muttaqīn bi-sharḥ asrār iḥyā' ʿulūm al-dīn (wa-bi-hāmish Kitāb al-Imlā' ʿan ishkālāt al-Iḥyā' lil-Ghazālī)*, 10 vols., Beirut n. d. (after 1970, reprint of Egypt 1311/1894).

al-Zayyaat, Montasser: *The Road to Al-Qaeda. The Story of bin Laaden's Right-Hand Man*, London 2002.

Zebiri, Kate: *Muslims and Christians Face to Face*, Oxford 1997.

Zymner, Rüdiger: Gattungen aus literaturwissenschaftlicher Sicht, in: Stephan Conermann (ed.): *Was sind Genres? Nicht-abendländische Kategorisierungen von Gattungen*, Berlin 2011, pp. 7–21.

Index